Basic
Accounting
for
Managerial
and
Financial
Control

Basic Accounting for Managerial and Financial Control

Albert Slavin NORTHEASTERN UNIVERSITY

Isaac N. Reynolds UNIVERSITY OF NORTH CAROLINA

Lawrence H. Malchman NORTHEASTERN UNIVERSITY

Holt, Rinehart and Winston, Inc.

NEW YORK   CHICAGO   SAN FRANCISCO   ATLANTA

DALLAS   MONTREAL   TORONTO   LONDON

Copyright © 1968 by Holt, Rinehart and Winston, Inc.
All rights reserved
Library of Congress Catalog Card Number: 68-10179
03-064890-4
0123   41   987654
Printed in the United States of America

Preface

This book is intended for use primarily in the first-year basic accounting course. It is arranged, however, to meet several needs. For the first-year basic accounting course, every chapter can be used. For a graduate level MBA survey course, Chapters 1–5 and 8–24, with some deletions in certain chapters, constitute a high-level course. For those many schools which teach only one course in elementary accounting, Chapters 1–6 and 8–14 provide excellent coverage of basic accounting. By carefully integrating the managerial uses of accounting with the traditional subject matter of financial accounting, the book provides students of business administration with the basic concepts and uses of accounting, and accounting majors with a broad foundation for advanced study. The primary objective of the text is to present the managerial and financial uses of accounting concomitantly with fundamental accounting practices and theory.

The emphasis on procedural details is reduced, thereby providing needed time and space for a continuing development of the uses of accounting as an aid in the formulation and administration of management policies and controls, financial management and analysis, and budgetary controls and procedures. Several of these areas are not included in the typical elementary text. The text attempts from the outset to stress the analysis and interpretation of financial statements as well as managerial accounting concepts, principles, and standards. Citations from the publications of the American Accounting Association and the American Institute of Certified Public Accountants have been interwoven with the pertinent text discussions.

The book is divided into four parts:

    I. Basic Concepts and Methodology: Service and Merchandising Business
   II. Income Measurement and Valuation Problems Related to Sources and Uses of Invested Capital
  III. Financial Reporting: Analysis and Interpretive Problems
  IV. Cost Accumulation, Cost Control, and Financial Planning

Part I (Chapters 1–6) covers the basic accounting cycle, introduces the various ways of processing a mass of data, and includes a discussion of automatic data processing.

Part II (Chapters 7–16) covers short-term business financing; the accounting for cash; the measurement and control of receivables, inventory, and plant and equipment; contributed capital; and managerial and financial debt and investment decisions.

Part III (Chapters 17–18) covers corporate financial reporting and sources and uses of funds.

Part IV (Chapters 19–24) introduces cost accumulation and control for general merchandising operations, job order and process cost systems, standard costs and direct costing, cost control in managerial decisions, capital budgeting, and federal income taxes.

The end-of-chapter material is divided into five parts: (1) questions for class discussion, (2) short exercises, (3) class demonstration problems designed for the use of the instructor, (4) problems, and (5) case problems. The demonstration problems, averaging three to a chapter, exemplify the high lights of each chapter. The questions and exercises are designed for either class discussion or for outside assignment; they test the student's understanding of the chapter contents. The problems stress both theory and practice and are graded as to level of difficulty and approximate completion time. The case problems are also correlated to the chapter material but are set within a broader business background and furnish a specific business case situation for in-depth analysis and class discussion.

The optional self-study guide, by Virginia Nabors, C.P.A., not only tests the student's comprehension of the text, but also reduces the amount of class time required to cover the individual chapters. Self-testing quizzes and short exercises are included in the self-study guide as a supplementary aid to an understanding of the text discussions. Also available are working papers for the exercises and problems. A short practice set, complete with narrative and working papers, furnishes a review of the fundamentals established in Part I.

In the text, the selective use of color, the marginal notations underscoring accounting concepts, the chapter summaries, the comprehensive index, and the unusually wide-page margins greatly enhance the usefulness of the book to the student. The discussions and problems in the text and all the supplementary materials have been classroom tested over a sustained period by the authors.

The authors are indebted to the staff of Holt, Rinehart and Winston for their invaluable editorial assistance; to Dr. Willard E. Stone for his instructive and detailed criticism of the original manuscript; to Leon Ennis, C.P.A., who contributed many of the case problems; and to Miss Virginia Nabors, who prepared the objective quizzes. We also wish to thank our many students and colleagues, too numerous to name separately here, for their valuable comments and criticisms.

Boston, Massachusetts
Chapel Hill, North Carolina
January 1968

Albert Slavin
Isaac N. Reynolds
Lawrence H. Malchman

Contents

Preface   v

Part One   **Basic Concepts and Methodology:**
                  Service and Merchandising Businesses

Chapter One   The Accounting Equation and the Statement
              of Financial Position   3

Accounting and Its Functions   3
The Entity Concept   4
Assets   4
Equities: Liabilities and Owner's Equity   5
The Accounting Equation   5
The Statement of Financial Position   6
Summary   16

Chapter Two   Basic Methodology—Position Statement Accounts   25

Preparation of a Statement of Financial
         Position after Each Transaction   26
Expansion of the Accounting Equation   29
A Separate Page for Each Component of the Accounting Equation   30
Division of Separate Pages into Columns—Creation of Accounts   31
Tools of Accounting   34
Development of the General Journal and Posting   36
The Trial Balance   41
Procedures Applicable to a Single Proprietorship   42
Summary   43

ix

Chapter Three   Basic Methodology—
                     Income Statement Accounts   59
  Revenues   59
  Expenses   60
  Basic Operating Concepts   61
  Dividends   62
  Expanded Rules for Debits and Credits   63
  The General Ledger and Subsidiary Ledgers   64
  The Accounting Sequence   65
  Procedures Applicable to a Single Proprietorship   87
  Interrelationship of the Financial Statements   90
  Summary   91

Chapter Four   The End-of-Period Process   107
  Accounting Methods   107
  The Need for Adjusting Entries   108
  The Process of Recording Adjustments   109
  The Worksheet   119
  Recording the Adjustments in the General Journal   127
  The Result of Adjusting Entries   127
  Closing Entries Recorded Directly from the Worksheet   129
  The General Ledger   130
  The Post-Closing Trial Balance   134
  The Accounting Cycle   134
  The Purpose of Split Entries   136
  Analyzing the Financial Statements   137
  Equity Ratios   138
  Summary   138

Chapter Five   Merchandising—Determining and Interpreting
                     the Results of Operations   157
  Accounts for a Merchandising Business   157
  The Functions of the Merchandise Accounts   161
  Cost of Goods Sold and Gross Margin on Sales   164
  The Operating Expense Accounts   166
  Other Revenue and Other Expenses   166
  The Completion of the Worksheet   167
  The Completed Financial Statements   169
  Closing Entries   171
  Interim Financial Statements   171
  Managerial Ratio Analysis   172
  Uncollectible Accounts   176
  Cash Discounts—Implications to Management   177
  Trade Discounts   177
  Management Control—The Exception Principle   177
  Summary   179

Chapter Six Special Journals
and Automatic Data Processing Methods 197
Special Journals 198
Automatic Data Processing 217
Summary 222

Part Two **Income Measurement and Valuation Problems
Related to Sources and Uses
of Invested Capital**

Chapter Seven Short-Term Business Financing 247
Promissory Notes 247
Notes Receivable Financing Problem 257
Discounting Customers' Notes Receivable 262
Drafts 266
The Cost of Borrowing Money 268
Full Disclosure 269
Summary 270

Chapter Eight Controlling and Forecasting Cash 285
Internal Control 285
Management Controls—Cash Forecasts 296
Summary 299

Chapter Nine The Measurement and Control of Receivables 313
Sources and Classification of Receivables 313
Recognition of Losses on Uncollectible Accounts 314
Accounts Receivable—Managerial Analysis 324
Internal Control—Accounts Receivable 325
Summary 325

Chapter Ten The Measurement and Control of Inventory 339
The Importance of Inventory Valuation 339
The Basis of Inventory Valuation 340
Specific Identification Costing 348
Perpetual and Periodic Inventory Methods Compared 349
Inventory Valuation Methods Compared and Analyzed 350
Lower of Cost or Market (LCM) 352
Position Statement Disclosure—Inventory 355
The Gross Margin Method of Estimating Inventories 355
Retail Method of Estimating Inventories 357
Markon Computations 358
Consistency in the Application of Procedures 359
Inventory Control 359
Periodic Physical Inventories—Special Considerations 361
Summary 362

Chapter Eleven Plant and Equipment—Acquisition,
                    Depreciation, and Disposal   375

Cost of Plant and Equipment   375
Depreciation of Plant and Equipment   376
Depreciation Methods Compared—Management Considerations   383
Capital and Revenue Expenditures   384
Disposal of Plant and Equipment   385
Changing Depreciation Charges   390
Depletion of Natural Resources   391
Intangible Assets   392
Plant and Equipment—Managerial Analysis   393
Plant and Equipment Replacement—Management
        Considerations   395
Summary   396

Chapter Twelve Control of Cash Disbursements and Payroll   407

The Voucher System   407
The Role of Supporting Documents in the Accounting System   417
Managerial Control of Payroll   418
Summary   426

Chapter Thirteen Contributed Capital—Single Proprietorships,
                      Partnerships, and Corporations   441

Single Proprietorships   441
Partnerships   443
The Characteristics of a Corporation   450
Summary   464

Chapter Fourteen Dividends, Retained Earnings, and Treasury Stock   477

Contributed Capital   477
Revaluations   479
Retained Earnings   479
Dividends   481
Treasury Stock   489
Book Value of Capital Stock   492
Contributed Capital in the Statement of Financial Position   493
Summary   496

Chapter Fifteen Managerial Financial Decisions—Debt   509

Current Liabilities   509
Bonds Payable   510
Other Long-Term Liabilities   532
Summary   532

Chapter Sixteen Managerial Financial Decisions—Investments   545

Marketable Securities   545
Long-Term Investments   550

Managerial Analysis   556
Summary   557

Part Three   **Financial Reporting: Analysis
and Interpretive Problems**

Chapter Seventeen   Corporate Financial Reporting   567
Development of Financial Reporting to Outside Groups   567
Management Needs for Financial Data   568
The Purpose of Financial Statements   569
Interpretive Financial Statement Presentation   570
The Interpretation and Analysis of Financial Data   579
Financial Statement Analysis—Influences   590
Summary   590

Chapter Eighteen   Sources and Uses of Funds—Working Capital; Cash   611
Funds   611
The Funds Statement   611
The Funds Statement—Managerial Analysis   626
Alternative Definitions of Funds   627
Summary   631

Part Four   **Cost Accumulation, Cost Control,
and Financial Planning**

Chapter Nineteen   Cost Accumulation and Control—
General Manufacturing Operations   655
Raw Materials Used   655
Direct Labor   657
Manufacturing Overhead   658
Total Period Manufacturing Costs   661
The Work-in-Process Inventory   661
Finished Goods and Cost of Goods Sold   662
Manufacturing Summary   663
The Worksheet for a Manufacturing Company   665
Financial Statements   670
Manufacturing Accounting—Managerial Analysis   671
Summary   675

Chapter Twenty   Cost Accumulation and Control—Job Order
and Process Cost Systems   693
Cost Accounting Systems   693
General Accounting Compared with Cost Accumulation
for a Manufacturing Company   694
The Job Order Cost System   695
The Process Cost System   704
Summary   712

Chapter Twenty-One   Cost Accumulation and Control—
                        Standard Costs; Direct Costing   729
Standard Costs   729
Managerial Interpretation of Variances   738
Direct Costing   739
Summary   744

Chapter Twenty-Two   Special Cost Analysis and Control
                        in Management Decisions   755
Break-Even Analysis   756
Special Orders   764
Product Pricing   764
Deciding to Make or Buy   767
Department, Territory, or Product Abandonment   767
Summary   770

Chapter Twenty-Three   Capital Budgeting   783
Simple Interest   783
Compound Interest   783
Budgeting Capital Expenditures   788
Comparing Capital Expenditures   791
Limitations   798
Summary   799

Chapter Twenty-Four   Federal Income Taxes   807
The Federal Income Tax   807
The Individual Income Tax   808
The Partnership Informational Return   819
Corporate Income Taxes   819
Income Tax Planning   821
Differences between Business Income and Taxable Income   822
Financial Reporting Problems   823
Summary   824

Index   835

Part One

Basic Concepts and Methodology: Service and Merchandising Businesses

Chapter One

The Accounting Equation and the Statement of Financial Position

Accounting is the language of business; it provides the kinds of information that managers and other interested individuals must possess in order to make business decisions. Accounting is therefore of tremendous service to complex modern business.

Basic Accounting for Managerial and Financial Control is designed as an introduction to the field of accounting as a whole. The text starts with basic concepts and methodology; then shifts to specific data processing methods, income measurement, valuation problems related to the sources and uses of invested capital, and the analysis and interpretation of financial reports; and concludes with cost accumulation, cost control, and financial planning.

ACCOUNTING AND ITS FUNCTIONS

A basic methodology must rest upon sound philosophical postulates. Following the introduction and evaluation of a few technical terms, this chapter presents the classical model upon which the total methodological framework of accounting is built.

Accounting is typically defined rather narrowly as the process of recording changes, in terms of increases and decreases, in property and in the rights to property, and the analysis and interpretation of financial transactions. Specifically:

Accounting is the art of recording, classifying, and summarizing in a significant manner and in terms of money, transactions and events which are, in part at least, of a financial character, and interpreting the results thereof.[1]

---

[1] *Accounting Research and Terminology Bulletins,* Final Edition, 1961. New York: American Institute of Certified Public Accountants, Accounting Terminology Bulletin No. 1, "Review and Resumé," p. 9.

3

Recording means writing down, or *documenting*, business transactions, or exchanges of values, so that a complete record is available for presentation and interpretation.

Classifying is the process of arranging a large mass of data in a form useful to management. Classification of business data is accomplished in an orderly manner through the accounting system.

Summarizing is the process of reducing the total data arising from the activities of business into an understandable and useful amount of information. Summarizing involves the preparation of reports and statements from the classified data in which all important and material accounting information is disclosed.

Interpreting the results of operations is concerned with the explanation of the significance of the reports and statements to determine the financial position of the enterprise and the progress it has made. Comparisons of past and present statements, percentage analyses, and trend data are useful tools for this purpose.

A broader conception of accounting can be obtained by viewing its primary objectives. Accounting is a service mechanism with two basic functions: (1) to provide information about the stability and profitability of a business enterprise to all interested persons and (2) to protect the properties of the enterprise from errors in data and from misappropriations. The latter function is often called *internal control*.

THE ENTITY CONCEPT

In order to provide meaningful decision-making information about a business unit, the accountant must maintain a separate set of records for each business enterprise of an owner. The focal point of attention is not the owner but the *economic unit*, which has well-defined boundaries. For example, suppose that John Goodwin owns a grocery store, a hardware store, and a service station, and that in addition he has a car, a residence, some stocks and bonds, and other personal items of value. These are shown in a graphic form:

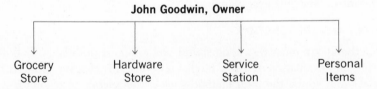

John Goodwin, Owner

| Grocery Store | Hardware Store | Service Station | Personal Items |

If the accountant's total attention is focused on John Goodwin, he may lose sight of the individual economic units. Thus, in this case, the accounting information for all Goodwin's activities lumped together is useless in making decisions for any single unit. ▶ In order to accomplish the accounting objectives mentioned in the preceding paragraph, a set of records must be provided for each of the individual business units, and the focal point of attention must be the individual unit rather than the owner. ◀ This is referred to as the *entity concept*.

Accounting Concept: Business Entity ◀

ASSETS

The *assets* of a business are everything of value found in the business. The word *value* is used here in the sense of future usefulness to a continuing business enterprise; it does not indicate the cost of replacing the asset or how much it would bring in if offered for sale. Cash, notes and accounts receivable (amounts owed to the business through transactions on credit), land, buildings, and high-grade, readily marketable stocks or bonds of other companies (*marketable securities*) are examples of assets in a business. An asset is recorded at its full cost even if it has not been fully paid for in cash; the amount of any debt or claim against the asset is shown as a *liability*.

EQUITIES: LIABILITIES AND OWNER'S EQUITY

The *equities* represent claims against, or rights in, the assets of a business. The two major classifications of individuals who have equities in a business are the *creditors* (liability holders) and the *owner*.

The liabilities of a business are everything owed to creditors. Liabilities represent the claims of the creditors of the business unit. *Accounts payable* and *notes payable*, which are amounts owed by the business through purchases on credit, are some liabilities that a business may have. Wages owed to employees is another example.

The *owner's equity* (*capital* and *proprietorship* are alternative terms) represents the proprietor's, the partners', or the stockholders' claims against the assets of a business, or the *excess* of all assets over all liabilities.

THE ACCOUNTING EQUATION

Since equities, by definition, represent the total claims against assets, then assets must equal equities. This relationship is shown:

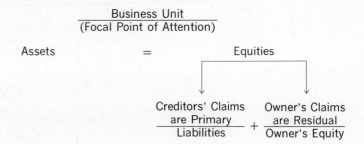

The equities of the unit are broken down into the *primary claims*, those of the creditors, and the *residual claims*, those of the owner. Since assets are derived primarily from these two sources, the truth of the equation is reinforced. The only remaining source is a *gift* of assets, which increases the owner's equity.

The following equation, then, is the *basic accounting equation*, which expresses the financial position of any business unit at all times.

Assets = Liabilities + Owner's Equity

Business assets owned equal sources of business assets. The equation must be modified slightly to indicate the particular kind of business organization: *single proprietorship, partnership,* or *corporation*. For example, in a corporation the equation would be:

Assets = Liabilities + Stockholders' Equity

and in a partnership the equation would be:

$$\text{Assets} = \text{Liabilities} + \text{Partners' Equity}$$

The various forms of business organization will be considered in more detail later in this chapter.

The equation may be restated for various analytical purposes in the following manner:

$$\text{Assets} - \text{Liabilities} = \text{Owner's Equity}$$

The use of this particular form of the equation will be discussed later.

The term *net assets* often is used in business; it may be expressed as follows:

$$\text{Total Assets} - \text{Total Liabilities} = \text{Net Assets}$$

The relationship expressed by the accounting equation is fundamental to the development of accounting records. ▶ In essence, bookkeeping is the process of ◀ recording changes in the terms of the equation during business operations. ◀

Accounting Concept:
Function of
Bookkeeping

THE STATEMENT OF FINANCIAL POSITION

The *statement of financial position,* or *position statement,* is an expression of the accounting equation. The statement of financial position summarizes the assets, liabilities, and owner's equity of a business unit as of a specific time. This statement is

Figure 1-1.
Account-Form Position Statement

ASSETS   =   LIABILITIES + STOCKHOLDERS' EQUITY

MURROW CLOTHING STORE
Statement of Financial Position
December 31, 1969

Assets			Liabilities and Stockholders' Equity		
Current Assets			Current Liabilities		
Cash	$ 325		Accounts Payable	$12,060	
Marketable Securities	1,900		Notes Payable	2,060	
Accounts Receivable	11,025		Accrued Wages		
Notes Receivable	2,520		Payable	970	
Merchandise Inventory	14,750		Total Current		
Prepaid Insurance	275		Liabilities		$15,090
Office Supplies	26		Long-Term Liabilities		
Store Supplies	89		Bank Loan Payable		
Total Current Assets		$30,910	(due June 1, 1972)	$ 4,000	
Plant and Equipment			Mortgage Payable	10,000	
Land	$ 3,000		Total Long-Term		
Building	10,000		Liabilities		14,000
Store Equipment	2,500		Total Liabilities		$29,090
Delivery Equipment	3,250		Stockholders' Equity		
Total Plant and			Capital Stock	$20,000	
Equipment		18,750	Retained Earnings	570	
			Total Stockholders'		
			Equity		20,570
			Total Liabilities and		
			Stockholders'		
Total Assets		$49,660	Equity		$49,660

often called a *balance sheet,* but the more descriptive term is used in this text. An *account form* of position statement is shown with the accounting equation on page 6.

A variant form of the same statement, the *report form,* is shown below. Both statements are good illustrations of the accounting equation.

Figure 1-2.
Report-Form Position Statement

MURROW CLOTHING STORE
Statement of Financial Position
December 31, 1969

Assets

Current Assets		
Cash	$ 325	
Marketable Securities	1,900	
Accounts Receivable	11,025	
Notes Receivable	2,520	
Merchandise Inventory	14,750	
Prepaid Insurance	275	
Office Supplies	26	
Store Supplies	89	
Total Current Assets		$30,910
Plant and Equipment		
Land	$ 3,000	
Building	10,000	
Store Equipment	2,500	
Delivery Equipment	3,250	
Total Plant and Equipment		18,750
Total Assets		$49,660

Liabilities and Stockholders' Equity

Current Liabilities		
Accounts Payable	$12,060	
Notes Payable	2,060	
Accrued Wages Payable	970	
Total Current Liabilities		$15,090
Long-Term Liabilities		
Bank Loan Payable (due June 1, 1972)	$ 4,000	
Mortgage Payable	10,000	
Total Long-Term Liabilities		14,000
Total Liabilities		$29,090
Stockholders' Equity		
Capital Stock	$20,000	
Retained Earnings	570	
Total Stockholders' Equity		20,570
Total Liabilities and Stockholders' Equity		$49,660

The heading of a statement of financial position usually contains three lines of information:

1. The name of the business
2. The name of the statement
3. The date of the statement

The date given in the example shows that it reveals the financial position of the firm as of the close of business on December 31, 1969.

Dollar signs are used on formal typed or printed statements at the top of each column of figures. A new column is created whenever a line is drawn for addition, subtraction, or other reasons. A double rule is drawn under any amount that is the final result of a series of calculations.

The Need for Classification in a Statement of Financial Position

Note that the assets and liabilities in the statement of financial position for the Murrow Clothing Store are *classified*. A financial statement should be classified so as to be of maximum value to an analyst, banker, creditor, employee, or other interested person; it can be made more easily understandable by the manner in which the items are arranged. The kind of classifications and the order of arrangement to be shown in the statement depend on tradition, the nature of the business activity, and the expected use of the document.

Classification of Assets—Current

Current assets consist of cash and other assets that are expected to be converted into cash and to be available for the operation of the business within one year. Current assets are usually listed in the order of their probable *liquidity*, or their expected conversion into cash. The current assets, listed in order of liquidity, of the Murrow Clothing Store are the following:

CASH. Cash is any item that a bank will accept as a deposit and that is immediately available and acceptable as a means of payment. Cash includes coins, currency, checks, bank drafts, money orders, and demand deposits in commercial banks.

MARKETABLE SECURITIES. Businesses that have a temporary excess of cash on hand and want to earn interest on it may buy promises to pay issued by other companies (usually referred to as *commercial paper*) or by governmental agencies or institutions (called *notes* or *bonds*). Many finance companies, for example, sell short-term notes that will usually mature within 60 days to six months. The United States government also issues short-term Treasury notes and certificates of indebtedness that are often acquired by businesses with excess cash to invest temporarily. Also, high-grade industrial bonds and stocks may be purchased as temporary investments.

ACCOUNTS RECEIVABLE. Accounts receivable represent the amounts due from customers for services rendered or for merchandise, or any asset, sold on credit terms (*open account*). A business with a limited number of customers could list them individually in the statement of financial position. If the debtors are numerous, however, the individual names are eliminated and the statement shows the total amount of accounts receivable in one figure. A record must be kept for each customer.

NOTES RECEIVABLE. A note receivable is a formal written promise by a customer to pay a fixed amount of money on demand or on a specific date. Since the note is usually transferable by endorsement to another party or to a bank, it represents an asset that can be converted readily into cash.

MERCHANDISE INVENTORY. Businesses that offer products for sale must have them readily available. All the merchandise on hand at any given moment is called the *merchandise inventory*. Merchandise inventories are found on retail store shelves and in stockrooms or warehouses.

PREPAID ITEMS. Prepaid items are current assets which have been acquired and not used up at the statement date. A physical inventory usually is taken of these assets at the statement date so that their cost may be shown. Some common prepaid items are described in the following paragraphs.

Prepaid Insurance. Every business must protect itself against hazards. Consequently, businesses take out insurance policies for protection. The cost of this type of security, which is listed on the statement, is called an insurance premium and is paid in advance. Insurance policies commonly are issued against such hazards as fire, burglary, personal injury, business interruption, and injury to employees (workmen's compensation).

Office Supplies. Supplies required in an office such as stamps, stationery, and typewriter and adding machine ribbons are grouped under the title Office Supplies and are current assets of the business.

Store Supplies. Store supplies include wrapping paper, twine, carbons, paper bags, and similar items used in a store. They are also classified as current assets.

No asset that will be used in the general operation of the business should be included in the merchandise inventory.

Classification of Assets—Plant and Equipment

Plant and equipment comprises assets used over a long period of time in the operation of the business. The caption "Equipment" may be used if the business does not own its land and building; that is, its *plant*. These assets are customarily listed on the statement of financial position according to the degree of permanency; the most permanent item is listed first. Some typical plant and equipment assets are the following:

LAND. Land is shown separately on the statement of financial position, although land and the buildings are usually sold together. Land and buildings are classified separately because the buildings will deteriorate through usage, whereas the land will not.

BUILDING. In order for the building to appear on the statement of financial position, it must be owned by the business.

STORE EQUIPMENT. Showcases, counters, and shelves are typical permanent items of store equipment used in selling the merchandise inventory.

DELIVERY EQUIPMENT. Delivery equipment consists of trucks and cars used for the delivery of products to the customer.

Classification of Liabilities—Current

The term *current liabilities* is used principally to designate obligations whose *liquidation* (payment or settlement) is reasonably expected to require the use of current assets or the creation (substitution) of other current liabilities.[2]

All liabilities to be paid within a one-year period are classified as current. In general, current liabilities are listed on the statement of financial position in their probable order of liquidation; those that, on the average, will be paid first are shown first, those to be paid next are next, and so on. Typical current liabilities are the following:

ACCOUNTS PAYABLE. Accounts payable represent amounts owed to creditors resulting from purchases on open account, or on credit. If creditors are few, their names may be listed separately on the statement of financial position. If creditors are numerous, the statement of financial position shows only the total amount of accounts payable. A separate record is kept for each creditor.

NOTES PAYABLE. A note payable is a formal written promise to pay money to a creditor for value received. A *trade note payable* arises from the purchase of merchandise or services used in the course of business. A note payable to a bank arises when a company borrows money from a bank for business use. Generally, these two items are *short-term* and are classified as current liabilities, unless the note is for more than one year.

ACCRUED LIABILITIES. Accrued wages payable and accrued interest payable are typical *accrued liabilities,* which are debts that are owed because of the passage of time but that will be paid in the future.

Classification of Liabilities—Long-Term

Debts that are not due for at least a year are called *long-term,* or *fixed,* liabilities. A mortgage payable is a typical long-term liability. If a part of a long-term liability is due within a year from the statement of financial position date, the amount of that part should be shown as a current liability.

---

[2] *Accounting Research and Terminology Bulletins,* Final Edition, 1961. New York: American Institute of Certified Public Accountants, Accounting Research Bulletin No. 43, pp. 21–22.

MORTGAGE PAYABLE. A mortgage payable is a debt owed by the business that is secured by a specific asset or assets. The legal document by which the debt is secured is called a *mortgage*. A business may arrange a long-term loan with a bank, for example, and give as security to the bank a mortgage on its land and building. If the business fails to meet the terms of payment of the mortgage, the bank can take necessary legal action to take possession of the asset, or to sell it and satisfy the mortgage claim from the proceeds of the sale. Any balance remaining from the sale of the asset reverts to the business.

BONDS PAYABLE. As a means of raising funds, corporations issue *bonds,* which are long-term promises to repay loans. These obligations may or may not be secured by assets of the borrowing company. Many corporations have excellent credit ratings and therefore do not need to offer specific security for loans.

Owner's Equity on the Statement of Financial Position

The form of a business organization determines the manner of reporting the owner's equity on the statement of financial position. The three common forms of business organizations are: (1) corporations, (2) single proprietorships, and (3) partnerships. The ownership interest in each of these organizational forms is disclosed in a slightly different manner on the statement of financial position.

A corporation is a separate legal entity, created by a *charter* from the state in which it is organized, that is owned by several *stockholders.* Each stockholder owns a certain portion of the corporation, expressed in *shares of stock. Stock certificates* are issued to him as evidence of his ownership. The *investments,* or contributions to the business, of all the stockholders are grouped under the term *capital stock.* Shares may be issued at *par,* which is the face value decided upon by the organizers and stated in the charter, or at a *premium* or *discount.*

The primary advantage of the corporate form of business to its owners is that the stockholders' personal assets cannot be taken by creditors to satisfy the debts of the business; only the assets of the business itself can be taken. There are also other significant legal advantages, which will be studied in later chapters. In turn, corporations are subject to special governmental regulation and taxation. The corporate form is the most important form of business ownership today; therefore, it is stressed throughout this text. Also, the use of the simple form of corporate ownership accentuates the entity concept of accounting. However, at the end of each introductory chapter the procedures applicable to the single proprietorship form of business organization are presented. Corporations and partnerships are discussed in detail in later chapters.

The profits of the corporation may be distributed to the stockholders in the form of *dividends,* or they may be retained in the corporation. The part that is kept is referred to as *retained earnings.* Retained earnings are not a part of the capital stock, but are a part of the total stockholders' equity. They represent the accumulated undistributed earnings of the corporation; that is, the total profits of the business from the date it was organized less the total dividends and losses that have been sustained during the same period. Retained earnings must be accounted for separately from the capital stock because of the legal restrictions placed upon the original capital contributions of corporations.

CORPORATION. The owners' equity section of a position statement for a corporation is shown:

Stockholders' Equity
    Capital Stock $20,000
    Retained Earnings   570
        Total Stockholders' Equity $20,570

SINGLE PROPRIETORSHIP. Many businesses are owned by individuals; they are referred to as *single proprietorships*. If a business is small and its operations are comparatively simple, the single-proprietorship form of ownership offers several advantages over the corporate form: The owner has a more direct control of the business, he does not have to report to several stockholders, and the business is not subject to the special regulations and taxes for corporations. But his personal assets can be taken as payment of the debts of the business. Of course, careful management will minimize the chances of such an event.

If Douglas Murrow owned the Murrow Clothing Store as a single proprietorship, his equity would be shown on the statement of financial position as follows:

Owner's Equity
    Douglas Murrow, Capital $20,570

The owner's equity for the single proprietorship is listed with the name of the proprietor, followed by the word "Capital." The total owner's equity may be shown as one item because there are no legal restrictions on withdrawals by a single proprietor as there are for the stockholders of a corporation.

PARTNERSHIP. Often several individuals find it advantageous to form a business by establishing a *partnership*. In this case, the owners are the *partners* of the business. The advantages of a partnership are similar to those of a single proprietorship, with the added advantages of a greater amount of capital from several partners and the different abilities that the partners can bring to the management of the business. The primary disadvantage of the partnership is that each partner is personally responsible for all the debts of the business.

If Douglas Murrow and John Wells owned the Murrow Clothing Store as partners, their equity would be shown on the statement of financial position as follows:

Partners' Equity
    Douglas Murrow, Capital $10,085
    John Wells, Capital   10,485
        Total Partners' Equity $20,570

Management Studies of the Statement of Financial Position

To provide information that will be of maximum assistance in decision making, an accountant must present financial data in a form and manner that make them meaningful and useful. The absolute amounts contained in the statement of financial position for the Murrow Clothing Store are quite useful to management, but they tell only part of the story. For example, a total current asset amount of $30,910 indicates a certain purchasing-power command over goods and services, but how adequate is this amount for the Murrow Clothing Store? The data begin to become more meaningful when they are compared with other related information of this or past years. The following relationships revealed by position statements are critical in making managerial decisions.

The Current Ratio

The relationship of current assets to current liabilities gives some indication of the firm's ability to pay its current debts as they mature. This relationship is called the *current ratio;* it is computed by dividing the current assets by the current liabilities. The current ratio of the Murrow Clothing Store is computed as follows:

Figure 1-3.

$$\frac{\text{Current Assets}}{\text{Current Liabilities}} = \frac{\$30,910}{\$15,090} = 2.05 \text{ to } 1$$

The Murrow Clothing Store has $2.05 of current assets for every $1 of current liabilities. This means that even if the current assets of the company were to shrink in value by as much as 50 percent, the short-term creditors could still be paid in full.

In the past, as a rule of thumb, a current ratio of 2 to 1 has been considered evidence of the satisfactory current financial condition of a company. Analysts, however, generally agree that no one ratio is sufficient and that certain other factors must be considered, such as the nature of the business, the season of the year, the composition of the specific items in the current assets category, and the quality of the management of the company.

Grantors of credit emphasize the relative convertibility of the current assets into cash. To illustrate, assume that the Amber Company and the Battle Company have the following current ratios:

	Amber Company	Battle Company
Current Assets		
Cash	$ 500	$ 2,000
Accounts Receivable	700	22,000
Merchandise Inventory	28,800	6,000
Total Current Assets	$30,000	$30,000
Current Liabilities		
Accounts Payable	$15,000	$15,000
Current Ratio	2:1	2:1

Although each company has a current ratio of 2 to 1, the Battle Company is apparently in a far better position to meet its obligations. The Amber Company first must sell its $28,800 merchandise inventory, then it must convert the resulting receivables into cash; or it can sell its inventory for cash as a single lot, probably for less than the stated value. The Battle Company has $24,000 in cash and receivables and only $6,000 in merchandise inventory, hence there is no conversion problem connected with the sale of inventory. The Amber Company thus may have a favorable current ratio but may be unable to pay its current liabilities due to an unfavorable distribution of the current assets.

Acid-Test Ratio

A supplementary test of the ability of a business to meet its current obligations is the acid-test ratio, which is expressed as follows:

$$\text{Acid-Test Ratio} = \frac{\text{Quick Assets}}{\text{Current Liabilities}}$$

Quick assets include only cash, readily marketable securities, and receivables. The acid-test ratio for the Murrow Clothing Store is computed as follows:

$$\frac{\text{Quick Assets}}{\text{Current Liabilities}} = \frac{(\$325 + \$1,900 + \$11,025 + \$2,520)}{\$15,090}$$

$$= \frac{\$15,770}{\$15,090}$$

$$= 1.05 \text{ to } 1$$

If the analyst is not satisfied with the current ratio as an indicator of liquidity, he may use the acid-test ratio, which does not consider merchandise inventory and prepaid items. If the quick assets are larger than the current liabilities (that is, if the acid-test ratio is better than 1 to 1), there is evidence of a strong credit position and assurance that the company is able to meet its currently maturing obligations.

Working Capital

A term frequently used in financial-statement analysis is *working capital*, or *circulating capital*. Working capital is the difference between the current assets and the current liabilities. The working capital of the Murrow Clothing Store is:

$$\text{Current Assets} - \text{Current Liabilities} = \text{Working Capital}$$
$$\$30,910 \quad - \quad \$15,090 \quad = \quad \$15,820$$

The business has an excess of $15,820 to use in operations after the current assets are converted into cash and the current liabilities are paid.

An interesting comparison may be made relative to working-capital analysis, assuming the following information:

	Line	Carson Company	Dickinson Company
Current Assets	(a)	$200,000	$800,000
Current Liabilities	(b)	100,000	600,000
Working Capital	(a − b)	$100,000	$200,000
Current Ratio	(a ÷ b)	2:1	1.33:1

The Dickinson Company has twice as much working capital as the Carson Company, but its debt-paying ability is not as satisfactory. The relationship between current assets and current liabilities may be more significant than their difference.

Working capital flows through the business in a regular pattern; this flow may be diagrammed as follows:

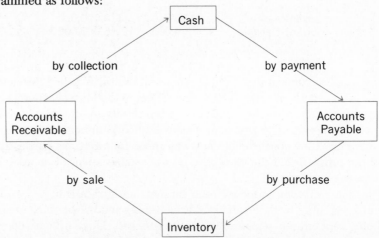

As funds flow into the business, the management of the Murrow Clothing Store must make decisions as to when, how much, and for what purpose the funds are to be used, or put back into the flow cycle. This is the point at which management must apply its skill in making effective use of available working capital.

Ratio Analysis—Limitations

A particular ratio may be satisfactory under one set of circumstances and entirely unsatisfactory under another set of circumstances. Ratios are in the nature of generalizations and reflect conditions that exist only at a particular time. The ratios change continually with the continuing operations of the business. Sole reliance on ratio analysis may at times give a misleading indication of financial condition. Often nonfinancial information must be analyzed in order to get a true picture, including the quality of the employees and employee-management relations. Understanding and correct interpretation of ratios, however, reduce the area over which subjective judgment must be exercised and thus aid the analyst in making sound decisions.

The ratios and comparisons discussed in this and subsequent chapters are valuable managerial aids, provided the user is aware of their limitations. The Murrow Clothing Store's current ratio of 2.05 to 1, computed in Figure 1-3, shows the relationship between two groups of items as of a given moment of time only. The ratio may fluctuate considerably during the course of the year. Furthermore, the ratio may have little meaning unless it is related to the entire business unit. It is like one small section of a painting, which has little meaning without the rest of the picture. If one states, for example, that Paul Clifford is an excellent student, we know very little about him. If we are told that he is 22 years of age, in the upper 5 percent of his class, president of Beta Gamma Sigma, and captain of the basketball team, we know a good deal more about him. Similarly, if we state that both the Atwater Company and the Excel Company have current ratios of 2 to 1, it does not mean too much, particularly if upon further investigation we find the following:

	Atwater Company	Excel Company
Current Assets	$10,000	$10,000,000
Current Liabilities	5,000	5,000,000

SUMMARY

Accounting is the process of recording the financial transactions of a business, classifying them in an orderly manner, summarizing them in the form of reports and statements useful to management, and interpreting the results and the significance of the statements and reports. The primary objectives of accounting are (a) to provide meaningful information about the business enterprise for interested parties and (b) to safeguard the properties of the enterprise by the establishment of an adequate and reliable system of accounting.

For data recording purposes, each business enterprise is to be considered a separate unit, or entity, with the affairs of the business and the personal affairs of the owners being kept entirely separate (the *entity concept*). Three primary components of the business entity about which accounting provides information are (a) *assets,* or the properties of the business, (b) *liabilities,* or the amounts that the business owes, and (c) *owners' equity,* or the claims that the owners have on the properties of the business.

The *accounting equation,* the fundamental model upon which accounting is built, states that assets equal equities. In an expanded form, this equation is referred to as the *statement of financial position,* or balance sheet, which summarizes the assets, liabilities, and owners' equity of a business entity at a specific point in time. To be of maximum use, the individual items reflected on this statement must be classified in an orderly and meaningful manner. Assets are generally classified as (a) *current assets,* or cash and other assets that will be converted to cash or will be consumed in the operations of the business within one year, and (b) *plant and equipment,* or physical assets that have a relatively long life and are used in the operation of the business. Liabilities are typically classified as (a) *current liabilities,* or obligations whose liquidation requires the use of a current asset or the creation of another current liability within a year, and (b) *long-term liabilities,* or obligations that are not due within the next year.

The three most common forms of business organization are *single proprietorships, partnerships,* and *corporations.*

For accounting information to be of maximum use, absolute amounts classified in a meaningful manner and analyses setting forth the significance of the information so classified must be provided. Three tools often used in analyzing accounting information are (a) the *current ratio,* which is computed by dividing the current assets by the current liabilities; (b) the *acid-test ratio,* which is computed by dividing the quick assets by the current liabilities; and (c) *working capital,* or the excess of current assets over current liabilities. These tools give some indication of the firm's ability to meet its current obligations as they mature.

☐ **QUESTIONS**

Q1–1. What are the major objectives of accounting?

Q1–2. What is the entity concept? Identify the ways in which this concept aids the accounting function.

Q1–3. Define and give three examples of each of the following terms:
   a. Assets
   b. Liabilities
   c. Owner's equity

Q1–4. What are current assets? Give five examples. In what order should these items be listed on the statement of financial position?

Q1–5. What is the purpose of the statement of financial position?

Q1–6. What is plant and equipment? Give five examples.

Q1–7. What are current liabilities? Give five examples.

Q1–8. Give the formula for:
   a. The current ratio
   b. The acid-test ratio
   c. Working capital

Q1–9. What is the major purpose of each item listed in Question 1–8?

Q1–10. On December 31, 1969, the Able Company had a current ratio of 3 to 1, and the Baker Company had a current ratio of 2 to 1. Is the Able Company in a better financial position to pay its accounts payable when they are due than the Baker Company is? Discuss.

☐ **EXERCISES**

E1–1. The books of the Ajax Company contain the following items:

Retained Earnings	$50,000
Cash	20,000
Capital Stock	75,000
Accounts Receivable	4,500
Accounts Payable	3,200
Prepaid Insurance	800

Select the current assets and prepare in good form the Current Assets section of the statement of financial position as of December 31, 1969.

E1–2. The books of the Barnes Company contain the following items:

Cash	$ 5,850
Land	10,000
John Barnes, Capital	100,000
Building	60,000
Bonds Payable (due July 1, 1989)	50,000
Delivery Equipment	10,000
Office Supplies	1,000

Select the plant and equipment items and prepare in good form the Plant and Equipment section of the statement of financial position as of December 31, 1969.

E1-3. The books of the Carson Company contain the following items:

Accounts Receivable	$ 3,420
Accounts Payable	2,860
Notes Receivable	1,950
Notes Payable	2,000
Accrued Wages Payable	1,230
Retained Earnings	42,680
Bonds Payable (due July 1, 1989)	30,000

Select the current liabilities and prepare in good form the Current Liabilities section of the statement of financial position as of December 31, 1969.

E1-4. The following condensed statement was prepared for the Dearborn Company as of December 31, 1969:

DEARBORN COMPANY

Statement of Financial Position

December 31, 1969

Assets

Current Assets	$ 20,000
Plant and Equipment	100,000
Total Assets	$120,000

Liabilities and Stockholders' Equity

Current Liabilities	$ 7,500
Long-Term Liabilities	20,000
Total Liabilities	$27,500
Stockholders' Equity	$ 92,500
Total Liabilities and Stockholders' Equity	$120,000

a. Compute: (1) the current ratio and (2) the working capital.

b. Explain the significance of each to management.

E1-5. Assume that the Dearborn Company (see Exercise E1-4) has the following current assets: cash, $2,000; marketable securities, $1,500; accounts receivable, $4,000; merchandise inventory, $10,000; and prepaid insurance, $2,500. Compute the acid-test ratio and explain its significance to management.

E1-6. Assume that a firm has total assets of $160,000 and total liabilities of $42,000 at the end of the year. Compute the owner's equity.

E1-7. Assume that a firm has current assets, $47,500; current liabilities, $15,500; long-term liabilities, $50,000; and stockholders' equity, $100,000 at the end of the year. Compute the amount of plant and equipment.

E1-8. Assume that a firm has the following items at the end of the year:

Total Assets	$300,000
Total Long-Term Liabilities	45,600
Capital Stock	100,000
Retained Earnings	32,500
Current Assets	50,000

Compute the amount of current liabilities.

E1–**9.** The following financial information is available for the Alberta Company as of December 31, 1969:

Marketable Securities	$10,000	Accounts Payable	$ 30,000
Accounts Receivable	40,000	Cash on Hand	2,000
Wages Payable	60,000	Cash in Bank	125,000
Buildings	60,000	Retained Earnings	?
Prepaid Insurance	1,000	Land	20,000
Inventories	80,000	Bonds Payable	150,000
Capital Stock	50,000		

Prepare a statement of financial position for the Alberta Company.

E1–**10.** The following statement of financial position was prepared by the bookkeeper of the Hoffman Company:

HOFFMAN COMPANY
Statement of Financial Position
For the Year Ending December 31, 1969

Assets

Current Assets		
Cash	$ 1,000	
Accounts Receivable	6,000	
Building	12,000	
Merchandise Inventory	3,000	
Total Current Assets		$22,000
Plant and Equipment		
Marketable Securities	$ 3,000	
Store Equipment	1,500	
Office Supplies	100	
Delivery Equipment	1,350	
Total Plant and Equipment		5,950
Total Assets		$27,950

Liabilities and Owner's Equity

Current Liabilities		
Accounts Payable	$ 5,600	
Notes Payable (due June 1, 1970)	2,000	
Notes Payable (due July 1, 1990)	1,000	
Total Current Liabilities		$ 8,600
Long-Term Liabilities		
Mortgage Payable (due May 1, 1991)	$ 8,000	
Accrued Wages and Salaries Payable	250	
Total Long-Term Liabilities		8,250
Total Liabilities		$16,850
Owner's Equity		
B. A. Hoffman, Capital		11,100
Total Liabilities and Assets		$27,950

List the errors in this statement.

☐ DEMONSTRATION PROBLEMS

DP1–**1.** (*Corporate account-form statement of financial position*) The following alphabetical list is taken from the records of the Johnson Company at December 31, 1969:

Accounts Payable	$ 25,000
Accounts Receivable	38,000
Building	300,000
Capital Stock	200,000
Cash	50,000
Delivery Equipment	40,000
Land	15,000
Merchandise Inventory	60,000
Mortgage Payable (due July 1, 1989)	180,000
Notes Payable	10,000
Notes Receivable	8,000
Prepaid Insurance	2,000
Retained Earnings	94,000
Wages Payable	4,000

Required: Prepare an account-form statement of financial position.

DP1–**2.** (*Liabilities and owner's equity—single-proprietorship statement of financial position*) Refer to Problem DP1–1. Assume that the Johnson Company is a single proprietorship, operated by John T. Johnson.

Required: Show how the right side of an account-form statement of financial position would appear.

DP1–**3.** (*Liabilities and partners' equity—partnership statement of financial position*) Again refer to Problem DP1–1. Assume that the Johnson Company is a partnership owned and operated by Ray M. Johnson and John T. Johnson, and that the two partners have equities as shown:

Ray M. Johnson	$120,000
John T. Johnson	174,000
Total	$294,000

Required: Show how the right side of the statement of financial position would appear.

DP1–**4.** (*Ratio analysis*) Using the data in Problem DP1–1, compute the current ratio, working capital, and acid-test ratio for the Johnson Company. Explain the significance of each to management.

☐ PROBLEMS

P1–**1.** On December 31, 1969, the assets, liabilities, and stockholders' equity of the Jason Company are as follows:

Assets (in alphabetical order)	
Accounts Receivable	$ 9,000
Building	50,000
Cash	20,000
Equipment	60,000
Land	10,000
Marketable Securities	45,000
Merchandise Inventory	20,000
Supplies	9,000

Liabilities (in alphabetical order)

Accounts Payable	10,000
Bonds Payable (due July 1, 1991)	45,000
Dividends Payable	4,000
Interest Payable	6,000

Stockholders' Equity

Capital Stock	150,000
Retained Earnings	?

Required: Prepare a properly classified account-form statement of financial position.

P1–2. The following is an alphabetical list of the assets, liabilities, and owner's equity of the Mitchell Company, a single proprietorship, as of December 31, 1969:

Accounts Payable	$ 5,500
Accounts Receivable	7,300
Building	100,000
Cash	65,000
Delivery Equipment	22,400
Land	10,600
Long-Term Notes Payable (due August 1, 1996)	75,000
Marketable Securities	4,800
Merchandise Inventory	33,500
Mortgage Payable (due March 1, 1981)	40,000
Notes Payable	5,250
Peter Mitchell, Capital	?
Prepaid Insurance	1,000
Salaries Payable	500

Required: Prepare a properly classified report-form statement of financial position.

P1–3. The following list contains all the current assets and current liabilities of the Lee Company as of December 31, 1969. The list also contains some noncurrent items.

Accounts Payable	$ 4,800
Accounts Receivable	7,200
Cash	10,500
Land	20,000
Marketable Securities	5,500
Merchandise Inventory	50,000
Mortgage Payable (due July 1, 1996)	75,000
Notes Payable (due July 1, 1970)	19,400
Prepaid Insurance	2,400
Salaries Payable	1,000

Required:

1. Compute the current ratio, the acid-test ratio, and the working capital.
2. Assume that you are the loan officer of a bank to which the Lee Company has applied for a 90-day loan of $15,000. Would you grant the loan? Why? Compute the current ratio, acid-test ratio, and working capital for the Lee Company immediately following the receipt of the loan.

P1–**4.** The following lists show selected statement totals for four different firms: A, B, C, and D. In each case, the amount is omitted for one total.

	A	B	C	D
Current Assets	$100,000	$ 72,000	$?	$ 20,000
Plant and Equipment	200,000	130,000	71,500	200,000
Current Liabilities	50,000	10,000	5,000	10,750
Long-term Liabilities	75,000	?	25,500	61,400
Capital Stock	175,000	50,000	100,000	?
Retained Earnings	?	20,000	6,500	10,850

Required: In each case, compute the missing figure.

P1–**5.** The assets, liabilities, and owner's equity of the Thomas Company as of December 31, 1969, are as follows:

Cash	$ 5,600
Accounts Receivable	15,200
Notes Receivable	3,000
Merchandise Inventory	5,600
Office Supplies	200
Prepaid Insurance	400
Store Equipment	3,500
Building	13,000
Land	5,000
Accounts Payable	10,000
Notes Payable	7,500
Mortgage Payable (due Feb. 1, 1982)	8,000
William J. Thomas, Capital	26,000

Required:

1. Prepare a report-form statement of financial position.
2. Compute the current ratio, the acid-test ratio, and the working capital.

CASE PROBLEM
Joseph Houston

Joseph Houston has been employed by small businesses such as grocery stores, drug stores, and service stations since his graduation from Central High School ten years ago. He has developed a good reputation among his various employers for his honesty, industriousness, and dependability. Many of his employers' customers have praised his friendliness, sincerity, and fairness in handling their transactions.

Houston has been nurturing the idea of having his own business; that dream is now materializing. He plans to lease a building and some equipment from Claude Wells. The building is on the outskirts of town but very near a developing middle-class residential area. Also, a relatively busy new highway, which connects the city with a nearby lake, is in front of the building. Houston believes that the building will be an excellent location for a combination service station, grocery, and soda fountain.

The building to be leased has adequate downstairs space for all the needs of the business, including a storage area. Also, the building contains a spacious five-room upstairs apartment that Houston plans to use as a home for his family of three (his wife and two children). A shady, grassy area is behind the building, and he plans to enclose it with a fence so that the children will have a safe place to play.

Houston has decided that the front of the building needs to be changed in order to make it more attractive and that the entire interior (downstairs and upstairs) needs painting. Since the building is made of brick, only the outside trim will require painting. All this work is to be performed by a local contractor.

The lease, which provides for the use of the building and lot, has a provision permitting the purchase of the premises or the renewal of the lease in five years. A deposit is required upon signing the lease and a fixed rental must be paid at the beginning of each month.

Much of the equipment needed by the service station and grocery is leased along with the building. However, arrangements must be made for supplementary equipment and for all the equipment for the soda fountain. Individual pieces of equipment may be either purchased or leased. Houston's preference is to purchase all the equipment if his personal savings and his available lines of credit permit.

Several years ago, Houston purchased an old pickup truck that he has used almost exclusively for fishing and hunting trips. In order to save money now, he plans to use this truck as needed in the operation of the service station. He will still use it for sporting trips when he can spare the time. Someday he hopes to buy a new truck for the station.

Houston's wife Alice has remarked about some of the advantages of their forthcoming living and working arrangements. She says it will be so much easier to get gas for the car and to have it serviced that she will surely not forget these needs as she usually does. Also, she will save time and money when shopping for groceries. It will be very convenient for the children to get ice cream and drinks, as all they will need to do is to go downstairs. She also plans to let one of the service station mechanics clean the children's yard occasionally when business at the station is slack. Alice also plans to help by working in the store for two or three hours each day, or whenever she is needed.

In view of the encouragement he has received from neighbors and the flow of automobile traffic in the area, Houston expects a large amount of business. Consequently, he plans to hire two employees to attend the service station during each of the two 8-hour shifts (7 AM to 11 PM). More will be hired when the need arises. The remainder of the business will be open from 9 AM to 7 PM; in the beginning he expects to employ one cashier, one stock attendant, one grocery attendant, and one soda-fountain attendant. He and Alice plan to work wherever they are needed, except that Alice will not work in the service station area. Houston will also supervise the entire business.

Required:

1. Identify the meaning of the entity concept.
2. Identify and discuss the relevance of this concept to Joseph Houston's plans.
3. Discuss the problems regarding the entity concept that Houston will undoubtedly encounter.
4. Of the expenditures that Houston will make while organizing and operating his business, which are properly classifiable as business expenditures and which as personal expenditures? Explain why you classified each one as you did.
5. Suggest some ways of resolving the difficulties or problems that you identified in Requirement 3.

Chapter Two
Basic Methodology— Position Statement Accounts

To obtain the data needed to prepare statements of financial position, an orderly accounting system must be developed. This chapter describes several possible systems, leading up to a discussion of the one in general use in modern business.

In this and the following two chapters, *service businesses*, which sell services rather than merchandise, will be used as examples. Service businesses are good first illustrations of the operation of an accounting system because they do not offer the added complications of the inventories required in *merchandising businesses*.

All businesses go through a period of organization, during which the owners make an investment, acquire plant and equipment, and get ready to operate. The transactions involved in the organization of the Whitside Realty Corporation follow.

1969

July 1 The Whitside Realty Corporation was organized by John Whitside, Ronald Raymond, and James Baker. The charter (proper legal authorization) was received from the Secretary of State, and capital stock in the amount of $50,000 was issued at par (sold for face amount) for cash; that is, the stockholders—Whitside, Raymond, and Baker—made an investment of $50,000 in the business. Whitside invested $40,000; Raymond, $6,000; and Baker, $4,000.

5 Purchased land and building for $30,000 in cash. The land was appraised at $5,000; the building, at $25,000.

10 Purchased furniture on account from the Jones Company for $8,000.

20 Paid the Jones Company $5,000 on account.

25 The Corporation found that part of the furniture was not of the type that it wanted. It sold furniture that had cost $1,800 to James Hill for $1,800 on account. Hill promised to pay this amount in thirty days.

31 Collected $1,000 from James Hill on account.

The following discussion is based on these transactions.

PREPARATION OF A STATEMENT OF FINANCIAL POSITION
AFTER EACH TRANSACTION

Since the statement of financial position is an expanded variation of the accounting equation, it is obvious that the total of the separate sides are always equal. A possible solution to the problem of accumulating data is the preparation of a statement of financial position immediately after each transaction.

Issuance of Capital Stock

The statement of financial position shown in Figure 2-1 would be prepared after the three stockholders incorporate their business and the capital stock of $50,000 is issued. (In this chapter, the account form of position statement is used to show the effect of each transaction on each side of the accounting equation.)

WHITSIDE REALTY CORPORATION
Statement of Financial Position
July 1, 1969

Assets		Liabilities and Stockholders' Equity	
Current Assets		Stockholders' Equity	
(+) Cash	$50,000	(+) Capital Stock	$50,000

Figure 2-1.
After Original Investment

This transaction involves an increase of an asset, Cash, accompanied by an increase in a stockholders' equity item, Capital Stock. The plus and minus signs show the direction of change of each item in the transaction; *they would not be part* of an actual statement.

Purchase of Land and Building

A statement of financial position prepared after the land and building are purchased appears in Figure 2-2.

WHITSIDE REALTY CORPORATION
Statement of Financial Position
July 5, 1969

Assets			Liabilities and Stockholders' Equity	
Current Assets			Stockholders' Equity	
(−) Cash		$20,000	Capital Stock	$50,000
Plant and Equipment				
(+) Land	$ 5,000			
(+) Building	25,000			
Total Plant and Equipment		30,000		
Total Assets		$50,000	Total Stockholders' Equity	$50,000

Figure 2-2.
After Purchase of Land and Building

This transaction involves increases of assets, Land and Building, accompanied by a decrease of an asset, Cash, with no change occurring in the stockholders' equity.

Purchase of Furniture on Account

The statement prepared after the Corporation purchases furniture on account from the Jones Company is shown in Figure 2-3.

WHITSIDE REALTY CORPORATION
Statement of Financial Position
July 10, 1969

Assets			Liabilities and Stockholders' Equity	
Current Assets			Current Liabilities	
Cash		$20,000	(+) Accounts Payable	$8,000
Plant and Equipment			Stockholders' Equity	
Land	$ 5,000		Capital Stock	50,000
Building	25,000			
(+) Furniture	8,000			
Total Plant and Equipment		38,000	Total Liabilities and	
Total Assets		$58,000	Stockholders' Equity	$58,000

Figure 2-3.
After Purchase of Furniture on Account

This transaction involves an increase of an asset, Furniture, accompanied by an increase of a liability, Accounts Payable, with no change occurring in the stockholders' equity.

Payment of Accounts Payable

The statement of financial position appearing in Figure 2-4 is prepared after the Corporation pays $5,000 in cash to the Jones Company on account:

WHITSIDE REALTY CORPORATION
Statement of Financial Position
July 20, 1969

Assets			Liabilities and Stockholders' Equity	
Current Assets			Current Liabilities	
(−) Cash		$15,000	(−) Accounts Payable	$ 3,000
Plant and Equipment			Stockholders' Equity	
Land	$ 5,000		Capital Stock	50,000
Building	25,000			
Furniture	8,000			
Total Plant and Equipment		$38,000	Total Liabilities and	
Total Assets		$53,000	Stockholders' Equity	$53,000

Figure 2-4.
After Partial Payment of Accounts Payable

The transaction reflected in this statement involves a decrease of a liability, Accounts Payable, accompanied by a decrease of an asset, Cash.

Sale of Furniture on Account

After the Corporation sells the furniture on account to James Hill, the statement of financial position shown in Figure 2-5 is prepared:

WHITSIDE REALTY CORPORATION
Statement of Financial Position
July 25, 1969

Assets			Liabilities and Stockholders' Equity	
Current Assets			**Current Liabilities**	
Cash	$15,000		Accounts Payable	$ 3,000
(+) Accounts Receivable	1,800			
Total Current Assets		$16,800	**Stockholders' Equity**	
			Capital Stock	50,000
Plant and Equipment				
Land	$ 5,000			
Building	25,000			
(−) Furniture	6,200			
Total Plant and Equipment		36,200	Total Liabilities and	
Total Assets		$53,000	Stockholders' Equity	$53,000

Figure 2-5. *After Sale of Furniture on Account*

1. The amount of money to be received from James Hill is reflected as an asset, Accounts Receivable. It is a current asset since it is collectible within a year.

2. This transaction involves an increase of an asset, Accounts Receivable, accompanied by a decrease of an asset, Furniture. It is similar in nature to the transaction of July 5 (Figure 2-2).

3. The furniture was sold at cost. If it had been sold at a price above its cost, a stockholders' equity item, Retained Earnings, would have been increased by the amount of the gain.

Collection of Accounts Receivable

After James Hill makes a payment of $1,000, the statement of financial position shown in Figure 2-6 is prepared.

WHITSIDE REALTY CORPORATION
Statement of Financial Position
July 31, 1969

Assets			Liabilities and Stockholders' Equity	
Current Assets			**Current Liabilities**	
(+) Cash	$16,000		Accounts Payable	$ 3,000
(−) Accounts Receivable	800		**Stockholders' Equity**	
Total Current Assets		$16,800	Capital Stock	50,000
Plant and Equipment				
Land	$ 5,000			
Building	25,000			
Furniture	6,200			
Total Plant and Equipment		36,200	Total Liabilities and	
Total Assets		$53,000	Stockholders' Equity	$53,000

Figure 2-6.
After Collection of Accounts Receivable

As in the preceding illustration, this transaction involves an increase of an asset, Cash, accompanied by a decrease of an asset, Accounts Receivable.

The method of accumulating accounting data illustrated thus far gives the desired results, but in most instances the time and expense involved would prohibit its use. In addition, a statement of financial position prepared after each transaction is not needed by those who use accounting information as a guide to action. A statement of financial position prepared at the end of each month is usually sufficient.

EXPANSION OF THE ACCOUNTING EQUATION

Since the procedure described in the foregoing section is cumbersome, a better methodology is called for. Using the basic accounting equation, developed in Chapter 1, it is possible to show how each transaction will affect the statement of financial position and yet have all six of the transactions combined in one document. In Figure 2-7, the balances are brought down after each transaction and form an equation from which a formal statement similar to Figure 2-6 could be prepared.

Figure 2-7.
*Expanded Accounting
Equation*

WHITSIDE REALTY CORPORATION
Expanded Accounting Equation Revealing Financial Position
For Month Ended July 31, 1969

Date	Business Transaction	Cash	+	Accounts Receivable	+	Land	+	Building	+ Furniture =	Accounts Payable	+ Capital Stock
								Assets		= *Liabilities* +	*Stockholders' Equity*
1969 July 1	Issued capital stock for $50,000 in cash.	+$50,000								=	+$50,000
5	Purchased land and building for $30,000 in cash. Land is appraised at $5,000; building, at $25,000.	−30,000				+$5,000		+$25,000			
	Balances	$20,000 +				$5,000 +		$25,000		=	$50,000
10	Purchased furniture on account from the Jones Company for $8,000.								+$8,000 =	+$8,000	
	Balances	$20,000 +				$5,000 +		$25,000 +	$8,000 =	$8,000 +	$50,000
20	Paid the Jones Company $5,000 on account.	−5,000								−5,000	
	Balances	$15,000 +				$5,000 +		$25,000 +	$8,000 =	$3,000 +	$50,000
25	Sold furniture at cost to James Hill for $1,800 on account.			+$1,800					−1,800		
	Balances	$15,000 +		$1,800 +		$5,000 +		$25,000 +	$6,200 =	$3,000 +	$50,000
31	Collected $1,000 from James Hill on account.	+1,000		−1,000							
	Balances	$16,000 +		$ 800 +		$5,000 +		$25,000 +	$6,200 =	$3,000 +	$50,000

After each transaction, the total of the Asset columns equals the total of the Liabilities and Stockholders' Equity columns. For example, after the July 25 transaction, the asset total of $53,000 ($15,000 + $1,800 + $5,000 + $25,000 + $6,200) equals the liabilities and stockholders' equity total of $53,000 ($3,000 + $50,000). A formal statement of financial position could be prepared from Figure 2-7 after the July 31 transaction by simply arranging the various assets, liabilities, and stockholders' equity items in the form illustrated in Figure 2-6.

Although this method tends to shorten the accounting process, it is unsuitable for most companies because it cannot easily be expanded to provide for a large number of asset and liability items. For example, it would be virtually impossible to use this procedure in a company that has 50 assets and 25 liabilities.

A SEPARATE PAGE FOR EACH COMPONENT OF THE ACCOUNTING EQUATION

An answer to the problem of an expanded number of assets and liabilities is to designate a separate page for each asset, liability, and stockholders' equity item. Using the six transactions of the Whitside Realty Corporation, this method may be illustrated as follows:

ASSET PAGES

	Cash	Page 101

1969		
July 1	Contribution of stockholders	+ $50,000
5	Purchase of land and building	− 30,000
20	Payment to Jones Company on account	− 5,000
31	Collection from James Hill	+ 1,000
	(Cash on hand $16,000)	

	Accounts Receivable (James Hill)	Page 111

1969		
July 25	Sold furniture on account	+ $1,800
31	Collection on account	− 1,000
	(Balance due $800)	

	Land	Page 151

1969		
July 5	Purchase of land	+ $5,000

	Building	Page 152

1969		
July 5	Purchase of Building	+ $25,000

Furniture	Page 157

1969	
July 10 Purchase of furniture on account	+ $8,000
20 Sale of furniture at cost	− 1,800
(Furniture on hand $6,200)	

LIABILITY PAGES

Accounts Payable (Jones Company)	Page 201

1969	
July 10 Purchased furniture on account	+ $8,000
20 Payment on account	− 5,000
(Balance due $3,000)	

STOCKHOLDERS' EQUITY PAGES

Capital Stock	Page 251

1969	
July 1 Issued capital stock to three stockholders	+ $50,000

A comment about the page numbering system should be made. The pages could be numbered 1, 2, 3, 4, 5, 6, 7; but if the numbers are to have a specific meaning —for example, 100–199 for assets, 200–249 for liabilities, and 250–299 for stockholders' equity items—and if expansion is contemplated (the insertion of new pages for new items), then the numbering system should be something like the one shown.

At the end of a designated period, the *balance*, or final amount, of each page may be obtained by adding the plus items and the minus items and subtracting the total of the minus items from the total of the plus items. These balances can then be arranged as a formal statement of financial position as shown in Figure 2-6.

This procedure does permit unlimited expansion, but the use of the plus and minus signs contributes to mathematical errors, and there is no economical way to run a mathematical check on the accuracy of the items contained in the accounting equation. Something else needs to be done to the system.

DIVISION OF SEPARATE PAGES INTO COLUMNS—CREATION OF ACCOUNTS

A possible solution to the problem is the division of the pages, referred to in accounting as *accounts*, into two sections by drawing a line down the middle of the page and using both sides to record financial information pertaining to the particular item for which the account is maintained. The accounting equation

Assets = Liabilities + Stockholders' Equity

suggests the following arrangement: Assets appear on the left side of the equation; therefore, the left side of the account is used to record increases of assets, and the opposite side, the right side, is used to record decreases. Similarly, since liabilities and the stockholders' equity appear on the right side of the accounting equation, the right side is used to record increases in liability and stockholders' equity accounts, and the opposite side, the left side, is used to record decreases.

A diagram of this kind of account is shown:

			Account Title				Account Number	
Date	Explanation	Amount	Date		Explanation	Amount		
	Use this side to record increases in assets and decreases in liability and stockholders' equity items.				Use this side to record decreases in assets and increases in liability and stockholders' equity items.			

Again using the six transactions of the Whitside Realty Corporation, the added feature of the accounting system is demonstrated. Before the information is placed in the accounts, each transaction is analyzed in the light of the foregoing suggestions for recording the information.

1969

July 1 The Whitside Realty Corporation was organized and capital stock was issued for cash in the amount of $50,000. Cash, an asset, is increased by $50,000, and Capital Stock, a stockholders' equity item, is likewise increased. The $50,000 is placed on the left side of the asset account, Cash, to indicate that it has been increased, and the same figure is placed on the right side of the Stockholders' Equity account to indicate that it also has been increased.

5 Purchased land and building for $30,000 in cash. The land was appraised at $5,000; the building, at $25,000. Both land and building are assets; thus, the $5,000 and the $25,000 are placed on the left sides of the Land and Building accounts, respectively, to reflect increases. The Cash account is decreased by $30,000; thus, this amount is placed on the right side of the Cash account.

10 Purchased furniture on account from the Jones Company for $8,000. The asset Furniture is increased by $8,000; this amount is placed on the left side of the Furniture account. A liability account, Accounts Payable, is increased by the amount due the Jones Company; $8,000 is placed on the right side of the Accounts Payable account to indicate that it has been increased.

20 Paid the Jones Company $5,000 on account. The liability Accounts Payable is decreased and the asset Cash is also decreased. The $5,000 is placed on the left side of the Accounts Payable account to record the decrease; the same figure is placed on the right side of the asset account, Cash, to reflect the decrease.

25 Sold furniture that cost $1,800 to James Hill for $1,800 on account. The asset Accounts Receivable is increased by $1,800 and the asset Furniture is decreased by $1,800. The increase in the asset Accounts Receivable is shown by placing the amount on the left side of the Accounts Receivable account; and the decrease in the asset Furniture is shown by placing the amount on the right side of the Furniture account.

31 Collected $1,000 from James Hill on account. The asset Cash is increased by $1,000; the asset Accounts Receivable is decreased by $1,000. The increase of the asset Cash is

shown by placing the $1,000 on the left side of the cash account; the decrease of the asset Accounts Receivable is shown by placing the $1,000 on the right side of the Accounts Receivable account.

These transactions would appear in the accounts as shown:

Cash   Acct. No. 101

Date		Explanation	Amount	Date		Explanation	Amount
1969				1969			
July	1	Issuance of Capital Stock	50,000	July	5	Purch. of land & bldg.	30,000
	31	Collection from Hill	1,000		20	Payment to Jones Co.	5,000
		(16,000)	51,000				35,000

Accounts Receivable (James Hill)   Acct. No. 111

Date		Explanation	Amount	Date		Explanation	Amount
1969				1969			
July	25	Sold furn. on acct.	1,800	July	31	Collection on acct.	1,000
		(800)					

Land   Acct. No. 151

Date		Explanation	Amount	Date		Explanation	Amount
1969							
July	5	Purchase land	5,000				

Building   Acct. No. 152

Date		Explanation	Amount	Date		Explanation	Amount
1969							
July	5	Purchased building	25,000				

Furniture   Acct. No. 157

Date		Explanation	Amount	Date		Explanation	Amount
1969				1969			
July	10	Purchased furn. on acct.	8,000	July	25	Sold furn. on acct.	1,800
		(6,200)					

Account Payables (Jones Company)   Acct. No. 201

Date		Explanation	Amount	Date		Explanation	Amount
1969				1969			
July	20	Paid on acct.	5,000	July	10	Purch. furn. on acct.	8,000
						(3,000)	

	Capital Stock				Acct. No. 251	
Date	Explanation	Amount	Date		Explanation	Amount
			1969 July	1	Issued for cash	50,000

After all the information is recorded, the accounts are *footed;* that is, each amount column containing more than one entry is totaled in small pencil figures under the last amount on each side—see how the Cash account is handled. Then the balance of each account is determined by subtracting the smaller amount from the larger; the balance is then placed in the Explanation column of the side with the larger amount. As a check on the accuracy of the work in relation to the accounting equation, the total of the balances on the left sides of the accounts is compared to the total of the balances on the right sides. If the totals agree, it is presumed that the accounting is correct up to this point. This listing of account balances is called a *trial balance,* illustrated in Figure 2-8.

WHITSIDE REALTY CORPORATION
Trial Balance
July 31, 1969

Acct. No.	Account Title	Left-Side Balances	Right-Side Balances
101	Cash	$16,000	
111	Accounts Receivable	800	
151	Land	5,000	
152	Building	25,000	
157	Furniture	6,200	
201	Accounts Payable		$ 3,000
251	Capital Stock		50,000
	Totals	$53,000	$53,000

Figure 2-8.
Trial Balance

After the trial balance is found to be correct, a statement of financial position similar to Figure 2-6 can be prepared.

TOOLS OF ACCOUNTING

Before the final stage of the basic accounting methodology is discussed, the following accounting tools should be considered:

1. The T account
2. Debits and credits
3. The formal account

The T Account

The simplest form of any account is called a T account because of its shape. Owing to its simplicity, this form best clarifies the effects of transactions on a given account.

As indicated in the preceding section, each account consists of a left side and a right side, with the title of the account written across the top. The left side of an account is called the *debit* side, and the right side of an account is called the *credit* side.

Account Title

DEBIT (left side)	CREDIT (right side)

The terms debit and credit originally had a more specific meaning, related to *debtor* and *creditor* accounts; today they may be used as nouns, verbs, or adjectives depending upon whether one is talking about an amount on the left side (*a debit*) or right side (*a credit*), the process of placing an amount on the left side (*to debit*) or the right side (*to credit*), or the characteristics of information on the left side (*a debit entry*) or the right side (*a credit entry*).

Substituting the terms debit and credit for the longer analytical description in the preceding section, the following rules may be stated:

Debit to record:	Credit to record:
an increase of an asset	a decrease of an asset
a decrease of a liability	an increase of a liability
a decrease in the stockholders' equity	an increase in the stockholders' equity

The relationship of the rules of debit and credit to the statement of financial position and to the accounting equation may be illustrated as follows:

Assets (Property Owned by a Business)			Liabilities (Creditors' Claims to Assets)			Stockholders' Equity (Owners' Claims to Assets)	
Debit Increase	Credit Decrease	=	Debit Decrease	Credit Increase	+	Debit Decrease	Credit Increase

The abbreviation for credit is *Cr.;* for debit it is *Dr.*

The Formal Ledger Account

In actual business practice, the T account is expanded to a formal *ledger account.* A ledger account is a statistical device used for sorting accounting information into homogeneous groupings; it typically consists of two sides, with columns on each side for (1) the date, (2) an explanation, (3) the page number of the source from which the amount was transferred (called the *folio column*), and (4) the amount. A standard form of the ledger account is shown; the folio column is indicated by an F.

				Cash			Acct. No. 101	
Date	Explanation	F	Debit	Date	Explanation	F	Credit

A variation of the T form is the three-money-column form, with Debit, Credit, and Balance columns. After each entry, the balance of the account may be computed and entered in the Balance column. This form is useful when frequent reference is made to the balance of the account.

A three-money-column account form is shown:

				Cash			Acct. No. 101
Date	Explanation	F	Debit	Credit	Balance

The book that contains all the accounts of a business is called the *ledger*.

DEVELOPMENT OF THE GENERAL JOURNAL AND POSTING

In the preceding sections of this chapter, the six transactions of the Whitside Realty Corporation were analyzed in terms of their effect on asset, liability, and stockholders' equity accounts, and the information was entered directly into the accounts. Records can be kept in this manner; however, most businesses need more detailed information as well as a means of ensuring a properly functioning and systematic procedure for the recording of transactions. The desired additional information includes a chronological record of transactions and a complete history of each transaction recorded *in one place*. It is often necessary to view a transaction in its entirety, including reference to the underlying documents and supporting papers. Since every entry consists of at least one debit and one credit, the transaction is recorded on different ledger pages. If the ledger contains many accounts, it may be difficult to reconstruct the complete transaction.

The recording process is commonly divided into two parts:

1. *Journalizing*, or recording transactions in a book called a *journal*. The record of a transaction in the journal is called a *journal entry*.

2. *Posting*, or transferring amounts in the journal to the correct accounts in the ledger.

Entering Transactions in the Journal

The following entry, in the basic form of a journal, the *general journal,* shows the July 1 transaction of the Whitside Realty Corporation:

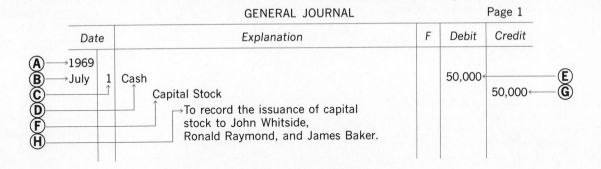

(A) The year is written in small figures at the top of the Date column. It should be written in that position on every page of the journal.

(B) The month of the first transaction recorded on this page is entered. It is not necessary to write the month again on this page unless it changes.

(C) The day of each transaction is entered.

(D) The title of the account debited is placed in the Explanation column against the date line. In order to eliminate confusion, it is important that the account title written in the journal entry should be the exact title of the account as it appears in the ledger.

(E) The amount of the debit is entered in the Debit money column.

(F) The title of the account credited is indented approximately one-half inch from the Date column.

(G) The amount of the credit is entered in the Credit money column.

(H) The explanation is entered on the next line, indented an additional one-half inch. The explanation should contain all the essential information as well as a reference to the source document from which the information was obtained—inspection report, receiving report, checkbook, and so on. (Since source documents are not illustrated in the first part of this text, the explanations of the illustrative journal entries do not always contain references to such documents.)

Posting from the General Journal

It should be emphasized that the journal does not *replace* the ledger account. The journal is called a *book of original entry* because it is necessary first to journalize the transaction and then to post to the proper accounts in the ledger (the *book of final entry*).

Figure 2-9 illustrates the posting of the July 1 entry from the general journal of the Corporation to its ledger. Posting normally should be done once a day.

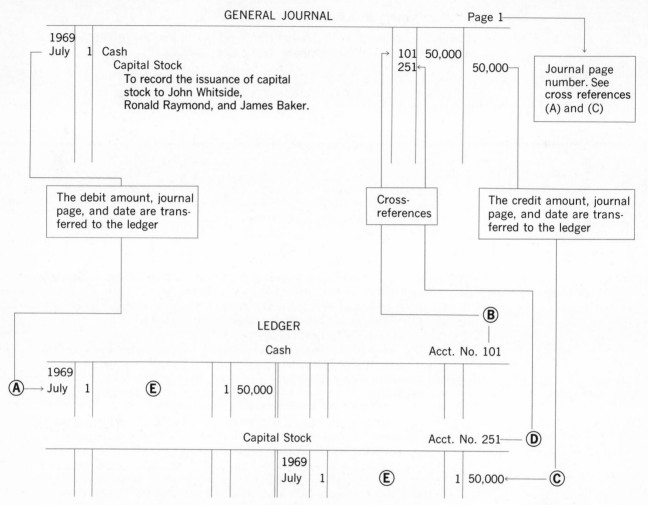

Figure 2-9.
Posting Flow Chart

Ⓐ The debit amount, $50,000; the journal page, 1; and the date, July 1, are entered on the debit side of the Cash account in the ledger. The year, 1969, is written at the top of the Date column. Dollar signs are not used in journals or ledgers.

Ⓑ The ledger account number for the debit entry, 101, is entered in the folio (F) column of the journal to cross-reference the journal and ledger.

Ⓒ The credit amount, $50,000; the journal page, 1; and the date, July 1, are entered on the credit side of the Capital Stock account in the ledger. The year, 1969, is written at the top of the Date column.

Ⓓ The ledger account number for the credit entry, 251, is entered in the folio column of the journal to complete the cross-referencing. It follows that the cross-reference in the journal also indicates that the posting to the ledger has been completed.

Ⓔ It should be observed that explanations are not usually used in the Explanation columns of the ledger accounts. The cross-reference to the journal page from which the information was recorded permits any interested individual to quickly find a complete story of the transaction. Short explanations are used in the ledger accounts only when it is deemed that they will be especially useful in particular transactions.

The Accounting Sequence for the Whitside Realty Corporation

The stage of accounting methodology used in actual practice is illustrated with the six transactions of the Whitside Realty Corporation. The steps in the accounting sequence are:

1. Journalizing
2. Posting
3. Preparing a trial balance
4. Preparing a statement of financial position

JOURNALIZING. The six transactions of the Whitside Realty Corporation appear in the general journal as follows:

GENERAL JOURNAL   Page 1

1969					
July	1	Cash	101	50,000	
		Capital Stock	251		50,000
		To record the issuance of capital stock to John Whitside, Ronald Raymond, and James Baker.			
	5	Land	151	5,000	
		Building	152	25,000	
		Cash	101		30,000
		To record purchase of land and building for cash.			
	10	Furniture	157	8,000	
		Accounts Payable—Jones Company	201		8,000
		To record purchase of furniture on account.			
	20	Accounts Payable—Jones Company	201	5,000	
		Cash	101		5,000
		To record payment on account.			
	25	Accounts Receivable—James Hill	111	1,800	
		Furniture	157		1,800
		To record sale of furniture at cost on account.			
	31	Cash	101	1,000	
		Accounts Receivable—James Hill	111		1,000
		To record collection on account.			

POSTING. The transactions are posted from page 1 of the general journal to the ledger accounts shown. The cross-references are entered in both the journal and the accounts.

LEDGER

Cash — Acct. No. 101

Date			Ref	Amount	Date			Ref	Amount
1969					1969				
July	1		1	50,000	July	5		1	30,000
	31	16,000	1	1,000		20		1	5,000
				51,000					35,000

Accounts Receivable—James Hill — Acct. No. 111

Date			Ref	Amount	Date			Ref	Amount
1969					1969				
July	25	800	1	1,800	July	31		1	1,000

Land — Acct. No. 151

Date			Ref	Amount	Date			Ref	Amount
1969									
July	5		1	5,000					

Building — Acct. No. 152

Date			Ref	Amount	Date			Ref	Amount
1969									
July	5		1	25,000					

Furniture — Acct. No. 157

Date			Ref	Amount	Date			Ref	Amount
1969					1969				
July	10	6,200	1	8,000	July	25		1	1,800

Accounts Payable—Jones Company — Acct. No. 201

Date			Ref	Amount	Date			Ref	Amount
1969					1969				
July	20		1	5,000	July	10	3,000	1	8,000

Capital Stock — Acct. No. 251

Date			Ref	Amount	Date			Ref	Amount
					1969				
					July	1		1	50,000

After all the journal entries are posted, the accountant foots each account as shown.

The system under discussion is called *double-entry accounting* because it requires that each record of a transaction have debits and credits of equal amount. Every transaction does not necessarily have a single debit and a single credit. For example, the July 5 entry of the Corporation involves two debits totaling $30,000 and one credit of $30,000. This is called a *compound entry*. Regardless of the number of accounts debited and credited in a single transaction, the total amount of all the debits and the total amount of all the credits must be equal. It follows that the totals of the debit and credit balances in all the accounts must also be equal.

THE TRIAL BALANCE

As stated previously, it is customary to prepare a trial balance to test the equality of the debit and credit balances in the ledger before a formal statement of financial position is prepared. The July 31, 1969, trial balance of the Whitside Realty Corporation is shown:

WHITSIDE REALTY CORPORATION
Trial Balance
July 31, 1969

Acct. No.	Account Title	Debits	Credits
101	Cash	$16,000	
111	Accounts Receivable	800	
151	Land	5,000	
152	Building	25,000	
157	Furniture	6,200	
201	Accounts Payable		$ 3,000
251	Capital Stock		50,000
	Totals	$53,000	$53,000

Although the trial balance proves the equality of debits and credits, this does not mean that the accounting is always proved to be correct. A full transaction could be omitted, the debit and credit amounts of an entry could be identically incorrect, a wrong account could be debited or credited, or both the debit and credit amounts for a given transaction could be posted twice. However, if the trial balance is in balance, the accountant considers this strong presumptive evidence of accuracy and proceeds from that point.

The trial balance is useful to the accountant in preparing periodic financial statements. The accountant could prepare a statement of financial position directly from the accounts, as was done in a previous stage, but the trial balance furnishes a convenient summary of the information used in the preparation of the statement of financial position.

If a trial balance does not balance, the following steps should be followed in the indicated sequence to locate the error.

1. Find the difference between the trial balance totals.
2. Examine the trial balance for balances that may be in the wrong column.
3. Re-add the trial balance columns.
4. Check the trial balance figures against those appearing in the ledger to see whether the amounts correspond and whether they have been entered in the proper columns.
5. Check the additions on each side of each ledger account and recompute the balances.
6. Check postings from journal to ledger.

The trial balance may not balance because of a single error. Time and effort may be saved by applying the following special tests after Step 1:

1. Errors in the amount of $0.01, $0.10, $1, $10, $100, and so on, may be due to errors in addition or subtraction.
2. If the trial balance difference is divisible by 2, the error may be due to a debit amount entered as a credit amount, or vice versa.
3. If the trial balance difference is divisible by 9 or 99, the error may be due to a transposition of figures ($83.41 posted as $38.41) or a slide ($1.05 posted as $105.00).

Statement of Financial Position

The next step in the accounting sequence is the preparation of the formal statement of financial position for the Whitside Realty Corporation (Figure 2-10). Note that Figure 2-10 is the same as Figure 2-6.

WHITSIDE REALTY CORPORATION
Statement of Financial Position
July 31, 1969

Assets			Liabilities and Stockholders' Equity	
Current Assets			Current Liabilities	
Cash	$16,000		Accounts Payable	$ 3,000
Accounts Receivable	800		Stockholders' Equity	
Total Current Assets		$16,800	Capital Stock	50,000
Plant and Equipment				
Land	$ 5,000			
Building	25,000			
Furniture	6,200			
Total Plant and Equipment		36,200	Total Liabilities and	
Total Assets		$53,000	Stockholders' Equity	$53,000

Figure 2-10.
Formal Statement of Financial Position

PROCEDURES APPLICABLE TO A SINGLE PROPRIETORSHIP

Many of small service businesses are single proprietorships. Among these are professional offices conducted by doctors, lawyers, accountants, engineers, and so on. The only difference between the single-proprietorship form of business organization and that of the corporation relative to the example of the Whitside Realty Corporation is the investment by the owners. If John Whitside had created a single-proprietorship form of realty business and had invested $50,000 in cash, the following journal entry would have been made:

GENERAL JOURNAL   Page 1

1969					
July	1	Cash		50,000	
		John Whitside, Capital			50,000
		To record investment by proprietor to form a realty business to be called the Whitside Realty Company.			

All the other entries would be recorded in the same way regardless of the form of business organization. The statement of financial position prepared at July 31, 1969, for the Whitside Realty Company, a single proprietorship, would be similar to Figure 2-10 with the exception of the owner's equity section, which would appear as follows:

Owner's Equity
John Whitside, Capital $50,000

SUMMARY

To fulfill the function of providing timely and meaningful information to management and other interested parties, accounting must provide an effective system for recording the various business transactions and for summarizing these transactions in useful statements and reports.

Since each business transaction has an effect on the statement of financial position, a new statement could be prepared after each transaction. This method is costly and inefficient. The use of an expanded accounting equation to accumulate data from which a statement of financial position can be prepared at the appropriate time is impractical because of the number of accounts normally maintained by a concern. Separate pages maintained for asset, liability, and owner's equity items permit unlimited expansion but the process is susceptible to arithmetical errors. An *account*, formed by dividing a page into two sections by a vertical line, is a device for recording the increases and decreases in an individual asset, liability, or owner's equity item in a systematic and orderly manner. The left side of an account is called the *debit* side and the right side is called the *credit* side. A debit entry records an increase in an asset account or a decrease in a liability or owner's equity account. A credit entry records a decrease in an asset account or an increase in a liability or owner's equity account. A book that contains a group of accounts is referred to as a *ledger*.

Because of the difficulty of recreating transactions when they are recorded only in accounts, each transaction is first listed in chronological order in a book of original entry called a *journal*. After an entry is recorded in the journal, each debit and credit amount is transferred from the journal to the related account in the ledger, a process known as *posting*. After all the entries for a specified period are recorded in the journal and posted to the ledger accounts, the balances of the accounts are computed and listed on a *trial balance*, which is a check of the equality of the debit and credit balances in the ledger. A statement of financial position can then be easily prepared from the trial balance.

The only difference between the single proprietorship and the corporation relative to the transactions discussed is the recording of the investment by the owners. In a corporation, the investment is credited to Capital Stock, whereas in the single proprietorship it is credited to the proprietor's capital account.

☐   **QUESTIONS**

Q2–**1.** What is a business transaction? Give eight examples.

Q2–**2.** In practice, why is a statement of financial position not prepared after the occurrence of each transaction?

Q2–**3.** What is the difference between the terms *debit* and *credit*?

Q2-**4.** What is the function of (a) the general journal? (b) the ledger?

Q2-**5.** A balanced trial balance is a correct trial balance. Discuss.

Q2-**6.** Robert Hanson purchased furniture on account from the Jones Company. Hanson debited the Furniture account for $800, and erroneously credited the Accounts Receivable account for $800.

    a. What effect would the error have on the debit and credit total of the trial balance taken at the end of the period?

    b. What accounts in the trial balance would be incorrectly stated?

Q2-**7.** What does the term *ledger account* mean? Indicate two forms of the account. State the reasons and circumstances for using each form.

Q2-**8.** Why are statements of financial position classified as to assets and liabilities?

Q2-**9.** Give an example of a transaction that would result in:

    a. An increase of an asset accompanied by an increase in the owner's equity.

    b. An increase of an asset accompanied by an increase of a liability.

    c. An increase of an asset accompanied by a decrease of an asset.

    d. A decrease of an asset accompanied by a decrease of a liability.

☐ **EXERCISES**

E2-**1.** The Batson Corporation engaged in the following transactions during the first week of operations:

1969

May   1   Issued capital stock at par to the four incorporators for $20,000 in cash.

       3   Purchased office equipment from Black and Sons for $4,000 on account.

       5   Purchased land for a future building site at a cost of $20,000; paid $5,000 down and issued a mortgage note payable in ten years for the balance.

Prepare a classified account-form statement of financial position after each transaction.

E2-**2.** The following T accounts were taken from the ledger of the Ritson Company:

Cash

1969		1969	
June 20	25,000	June 23	4,000
		30	2,000
		30	16,000

Marketable Securities (U.S. Treasury Notes)

1969			
June 30	2,000		

Office Supplies

1969		
June 23	4,000	

Land

1969		
June 30	5,000	

Building

1969		
June 30	15,000	

Mortgage Payable

	1969	
	June 30	4,000

Capital Stock

	1969	
	June 20	25,000

Analyze these accounts and describe each transaction.

E2-3. The following transactions are among those of the Philips Corporation for 1969:

1969

Nov. 2   The Philips Corporation was incorporated and capital stock with a par value of $90,000 was issued for cash.

8   Purchased a plot of land for $15,000 in cash.

11   Purchased a cabin at a nearby location and moved it to the land owned by the Corporation. The cabin will serve as a business office. The total cash paid by the Corporation was $6,000.

30   Invested $4,000 in marketable securities (U.S. government bonds).

Journalize the transactions and post to ledger accounts. (Assign appropriate numbers to accounts.)

E2-4. The following statements of financial position were prepared immediately following each of three transactions engaged in by the Catwaller Company:

CATWALLER COMPANY
Statement of Financial Position
July 1, 1969

Assets		**Owner's Equity**	
Current Assets		Owner's Equity	
Cash	$25,000	John Catwaller, Capital	$25,000

CATWALLER COMPANY
Statement of Financial Position
July 3, 1969

Assets			**Liabilities and Owner's Equity**	
Current Assets			Long-Term Liabilities	
Cash		$19,000	Mortgage Payable	$49,000
Plant and Equipment			Owner's Equity	
Land	$ 5,000		John Catwaller, Capital	25,000
Building	50,000			
Total Plant and Equipment		55,000		
Total Assets		$74,000	Total Liabilities and Owner's Equity	$74,000

CATWALLER COMPANY
Statement of Financial Position
July 5, 1969

Assets			**Liabilities and Owner's Equity**	
Current Assets			Current Liabilities	
Cash	$19,000		Accounts Payable	$ 1,000
Office Supplies	1,000		Long-Term Liabilities	
Total Current Assets		$20,000	Mortgage Payable	49,000
Plant and Equipment			Total Liabilities	$50,000
Land	$ 5,000		Owner's Equity	
Building	50,000		John Catwaller, Capital	25,000
Total Plant and Equipment		55,000		
Total Assets		$75,000	Total Liabilities and Owner's Equity	$75,000

Date and describe each transaction.

E2-5. The following are among the transactions of the Ace Corporation:

1969

Dec. 1 Capital stock of $9,000 par value was issued for cash.

    4 Purchased land for $6,000 in cash.

8   Purchased marketable securities (U.S. government bonds) for $1,500 in cash.

14   Purchased service supplies from White & Son Company for $515 on account.

18   Sold the land for $6,000 in cash.

31   Paid $515 to White & Son Company on account (provide account numbers).

Journalize the transactions, post to T accounts, and prepare a trial balance. (Assign appropriate numbers to accounts.)

E2-6. The following trial balance was prepared by the Jay Deuce Company. The trial balance is not in balance and the accounts are not in the proper order, but the account balances are correct.

JAY DEUCE COMPANY
Trial Balance
December 31, 1969

Account Title	Debits	Credits
Cash	$50,000	
Jay Deuce, Capital		$ 75,000
Accounts Payable	10,000	
Notes Payable	5,000	
Land		4,000
Building		60,000
Accounts Receivable		7,000
Notes Receivable		6,000
Service Supplies	3,000	
Mortgage Payable		40,000
Totals	$68,000	$192,000

1. Prepare a corrected trial balance showing the accounts in proper order.
2. Prepare a classified report-form statement of financial position.

E2-7. The Roger McGrath Company had the following ledger accounts at November 30, 1969:

Cash		Acct. No. 101
50,000		3,000
400		1,000
		2,500

Notes Receivable		Acct. No. 112
1,500		400

Service Supplies		Acct. No. 161
4,000		1,500

Land		Acct. No. 151
10,000		

Accounts Payable		Acct. No. 201
2,500		7,000
		3,000

Roger McGrath, Capital		Acct. No. 251
		50,000

1. Compute the account balances.
2. Prepare a trial balance.
3. Prepare an account-form statement of financial position.

E2–8. The following transactions were engaged in by the Carolina Corporation.

1969

Feb. 1 Received a charter and issued all authorized capital stock at par for $100,000 in cash.

2 Purchased land and buildings for $10,000 in cash and a 20-year mortgage payable for $50,000. The land was appraised at $8,000 and the building at $52,000.

3 Purchased service supplies from the Belk Company for $4,000 on account.

28 Sold a portion of the lot purchased on February 2 for its approximate cost

of $3,500. The buyer, the Gulf Sands Company, paid $1,200 in cash and issued a 90-day note for $2,300.

1. Journalize the transactions.
2. Post to formal ledger accounts. (Assign appropriate numbers to accounts.)
3. Take a trial balance.
4. Prepare a classified account-form statement of financial position.

☐ **DEMONSTRATION PROBLEMS**

DP2-**1.** (*Development of an accounting system—corporation*) The following transactions occurred at the Eagle Company during its first month of operations:

1969

March 1 Received a corporate charter and issued all its authorized stock for $75,000 in cash.

2 Purchased land and building for $40,000. The Company paid $10,000 in cash and issued a 20-year mortgage payable for the balance. The land was appraised at $12,000 and the building at $28,000.

3 Purchased furniture from the Garwood Company for $7,500 on account.

15 Paid the Garwood Company $2,500 on account.

20 Sold a portion of the land purchased on March 2 at its approximate cost of $4,500 to the Hill Realty Company on account.

31 Received $2,000 in cash and a 90-day note for $2,500 from the Hill Realty Company.

Required:

Using these six transactions, illustrate the five stages discussed in the text:

1. Prepare a statement of financial position after each transaction.
2. Record the transactions in an expanded accounting equation.
3. Record the transactions on separate pages, not divided.
4. Record the transactions on separate pages, divided into Debit and Credit columns.
5. Journalize the transactions, post to formal ledger accounts, take a trial balance, and prepare a classified account-form statement of financial position.

DP2-**2.** (*Transactions peculiar to single proprietorships*) Assume that the Eagle Company in Problem DP2-1 is a single proprietorship owned and operated by Robert Eagle.

Required: Which transactions would be different under this assumption? Journalize the transactions.

DP2-**3.** (*Development of an accounting system—single proprietorship*) Dr. Thomas Eastman prepared to open a dental office and engaged in the following transactions:

1969

July 1 Opened a bank account, under the business name of Dr. Thomas B. Eastman, in the amount of $30,000.

2 Purchased land and building for $20,000. Paid $5,000 in cash and issued a 10-year mortgage payable for the balance. The land was appraised at $3,500; the building, at $16,500.

3 Purchased dental equipment and furniture from the Perro Company for $7,500 on account.

12 Dr. Eastman wrote a check on his personal bank account (not his business account) for $2,500 in part payment of the Perro Company account.

15 It was discovered that part of the furniture purchased on July 3 was not satisfactory for his office needs, so Dr. Eastman sold it on account to an attorney, Samuel Shaffner, at its cost of $1,000.

31 Received $800 from Shaffner on account.

Required:

Using these six transactions, illustrate the five stages discussed in the text.

1. Prepare a statement of financial position after each transaction.
2. Record the transactions in an expanded accounting equation.
3. Record the transactions on separate pages, not divided. (Number pages.)
4. Record the transactions on separate pages, divided into Debit and Credit columns.
5. Journalize the six transactions, post to formal ledger accounts, take a trial balance, and prepare a report-form statement of financial position.

☐ PROBLEMS

P2–1. The transactions of the newly organized Services, Inc., for the week of April 1 to 6, 1969, are given:

1969

April 1 Received a charter and issued all its authorized capital stock at par for $100,000 in cash.

2 Purchased land and building at a cost of $90,000. Paid $20,000 in cash and issued a 20-year mortgage payable for the balance. The land is appraised at $18,000; the building, at $72,000.

3 Purchased furniture for $2,000 from the Comfort Chair Company on account.

4 Purchased office supplies (stationery, stamps, and envelopes) for $800 in cash.

5 Some of the furniture was found to be defective and was returned to the Comfort Chair Company. The account was reduced by $350.

6 Paid the balance due the Comfort Chair Company.

Required:

Prepare a classified statement of financial position after each transaction.

P2–2. Successive statements of financial position for the Hill Clinic are given after each of six transactions.

HILL CLINIC
Statement of Financial Position
August 1, 1969

Assets		**Liabilities and Owner's Equity**	
Current Assets		Owner's Equity	
Cash	$65,000	Benjamin Hill, Capital	$65,000

HILL CLINIC
Statement of Financial Position
August 2, 1969

Assets			**Liabilities and Owner's Equity**	
Current Assets			Long-Term Liabilities	
Cash		$ 58,000	Mortgage Payable	$ 43,000
Plant and Equipment			Owner's Equity	
Land	$ 7,500		Benjamin Hill, Capital	65,000
Building	42,500	50,000	Total Liabilities and	
Total Assets		$108,000	Owner's Equity	$108,000

HILL CLINIC
Statement of Financial Position
August 3, 1969

Assets			**Liabilities and Owner's Equity**	
Current Assets			Current Liabilities	
Cash	$58,000		Accounts Payable	$ 3,000
Medical Supplies	3,000	$ 61,000	Long-Term Liabilities	
Plant and Equipment			Mortgage Payable	43,000
Land	$ 7,500		Total Liabilities	$ 46,000
Building	42,500	50,000	Owner's Equity	
			Benjamin Hill, Capital	65,000
			Total Liabilities and	
Total Assets		$111,000	Owner's Equity	$111,000

HILL CLINIC
Statement of Financial Position
August 4, 1969

Assets			**Liabilities and Owner's Equity**	
Current Assets			Current Liabilities	
Cash	$58,000		Accounts Payable	$ 3,000
Notes Receivable	1,500		Long-Term Liabilities	
Medical Supplies	3,000	$ 62,500	Mortgage Payable	43,000
Plant and Equipment			Total Liabilities	$ 46,000
Land	$ 6,000		Owner's Equity	
Building	42,500	48,500	Benjamin Hill, Capital	65,000
			Total Liabilities and	
Total Assets		$111,000	Owner's Equity	$111,000

HILL CLINIC
Statement of Financial Position
August 5, 1969

Assets			**Liabilities and Owner's Equity**	
Current Assets			Current Liabilities	
Cash	$58,000		Accounts Payable	$ 1,000
Notes Receivable	1,500		Long-Term Liabilities	
Medical Supplies	3,000	$ 62,500	Mortgage Payable	43,000
Plant and Equipment			Total Liabilities	$ 44,000
Land	$ 6,000		Owner's Equity	
Building	42,500	48,500	Benjamin Hill, Capital	67,000
			Total Liabilities and	
Total Assets		$111,000	Owner's Equity	$111,000

HILL CLINIC
Statement of Financial Position
August 7, 1969

Assets			**Liabilities and Owner's Equity**	
Current Assets			Current Liabilities	
Cash	$59,500		Accounts Payable	$ 1,000
Medical Supplies	3,000	$ 62,500	Long-Term Liabilities	
Plant and Equipment			Mortgage Payable	43,000
Land	$ 6,000		Total Liabilities	$ 44,000
Building	42,500	48,500	Owner's Equity	
			Benjamin Hill, Capital	67,000
			Total Liabilities and	
Total Assets		$111,000	Owner's Equity	$111,000

Required:

Study the successive statements of financial position to determine what transactions have occurred. Prepare a list of these transactions, giving the date and description of each.

P2-3. The following account numbers and titles were designed for the Hawaii Car Rental System, a single proprietorship:

101	Cash
111	Accounts Receivable
120	Land
130	Building
140	Automobiles
150	Office Equipment
300	Accounts Payable
310	Notes Payable
500	Charles Newsome, Capital

During the first month of operation the following transactions occurred:

1969

Jan. 1   Newsome deposited $90,000 in cash in a bank account in the name of the business, Hawaii Car Rental System, a single proprietorship.

3   Purchased land for $5,000 and a building on the lot for $30,000. A cash payment of $15,000 was made, and a promissory note was issued for the balance.

4   Purchased 15 new automobiles at $2,300 each from the Allied Motor Company. A down payment of $20,000 in cash was made; the balance was promised to be paid in 30 days.

5   Sold one automobile to one of the Company's employees at cost. The employee paid $1,000 in cash and agreed to pay the balance within 30 days.

6   One automobile proved to be defective and was returned to the Allied Motor Company. The amount due was reduced by $2,300.

11   Purchased a cash register and office desks for $1,850 in cash.

31   Paid $6,000 in cash to the Allied Motor Company on account.

Required:

1. Journalize the transactions.
2. Post to T accounts (provide account numbers).

P2–4. The transactions listed are those of the Sanders Company, which was organized on January 1, 1969.

1969

Jan. 1   Capital stock with a par value of $20,000 was issued for cash.

4   Purchased land for $4,000 in cash.

6   Purchased repair parts from George Wilson for $1,000 on account.

8   Purchased a more suitable piece of land for $5,000 in cash.

11   Sold the land acquired on January 4 for $4,000. The buyer, Peter Lorence, agreed to pay for the land within 10 days.

19   Paid George Wilson $1,000 on account.

20   Received $4,000 from Peter Lorence.

27   Purchased additional repair parts for $700 in cash.

31   Invested $3,000 in cash in marketable securities (U.S. government bonds).

Required:

1. Journalize these transactions.
2. Post to ledger accounts. (Assign numbers to accounts.)
3. Prepare a trial balance.

P2–5. The Grant Stenographic Service, a newly formed company owned and operated by Arthur Grant, plans to provide typing, duplicating, and stenographic services to the tenants of the office building it owns and to other clients. The ledger accounts as of October 31, 1969, are not in the proper order.

Cash		Land	
65,000	53,200	10,000	
	1,500		
	450		
	1,050		
	300		
	125		

Office Supplies		Accounts Payable	
100		125	435
450		110	110

Maintenance Supplies		Mortgage Payable	
500			50,000
435			

Prepaid Insurance		Arthur Grant, Capital	
1,500			64,700

Machine		Delivery Equipment	
20,000		1,050	

Building		Office Equipment	
72,000		600	

Required:

1. Determine the account balances and prepare a trial balance as of October 31, 1969, in the proper order.
2. Prepare a statement of financial position.

P2-6. The Baxter Garage was incorporated on March 20, 1969. During the first several days of operations, its part-time bookkeeper (a high school student who had a few months' instruction in bookkeeping) recorded the transactions and rendered the following unbalanced trial balance as of March 31, 1969:

BAXTER GARAGE
Trial Balance
March 31, 1969

Account Title	Debit	Credit
Accounts Payable	$ 8,550	
Accounts Receivable		$10,000
Building	50,000	
Capital Stock	75,000	
Cash	15,500	
Furniture	6,000	
Land		12,000
Marketable Securities		9,600
Mortgage Payable		20,000
Notes Payable	10,350	
Notes Receivable		8,000
Service Supplies	2,800	
Totals	$168,200	$59,600

Required:

1. Assuming that the amounts are correct but that the bookkeeper did not understand the proper debit-credit position of some accounts, prepare a trial balance showing the accounts in correct statement of financial position order.
2. Prepare a report-form statement of financial position.

P2-**7.** The Booker Corporation has been operating for a period of years. In September 1969 the accountant of the company disappeared, taking the records with him.

You are hired to reconstruct the accounting records, and with this in mind you make an inventory of all company assets. By checking with banks, counting the materials on hand, investigating the ownership of buildings and equipment, and so on, you develop the following information as of October 31, 1969:

Account Title	Balance
Land	$15,000
Equipment	25,000
Buildings	20,000
Accounts Receivable	10,000
Marketable Securities	5,000
Inventories	14,000
Cash on Hand	3,000
Cash in Banks	53,000

Statements from creditors and unpaid invoices found in the office indicate that $40,000 is owed to trade creditors. There is a $10,000 long-term mortgage (30 years) outstanding.

Interviews with the board of directors and a check of the capital stock record book indicate that there are 1,000 shares of capital stock outstanding and that the stockholders have contributed $30,000 to the corporation. No record is available regarding past retained earnings.

Required: Prepare a trial balance and a statement of financial position as of October 31, 1969.

P2–**8.** Accounts included in the trial balance of the Weil Brocher Company as of September 30, 1969, were as follows:

Acct. No.	Account Title	Balance
101	Cash	$14,215
111	Accounts Receivable	11,785
150	Office Supplies	1,220
200	Land	?
250	Building	?
300	Furniture and Fixtures	8,000
350	Machines	60,000
400	Delivery Equipment	3,210
600	Accounts Payable	3,750
650	Notes Payable	25,000
700	Taxes Payable	103
800	Weil Brocher, Capital	?

Land and building were acquired at a cost of $30,000. It was determined that one-third of the total cost should be applied to the cost of land.

The following transactions were completed during the month of October:

1969

Oct. 2 Paid in full a liability of $110 to the Dupont Company.

3 Collected in full an account receivable of $670 from the Riverside Mills Corporation.

4 Purchased office supplies from the Philip Corporation for $400 on account.

8 Brocher made an additional investment of $16,000 in cash in the business.

10 Collected $1,000 from the Johnson Company on account.

11 Purchased a machine from the New Business Machine Company for $22,000; a cash payment of $2,000 was made, the balance to be paid within 30 days.

15 Paid in full a liability of $400 to the Pace Company.

20 Paid $10,000 in cash to the New Business Machine Company in partial settlement of the liability of October 11. Issued a note payable for the balance.

31 Collected in full an account receivable of $300 from the Durham Company.

Required:

1. Journalize these transactions.
2. Transfer the balances of September 30, 1969, to ledger accounts, post the October entries, and determine the new balances.
3. Prepare a trial balance as of October 31, 1969.
4. Prepare a statement of financial position.
5. Compute the following:
   a. Working capital
   b. Current ratio
   c. Acid-test ratio

CASE PROBLEM
Precision Recordkeepers, Inc.

William Jackson has completed the arrangements for opening a new business, Precision Recordkeepers, Inc., an electronic data processing (EDP) center. Since Jackson decided to open the center, he has been required to make numerous business decisions and to spend much time and money on the arrangements. However, Jackson is very pleased that everything has proceeded smoothly and that tomorrow morning at 9 o'clock (May 1) the business will officially open as scheduled.

Jackson is now reviewing the records with Wallace Jones, the company treasurer, and they are trying to determine how the firm stands just before operations begin. The business checkbook contains the following entries:

Deposits to account of Precision Recordkeepers, Inc.:

April 27	Received from issuance of 10,000 shares of capital stock	$10,000
28	Received from issuance of 800 shares of capital stock	800
29	Received from William Jackson on loan	3,300
30	Received from bank on loan (issued a note)	1,800
	Total deposits	$15,900

Checks issued on the Gibraltar Bank & Trust Company:

April 27	Rental deposit paid to landlord	$ 150	
27	Payment of rent on office space for the month of May	150	
28	Insurance for one year beginning April 30	350	
28	Payment for purchase of office furniture	1,350	
29	Payment for office supplies	1,200	
30	Deposit paid to lessor of EDP equipment	3,000	
30	Payment for rental of EDP equipment for the month of May	1,500	
	Total payments		7,700
	Balance on deposit, April 30		$ 8,200

They are pleased that the firm has this much cash, but they do not know how long it will last. They are aware of the following unpaid bills:

Balance due on purchase of office furniture (due in two equal payments on June 1 and July 1)	$ 650
Amount due as one month's rental on leased equipment (due May 30)	1,500
Unpaid invoices on supplies purchases (due in three equal payments on June 1, July 1, and August 1)	400
Payment of second month's office rental (due May 27)	150
Amount owed to Jackson (due whenever the company can repay) at a 5% annual interest rate)	3,300
Amount owed to bank (due November 1 at a 6% annual interest rate)	1,800

While they are computing the firm's status, they make the following notes:

1. The deposit paid to the landlord will be returned in 10 years if the lease is not renewed at that time.
2. The leased equipment can be used as long as the rental is paid each month. The deposit is forfeited unless the equipment is used (and the rental is paid) for at least 24 months.
3. The insurance is for fire and public liability coverage from April 30 through the following April 29 (one year).
4. All employees begin working tomorrow. The total weekly payroll should be about $500.

Required:

1. Prepare a properly classified statement of financial position for Precision Recordkeepers, Inc., as of April 30.
2. Give your reasons for including or excluding each item of information presented in the problem.
3. Explain what a statement of financial position is and what function it serves.
4. Explain why you arranged the items on the statement as you did.
5. Jackson also wishes to know what the items "on the left" have in common since they do not appear to be closely related. Answer this question for items "on the left" and also for items "on the right."

Chapter Three

Basic Methodology— Income Statement Accounts

In the previous chapter, changes in the stockholders' equity caused by stockholder investments were discussed. Other changes may be caused by *revenues, expenses,* and *dividends* to stockholders. These changes, and the statements on which they are reflected, are explained in this chapter.

REVENUES

The term *revenue* describes the source of inflows of assets received in exchange for services rendered, sales of products or merchandise, gains from sales or exchanges of assets other than stock in trade, and earnings from interest and dividends on investments. It does not include increases arising from owners' contributions or from borrowed funds. For revenue to be earned, it does not have to be collected immediately in cash; it is sufficient that claims for cash on customers or clients exist.

Revenue accounts are created to accumulate the amounts earned during a specified period of time; the typical accounting period is one year. Often, however, progressive statements are prepared each month for the information of the management. The title of a revenue account should indicate the nature of the particular revenue; examples are Commissions Earned, Sales, Interest Earned, Dividends Earned, Accounting Fees Earned, and Garage Repair Revenue.

Revenue accounts are *credited* to record *increases;* the particular asset that is received is *debited.* To illustrate the journalizing of revenue transactions, several companies that earned different kinds of revenue are considered.

First, suppose that on August 1, 1969, the Whitside Realty Corporation sells a house and lot and receives a commission of $500 in cash; this can be recorded as follows:

GENERAL JOURNAL   Page 1

1969					
Aug.	1	Cash		500	
		Commissions Earned			500
		To record receipt of commission on sale of			
		house and lot.			

Next, assume that on July 30, 1969, I. N. Malvin, CPA, bills the Anderson Company for $1,000 for an annual audit that he had performed; his journal entry might look like this:

GENERAL JOURNAL   Page 1

1969					
July	30	Accounts Receivable		1,000	
		Accounting Fees Earned			1,000
		To record billing of following client for audit			
		performed: Anderson Company $1,000			

Suppose that on January 2, 1969, the Georgetown Rental Agency receives $750 in cash for January rent:

GENERAL JOURNAL   Page 1

1969					
Jan.	2	Cash		750	
		Rent Earned			750
		To record rental receipts for month of			
		January, 1969.			

EXPENSES

Expenses are costs of the materials used and services received during a specified period and used in the production of revenue during that same period. Examples of *expense accounts* are Salaries Expense, Rent Expense, and Office Expense. Expenses are recorded by a debit to the appropriate expense account and a credit to the Cash account, to a liability account, or possibly to some other type of account.

With a few special exceptions, which will be considered in later chapters, expenses are recorded when they are paid. The recording process for expenses is illustrated by the following transactions, which took place at the Mason Company.

1969

Jan. 2 Paid $400 in rent for the month of January.

   10 Purchased an advertisement in the local newspaper for $75 in cash.

   15 Paid semimonthly salaries of $600.

   20 Had some office machinery repaired at a cost of $45.

These transactions are recorded in the general journal as follows:

GENERAL JOURNAL   Page 1

1969				
Jan.	2	Rent Expense	400	
		Cash		400
		To record payment of rent for month of January, 1969.		
	10	Advertising Expense	75	
		Cash		75
		To record payment for advertising.		
	15	Salaries Expense	600	
		Cash		600
		To record payment of semimonthly salaries.		
	20	Repairs Expense—Office Equipment	45	
		Cash		45
		To record payment of repairs to office equipment.		

BASIC OPERATING CONCEPTS

Accounting Concept: Measurement of Net Income ▶

▶ The total expenses for a period are deducted from the total revenues to measure the *net income* (profit) for the period, which in turn reflects the increase in the stockholders' equity resulting from business operations. ◀ This may be expressed in equation form:

Total Revenues − Total Expenses = Net Income

If the expenses for a period exceed the revenues for that period, a *net loss* results, and the stockholders' equity is decreased. The equation now becomes

Total Expenses − Total Revenues = Net Loss

Accounting Concept: Expenses Compared with Costs ▶

▶ It is necessary to distinguish between an *expense* and a *cost*. A *cost* is the amount paid or payable in either cash or the equivalent, for goods, services, or other assets purchased. When a cost no longer has asset status; that is, when its potential to produce revenue is lost; it is said to be expired and thus to have become an *expense*. ◀ From this statement the following conclusions are warranted:

Expenses = Expired Costs (used up in producing revenue)
Assets = Unexpired Costs (to be used to produce future revenue)

For example, rent paid in advance for three months is an asset, Prepaid Rent. As time passes, this becomes Rent Expense. The required adjusting process is discussed in detail in the next chapter.

A *disbursement* is a payment in cash or by check. Hence, a machine may be acquired at a cost of $10,000; the transaction is completed by a disbursement in the form of a check for $10,000; and as the machine is used in operations it loses part of its service value, or *depreciates*. This is an element of expense, Depreciation Expense.

Basically, the purpose of operating a business is to make a profit. A profit, or net income, results when more is received from a customer for a service rendered than the total expense of that service to the business; a loss is incurred when the expense of a service to the enterprise is more than it receives from the customer for the service rendered.

Most businesses cannot keep the detailed records necessary to indicate the expense of each service rendered and therefore cannot determine the net income or net loss from each transaction. Even when it is possible, the clerical costs involved in getting the information would not justify the end result. For example, a lawyer bills his client for $1,000 for services performed. How much did it cost the lawyer to perform the service and how much net income did he make on this *one* transaction? The lawyer might total the number of hours he devoted to the case and arrive at an expense in terms of time spent. But how about the rent for his office? the secretary's salary? the telephone bill? the electricity bill?

Since the determination of each expense involved in rendering service for a particular client would require a considerable amount of recordkeeping, accounting has evolved another and easier method of accomplishing the same result. No attempt is made to determine the cost of each service; instead, records of revenue and expense are kept for a period of time. ▶ At the end of the period, the expenses are matched against the revenue to determine the net income or net loss for that period. This information is contained in a financial statement called an *income statement*, discussed and illustrated later in this chapter. ◀

Accounting Concept: Matching of Expenses against Revenue for a ◀ *Time Period*

DIVIDENDS

Dividends are distributions of net income regardless of whether that income is earned in the current period or in past periods. Although dividends reduce the stockholders' equity, they are *not* expenses; they are not declared and paid for the purpose of producing revenue. A dividend may be recorded by a debit to a special Dividends account and a credit to Cash, or to a liability account if it is to be paid at a date subsequent to the date of declaration. For example, suppose that the Zephran Corporation declared and paid a regular quarterly cash dividend of $1,000 to its stockholders on November 10, 1969; this transaction would be recorded in the general journal of the Zephran Corporation as follows:

GENERAL JOURNAL   Page 1

1969				
Nov.	10	Dividends	1,000	
		Cash		1,000
		To record declaration and payment of fourth quarterly dividend.		

EXPANDED RULES FOR DEBITS AND CREDITS

Since new types of accounts have been introduced, the rules for debiting and crediting accounts are expanded and restated:

Debit in order to record:

1. An increase of an asset
2. An increase of an expense
3. An increase of dividends
4. A decrease of a liability
5. A decrease in the stockholders' equity
6. A decrease of revenue

Credit in order to record:

1. A decrease of an asset
2. A decrease of an expense
3. A decrease of dividends
4. An increase of a liability
5. An increase in the stockholders' equity
6. An increase in revenue

The relationship of the rules of debits and credits to the accounting equation may be diagrammed as follows:

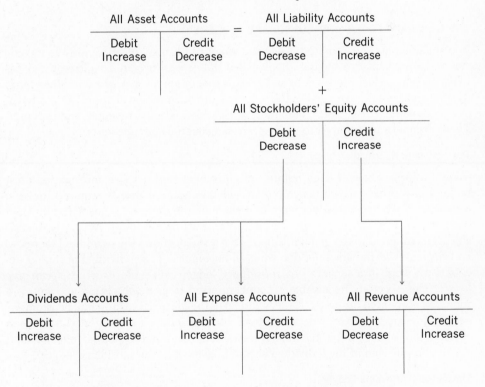

EXPANDED ACCOUNTING EQUATION

It is evident from the expanded accounting equation that a *decrease* in the stockholders' equity is debited. Note that when the decrease in the stockholders' equity is recorded in an expense account, the expense account is *increased* (debited); that is, the expense account is designed to *accumulate* a decrease that is later transferred to the stockholders' equity accounts. The specific relationship between the expense accounts and the stockholders' equity accounts is further illustrated as follows:

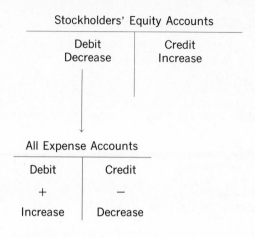

Stockholders' Equity Accounts

Debit Decrease	Credit Increase

Increases in expenses result in stockholders' equity decreases; the plus sign (+) indicates the accumulation of periodic decreases in the stockholders' equity

All Expense Accounts

Debit	Credit
+	−
Increase	Decrease

THE GENERAL LEDGER AND SUBSIDIARY LEDGERS

Accounts that are incorporated in the statement of financial position and the income statement are kept in a separate book called the *general ledger.* This ledger may actually be a loose-leaf binder, a bound book, cards in open trays, or some other form. Accounts are usually arranged in the sequence in which they will appear in the financial statements; that is, assets, liabilities, stockholders' equity, revenue, and expenses. These accounts are referred to collectively as *general ledger accounts.*

The Accounts Receivable Ledger

Many businesses have a large number of customers, and detailed information must be kept of transactions with each one. A separate account thus is required for each customer. If the general ledger were to include all the customers' accounts, it would become too large and unwieldy. Consequently, only one account, Accounts Receivable, is maintained in the general ledger. This account shows the combined increases and decreases in the amounts due from all customers. The individual customer accounts are kept in a separate, or *subsidiary*, ledger called the *accounts receivable ledger.* The Accounts Receivable account, referred to as a controlling account, is a summary account in the general ledger and takes the place of the individual customers' accounts in the subsidiary ledger. After all the transactions for the period have been entered, the balance of the Accounts Receivable account in the general ledger should be equal to the sum of the individual account balances in the subsidiary ledger.

The Accounts Payable Ledger

Many businesses have a large number of individual creditors. Consequently, only one account, Accounts Payable, is kept in the general ledger. This account shows the increases and decreases in amounts due to creditors. The individual creditors' accounts are kept in a subsidiary ledger called the *accounts payable ledger.* Accounts Payable, another controlling account, is a summary account in the general ledger. This account takes the place of the individual creditors' accounts kept in the subsidiary ledger. After all the transactions for the period have been entered, the balance of the Accounts Payable account in the general ledger should be equal to the sum of the individual account balances in the subsidiary ledger.

Controlling Accounts

As mentioned above, the Accounts Receivable and Accounts Payable accounts appearing in the general ledger are referred to as controlling accounts. A controlling account, by definition, is any account in the general ledger that controls or is supported by a number of other accounts in a separate ledger. These accounts contain summary totals of many transactions, the details of which appear in subsidiary ledgers. The accounts receivable ledger is sometimes referred to as the *customers' ledger;* the accounts payable ledger, as the *creditors' ledger.* Other controlling accounts and their appropriate subsidiary ledgers may be established when enough homogeneous general ledger accounts are created to make it necessary to relegate these accounts to a separate ledger.

Posting to the General Ledger and the Subsidiary Ledgers

To illustrate the method of posting from the general journal to the general and subsidiary ledgers, the following transaction is considered:

On August 1, 1969, Bookkeeping Services, Inc., billed the following clients for professional services performed:

Jay Johnson	$550
O. M. Omar	120
C. W. Wayne	230

This information is recorded and posted as indicated in Figure 3-1 (see page 66).

Entries to the Accounts Payable controlling account and the accounts payable ledger are handled similarly.

THE ACCOUNTING SEQUENCE

Ten steps in the accounting sequence are illustrated through the example of a newly incorporated business called the Nelson Garage. These steps are: (1) selecting a chart of accounts, (2) journalizing the transactions, (3) posting to the general and subsidiary ledgers, (4) preparing a trial balance, (5) preparing a schedule of accounts receivable, (6) preparing a schedule of accounts payable, (7) preparing the financial statements, (8) closing and ruling the revenue and expense accounts, (9) balancing and ruling the position-statement accounts, and (10) taking a post-closing trial balance. An explanation of each step in the sequence is presented along with the accounting procedure for that step.

Selecting a Chart of Accounts

The first step in establishing an efficient accounting system that will satisfy the needs of management, governmental agencies, and other interested groups is the construction of a *chart of accounts.* A separate account should be set up for each item that appears in the financial statements, to make the statements easier to prepare. The classification and the order of the items in the chart of accounts corresponds to those of the statements.

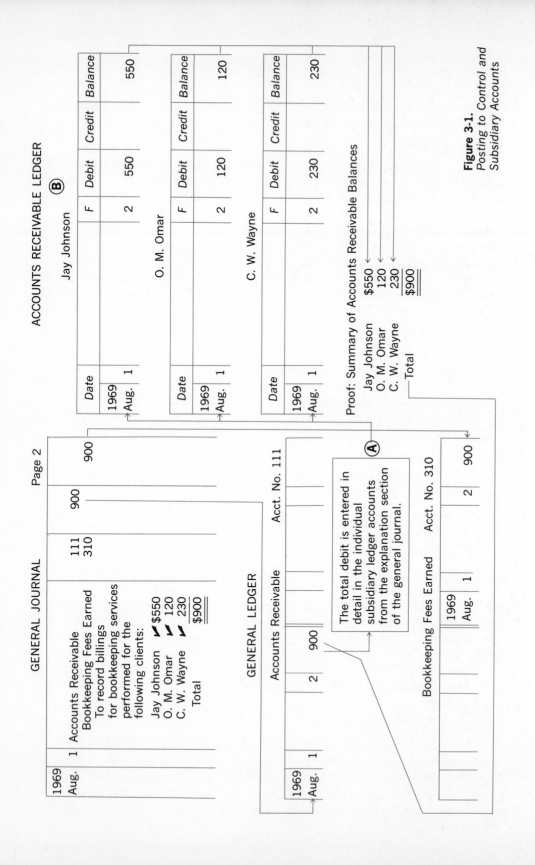

Figure 3-1.
Posting to Control and Subsidiary Accounts

(A) Figure 3-1 shows the detailed posting of the $900 debit to the Accounts Receivable account in the general ledger and to the subsidiary ledger accounts. Each customer is debited for the amount shown in the explanation of the general journal entry; the balance is extended to the Balance column; the journal page number is entered in the folio (F) column; and the date is entered. After each posting has been completed, a check mark (✔) is entered to the left of each amount in the Explanation column of the general journal to indicate that the amount has been posted to the proper subsidiary ledger account. A check mark is used, rather than a page number, because subsidiary accounts are generally not numbered but are kept in alphabetical order.

After only a cursory study, it may seem that this dual accounting for accounts receivable would result in double debits that will be incorrectly reflected in the trial balance. Note carefully, however, that only one debit goes into the Accounts Receivable controlling account for later incorporation in the trial balance. The amounts entered in the accounts receivable ledger will not go in the trial balance, but the total of the uncollected balances at the end of a period will be compared with the single balance of the Accounts Receivable controlling account as a check on the accuracy of both the accounts receivable ledger and the Accounts Receivable controlling account in the general ledger.

(B) It should be observed that the balance form of ledger account is used for the accounts receivable ledger. This particular form is customarily used in subsidiary ledgers for two reasons:

1. The balances have to be referred to quite often.
2. The form is adaptable to machine accounting, which is frequently employed for accounts receivable accounting.

Account titles should be carefully selected to suit the needs of the business, and should indicate clearly and precisely the nature of the accounts to ensure proper recording of transactions. However, titles are not standardized; for example one accountant may use Unexpired Insurance and another Prepaid Insurance Premiums in the same context.

The accountant of the Nelson Garage, expecting the company to grow rapidly, sets up the following chart of accounts—the accounts that he expects to use during the first month of operations are listed, with numbers skipped to provide for future expansion.

NELSON GARAGE
Chart of Accounts

Statement of Financial Position Accounts
Assets (100–299)

Current Assets (100–199)

    101 Cash
    121 Accounts Receivable
    131 Garage Parts and Supplies
    141 Prepaid Insurance

Plant and Equipment (200–299)

    201 Land
    221 Automotive Tools and Equipment

Liabilities and Stockholders' Equity (300–499)

Current Liabilities (300–399)
    301 Accounts Payable
    302 Notes Payable
Stockholders' Equity (400–499)
    401 Capital Stock
    411 Retained Earnings
    421 Dividends

Income Statement Accounts (500–999)

Revenue (500–599)
    501 Garage Repair Revenue
Expenses (600–699)
    601 Rent Expense—Garage Building
    602 Rent Expense—Automotive Tools and Equipment
    604 Salaries Expense
    608 Electricity and Water Expense
    609 Garage Parts and Supplies Used
Clearing and Summary Accounts (900–999)
    901 Revenue and Expense Summary

In this example, a three-digit system is used to number the accounts; a larger business with a number of departments or branches may use four or more digits. Notice that Accounts 100–299 represent assets; Accounts 300–499 represent liabilities and stockholders' (owner's) equity, and that Accounts 500–999 represent income statement accounts. The more detailed breakdown for current assets, plant and equipment, current liabilities, and so on, can be seen in the chart. As was stated previously, the gaps between the assigned account numbers allow for additional accounts as they are needed by the business for recording purposes.

Analyzing Transactions and Journalizing

The transactions of the Nelson Garage that occurred during the month of January, 1969, are given. Before making entries in the journal, the accountant must analyze each transaction in terms of the basic system of debits and credits that has already been outlined. Following each transaction listed, a description of the analytical thinking that must precede the journalizing of each transaction is given as a guide to future action.

1969
Jan. 2   The charter for the Nelson Garage was received on this date, and all the authorized capital stock was issued to three stockholders at par for $30,000 in cash. An asset, cash, is received; to record an increase of an asset, it must be debited; therefore, the Cash account is debited for $30,000. The stockholders have a claim against the business; the increase in the stockholders' equity account, Capital Stock, is shown by a credit to that account.

      3   Rented a temporary garage and paid $300 for rent for January. Since all the rent will have expired by the time the financial statements are prepared, it is considered an expense of the month of January. An increase of an expense account is recorded by a debit; therefore, the Rent Expense–Garage Building account is debited. The decrease of the asset cash is recorded by a credit to Cash. A single rent account may be sufficient for all rented buildings and equipment. In this case, the accountant felt that managerial analyses required a separate Rent Expense account for the garage building.

1969

Jan. 4 Rented automotive tools and equipment pending purchase of its own. Rent in the amount of $80 was paid for January. As in the preceding transaction, all this rent will have expired before the financial statements are prepared; and therefore it is considered an expense of January. An increase of an expense account is recorded by a debit—in this case to Rent Expense—Automotive Tools and Equipment. The decrease of the asset cash is recorded by a credit to Cash. Again, a single Rent Expense account may have been sufficient.

5 Purchased garage parts and supplies from the Southern Supply Company for $400 on account. The Garage Parts and Supplies account is an asset and is increased by the transaction; the increase in the asset is shown by a debit to Garage Parts and Supplies. Since the purchase was on credit, a liability is created. To record the increase in the liability, the Accounts Payable account is credited. The amount payable to the particular creditor, the Southern Supply Company, must be shown in the books. A note should be made in the Explanation column of the journal to the effect that the creditor is the Southern Supply Company, so that the amount can be posted to the accounts payable ledger.

6 Performed garage repairs for several cash customers; received $1,000 in cash. Cash, an asset, is received; to record the increase of the asset the Cash account must be debited. The particular source of this asset is a revenue. To record an increase in the revenue, Garage Repairs Revenue is credited.

10 Purchased land as a prospective building site for $10,000. Paid $4,000 in cash and issued a one-year note for the balance. Land, an asset, is received; to record the increase of the asset, the Land account is debited for $10,000. Cash, an asset, is decreased by the $4,000 payment; to record the decrease, the Cash account is credited for $4,000. In addition, a liability for $6,000 is created. Since a written promise to pay is given, the liability created is called Notes Payable; to record the increase of the liability, the Notes Payable account is credited for $6,000.

12 Made repairs on George Shipman's car for $40. Shipman asked that a charge account be opened in his name; he promises to settle the account within 30 days. This was authorized by the service manager. A claim against Shipman is received. This claim is an asset, Accounts Receivable. To record the increase of the asset, the Accounts Receivable account is debited. The particular source of this asset is a revenue. To record the increase in the revenue, Garage Repairs Revenue is credited. Also, a record of the individual claim against Shipman must be maintained. To show this and to permit posting to the accounts receivable ledger, a note of the amount along with Shipman's name is made in the Explanation column of the journal.

15 Paid $800 in salaries for first half of month. The amount of salaries paid applied entirely to the month of January; an expense account, Salaries Expense, is increased. The Salaries Expense account is debited to show the increase. The asset cash is decreased and is therefore credited.

20 Performed garage repairs for cash customers for $2,000. The asset cash is increased, and therefore the Cash account debited. The source of the asset is a revenue; Garage Repairs Revenue is increased and is therefore credited.

25 Repairs were made on Jay Munson's truck for $60. A charge account was opened in his name. The asset Accounts Receivable is increased and is therefore debited. The particular source of the asset is a revenue; Garage Repairs Revenue is increased and is therefore credited. To record the claim against Jay Munson, a note is made of his name and the amount in the Explanation column of the journal. From this note, postings can be made to the accounts receivable ledger.

1969

Jan. 28   Made repairs on Robert Batson's car for $120. A charge account was opened in his name. This transaction is similar to the transaction of January 25. The asset Accounts Receivable is debited to reflect an increase; Garage Repair Revenue is credited to show an increase in the revenue account.

29   Purchased garage parts and supplies from the Delco Supply House for $250 on account. The Garage Parts and Supplies account is debited to show an increase in the asset; Accounts Payable account is credited to reflect an increase in the liability. In addition, a note of the creditor's name and the amount due is made in the Explanation column of the journal so that a separate posting may be made to the accounts payable ledger.

30   Paid the Southern Supply Company $300 on account. This transaction reduces a liability; the liability, Accounts Payable, is debited to show the decrease. An asset is decreased; the asset account, Cash, is credited to show the decrease. The Southern Supply Company's account in the accounts payable ledger must also be debited to show the decrease; therefore, a note is made in the Explanation column of the journal.

31   Paid electricity and water bills for January, totaling $80. An expense is created by this transaction. The Electricity and Water Expense account is debited to reflect the increase. The asset Cash account is credited to show the decrease.

31   Made garage repairs for cash customers for $1,800. The asset Cash is increased; the account is debited to reflect the increase. The Garage Repairs Revenue account is likewise increased; it is credited.

31   Paid $900 in salaries for the last half of the month. The Salaries Expense account is increased; it is debited to show the increase. The asset Cash account is decreased; it is credited to reflect the decrease.

31   Paid a $300 cash dividend to the three stockholders. This cash payment does not involve an expense; a dividend is considered distribution of income. Therefore, it reduces the stockholders' equity account, Retained Earnings; but rather than show the decrease as a debit to Retained Earnings, a special Dividends account is opened. This account is debited to show an increase in dividends. The Retained Earnings account, in turn, will be decreased when the Dividends account is transferred to Retained Earnings at the end of the period. The asset Cash account is decreased; it is credited to show the decrease.

31   Purchased automotive tools and equipment for $4,000 in cash. The list price was $5,000. The asset Automotive Tools and Equipment account is increased; it is debited to reflect the increase. ▶ The figure $4,000 is used because of the generally accepted accounting principle that assets should be recorded at cost. Cost is objectively determinable, being the result of an arm's-length transaction between a seller and a buyer. Value, on the other hand, often means all things to all men. ◀ Since cash was disbursed, the asset Cash account is credited to show the decrease.

Accounting Concept: Basis for Recording ◀ *Assets: Cost*

31   Paid a premium of $600 on a 12-month comprehensive insurance policy; the policy becomes effective on February 1, 1969. Since this prepayment benefits twelve accounting periods of one month each, it is considered an asset. The asset Prepaid Insurance account is debited to show that it is increased. The asset Cash account is credited to show a decrease.

31   Received a check for $10 from George Shipman as part payment of his account. The asset Cash account is debited to show the increase. Another asset account, Accounts Receivable, is decreased; it is credited to show the decrease. In addition, Shipman's

account in the accounts receivable ledger must be decreased. A note is made in the Explanation column of the journal so that the $10 amount may be posted as a credit to Shipman's account.

31 Took a physical inventory of garage parts and supplies; it showed that there were parts and supplies costing $375 on hand, thus indicating that $275 (January 5 purchase $400, plus January 29 purchase $250, minus inventory, $375) worth of garage parts and supplies had been used, becoming an expense. Originally, as parts and supplies were purchased, they were debited to an asset account. Now, as the amount used becomes known, an entry is made debiting an expense account, Garage Parts and Supplies Used, to show that the expense account has been increased, and crediting an asset account, Garage Parts and Supplies, to show that the asset account has been decreased. (This type of transaction is normally recorded in an *adjusting entry,* explained in Chapter 4. It is presented here to broaden the scope of this problem.)

The results of this analytical reasoning are presented in the following general journal. Note that space is left between entries to ensure that they are separate and distinct.

GENERAL JOURNAL   Page 1

1969					
Jan.	2	Cash	101	30,000	
		Capital Stock	401		30,000
		To record issuance of capital stock for cash.			
	3	Rent Expense—Garage Building	601	300	
		Cash	101		300
		To record payment of rent on garage building for month of January, 1969.			
	4	Rent Expense—Automotive Tools and Equip.	602	80	
		Cash	101		80
		To record payment of rent for automotive tools and equipment for month of January, 1969.			
	5	Garage Parts and Supplies	131	400	
		Accounts Payable	301		400
		To record purchase of parts and supplies on account:			
		Southern Supply Co. ✔ $400			
	6	Cash	101	1,000	
		Garage Repair Revenue	501		1,000
		To record collections from cash customers for services rendered			
	10	Land	201	10,000	
		Cash	101		4,000
		Notes Payable	302		6,000
		To record purchase of land.			
	12	Accounts Receivable	121	40	
		Garage Repair Revenue	501		40
		To record billing for repairs rendered:			
		George Shipman ✔ $40			

GENERAL JOURNAL   Page 1 (cont.)

Jan.	15	Salaries Expense	604	800	
		Cash	101		800
		To record payment of semimonthly salaries.			

GENERAL JOURNAL   Page 2

1969					
Jan.	20	Cash	101	2,000	
		Garage Repair Revenue	501		2,000
		To record collections from cash customers for services rendered.			
	25	Accounts Receivable	121	60	
		Garage Repair Revenue	501		60
		To record billing for repair services rendered: Jay Munson ✔ $60			
	28	Accounts Receivable	121	120	
		Garage Repair Revenue	501		120
		To record billing for repair services rendered: Robert Batson ✔ $120			
	29	Garage Parts and Supplies	131	250	
		Accounts Payable	301		250
		To record purchase of parts and supplies on account: Delco Supply House ✔ $250			
	30	Accounts Payable	301	300	
		Cash	101		300
		To record payment: Southern Supply Company ✔ $300			
	31	Electricity and Water Expense	608	80	
		Cash	101		80
		To record payment of electricity and water bills for month of January.			
	31	Cash	101	1,800	
		Garage Repair Revenue	501		1,800
		To record collections from cash customers for services rendered.			
	31	Salaries Expense	604	900	
		Cash	101		900
		To record payment of salaries for last half of January.			
	31	Dividends	421	300	
		Cash	101		300
		To record payment of dividends to stockholders.			

GENERAL JOURNAL   Page 3

1969					
Jan.	31	Automotive Tools and Equipment	221	4,000	
		Cash	101		4,000
		To record purchase of tools and equipment at a cost of $4,000 (list price, $5,000).			
	31	Prepaid Insurance	141	600	
		Cash	101		600
		To record payment of insurance premium for 12 months. Insurance is effective February 1, 1969.			
	31	Cash	101	10	
		Accounts Receivable	121		10
		To record collection to apply on account: George Shipman ✔ $10			
	31	Garage Parts and Supplies Used	609	275	
		Garage Parts and Supplies	131		275
		To record cost of parts and supplies used during month of January.			

Posting to the Ledgers

As the transactions are posted to the ledger, the account numbers are entered in the general journal folio (F) column. At the same time, the number of the journal page from which the entry is posted is entered in the folio (F) column of the ledger account.

The timing of the posting process is a matter of personal preference and expediency. All postings, however, must be completed before financial statements can be prepared. It is advisable to keep accounts with customers and creditors up to date, so that the account balances are readily available. Because of this, it is probably the best rule to post from the journal to the ledgers on a daily basis.

The three posted ledgers are shown:

GENERAL LEDGER

Cash   Acct. No. 101

1969					1969			
Jan.	2		1	30,000	Jan.	3	1	300
	6		1	1,000		4	1	80
	20		2	2,000		10	1	4,000
	31		2	1,800		15	1	800
	31	23,450	3	10		30	2	300
				34,810		31	2	80
						31	2	900
						31	2	300
						31	3	4,000
						31	3	600
								11,360

GENERAL LEDGER (Cont.)

Accounts Receivable — Acct. No. 121

1969						1969					
Jan.	12			1	40	Jan.	31			3	10
	25			2	60						
	28		210	2	120						
					220						

Garage Parts and Supplies — Acct. No. 131

1969						1969					
Jan.	5			1	400	Jan.	31			3	275
	29		375	2	250						
					650						

Prepaid Insurance — Acct. No. 141

1969					
Jan.	31			3	600

Land — Acct. No. 201

1969					
Jan.	10			1	10,000

Automotive Tools and Equipment — Acct. No. 221

1969					
Jan.	31			3	4,000

Accounts Payable — Acct. No. 301

1969						1969					
Jan.	30			2	300	Jan.	5			1	400
							29		350	2	250
											650

Notes Payable — Acct. No. 302

						1969					
						Jan.	10			1	6,000

Capital Stock — Acct. No. 401

						1969					
						Jan.	2			1	30,000

GENERAL LEDGER (Cont.)

Retained Earnings   Acct. No. 411

Dividends   Acct. No. 421

1969				
Jan.	31		2	300

Garage Repair Revenue   Acct. No. 501

				1969				
				Jan.	6		1	1,000
					12		1	40
					20		2	2,000
					25		2	60
					28		2	120
					31		2	1,800
								5,020

Rent Expense—Garage Building   Acct. No. 601

1969				
Jan.	3		1	300

Rent Expense—Automotive Tools and Equipment   Acct. No. 602

1969				
Jan.	4		1	80

Salaries Expense   Acct. No. 604

1969				
Jan.	15		1	800
	31		2	900
				1,700

Electricity and Water Expense   Acct. No. 608

1969				
Jan.	31		2	80

GENERAL LEDGER (Cont.)

Garage Parts and Supplies Used   Acct. No. 609

1969									
Jan.	31		3	275					

Revenue and Expense Summary   Acct. No. 901

ACCOUNTS RECEIVABLE LEDGER

Robert Batson

1969					
Jan.	28		2	120	120

Jay Munson

1969					
Jan.	25		2	60	60

George Shipman

1969					
Jan.	12		1	40	40
	31		3		10	30

ACCOUNTS PAYABLE LEDGER

Delco Supply House

1969					
Jan.	29		2		250	250

Southern Supply Company

1969					
Jan.	5		1		400	400
	30		2	300		100

Preparing a Trial Balance

After the accounts in the general ledger are footed and the balances are obtained, the following trial balance is taken:

NELSON GARAGE
Trial Balance
January 31, 1969

Acct. No.	Account Title	Debits	Credits
101	Cash	$23,450	
121	Accounts Receivable	210	
131	Garage Parts and Supplies	375	
141	Prepaid Insurance	600	
201	Land	10,000	
221	Automotive Tools and Equipment	4,000	
301	Accounts Payable		$ 350
302	Notes Payable		6,000
401	Capital Stock		30,000
421	Dividends	300	
501	Garage Repair Revenue		5,020
601	Rent Expense—Garage Building	300	
602	Rent Expense—Automotive Tools and Equipment	80	
604	Salaries Expense	1,700	
608	Electricity and Water Expense	80	
609	Garage Parts and Supplies Used	275	
	Totals	$41,370	$41,370

Preparing a Schedule of Accounts Receivable

The fact that the trial balance is in balance is presumptive evidence of accuracy of the accounting up to this point; the accountant therefore takes the next step, that of preparing a *schedule of accounts receivable*.

At the end of a designated accounting period (one month in this example), the total of all the balances of customers' accounts should agree with the balance of the Accounts Receivable controlling account in the general ledger. A schedule of accounts receivable usually is prepared to check this agreement. The schedule of accounts receivable taken from the Nelson Garage's accounts receivable ledger shows that the total of all customers' accounts is $210, which agrees with the balance of the Accounts Receivable controlling account:

NELSON GARAGE
Schedule of Accounts Receivable
January 31, 1969

Robert Batson	$120
Jay Munson	60
George Shipman	30
Total Accounts Receivable	$210

Preparing a Schedule of Accounts Payable

The next step is similar to the preceding one; it involves the preparation of a *schedule of accounts payable*.

At the end of the accounting period, the total of the balances of the individual creditors' accounts should equal the balance of the Accounts Payable controlling account. The schedule of accounts payable taken from the Nelson Garage's accounts payable ledger shows that the total of the creditors' accounts is $350, which agrees with the balance of the Accounts Payable controlling account.

NELSON GARAGE
Schedule of Accounts Payable
January 31, 1969

Delco Supply House	$250
Southern Supply Company	100
Total Accounts Payable	$350

Preparing the Financial Statements from the Trial Balance

The income statement, the statement of retained earnings, and the statement of financial position are usually prepared at the end of an accounting period. The first two have not yet been illustrated.

THE INCOME STATEMENT. The income statement shown in Figure 3-2 was prepared from the trial balance of the Nelson Garage.

The heading of the income statement gives:

1. The name of the business
2. The name of the statement
3. The period covered by the statement

NELSON GARAGE
Income Statement
For Month Ended January 31, 1969

Figure 3-2.
Income Statement

Revenue		
Garage Repair Revenue		$5,020
Expenses		
Rent Expense—Garage Building	$ 300	
Rent Expense—Automotive Tools and Equipment	80	
Salaries Expense	1,700	
Electricity and Water Expense	80	
Garage Parts and Supplies Used	275	
Total Expenses		2,435
Net Income		$2,585

It is important that the period covered be specified clearly. The date January 31, 1969, is not sufficient; alone, it does not indicate whether the net income of $2,585 was earned in one day, one month, or one year ending January 31, 1969. Certainly, the analyst must know how long a period of time it took for the firm to earn the $2,585.

The determination of net income for the Nelson Garage at this level should not be interpreted as being definitive. For example, a corporation is subject to income taxes; but the accounting for income taxes and certain other more complex problems are deferred to later chapters.

There is no standard order for listing accounts in the income statement.

THE STATEMENT OF RETAINED EARNINGS. Since the corporation is a creature of the law, there are certain legal restrictions on it, including a requirement that the net income retained in a business be recorded separately from the Capital Stock account. The typical title of the account used to accumulate this information is Retained Earnings. *The statement of retained earnings* shows the changes in that part of the stockholders' equity designated as retained earnings; it should cover the same period as the income statement. Since by definition retained earnings are the accumulation of all past net income less any dividends paid out, it follows that net income and dividends for a period must be reflected in the statement. The first end-of-period statement of retained earnings of the Nelson Garage is shown in Figure 3-3.

Figure 3-3.
Statement of Retained Earnings for New Business

NELSON GARAGE
Statement of Retained Earnings
For Month Ended January 31, 1969

Net Income for January, 1969	$2,585
Deduct Dividends	300
Retained Earnings, January 31, 1969	$2,285

The heading of the statement of retained earnings is similar to that of the income statement.

For a business that has been in existence prior to the current period, there would be an additional item in the statement of retained earnings, the beginning-of-period balance. For example, the statement of the Bebol Company is shown in Figure 3-4.

Figure 3-4.
Complete Statement of Retained Earnings

BEBOL COMPANY
Statement of Retained Earnings
For Month Ended January 31, 1969

Retained Earnings, January 1, 1969	$5,000,000
Add Net Income for January, 1969	400,000
Total	$5,400,000
Deduct Dividends	300,000
Retained Earnings, January 31, 1969	$5,100,000

THE STATEMENT OF FINANCIAL POSITION. Since the retained earnings of the Nelson Garage, as of January 31, 1969, have now been determined (Figure 3-3), it is possible to prepare the formal statement of financial position, shown in Figure 3-5.

NELSON GARAGE
Statement of Financial Position
January 31, 1969

Assets			Liabilities and Stockholders' Equity		
Assets			**Liabilities and Stockholders' Equity**		
Current Assets			Current Liabilities		
Cash	$23,450		Accounts Payable	$ 350	
Accounts Receivable	210		Notes Payable	6,000	
Garage Parts and Supplies	375		Total Current Liabilities		$ 6,350
Prepaid Insurance	600		Stockholders' Equity		
Total Current Assets		$24,635	Capital Stock	$30,000	
Plant and Equipment			Retained Earnings	2,285	
Land	$10,000		Total Stockholders'		
Automotive Tools and Equipment	4,000		Equity		32,285
Total Plant and Equipment		14,000	Total Liabilities and		
Total Assets		$38,635	Stockholders' Equity		$38,635

Figure 3-5.
Formal Statement of Financial Position

Note that the heading of the statement of financial position contains the single date *January 31, 1969*. This statement reveals the financial position as of the close of business on January 31. It is analogous to a still photograph, whereas the income statement and statement of retained earnings are like moving pictures—they show the changes that have taken place during a specific period.

Closing and Ruling the Revenue and Expense Accounts

The revenue, expense, and dividends accounts are used to measure part of the changes that take place in retained earnings during a specified period of time. For this reason, these accounts are often called *temporary owner's equity accounts*, or *nominal accounts*. At the end of an accounting period, these accounts must be emptied—or *closed*—so that they may be used to accumulate the changes in retained earnings for the next period. Therefore, *closing entries* are made to transfer the final effects of the temporary stockholders' equity accounts to the Retained Earnings account, which is a *permanent*, or *real*, account. The term *real* is applied to the accounts that appear in the statement of financial position; these accounts are not closed at the end of a period.

THE CLOSING PROCEDURE. To simplify the transfer of revenue and expense account balances, an intermediate *summary account*, called Revenue and Expense Summary, is used. The balances of all revenue and expense accounts are transferred to this account. The Revenue and Expense Summary account, the balance of which reveals the net income or loss for the period, is then closed by transferring its balance to the Retained Earnings account, a part of the stockholders' equity. This action is justified because net income or net loss accrues to the owners. Since the Dividends account is not an expense account, it is not closed to the Revenue and Expense Summary account; rather, it is closed directly to the Retained Earnings account. After the revenue and expense accounts are closed, they are ruled to indicate that they have zero balances and that they are now available to accumulate information for measuring the changes in retained earnings in the next accounting period.

The closing procedure is illustrated in Figure 3-6.

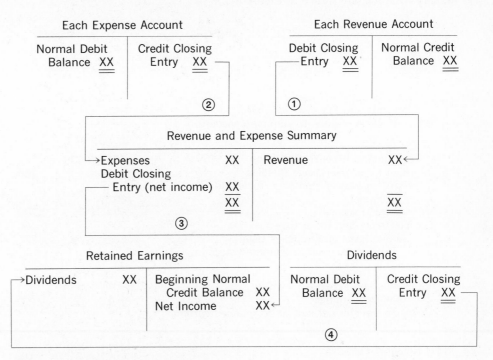

Figure 3-6.
The Closing Procedure

Entry ①—The revenue accounts are closed.
Entry ②—The expense accounts are closed.
Entry ③—The Revenue and Expense Summary account is closed.
Entry ④—The Dividends account is closed.

The caption *Closing Entries* is written in the middle of the first unused line in the general journal under the transactions of the period, and the closing entries are begun directly under that. They are posted immediately to the general ledger. As indicated in Figure 3-6, the closing entries are made in the following sequence:

Entry 1. All the revenue accounts are debited in a compound entry, and the sum of the revenue items is credited to the Revenue and Expense Summary account.

Entry 2. All the expense accounts are credited in a second compound entry, and the sum of the expense items is debited to the Revenue and Expense Summary account.

Entry 3. After entries 1 and 2 are posted, a credit balance in the Revenue and Expense Summary account represents net income; a debit balance, net loss. The balance of the account is transferred to the Retained Earnings account.

Entry 4. The Dividends account is closed directly to the Retained Earnings account by a debit to Retained Earnings and a credit to Dividends.

Unlike regular transaction entries, which require analysis and judgment, the closing process is purely mechanical and involves only the shifting and summarizing of previously determined amounts. The closing journal entries of the Nelson Garage on January 31, 1969, are shown in Figure 3-7.

GENERAL JOURNAL   Page 4   **Figure 3-7.**
Closing Entries

		Closing Entries			
1969		①			
Jan.	31	Garage Repair Revenue	501	5,020	
		Revenue and Expense Summary	901		5,020
		To close revenue to summary account.			
		②			
	31	Revenue and Expense Summary	901	2,435	
		Rent Expense—Garage Building	601		300
		Rent Expense—Automotive Tools and Equipment	602		80
		Salaries Expense	604		1,700
		Electricity and Water Expense	608		80
		Garage Parts and Supplies Used	609		275
		To close expenses to summary account.			
		③			
	31	Revenue and Expense Summary	901	2,585	
		Retained Earnings	411		2,585
		To transfer net income to retained earnings.			
		④			
	31	Retained Earnings	411	300	
		Dividends	421		300
		To close dividends to retained earnings.			

The closing journal entries are posted to the ledger accounts indicated in the journal (see Figures 3-8 and 3-9). Closing entries are indicated by the words *Closing Entry* in the Explanation columns of the nominal accounts, as shown in Figure 3-8.

RULING THE CLOSED NOMINAL ACCOUNTS. After the closing entries have been posted, the temporary stockholders' equity accounts consist of equal debit and credit totals; that is, they have zero balances. These accounts (revenue, expense, and dividend) are ruled to separate the amounts entered during one accounting period from the amounts to be entered during the next. Each side is totaled; and the equal debit and credit totals are written on the first available full line. Double rules are then drawn across all the columns, except the Explanation columns, to signify that the accounts have a zero balance. If an account has only one debit and one credit, it is unnecessary to foot the account; double rules are drawn below the individual amounts. Figure 3-8 shows the posting of the closing entries and the ruling of the nominal accounts.

GENERAL LEDGER

Figure 3-8.
*The Nominal Accounts
Are Closed and Ruled*

Dividends — Acct. No. 421

1969					1969				
Jan.	31		2	300	Jan.	31	Closing Entry	4	300

Garage Repair Revenue — Acct. No. 501

1969					1969				
Jan.	31	Closing Entry	4	5,020	Jan.	6		1	1,000
						12		1	40
						20		2	2,000
						25		2	60
						28		2	120
						31		2	1,800
									5,020
				5,020					5,020

Rent Expense—Garage Building — Acct. No. 601

1969					1969				
Jan.	3		1	300	Jan.	31	Closing Entry	4	300

Rent Expense—Automotive Tools and Equipment — Acct. No. 602

1969					1969				
Jan.	4		1	80	Jan.	31	Closing Entry	4	80

Salaries Expense — Acct. No. 604

1969					1969				
Jan.	15		1	800	Jan.	31	Closing Entry	4	1,700
	31		2	900					
				1,700					
				1,700					1,700

Electricity and Water Expense — Acct. No. 608

1969					1969				
Jan.	31		2	80	Jan.	31	Closing Entry	4	80

Garage Parts and Supplies Used — Acct. No. 609

1969					1969				
Jan.	31		3	275	Jan.	31	Closing Entry	4	275

Revenue and Expense Summary — Acct. No. 901

1969					1969				
Jan.	31	Expenses	4	2,435	Jan.	31	Revenue	4	5,020
	31	Closing Entry	4	2,585					
				5,020					
				5,020					5,020

Balancing and Ruling the Open Real Accounts

To simplify computations in the statement of financial position accounts during the following accounting period, and to set apart the amounts from each accounting period, it is customary to bring down the balances of the real accounts, which are still open. The procedure is as follows:

1. The balance of the account is computed. The amount is transferred to the money column on the opposite side, dated as of the last day of the accounting period. The word *Balance* is entered in the Explanation column, and a check mark is placed in the folio (F) column.
2. The equal debit and credit footings are entered on the next unused full line.
3. Double rules are drawn across all the columns, except the Explanation columns.
4. The balance is written under the rules on the appropriate side, dated as of the first day of the new accounting period. The word *Balance* is written in the Explanation column, and a check mark is placed in the folio (F) column. It is not necessary to balance and rule an account that contains only one amount. Balancing an account, unlike adjusting and closing, does not involve journalizing or posting since the balance of the account does not change.

The real accounts of the Nelson Garage are shown in Figure 3-9. Note the placement of rules and balances.

GENERAL LEDGER

Cash   Acct. No. 101

Figure 3-9.
The Real Accounts Are Balanced and Ruled

1969						1969					
Jan.	2			1	30,000	Jan.	3		1		300
	6			1	1,000		4		1		80
	20			2	2,000		10		1		4,000
	31			2	1,800		15		1		800
	31		23,450	3	10		30		2		300
							31		2		80
							31		2		900
							31		2		300
							31		3		4,000
							31		3		600
							31	Balance	✔		23,450
					34,810						34,810
1969											
Feb.	1	Balance		✔	23,450						

Accounts Receivable — Acct. No. 121

1969					1969				
Jan.	12		1	40	Jan.	31		3	10
	25		2	60		31	Balance	✔	210
	28	210	2	120					
				220					220
1969									
Feb.	1	Balance	✔	210					

Garage Parts and Supplies — Acct. No. 131

1969					1969				
Jan.	5		1	400	Jan.	31		3	275
	29		2	250		31	Balance	✔	375
		375		650					650
1969									
Feb.	1	Balance	✔	375					

Prepaid Insurance — Acct. No. 141

1969				
Jan.	31		3	600

Land — Acct. No. 201

1969				
Jan.	10		1	10,000

Automotive Tools and Equipment — Acct. No. 221

1969				
Jan.	31		3	4,000

Accounts Payable — Acct. No. 301

1969					1969				
Jan.	30		2	300	Jan.	5		1	400
	31	Balance	✔	350		29	350	2	250
				650					650
					1969				
					Feb.	1	Balance	✔	350

Notes Payable — Acct. No. 302

					1969				
					Jan.	10		1	6,000

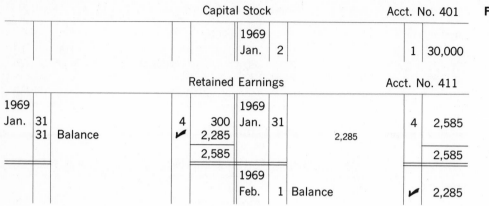

Figure 3-9 (cont.)

Taking a Post-Closing Trial Balance

After the closing entries have been posted, and the accounts are ruled and balanced, a *post-closing trial balance* is taken from the general ledger. Since the only accounts with open balances are the real accounts, the accounts and amounts in the post-closing trial balance are the same as in the statement of financial position. The post-closing trial balance tests the debit and credit equilibrium of the general ledger before the accounts are used during the next accounting period. Its use, however, is optional, and a comparison of the general ledger account balances with the statement of financial position will serve the same purpose. In any case, it is absolutely essential to start a new period with the accounts in proper balance; even though the trial balance at the end of the new period would indicate an error, errors made in previous accounting periods are very difficult to trace.

The post-closing trial balance of the Nelson Garage is shown:

NELSON GARAGE
Post-Closing Trial Balance
January 31, 1969

Acct. No.	Account Title	Debits	Credits
101	Cash	$23,450	
121	Accounts Receivable	210	
131	Garage Parts and Supplies	375	
141	Prepaid Insurance	600	
201	Land	10,000	
221	Automotive Tools and Equipment	4,000	
301	Accounts Payable		$ 350
302	Notes Payable		6,000
401	Capital Stock		30,000
411	Retained Earnings		2,285
	Totals	$38,635	$38,635

PROCEDURES APPLICABLE TO A SINGLE PROPRIETORSHIP

Since many service-type businesses are single proprietorships, the procedures discussed in this chapter that affect this form of business organization must be considered. If the Nelson Garage had been started by John Nelson as a single proprietorship, the following accounting differences would apply:

On January 2, 1969, Nelson would make the entire investment of $30,000, instead of three stockholders making an investment in a corporation. This investment by the single proprietor would be recorded in the journal as follows:

GENERAL JOURNAL   Page 1

1969				
Jan.	2	Cash	30,000	
		John Nelson, Capital		30,000
		To record investment by proprietor in a business		
		to be called the Nelson Garage.		

The only other regular transaction that would be recorded differently in a single proprietorship is the dividend paid by the corporation on January 31, 1969. A comparable situation in the case of the single proprietor would be his withdrawal of cash (or some other asset) in *anticipation* of the net income that he expects to earn. If Nelson withdraws $300, the transaction would be recorded as follows:

GENERAL JOURNAL   Page 1

1969				
Jan.	31	John Nelson, Drawing	300	
		Cash		300
		To record withdrawal by proprietor in anticipation		
		of earned income.		

A special account, *John Nelson, Drawing,* would be debited for all withdrawals in anticipation of income, and Cash would be credited; at the end of the period the drawing account would be credited for the net income that is actually earned.

All the other regular transactions of the Nelson Garage would be recorded in exactly the same manner for a single proprietorship as for a corporation.

The only other recording difference between the two forms of business organization is in the closing process. After the revenue and expense accounts are closed, the Revenue and Expense Summary and John Nelson, Drawing accounts will appear as follows:

Revenue and Expense Summary		John Nelson, Drawing
Expenses 2,435 | Revenue 5,020		300
2,585		

The following entries are made in the journal of the single proprietorship to complete the closing process:

GENERAL JOURNAL   Page 4

1969		Closing Entries for a Single Proprietorship		
Jan.	31	Revenue and Expense Summary	2,585	
		John Nelson, Drawing		2,585
		To close net income to Drawing account.		
	31	John Nelson, Drawing	2,285	
		John Nelson, Capital		2,285
		To close balance of Drawing account to capital.		

The effect of these entries is shown in the following T accounts:

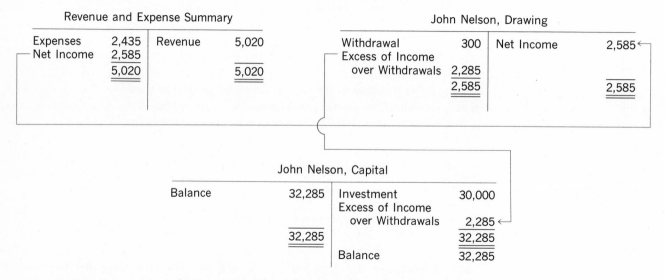

Revenue and Expense Summary			
Expenses	2,435	Revenue	5,020
Net Income	2,585		
	5,020		5,020

John Nelson, Drawing			
Withdrawal	300	Net Income	2,585
Excess of Income over Withdrawals	2,285		
	2,585		2,585

John Nelson, Capital		
Balance	32,285	Investment	30,000
		Excess of Income over Withdrawals	2,285
	32,285		32,285
		Balance	32,285

The net income, or net loss, is transferred to the proprietor's drawing account. This is consistent with the analysis of the withdrawal; since the drawing account is debited for withdrawals in anticipation of income, it should also be credited with the net income actually earned during the period. If the resulting balance of the account is a credit, it indicates that earnings have exceeded withdrawals, so that additional withdrawals can be made. A debit balance indicates an excess of withdrawals over earnings and the possible need for additional investments to cover the deficiency.

Since there are no such legal restrictions on the earnings of a single proprietorship as there are on those of a corporation, the balance of the drawing account is usually closed into the proprietor's capital account at the end of the accounting period.

The statement of financial position of a single proprietorship would be the same as that of a corporation, except for the Owner's Equity section. For a single proprietorship, this section appears as shown:

Owner's Equity
  John Nelson, Capital   <u>$32,285</u>

Since no Retained Earnings account is required for a single proprietorship, a statement of retained earnings would not be prepared; instead, a statement of owner's equity would be made. The statement of owner's equity for the Nelson Garage as a single proprietorship owned and operated by John Nelson is shown:

NELSON GARAGE
Statement of Owner's Equity
For the Month Ended January 31, 1969

John Nelson, Original Investment, January 2, 1969	$30,000
Add Net Income for January, 1969	2,585
Total	$32,585
Deduct Withdrawals	300
John Nelson, Capital, January 31, 1969	$32,285

A statement of owner's equity for a single proprietorship with a beginning balance and an additional investment during January is shown:

JAMES CLARK SERVICES
Statement of Owner's Equity
For the Month Ended January 31, 1969

James Clark, Capital, January 1, 1969	$500,000
Add Net Income for January, 1969	100,000
Additional Investment	200,000
Total	$800,000
Deduct Withdrawals	50,000
James Clark, Capital, January 31, 1969	$750,000

INTERRELATIONSHIP OF THE FINANCIAL STATEMENTS

There is a significant interrelationship between the statement of financial position, the statement of retained earnings, and the income statement, as illustrated in Figure 3-10. The income statement shows the net amount remaining after revenues have been matched with expenses for a given period. This amount, the net income, is transferred to the statement of retained earnings, which shows part of the changes that have taken place in stockholders' equity as a result of the operations of a period. The end-of-the period balance of retained earnings is transferred to the end-of-period statement of financial position, which presents information as of a moment of time; that is, at the end of the accounting period. The income statement and the statement of retained earnings help to account for the changes in the stockholders' equity during the interval between statements of financial position.

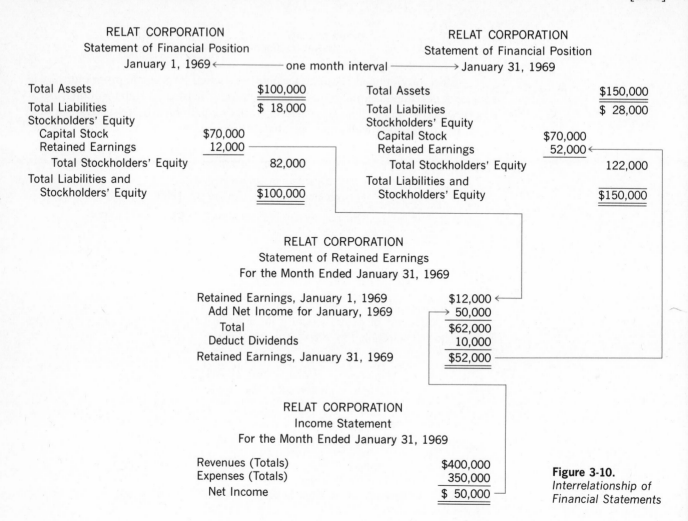

Figure 3-10.
*Interrelationship of
Financial Statements*

Summary totals are used so that the statements can be presented on one page. This procedure is not acceptable for the problems; details should be given on all statements.

1. The date of the first statement of financial position is also the beginning date of the statement of retained earnings and the income statement. (*For the Month Ended January 31, 1969*, means the period beginning January 1 and ending January 31.)
2. The date of the second statement of financial position (January 31, 1969) is also the ending date of the statement of retained earnings and the income statement.

3. The retained earnings in the first statement of financial position ($12,000) is the same as the beginning amount in the statement of retained earnings.
4. The net income ($50,000) is transferred from the income statement to the statement of retained earnings.
5. The end-of-period retained earnings ($52,000) is transferred from the statement of retained earnings to the statement of financial position dated January 31, 1969.

SUMMARY

Revenue describes the source of the inflow of assets resulting from services rendered, sales of products or merchandise, gains from sales or exchanges of assets other than stock in trade, and earnings from interest and dividends on investments. *Expenses* are the costs of goods and services used in the production of revenue. A debit records an increase in an expense and a decrease in revenue; whereas a credit records an increase in revenue and a decrease in an expense. *Net income* is the excess of total revenue over total expenses for a specified period of time. It reflects the increase in the owner's equity resulting from business operations. A *net loss* is the excess of total expenses over total revenue for a definite time period. It reflects the decrease in owner's equity resulting from business operations. *Dividends* are distributions of net income, earned in the current period or a prior period, to stockholders. Thus, dividends reduce the owner's equity. A debit records an increase in dividends and a credit records a decrease in dividends.

A *chart of accounts* is a classified listing of all the accounts used by a firm. The *general ledger* contains the statement of financial position and income statement accounts. When there is a large number of homogenous accounts (such as customer's accounts) in the general ledger, a *subsidiary ledger* can be opened to maintain the individual accounts. A *controlling account* in the general ledger summarizes the changes recorded in the subsidiary ledger. A transaction involving a controlling account must be posted to the general ledger and to the appropriate account in the related subsidiary ledger.

The accounting sequence discussed may be summarized as follows: (a) at the end of an accounting period, after all the transactions have been properly recorded and posted and the balances of the accounts have been obtained, a trial balance is taken. (b) After this step, a schedule listing the balances of the individual accounts of each subsidiary ledger is compiled; the total of these balances as shown on the schedule should agree with the related controlling account in the general ledger. (c) An *income statement*, which summarizes the expenses and revenue for a specific time period, showing the net income or net loss accruing to the owners; a *statement of retained earnings*, which shows the changes in that part of stockholder's equity designated as retained earnings; and a *statement of financial position* are prepared from the trial balance. (d) The revenue and expense accounts are closed to the Revenue and Expense Summary account, which is then closed to the Retained Earnings account. The Dividends account is also closed to the Retained Earnings account. The revenue, expense, and dividends accounts are set up to measure part of the changes that take place in Retained Earnings during a specified period of time and therefore must be closed, or emptied, at the end of that accounting period. (e) After the closing entries are posted and the accounts are balanced and ruled, a *post-closing trial balance* is prepared to test the equality of debits and credits before the accounts are used during the next accounting period.

In a single proprietorship, a drawing account is debited for all withdrawals of earnings. At the end of an accounting period, the Revenue and Expense Summary account is closed to the drawing account and the drawing account is closed to the proprietor's capital account. In a single proprietorship, a *statement of owner's equity* replaces the statement of retained earnings prepared in a corporation. It shows the changes that have taken place in the proprietor's capital account over a specified period of time.

□ **QUESTIONS**

Q3–1. Define the term *revenue*. Does the receipt of cash by a business indicate that revenue has been earned? Explain. List ten small businesses and professions, and name the major source of revenue for each.

Q3–2. Define the term *expense*. Does the payment of cash by a business indicate that an expense has been incurred? Explain. Distinguish between a dividend and an expense.

Q3–3. The accountant for J. A. Williams, owner of a parking-lot business, listed the parking lot at a cost of $10,000 on the financial position statement. Williams argues that this amount should be $18,000 because he has recently been offered $18,000 for the lot. Discuss.

Q3–4. What item is common to each of the following: (1) the income statement and the statement of owner's equity; (2) the statement of owner's equity and the statement of financial position as of the beginning of an accounting period; and (3) the statement of owner's equity and the statement of financial position as of the end of an accounting period?

Q3–5. Robert Hanlon purchased electrical supplies on account from the Wilson Company for $350, and from Jackson, Inc., for $100. Hanlon debited Electrical Supplies, $450, and erroneously credited Accounts Receivable for $450 in the general ledger. The credit postings to the accounts payable ledger were properly made.
  a. What effect would the error have on the debit and credit totals of the trial balance taken at the end of the month?
  b. What accounts in the trial balance would be incorrectly stated?
  c. Would the error be discovered? How?

Q3–6. List the advantages to management of a division of the general and subsidiary ledgers and the use of controlling accounts. Is it equally advantageous to exclude the schedules of accounts receivable and accounts payable from the general ledger trial balance? Explain.

Q3–7. The following transaction occurred on June 15, 1969:

Received bills representing charges for truck maintenance and repairs as follows: Beacon Hill Garage, $150; Uptown Garage, $225.

Showing the proper general journal and general and subsidiary ledger accounts, prepare flow charts as shown in Figure 3-1 to illustrate posting from the general journal to the general ledger and the accounts payable ledger.

Q3–**8.** Assume that your firm has 1000 charge customers.
   a. Why would you want to keep your posting up to date?
   b. Is it true that posting depends on previous journalizing?
   c. Does journalizing, in turn, depend on earlier procedures in the complete accounting system? Explain.

Q3–**9.** What is the purpose of closing the books? Using T accounts for Revenue, Expenses, Dividends, Revenue and Expense Summary, and Retained Earnings, diagram the closing process.

Q3–**10.** Distinguish between single-proprietorship and corporate accounting for investments and withdrawals, giving examples.

Q3–**11.** Draw a diagram showing the interrelationship of the statement of financial position, statement of retained earnings, and income statement.

Q3–**12.** The balance of retained earnings of the Hanson Company on December 31, 1969, was $1,000 less than on December 31, 1968. Give two possible reasons for the decrease.

□ **EXERCISES**

E3–**1.** The following cash receipt transactions occurred at the Ababa Realty Corporation during the month of July, 1969:

1969
July 1   Issued capital stock for $50,000 in cash.
      7   Received a commission of $1,200 from the sale of a house and lot.
      8   Received $2,500 in cash from the issuance of a note payable to a bank.
     13   Received $750 in interest from U.S. government bonds.
     20   Received $250 in cash for rent of part of a building for July, 1969.

Journalize the revenue transactions only.

E3–**2.** The following were among the cash payment transactions at the Ballow Garage during the month of September, 1969:

1969
Sept. 3   Paid $3,000 for a truck.
       7   Paid $760 for salaries for the month.
       9   Paid $2,000 in settlement of an account.
      12   Paid $350 for a typewriter.
      16   Declared and paid a $1,000 cash dividend to stockholders.
      22   Paid $175 for rent of the office for September.

Journalize the expense transactions only.

E3–**3.** The October, 1969, transactions of the Baker Travel Service are given:

1969
Oct. 1   Paid $160 for an advertisement in the Travel section of the New York Times.
      2   Arranged a round-the-world trip for Mr. and Mrs. Hooker J. Sander. A

commission of $250 in cash was collected from the steamship company.

3 Arranged fly-now, pay-later European trips for several clients. The Transatlantic Airway System agreed to a commission of $600 for services rendered, payment to be made at the end of the month.

4 Another advertisement was placed in the New York Times for $250, payment to be made in 10 days.

16 Benjamin K. Baker, owner of the Baker Travel Service, withdrew $350 from the business for his personal use.

19 Collected $600 from the Transatlantic Airway System.

Following the example given for the October 1 transaction, analyze each transaction and prepare the necessary journal entry.

Example:

Oct. 1 (a) Advertising is an operating expense. Expenses are recorded by debits. Debit Advertising Expense for $160.

(b) The asset Cash was decreased. Decreases of assets are recorded by credits. Credit Cash for $160.

(c) Journal entry:
Advertising Expense $160
    Cash $160

E3–4. The Cash account in the general ledger of Graham's Repair Shop is given:

Cash   Acct. No. 101

(1)	1,000	(3)	600
(2)	400	(5)	500
(4)	500		

Item 1 is Graham's original investment on June 1. Items 2 and 4 are cash receipts, and Items 3 and 5 are cash payments made during June.

a. What is the balance of the account to be shown in the trial balance as of the end of June?

b. Will Graham's income statement for the month of June reflect a net loss of $200—the excess of payments ($1,100) over receipts other than the original investment ($900)? Explain.

E3–5. The following transactions occurred at the Adams Rug Cleaning Company:

1969

Sept. 1 Billed customers for $285 for rug cleaning work, as follows:

Charles Abbott	$ 75
Morgan Hooley	120
Arthur Rogers	90
Total	$285

30 Received $135 on account from the following customers:

Charles Abbott	$ 25
Morgan Hooley	60
Arthur Rogers	50
Total	$135

a. Prepare general journal entries to record the transactions.
b. Post to general ledger and accounts receivable ledger accounts. (Assign appropriate numbers to general ledger accounts.)
c. Prepare a schedule of accounts receivable.

E3-6. On July 1, 1969, the Astor Plumbing Company purchased plumbing supplies on account as follows:

Allan Company	$ 300
Jackson Company	100
Warren, Inc.	600
Total	$1,000

On July 15, 1969, the Astor Plumbing Company paid its creditors as follows:

Allan Company	$200
Jackson Company	40
Warren, Inc.	150
Total	$390

a. Prepare general journal entries to record the transactions.
b. Post to general ledger and accounts payable ledger accounts. (Assign appropriate numbers to general ledger accounts.)
c. Prepare a schedule of accounts payable.

E3-7. As of December 31, 1969, the ledger of the Deason Company contained the following accounts and account balances, among others: Cash, $50,000; Accounts Receivable, $10,000; Retained Earnings, $62,500; Commissions Earned, $50,000; Rent Earned, $6,000; Salaries Expense, $35,000; Office Expense, $5,000; Miscellaneous Expense, $12,000; Dividends, $6,000. (All the nominal accounts are included.)

Journalize the closing entries.

E3-8. Financial information for three different corporations is given:

a. Net income for 1969	$ 22,800
Retained earnings at beginning of year	100,000
Dividends declared and paid in 1969	15,000
Retained earnings at end of year	?
b. Net income for 1969	$?
Retained earnings at beginning of year	160,000
Dividends declared and paid in 1969	20,000
Retained earnings at end of year	155,000
c. Net loss sustained in 1969	$ 5,000
Retained earnings at beginning of year	?
Dividends declared and paid in 1969	7,600
Retained earnings at end of year	265,000

Supply the missing figures.

E3-9. Financial information for three different single proprietorships is given:

a. Net income for 1969	$50,000
Owner's equity at the beginning of year	?
Owner's equity at the end of year	95,000
Withdrawals by owner during 1969	8,500

b. Net income for 1969 $?
    Owner's equity at beginning of year   70,000
    Owner's equity at end of year   68,000
    Withdrawals by owner during 1969   6,200

c. Net loss sustained in 1969 $ 7,800
    Owner's equity at beginning of year   30,000
    Owner's equity at end of year   19,800
    Withdrawals by owner during 1969   ?

Supply the missing figures. (Assume that no additional investments were made during 1969).

E3–10. Some of the possible effects of a transaction are listed:

(1) an asset increase accompanied by an asset decrease
(2) an asset increase accompanied by an owner's equity increase
(3) an asset increase accompanied by a liability increase
(4) an asset increase accompanied by a revenue increase
(5) an asset decrease accompanied by a liability decrease
(6) an asset decrease accompanied by owner equity decrease
(7) an asset decrease accompanied by an expense increase
(8) an expense increase accompanied by a liability increase

Using the identifying numbers to the left of the listed combinations, indicate the effect of each of the following transactions:

Example: Issued capital stock for cash. Answer: (2)

a. Paid an account payable.
b. Borrowed money from a bank and issued a note.
c. Collected an account receivable.
d. Collected a commission on a sale made today.
e. Paid for an ad in a newspaper.

□ **DEMONSTRATION PROBLEMS**

DP3–1. (*Journalizing, posting, trial balance, and schedule of accounts receivable*) The chart of accounts of the White Corporation includes the following accounts and identifying numbers: Cash, 101; Accounts Receivable, 111; Cleaning Supplies, 135; Store Equipment, 164; Capital Stock, 251; Cleaning Revenue, 301; Miscellaneous General Expense, 712; Wages Expense, 714.

1969

Dec. 1   Issued capital stock for $3,000 in cash to start a cleaning business.

     3   Purchased store equipment for $800 in cash.

   10   Paid $50 in cash for cleaning supplies.

   15   Billed the following customers for cleaning work for the first half of month:

               G. Jamieson $125
               W. Nixon   100
               J. Zarba   50

   15   Paid $200 in salaries.

   21   Paid $90 for miscellaneous general expenses.

Dec. 26   Received cash from the following customers to apply on account:

G. Jamieson $100
W. Nixon   60
J. Zarba   25

31   Paid $250 in salaries.

31   Billed the following customers for cleaning work for the second half of the month:

G. Jamieson $190
J. Zarba   80

31   Received $420 from cash customers for the month.

Required: 1. Journalize the transactions.
           2. Open accounts and post from the journal to the appropriate ledgers. (Assign appropriate numbers to general ledger accounts.)
           3. Take a trial balance.
           4. Prepare a schedule of accounts receivable.

DP3–2. (*Journalizing, posting, and statements*) Dr. Richard T. Taylor opened an office for the general practice of dentistry. During the month of October, 1969, the following transactions occurred.

1969

Oct. 1   Invested $2,000 in the business.

3   Purchased dental supplies on account, as follows:

Safety Dental Supply Company $350
Sanitary Supply Company   400

3   Paid $300 for the October rent.

7   Paid $200 for miscellaneous general expenses.

9   Received $1,200 in cash for professional services rendered.

10   Purchased office equipment from Dental Equipment Company for $5,000 on account.

15   Paid $200 to the Safety Dental Supply Company on account, and $300 to the Sanitary Supply Company.

26   Mailed statements to the following clients for services rendered:

R. Beale $45
P. Witty   75

31   Paid $1,000 in cash and issued a note payable for $4,000 to the Dental Equipment Company.

31   Received $20 in cash from R. Beale and $50 from P. Witty.

Required: 1. Journalize the transactions.
           2. Post to the general ledger, accounts receivable ledger, and accounts payable ledger. (Assign numbers to the general ledger accounts).
           3. Take a trial balance.
           4. Prepare schedules of accounts receivable and accounts payable as of October 31, 1969.

5. Prepare an income statement, a statement of owner's equity, and a statement of financial position.
6. Journalize the closing entries and post them.
7. Prepare a post-closing trial balance.

DP3–**3.** (*Closing entries and post-closing trial balance*) The trial balance of the Citterow Corporation on December 31, 1969, is given:

CITTEROW CORPORATION
Trial Balance
December 31, 1969

Acct. No.	Account Title	Debits	Credits
101	Cash	$50,000	
111	Accounts Receivable	4,000	
121	Supplies	1,800	
221	Equipment	20,000	
301	Accounts Payable		$ 4,000
401	Capital Stock		50,000
411	Retained Earnings, January 1, 1969		14,850
421	Dividends	2,000	
501	Commissions Earned		15,000
511	Rent Earned		5,000
601	Salaries Expense	6,700	
602	Advertising Expense	1,000	
603	Supplies Used	1,600	
604	Miscellaneous Expense	1,750	
	Totals	$88,850	$88,850

Required: 1. Set up T accounts for Retained Earnings, Dividends, and each revenue and expense account listed in the trial balance. Enter the account balances.
2. Journalize the closing entries and post to the T accounts.
3. Prepare a post-closing trial balance.

☐ **PROBLEMS**

P3–**1.** After obtaining his law degree, John MacPherson decided to open his own office. Transactions for the month of March, 1969, were:

1969

March 1 Deposited $5,000 in a checking account under the business name, John MacPherson, Attorney-at-Law.

3 Paid $150 for the first month's rent on his office.

5 Purchased office equipment for $720. Paid $220 in cash and issued a note payable for the balance.

6 Paid $120 for a one-year insurance policy on the office equipment, effective March 1, 1969.

7 Paid $100 in cash for office supplies.

8 Billed the following clients for services rendered:

J. Bates	$100
S. Canner	50
C. Faler	50

March 10   Withdrew $300 for personal use.

15   Received cash from the following clients:

J. Bates $50
S. Canner   50

18   Received $500 in cash for services rendered not previously billed.

31   Paid $375 for miscellaneous general expenses for March.

Required: Journalize the transactions.

P3-2. John Long, a master electrician, completed the following transactions during the month of August, 1969:

1969

Aug. 1   Transferred $16,000 from his personal savings and opened a business checking account.

1   Paid $250 for rent for the month.

1   Paid $2,000 in cash for store equipment to the Best Equipment Company.

1   Purchased electrical supplies for $1,500 on account, as follows:

Ray Electrical Supply Company $1,100
Mystic Wire Company   300
Burnett Supply Company   100

2   Paid a $200 premium on a one-year comprehensive insurance policy, effective August 1, 1969.

4   Purchased a truck for $3,100 from Bennett Motor Company, giving $1,100 in cash and a note payable for the balance.

8   Received $800 in cash for a completed wiring job.

12   Paid the following creditors:

Ray Electrical Supply Company $400
Mystic Wire Company   200
Burnett Supply Company   50

15   Invested an additional $2,000 in cash in the business.

20   Received $60 in cash for the rental of his truck.

23   Received $400 in cash for a completed wiring job.

26   Paid $30 for telephone service.

27   Paid $165 for gas, oil, and other truck expenses.

28   Withdrew $250 for personal use.

30   Paid the *Weekly Mercury* $25 for advertising space.

31   Billed customers for completed work, as follows:

Arlex Company $95
Raymond Wills   60
James Phillips   45

Required: 1. Open the following accounts in the general ledger: Cash 101, Accounts Receivable 111, Electrical Supplies 135, Prepaid Insurance 140, Truck 162, Store Equipment 164, Accounts Payable 201, Notes Payable 204, John Long, Capital 251, John Long, Drawing 252, Electrical Service Revenue 301, Rental Revenue 302, Advertising Expense 618, Rent Expense 703, Telephone and Telegraph Expense 709, Truck Expense 710.

2. Open customers' accounts in the accounts receivable ledger.
3. Open creditors' accounts in the accounts payable ledger.
4. Record all the transactions in the general journal.
5. Post from the general journal to the appropriate ledgers.
6. Prepare a trial balance from the general ledger.
7. Prepare a schedule of accounts receivable.
8. Prepare a schedule of accounts payable.

P3–3. The Sevran Service and Repair Tool Shop was incorporated on September 1, 1969, and capital stock was issued for $20,000 in cash. During the month of September, the Corporation completed the following transactions:

1969

Sept. 1 Paid a $300 premium on a one-year comprehensive insurance policy, effective September 1, 1969.

1 Paid $450 for the September rent.

2 Purchased store equipment for $2,000 in cash.

2 Purchased shop supplies on account as follows:

Alex Supply Company	$1,200
Cambridge Supply House	600
Mystic Tool Company	400

5 Purchased an automobile for $3,100 from Hosmer's Motor Company, giving $800 in cash and a note payable for the balance.

9 Received $600 in cash for servicing and repairing tools.

10 Paid $50 in cash for advertising space in the *Cambridge Weekly*.

15 Paid cash for gas, oil, and other automobile expenses for two weeks, $68.

15 Paid $1,700 to the following creditors:

Alex Supply Company	$900
Cambridge Supply House	500
Mystic Tool Company	300

18 Received $800 in cash for repairing tools.

20 Paid $500 in cash on the note given for the purchase of the automobile.

21 Declared and paid a $250 dividend.

22 Paid $35 for telephone service.

23 Paid $18 for a new battery for the automobile. (Debit Automobile Expense).

24 Billed customers $500 for service and repair work, as follows:

Harris Jones	$225
William Meserve	175
Patrick Robinson	100

25 Paid $15 for cleaning the shop.

25 Received $450 in cash for servicing tools.

26 Purchased additional shop supplies on account, as follows:

| Alex Supply Company | $225 |
| Cambridge Supply House | 150 |

27 Paid $58 for electric service.

28 Purchased a typewriter and an adding machine for $450.

29 Received $325 on account from the following customers:

Harris Jones	$100
William Meserve	150
Patrick Robinson	75

Sept. 30   Paid $55 for gas, oil, and other automobile expenses for two weeks.

   30   Received $350 from customers for repair work not previously billed.

   30   Paid $100 in cash for advertising space in a local magazine.

   30   Received a promissory note from Harris Jones for the balance due on his account.

Required: 1. Open the following accounts in the general ledger: Cash, 101; Accounts Receivable, 111; Notes Receivable, 115; Shop Supplies, 136; Prepaid Insurance, 140; Automobile, 162; Store Equipment, 164; Office Equipment, 165; Accounts Payable, 201; Notes Payable, 204; Capital Stock, 251; Dividends, 252; Repair Service Revenue, 301; Advertising Expense, 618; Rent Expense, 703; Heat and Light Expense, 705; Telephone and Telegraph Expense, 709; Automobile Expense, 710; Miscellaneous General Expense, 712.
2. Open customers' accounts in the accounts receivable ledger.
3. Open creditors' accounts in the accounts payable ledger.
4. Record all the transactions in the general journal.
5. Post to the appropriate ledgers.
6. Prepare a trial balance.
7. Prepare a schedule of accounts receivable.
8. Prepare a schedule of accounts payable.

P3–**4.** The trial balance of the Detter Parking Lot shows the accounts in alphabetical order:

DETTER PARKING LOT
Trial Balance
December 31, 1969

Account Title	Debits	Credits
Accounts Payable		$ 1,000
Accounts Receivable	$ 6,500	
Cash	21,800	
Capital Stock		20,000
Dividends	950	
Equipment Maintenance Expense	1,200	
Heat and Light Expense	800	
Interest Earned		600
Land	5,000	
Notes Payable		2,000
Notes Receivable	1,500	
Parking Fees Earned		19,650
Salaries	4,500	
Retained Earnings, January 1, 1969		1,250
Supplies on Hand	700	
Supplies Used	1,450	
Telephone Expense	100	
Totals	$44,500	$44,500

Required: 1. Prepare a trial balance in proper statement order.
2. Prepare an income statement, a statement of retained earnings, and a statement of financial position.
3. Journalize the closing entries.

P3-5. The following statements have been prepared for the E. Hooker Company:

E. HOOKER COMPANY
Income Statement
For the Month Ended January 31, 1969

Revenue		
Storage Fees		$2,485
Expenses		
Office Rent Expense	$ 300	
Salaries Expense	1,000	
Miscellaneous Expenses	335	1,635
Net Income		$ 850

E. HOOKER COMPANY
Statement of Financial Position
January 31, 1969

Assets			**Liabilities and Stockholders' Equity**		
Current Assets			Current Liabilities		
Cash	$1,000		Accounts Payable		$ 300
Repair Parts	500		Stockholders' Equity		
Total Current Assets		$1,500	Capital Stock	$3,000	
Plant and Equipment			Retained Earnings	1,700	
Land	$1,000		Total Stockholders' Equity		4,700
Building	2,500				
Total Plant and Equipment		3,500	Total Liabilities and		
Total Assets		$5,000	Stockholders' Equity		$5,000

During January, the Company declared and paid a dividend of $100.

Required: Prepare a statement of retained earnings for the E. Hooker Company for the month of January, 1969, and the closing entries as of January 31, 1969.

P3-6. Harold Fine, a master plumber, opened his own shop. During the month of March, 1969, he completed the following transactions.

1969

March 1 Invested $3,000 in cash in the business.

2 Paid $50 rent for the month of March.

4 Purchased plumbing supplies on account, as follows:

Rice Plumbing Company	$250
Massachusetts Plumbing Company	500
Plumbers, Inc.	150

March 6 Purchased a used truck for $2,016 from the Barrs Motor Company, giving $216 in cash and a note payable for the balance.

9 Paid $600 in cash for shop equipment.

10 Paid $180 in cash for a one-year insurance policy on the shop equipment and truck, effective March 10, 1969.

14 Received $350 for a completed plumbing job.

18 Paid creditors on account, as follows:

Rice Plumbing Company	$20
Massachusetts Plumbing Company	30
Plumbers, Inc.	15

20 Fine withdrew $175 for his personal use.

Use the following account numbers and titles:

11	Cash	55	Notes Payable
15	Accounts Receivable	61	Harold Fine, Capital
21	Plumbing Supplies	62	Harold Fine, Drawing
31	Prepaid Insurance	71	Rental Revenue
41	Truck	81	Plumbing Revenue
45	Shop Equipment	91	Rent Expense
51	Accounts Payable	92	Telephone and Telegraph Expense

Required: 1. Journalize the transactions.
2. Post to the appropriate ledger accounts.
3. Take a trial balance.
4. Prepare schedule of accounts payable.

P3-7. The following transactions occurred during January, 1969, at the David Roof Repair Company.

1969

Jan. 1 Issued capital stock for $10,000 in cash.

5 Paid $200 for two days' rental of a derrick and pulley assembly used on a repair job.

9 Purchased U.S. government bonds for $4,000 in cash.

11 Collected $1,300 on completion of roofing repair work.

20 Signed an agreement with Hampton College to repair dormitory roofs for $3,000. The work is to be completed during February and March.

25 Paid a cash dividend of $250 to stockholders.

28 Paid $450 for repair materials used on jobs during the month.

30 Paid $1,800 in salaries and wages.

31 Completed roofing repair work for Willard J. Evans in the amount of $1,600. Evans promised to pay for the work on February 10.

Use the following account titles and numbers:

11	Cash	41	Repair Service Revenue
15	Marketable Securities	51	Salaries and Wages Expense
18	Accounts Receivable	53	Repair Materials Expense
31	Capital Stock	55	Rental Expense
32	Retained Earnings	61	Revenue and Expense Summary
33	Dividends		

Required: 1. Journalize the transactions.
2. Post to general ledger accounts.
3. Take a trial balance.
4. Prepare an income statement, a statement of retained earnings, and a statement of financial position.
5. Prepare and post the closing entries.
6. Rule the accounts that have no balances.
7. Take a post-closing trial balance.

P3–**8.** The following information is taken from the books of the Grant Company:

GRANT COMPANY
Statement of Retained Earnings
For the Year Ended December 31, 1969

Retained Earnings, January 1, 1969	$ 50,000
Net Income for 1969	100,000
Total	$150,000
Deduct Dividends	35,000
Retained Earnings, December 31, 1969	$115,000

The expenses for 1969 were: Salaries, $40,000; Advertising Expense, $10,000; Office Expense, $8,000; and Miscellaneous Expense, $18,000. The revenue came from only one source, Commissions Earned.

Required: Prepare a formal income statement for the Grant Company. Show your computations of the amounts that are not given.

CASE PROBLEM
Reliable Appliance Service, Inc.

Since starting his own firm, the Reliable Appliance Service, Inc., last January, Fredric Clark has been very pleased with the volume of business and the prospect of even more business in the future. He had several years of experience in electrical appliance and refrigeration work, so he decided to set up a corporation to service electrical and refrigeration appliances such as television sets, radios, air conditioners, refrigerators, ranges, fans, and irons.

The first year of operations has now ended, and Clark and the other corporate officers want to know how well the firm has done during that period. They know from the statement of financial position how they stood last January 1.

RELIABLE APPLIANCE SERVICE, INC.
Statement of Financial Position
January 1, 1969

Assets		**Liabilities and Stockholders' Equity**	
Current Assets		Current Liabilities	
Cash	$4,500	Note Payable to Bank	$1,000
Shop Supplies	300	Stockholders' Equity	
Total Current Assets	$4,800	Capital Stock	$10,000
Plant and Equipment			
Equipment	$ 3,500		
Delivery truck	2,700		
Total Plant and Equipment	$ 6,200	Total Liabilities and	
Total Assets	$11,000	Stockholders' Equity	$11,000

Even though the Company accountant has kept very accurate records throughout the year, Clark wishes to check the work, so he begins by reviewing the checkbook, cancelled checks, and deposit book. He lists the following transactions in summary form:

Deposits

Money collected from cash customers	$19,000
Money collected from customers on account	2,500
Money received for capital stock	1,000
Money borrowed from Mrs. Fredric Clark	500
Total deposits	$23,000

Checks written

Payments to employees for salaries and wages	$10,000
Payments to vendors for shop supplies	1,750
Payments to bank on note payable (includes $30 interest)	1,030
Payments for delivery truck expenses	600
Payments to corporate officers for salary	8,500
Payments to landlord for building rental	1,440
Total checks	$23,320

Next, he adds up the sales tickets prepared during the year for work that was done for customers. He finds that the volume of business done was $23,200. Also, he sees that the amount these customers still owe the firm totals $1,700. (Note that the amounts collected, $19,000 + $2,500, plus the amounts not collected, $1,700, equal the total sales volume, $23,200.)

He also considers the amounts that the firm owes but has not paid: $175 for shop supplies and $20 for gas used in the delivery truck.

Of the shop supplies that have been available for use during the year (the beginning amount, $300, plus the amounts purchased, $1,750 plus $175), Clark notes from other records that $400 worth has not been used. Checking the closing entries in the journal, he finds a debit to Depreciation Expense for $750 and a credit to Accumulated Depreciation for the same amount. (Adjustments for depreciation are discussed in Chapter 4.)

Required: 1. Prepare a properly classified income statement for the year ended December 31, 1969. (Place the asset, liability, and stockholders' equity balances as of January 1 in T accounts. Use the other data accumulated by Clark to bring the T accounts up to date as of December 31. Then select the titles and amounts that will appear on the income statement from the T accounts.)

2. Give your reasons for including or excluding each title and amount in the T accounts.

3. Explain what an income statement is and what function it serves.

4. Explain why you arranged the items on the statement as you did.

5. Explain and diagram the steps that the company accountant must have followed.

6. Reconstruct in summary form the journal entries that (if posted) would bring the beginning general ledger balances up to date.

7. Explain the relationship between a statement of financial position and an income statement.

Chapter Four

The End-of-Period Process

A complete but simple example, the transactions of the Nelson Garage, was used in Chapter 3. A similar but more complex example is used in this chapter to introduce the following elements: (1) adjustments—continuous transactions that, for convenience, are not recorded until the end of the period, (2) the worksheet—an orderly method of collecting information for the preparation of formal financial statements, and (3) further managerial analysis.

ACCOUNTING METHODS

Two accounting methods are usually used: the *cash basis* and the *accrual basis*.

The Cash Basis

Under the cash basis of accounting, revenue is recognized when payment is received and is recorded at that time. Expenses are recognized in the period of payment. Hence, recognition of revenue and expenses during an accounting period is based on an inflow and outflow of cash—a matching of cash receipts and cash disbursements to determine operating results during an accounting period. This method of accounting is obviously simple in application, but in most cases it does not properly measure net income because, for example, it does not recognize credit sales as revenue and credit purchases as expenses until actual payment is made. Hence, it matches only some of the revenues and expenses for a given period. There are instances, however, particularly in small professional and service businesses, in which the cash basis of accounting is used with acceptable results. Hybrid systems, or modifications of the cash basis system, are often found in practice.

The Accrual Basis

The accrual basis of accounting is founded on the principle that, to properly measure the net income of a business for a given period of time, it is essential that all the revenue earned during that period and all the related expenses assignable to the period be considered. Revenues are recognized at the time of sale, and expenses are usually recognized at the time of incurrence. ▶ This process of matching the revenue of a period with the expenses of that period, regardless of when, whether, or how much cash has been received or paid, is the central goal of the accrual basis of accounting and underlies all the discussions in this text. ◀

Accounting Concept:
Matching Revenue and
◀ *Expenses*

The difference in net income resulting from the use of each method is best illustrated by an example. The Dee Company, which does landscape gardening, performed work during August for which it charged $1,000. It received $600 on August 15 and $400 on September 10. Wages (the only expense) of $550 were paid on August 31. No work was performed during September.

	Cash Basis		Accrual Basis	
	August	September	August	September
Revenue	$600	$400	$1,000	$-0-
Expense	550	-0-	550	-0-
Net Income	$ 50	$400	$ 450	$-0-

The accrual basis of accounting gives more useful results because revenue is reflected in the period to which it properly belongs; that is, the period in which it was earned. Net income is the difference between revenue earned and expenses incurred during the accounting period. The accrual method, by matching expenses incurred with revenue earned for the period, presents the true net income. Since the accrual basis of accounting results in more accurate financial statements, most businesses use it.

THE NEED FOR ADJUSTING ENTRIES

During the accounting period, regular business transactions are recorded as they occur. At the end of the period, the accountant may find that the ledger accounts are incomplete: some new accounts must be brought into the books and other accounts must be brought up to date. The journal entries necessary to accomplish this are referred to as *adjusting entries*. Periodic adjustment of the ledger accounts is indispensable if the financial statements are to reflect the true position of the company—its assets and equities—as of the end of the period, and the results of its operations—revenue earned and expenses incurred—during the period.

It is impractical and sometimes impossible to record the day-to-day changes in certain accounts. For example, when the premium payment is made on an insurance policy, the asset Prepaid Insurance is debited. At the end of the accounting period, however, only part of the balance of the Prepaid Insurance account represents an asset. The amount that has expired with the passage of time is an expense because it represents the cost of insurance protection. At the end of the accounting period, therefore, Prepaid Insurance contains both an asset and an expense element. An adjustment is necessary to record the correct amount of Insurance Expense and to reduce Prepaid Insurance. Any account that contains two such distinct elements is referred to as a *mixed account.*

An adjusting entry may be required to record previously unrecorded data. Assume, for example, that a company paid wages on March 28 for the two-week period that ended on that date. However, the employees worked on March 29, 30, and 31. If March 31 is the end of the accounting period, recognition must be given to this unrecorded but incurred expense as well as to the corresponding increase in liabilities, so that the financial statements may show the liability and the proper assignment of the expense to the period.

Adjusting entries may be entered initially in the worksheet with formal recording in the journal deferred until the closing entries are made, or they may be recorded in the journal first and then applied to the worksheet.

A distinction must be made between adjusting entries and entries that record regular business transactions. Regular business transactions start and complete their cycles within an accounting period. Adjusting entries deal with the transactions that transpire continuously. It is neither feasible nor necessary to record these continuing changes during the period; rather, they are recorded at the end of each accounting period by means of summary adjusting entries. The nature of the adjusting entries varies. The adjusting entry for wages, for example, records a change that has already taken place; the increase in a liability incurred but unrecorded. The adjusting entry for Supplies Expense, on the other hand, recognizes the partial consumption of an item that was recorded at the time of acquisition in an asset account.

THE PROCESS OF RECORDING ADJUSTMENTS

The Connolly Trucking Company started business on June 1, 1969. As a convenience in illustrating the end-of-period procedures, it is assumed that the books are closed on June 30 (books are customarily closed annually). The trial balance taken from the Connolly Trucking Company's general ledger is shown in Figure 4-1.

The adjusting entries are illustrated by T accounts. The separate discussion of each adjusting entry is identified by the letter used to cross-reference the debit and credit adjustments in the Adjustments columns of the *worksheet*, shown in Figure 4-4. In addition, amounts taken from the trial balance are shown in the T accounts to highlight the effect of each adjusting entry. A journal entry must be made for each adjustment. This is shown in Figure 4-10.

Adjusting the Mixed Accounts—Asset and Expense

There are three steps in adjusting the mixed accounts:

1. Determining the balance of each account to be adjusted
2. Determining the amount of the asset or expense elements in each account
3. Recording the adjusting entries.

CONNOLLY TRUCKING COMPANY
Trial Balance
June 30, 1969

Acct. No.	Account Title	Debit	Credit
101	Cash	$ 5,250	
111	Accounts Receivable	550	
112	Notes Receivable	1,440	
131	Office Supplies	230	
141	Prepaid Insurance	2,160	
142	Prepaid Rent	1,500	
201	Office Equipment	1,400	
211	Trucks	13,000	
301	Accounts Payable		$ 200
302	Notes Payable		8,000
321	Unearned Rent		600
401	Capital Stock		12,000
402	Dividends	500	
501	Trucking Revenue		7,465
601	Heat and Light Expense	40	
602	Maintenance and Repairs Expense	375	
603	Telephone and Telegraph Expense	95	
604	Gas and Oil Expense	525	
605	Wages Expense	1,200	
	Totals	$28,265	$28,265

Figure 4-1.
Trial Balance

(a)

On June 1, the Connolly Trucking Company paid $1,500 in cash for three month's rent.

Step 1. The general ledger shows the following balance in the account:

Prepaid Rent (mixed)		Acct. No. 142
June 1	$1,500	

Step 2. The amount of expense applicable to the month of June is $500 ($1,500 ÷ 3 mo.). On June 30, therefore, Prepaid Rent is a mixed account consisting of:

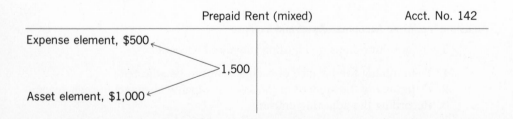

Prepaid Rent (mixed)		Acct. No. 142
Expense element, $500 ⟍		
⟩ 1,500		
Asset element, $1,000 ⟋		

Step 3. The required adjusting entry is a $500 debit to Rent Expense and a corresponding credit to Prepaid Rent. The expense element is thus removed from the mixed account, as shown:

Prepaid Rent (asset)		Acct. No. 142	
June 1	1,500	June 30 (adjustment)	500

Rent Expense (expense)		Acct. No. 606	
June 30 (adjustment)	500		

Prepaid Rent ($1,000) is classified in the statement of financial position as a current asset, and Rent Expense ($500) appears in the income statement as an expense.

(b)

The Connolly Trucking Company paid a premium of $2,160 for a comprehensive three-year insurance policy, effective June 1, 1969.

Step 1. Prepaid Insurance, before adjustment, shows a balance of $2,160. The title Prepaid Insurance classifies it as basically an asset account, but it is in fact a mixed account.

Step 2. An analysis of the account shows that the expense element for the month of June is $60 ($2,160 ÷ 36 mo.), and that the unused portion of $2,100 is the asset prepayment benefiting future periods.

Step 3. An adjusting entry for $60 is required, debiting Insurance Expense to increase the expense account and crediting Prepaid Insurance to decrease the asset account.

Prepaid Insurance (asset)		Acct. No. 141	
June 1	2,160	June 30 (adjustment)	60

Insurance Expense (expense)		Acct. No. 607	
June 30 (adjustment)	60		

Prepaid Insurance ($2,100) is classified in the statement of financial position as a current asset, and Insurance Expense ($60) appears in the income statement as an expense.

(c)

Step 1. On the trial balance (Figure 4-1), Office Supplies has a debit balance of $230, representing a purchase made on June 6.

Step 2. The inventory taken on June 30 showed $60 worth of unused supplies; therefore, the expense element is $170 ($230 − $60).

Step 3. The expense of $170 needs to be removed by an adjusting entry from the mixed account and transferred to a separate expense account.

Office Supplies (asset)		Acct. No. 131	
June 6	230	June 30 (adjustment)	170

Office Supplies Expense (expense)		Acct. No. 608	
June 30 (adjustment)	170		

Office Supplies ($60) is classified in the statement of financial position as a current asset and Office Supplies Expense ($170) appears in the income statement as an expense.

Adjusting the Mixed Accounts—Liability and Revenue

The same three steps are followed in adjusting mixed liability accounts and revenue accounts.

(d)

On June 1, the Connolly Trucking Company signed a contract for the use of its trucks on a part-time basis and received an advance payment of $600 for six months' rent. At that time, Cash was debited and a liability account, Unearned Rent, was credited for $600. On June 30, only the portion earned in the month of June is transferred from Unearned Rent to Rent Earned; the unearned portion remains in Unearned Rent as a liability because the Connolly Trucking Company must provide the use of its truck on a part-time basis for another five months.

Step 1. The amount in the T account is taken from the trial balance, Figure 4-1:

Unearned Rent (mixed)		Acct. No. 321	
		June 1	600

Step 2. The rent actually earned in June is $100 ($600 ÷ 6 mo.); on June 30, Unearned Rent, a mixed account, consists of:

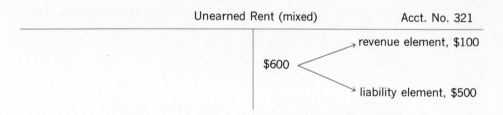

Unearned Rent (mixed)		Acct. No. 321
	$600	revenue element, $100
		liability element, $500

Step 3. The necessary adjusting entry is a debit to Unearned Rent and a credit to Rent Earned for $100. The revenue element is removed from the mixed account as follows:

Unearned Rent (liability)			Acct. No. 321
June 30 (adjustment)	100	June 1	600

Rent Earned (revenue)		Acct. No. 511
	June 30 (adjustment)	100

Rent Earned ($100) appears in the income statement as a revenue item, and Unearned Rent ($500) appears in the statement of financial position as a current liability.

Recording Asset Expirations and Unrecorded Data

The remaining adjusting entries record asset expirations and previously unrecorded expense and revenue items that should be shown in the financial statements. Three steps similar to those for mixed accounts are followed.

(e)

Step 1. The trial balance, Figure 4-1, shows a balance in the Office Equipment account of $1,400.

Step 2. The equipment, acquired on June 1, is estimated to have a useful life of ten years, or 120 months, and a *salvage value* of $200 at the end of that period. Salvage, or *residual*, value is the estimated price for which an asset may be sold when it is no longer serviceable to the business. In effect, the use of office equipment for ten years has been purchased at a net cost of $1,200 ($1,400 − $200). A portion of this cost expires in each accounting period during the useful life of the equipment. ▶ This periodic expired cost, called *depreciation expense*, requires no periodic cash outlay, but nevertheless is a continuous expense of operating the business. The portion of the cost of an asset assigned to the accounting period is called *depreciation*. There are a number of methods that may be used in calculating the periodic depreciation charge. ◀ Depreciation expense for the month of June is computed in this case by using the *straight-line method*, in which a uniform portion of the cost is assigned to each period.

Accounting Concept:
◀ *Depreciation*

$$\frac{\text{Cost} - \text{Salvage Value}}{\text{Estimated Months of Useful Life}} = \text{Depreciation for Month}$$

The depreciation expense for the office equipment in June is computed at $10.

$$\frac{\$1,400 - \$200}{120} = \$10$$

Step 3. An adjusting entry is made, debiting Depreciation Expense–Office Equipment (a new account) and crediting Accumulated Depreciation–Office Equipment (another new account) for $10. The latter is called an *asset valuation account* because its balance is deducted from Office Equipment to show the *book value,* or *carrying value,* of the asset. Office Equipment could be credited directly because the depreciation represents a decrease in the asset; but this procedure is undesirable because it fails to disclose information that is useful to management. Depreciation is an estimate; it is informative to keep asset costs separate from estimated reductions in cost. When separate accounts are used, the original cost and the accumulated depreciation can be determined readily. The June 30 adjusting entry is:

Depreciation Expense—Office Equipment (expense)	Acct. No. 609
June 30 (adjustment) 10	

Accumulated Depreciation—Office Equipment (asset valuation)	Acct. No. 201A
	June 30 (adjustment) 10

In the statement of financial position (Figure 4-8), the asset valuation account (also referred to as a *contra account*) Accumulated Depreciation–Office Equipment is deducted from Office Equipment; the remainder is the *undepreciated cost;* that is, the portion of the cost of the asset that is not yet charged to expense. Depreciation Expense–Office Equipment ($10) is shown in the income statement as an expense.

(f)

Step 1. On June 1, the Connolly Trucking Company purchased two trucks for business use, each costing $6,500. Since the useful life of the trucks is limited, a portion of the cost is allocable to the month of June. It is estimated that their useful life is five years, or 60 months, at the end of which time each truck will have a salvage value of $500.

Step 2. The computation and recording of the depreciation expense for the trucks is similar to that for the office equipment. The depreciation expense for June for the two trucks is calculated by the straight-line method as follows:

$$\frac{\text{Cost of \$6,500} - \text{salvage value of \$500}}{\text{60 months}}$$
$$= \$100 \text{ Depreciation per month for each truck, or \$200 for two trucks}$$

Step 3. The following adjusting entry is made on June 30:

Depreciation Expense—Trucks (expense)		Acct. No. 610
June 30 (adjustment)	200	

Accumulated Depreciation—Trucks (asset valuation)		Acct. No. 211A
	June 30 (adjustment)	200

The classification of these accounts in the financial statements is shown in Figures 4-7 and 4-8.

The Accumulated Depreciation accounts are used to accumulate the periodic charges made to expense and to segregate the deduction for the asset valuation. Depreciation Expense shows the expired cost for the accounting period and is closed along with the other expense accounts in an entry that transfers the total expense to Revenue and Expense Summary. Assume that the same adjusting entry for trucks is made on July 31. After it is posted, the general ledger T accounts for Trucks, Depreciation Expense–Trucks, and Accumulated Depreciation–Trucks appear as follows:

Trucks		Acct. No. 211
June 1	13,000	

Accumulated Depreciation—Trucks   Acct. No. 211A

| | | June 30 | 200 |
| | | July 31 | 200 |

Depreciation Expense–Trucks   Acct. No. 610

| June 30 (adjusting entry) | 200 | June 30 (closing entry) | 200 |
| July 31 (adjusting entry) | 200 | | |

The cost of the trucks and the accumulated depreciation are shown on the statement of financial position at July 31 as follows:

Equipment
    Trucks $13,000
    Deduct Accumulated Depreciation–Trucks   400 $12,600

(g)

Step 1. Wages Expense contains two debits of $600 each, representing wages paid biweekly to employees through June 27.

Step 2. The employees earned wages of $150 for work on June 28, 29, and 30, the last three days of the accounting period. Although the company will not pay the employees again until July 11, it has nevertheless incurred $150 of wages expense for these three days, and a $150 liability exists as of June 30.

Step 3. The adjusting entry is a debit to Wages Expense and a credit to Accrued Wages Payable for $150.

Wages Expense (expense)   Acct. No. 605

June 13	600		
27	600		
30 (adjustment)	150		

Accrued Wages Payable (liability)   Acct. No. 311

| | | June 30 (adjustment) | 150 |

Wages Expense ($1,350) is shown in the income statement as an expense; Accrued Wages Payable ($150) is shown in the statement of financial position as a current liability.

(h)

Step 1. On June 12, the Connolly Trucking Company borrowed $8,000 from the bank and signed a 45-day, 6-percent interest-bearing note payable. This transaction was recorded in the general journal by debiting Cash and crediting Notes Payable for $8,000.

Step 2. The cost of the use of the $8,000—interest expense—continues throughout the 45 days because interest expense accumulates with the passage of time. The total interest expense plus the $8,000 principal amount will be paid to the bank on July 27, the *maturity*, or due, date. However, unpaid interest expense on an interest-bearing note payable for the 18-day period from June 12 through June 30 must be recognized by an adjusting entry debiting Interest Expense and crediting Accrued Interest Payable for $24.

The formula for computing interest is:

Figure 4-2.
Interest Formula

$$\text{Principal} \times \text{Interest Rate} \times \frac{\text{Elapsed Time in Days}}{360} = \text{Interest}$$

The unpaid interest expense accrued on June 30 is computed as follows:

$$\$8,000 \times 0.06 \times \frac{18}{360} = \$24$$

The principal multiplied by the interest rate equals the total interest for one year ($8,000 × 0.06 = $480); the interest for a year ($480) multiplied by the elapsed fraction of a year ($\frac{18}{360}$ or $\frac{1}{20}$) is the interest expense for 18 days ($480 × 1/20), or $24. The use of 360 days in the formula is consistent with commercial practice, the primary reason being simplicity of calculation.

Step 3. The adjusting entry debits Interest Expense and credits Accrued Interest Payable for $24. After the entry has been posted, the accounts in the general ledger appear as follows:

Interest Expense (expense)		Acct. No. 611
June 30 (adjustment)	24	

Accrued Interest Payable (liability)		Acct. No. 303
	June 30 (adjustment)	24

Interest Expense ($24) is reported as an expense in the income statement; Accrued Interest Payable ($24) appears as a current liability in the statement of financial position. This entry gives rise to an *accrued liability*, or *accrued expense*. These terms refer to the liability for an expense incurred during one accounting period but payable in a future accounting period. Expenses incurred for which invoices have not yet been received—telephone, heat, light, water, and so on—are also in this category. These may be recorded by debits to appropriate expense accounts and a credit to Accrued Accounts Payable.

(i)

Step 1. The Connolly Trucking Company loaned $1,440 to one of its customers, who signed a 30-day, 5-percent interest-bearing note dated June 10. An entry was made debiting Notes Receivable and crediting Cash for $1,440.

Step 2. The company earned interest on the loan for 20 days in June (June 10 through June 30); it will be received on the maturity date, July 10, when the amount due (principal plus total interest) is paid by the customer. Interest earned, like interest expense, accrues with the passage of time. The 20 days interest earned by June 30 is recorded by an adjusting entry debiting Accrued Interest Receivable and crediting Interest Earned for $4. Using the formula shown in Figure 4-2, the computation of the interest is:

$$\$1,440 \times .05 \times \frac{20}{360} = \$4$$

Step 3. The adjusting entry debits Accrued Interest Receivable and credits Interest Earned for $4. After posting adjusting entry (i) the accounts in the general ledger appear as follows:

Accrued Interest Receivable (asset)		Acct. No. 113	
June 30 (adjustment)	4		

Interest Earned (revenue)		Acct. No. 521	
		June 30 (adjustment)	4

Accrued Interest Receivable ($4) is a current asset in the statement of financial position. Interest Earned is a revenue item in the income statement. An adjusting entry of this type gives rise to *accrued assets* and *accrued revenue*.

(j)

A single proprietor or a partner combines his net income from his proprietorship or partnership interest with his income from other sources and computes his tax as an individual taxpayer; he does not pay a tax on his business entity as such. A corporation, however, is taxed as a separate entity, and its financial statements must show the tax and the liability for the tax.

Step 1. It is difficult to determine precisely the tax related to the taxable income for the month of June because the annual taxable income, on which the tax is based, is not yet known. Nevertheless, the business must make the best possible estimate.

Step 2. The Connolly Trucking Company estimates its income taxes for the month of June to be $1,900.

Step 3. The adjusting entry is a debit to Income Tax Expense and a credit to Income Taxes Payable as shown:

Income Tax Expense (expense)		Acct. No. 611	
June 30 (adjustment)	1,900		

Income Taxes Payable (liability)		Acct. No. 331	
		June 30 (adjustment)	1,900

The income tax expense of $1,900 appears in the income statement; it is deducted from net income before income taxes to determine net income after income taxes (Figure 4-7); Income Taxes Payable appears in the statement of financial position as a current liability.

THE WORKSHEET

The worksheet is a device used by the accountant to facilitate the preparation of the formal financial statements; it is not a substitute for the financial statements. Although the worksheet is not indispensable, it would be difficult in most instances to prepare the statements directly from the journals and ledgers since that would often require consolidating material from books, cards, and other documents. The worksheet bridges the gap between the accounting records and the formal statements and serves as a convenient device to calculate the effect of the adjustments and to determine the net income, or net loss, before the adjustments are formally entered in the books and posted to the ledger. It furnishes the accountant with a preview of the final statements. Many businesses do not formally close their books at the end of every accounting period; thus the worksheet substitutes for the formal procedure of recording and posting the usual adjusting and closing entries.

Preparing the Worksheet

There are four steps in the preparation of the worksheet:

Step 1. The worksheet is headed to show the name of the company, the name of the statement, and the accounting period; the column headings are entered; the trial balance account titles and amounts are entered either directly from the general ledger or from a prepared listing, if available. The account titles are entered in the space provided and the amounts are entered in the first pair of money columns. The worksheet of the Connolly Trucking Company after completion of Step 1 appears in Figure 4-3.

CONNOLLY TRUCKING COMPANY
Worksheet
For the Month Ended June 30, 1969

Acct. No.	Account Title	Trial Balance		Adjustments		Adjusted Trial Balance		Income Statement		Position Statement	
		Dr.	Cr.	Dr.	Cr.	Dr.	Cr.	Dr.	Cr.	Dr.	Cr.
101	Cash	5,250									
111	Accounts Receivable	550									
112	Notes Receivable	1,440									
131	Office Supplies	230									
141	Prepaid Insurance	2,160									
142	Prepaid Rent	1,500									
201	Office Equipment	1,400									
211	Trucks	13,000									
301	Accounts Payable		200								
302	Notes Payable		8,000								
321	Unearned Rent		600								
401	Capital Stock		12,000								
402	Dividends	500									
501	Trucking Revenue		7,465								
601	Heat and Light Expense	40									
602	Maintenance and Repairs Expense	375									
603	Telephone and Telegraph Expense	95									
604	Gas and Oil Expense	525									
605	Wages Expense	1,200									
	Totals	28,265	28,265								

Trial balance before adjustments.

Figure 4-3.
Worksheet, Step 1

Step 2. The adjustments are keyed for identification (cross-referencing) as they are entered in the Adjustments columns. Any additional accounts required by the adjusting entries are added below the trial balance. (Alternatively, they may be listed in sequence with the other accounts without amounts in the Trial Balance columns.) In Entry *a*, for example, Rent Expense is debited for $500. Since this account does not appear in the trial balance, the title is written on the line immediately below the trial balance totals and the amount is entered directly in the Adjustments Debit column on the same line; the $500 also is entered in the Adjustments Credit column opposite Prepaid Rent. In this adjustment, only one of the accounts involved had to be written in below the trial balance. In Entry *e*, however, both the debited and credited accounts had to be written in. After all the adjustments are entered, the Adjustments columns are added as a proof of their equality. The worksheet following the completion of Step 2 is illustrated in Figure 4-4.

CONNOLLY TRUCKING COMPANY
Worksheet
For the Month Ended June 30, 1969

Acct. No.	Account Title	Trial Balance Dr.	Trial Balance Cr.	Adjustments Dr.	Adjustments Cr.	Adjusted Trial Balance Dr.	Adjusted Trial Balance Cr.	Income Statement Dr.	Income Statement Cr.	Position Statement Dr.	Position Statement Cr.
101	Cash	5,250									
111	Accounts Receivable	550									
112	Notes Receivable	1,440									
131	Office Supplies	230			(c) 170						
141	Prepaid Insurance	2,160			(b) 60						
142	Prepaid Rent	1,500			(a) 500						
201	Office Equipment	1,400									
211	Trucks	13,000									
301	Accounts Payable		200								
302	Notes Payable		8,000								
321	Unearned Rent		600	(d) 100							
401	Capital Stock		12,000								
402	Dividends	500									
501	Trucking Revenue		7,465								
601	Heat and Light Expense	40									
602	Maintenance and Repairs Expense	375									
603	Telephone and Telegraph Expense	95									
604	Gas and Oil Expense	525									
605	Wages Expense	1,200		(g) 150							
		28,265	28,265								
606	Rent Expense			(a) 500							
607	Insurance Expense			(b) 60							
608	Office Supplies Expense			(c) 170							
511	Rent Earned				(d) 100						
609	Depreciation Expense–Office Equipment			(e) 10							
201A	Accumulated Depreciation–Office Equipment				(e) 10						
610	Depreciation Expense–Trucks			(f) 200							
211A	Accumulated Depreciation–Trucks				(f) 200						
311	Accrued Wages Payable				(g) 150						
611	Interest Expense			(h) 24							
303	Accrued Interest Payable				(h) 24						
113	Accrued Interest Receivable			(i) 4							
521	Interest Earned				(i) 4						
612	Income Tax Expense			(j) 1,900							
331	Income Taxes Payable				(j) 1,900						
				3,118	3,118						

Letters are used to cross-reference the debit and credit adjustments.

Additional accounts for the adjustments

Adjustments are entered in these columns

Figure 4-4.
Worksheet, Step 2

Step 3. The amounts extended to the Adjusted Trial Balance columns result from combining the amounts in the Trial Balance columns with the amounts in the Adjustments columns as follows:

a. If there are no adjustments to an account, a debit trial balance amount is extended to the Debit column of the adjusted trial balance, and a credit trial balance amount is extended to the Credit column of the adjusted trial balance.

b. If the account in the trial balance has a debit balance, add its debit adjustments and subtract its credit adjustments. The balance, if a debit, is extended to the Adjusted Trial Balance Debit column; if a credit, it is extended to the Credit column.

c. If the account in the trial balance has a credit balance, add its credit adjustments and subtract its debit adjustments. The adjusted balance is extended to the proper Adjusted Trial Balance column.

d. For the accounts listed below the trial balance totals, the adjustment amount is extended directly to the appropriate Adjusted Trial Balance column.

Upon completion of Step 3, the account balances will be the same as the balances of the accounts in the general ledger after the adjusting entries have been journalized and posted. Each line on the worksheet represents a general ledger account and functions in the same manner as to the debit and credit position. For example, after adjustment the Prepaid Rent account appears in the general ledger as follows:

Prepaid Rent			Acct. No. 142
June 1	1,500	June 30 (adjusting entry)	500

The balance is a debit of $1,000, which is the amount shown opposite Prepaid Rent in the Adjusted Trial Balance Debit column of the worksheet.

The worksheet following the completion of Step 3 is shown in Figure 4-5.

Step 4. The amounts in the Adjusted Trial Balance columns are extended either to the Income Statement columns or to the Position Statement columns, depending on their statement classification. Expense and revenue accounts are entered in the Income Statement columns; asset, liability, and stockholders' equity accounts are entered in the Position Statement columns. The four columns then are footed. The difference between the totals of the Income Statement columns is the net income, or net loss, for the period; a net income is indicated if the total of the Credit column exceeds the total of the Debit column. The excess is entered in the Income Statement Debit column and in the Position Statement Credit column just below the column totals. This procedure records on the worksheet the increase in the stockholders' equity resulting from an excess of revenue over expenses during the period. A net loss is indicated if the total of the Income Statement Debit column exceeds that of the Income Statement Credit column. A loss is shown on the worksheet in the Income

CONNOLLY TRUCKING COMPANY
Worksheet
For the Month Ended June 30, 1969

Acct. No.	Account Title	Trial Balance		Adjustments		Adjusted Trial Balance		Income Statement		Position Statement	
		Dr.	Cr.	Dr.	Cr.	Dr.	Cr.	Dr.	Cr.	Dr.	Cr.
101	Cash	5,250				5,250					
111	Accounts Receivable	550				550					
112	Notes Receivable	1,440				1,440					
131	Office Supplies	230			(c) 170	60					
141	Prepaid Insurance	2,160			(b) 60	2,100					
142	Prepaid Rent	1,500			(a) 500	1,000					
201	Office Equipment	1,400				1,400					
211	Trucks	13,000				13,000					
301	Accounts Payable		200				200				
302	Notes Payable		8,000				8,000				
321	Unearned Rent		600	(d) 100			500				
401	Capital Stock		12,000				12,000				
402	Dividends	500				500					
501	Trucking Revenue		7,465				7,465				
601	Heat and Light Expense	40				40					
602	Maintenance and Repairs Expense	375				375					
603	Telephone and Telegraph Expense	95				95					
604	Gas and Oil Expense	525				525					
605	Wages Expense	1,200		(g) 150		1,350					
		28,265	28,265								
606	Rent Expense			(a) 500		500					
607	Insurance Expense			(b) 60		60					
608	Office Supplies Expense			(c) 170		170					
511	Rent Earned				(d) 100		100				
609	Depreciation Expense–Office Equipment			(e) 10		10					
201A	Accumulated Depreciation–Office Equipment				(e) 10		10				
610	Depreciation Expense–Trucks			(f) 200		200					
211A	Accumulated Depreciation–Trucks				(f) 200		200				
311	Accrued Wages Payable				(g) 150		150				
611	Interest Expense			(h) 24		24					
303	Accrued Interest Payable				(h) 24		24				
113	Accrued Interest Receivable			(i) 4		4					
521	Interest Earned				(i) 4		4				
612	Income Tax Expense			(j) 1,900		1,900					
331	Income Taxes Payable				(j) 1,900		1,900				
				3,118	3,118	30,553	30,553				

Balances from the trial balance, adjusted by the amounts in Adjustments columns, are extended here.

Figure 4-5.
Worksheet, Step 3

Statement Credit column and the Position Statement Debit column just below the column totals. The designation Net Income or Net Loss for the Month, whichever is pertinent, is entered in the Account Title column on the same line. The worksheet following the completion of Step 4 is illustrated in Figure 4-6.

If the differences between the Income Statement Debit and Credit columns (net income) and the Position Statement Debit and Credit columns are not the same,

CONNOLLY TRUCKING COMPANY
Worksheet
For the Month Ended June 30, 1969

Acct. No.	Account Title	Trial Balance		Adjustments		Adjusted Trial Balance		Income Statement		Position Statement	
		Dr.	Cr.	Dr.	Cr.	Dr.	Cr.	Dr.	Cr.	Dr.	Cr.
101	Cash	5,250				5,250				5,250	
111	Accounts Receivable	550				550				550	
112	Notes Receivable	1,440				1,440				1,440	
131	Office Supplies	230			(c) 170	60				60	
141	Prepaid Insurance	2,160			(b) 60	2,100				2,100	
142	Prepaid Rent	1,500			(a) 500	1,000				1,000	
201	Office Equipment	1,400				1,400				1,400	
211	Trucks	13,000				13,000				13,000	
301	Accounts Payable		200				200				200
302	Notes Payable		8,000				8,000				8,000
321	Unearned Rent		600	(d) 100			500				500
401	Capital Stock		12,000				12,000				12,000
402	Dividends	500				500				500	
501	Trucking Revenue		7,465				7,465		7,465		
601	Heat and Light Expense	40				40		40			
602	Maintenance and Repairs Expense	375				375		375			
603	Telephone and Telegraph Expense	95				95		95			
604	Gas and Oil Expense	525				525		525			
605	Wages Expense	1,200		(g) 150		1,350		1,350			
		28,265	28,265								
606	Rent Expense			(a) 500		500		500			
607	Insurance Expense			(b) 60		60		60			
608	Office Supplies Expense			(c) 170		170		170			
511	Rent Earned				(d) 100		100		100		
609	Depreciation Expense–Office Equipment			(e) 10		10		10			
201A	Accumulated Depreciation–Office Equipment				(e) 10		10				10
610	Depreciation Expense–Trucks			(f) 200		200		200			
211A	Accumulated Depreciation–Trucks				(f) 200		200				200
311	Accrued Wages Payable				(g) 150		150				150
611	Interest Expense			(h) 24		24		24			
303	Accrued Interest Payable				(h) 24		24				24
113	Accrued Interest Receivable			(i) 4		4				4	
521	Interest Earned				(i) 4		4		4		
612	Income Tax Expense			(j) 1,900		1,900		1,900			
331	Income Taxes Payable				(j) 1,900		1,900				1,900
				3,118	3,118	30,553	30,553	5,249	7,569	25,304	22,984
	Net Income for the Month							2,320			2,320
								7,569	7,569	25,304	25,304

The difference between the Income Statement columns is net income.

Net income is transferred to the Position Statement Credit column.

Figure 4-6.
Worksheet, Step 4

an error has been made. The totaling and ruling of the last four columns of the worksheet (Step 4) is illustrated in Figure 4-6. Note that balancing the last four columns provides only a limited proof of the accuracy of the worksheet—proof that the equality of debits and credits has been maintained throughout its preparation. The extension of the Cash account debit into the Income Statement Debit column, for example, would not destroy the debit-credit relationship of the worksheet, although statements prepared from that worksheet would be inaccurate. Note also that the total of the Position Statement Debit column need not correspond with the total assets reported in the statement. Accumulated Depreciation–Trucks, for example, is extended to the Position Statement Credit column because it represents a position statement account with a credit balance. It is neither an asset nor a liability, but rather a deduction from Trucks, which is extended into the Position Statement Debit column. Since plus and minus symbols are not used on the worksheet, a deduction from an amount in a Debit column is effected by positioning the item to be deducted in the credit column.

The worksheet may be varied in form—particularly with respect to the number of columns—to meet specific needs of the user. In Figure 5-3, for example, the columns for the adjusted trial balance are omitted.

The Preparation of Financial Statements from the Worksheet

The income statement is prepared from the amounts in the Income Statement columns of the worksheet; the statement of financial position and the statement of retained earnings are prepared from the amounts in the Position Statement columns of the worksheet. In preparing the financial statements, care should be taken to use each amount just once, and in its proper debit and credit relationship. It is not em-

Figure 4-7.
Income Statement

CONNOLLY TRUCKING COMPANY   Exhibit A
Income Statement
For the Month Ended June 30, 1969

			Percent
Revenue			
Trucking Revenue		$7,465	
Interest Earned		4	
Rent Earned		100	
Total Revenues		$7,569	100.0
Expenses			
Heat and Light Expense	$ 40		.5
Maintenance and Repairs Expense	375		5.0
Telephone and Telegraph Expense	95		1.3
Gas and Oil Expense	525		6.9
Wages Expense	1,350		17.8
Rent Expense	500		6.6
Insurance Expense	60		.8
Office Supplies Expense	170		2.3
Depreciation Expense–Office Equipment	10		.1
Depreciation Expense–Trucks	200		2.6
Interest Expense	24		.3
Total Expenses		3,349	44.2
Net Income Before Income Taxes		$4,220	55.8
Income Tax Expense		1,900	25.1
Net Income After Income Taxes—To Exhibit C		$2,320	30.7

phasized by the statements, but the relationship is present. In the statement of financial position, for example, Accumulated Depreciation–Trucks, with a credit balance of $200, is deducted from Trucks, which has a debit balance. Net income (or loss) appears in both the income statement and the statement of retained earnings.

The financial statements of the Connolly Trucking Company for June are shown in Figures 4-7, 4-8, and 4-9. The computation and significance of the items in the Percent columns are discussed later in this chapter. The designations used to identify and cross-reference the financial statements are:

Exhibit A for the income statement
Exhibit B for the statement of financial position
Exhibit C for the statement of retained earnings

CONNOLLY TRUCKING COMPANY   Exhibit B

Statement of Financial Position

June 30, 1969

Figure 4-8.
Statement of Financial Position

Assets

			Percent
Current Assets			
Cash		$ 5,250	21.3
Accounts Receivable		550	2.2
Notes Receivable		1,440	5.9
Accrued Interest Receivable		4	–0–
Office Supplies		60	.2
Prepaid Insurance		2,100	8.5
Prepaid Rent		1,000	4.1
Total Current Assets		$10,404	42.2
Equipment			
Office Equipment	$ 1,400		
Accumulated Depreciation	10	$ 1,390	5.7
Trucks	$13,000		
Accumulated Depreciation	200	12,800	52.1
Total Equipment		14,190	57.8
Total Assets		$24,594	100.0

Liabilities and Stockholders' Equity

Current Liabilities			
Accounts Payable		$ 200	.8
Notes Payable		8,000	32.5
Accrued Interest Payable		24	.1
Accrued Wages Payable		150	.6
Unearned Rent		500	2.1
Income Taxes Payable		1,900	7.7
Total Current Liabilities		$10,774	43.8
Stockholders' Equity			
Capital Stock	$12,000		
Retained Earnings—Exhibit C	1,820		
Total Stockholders' Equity		13,820	56.2
Total Liabilities and Stockholders' Equity		$24,594	100.0

Statement of Retained Earnings
For the Month Ended June 30, 1969

Figure 4-9.
Statement of
Retained Earnings

Net Income for Month of June, 1969—Exhibit A	$2,320
Deduct Dividends	500
Retained Earnings, June 30, 1969—To Exhibit B	$1,820

Since the Company was organized on June 1, 1969, it had no beginning balance in the Retained Earnings account; therefore, this item does not appear in the statement.

RECORDING THE ADJUSTMENTS IN THE GENERAL JOURNAL

After the financial statements have been prepared, the adjusting entries are first recorded in the general journal and then posted to the general ledger. The adjusting entries are taken directly from the Adjustments columns of the worksheet and dated as of the last day of the accounting period. The caption Adjusting Entries is written in the general journal on the line following the last regular general journal entry. After the adjusting entries have been posted, the general ledger account balances will correspond with the amounts in the Adjusted Trial Balance columns of the worksheet. The adjusting entries of the Connolly Trucking Company are shown in Figure 4-10.

THE RESULT OF ADJUSTING ENTRIES

When all the adjusting entries are recorded in the journal and posted to the general ledger, the mixed elements in the accounts have been eliminated. Accounts consisting of asset and expense elements and accounts containing liability and revenue elements are adjusted so that each element is recorded in a separate account: advance payments for goods and services to be consumed in the future are shown in the appropriate asset accounts; advance receipts for future revenue are shown in liability accounts; and all other supplementary data not previously recorded but necessary

Accounting Concept:
Fair Presentation and
Full Disclosure ▶

for the preparation of financial statements are available in the ledger. ▶ The general ledger contains all the accounts and amounts—expense, revenue, asset, liability, and stockholders' equity—necessary for the fair presentation of the financial position of the company as of the end of the accounting period and the results of its operations for the period then ended. Failure to adjust a mixed account results in incorrect financial statements; failure to disclose all information may result in misleading financial

Accounting Concept:
Materiality ▶

statements. ◀ ▶ The need for adjustment, however, and the need for full disclosure do not apply to insignificant, immaterial, or trivial matters. ◀ The box of paper clips in the bookkeeper's desk as of the position-statement date is an asset of the company, although it has been charged to expense. It is possible, but impractical, to ascertain the asset value of the unused clips and make a corresponding adjusting entry. Because of the insignificance of the unused paper clips, failure to make the adjustment will have no material effect on the financial statements and cannot mislead the user of such statements. A similar situation exists with respect to other items of supply or services.

GENERAL JOURNAL   Page 4

1969				
		Adjusting Entries		
June	30	Rent Expense	606	500	
		Prepaid Rent	142		500
		To record rent expense for June.			
	30	Insurance Expense	607	60	
		Prepaid Insurance	141		60
		To record insurance expense for June.			
	30	Office Supplies Expense	608	170	
		Office Supplies	131		170
		To record supplies used during June.			
	30	Unearned Rent	321	100	
		Rent Earned	511		100
		To record revenue earned from rental of trucks during June.			
	30	Depreciation Expense–Office Equipment	609	10	
		Accumulated Depreciation–Office Equipment	201A		10
		To record the depreciation for June.			
	30	Depreciation Expense–Trucks	610	200	
		Accumulated Depreciation–Trucks	211A		200
		To record the depreciation for June.			
	30	Wages Expense	605	150	
		Accrued Wages Payable	311		150
		To record wages expense accrued during June.			

Figure 4-10.
Adjusting Entries

GENERAL JOURNAL   Page 5

1969				
June	30	Interest Expense	611	24	
		Accrued Interest Payable	303		24
		To record interest expense accrued during June.			
	30	Accrued Interest Receivable	113	4	
		Interest Earned	521		4
		To record interest revenue accrued during June.			
	30	Income Tax Expense	612	1900	
		Income Taxes Payable	331		1900
		To record estimated taxes for June.			

The accountant is faced with the problem of determining the line between what is material and what is immaterial—making a value judgment. An item costing $100 may be material in a small business, whereas an item costing $1,000 may be insignificant in a multimillion-dollar business. It is not misleading to combine several insignificant items of expense or revenue into one account; it is misleading, however, to combine a significant loss from a lawsuit with an operating expense account. It may be necessary to disclose an item of an essential nature, regardless of its amount.

CLOSING ENTRIES RECORDED DIRECTLY FROM THE WORKSHEET

The caption *Closing Entries* is written in the middle of the first unused line on the journal page under the adjusting entries. The closing entries are recorded (Figure 4-11) and are then posted to the general ledger. They are made directly from the worksheet in the following sequence:

Entry 1. Each account in the Income Statement Credit column is debited, and the sum of the debits is credited to the Revenue and Expense Summary account.

Entry 2. Each account in the Income Statement Debit column is credited, and the sum of the credits is debited to the Revenue and Expense Summary account.

Entry 3. The balance of Revenue and Expense Summary, which, after posting Entries 1 and 2, represents the net income or the net loss as shown on the worksheet, is transferred to Retained Earnings.

Entry 4. The balance of the Dividends account is closed into Retained Earnings. The amount of this entry is the amount on the Dividends account line in the Position Statement Debit column of the worksheet.

GENERAL JOURNAL   Page 5

Figure 4-11.
Closing Entries

1969				
		Closing Entries		
June 30	Trucking Revenue	501	7,465	
	Rent Earned	511	100	
	Interest Earned	521	4	
	Revenue and Expense Summary	902		7,569
	To close.			
30	Revenue and Expense Summary	902	5,249	
	Heat and Light Expense	601		40
	Maintenance and Repairs Expense	602		375
	Telephone and Telegraph Expense	603		95
	Gas and Oil Expense	604		525
	Wages Expense	605		1,350
	Rent Expense	606		500
	Insurance Expense	607		60
	Office Supplies Expense	608		170
	Depreciation Expense–Office Equipment	609		10
	Depreciation Expense–Trucks	610		200
	Interest Expense	611		24
	Income Tax Expense	612		1,900
	To close.			
30	Revenue and Expense Summary	902	2,320	
	Retained Earnings	403		2,320
	To transfer net income to			
	Retained Earnings.			
30	Retained Earnings	403	500	
	Dividends	402		500
	To close.			

THE GENERAL LEDGER

The general ledger of the Connolly Trucking Company is reproduced after the adjusting entries and the closing entries have been posted. In reproducing the general ledger, exact dates are used when the information is given in the previous discussion. Otherwise the date of June 30 and the balance of the account as taken from the trial balance in Figure 4-1 are inserted because the detailed transactions were omitted from this example. The symbols *T.B.* for trial balance, *A.E.* for adjusting entry, and *C.E.* for closing entry are shown in the Explanation column as an aid in tracing the amounts to their sources. A check mark indicates that the amount was not posted from the journal.

GENERAL LEDGER

Cash   Acct. No. 101

1969								
June	30	T.B.	✔	5,250				

Accounts Receivable   Acct. No. 111

1969								
June	30	T.B.	✔	550				

Notes Receivable   Acct. No. 112

1969								
June	10	T.B.	✔	1,440				

Accrued Interest Receivable   Acct. No. 113

1969								
June	30	A.E.	5	4				

Office Supplies   Acct. No. 131

1969					1969				
June	6	T.B.	✔	230	June	30	A.E.	4	170
						30	Balance	✔	60
				230					230
1969									
July	1	Balance	✔	60					

Prepaid Insurance   Acct. No. 141

1969					1969				
June	1	T.B.	✔	2,160	June	30	A.E.	4	60
						30	Balance	✔	2,100
				2,160					2,160
1969									
July	1	Balance	✔	2,100					

Prepaid Rent   Acct. No. 142

1969					1969					
June	1	T.B.	✔	1,500	June	30	A.E.		4	500
						30	Balance		✔	1,000
				1,500						1,500
1969										
July	1	Balance	✔	1,000						

Office Equipment   Acct. No. 201

1969				
June	1	T.B.	✔	1,400

Accumulated Depreciation–Office Equipment   Acct. No. 201A

					1969					
					June	30	A.E.		4	10

Trucks   Acct. No. 211

1969				
June	1	T.B.	✔	13,000

Accumulated Depreciation–Trucks   Acct. No. 211A

					1969					
					June	30	A.E.		4	200

Accounts Payable   Acct. No. 301

					1969					
					June	30	T.B.		✔	200

Notes Payable   Acct. No. 302

					1969					
					June	12	T.B.		✔	8,000

Accrued Interest Payable   Acct. No. 303

					1969					
					June	30	A.E.		5	24

Accrued Wages Payable   Acct. No. 311

					1969					
					June	30	A.E.		4	150

Unearned Rent — Acct. No. 321

1969					1969				
June	30	A.E.	4	100	June	1	T.B.	✔	600
	30	Balance	✔	500					
				600					600
					1969				
					July	1	Balance	✔	500

Income Taxes Payable — Acct. No. 331

					1969				
					June	30	A.E.	5	1,900

Capital Stock — Acct. No. 401

					1969				
					June	1	T.B.	✔	12,000

Retained Earnings — Acct. No. 403

1969					1969				
June	30	C.E.	5	500	June	30	C.E.	5	2,320
	30	Balance	✔	1,820					
				2,320					2,320
					1969				
					July	1	Balance	✔	1,820

Dividends — Acct. No. 402

1969					1969				
June	30	T.B.	✔	500	June	30	C.E.	5	500

Trucking Revenue — Acct. No. 501

1969					1969				
June	30	C.E.	5	7,465	June	30	T.B.	✔	7,465

Interest Earned — Acct. No. 521

1969					1969				
June	30	C.E.	5	4	June	30	A.E.	5	4

Rent Earned — Acct. No. 511

1969					1969				
June	30	C.E.	5	100	June	30	A.E.	4	100

Heat and Light Expense   Acct. No. 601

1969					1969					
June	30	T.B.	✔	40	June	30	C.E.		5	40

Maintenance and Repairs Expense   Acct. No. 602

1969					1969					
June	30	T.B.	✔	375	June	30	C.E.		5	375

Telephone and Telegraph Expense   Acct. No. 603

1969					1969					
June	30	T.B.	✔	95	June	30	C.E.		5	95

Gas and Oil Expense   Acct. No. 604

1969					1969					
June	30	T.B.	✔	525	June	30	C.E.		5	525

Wages Expense   Acct. No. 605

1969					1969					
June	13		✔	600	June	30	C.E.		5	1,350
	27		✔	600						
	30	A.E.	4	150						
				1,350						1,350

Rent Expense   Acct. No. 606

1969					1969					
June	30	A.E.	4	500	June	30	C.E.		5	500

Insurance Expense   Acct. No. 607

1969					1969					
June	30	A.E.	4	60	June	30	C.E.		5	60

Office Supplies Expense   Acct. No. 608

1969					1969					
June	30	A.E.	4	170	June	30	C.E.		5	170

Depreciation Expense–Office Equipment   Acct. No. 609

1969					1969				
June	30	A.E.	4	10	June	30	C.E.	5	10

Depreciation Expense–Trucks   Acct. No. 610

1969					1969				
June	30	A.E.	4	200	June	30	C.E.	5	200

Interest Expense   Acct. No. 611

1969					1969				
June	30	A.E.	5	24	June	30	C.E.	5	24

Income Tax Expense   Acct. No. 612

1969					1969				
June	30	A.E.	5	1,900	June	30	C.E.	5	1,900

Revenue and Expense Summary   Acct. No. 902

1969					1969				
June	30	C.E.	5	5,249	June	30	C.E.	5	7,569
	30	C.E.	5	2,320					
				7,569					7,569

THE POST-CLOSING TRIAL BALANCE

The post-closing trial balance of the Connolly Trucking Company, taken from the general ledger, is shown in Figure 4-12.

THE ACCOUNTING CYCLE

In this and the preceding chapter, the complete *accounting cycle* of a business concern has been presented. The cycle consists of a series of steps, as follows:

1. *Journalizing,* which consists of analyzing and recording transactions in chronological order in the journal.
2. *Posting,* which is transferring debits and credits to the appropriate ledgers and to the proper accounts in the ledgers.
3. *Preparing a trial balance,* or summarizing the general ledger accounts to test the equality of debits and credits.
4. *Preparing a schedule of accounts receivable,* which is summarizing the accounts receivable ledger accounts and reconciling the total with the balance of the Accounts Receivable controlling account in the general ledger.

CONNOLLY TRUCKING COMPANY
Post-Closing Trial Balance
June 30, 1969

Figure 4-12.
Post-Closing
Trial Balance

101	Cash	$ 5,250	
111	Accounts Receivable	550	
112	Notes Receivable	1,440	
113	Accrued Interest Receivable	4	
131	Office Supplies	60	
141	Prepaid Insurance	2,100	
142	Prepaid Rent	1,000	
201	Office Equipment	1,400	
201A	Accumulated Depreciation–Office Equipment		$ 10
211	Trucks	13,000	
211A	Accumulated Depreciation–Trucks		200
301	Accounts Payable		200
302	Notes Payable		8,000
303	Accrued Interest Payable		24
311	Accrued Wages Payable		150
321	Unearned Rent		500
331	Income Taxes Payable		1,900
401	Capital Stock		12,000
403	Retained Earnings		1,820
	Totals	$24,804	$24,804

5. *Preparing a schedule of accounts payable,* which is summarizing the accounts payable ledger accounts and reconciling the total with the balance of the Accounts Payable controlling account in the general ledger.

6. *Preparing the worksheet,* or assembling and classifying information in columnar form to facilitate the preparation of financial statements.

7. *Preparing the financial statements* from the worksheet; these are the income statement, statement of financial position, and statement of retained earnings.

8. *Adjusting the books,* or recording and posting the adjusting entries from the worksheet.

9. *Closing the books,* which is recording and posting the closing entries from the income statement columns of the worksheet.

10. *Balancing and ruling the real accounts* and bringing the balances forward for the new accounting period.

11. *Taking a post-closing trial balance,* or totaling the open account balances to prove the equality of the debits and credits in the general ledger.

12. *Analyzing and interpreting the financial statements* by developing percentages, ratios, and other indicators, to make the statements more meaningful.

THE PURPOSE OF SPLIT ENTRIES

The adjusting entries are recorded in the general journal and posted to the general ledger. Three of the adjusting entries—g, h, and i—involve the accrual of previously unrecorded revenue or expense items assignable to June and require a split form of entry in July when the transaction cycle culminates in the receipt or payment of cash.

Paying the Accrued Wages Payable

The next regular payday at the Connolly Trucking Company is on July 11. On July 1, Wages Expense had a zero balance as a result of the closing entries on June 30. Assuming that the biweekly wages again amounted to $600, the entry on July 11 to record this payment is:

GENERAL JOURNAL   Page 5

1969				
July	11	Accrued Wages Payable	150	
		Wages Expense	450	
		Cash		600
		To record the payment of biweekly wages.		

The result of this entry is to split the biweekly wages of $600 so that $150, which was recognized as a June expense, is debited to Accrued Wages Payable and $450 is recorded as an expense in July. Accrued Wages Payable now has a zero balance.

Paying the Accrued Interest Payable

On the maturity date of the note payable, July 27 (45 days including 18 days accrued in June), the Connolly Trucking Company pays the bank $8,060, the maturity value. The amount consists of $8,000 principal plus $60, which is 45 days' interest at 6 percent on $8,000, calculated as follows:

$$\$8,000 \times .06 \times \frac{45}{360} = \$60$$

The entry to record the payment to the bank is:

GENERAL JOURNAL   Page 5

1969				
July	27	Notes Payable	8,000	
		Accrued Interest Payable	24	
		Interest Expense	36	
		Cash		8,060
		To record the payment of a note payable.		

The adjusting entry on June 30 allocated 18 days' interest expense ($24) on the note to the month of June. The July entry splits the total interest of $60 so that the $24 liability applicable to June is cancelled and the remaining $36 ($60 − $24) is recorded as interest expense for 27 days in July.

Receiving the Accrued Interest Receivable

On the maturity date of the note receivable, July 10 (30 days, including 20 days accrued in June), the Connolly Trucking Company receives the maturity value, $1,446. The maturity value is determined by adding to the principal, $1,440, 30 days' interest at 5 percent, or $6, computed as follows:

$$\$1,440 \times .05 \times \frac{30}{360} = \$6$$

The entry to record the receipt from the customer is:

GENERAL JOURNAL   Page 5

1969					
July	10	Cash		1,446	
		Notes Receivable			1,440
		Accrued Interest Receivable			4
		Interest Earned			2
		To record the collection of a note receivable.			

On June 30, the adjusting entry accrued 20 days' interest earned on the note, or $4, in June. The total interest earned of $6 is split by the July entry so that the $4 asset, Accrued Interest Receivable, is cancelled and the balance of $2 ($6 − $4) is entered as interest earned in July.

ANALYZING THE FINANCIAL STATEMENTS

The financial statements are not ends in themselves. Additional information and insight about the business may be obtained by analyzing the relationships within and between the statements to make them more meaningful to management, creditors, and other interested persons. For this purpose percentages are useful.

A percentage analysis of the income statement and statement of financial position of the Connolly Trucking Company is shown in Figure 4-7 and Figure 4-8. In the income statement, the total revenue ($7,569) is 100 percent. Each expense item is expressed as a percentage of the total revenue. The reader can see the distribution of each revenue dollar; that is, the percentage of revenue that has been absorbed by each expense item. Rent Expense, for example, absorbed 6.6 cents of each revenue dollar, and 25.1 cents of each revenue dollar was absorbed by income tax expense.

In the statement of financial position, the total asset amount is used as the base (100 percent), and the percentage of each asset to the total assets is determined by dividing the individual asset by the total assets. Similarly, the percentage of each liability and stockholders' equity item is expressed as a percentage of the total liabilities and stockholders' equity, and is computed by dividing the individual items by the amount of total liabilities and stockholders' equity. Thus:

$$\frac{\text{Cash}}{\text{Total Assets}} = \frac{\$5,250}{\$24,594} = 21.3\%$$

$$\frac{\text{Notes Payable}}{\text{Total Liabilities and Stockholders' Equity}} = \frac{\$8,000}{\$24,594} = 32.5\%$$

Percentage computations also are made to show the relationship of subtotals to the related totals. The analysis shows that total current assets are 42.2 percent of total assets, and total current liabilities are 43.8 percent of total liabilities and stockholders' equity.

EQUITY RATIOS

A significant measure of the stability of a business is the percentage relationship of the equities of the creditors and the owners in the total assets. These equity ratios for the Connolly Trucking Company are computed as follows:

1. Creditors' interest in assets:

$$\frac{\text{Total Liabilities}}{\text{Total Assets}} = \frac{\$10,774}{\$24,594} = 43.8\%$$

2. Stockholders' interest in assets:

$$\frac{\text{Total Stockholders' Equity}}{\text{Total Assets}} = \frac{\$13,820}{\$24,594} = 56.2\%$$

The creditors have an equity of 43.8 cents and the stockholders have an equity of 56.2 cents of each asset dollar. Many analysts consider the equity ratios equal in importance to the current ratio as indicators of credit strength and sound management. There are no universally accepted percentage relationships to serve as guides for the equity ratios, but it is generally felt that the larger the owner's equity, the stronger the financial condition of the business. A company may, for example, borrow money on a long-term note for working capital purposes. The loan increases the current assets and creates a more favorable current ratio; but it also reduces the stockholders' equity ratio, signaling a possible overdependence on outside sources for financial needs.

SUMMARY

The cash basis and the accrual basis both may be used in an accounting system. By the cash basis, revenue is considered to be earned and is recorded when payment is received; expenses are considered to have been incurred and are recorded only at the time of payment. Accrual accounting is based on the principle that revenue is realized at the time of the sale and expenses are recognized at the time they are incurred. The timing of the cash receipt or cash payment is irrelevant to this matching process.

The proper allocation of the accounts is deferred to the end of the accounting period, at which time the accountant may find that some new accounts must be brought into the books and other accounts brought up to date. This periodic adjustment of the ledger is accomplished by making adjusting entries, which are necessary whenever financial statements are to be prepared.

Adjustments are needed under the following conditions:

1. When an account contains both an asset and an expense element; for example, when a portion of the insurance premiums previously debited to Prepaid Insurance have expired.
2. When previously unrecorded data are to be entered; for example, on recognition of the incurred expense and corresponding liability for amounts due employees for services received but not recorded.
3. When amounts previously received and recorded in a liability account are earned; for example, when an amount is transferred from Unearned Rent to Rent Earned.
4. When previously unrecorded revenue and asset increases are recognized; for example, Interest Earned and Accrued Interest Receivable on an outstanding interest-bearing note from a customer.

The worksheet is an orderly means of collecting information for the preparation of formal financial statements. It may be varied in form, especially in the number of columns. The steps in its preparation consist of (1) entering the trial balance in the Trial Balance columns, (2) entering the adjusting entries in the Adjustments columns, (3) extending the combined amounts to the Adjusted Trial Balance columns, (4) extending the amounts in the Adjusted Trial Balance columns to either the Income Statement or the Position Statement columns, depending on their statement classification, (5) footing the columns and entering the excess—the net income or net loss for the period—below the column totals.

The steps in the accounting cycle are (1) journalizing, (2) posting, (3) preparing a trial balance, (4) preparing a schedule of accounts receivable, (5) preparing a schedule of accounts payable, (6) preparing the worksheet, (7) preparing the financial statements, (8) adjusting the books, (9) closing the books, (10) balancing and ruling the accounts, (11) taking a post-closing trial balance, and (12) analyzing and interpreting the financial statements.

☐ QUESTIONS

Q4–1. (a) What are the essential differences between the cash basis and the accrual basis of accounting? (b) Under what conditions is it appropriate to use the cash basis? (c) Under what conditions is it inappropriate to use the cash basis?

Q4–2. (a) What purpose is served by adjusting entries? (b) What events make them necessary? (c) How do they affect the work of the accountant? (d) How does the time period covered by the income statement affect the adjusting entries? (e) How do adjusting entries differ from other entries? (f) What is a mixed account? (g) What are the results of the adjusting entries?

Q4–3. (a) What is the purpose and function of the worksheet? (b) Can the work of the accountant be completed without the use of the worksheet? (c) Where do the amounts on the worksheet come from? (d) What determines the number of columns to be used in the preparation of a worksheet? (e) Why are the parts of each entry in the Adjustments columns cross-referenced with either numbers or letters? (f) How is the amount to be extended into another column determined? (g) What determines the column into which an amount is to be extended? (h) Is the worksheet fool-proof? (i) Does the worksheet eliminate the need for formal financial statements? (j) Does the worksheet eliminate the need for recording the adjusting entries on the books?

Q4–**4.** (a) Do you agree with the statement that "items of little or no consequence may be dealt with as expediency may suggest"? (b) Do you agree with the statement that "problems of materiality are easily resolved and, in any case, are not very important"?

Q4–**5.** (a) What is meant by the accounting cycle? (b) What are the steps in the complete cycle? (c) Is it possible for the bookkeeper to vary the sequence in which he performs the steps of the cycle?

Q4–**6.** Is it possible to prepare the formal financial statements from a four-column work-sheet consisting of the trial balance amounts and all the necessary adjustments?

Q4–**7.** What is the purpose and function of the Percent columns in the financial statements?

Q4–**8.** (a) When would the amounts for Depreciation Expense and for Accumulated Depreciation in the adjusted trial balance be the same? (b) When would these amounts be different?

☐ **EXERCISES**

E4–**1.** Joseph De Roche, an electrician, prepares monthly financial statements. The following transactions occurred during December, 1969:

1969
December 15   Billed customers $900 for services rendered this month.
        17   Purchased $550 worth of electrical supplies on account.
        31   Received $410 in cash from customers billed on December 15.
        31   Paid $300 on account for electrical supplies purchased on December 17.

The electrical supplies inventory on December 31 was $90. Journalize the transactions, assuming that De Roche keeps his books (a) on the cash basis; (b) on the accrual basis. (c) What is the net income on the cash basis? on the accrual basis? (d) Which method should De Roche use? Why?

E4–**2.** The Ajax Company purchased a new truck on January 1, 1969, for $5,200. It had an estimated useful life of four years and a trade-in value at the end of that time of $400. (a) What is the depreciation expense for 1969? (b) What is the balance in the Accumulated Depreciation–Delivery Equipment account at the end of 1969? 1970? (c) What will the carrying value of the truck be in the statement of financial position of December 31, 1969? December 31, 1970? (d) Why is depreciation expense credited to Accumulated Depreciation–Delivery Equipment rather than directly to Delivery Equipment?

E4–**3.** The trial balance of the Bell Company on December 31, 1969 included the following account balances before adjustments:

Prepaid Insurance	$ 600
Prepaid Advertising Supplies	800
Prepaid Rent	1,200
Office Supplies	1,500
Office Equipment	3,300

Data for adjustments on December 31, 1969, were:

a. On November 1, 1969, the Company purchased a two-year comprehensive insurance policy for $600.

      b. Advertising supplies on hand totaled $300.

      c. On September 1, 1969, the Company paid one year's rent in advance.

      d. The office supplies inventory was $720.

      e. The office equipment was purchased on July 1, 1969, and has an estimated useful life of 10 years and a salvage value of $300.

      Make the adjusting entries.

E4–4. The Wilson Company employs three sales clerks at a weekly salary of $100 each. They are paid on Friday, the last day of a five-day workweek. Make the adjusting entry, assuming that the accounting period ended on Tuesday.

E4–5. The statements of financial position of the Durning Company as of December 31, 1969 and 1970, showed Office Supplies at $1,350 and $1,500, respectively. During 1970, office supplies totaling $2,200 were purchased. What was the Office Supplies Expense for the year 1970?

E4–6. The balances of the Prepaid Insurance account of the Barth Company were:

December 31, 1969	$930
December 31, 1970	520

      The income statement for 1970 showed insurance expense of $1,100. What were the expenditures for insurance premiums during 1970?

E4–7. Make the additional closing entries indicated by the following accounts:

John Sobel, Capital		John Sobel, Drawing	
	30,000	10,000	

Revenue and Expense Summary	
125,000	150,000

E4–8. The Johnson Company's adjusted trial balance, taken from the worksheet for the year ended December 31, 1969, was as follows:

Cash	$ 5,700	
Accounts Receivable	11,400	
Machinery and Equipment	32,900	
Accumulated Depreciation		$12,000
Accounts Payable		3,040
Notes Payable		7,600
William Johnson, Capital		22,360
William Johnson, Drawing	5,000	
Service Revenue		50,000
Heat and Light	1,000	
Wages Expense	35,000	
Depreciation Expense	4,000	
Totals	$95,000	$95,000

(a) Enter the adjusted trial balance on a worksheet; (b) complete the worksheet; (c) prepare an income statement with a Percent column, a statement of financial position with a Percent column, a statement of owner's equity, and the closing entries.

E4-**9**. The Home Magazine Company credited Subscription Revenue for $18,000 received from subscribers to its new monthly magazine. All subscriptions were for 12 issues. The initial issue was mailed during October, 1969. Make the adjusting entry on December 31, 1969.

E4-**10**. Make the end-of-year adjusting entries for the Richard Hale Company for the following items:

    a. The debit balance of the Prepaid Insurance account is $720. Of this amount, $600 is expired.

    b. Accrued salaries and wages payable total $150.

    c. The Office Supplies account has a debit balance of $180; $30 worth is on hand.

    d. Depreciation on store equipment is $200; on office equipment, $175.

    e. Accrued interest receivable is $95.

    f. Accrued interest payable is $60.

    g. Unearned Rent has a credit balance of $2,600, of which $2,400 was earned during the past year.

E4-**11**. From the account balances given, prepare the adjusting entries:

Account	Amount in Trial Balance	Balance After Adjustment
Prepaid Insurance	$1,800	$ 600
Prepaid Interest	200	50
Unearned Rent	700	200
Accumulated Depreciation–Building	7,000	10,000
Salaries and Wages Payable	–0–	450
Accrued Interest Receivable	–0–	110
Accrued Interest Payable	–0–	90

E4-**12**. The Swift Company debits the cost of all office supplies purchased to Office Supplies Expense. Office supplies inventories were:

                January 1, 1969 $820

                December 31, 1969   570

Supplies used during the year totalled $2,570. What was the cost of office supplies purchased during 1969?

E4-**13**. The Finn Company issued a 60-day, 6-percent note for $500, dated July 1, to a supplier of merchandise. On July 16, the company received a 30-day, 4-percent note for $750 from a customer. Make the necessary adjusting entries on July 31.

E4-**14**. The income statement of the Cunningham Company for the three-month period ended March 31, 1969 shows net income before income taxes of $20,000. Assuming an income tax rate of 48 percent, make the necessary adjusting entry.

E4-**15**. Upon examining the books and records of the Foley Company on December 31, 1969, you find the following:

a. The inventory of office supplies on hand is $150. Some partially filled cans of duplicating fluid valued at $3.50 were not inventoried.

b. Included in Miscellaneous Expense was a charge of $500 for uninsured losses from a fire.

Indicate the adjustments, if any, that should be made, and why.

E4–**16.** The Smith Company received a 30-day, 6-percent note for $500 from a customer on September 15. On September 20, the company borrowed $1,800 from the bank on its own 30-day, 6-percent note. Make entries to adjust the books on September 30, and to record the collection and payment of the notes on their respective due dates.

E4–**17.** The statement of financial position of the Masters Company at December 31, 1969, shows the following totals:

Current assets	$13,000
Total assets	40,000
Current liabilities	6,000
Total liabilities	16,000

Prepare analyses that will make these summary totals more meaningful to a reader of the statement.

☐ **DEMONSTRATION PROBLEMS**

DP4–**1.** (*Worksheet*) The general ledger of Bowlarama, Inc., showed the following balances at December 31, 1969. The books are closed annually on December 31. The company obtains revenue from its bowling alleys and from a refreshments stand that is leased on a concession basis.

Cash	$ 9,000
Bowling Supplies	7,200
Prepaid Insurance	6,000
Prepaid Rent	6,500
Bowling Equipment	50,000
Accumulated Depreciation	12,250
Mortgage Payable	28,000
Capital Stock	5,000
Retained Earnings	8,220
Dividends	7,200
Bowling Revenue	45,600
Concession Revenue	5,750
Wages Expense	13,000
Repair Expense	2,625
Heat and Light Expense	2,100
Telephone and Telegraph Expense	275
Miscellaneous Expense	920

Supplementary data:

1. Bowling supplies on hand based on physical count totaled $525.

2. The balance of the Prepaid Insurance account represents the premium on a three-year insurance policy, effective January 1, 1969.

3. Rent expense for the year was $6,000.

4. The bowling equipment has an expected useful life of 10 years and salvage value of $1,000. No equipment was acquired during the year.

5. Salaries earned by employees but unpaid on December 31 were $125.

Required: 1. Record the trial balance on a worksheet.
2. Complete the worksheet.
3. Why is the difference between the totals of the Income Statement columns and the totals of the Position Statement columns the same amount?

DP4-2. (*Adjusting entries*) Certain unadjusted account balances from the trial balance of the Fox Company, a systems consulting firm, for the year ended December 31, 1969, are given:

Account Title	Debit	Credit
Accounts Receivable	$20,000	
Notes Receivable	9,000	
Prepaid Insurance	1,080	
Office Supplies	620	
Automobiles	10,000	
Accumulated Depreciation–Automobiles		$ 2,000
Notes Payable		3,000
Revenue–Consulting Fees		240,000
Advertising Expense	900	
Rent Expense	20,000	
Salaries Expense	24,500	
Property Taxes Expense	1,675	
Heat and Light Expense	1,200	
Interest Earned		300
Rent Earned		1,200

Adjustment data on December 31 are as follows:

1. Office supplies on hand totaled $50.
2. Depreciation for the year was $1,000.
3. Estimated heat and light expense not recorded was $125.
4. Of the amount shown for Interest Earned, $100 was unearned as of December 31, 1969.
5. The balance of the Prepaid Insurance account consists of $360 for the premium on a three-year policy dated July 1, 1969, and $720 for premiums on a three-year policy dated January 1, 1969.
6. Advertising supplies on hand were $70.
7. The balance of the notes payable account represents a 6-percent interest bearing note dated January 1, 1969, due July 1, 1970.
8. The rent is $2,000 a month.
9. Salaries earned but not paid were $650.
10. Property taxes accrued were $95.
11. On January 1, 1969 the Fox Company subleased a section of its rented space. The lease with the tenant specifies a minimum yearly rental of $1,200 payable in 12 installments at the beginning of each month. The maximum annual rental is 5-percent of sales. The rental adjustment, if any, is due on January 15. The tenant reported sales of $26,500 for 1969.
12. Included in Revenue–Consulting Fees are advance payments of $7,500 by clients for services to be rendered early in 1970.

Required: From the information given, (a) record the adjusting entries, (b) indicate the financial statement classification of each account in each entry, and (c) show the amount reported on the financial statements. Present the data in schedule form as shown (Item 1 is done as an example):

Item No.	Adjusting Journal Entries December 31, 1969	Dr.	Cr.	Financial Statement Classification	Amount Reported on Financial Statement
1	Office Supplies Exp. Office Supplies	570	570	Expenses Current Assets	$570 50

DP4–3. (Financial statements; closing entries) Bourne Decorators' adjusted trial balance, taken from the worksheet for the month ended July 31, 1969, was as follows:

Cash	$ 600	
Accounts Receivable	900	
Decorating Supplies	2,000	
Prepaid Insurance	1,200	
Building	10,000	
Accumulated Depreciation–Building		$ 5,700
Land	3,000	
Accounts Payable		2,000
Note Payable		1,200
Bank Loan Payable (due June 1, 1971)		3,600
Capital Stock		1,500
Retained Earnings		690
Dividends	475	
Service Revenue		7,950
Heat and Light Expense	120	
Telephone and Telegraph Expense	40	
Wages Expense	800	
Decorating Supplies Expense	3,200	
Insurance Expense	160	
Depreciation Expense–Building	240	
Income Tax Expense	750	
Accrued Wages Payable		70
Interest Expense	25	
Accrued Interest Payable		50
Income Taxes Payable		750
Totals	$23,510	$23,510

Required: 1. An income statement with a Percent column
2. A position statement with a Percent column
3. A statement of retained earnings
4. Closing entries
5. The Company needs additional cash to increase its volume of business. Suggest alternative means of raising money and the advantages and disadvantages of each alternative.

□ PROBLEMS

P4-1. Neal Stone, a Certified Public Accountant, began practice on July 1, 1969. He kept his accounts on the accrual basis. At the end of the year, the following adjusted trial balance was taken from his worksheet:

Cash	$ 250	
Accounts Receivable	1,300	
Office Supplies	50	
Accrued Salaries Payable		$ 40
Neal Stone, Capital		1,400
Neal Stone, Drawing	3,400	
Professional Fees		8,300
Rent Expense	1,200	
Insurance Expense	150	
Office Salaries Expense	3,100	
Miscellaneous Expense	290	
Totals	$9,740	$9,740

An examination of the worksheet shows the following adjustments:

Office Salaries Expense	40	
Accrued Salaries Payable		40
Miscellaneous Expense	30	
Office Supplies		30

Required: 1. Prepare an income statement to determine Stone's net income on the accrual basis of accounting.
2. Prepare an income statement to determine Stone's net income on the cash basis of accounting.
3. Which method of accounting should Stone use? Why?

P4-2. Following is the trial balance of the Self-Parking Corporation for the month of May, 1969, the first month of operations.

SELF-PARKING CORPORATION
Trial Balance
May 31, 1969

Cash	$2,400	
Accounts Receivable	800	
Garage Supplies	450	
Prepaid Insurance	325	
Accounts Payable		$ 85
Capital Stock		3,600
Dividends	350	
Garage Revenue		1,200
Advertising Expense	125	
Miscellaneous Expenses	230	
Telephone and Telegraph Expense	75	
Wages Expense	130	
Totals	$4,885	$4,885

Supplementary data on May 31 were:

1. Garage supplies on hand were $300.
2. Expired insurance was $250.
3. Wages earned by employees but not paid were $70.

Required: 1. Record the trial balance on a worksheet.
2. Complete the worksheet for the month of May.
3. Determine the net income for the month on the cash basis of accounting.

P4-3. Listed below are the account balances taken from the Trial Balance and Adjusted Trial Balance columns of the worksheet of the Fowler Company for the 12-month period ended June 30, 1969, the first year of operations.

Account Title	Trial Balance	Adjusted Trial Balance
Cash	$ 1,200	$ 1,200
Accounts Receivable	2,000	2,000
Office Supplies	1,750	500
Store Supplies	1,500	100
Prepaid Insurance	1,800	600
Prepaid Rent	2,400	600
Equipment	20,600	20,600
Accounts Payable	7,000	7,000
Capital Stock	19,650	19,650
Dividends	3,500	3,500
Service Revenue	15,500	15,500
Wages Expense	5,500	5,570
Miscellaneous Expense	1,900	1,900
Office Supplies Expense		1,250
Store Supplies Expense		1,400
Insurance Expense		1,200
Rent Expense		1,800
Depreciation Expense–Equipment		2,000
Accumulated Depreciation–Equipment		2,000
Accrued Wages Payable		70

Required: Reconstruct the Trial Balance, Adjustments, and Adjusted Trial Balance columns of the worksheet.

P4-4. Selected transactions of the Eastern Sales Company for 1969 are given:

January   1   Purchased a four-year insurance policy for $3,600.

July   1   Bought two trucks for $11,500. The trucks are expected to last five years, at the end of which time their salvage value will be $750 each.

December 31 Paid $900 rent for the three-month period ending March 31, 1970.

         31 Purchased office supplies for $350.

Required: 1. Make journal entries to record the transactions.
2. Make the adjusting entries as of December 31, 1969. The company closes its books annually on December 31.

3. What adjusting entries would be made if the Eastern Sales Company was on the cash basis?

P4–5. Certain account balances from the trial balance of the Dunn Company as of June 30, 1969, the end of its fiscal year, are given:

Account Title	Debit	Credit
Office Supplies	$ 350	
Prepaid Insurance	3,600	
Prepaid Advertising	4,200	
Unearned Rent		$ 600
Rent Expense	2,000	

Examination of the records as of June 30 shows the following:

1. Office supplies on hand totaled $75.
2. A three-year comprehensive insurance policy was purchased on July 1, 1968 at a premium cost of $3,600.
3. The monthly rent expense is $200.
4. Included in Prepaid Advertising is a payment of $200 for ads to appear during July, 1969. The balance is for ads that appeared in prior months.
5. A portion of the floor space was subleased at $50 a month on September 1, 1968. The tenant paid a year's rent in advance on signing the lease.

Required: Record the adjusting entries as of June 30, 1969. The books are closed annually.

P4–6. Following is the trial balance of the Andersen Print Company at October 31, 1969. The Company began operations on September 1, 1969. Its fiscal year ends on October 31.

ANDERSEN PRINT COMPANY
Trial Balance
October 31, 1969

Account Title	Debit	Credit
Cash	$ 6,100	
Notes Receivable	2,000	
Accounts Receivable	3,400	
Office Supplies	750	
Printing Supplies	1,000	
Prepaid Rent	2,400	
Printing Equipment	12,000	
Accounts Payable		$ 3,600
Notes Payable		2,200
Lars Andersen, Capital		16,000
Lars Andersen, Drawing	500	
Printing Revenue		8,335
Heat and Light Expense	80	
Telephone Expense	45	
Maintenance Expense	260	
Wages Expense	1,600	
Totals	$30,135	$30,135

Other data:

1. A physical count shows that (a) office supplies on hand total $375 and (b) printing supplies on hand are $600.
2. The monthly rental is $600.
3. Printing equipment acquired on September 1 has an estimated useful life of five years and a salvage value of $1,200.
4. Wages of employees earned but not paid are $300.
5. The note payable is a one-year note, signed on September 1, and bears interest at 6 percent.
6. The notes receivable account represents a 60-day 5-percent interest-bearing note signed by a customer on October 1.

Required: 1. Prepare adjusting entries.
2. Why did Andersen accept the note from the customer?

P4–7. After analyzing the accounts and other records of Burnham, Inc., the following information is made available for the year ended December 31, 1969:

1. The Office Supplies account has a debit balance of $350. Office supplies on hand at December 31 total $110.
2. The Prepaid Rent account has a debit balance of $5,200. Included in this amount is $400 paid in December for the succeeding January; $4,800 has expired.
3. The Prepaid Insurance account has a debit balance of $1,380. It consists of the following policies purchased during 1969:

Policy No.	Date of Policy	Life of Policy	Premiums
A 5321	January 1	3 years	$960
E 452	April 1	2 years	240
X 321	August 1	1 year	180

4. The Prepaid Advertising account has a debit balance of $1,200. Included in this amount is $200 paid to a local monthly magazine for advertising space in its January and February, 1970, issues.
5. At the close of the year three notes receivable were on hand, as follows:

Date	Face Value	Time of Note	Interest Rate
November 16	$5,500	90 days	4 percent
December 4	3,000	60 days	6 percent
December 10	2,500	30 days	none

6. At the close of the year two notes payable were outstanding, as follows:

Date	Face Value	Time of Note	Interest Rate
September 15	$8,000	180 days	6 percent
November 3	5,000	90 days	4 percent

7. Salaries and wages accrued totaled $1,020.
8. The Rent Earned account has a credit balance of $7,200. This amount represents payment on a one-year lease effective May 1, 1969.
9. The Store Equipment account has a debit balance of $11,500. The equipment

has an estimated useful life of 10 years and a salvage value of $1,000. All store equipment was acquired prior to January 1, 1969.

10. The Truck account has a debit balance of $5,000. The truck was purchased on June 15, 1968, and has an estimated life of five years and salvage value of approximately $400.

11. Property taxes accrued were $850.

12. Estimated income taxes for the year were $2,500.

Required: Prepare the adjusting journal entries required at December 31.

P4-**8.** The bookkeeper for the Rae Company prepared the following condensed income statement for the year ended December 31, 1969, and the condensed statement of financial position as of that date.

Income Statement

Revenue from Services		$30,500
Operating Expenses		
Insurance Expense	$ 1,050	
Miscellaneous Expense	3,800	
Office Supplies Expense	350	
Wages Expense	12,000	17,200
Net Income		$13,300

Statement of Financial Position
Assets

Cash	$ 2,500
Accounts Receivable	8,400
Equipment	30,500
Total Assets	$41,400

Liabilities and Owner's Equity

Accounts Payable	$ 8,400
Stanley Rae, Capital	33,000
Total Liabilities and Owner's Equity	$41,400

The following items were overlooked entirely by the bookkeeper in the preparation of the statements:

1. The depreciation of equipment (acquired January 1, 1969): estimated life, 10 years; no salvage value

2. Wages earned but unpaid, $600

3. Office supplies on hand, $125 (purchases during 1969 were debited to Office Supplies Expense)

4. Unexpired insurance premiums, $425

5. Heat and light invoices for December, $225

Required: 1. What adjustments are needed?
2. Prepare revised financial statements.
3. Prepare a schedule reconciling the revised amount of owner's equity with the amount shown in the original statement.

P4-**9.** On August 1, 1969, Irving Baker opened a repair shop. During August, the following transactions were completed:

1969

August 1 Transferred $750 from his personal savings account to a checking account under the name of Baker's Fixit Shop.

2 Paid $50 for office supplies.

3 Purchased second-hand office equipment for $150 in cash.

4 Issued a check for $50 for August rent.

5 Paid a premium of $24 for an insurance policy on the equipment, effective August 1.

6 Purchased supplies on account to be used in repair work, as follows:

Andrews Supply Company	$ 35
House of Berezin	20
Bonica's, Inc.	30
Fixit Supply Company	60
Total	$145

17 Received $950 for repair work completed.

20 Additional repair work was completed, and bills were sent out, as follows:

William Curtis	$ 35
Leo Bonner and Company	105
Peter Kent	60
Arnold Johnson	28
Total	$228

22 Paid $20 for the telephone service for the month.

25 Paid the following creditors:

Andrews Supply Company	$20
Fixit Supply Company	30
Bonica's, Inc.	10
House of Berezin	10
Total	$70

27 Received cash from customers to apply on account, as follows:

Peter Kent	$20
Arnold Johnson	10
Leo Bonner and Company	50
William Curtis	10
Total	$90

30 Baker withdrew $300 in cash for his personal use.

Supplementary adjustment data as of August 31, 1969, were:

1. The insurance premium paid on August 5 is for one year.
2. A physical count shows that (a) office supplies on hand total $25, and (b) repair supplies on hand are $65.

3. The office equipment has an estimated useful life of five years with no salvage value.

Required: 1. Open the following accounts in the general ledger: Cash, 101; Accounts Receivable, 111; Office Supplies, 136; Repair Supplies, 137; Prepaid Insurance, 140; Office Equipment, 163; Accumulated Depreciation–Office Equipment, 163A; Accounts Payable, 201; Irving Baker, Capital, 251; Irving Baker, Drawing, 252; Repair Revenue, 301; Insurance Expense, 702; Rent Expense, 703; Office Supplies Expense, 708; Telephone and Telegraph Expense, 709; Repair Supplies Expense, 712; Depreciation Expense–Office Equipment, 717; Revenue and Expense Summary, 902.

2. Open accounts in the accounts receivable ledger for Leo Bonner and Company, William Curtis, Arnold Johnson, and Peter Kent.

3. Open accounts in the accounts payable ledger for the Andrews Supply Company; Bonica's, Inc.; the Fixit Supply Company; and the House of Berezin.

4. Record all the transactions in the general journal, post to the appropriate ledgers and enter the general ledger account balances directly in the Trial Balance columns of the worksheet.

5. Enter the adjustment data in the Adjustments columns of the worksheet.

6. Complete the worksheet.

7. Prepare an income statement, a statement of financial position, and a statement of owner's equity (include percentage analyses and equity ratios).

8. Prepare a schedule of accounts receivable.

9. Prepare a schedule of accounts payable.

10. Prepare adjusting journal entries in the general journal.

11. Post the adjusting journal entries from the general journal to the general ledger.

12. Prepare closing entries in the general journal and post to the general ledger.

13. Balance and rule the accounts.

14. Prepare a post-closing trial balance.

P4–10. The closing entries and post-closing trial balance of the Faulkner Realty Company, as of December 31, 1969, are given on page 153. A yearly accounting period is used. Thomas Faulkner, the proprietor, had a capital balance of $10,000 on January 1, 1969; he made one additional investment during the year.

Required: 1. An income statement for 1969.

2. A statement of owner's equity.

3. Faulkner believes that the income statement should show a deduction of a reasonable amount for his services to the business. Comment.

GENERAL JOURNAL   Page 12

			Closing Entries		
1969					
Dec.	31	Rental Revenue		5,500	
		Commission Revenue		21,600	
		Revenue and Expense Summary			27,100
	31	Revenue and Expense Summary		20,050	
		Rent Expense			1,800
		Insurance Expense			400
		Supplies Expense			150
		Commission Expense			16,500
		Depreciation Expense–Office Equipment			1,000
		Miscellaneous Expense			200
	31	Revenue and Expense Summary		7,050	
		Thomas Faulkner, Drawing			7,050
	31	Thomas Faulkner, Drawing		2,050	
		Thomas Faulkner, Capital			2,050

FAULKNER REALTY COMPANY
Post-Closing Trial Balance
December 31, 1969

Account Title	Debit	Credit
Cash	$ 300	
Office Supplies	150	
Prepaid Insurance	1,600	
Office Equipment	16,000	
Accumulated Depreciation–Office Equipment		$ 2,000
Bank Loans Payable		1,000
Thomas Faulkner, Capital		15,050
Totals	$18,050	$18,050

CASE PROBLEM
The Newtown Reporter, Inc.

The Newtown Reporter, Inc., a small-town tri-weekly newspaper, was founded by Barry Wright and began operations on September 1, 1968. The date is now August 31, 1969, and the Company bookkeeper wishes to adjust and close the books in order to prepare an income statement and a statement of financial position. As a local certified public accountant, you have been asked to offer recommendations as to what adjusting and closing entries are necessary.

After talking with Wright about your very limited responsibilities, you ask the bookkeeper to let you see the Company statement of financial position as of September 1, 1968 (the opening day), and the (unadjusted) trial balance as of today (August 31, 1969, the end of the first year's operations). He shows you the statement of financial position given on page 154 and the trial balance given on page 155.

THE NEWTOWN REPORTER, INC.
Statement of Financial Position
September 1, 1968

Assets			**Liabilities and Stockholders' Equity**		
Current Assets			Current Liabilities		
Cash	$ 6,000		Accounts Payable	$2,000	
Accounts Receivable–Advertisers	1,200		Notes Payable	2,400	
Accounts Receivable–Subscribers	800		Unearned Advertising	1,200	
Supplies Inventory	2,500		Unearned Subscriptions	800	
Total Current Assets		$ 10,500	Total Current Liabilities		$ 6,400
Land and Depreciable Assets			Long-Term Liabilities		
Land	$15,000		Mortgage Payable		50,000
Building	60,000		Stockholders' Equity		
Printing Equipment	20,000		Capital Stock		52,100
Office Equipment	3,000				
Total land and Depreciable Assets		$ 98,000	Total Liabilities and		
Total Assets		$108,500	Stockholders' Equity		$108,500

When the firm started operations, you suggested what general ledger account titles would be desirable, and you notice that the bookkeeper has placed all these titles on the trial balance, including those with zero balances.

During a discussion period with Wright and his bookkeeper, you make the following notes:

1. The supplies inventory consists of items that cost $2,850.
2. The building has an estimated useful life of 50 years.
3. The printing equipment has an estimated useful life of 11 years and an estimated salvage value of $2,400.
4. The office equipment has an estimated useful life of 10 years and an estimated salvage value of $300.
5. Interest of $9 on the 6-percent note payable for the month of August will be paid on September 1, when the regular $50 payment is made.
6. Unearned advertising as of August 31 is determined to be $450.
7. Unearned subscriptions as of August 31 are determined to be $2,800.
8. Salaries and wages that have been earned by employees but are not due to be paid to them until the next payday (in September) amount to $325.
9. Interest of $199 on the 5-percent mortgage payable for the month of August will be paid on September 1, when the regular $200 payment is made.
10. The Company's insurance coverage is provided by a single comprehensive 24-month policy that began on last September 1.

Required: 1. Prepare the adjusting journal entries that you would recommend.
2. Prepare the closing journal entries that you would recommend.
3. Explain to Wright and his bookkeeper the function of *each* journal entry that you recommend. (Note: Be sure to justify your inclusion of each part of each entry.)
4. Explain to Wright the difference between cash and retained earnings.

5. Explain to Wright what is meant by:
   a. Accumulated depreciation
   b. Unearned subscriptions
   c. Accrued accounts payable
   d. Revenue and expense summary

THE NEWTOWN REPORTER, INC.

Trial Balance

August 31, 1969

Account Title	Debits	Credits
Cash	$ 12,000	
Accounts Receivable–Advertisers	2,500	
Accounts Receivable–Subscribers	1,100	
Unexpired Insurance	–0–	
Supplies Inventory	2,500	
Land	15,000	
Building	60,000	
Accumulated Depreciation–Building		–0–
Printing Equipment	20,000	
Accumulated Depreciation–Printing Equipment		–0–
Office Equipment	3,000	
Accumulated Depreciation–Office Equipment		–0–
Accounts Payable		$ 2,600
Notes Payable, 6 percent		1,800
Unearned Advertising		1,200
Unearned Subscriptions		800
Accrued Salaries and Wages Payable		–0–
Accrued Interest Payable		–0–
Mortgage Payable, 5 percent		47,600
Capital Stock		52,100
Retained Earnings		–0–
Revenue and Expense Summary	–0–	–0–
Advertising Revenue		37,900
Subscriptions Revenue		32,700
Depreciation Expense–Building	–0–	
Depreciation Expense–Printing Equipment	–0–	
Depreciation Expense–Office Equipment	–0–	
Interest Expense	2,365	
Insurance Expense	1,800	
Promotional Expense	4,300	
Salaries and Wages Expense	33,475	
Supplies Expense	15,800	
Utilities Expense	2,860	
Totals	$176,700	$176,700

Chapter Five

Merchandising— Determining and Interpreting the Results of Operations

Accounting for businesses that render a service to customers or clients has been discussed up to this point. In this and subsequent chapters, accounting for businesses that buy and sell *merchandise*, or goods, is examined. The principles developed thus far, however, apply to all types of business enterprise, whether service, merchandising, or manufacturing.

ACCOUNTS FOR A MERCHANDISING BUSINESS

The principal difference in the accounts of a merchandising business from those of a service business is that a merchandising business has to account for the purchase of goods, their handling, and their sale—it has to account not only for operating expenses but also for the *cost of goods* that it has sold. The income statement for a merchandising business, therefore, shows an operating income only if the goods are sold for more than their cost plus all other expenses necessary in operating the business. Since a merchandising business is involved in many activities that are not found in service businesses, additional accounts are needed to report the financial position and operating results of the enterprise. By using separate accounts, detailed information is made available; by combining some of these accounts, additional useful information is made available. The functions of the merchandising accounts and their classifications in the financial statements are discussed and illustrated in this chapter.

The Sales Account

A sale of merchandise, like a sale of service, is recorded by a credit to a revenue account, as shown:

TRANSACTION:

Sold merchandise for $200 on account.

JOURNAL ENTRY:

Accounts Receivable	200	
Sales		200

The debit to Accounts Receivable (or to Cash if the sale is for cash) records an increase in an asset. The credit to Sales, a revenue account, records an increase in the stockholders' equity. This credit constitutes a recovery of the cost of the merchandise sold as well as the profit. However, each individual sale cannot be divided into a return of cost and a profit. To do so would require such extensive records as to make the accounting impracticable. Therefore, the entire sales price of the goods is recorded as revenue and the entire cost of goods purchased and sold becomes a deduction from revenue.

The Sales Returns and Allowances Account

A customer may return merchandise because it is not exactly what he ordered; or the customer may be entitled to a reduction of the price, or *allowance*, for defective or broken goods that he retains. The effect of the entry to record a return or allowance is the opposite of a sale; that is, either Cash or the customer's account is credited, and Sales Returns and Allowances is debited. The latter account is used, rather than Sales, so that a record may be available of the amount of returns and allowances.

TRANSACTION:
   The customer returned $10 of the merchandise (see the previous transaction).

JOURNAL ENTRY:

Sales Returns and Allowances	10	
Accounts Receivable		10

The Sales Discounts Account

The customer may be allowed a *discount*, or reduction in price, if he pays within a limited period of time. Since the effect of a discount is to reduce the amount actually received from the sale, Sales Discounts is debited for the amount of the discount. Sales Discounts is a contra account to Sales and is used for the same reason that prompts the use of Sales Returns and Allowances—to supply management with valuable information about the business. When discounts are offered, the customer is in fact being offered the choice of paying (1) the full amount of the invoice or (2) the full amount reduced by the amount of the discount. The seller, however, does not know at the time of the sale whether the customer is going to avail himself of the discount. The customer is charged, therefore, with the full amount of the sale. If the customer pays within the discount period, payment is recorded under the *gross price method* as shown.

TRANSACTION:
   The customer (see the previous transactions) paid his invoice within the discount period, deducting the 2-percent sales discount.

JOURNAL ENTRY:

Cash	186.20	
Sales Discounts	3.80	
Accounts Receivable		190.00

COMPUTATION:

Gross sale price	$200.00
Merchandise returned	10.00
	$190.00
2% discount	3.80
Cash received	$186.20

An alternative procedure, the *net price method,* is discussed later in this chapter.

The following partial income statement of the King Corporation, whose accounts are used for illustrative purposes in this chapter, shows the classification of the Sales and contra Sales accounts.

KING CORPORATION   Exhibit A
Income Statement
For the Year Ended December 31, 1969

Sales Revenue		
Sales		$124,200
Deduct Sales Returns and Allowances	$2,400	
Sales Discounts	1,800	4,200
Net Sales Revenue		$120,000

The Purchases Account

It is customary in a merchandising business to use a separate Purchases account for all merchandise bought for resale. The account is not used for the purchase of operating supplies, for example, or for store equipment used in operations. The Purchases account is debited for the cost of the goods bought, shown on a document from the seller called an *invoice,* and therefore provides a record of the cost of the goods purchased during the period—not a record of the goods on hand. During the year, Purchases will always have a debit balance; the usual credits to the account are to close the account or to correct errors requiring offsetting debits to some other account(s).

TRANSACTION:
    Purchased merchandise for $800 on account.

JOURNAL ENTRY:

Purchases	800	
Accounts Payable		800

The Transportation In Account

The invoice price of goods may include the cost of transporting the goods from the seller's place of business to that of the buyer. If so, no separation is made, and the entire purchase price is debited to Purchases. If the cost of transportation is not included, the carrier is paid directly by the buyer, who debits the amount to Transportation In. This account is added to Purchases in the income statement to determine the *delivered cost of merchandise.*

The following terms are used in connection with the transportation of merchandise:

F.O.B. (free on board) *destination* means that the seller pays the freight cost to the buyer's location. (Sometimes the buyer pays the cost and deducts the amount from his payment to the seller.)

F.O.B. *shipping point* means that the buyer pays the freight cost from the point of shipment to the destination.

TRANSACTION:

Freight charges of $50 were paid upon delivery of merchandise (see the previous transaction); terms of the purchase were F.O.B. shipping point.

JOURNAL ENTRY:

Transportation In	50	
Cash		50

The Purchase Returns and Allowances Account

Goods bought for resale may be defective, broken, or not of the quality ordered. Either they may be returned for credit, or the seller may make an adjustment by reducing the original price.

TRANSACTION:

Returned $100 worth of defective merchandise to the vendor.

JOURNAL ENTRY:

Accounts Payable	100	
Purchase Returns and Allowances		100

Purchase Returns and Allowances is a contra account to Purchases. The same result could be accomplished by crediting Purchases, but it is useful to management to have the books show total Purchases as well as total Purchase Returns and Allowances. Analysis of the Purchase Returns and Allowances account may indicate the need for changes in the procedures of ordering and handling merchandise.

The Purchase Discounts Account

The Purchase Discounts account is used to record deductions from the purchase price of goods for payment made within the discount period specified by the seller. At the time of the purchase, the buyer may not know whether he will avail himself of the discount; the account with the seller (Accounts Payable) is therefore credited for the gross purchase price. As in the case of merchandise sales, an alternative procedure, the *net price method,* is discussed later in the chapter.

TRANSACTION:

Paid for merchandise (see the previous transactions) within the discount period and deducted the allowed discount of 1 percent.

JOURNAL ENTRY:

Accounts Payable	700	
Cash		693
Purchase Discounts		7

COMPUTATION:

Gross purchase	$800
Merchandise returned	100
	$700
1% discount	7
Cash paid	$693

The Merchandise Inventory Account

Merchandise purchased is recorded at cost in Purchases; merchandise sold is recorded at selling price in Sales. Therefore, an account is needed to show the merchandise actually on hand at the end of the accounting period. The amount is determined by making a list of the goods on hand, usually based on an actual count showing physical quantities and their cost. This *ending inventory* is entered in the books and becomes the beginning inventory of the next period. The amount in the ledger account will not be changed until the end of the next accounting period because the Merchandise Inventory account is not used during the period. Since the account remains open, its balance—the beginning inventory—appears in the trial balance at the end of the period and is transferred to Revenue and Expense Summary when the books are closed. Concurrently, the new ending merchandise inventory is entered as a debit to Merchandise Inventory and a credit to Revenue and Expense Summary. After the closing entries are posted, the Merchandise Inventory account in the general ledger of the King Corporation appears as shown:

Merchandise Inventory   Acct. No. 121

1968				1969			
Dec. 31	(A)	15,400		Dec. 31	C.E.	(B)	15,400
1969							
Dec. 31	(C)	11,480					

(A) The debit amount of $15,400 is the cost of the merchandise inventory on hand at December 31, 1968 (the beginning inventory).

(B) The credit posting of $15,400 closes the account temporarily and transfers the balance to Revenue and Expense Summary.

(C) The debit posting of $11,480 is the cost of the merchandise inventory on hand at December 31, 1969 (the ending inventory); this amount will remain unchanged in the account until the books are closed again on December 31, 1970.

THE FUNCTIONS OF THE MERCHANDISE ACCOUNTS

The following T accounts define the functions of the merchandise accounts and their locations in the financial statements. The accounts are presented in their income statement sequence. The description *Balance* in each account refers to the balance before the closing entries have been posted. After the closing entries are posted, all the merchandise accounts, except Merchandise Inventory, are closed.

Sales

Debited	Credited
At the end of the accounting period to close the account.	During the accounting period for the sales price of goods sold.
	Balance
	A credit representing cumulative sales for the period to date.
	Statement classification
	In the income statement, the first item under sales revenue.

Sales Returns and Allowances

Debited	Credited
During the accounting period for un-wanted merchandise returned by customer and allowances for defective or broken goods.	At the end of the accounting period to close the account.
Balance	
A debit representing cumulative sales returns and allowances for the period to date.	
Statement classification	
In the income statement, a deduction from sales revenue.	

Sales Discounts

Debited	Credited
During the accounting period for the amounts that the customers may deduct from the gross sales price if payment is made within the period established by the seller.	At the end of the accounting period to close the account.
Balance	
A debit representing cumulative sales discounts allowed for the period to date.	
Statement classification	
In the income statement, a deduction from sales revenue.	

Merchandise Inventory

Debited	Credited
At the end of each accounting period for the merchandise actually on hand.	At the end of each accounting period for merchandise that was on hand at the beginning of the period, in order to remove the old inventory from the account.

Balance

A debit representing the cost of goods on hand at the beginning of the period.

Statement classification

1. In the position statement, under current assets.
2. In the income statement, in the cost of goods sold section, the beginning inventory is added to Purchases and the ending inventory is subtracted from the cost of merchandise available for sale.

Purchases

Debited	Credited
During the accounting period for the purchase price of goods bought for resale.	At the end of the accounting period to close the account.

Balance

A debit representing cumulative purchases for the period to date.

Statement classification

In the income statement, added to the beginning inventory under the Cost of Goods Sold.

Transportation In

Debited	Credited
During the accounting period for delivery costs—freight or cartage—on merchandise purchases.	At the end of the accounting period to close the account.

Balance

A debit representing cumulative costs for the period to date incurred by the buyer for the delivery of merchandise.

Statement classification

In the income statement, in the cost of goods sold section, added to Purchases.

Purchase Returns and Allowances

Debited	Credited
At the end of the accounting period to close the account.	During the accounting period for unwanted merchandise returned by the buyer to the seller or allowances received for defective or broken merchandise.
	Balance
	A credit representing cumulative purchase returns and allowances for the period to date.
	Statement classification
	In the income statement, in the cost of goods sold section, as a deduction from the gross cost of merchandise purchased.

Purchase Discounts

Debited	Credited
At the end of the accounting period to close the account.	During the accounting period for the amounts that the buyer may deduct from the gross purchase price of merchandise if payment is made within the period established by the seller.
	Balance
	A credit representing cumulative purchase discounts taken for the period to date.
	Statement classification
	In the income statement, in the cost of goods sold section, as a deduction from the gross cost of merchandise purchased.

COST OF GOODS SOLD AND GROSS MARGIN ON SALES

The cost of goods sold is the difference between the cost of the goods available for sale during a period and the cost of the unsold goods on hand at the end of the period. The term does not identify an active account for the recording of transactions but rather the result of adding and subtracting the balances of several accounts. The computation is shown:

Cost of Goods Sold = Beginning Inventory + Net Purchases − Ending Inventory

Net purchases is the total cost of purchases, plus transportation in, less returns, allowances, and discounts.

The income statement of the King Corporation is shown in Figure 5-1. It was prepared from the worksheet in Figure 5-3.

Figure 5-1.   KING CORPORATION   Exhibit A
Income Statement   Income Statement
                               For Year Ended December 31, 1969

				Percent
Gross Sales Revenue			$124,200	
Deduct: Sales Returns and Allowances		$ 2,400		
Sales Discounts		1,800	4,200	
Net Sales Revenue			$120,000	100.0
Cost of Goods Sold				
Merchandise Inventory, January 1, 1969			$15,400	
Purchases		$63,580		
Transportation In		4,800		
Gross Purchases		$68,380		
Deduct: Purchase Returns and Allowances	$1,500			
Purchase Discounts	3,600	5,100		
Net Purchases			63,280	
Cost of Merchandise Available for Sale			$78,680	
Deduct Merchandise Inventory, December 31, 1969			11,480	
Cost of Goods Sold			67,200	56.0
Gross Margin on Sales			$ 52,800	44.0
Deduct Operating Expenses				
Selling Expenses				
Salesmen's Salaries Expense		$12,000		10.0
Transportation Out Expense		2,400		2.0
Advertising Expense		3,000		2.5
Total Selling Expenses			$17,400	14.5
General and Administrative Expenses				
Rent Expense		$ 6,000		5.0
Property Tax Expense		7,800		6.5
Heat and Light Expense		2,160		1.8
Miscellaneous General Expense		480		.4
Insurance Expense		1,920		1.6
Supplies Expense		2,040		1.7
Depreciation Expense–Machinery and Equipment		3,600		3.0
Total General and Administrative Expenses			24,000	20.0
Total Operating Expenses			41,400	34.5
Net Operating Margin			$ 11,400	9.5
Other Revenue				
Interest Earned		$ 125		
Rent Earned		300	$ 425	
Other Expenses				
Interest Expense		$ 75		
Loss on Sale of Equipment		100	175	250
Net Income Before Income Taxes			$ 11,650	
Income Taxes			5,825	
Net Income			$ 5,825	

The income statement of the King Corporation shows all the accounts needed to derive the cost of goods sold of $67,200.

The *gross margin on sales* of $52,800 is what is left after the cost of goods sold of $67,200 is deducted from the net sales revenue of $120,000. The term *gross* indicates that the operating expenses necessary to the conduct of the business must still be deducted to arrive at the *net operating margin.* If the gross margin on sales is less than the operating expenses, the difference is a net operating loss for the period.

THE OPERATING EXPENSE ACCOUNTS

Operating expenses are salaries, postage, telephone and telegraph, heat and light, insurance, advertising, and any other costs incurred for goods or services used in operating the business. The breakdown of operating expenses into a number of detailed accounts facilitates analyses and comparisons that aid in the management of the business. The amount of detail shown depends on the size and type of the business and on the needs and wishes of the management.

The operating expenses are often subdivided into *selling* and *general and administrative.* The expenses incurred in packaging the product, advertising it, making the sale, and delivering the product are classified as selling expenses. Salesmen's salaries, commissions, and supplies used in the Sales department are examples of expenses incurred in making the sale. Expenses of delivering the product include freight paid by the seller (transportation out) and the expense of operating motor vehicles. Expenses such as rent, taxes, and insurance, to the extent that they are incurred in selling the product, are also classified as selling expenses. All other expenses are classified as general and administrative, including office expenses, executive salaries, and the portion of rent, taxes, and insurance applicable to the administrative function of the business. The expenses that are common to both selling and administrative functions may be apportioned on some equitable basis. If an apportionment is not practicable, the account should be classified under the function it serves most broadly. In Figure 5-1, the operating expense accounts that are entirely related to selling are classified as such; all the others are classified as general and administrative. The total operating expenses of $41,400 are deducted from the gross margin on sales of $52,800 to arrive at the net operating margin of $11,400.

If the operating expense accounts in the general ledger are too numerous, it is advisable to remove them to subsidiary selling expense and general and administrative expense ledgers. Two controlling accounts are substituted in the general ledger—Selling Expense and General and Administrative Expense—in place of the accounts that have been removed. The function of controlling accounts was explained in Chapter 3.

OTHER REVENUE AND OTHER EXPENSES

Items of a nonrecurring nature that do not arise from the regular operations of the business are not used to determine the net operating margin; rather, they are added to or deducted from the net operating margin to arrive at net income. One reason for this is to enable the operating margin to be compared with those of prior statements or statements of other companies. The inclusion of extraneous items in arriving at the net operating margin would distort the comparison, since not all the statements would include comparable items. For example, a company may show a profit from its regular business operations but, owing to a loss from the sale of unused equipment, show a net loss for the period. For comparative purposes, either with prior years' statements of the same company or with statements of other companies, the loss from the sale of the equipment—an occasional event—is shown after the net operating margin. Interest expense and other expenses of a nonrecurring nature are excluded in arriving at the net operating margin for the same reason.

The Other Revenue and Other Expenses sections of the income statement serve a valuable function; they enable the derivation of the net operating margin undistorted by extraneous items and link the net operating margin for the period with the net income for that period. Some accountants report unusual and nonrecurring gains and losses in the statement of retained earnings rather than in the income statement. This is shown in Chapter 17.

Other Revenue

Some common examples of items classified as other revenue are gains from the sale of securities, dividends on shares of stock owned, gains from a settlement with an insurance company for fire damage, and gains from the sale of plant and equipment. In Figure 5-1, the King Corporation shows $125 in interest earned and $300 in rent earned under Other Revenue.

Other Expenses

Nonoperating expenses such as interest on money borrowed from the bank or notes given to creditors for the purchase of merchandise, uninsured property losses, or losses from the sale of plant and equipment are shown under other expenses. In the income statement in Figure 5-1, the King Corporation shows $75 in interest expense and $100 from a loss on a sale of equipment under Other Expenses.

The King Corporation added $250, the excess of other revenue over other expenses, to the net operating margin. If other expenses exceed other revenue, the expenses are listed first and the excess is deducted from the net operating margin.

In the absence of other revenue or other expenses, net operating margin becomes net income and net operating loss becomes net loss.

THE COMPLETION OF THE WORKSHEET

The procedure for completing the worksheet in a merchandising business is similar to that in a service business, with the obvious exception of the handling of the merchandise inventories.

At the end of the period, the balance of the Merchandise Inventory account, the beginning inventory of $15,400, is extended to the Income Statement Debit column of the worksheet because it is part of the cost of merchandise available for sale. The ending inventory, $11,480, is shown in the Income Statement Credit column because it is a deduction from the cost of merchandise available for sale and in the Position Statement Debit column because it is an asset. This treatment, which preserves the equality of debits and credits in the worksheet, is shown in Figure 5-2.

KING CORPORATION
Partial Worksheet
For the Year Ended December 31, 1969

Figure 5-2.
Partial Worksheet

Name of Account	Trial Balance		Income Statement		Position Statement	
	Dr.	Cr.	Dr.	Cr.	Dr.	Cr.
Cash						
Accounts Receivable						
Merchandise Inventory	15,400		15,400	11,480	11,480	

The beginning inventory in the trial balance is extended to the Income Statement Debit column.	The ending inventory is shown in the Income Statement Credit column.	The ending inventory is also entered in the Position Statement Debit column.

The worksheet of the King Corporation is shown in Figure 5-3. There are a number of possible variations in the form; for instance, the Adjusted Trial Balance columns are omitted in this example. The combined Trial Balance and Adjustment column amounts are extended directly to the proper Income Statement or Position Statement columns.

Trial Balance Columns

The account balances in the trial balance are taken from the general ledger of the King Corporation as of December 31, 1969.

Adjustment Columns

Supplementary records show the following information as of December 31, 1969:

   a. Insurance that has expired is $1,920.
   b. Office supplies on hand total $1,200.
   c. Depreciation on machinery and equipment is computed at $3,600.
   d. Income tax expense is estimated to be $5,825.

Income Statement Columns

All the account balances that enter into the measurement of net income are extended to the Income Statement columns. The income statement accounts that enter into the determination of gross margin are shown in Figure 5-4.

The computation is accomplished on the formal income statement (Figure 5-1), resulting in a gross margin on sales of $52,800. The difference between the column totals in Figure 5-4 ($140,780 − $87,980 = $52,800) is the same as the gross margin on sales because all the accounts that enter into the determination of the gross margin are listed. Similar examples could be made from the other sections of the income and position statements.

KING CORPORATION
Worksheet
For the Year Ended December 31, 1969

Acct. No.	Account Title	Trial Balance Dr.	Trial Balance Cr.	Adjustments Dr.	Adjustments Cr.	Income Statement Dr.	Income Statement Cr.	Position Statement Dr.	Position Statement Cr.
101	Cash	7,200						7,200	
111	Accounts Receivable	40,800						40,800	
121	Merchandise Inventory	15,400				15,400	11,480	11,480	
131	Office Supplies	3,240			(b) 2,040			1,200	
141	Prepaid Insurance	3,740			(a) 1,920			1,820	
151	Machinery and Equipment	70,100						70,100	
151A	Accumulated Depreciation–Machinery and Equipment		7,200		(c) 3,600				10,800
201	Accounts Payable		17,700						17,700
202	Notes Payable		7,300						7,300
221	Mortgage Payable		20,000						20,000
301	Capital Stock		60,000						60,000
302	Retained Earnings		5,150						5,150
401	Sales Revenue		124,200				124,200		
402	Sales Returns and Allowances	2,400				2,400			
403	Sales Discounts	1,800				1,800			
501	Purchases	63,580				63,580			
502	Transportation In	4,800				4,800			
503	Purchase Returns and Allowances		1,500				1,500		
504	Purchase Discounts		3,600				3,600		
601	Salesmen's Salaries Expense	12,000				12,000			
602	Transportation Out Expense	2,400				2,400			
603	Advertising Expense	3,000				3,000			
701	Rent Expense	6,000				6,000			
702	Property Tax Expense	7,800				7,800			
703	Heat and Light Expense	2,160				2,160			
704	Miscellaneous General Expense	480				480			
801	Interest Earned		125				125		
802	Rent Earned		300				300		
821	Interest Expense	75				75			
822	Loss on Sale of Equipment	100				100			
		247,075	247,075						
705	Insurance Expense			(a) 1,920		1,920			
706	Office Supplies Expense			(b) 2,040		2,040			
707	Depreciation Expense–Machinery and Equipment			(c) 3,600		3,600			
708	Income Tax Expense			(d) 5,825		5,825			
709	Income Taxes Payable				(d) 5,825				5,825
				13,385	13,385	135,380	141,205	132,600	126,775
	Net Income for the Year					5,825			5,825
						141,205	141,205	132,600	132,600

Figure 5-3.
Worksheet

Position Statement Columns

All the amounts that are used to prepare the statements of financial position and retained earnings are extended to the Position Statement columns.

THE COMPLETED FINANCIAL STATEMENTS

Figure 5-5 shows the classified statement of financial position and Figure 5-6 shows the statement of retained earnings. These statements and the income statement (Figure 5-1) were prepared after the completion of the worksheet.

Acct. No.	Account Title	Income Statement	
		Dr.	Cr.
121	Merchandise Inventory	15,400	11,480
401	Sales Revenue		124,200
402	Sales Returns and Allowances	2,400	
403	Sales Discounts	1,800	
501	Purchases	63,580	
502	Transportation In	4,800	
503	Purchase Returns and Allowances		1,500
504	Purchase Discounts		3,600
	Totals	87,980	140,780

Figure 5-4.
Abstract from the Worksheet

KING CORPORATION   Exhibit B
Statement of Financial Position
December 31, 1969

Figure 5-5.
Statement of Financial Position

Assets

			Percent
Current Assets			
Cash	$ 7,200		5.9
Accounts Receivable	40,800		33.5
Merchandise Inventory	11,480		9.4
Office Supplies	1,200		1.0
Prepaid Insurance	1,820		1.5
Total Current Assets		$ 62,500	51.3
Plant and Equipment			
Machinery and Equipment	$70,100		
Deduct Accumulated Depreciation	10,800		
Total Plant and Equipment		59,300	48.7
Total Assets		$121,800	100.0

Liabilities and Stockholders' Equity

Current Liabilities			
Accounts Payable	$17,700		14.5
Notes Payable	7,300		6.0
Income Taxes Payable	5,825		4.8
Total Current Liabilities		$ 30,825	25.3
Long-Term Liabilities			
Mortgage Payable		20,000	16.4
Total Liabilities		$ 50,825	41.7
Stockholders' Equity			
Capital Stock	$60,000		
Retained Earnings–Exhibit C	10,975		
Total Stockholders' Equity		70,975	58.3
Total Liabilities and Stockholders' Equity		$121,800	100.0

Figure 5-6.
Statement of Retained Earnings

KING CORPORATION   Exhibit C
Statement of Retained Earnings
For Year Ended December 31, 1969

Retained Earnings, January 1, 1969	$ 5,150
Add Net Income for the Year—Exhibit A	5,825
Retained Earnings, December 31, 1969	$10,975

CLOSING ENTRIES

The procedure for recording the closing entries in a merchandising business is essentially the same as in a service business. The closing entries, including the closing of the beginning merchandise inventory and the recording of the ending inventory, are shown in Figure 5-7. After the closing entries are posted, all the revenue and expense accounts have zero balances. The remaining accounts—the open position statement accounts—are ruled and balanced, and a post-closing trial balance is prepared.

The King Corporation did not declare any dividends during the year. If dividends had been declared, another closing entry would be made, debiting Retained Earnings and crediting Dividends to close the Dividends account. The dividends would also be shown on the statement of retained earnings.

INTERIM FINANCIAL STATEMENTS

Financial statements are prepared at least once a year, at which time the adjusting and closing entries are recorded and posted to the general ledger. The closing of the books at intervals of less than one year is not customary but has been assumed in this text as a convenience in illustrating the periodic summary. Financial statements, however, may be prepared at frequent intervals—monthly or quarterly—without the formal recording and posting of the adjusting and closing entries.

Financial statements may be produced at regular or intermittent intervals during the accounting period for external reasons, such as the establishment of credit for a bank loan, or for the internal use of managers and stockholders. They are referred to as *interim statements* and are prepared with the aid of the worksheet. The general ledger account balances as of the end of the interim period are entered on the worksheet, the adjustments are listed, the adjusted balances are extended to the appropriate Income Statement and Position Statement columns, and formal statements are prepared.

The amounts in the Trial Balance columns of the worksheet represent the cumulative general ledger totals for the year to date and the adjustments are for the same interval; hence, the amounts in the interim income statement are for the year to date. However, if monthly income statements are desired, the amounts on the statements for the previous months are deducted from the amounts on the current statement, thereby providing year-to-date figures as well as results of the current period. The amounts in the Position Statement columns of the worksheet are the correct amounts for the statement of financial position as of the close of the current period.

GENERAL JOURNAL   Page 12

Figure 5-7.
General Journal—
Closing Entries

1969					
Dec.	31	Merchandise Inventory	121	11,480	
		Sales Revenue	401	124,200	
		Purchase Returns and Allowances	503	1,500	
		Purchase Discounts	504	3,600	
		Interest Earned	801	125	
		Rent Earned	802	300	
		Revenue and Expense Summary	901		141,205
		To record the ending inventory and close the revenue accounts.			
	31	Revenue and Expense Summary	901	135,380	
		Merchandise Inventory	121		15,400
		Sales Returns and Allowances	402		2,400
		Sales Discounts	403		1,800
		Purchases	501		63,580
		Transportation In	502		4,800
		Salesmen's Salaries Expense	601		12,000
		Transportation Out Expense	602		2,400
		Advertising Expense	603		3,000
		Rent Expense	701		6,000
		Property Tax Expense	702		7,800
		Heat and Light Expense	703		2,160
		Miscellaneous General Expense	704		480
		Insurance Expense	705		1,920
		Office Supplies Expense	706		2,040
		Depreciation Expense– Machinery and Equipment	707		3,600
		Income Tax Expense	708		5,825
		Interest Expense	821		75
		Loss on Sale of Equipment	822		100
		To close the beginning inventory and the expense accounts.			
	31	Revenue and Expense Summary	901	5,825	
		Retained Earnings	302		5,825
		To transfer net income to Retained Earnings.			

The preparation of interim statements requires a determination of the cost of the merchandise on hand. Taking a detailed physical inventory, however, is costly and time-consuming and may not be necessary. Alternative methods of determining the ending inventory, such as the gross margin method of inventory valuation and the perpetual inventory system, are discussed in Chapter 10.

MANAGERIAL RATIO ANALYSIS

The financial statements of the King Corporation are analyzed to illustrate some additional ratios commonly used by the management in the analysis of the financial statements. The following amounts used in the illustrations are taken from the prior year's statement of financial position:

Stockholders' equity	$93,200
Total liabilities	58,600
Current assets	71,500
Current liabilities	29,000

Figures are rounded when it is necessary.

Rate of Return on Stockholders' Equity

The relationship between earnings and the stockholders' investment is a significant measure of the profitability of a business. The rate of return on the stockholders' equity is computed as shown:

Net income for the year 1969	Ⓐ	$ 5,825
Average stockholders' equity		
Balance, January 1, 1969	Ⓑ	$ 93,200
Balance, December 31, 1969	Ⓒ	70,975
Total	Ⓓ	$164,175
Average (Line D ÷ 2)	Ⓔ	$ 82,088
Rate of return on stockholders' equity (Line A ÷ Line E)		7.1%

Earnings for 1969 were 7.1 cents for each dollar of the stockholders' equity. The average stockholders' equity is computed so that the computation is not based on either the beginning-of-year or the end-of-year stockholders' equity. A further refinement is to compute the average by using the month-end balance for each month in the period covered by the analysis. This practice should be followed for any ratios involving amounts that fluctuate during the period to avoid distortion.

Rate of Return on Total Equities

The relationship of the earnings of a corporation to its total resources is another important indication of profitability. It is computed as shown:

Net income for the year 1969		Ⓐ	$ 5,825
Average total liabilities:			
Balance, January 1, 1969	$ 58,600		
Balance, December 31, 1969 (Fig. 5-5)	50,825		
Total	$109,425		
Average total liabilities ($109,425 ÷ 2)		Ⓑ	$ 54,713
Average stockholders' equity (above)		Ⓒ	82,088
Total average equities		Ⓓ	$136,801
Rate of return on total equities (Line A ÷ Line D)		Ⓔ	4.3%

The King Corporation earned 4.3 cents for each dollar invested in the company—whether by outside creditors or by stockholders. Since total equities are equal to total assets, it also may be said that the King Corporation earned 4.3 cents on each dollar of assets used in the business.

Operating Ratio

An indication of the amount expended during a period in relationship to the revenue of the period is important to management. The computation is shown:

Net sales revenue	Ⓐ	$120,000
Cost of goods sold	Ⓑ	$ 67,200
Total operating expenses	Ⓒ	41,400
Total revenue deductions	Ⓓ	$108,600
Operating ratio (Line D ÷ Line A)		90.5%

The operating ratio shows that 90.5 cents of each sales dollar was absorbed by the operations of the King Corporation, or that costs and expenses of 90.5 cents were incurred to generate a dollar of sales revenue.

Net Operating Margin Ratio

The net operating margin ratio is a complement of the operating ratio; it shows the relationship of the net operating margin to sales (other revenue and other expenses are excluded).

$$\frac{\text{Net Operating Margin}}{\text{Net Sales Revenue}} = \frac{\$11,400}{\$120,000} = 9.5\%$$

The King Corporation earned 9.5 cents for each dollar of net sales. This ratio must be considered together with the rate of return on the stockholders' equity in appraising the earning power of a business. A high net operating margin ratio is not necessarily a favorable indication if it is accompanied by a low rate of return on the stockholders' equity.

Turnover of Merchandise Inventory

The quantity of goods to be kept on hand is a major business decision. It is considered good management to carry as little as possible and to turn it over as rapidly as possible. Good management must guard against excessive inventories, the consequences of which could be an abnormal drain on working capital leading to financial difficulties. The greater the inventory, the greater is the amount of money tied up, extra space required, and extra handling costs, as well as an increased possibility of loss through shrinkage, style changes, or other factors. Inadequate inventories, on the other hand, may result in higher costs due to buying in smaller quantities and the possible loss of business if what the customer wants is not on hand. Good management, therefore, requires a careful evaluation of all these factors in establishing inventory levels.

One of the ratios used in inventory analysis is the inventory turnover—the relationship between inventory and either net sales or cost of goods sold. Since the net sales figure is given at selling price and the inventory is given at cost, the ratio is computed by dividing the cost of goods sold rather than net sales by the average inventory. The figure used may be the average of the beginning and ending inventories of the period or, preferably, the average for the month involved to minimize the effect of seasonal fluctuations. Although high turnover is usually a sign of good management, this ratio varies widely from one industry to another. A wholesaler of automobile parts and accessories may average five inventory turnovers per year as compared with thirty-five or more for a wholesaler of meat and poultry. Also, a high-volume, low-margin business would have to turn over its inventory more often than a similar business having a low-volume, high-margin policy.

The inventory turnover is computed as shown:

Cost of goods sold	(A)	$67,200
Average merchandise inventory:		
January 1, 1969	(B)	$15,400
December 31, 1969	(C)	11,480
Total	(D)	$26,880
Average (Line D ÷ 2)	(E)	$13,440
Turnover of inventory (Line A ÷ Line E)		5.0

The King Corporation sold and replaced its merchandise inventory five times during the year; that is, the cost of merchandise sold was five times greater than the average cost of merchandise on hand.

Working Capital Turnover

The relationship between working capital and sales tests the efficiency with which the working capital is used. The computation is made as shown:

	January 1, 1969	December 31, 1969
Average working capital:		
Current assets	$71,500	$62,500
Current liabilities	29,000	30,825
Working capital	$42,500	$31,675
Average working capital		
($42,500 + $31,675 = $74,175 ÷ 2)		$ 37,088
Net sales revenue		$120,000
Working capital turnover ($120,000 ÷ $37,088)		3.24

The King Corporation sold $3.24 worth of merchandise for each dollar of working capital. Care must be used in drawing any conclusions from this ratio because of the number of continuously changing elements (current assets, current liabilities, and sales) that it interrelates.

Percentage Analysis—King Corporation

The ratio of each revenue deduction to net revenue, each asset to total assets, each equity to total equities, and the several subtotals to the related totals is also significant. These percentages may be determined readily from the Percent columns of the King Corporation statements and are therefore not reproduced here. This form of analysis is called *vertical analysis* because the percentages relate to amounts usually shown in columnar statement form.

In Figure 5-1, the amounts of the items listed under other revenue and other expenses are not converted to percentages of net sales revenue because they are not part of the normal operating business cycle and there is no direct relationship between these amounts and net sales revenue.

The Percent column in the income statement of the King Corporation is a *common-size* income statement—each item is stated as a percentage of net sales revenue. It is also called a *dollar* statement because it is identical in proportion to the common-size statement. For example, the distribution of the net sales dollar in Figure 5-1 may be expressed as follows.

Cost of Goods Sold	$ .560
Selling Expenses	.145
General and Administrative Expenses	.200
Net Operating Margin	.095
Net Sales Revenue	$1.000

In addition to the analyses already illustrated and discussed, other ratios and percentages furnish useful managerial information. Some relationships of the King Corporation are given:

$$\text{Sales returns and allowances to sales revenue} = \frac{\$2,400}{\$124,200} = 1.9\%$$

$$\text{Sales discounts to sales revenue} = \frac{\$1,800}{\$124,200} = 1.5\%$$

$$\text{Purchase returns and allowances to purchases} = \frac{\$1,500}{\$63,580} = 2.4\%$$

$$\text{Purchase discounts to purchases} = \frac{\$3,600}{\$63,580} = 5.7\%$$

These ratios serve as tools for controlling various accounts. If, for example, sales returns and allowances has previously been approximately 1/2 of 1 percent, then management ought to determine the causes of the increase to 1.9 percent.

UNCOLLECTIBLE ACCOUNTS

To measure properly the bad debt losses attributable to sales of a given period and the net realizable value of Accounts Receivable which should be shown on the statement of financial position, it is necessary to make the following end-of-period adjusting entry:

Bad Debts Expense	500	
Allowance for Doubtful Accounts		500
To record the bad debt expense for the year.		

Bad Debts Expense is shown on the income statement as a general and administrative expense and Allowance for Doubtful Accounts is shown on the statement of financial position as follows:

Accounts Receivable	$7,500	
Deduct Allowance for Doubtful Accounts	500	$7,000

When an account is discovered to be uncollectible, it is written off against Allowance for Doubtful Accounts as follows:

Allowance for Doubtful Accounts	75	
Accounts Receivable—James Dunker		75
To write off the uncollectible account of James Dunker.		

A more detailed discussion of the accounting for bad debts and uncollectible accounts is deferred to Chapter 9.

CASH DISCOUNTS—IMPLICATIONS TO MANAGEMENT

Cash discounts are computed on the net sales price; the conditions of payment are stated on the invoice. Some typical conditions are:

Net cash	Payment is due in full upon delivery of the goods.
Net 30, or n/30	The full amount shown on the invoice is due within 30 days from the date of the invoice.
2/10, n/30	A 2-percent discount may be taken, provided payment is made within 10 days from the invoice date; otherwise the full invoice price is due in 30 days.
2/EOM, n/60	A 2-percent discount may be taken, provided payment is made by the end of the month (EOM) in which the goods are billed; the full amount is due in 60 days from the end of the month.
1/10 prox, n/60 or 1/10 EOM, n/60	A 1-percent discount may be taken, provided payment is made by the tenth of the following month; the full amount is due in 60 days from the end of the month. *Prox* is an abbreviation of *proximal,* or nearest. These terms are designed for buyers who prefer making payments during the first ten days of the month to spreading them throughout.

When the terms of the sale—or of the purchase—are, for example, 2/10, n/30, it is important to recognize the magnitude of the discount offered. This can be done best if the discount is converted into its equivalent annual interest rate. If the buyer of merchandise pays within 10 days from the date shown on the invoice, he may deduct 2 percent from the invoice price, or he may take an additional 20 days, or 30 days in all, before paying. The cost of the additional 20 days is high, however, because the loss of the 2-percent discount amounts to 1/10 of 1 percent per day ($2\% \div 20$), or 36 percent per 360-day year ($0.1\% \times 360$). The prudent businessman should, therefore, take all cash discounts, even if he has to borrow the money to do so.

TRADE DISCOUNTS

Another type of discount is the *trade discount,* which, unlike the cash discount, is not recorded in the accounts. A trade discount is a percentage reduction from a list price. The seller prints a catalog in which the prices of the various articles are shown. The actual price charged may differ from the list price because of the class of buyer (wholesalers, retailers, and so on), the quantity ordered, or changes in the catalog. The granting of trade discounts eliminates the need for frequent reprinting of catalogs or printing different lists for different classes of buyers. If more than one discount is given—a so-called *chain discount*—each discount is applied successively to arrive at the invoice price. Thus, the actual price of an item listed at $300 less trade discounts of 20 percent, 10 percent, and 5 percent is $205.20.

MANAGEMENT CONTROL—THE EXCEPTION PRINCIPLE

The control principle of management by exception involves isolating those amounts or accounts that indicate operating inefficiencies and focus attention on the areas that might require corrective action. Since only exceptions from the norm require such corrective action, management's task is simplified and expedited by separating from the mass of data the exceptional items for further study.

The alternative method for recording cash discounts—the net price method—illustrates the principle of management by exception. Under the gross price procedure discussed earlier in this chapter, the volume of discounts granted or taken is accumulated in the Sales Discounts and Purchases Discounts accounts. Management is interested primarily, however, not in the amount of discounts taken—since it assumes that all available discounts are taken—but rather in the exceptions; that is, the discounts not taken.

Sales Discounts Not Taken

Assume that a $1,000 sale is made on April 1, with terms of 2/10, n/30, and that payment is received on April 10. The entries, recorded net of discount, are:

```
1969
Apr.  1   Accounts Receivable            980
             Sales                                    980
      10   Cash                           980
             Accounts Receivable                      980
```

If the payment was received on April 25, the entry would be:

```
1969
Apr. 25   Cash                         1,000
             Accounts Receivable                      980
             Sales Discounts Not Taken                 20
```

Sales Discounts Not Taken is classified as other revenue in the income statement.

Management should make a careful analysis of Sales Discounts Not Taken. A customer who fails to take advantage of discount terms of 2/10, n/30, for example, is foregoing savings equivalent to an annual rate of 36 percent. This indicates an unwillingness or an inability to pay debts promptly, significant information in granting credit or evaluating possible losses from uncollectible accounts.

Purchases Discounts Lost

The rationale for the alternative method of recording purchase discounts under the net price method is the same as for the recording of sales discounts. Purchases are recorded at net price, and discounts lost are entered in a special account.

To illustrate the accounting for discounts lost by the net price method, assume that a purchase of $5,000 in merchandise is received on July 1, with terms of 2/10, n/30, and that the invoice is paid on July 10. Purchases and Accounts Payable are recorded *net of discount*, as shown:

```
1969
July  1   Purchases                    4,900
             Accounts Payable                       4,900
      10   Accounts Payable             4,900
             Cash                                    4,900
```

If the invoice was not paid until July 15, the entries would be:

```
1969
July  1   Purchases                        4,900
              Accounts Payable                             4,900

     15   Accounts Payable                 4,900
          Purchases Discounts Lost           100
              Cash                                         5,000
```

Under the net price procedure, the debit to Purchases is $4,900 whether or not the discount is lost, and the loss of $100 appears in a separate general and administrative expense account, isolating the amount for the detection of possible laxities in procedures. The loss of available discounts may indicate a weakness in the organization, such as lack of bank credit or slowness in processing invoices for payment. The cost of goods purchased is not increased when discounts are lost; the amount is classified under other expenses.

There are some disadvantages to recording purchases at the net price: (1) the amount of discounts taken is not reported separately in the income statement; (2) statements from creditors do not agree with the net amounts recorded in the accounts payable ledger; (3) the amounts entered on individual inventory record cards may not agree with the net amounts entered as purchases since the inventory is carried at cost; (4) the additional information may not justify the increased clerical costs and inconveniences; (5) an adjusting entry is needed at the end of the period to record lapsed discounts by debiting Purchase Discounts Lost and crediting Accounts Payable.

SUMMARY

Additional accounts are needed to report the financial position and operating results of a business that buys and sells merchandise. These accounts—either singly or in combination—provide additional useful information.

Net sales revenue is determined from the Sales account less the Sales Returns and Allowances and the Sales Discount accounts. The net cost of goods purchased is determined from the Purchases and Transportation In accounts less the Purchases Returns and Allowances and Purchases Discounts accounts. The cost of goods sold is equal to beginning inventory plus net purchases minus ending inventory. The gross margin is the difference between the net sales and the cost of goods sold. The operating expenses—subdivided into selling and general and administrative—are deducted from the gross margin on sales to arrive at the net operating margin. Items of a nonrecurring nature are recorded in separate accounts and classified under Other Revenue and Other Expenses and their difference is added to or deducted from the net operating margin to arrive at net income for the period.

Again, the worksheet is used to facilitate the preparation of the financial statements. The income statement accounts that enter into the determination of gross margin are extended to the Income Statement columns. The beginning inventory in the Trial Balance Debit column is extended to the Income Statement Debit column;

the ending inventory is entered directly into the Income Statement Credit column and the Position Statement Debit column.

Significant information is made available to management by certain ratios and by showing the percentage distributions of the financial statement items. Ratios such as the rate of return on the stockholders' equity, the rate of return on the total equities, and the net operating margin ratio focus on the profitability of the company. The operating ratio and the turnover of merchandise inventory emphasize the effectiveness of a company's inventory management policies and the level of costs and expenses required to generate a dollar of sales revenue.

The principle of management by exception involves isolating those amounts or accounts that indicate operating inefficiencies. Management's task is simplified and expedited by separating from the mass of data only the exceptional items for further study. This is illustrated by the practice of recording sales and purchases at net amounts and recording sales discounts not taken and purchases discounts lost in separate accounts.

☐ QUESTIONS

Q5–1. (a) What is the function of the Sales account? (b) the Sales Returns and Allowances account? (c) the Sales Discount account?

Q5–2. (a) What is the function of the Purchases account? (b) the Purchase Returns and Allowances account? (c) the Purchase Discounts account? (d) the Transportation In account?

Q5–3. (a) What is the function of the Merchandise Inventory account? (b) How is its amount determined? (c) In which columns of the worksheet is the beginning inventory shown? (d) the ending inventory?

Q5–4. (a) How is the cost of goods sold determined? (b) Why isn't the cost of goods sold recorded at the time of the sale? (c) What is the relationship between the cost of goods sold and the gross margin on sales?

Q5–5. Why is it desirable to show the following items separately on the income statement: (a) operating expenses and other expenses? (b) net operating margin and other revenue?

Q5–6. (a) What is the purpose of interim statements? (b) For whom are they prepared? (c) How are they prepared? (d) What special problems do they create?

Q5–7. Is it true that (a) management need not concern itself with the normal results but only with the exceptions? (b) only the big exceptions require corrective action? (c) The alternative method for recording cash discounts illustrates the principle of management by exception. Can you think of any other alternative recording methods that further illustrate this principle? (d) What are the disadvantages of recording purchases at the net price?

Q5–8. (a) What is meant by *inventory turnover*? (b) "The greater the turnover of inventory, the greater the gross margin on sales." Is this statement correct? Explain. (c) What is the significance to management of the turnover of merchandise inventory? (d) Is there an advantage in using monthly inventories to compute the turnover?

Q5–9. What ratios or percentages would aid in answering the following questions: (a) Is the net income satisfactory? (b) Are the operating expenses excessive? (c) Does the net income represent a reasonable return on the company's total resources? (d) Does the net income represent a reasonable return on the stockholders' equity? (e) Is the company maintaining an efficient relationship between working capital and sales? (f) Are the total selling expenses excessive? (g) Is the merchandise on hand excessive?

Q5–**10.** Assume that a merchandise transaction was made on September 4. In each case, determine the latest possible payment date to allow the discount deduction. (a) 1/10, n/30; (b) 2/EOM, n/60; (c) 1/10 EOM, n/60.

Q5–**11.** Discuss the significance of each of the following: (a) the rate of return on stockholders' equity; (b) the rate of return on total equities; (c) the operating ratio; (d) the turnover of inventory; and (e) the working capital turnover.

Q5–**12.** (a) Distinguish between a cash discount and a trade discount. (b) Why are trade discounts used in quoting prices? (c) What are the advantages, if any, of recording purchases of merchandise at the invoice amount less cash discount, or net, over recording the full, or gross, invoice amount? (d) Explain the term *2/10, n/30*. (e) Discuss and illustrate alternative income statement presentations of Purchases Discounts and Sales Discounts.

☐ **EXERCISES**

E5–**1.** During the year 1969, the Hobart Sales Company purchased merchandise costing $13,500. Calculate the cost of goods sold for the year under each of the following assumptions regarding the beginning and ending merchandise inventory balances:

 a. No beginning or ending inventory
 b. A beginning inventory of $12,000; no ending inventory
 c. A beginning inventory of $15,000 and an ending inventory of $19,000
 d. No beginning inventory; an ending inventory of $4,000

E5–**2.** From the following information taken from the books of the Wilson Company, prepare a partial income statement through gross margin on sales:

Merchandise Inventory, January 1, 1969	$ 1,500
Merchandise Inventory, January 31, 1969	1,100
Sales	12,400
Transportation In	450
Purchase Discounts	370
Sales Returns and Allowances	230
Purchases	6,300
Sales Discounts	150
Purchase Returns and Allowances	110

E5–**3.** Journalize the following transactions on the books of the buyer and the seller.

 a. On June 1, the Atkins Manufacturing Company in New York sold merchandise to the Smith Company in Boston for $800; terms 2/10, n/30, F.O.B. destination. The Smith Company paid $50 freight on the shipment. On June 5, the Smith Company returned some unsatisfactory merchandise and received credit for $25. On June 10, the Smith Company mailed a check to the Atkins Manufacturing Company for the net amount due.
 b. Assume the same facts as in a., except that the terms were F.O.B. shipping point.

E5–**4.** The accounts and balances in the Income Statement columns of Thomas Kent's worksheet for the year ended December 31, 1969 are given:

Account Title	Income Statement	
	Dr.	Cr.
Merchandise Inventory	5,000	5,500
Sales		15,300
Sales Returns and Allowances	50	
Sales Discounts	350	
Purchases	8,000	
Transportation In	200	
Purchase Returns and Allowances		100
Purchase Discounts		500
Selling Expenses	1,800	
General Expenses	3,000	
Totals	18,400	21,400
Net Income	3,000	
	21,400	21,400

The Position Statement Debit column of the worksheet showed $800 for Thomas Kent, Drawing. (a) Journalize the closing entries. (b) Show the Merchandise Inventory and Revenue and Expense Summary accounts after the closing entries have been posted. (c) What difference, if any, is there between the closing entries of a trading business and those of a nontrading business? (d) May the Revenue and Expense Summary account be eliminated? Explain.

E5–**5.** On November 5, Robert Gayton, who uses the net price procedure, purchased merchandise for $2,000; terms 2/10, n/30. The invoice was paid on December 1. (a) Record the purchase and the payment of the invoice. (b) Is the net cost of merchandise the same under both the gross and the net procedure? Show your computations. (c) Assume that Gayton takes advantage of all purchase discounts. Is there any advantage in his using the gross price method of recording the purchase of merchandise?

E5–**6.** John MacPhee, who uses the net price procedure, sold merchandise on June 1 for $3,000; terms 1/10, n/30. The customer paid the invoice on June 20. (a) Record the sale and the collection of the account receivable. (b) Would net sales revenue be the same under both the gross and the net procedure? Show your computations. (c) Compare and contrast the significance to management of the Sales Discounts Not Taken account and the Sales Discount account.

E5–**7.** The Arthur Marlin Company grants customer discounts on partial payments made within the discount period. On May 5, the Company sold merchandise to Paul Kandar for $800; terms 3/10, n/30. On May 15, the Company received $500 to apply on account; on June 4, a check was received for the balance of the invoice. (a) Record the transactions for the Arthur Marlin Company using (1) the net price procedure and (2) the gross price procedure. (b) Make the corresponding journal entries for Paul Kandar.

E5–**8.** The following information is taken from John Singleton's books as of December 31, 1969:

Trial Balance		Adjustment Data	
1. Prepaid Insurance	$1,200	Expired Insurance	$1,000
2. Rent Expense	4,800	Rent paid in advance	800
3. Wages Expense	8,700	Accrued wages	300
4. Interest Expense	150	Accrued interest	50
5. Unearned Rent	3,600	Rent earned	3,300
6. Interest Earned	1,200	Unearned interest	200

For each account: (a) prepare the adjusting entry; (b) state the amount to be shown in the income statement; (c) state the amount to be shown in the statement of financial position.

E5–**9.** The following items are taken from John Deal's trial balance on December 31. The books are closed annually on December 31. All the store equipment was acquired three years ago.

	Debit	Credit
Notes Receivable (90-day, 4% note, dated December 1)	$ 3,000	
Prepaid Insurance (one-year policy, dated May 1)	360	
Prepaid Rent (payable one year in advance on April 1)	4,800	
Store Equipment (10-year life; salvage value $500)	12,500	
Notes Payable (120-day, 6% note, dated November 1)		$2,000
Rent Earned (one-year lease commencing August 1)		2,400

Prepare the adjusting entries.

E5–**10.** Complete the partial worksheet given:

Account Title	Trial Balance			Income Statement		Position Statement	
	Dr.	Cr.		Dr.	Cr.	Dr.	Cr.
Cash	4,000					4,000	
Accounts Receivable	11,000					11,000	
Merchandise Inventory							
Beginning inventory	$ 9,000						
Ending inventory	12,000						

E5–**11.** The following information was taken from the financial statements of the Gill Company.

	December 31, 1968	December 31, 1969
Net income		$ 5,000
Stockholders' equity	$48,000	53,000
Total liabilities	42,000	40,000
Cost of goods sold		60,000
Total operating expenses		45,000
Merchandise inventory	16,000	14,000
Current assets	37,000	39,000
Sales revenue		114,000
Sales discounts		1,000
Sales returns and allowances		3,000
Current liabilities	19,000	13,000

   a. Compute the following ratios:
     1. The rate of return on the stockholders' equity
     2. The rate of return on the total equities
     3. The operating ratio
     4. The net operating margin ratio
     5. The turnover of merchandise inventory
     6. The working capital turnover
   b. What are the implications of each ratio?
   c. As a bank officer, would you approve a request by the Company for a two-year loan for $5,000?

E5–12. From the following information, prepare a partial income statement for the Hansen Company.

Net operating margin	$5,500
Gain from the sale of a truck	200
Interest paid on bank loan	100
Loss from theft (uninsured)	300
Payment for land taken under eminent domain	700
Rent earned from leasing facilities	400

E5–13. Record the following transactions:

   a. A check for $1,960 was issued in payment for equipment purchased 26 days ago; terms 2/30, n/60. The equipment was entered on the books at the invoice price.
   b. A $245 collection was received on account from T. Hobbs. The customer had incorrectly taken a 2-percent discount after the expiration of the discount period.
   c. A freight charge of $105 was paid on the equipment.

E5–14. The Ward Plastic Company closes its books annually on December 31. An examination of its insurance policies shows:

Policy No.	Unexpired Premium—January 1, 1969	Remaining Life—January 1, 1969
3954	$126	21 months
4872	98	14 months
670	48	6 months

The policies purchased during 1969 were:

Policy No.	Date of Policy	Life of Policy	Prepaid Premium
65412	March 1	2 years	$144
8941	August 1	3 years	180
4624	November 1	5 years	420

   a. What was the balance of the Prepaid Insurance account as of January 1, 1969? The Ward Plastic Company debits Prepaid Insurance for all purchases of insurance policies.
   b. What was the adjusting entry necessary on December 31, 1969?
   c. Reproduce the T accounts for Prepaid Insurance and Insurance Expense as they would appear in the general ledger after the closing entries have been posted on December 31, 1969.

    d. Assuming that no additional premiums are paid during 1970, what will be the adjusting entry on December 31, 1970?

E5–15. On January 1, 1967, the Fenmore Company entered into a ten-year lease for the rental of a factory from the Kane Investment Corporation. The terms of the lease provided for a rental adjustment whereby the Fenmore Company would pay the Kane Investment Corporation for any increase in real estate taxes in excess of a base assessment of $100,000 and a tax rate of $57 per $1,000 of assessed valuation.

    Make the adjusting entries for the Fenmore Company for 1967, 1968, and 1969, assuming the following:

Year	Assessment	Tax Rate Per $1,000
1967	$100,000	$60
1968	100,000	62
1969	105,000	63

E5–16. The statement of financial position of the Deacon Company at December 31, 1968, showed:

Accrued Interest Receivable	$2,650
Unearned Interest Revenue	380

During 1969, interest collected in cash amounted to $6,240. The statement of financial position at December 31, 1969, showed:

Accrued Interest Receivable	$2,960
Unearned Interest Revenue	250

    Compute the amount of interest earned that should appear on the income statement for 1969.

E5–17. The following information was taken from the records of the Milton Company at September 30, 1969, the end of the fiscal year:

    a. On April 1, $3,360 was collected as subscription revenue for one year; Unearned Subscription Revenue was credited.

    b. On March 1, 1969, a one-year, 5-percent note for $3,000 was received from a customer.

    c. The Company has a 4-percent mortgage note payable outstanding with a face value of $500,000. The interest on this note is payable semiannually on March 1 and September 1.

    d. The store supplies inventory on September 30, 1968, was $6,250. Acquisitions of $17,750 for the year were charged to Stores Supplies; a physical count on September 30, 1969, disclosed store supplies costing $8,500 on hand.

    Make the adjusting entries.

☐ **DEMONSTRATION PROBLEMS**

DP5–1. (*Cash discounts: gross and net price methods*) The following transactions were completed by the Hudson Company during November, 1969:

1969

Nov. 1   Sold merchandise on account to the Abel Company for $700; terms 2/10, n/30.

      5   Purchased merchandise from the Jones Company for $800; terms 1½/10, n/30.

1969

Nov. 6 Purchased merchandise on account from the Fox Corporation for $650; terms 1/10, n/30, F.O.B. shipping point.

6 Sold merchandise to the Hancock Corporation for $1,000; terms 1/10, n/30.

10 Paid freight charges of $20 on the merchandise purchased from the Fox Corporation.

11 Received payment from the Abel Company, less the cash discount.

12 Received a $50 credit (gross amount) for defective merchandise returned to the Fox Corporation.

15 Paid the Fox Corporation.

25 Paid the Jones Company. Received payment from the Hancock Corporation.

Required: 1a. Journalize the transactions, using the gross price method.

b. Prepare the cost of goods sold section of the income statement. Assume the following inventories: November 1, $500; November 30, $850.

2a. Journalize the transactions, using the net price method.

b. Prepare the cost of goods sold section of the income statement. Assume inventories as in 1(b).

3a. When invoices are recorded at the net amount, certain useful information becomes available to management. Explain.

b. Discuss the significance of cash discounts to (1) the buyer and (2) the seller.

DP5-2. (*Worksheet and financial statements*) The trial balance of the Savran Company for the year 1969 is shown:

SAVRAN COMPANY
Trial Balance
December 31, 1969

Account Title	Debit	Credit
Cash	$ 38,250	
Accounts Receivable	166,500	
Merchandise Inventory	50,000	
Office Supplies	21,000	
Prepaid Insurance	23,100	
Store Equipment	217,750	
Accumulated Depreciation–Store Equipment		$ 35,200
Accounts Payable		57,000
Notes Payable		31,500
Capital Stock		259,100
Retained Earnings		60,000
Dividends	20,000	
Sales		499,200
Sales Returns and Allowances	10,000	
Sales Discounts	9,200	
Purchases	295,000	
Transportation In	15,000	

Purchase Returns and Allowances		6,000
Purchase Discounts		9,000
Salesmen's Salaries Expense	38,400	
Transportation Out Expense	4,800	
Advertising Expense	14,400	
Rent Expense	19,200	
Heat and Light Expense	7,200	
Miscellaneous Expense	7,200	
Totals	$957,000	$957,000

Supplementary data on December 31, 1969, is given:

a. Merchandise inventory, $45,000.
b. Unexpired insurance, $13,500.
c. Office supplies on hand, $9,000.
d. Depreciation on store equipment, $4,800.
e. Estimated income taxes for the year, $24,000.

Required: 1. Complete the worksheet.
2. Prepare an income statement with a percent analysis.
3. Prepare a position statement with a percent analysis.
4. Prepare a statement of retained earnings.
5. Explain the significance of the percent analyses.

DP5-3. (*Financial statement analysis*) The statement of financial position of the Cavanagh Company as of December 31, 1969 is shown:

CAVANAGH COMPANY
Statement of Financial Position
December 31, 1969

Assets

Current Assets		
Cash	$20,000	
Marketable Securities	10,000	
Accounts Receivable	20,000	
Notes Receivable	6,000	
Merchandise Inventory	40,000	
Prepaid Insurance	4,000	
Total Current Assets		$100,000
Plant and Equipment		
Store Equipment	$65,000	
Deduct Accumulated Depreciation	15,000	
Total Plant and Equipment		50,000
Total Assets		$150,000

Liabilities and Owner's Equity

Current Liabilities		
Accounts Payable	$19,000	
Notes Payable	16,000	
Accrued Wages Payable	5,000	
Total Current Liabilities		$ 40,000
Long-Term Liabilities		
Mortgage Payable (due December 31, 1973)		70,000
T. Cavanagh, Capital		40,000
Total Liabilities and Owner's Equity		$150,000

Additional data is given:

T. Cavanagh, Capital, January 1, 1969	$ 30,000
Net sales	120,000
Net income	12,000
Cost of goods sold	60,000
Merchandise inventory, January 1, 1969	50,000
Total operating expenses	48,000

Required: 1. Compute the following (show all your computations): (a) Current ratio (b) Working capital turnover (c) Operating ratio (d) Acid-test ratio (e) Rate of return on the owner's equity (f) Turnover of merchandise inventory (g) Net operating margin ratio.

2. Explain the significance of the ratios to: (a) Cavanagh (b) The holder of the mortgage (c) The holder of the note payable

3. What additional data are needed for a more comprehensive analysis of Cavanagh's financial statements?

DP5–4. The following account balances were taken from the Income Statement columns of Robert Faler's worksheet for the year ended December 31, 1969.

Account Title	Income Statement	
	Debit	Credit
Merchandise Inventory	7,800	8,500
Sales		23,100
Sales Returns and Allowances	275	
Sales Discounts	450	
Purchases	7,115	
Transportation In	375	
Purchase Returns and Allowances		225
Purchases Discounts		640
Selling Expenses	1,700	
General Expenses	3,600	
Totals	21,315	32,465
Net Income	11,150	
	32,465	32,465

The Position Statement Debit column showed a balance in the R. Faler, Drawing account of $3,500.

Required: Prepare closing journal entries.

PROBLEMS

P5–1. The accountant of the John Baker Corporation prepared the following trial balance at December 31, 1969:

JOHN BAKER CORPORATION
Trial Balance
December 31, 1969

Account Title	Debit	Credit
Cash	$ 1,500	
Accounts Receivable	48,700	
Prepaid Insurance	2,500	
Merchandise Inventory	55,000	
Store Equipment	30,400	
Accumulated Depreciation–Store Equipment		$ 6,000
Accounts Payable		9,000
Notes Payable		20,000
Capital Stock		50,000
Retained Earnings		11,000
Dividends	10,400	
Sales		182,000
Purchases	85,000	
Advertising Expense	3,700	
Miscellaneous Selling Expense	4,000	
Wages Expense	29,000	
Miscellaneous General Expense	5,900	
Rent Expense	2,400	
Interest Expense	500	
Interest Earned		300
Rent Earned		700
Totals	$279,000	$279,000

Additional data are given:

1. Included in Advertising Expense is a charge of $750 for space in the January, 1970, issue of a monthly periodical.

2. The Prepaid Insurance account consists of premiums paid on the following policies:

Policy No.	Date of Policy	Life of Policy	Premium
A938	January 1, 1969	6 months	$ 400
J672	September 1, 1969	3 years	1,800
N531	October 1, 1969	1 year	300
Total			$2,500

3. The Store Equipment account consists of the following acquisitions:

Purchase Date	Cost	Useful Life	Salvage Value
Prior to January 1, 1969	$22,000	10 years	$2,000
June 1, 1969	1,400	10 years	200
July 1, 1969	1,000	5 years	100
September 1, 1969	6,000	15 years	600
Total	$30,400		

4. A physical count of store supplies shows $200 worth on hand at December 31, 1969. At the time of purchase, Miscellaneous General Expense was debited.
5. On October 1, the Baker Corporation rented some of its equipment to the Jones Company for eight months under the following terms: $175 per month payable in two payments of $700 each on October 1, 1969, and February 1, 1970.
6. Wages earned by employees but unpaid on December 31, 1969 totaled $480.
7. Property taxes of $300 for 1969 are unpaid.
8. An invoice of $300 from the Packing Materials Company, dated December 14, 1969, for shipping cartons is discovered and is to be recorded as a Miscellaneous Selling Expense.
9. Shipping cartons on hand at December 31 were worth $350.
10. The Notes Payable account consists of a 90-day, 6-percent note dated November 1, 1969, issued to a bank.
11. The merchandise inventory at December 31, 1969 was $40,000. Income taxes for the year were estimated at $11,500.

Required: In schedule form given, show:

 a. The adjusting entries
 b. The section of the position statement affected by the adjusting entry
 c. The section of the income statement affected by the adjusting entry
 d. The amount reported on the appropriate financial statement

Item 1 has been entered as an example.

Item	Explanation	Adjusting Entries		Financial Statement Classification	Amount Reported on Financial Statement
		Dr.	Cr.		
1	Prepaid Advertising Advertising Expense	750	750	Current Asset (PS) Selling Expense (IS)	750 2,950
2					
3					
4					
5					

P5-2. The trial balance of the Blade Corporation as of March 31, 1969, is shown:

BLADE CORPORATION
Trial Balance
March 31, 1969

Account Title	Debit	Credit
Cash	$ 7,500	
Accounts Receivable	14,300	
Notes Receivable	1,525	
Merchandise Inventory, January 1, 1969	21,200	
Prepaid Insurance	850	
Prepaid Rent	4,200	
Office Supplies	190	
Store Equipment	2,500	
Accumulated Depreciation–Store Equipment		$ 1,600
Delivery Equipment	4,500	
Accumulated Depreciation–Delivery Equipment		1,560
Accounts Payable		8,950
Notes Payable		4,200
Capital Stock		25,000
Retained Earnings		10,610
Dividends	2,600	
Sales		107,095
Sales Returns and Allowances	3,175	
Sales Discounts	1,295	
Purchases	77,050	
Purchase Returns and Allowances		2,290
Transportation In	1,635	
Advertising Expense	5,540	
Miscellaneous General Expense	635	
Salesmen's Salaries Expense	7,950	
General Selling Expense	4,660	
Totals	$161,305	$161,305

Additional information on March 31 is given:

a. Merchandise inventory	$20,500
b. Insurance expired during the three-month period	240
c. The Prepaid Rent represents a payment made for the first six months of 1969.	
d. Office supplies inventory	55
e. Depreciation of store equipment	60
f. Depreciation of delivery equipment	250
g. Estimated income taxes for the period	800

Required: 1. Prepare a worksheet for the three months ended March 31, 1969.

          2. After you complete the worksheet, but before preparing the formal financial statements, the bookkeeper of the Blade Corporation informs you that (a) $250 in cash received from a customer to apply on account was credited in error to Sales and (b) a $100 account sale made on March 31 was recorded as of April 1. What additional adjustments would you make? How will they affect the financial statements?

P5-**3.** The following information was taken from the general ledger of the Davis Corporation on December 31, 1969.

Account Title	Amount
Cash	$ 7,000
Marketable Securities	18,600
Accounts Receivable	41,000
Notes Receivable	7,000
Accrued Interest Receivable	–0–
Merchandise Inventory, January 1, 1969	50,000
Store Supplies	–0–
Advertising Supplies	–0–
Prepaid Insurance	2,500
Store Equipment	40,500
Accumulated Depreciation—Store Equipment	10,000
Accounts Payable	22,000
Notes Payable	23,000
Accrued Interest Payable	–0–
Accrued Wages Payable	–0–
Income Taxes Payable	–0–
Accrued Mortgage Interest Payable	–0–
Unearned Rent	–0–
Mortgage Payable (due 1973)	15,000
Capital Stock	50,000
Retained Earnings	15,000
Dividends	5,500
Sales	250,000
Purchases	141,500
Transportation In	2,500
Advertising Expense	4,900
Miscellaneous Selling Expense	7,500
Depreciation Expense–Store Equipment	–0–
Heat, Light, and Power Expense	5,000
Insurance Expense	–0–
Miscellaneous General Expense	8,800
Income Tax Expense	–0–
Rent Expense	4,800
Wages Expense	38,000
Interest Expense	1,500
Interest Earned	400
Rent Earned	1,200
Revenue and Expense Summary	–0–

Data for the end-of-period adjustments are as follows:

a. The Prepaid Insurance account consists of the following:

Policy Number	Date of Policy	Life of Policy	Premiums
A648	January 1, 1969	3 Years	$1,500
P832	October 1, 1969	2 Years	1,000

b. The Notes Receivable account consists of a 60-day, 6-percent note dated December 1, 1969, for $7,000.

c. The Notes Payable account consists of a 90-day, 6-percent note dated November 16, 1969.

d. Purchases of store equipment were as follows:

Purchase Date	Cost	Useful Life	Salvage Value
January 1, 1969	$22,000	10 years	$2,000
April 1, 1969	10,000	20 years	–0–
July 1, 1969	8,500	8 years	500

e. Wages earned by employees but unpaid as of December 31, 1969, totaled $500.

f. Income taxes for the year were estimated at $3,500.

g. On October 1, 1969, the Davis Corporation rented some store equipment to the O'Leary Company for 12 months and received a check for $1,200 representing the entire year's rental fee.

h. Interest on the mortgage payable is $800 per year, paid in semiannual installments on April 1 and October 1.

i. Inventories on December 31, 1969, were:

Merchandise	$34,000
Advertising supplies	900
Store supplies (the original debit was made to Miscellaneous General Expense)	200

Required: 1. Prepare a worksheet for the year ended December 31, 1969.

2. Prepare (a) an income statement, (b) a statement of financial position, and (c) a statement of retained earnings.

3. Prepare the closing entries.

P5-4. The following balances, arranged in alphabetical order, were taken from the Adjusted Trial Balance columns of the worksheet of the Black Corporation for the fiscal year ended June 30, 1969. The inventory on that date was $21,800.

Accounts Payable	$ 7,520
Accounts Receivable	10,500
Accumulated Depreciation–Delivery Equipment	3,500
Advertising Expense	1,100
Capital Stock	38,000
Cash	3,000
Delivery Equipment	10,500
Delivery Expense	2,200
Depreciation Expense–Delivery Equipment	1,650
Dividends	2,000
Gain on Disposal of Marketable Securities	350
Heat and Light Expense	890
Income Tax Expense	2,150
Income Taxes Payable	2,150
Insurance Expense	1,720
Interest Earned	250
Interest Expense	160
Loss on Disposal of Land	200
Marketable Securities	21,830
Merchandise Inventory, July 1, 1968	22,400
Notes Payable	2,000
Office Supplies	705

Prepaid Advertising	900
Prepaid Insurance	1,420
Purchases	59,700
Purchase Discounts	725
Purchase Returns and Allowances	1,230
Rent Earned	1,800
Rent Expense	2,500
Retained Earnings	10,000
Sales	91,500
Sales Discounts	1,600
Sales Returns and Allowances	4,300
Salesmen's Salaries Expense	6,300
Transportation In	1,300

Required: 1. Prepare an income statement for the year ended June 30, 1969.

2. Prepare a statement of financial position as of June 30, 1969.

3. Prepare a statement of retained earnings for the year ended June 30, 1969.

CASE PROBLEM
Wilde Furniture Company, Inc.

The firm of King and Reese, Certified Public Accountants, has employed you as a staff accountant. One of your first assignments is to assist in the audit of the records of the Wilde Furniture Company, a large furniture retailer. During the course of your work, you notice that the firm made a large single purchase of merchandise and display equipment during the past year. You are told by the Company bookkeeper that all the items were purchased at only a fraction of what they would have cost if they had been purchased in the usual way. Hillard Originals, Inc., a furniture manufacturer on the Coast, went bankrupt; the purchasing agent of the Company flew to the plant with an attorney, made an examination, and took the necessary steps to purchase the items wanted.

You determine that the following extra costs to this purchase were incurred:

Round-trip airplane fares for purchasing agent and attorney	$510
Reimbursement for rooms and meals	75
Telephone calls to confer with Company president	15
Fee paid to attorney, who is not a regular employee	300
Storage charges (after purchase but before shipment)	200
Shipping charges	800

The amount paid to the trustee of the bankrupt company for the merchandise and display equipment was $110,000. You ascertain that if these same items had been purchased through regular channels they would have cost about $200,000, with about 90 percent of this amount being for merchandise and the balance for the display equipment.

An examination of the journal entries recording the payment for all these items shows the following information:

Purchasing Expenses	(A)	1,900
Purchases	(B)	180,000
Display equipment	(C)	20,000
Cash	(D)	111,900
Retained Earnings	(E)	90,000

(A) $510 + $75 + $15 + $300 + $200 + $800 = $1,900
(B) 90% of $200,000 = $180,000
(C) 10% of $200,000 = $20,000
(D) $110,000 + $1,900 = $111,900
(E) $200,000 − $110,000 = $90,000

You ask the bookkeeper why the transaction was recorded as shown. He tells you that the president of the Company insisted that a profit of $90,000 had been made on the transaction, and that since they didn't know what the future held for the Company, it would be better to show some profit now. He also felt that if the merchandise and equipment are recorded for less than they are worth, the creditors, customers, and suppliers of the Company might conclude from looking at a statement of financial position that the Company was investing in cheap, inferior items. You tell the bookkeeper that accounting principles must be followed, but he believes that there is no need for principles; that each person should decide what is best for himself; and that, after all, 85 percent of the firm is owned by the president, Harold Wilde, and it is really only a large part of his personal life. He also thinks that accountants can solve the problem of income measurement just by seeing how much the cash balance changes during the year. If it increases, there is a profit; if it decreases, there is a loss.

Required: 1. Explain to the bookkeeper why there is a need for accounting principles.
2. Identify and briefly describe the principles that have been violated (a) by the journal entries recording the purchase of merchandise and equipment and (b) by the arguments of the president and the bookkeeper of the Company.
3. Present a brief counterargument for each statement with which you disagree, and present a brief supporting statement for each statement with which you agree.
4. What is the proper way to record the payment of $111,900?
5. Give the journal entries to correct the accounts.

Chapter Six

Special Journals and Automatic Data Processing Methods

As the frequency of similar transactions increases, some means of recording them, other than the two-column general journal illustrated in the preceding chapters, must be devised. The two-column journal is satisfactory for a small business and for teaching the fundamentals of the accounting process; but when this kind of journal is used, each entry must be posted individually to its general ledger accounts and, if subsidiary ledger accounts are involved, each entry must be posted twice. In essence, the data in the journal are repeated in detail in the ledger. A large business, with thousands of transactions occurring each day, must simplify and accelerate the processing of these data.

The particular accounting records and procedures should be designed to meet the needs of the individual business firm. For example, in a small firm that has a reasonable number of transactions but still few enough for one accountant to do all the work, several columns may be added to the general journal, one for each account that is used frequently, and the column totals can then be posted at the end of each month. If the number of transactions increases and the processing becomes physically impossible for one accountant to perform, it is necessary to group similar transactions into classes and use a *special journal* for recording each class. If the volume of transactions becomes enormous, it is perhaps necessary to use complex *accounting machines* in the processing of the accounting data.

In this chapter, the various ways of processing mass data are considered. First, the division of the general journal into special journals is described. Following the discussion of special journals, consideration is given to direct posting from business documents, the use of simple accounting machines, and a brief description of *automatic data processing*.

197

SPECIAL JOURNALS

When a business grows beyond a certain size, it may engage in several hundreds and possibly thousands of transactions every day. It becomes virtually impossible for one accountant to record all these transactions in one journal and post them to the general and subsidiary ledgers. With only one journal, it is extremely difficult to assign the recording and posting duties to more than one person. Rapid and efficient processing of the accounting data created by a large volume of transactions is helped by grouping like transactions into classes and by using a special journal to record each class. Thus, all sales of merchandise on account are recorded in a *sales journal,* all purchases of merchandise on account are recorded in a *purchases journal,* and so on. The number and kinds of journals used are influenced by the type of business and the information desired. The following chart gives the names, functions, and reference symbols of six special journals (like the general journal, referred to as books of original entry) in common use:

Journal	Kind of Transaction	Symbol
Sales journal	Sales of merchandise on account	S
Purchases journal	Purchases of merchandise on account	P
Cash receipts journal	Receipts of cash	CR
Cash disbursements journal	Payments of cash	CD
Sales returns and allowances journal	Credit granted to charge customers for returns or allowances	SR
Purchases returns and allowances journal	Credit received from vendors for returns or allowances	PR

The general journal is used for transactions requiring extensive explanations, transactions other than the six listed above, and adjusting and closing entries.

Special journals offer the following advantages:

1. Similar transactions are grouped in chronological order in one place. All credit sales of merchandise, for example, are entered in the sales journal.
2. The repeated writing of each account title—Sales, Purchases, Cash, and so on—is eliminated.
3. Postings are made from column footings in total only—rather than item by item—thereby reducing the volume of work. The general ledger is relieved of unnecessary detail since fewer postings are made. As a result of the fewer postings, the general ledger is more compact and easier to use, thus reducing the probability of error.
4. Bookkeeping duties may be divided up by function. For example, one person may enter information regarding charge sales, taken from *sales slips,* in the sales journal; a second person may post either from the sales journal or directly from the sales slips to the accounts receivable ledger; a third person may enter cash received from charge customers in the cash receipts journal and post to the accounts receivable ledger; and a fourth person may verify the accuracy of the work by comparing the accounts receivable

ledger with the Accounts Receivable controlling account in the general ledger. ˏ

Accounting Concept:
Essence of Internal Control ▶ This division of responsibilities not only facilitates and accelerates the work flow but also creates some protection against errors and the misappropriation of assets. ▶ An essential feature of *internal control*—the built-in safeguards for the protection of the assets of an enterprise—is the careful planning and supervision of the recordkeeping of a company and a division of the work so that no one employee has complete control both of an operation of the business and of the recording of that operation. ◀

The Sales Journal

All sales of merchandise on account are recorded in the sales journal. To illustrate the use of the sales journal, assume that the following transactions took place at the Hyde Park Company during June, 1969:

1969
June 1   Sold merchandise to J. C. Groton, $600; terms 2/10, n/30.

     14   Sold merchandise to F. T. Bedford, $400; terms 1/5, n/60.

     19   Sold merchandise to L. B. Concord, $300; terms 1/5, n/30.

     30   Sold merchandise to T. L. Ashby, $800; terms 2/10, n/30.

Figure 6-1.
Simple Sales Journal

SALES JOURNAL   Page 1

Date	Sales Slip No.	Account Debited	Terms	F	Amount
1969					
June 1	1	J. C. Groton	2/10, n/30		600
14	2	F. T. Bedford	1/5, n/60		400
19	3	L. B. Concord	1/5, n/30		300
30	4	T. L. Ashby	2/10, n/30		800
30		Accounts Receivable, Dr.—Sales, Cr.			2,100

When merchandise is sold on account, the transaction is recorded in the sales journal as follows:

1. The date of the transaction is entered in the Date column.
2. Sales slips or invoices are numbered in sequence; the numbers are entered in chronological order in the Sales Slip No. or Sales Invoice No. column.
3. The name of the customer to whom the sale was made is entered in the Account Debited column.
4. The terms of the sale are listed in the Terms column.
5. If the subsidiary ledger account has a folio, or reference number, it is entered in the folio (F) column when posting is complete; otherwise, a check mark is entered.
6. The amount of the sale is entered in the Amount column.

Each entry in the sales journal is a debit to the Accounts Receivable account and to the customer's account in the accounts receivable ledger and a credit to the Sales account. Expressed in the form of a two-column general journal entry, the entry for the sale made on June 1, for example, would be:

Accounts Receivable–J. C. Groton	600	
Sales		600

The transaction is not actually recorded in both the general journal and the sales journal. It is shown in this manner only to illustrate the difference between the two forms.

Each amount is posted separately as a debit to the accounts receivable ledger, supporting the single debit that is posted at the end of the month to the Accounts Receivable controlling account in the general ledger. Posting to the subsidiary ledger accounts is usually done daily. It is important to have the up-to-date balance of each customer's account readily available so that requests for this information from the customer, the credit department, or others may be readily fufilled.

The daily posting is usually done in the following sequence:

1. The amount of the sale is posted to the Debit column of the account and is added to the balance, if any, in the Balance column.
2. The journal symbol (S1) is written in the folio (F) column.
3. The date of the sale is recorded in the Date column.
4. A check mark is placed in the folio (F) column of the sales journal to indicate that the entry has been posted.

At the end of the month, the Amount column of the sales journal is footed. The total, the date of the transfer, and the sales journal page number are then posted to the debit side of the Accounts Receivable controlling account and the credit side of the Sales account in the general ledger. The general ledger account numbers are recorded in the sales journal immediately below the footing. To minimize errors, a systematic procedure should be followed in posting. The following sequence is suggested:

Debit posting:
1. The amount is posted to the Debit money column of the Accounts Receivable account in the general ledger.
2. The journal symbol (S1) is written in the folio (F) column of the account.
3. The date is recorded in the Date column.
4. The Accounts Receivable account number is written in parentheses below and to the left of the double rule in the Amount column of the journal.

Credit posting:
5. The amount is posted to the Credit money column of the Sales account in the general ledger.
6. The journal symbol (S1) is written in the folio (F) column of the account.
7. The date is recorded in the Date column.
8. The Sales account number is written in parentheses below the double rule in the Amount column of the journal, to the right of the debit posting reference number.

Postings from the sales journal of the Hyde Park Company for the month of June, 1969, are shown in Figure 6-2.

Figure 6-2.
Posting Flow from the Sales Journal

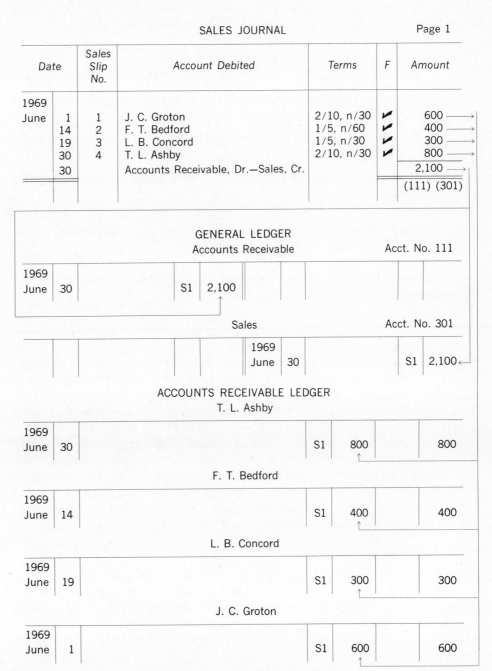

SALES JOURNAL   Page 1

Date	Sales Slip No.	Account Debited	Terms	F	Amount
1969 June	1	J. C. Groton	2/10, n/30	✔	600 →
14	2	F. T. Bedford	1/5, n/60	✔	400 →
19	3	L. B. Concord	1/5, n/30	✔	300 →
30	4	T. L. Ashby	2/10, n/30	✔	800 →
30		Accounts Receivable, Dr.—Sales, Cr.			2,100 →
					(111) (301)

GENERAL LEDGER
Accounts Receivable   Acct. No. 111

| 1969 June | 30 | | S1 | 2,100 | | | |

Sales   Acct. No. 301

| | | | 1969 June | 30 | | S1 | 2,100 ← |

ACCOUNTS RECEIVABLE LEDGER
T. L. Ashby

| 1969 June | 30 | | S1 | 800 | 800 |

F. T. Bedford

| 1969 June | 14 | | S1 | 400 | 400 |

L. B. Concord

| 1969 June | 19 | | S1 | 300 | 300 |

J. C. Groton

| 1969 June | 1 | | S1 | 600 | 600 |

The Purchases Journal

The relationship of the purchases journal and the accounts payable ledger is similar to that of the sales journal and the accounts receivable ledger. All purchases of merchandise on account are recorded in the purchases journal. The transactions of the Hyde Park Company during June, 1969, illustrate the use of this journal.

1969

June 3   Purchased merchandise from Pepperell, Inc., $900; terms 2/10, n/20.

      8   Purchased merchandise from The Weston Supply Company, $400; terms 2/10, n/60.

   16   Purchased merchandise from The Sherborn Trading Company, $500; terms 3/5, n/30.

   28   Purchased merchandise from The Hudson Company, $700; terms 1/20, n/60.

Figure 6-3 shows how these transactions are recorded in the purchases journal and posted to the general and subsidiary ledger accounts.

Expressed as a two-column general journal entry, the first entry in the purchases journal would be:

```
Purchases                              900
      Accounts Payable–Pepperell, Inc.         900
```

The transaction is not actually recorded in both the general journal and the purchases journal. It is shown in this manner to illustrate the difference between the two recording forms.

Each transaction is posted separately as a credit to the accounts payable ledger to support the credit posted at the end of the month to the Accounts Payable controlling account in the general ledger. Transactions are usually posted to the subsidiary ledger daily. The date of the entry in the subsidiary ledger account is the invoice date, which is significant in determining if a discount may be taken. At the end of the month, the Amount column of the purchases journal is footed. This total is posted to the Purchases account in the general ledger as a debit. The same total is posted to the Accounts Payable controlling account in the general ledger as a credit.

The Cash Receipts Journal

All transactions involving the receipt of cash are entered in the cash receipts journal. A simple multicolumn cash receipts journal form is illustrated in Figure 6-4. The column headings typically provide the necessary flexibility to record cash receipts from customers or any other source and to record sales discounts. The form may be varied, particularly in the number and headings of the columns, to meet the needs of the individual business.

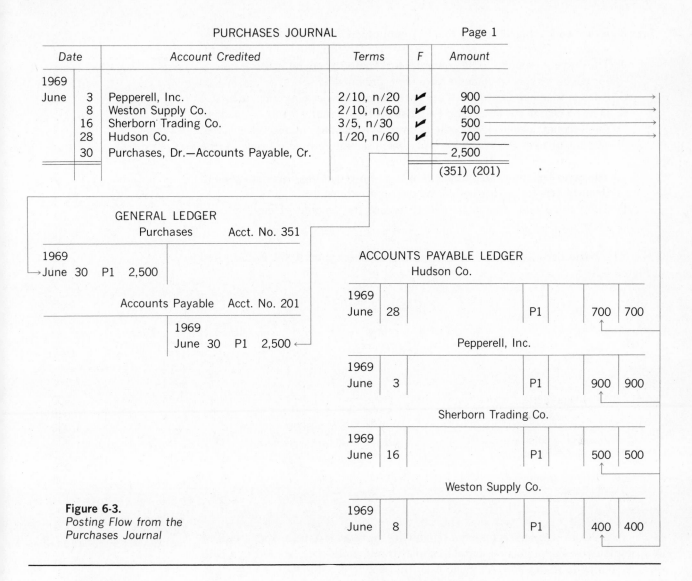

Figure 6-3.
*Posting Flow from the
Purchases Journal*

Figure 6-4.
*Column Headings of
the Cash Receipts
Journal*

CASH RECEIPTS JOURNAL

Date	Account Credited	F	Other Accounts Cr.	Sales Cr.	Accounts Receivable Cr.	Sales Discounts Dr.	Cash Dr.

Explanations of the various columns are:
1. The date of the transaction is entered in the Date column.
2. The name of the general or subsidiary ledger account to be credited is written in the Account Credited column.

3. A posting symbol indicating that the amount has been posted to the general ledger or the accounts receivable ledger is placed in the folio (F) column.
4. The Other Accounts Credit column is for credits to general ledger accounts for which no special columns have been provided.
5. Sales of merchandise for cash are entered in the Sales Credit column.
6. When a charge customer makes a payment on account, an entry is made in the Accounts Receivable Credit column. The amount entered is the actual amount of cash received plus any sales discounts properly taken by the customer.
7. The Sales Discounts Debit column is used for recording discounts granted to customers for paying within the discount period.
8. The Cash Debit column is used to record the amount of cash actually received.

The Hyde Park Company's cash receipts journal for June, 1969, is illustrated in Figure 6-5.

CASH RECEIPTS JOURNAL   Page 1

Date		Account Credited	F	Other Accounts Cr.	Sales Cr.	Accounts Receivable Cr.	Sales Discounts Dr.	Cash Dr.
1969								
June	1	Allen Young, Capital		2,500				2,500
	10	J. C. Groton				600	12	588
	15	Sales			1,000			1,000
	18	F. T. Bedford				400	4	396
	22	Notes Payable		600				600
	30	Sales			950			950
	30	L. B. Concord				100		100
	30	Totals		3,100	1,950	1,100	16	6,134

Figure 6-5.
Simple Cash Receipts Journal

In previous chapters, transactions involving the receipt of cash were recorded in a simple two-column general journal. Similar transactions are recorded in a cash receipts journal in Figure 6-5. Although each transaction is entered on a single line, the equality of debits and credits is still maintained through the use of multiple columns. The equivalent general journal entry is given to show the effect of the transaction; however, these transactions are not actually recorded in both the cash receipts journal and the general journal.

1969
June 1 Allen Young, the owner, invested $2,500 in the Hyde Park Company.

    Cash   2,500
        Allen Young, Capital   2,500

Cash is debited by entering the amount in the Cash Debit column. Since there is no special column for Allen Young, Capital, the amount is entered in the Other Accounts Credit column.

10   Received full payment from J. C. Groton.

Cash	588	
Sales Discounts	12	
Accounts Receivable		600

The sales journal shows that, on June 1, merchandise with an invoice price of $600 was sold to J. C. Groton; terms 2/10, n/30. Since payment was made within 10 days, Groton deducted $12 from the invoice price and paid $588. Entering the three amounts in the special columns as shown has the same effect on the general ledger as the explanatory general journal entry does. The customer's name is entered in the Account Credited column for posting to the accounts receivable ledger. If cash receipts from charge customers are numerous, a daily total may be entered from an adding machine tape; posting to the subsidiary ledger is done from supporting documents.

15   Cash sales for the first half of the month were $1,000.

Cash	1,000	
Sales		1,000

The word *Sales* is written in the Account Credited column to fill the space. However, it could be omitted since both the debit and the credit amount are entered in special columns.

18   Received full payment from F. T. Bedford.

Cash	396	
Sales Discounts	4	
Accounts Receivable		400

The sales journal shows that, on June 14, merchandise with an invoice price of $400 was sold to F. T. Bedford; terms 1/5, n/60. Since payment was made within five days, Bedford deducted $4 from the invoice amount and paid $396.

22   Borrowed $600 from the bank on a note payable.

Cash	600	
Notes Payable		600

Since there is no special column for the Notes Payable account, the amount is entered in the Other Accounts Credit column and the name of the account is written in the Account Credited column.

30   Cash sales for the last half of the month were $950.

Cash	950	
Sales		950

30   Received $100 from L. B. Concord on account.

Cash	100	
Accounts Receivable		100

The sales journal shows that, on June 19, merchandise with an invoice price of $300 was sold to L. B. Concord; terms 1/5, n/30. The Sales Discounts account is not involved in this partial payment because the discount period has expired.

At the end of the month, the columns in the cash receipts journal are footed. Since each line contains equal debits and credits, it follows that the total of the Debit column footings should equal the total of the Credit column footings. This equality should be proved for each special journal before the column totals are posted to the general ledger; otherwise, errors in the special journals may not be detected, the postings to the ledger will not be equal, the ledger will not have equal balances, and the trial balance will not balance. Moreover, the controlling accounts may not agree with their corresponding subsidiary ledgers. The cash receipts journal of the Hyde Park Company is proved as shown:

	Debits		Credits
Cash	$6,134	Accounts Receivable	$1,100
Sales Discounts	16	Sales	1,950
		Other Accounts	3,100
Total	$6,150	Total	$6,150

Postings from the cash receipts journal of the Hyde Park Company are shown in Figure 6-6.

Individual credit postings are made to the accounts receivable ledger to support the $1,100 credit posting to the Accounts Receivable controlling account in the general ledger. A check mark is entered in the folio (F) column of the cash receipts journal on the line of the entry to indicate that the item has been posted to the customer's account in the subsidiary ledger. Note that the balance of each account is either a debit or zero. Transactions have already been posted to these accounts from the sales journal.

The totals of the Cash Debit column ($6,134) and the Sales Discounts Debit column ($16) are posted to the respective general ledger accounts. The regular sequence for transferring an amount from a journal to a ledger is followed. The general ledger account number is entered in parentheses below the double rule in each column.

The Accounts Receivable account is credited for $1,100 and the Sales account is credited for $1,950. These postings are also dated June 30. A dash, or sometimes a check mark, is used in the folio (F) column on the line of the entry for a cash sale to indicate that the item does not require individual posting. The dash is preferred in a journal in which the check mark is used to indicate another function, as it is used in the cash receipts journal to indicate a posting to the subsidiary ledger.

The X below the double rule in the Other Accounts Credit column indicates that the column total is not to be posted to the general ledger. The total is not posted because the $2,500 credit to Allen Young, Capital, and the $600 credit to Notes Payable were posted separately during the month. The ledger page numbers of these

Date		Account Credited	F	Other Accounts Cr.	Sales Cr.	Accounts Receivable Cr.	Sales Discounts Dr.	Cash Dr.
1969								
June	1	Allen Young, Capital	251	2,500 →				2,500
	10	J. C. Groton	✔			600 →	12	588
	15	Sales	—		1,000			1,000
	18	F. T. Bedford	✔			400 →	4	396
	22	Notes Payable	205	600 →				600
	30	Sales	—		950			950
	30	L. B. Concord	✔			100 →		100
	30	Totals		3,100	1,950	1,100	16	6,134
				(X)	(301)	(111)	(311)	(101)

GENERAL LEDGER

Cash   Acct. No. 101

1969				
June	30	CR1	6,134	

Accounts Receivable   Acct. No. 111

1969					1969			
June	30	S1	2,100		June	30	CR1	1,100 ←

Notes Payable   Acct. No. 205

				1969			
				June	22	CR1	600 ←

Allen Young, Capital   Acct. No. 251

				1969			
				June	1	CR1	2,500 ←

Sales   Acct. No. 301

				1969			
				June	30	S1	2,100
					30	CR1	1,950 ←

Sales Discounts   Acct. No. 311

1969				
June	30	CR1	16	

ACCOUNTS RECEIVABLE LEDGER

F. T. Bedford

1969					
June	14	S1	400		400
	18	CR1		400	–0–

L. B. Concord

1969					
June	19	S1	300		300
	30	CR1		100	200

J. C. Groton

1969					
June	1	S1	600		600
	10	CR1		600	–0–

Figure 6-6.
Posting Flow from the Cash Receipts Journal

accounts are entered in the folio (F) column of the journal when the posting is done. Note that account numbers 251 and 205 are written in the folio column of the cash receipts journal in Figure 6-6. Postings from the Other Accounts Credit column are dated as of the date of the entry.

The Cash Disbursements Journal

All transactions involving the payment of cash are entered in the cash disbursements journal. Most cash payments should be made by check. When payments in currency are required they may be recorded in a *petty cash journal,* discussed in a later chapter.

A typical cash disbursements journal is illustrated. The columns provide for recording cash payments, either to creditors or for any other purpose, and for recording purchases discounts.

CASH DISBURSEMENTS JOURNAL   Page 1

Date	Check No.	Account Debited	F	Other Accounts Dr.	Accounts Payable Dr.	Purchases Discounts Cr.	Cash Cr.

Explanations of the various columns are:
1. The date of the disbursement of cash is entered in the Date column.
2. Detailed information is initially recorded on the check stub, which bears the same number as the check. Entries in the cash disbursements journal then are made from the check stub and the check number is listed in the Check No. column.
3. The name of the general ledger or subsidiary ledger account to be debited is written in the Account Debited column.
4. A posting symbol indicating that the amount has been posted to the general ledger or the accounts payable ledger is placed in the folio (F) column.
5. The Other Accounts Debit column is for debits to general ledger accounts for which no special columns have been provided.
6. When a creditor is paid in full or on account, the amount is entered in the Accounts Payable Debit column. The amount entered is the actual amount of the check plus any purchases discounts taken.
7. The Purchases Discounts Credit column is used for recording discounts taken on invoices paid within the discount period.
8. The Cash Credit column is used to record the amount of the check issued.

The cash disbursements journal of the Hyde Park Company is illustrated in Figure 6-7.

Although each transaction is entered on a single line, the equality of debits and credits is maintained through the use of multiple columns. The equivalent general journal entry is given to show the effect of the transaction; however, these transactions are not actually recorded in both the cash receipts journal and the general journal.

CASH DISBURSEMENTS JOURNAL   Page 1

Date		Check No.	Account Debited	F	Other Accounts Dr.	Accounts Payable Dr.	Purchases Discounts Cr.	Cash Cr.
1969								
June	1	1	Rent Expense		150			150
	11	2	Pepperell, Inc.			900	18	882
	13	3	Weston Supply Co.			400	8	392
	15	4	Purchases		200			200
	30	5	Sherborn Trading Co.			300		300
	30	6	Allen Young, Drawing		400			400
	30	7	Miscellaneous General Expense		100			100
	30		Totals		850	1,600	26	2,424

Figure 6-7.
*Simple Cash
Disbursements Journal*

TRANSACTION:
June 1   Issued Check 1 in the amount of $150 for the June rent.

JOURNAL ENTRY:

Rent Expense	150	
Cash		150

TRANSACTION:
June 11   Paid Pepperell, Inc., in full.

JOURNAL ENTRY:

Accounts Payable	900	
Purchases Discounts		18
Cash		882

The purchases journal shows that, on June 3, merchandise with an invoice price of $900 was purchased from Pepperell, Inc.; terms 2/10, n/20. Since payment was made within 10 days, a 2-percent discount, or $18, is taken, and a check for $882 is issued. Entering the three amounts in the special columns has the same effect on the general ledger as the explanatory general journal entry would. The creditor's name is entered in the Account Debited column for posting to the accounts payable ledger.

TRANSACTION:
June 13   Paid the Weston Supply Co. in full.

JOURNAL ENTRY:

Accounts Payable	400	
Purchases Discounts		8
Cash		392

The explanation for this entry is similar to that for the entry of June 11.

TRANSACTION:
June 15   Purchased merchandise and issued a check for the full amount of the invoice.

JOURNAL ENTRY:

Purchases	200	
Cash		200

Purchases of merchandise on account are entered in the purchases journal. A company may occasionally purchase merchandise for cash, probably from another company with which no credit relationship exists. These cash purchases are recorded directly in the cash disbursements journal. If cash purchases of merchandise occur frequently, a special Purchases Debit column may be provided in the cash disbursements journal.

TRANSACTION:

June 30   Paid the Sherborn Trading Co. $300 on account.

JOURNAL ENTRY:

Accounts Payable	300	
Cash		300

Reference to the purchases journal shows that, on June 16, merchandise with an invoice price of $500 was purchased from the Sherborn Trading Company; terms 3/5, n/30. Since the discount period has expired, no discount is taken.

TRANSACTION:

June 30   Allen Young, the owner, withdrew $400 for his personal use in anticipation of earned income.

JOURNAL ENTRY:

Allen Young, Drawing	400	
Cash		400

Since there is no special column for personal withdrawals, the cash withdrawal is entered in the Other Accounts Debit column. If such withdrawals are numerous, a special column with the heading Allen Young, Drawing Debit could be provided.

TRANSACTION:

June 30   Issued Check 7 in the amount of $100 for miscellaneous general expenses.

JOURNAL ENTRY:

Miscellaneous General Expense	100	
Cash		100

The expense account is debited for various items purchased and consumed during the month.

Before the end-of-the-month postings are made, the columns of the cash disbursements journal should be footed, and the equality of debits and credits proved as shown:

	Debits		Credits
Other Accounts	$ 850	Purchases Discounts	$ 26
Accounts Payable	1,600	Cash	2,424
Total	$2,450	Total	$2,450

The total debit and total credit postings from this journal to the general ledger are equal.

Posting from the cash disbursements journal of the Hyde Park Company is shown in Figure 6-8.

Date		Check No.	Account Debited	F	Other Accounts Dr.	Accounts Payable Dr.	Purchases Discounts Cr.	Cash Cr.
1969								
June	1	1	Rent Expense	703	150 ←			150
	11	2	Pepperell, Inc.	✔		900 ←	18	882
	13	3	Weston Supply Co.	✔		400 ←	8	392
	15	4	Purchases	351	200 ←			200
	30	5	Sherborn Trading Co.	✔		300 ←		300
	30	6	Allen Young, Drawing	252	400 ←			400
	30	7	Misc. General Expense	712	100 ←			100
	30		Totals		850	1,600	26	2,424
					(X)	(201)	(365)	(101)

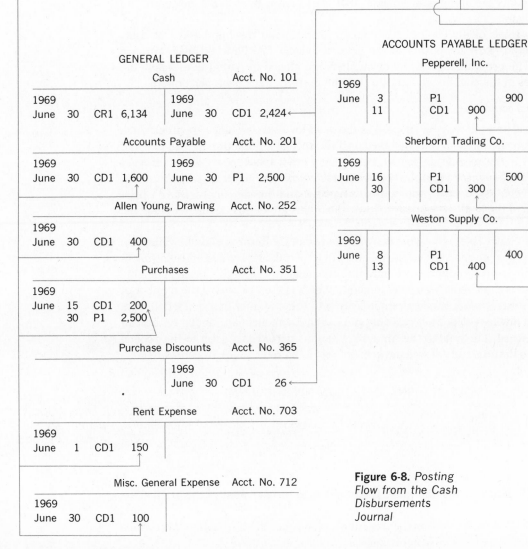

GENERAL LEDGER

Cash   Acct. No. 101

1969				1969			
June	30	CR1	6,134	June	30	CD1	2,424 ←

Accounts Payable   Acct. No. 201

1969				1969			
June	30	CD1	1,600	June	30	P1	2,500

Allen Young, Drawing   Acct. No. 252

1969			
June	30	CD1	400

Purchases   Acct. No. 351

1969			
June	15	CD1	200
	30	P1	2,500

Purchase Discounts   Acct. No. 365

				1969			
				June	30	CD1	26 ←

Rent Expense   Acct. No. 703

1969			
June	1	CD1	150

Misc. General Expense   Acct. No. 712

1969			
June	30	CD1	100

ACCOUNTS PAYABLE LEDGER

Pepperell, Inc.

1969						
June	3		P1		900	900
	11		CD1	900		-0-

Sherborn Trading Co.

1969						
June	16		P1		500	500
	30		CD1	300		200

Weston Supply Co.

1969						
June	8		P1		400	400
	13		CD1	400		-0-

Figure 6-8. *Posting Flow from the Cash Disbursements Journal*

The individual debit postings to the accounts payable ledger support the $1,600 debit posting to the Accounts Payable controlling account in the general ledger. A check mark in the folio (F) column of the cash disbursements journal indicates that the posting has been made to the supplier's account in the subsidiary ledger. Note that the balance of each account is either a credit or zero.

The Accounts Payable account is debited for $1,600 as of June 30.

The total of the Other Accounts Debit column is not posted because it is used to record debits to accounts for which no special columns have been provided; each amount must be posted separately. The numbers of these accounts—703, 351, 252, and 712—are entered in the folio (F) column. The X below the double rule in the Other Accounts Debit column indicates that the column total is not posted to the general ledger.

The totals of the Cash Credit column ($2,424) and the Purchases Discounts Credit column ($26) are posted to the general ledger. The basic posting steps are followed. The general ledger account numbers are placed in parentheses below the double rules in the columns to indicate that the postings have been performed.

Other Special Journals

Other special journals may be adopted as the need for them becomes apparent. Such a need is indicated if labor may be saved or if the special journal provides an element of flexibility in the accounting system. Examples of other special journals are the *sales returns and allowances journal,* the *purchases returns and allowances journal,* the *notes receivable register,* the *notes payable register,* and the *voucher register.* A brief explanation of the first two journals follows; the others are discussed in later chapters.

THE SALES RETURNS AND ALLOWANCES JOURNAL. Returns and allowances on merchandise sold on account may be recorded in a special sales returns and allowances journal. This journal, outlined in Figure 6-9, is similar to the sales journal. The only new column is the Credit Memo No. column, which is used to record the number of the *credit memorandum* issued as a notification to the customer of a deduction from the original invoice price. The recording and posting sequences are similar to those of the sales journal. The total of the Amount column is posted as a debit to the general ledger Sales Returns and Allowances account and as a credit to the Accounts Receivable account.

SALES RETURNS AND ALLOWANCES JOURNAL

Date	Credit Memo No.	Account Credited	F	Amount

Figure 6-9. Outline of Sales Returns and Allowances Journal

If the return or the allowance is granted after full payment of the original invoice, then:

1. If the adjustment is in the form of a cash refund, the transaction is recorded in the cash disbursements journal.

2. If the adjustment is to apply against a later sales to the customer, the transaction is recorded in the sales returns and allowances journal. The credit to the customer's account, in the absence of an off-setting debit, results in an account with a credit balance in the accounts receivable ledger. If the credit is not offset before the preparation of financial statements, the amount is classified in the statement of financial position as a current liability.

THE PURCHASES RETURNS AND ALLOWANCES JOURNAL. A separate journal may be maintained to record all purchases returns and allowances for which credit has been granted by the vendor. The form and the posting of the purchases returns and allowances journal, outlined in Figure 6-10, are similar to the purchases journal.

PURCHASES RETURNS AND ALLOWANCES JOURNAL

Figure 6-10.
Outline of Purchases Returns and Allowances Journal

Date	Account Debited	F	Amount

Postings to the individual subsidiary accounts are debits and are made daily. At the end of the month, the total of the Amount column is posted as a debit to Accounts Payable and a credit to Purchases Returns and Allowances.

Adapting Special Journals to Meet Special Needs

As a general principle, the accounting records and procedures of a firm should be designed to meet the particular needs of that firm. The special journals shown so far in this chapter emphasize the element of simplicity. In this section, two brief examples of ways in which the cash receipts journal and the cash disbursements journal may be adapted to meet specific needs are presented.

ADAPTING THE CASH RECEIPTS JOURNAL. If a cash receipts transaction requiring multiple debits and credits occurs, it may be cumbersome to record it in a cash receipts journal similar to the one illustrated in Figure 6-5. For example, suppose that on November 1, 1969, the Bell Corporation issues 5,000 shares of $100 par value capital stock to Anthony Shaw in exchange for land appraised at $20,000, a building appraised at $180,000, and $315,000 in cash; and that the Corporation assumes the liability for a mortgage payable of $15,000 that Shaw had issued on the land and building. If the simple cash receipts journal is used, the entry must be split—the receipt of the land and the building and the assumption of the mortgage payable are recorded in the general journal and the cash is recorded in the cash receipts journal. An entry split in this manner fails to tell the complete story of the transaction. One way to remedy this is to add to the cash receipts journal an Other Accounts section with Debit and Credit money columns. With this simple adaptation, the entry recording the issuance of the capital stock by the Bell Corporation would be made as shown in Figure 6-11.

CASH RECEIPTS JOURNAL
Page 11

Date		Description	Cash Dr.	Sales Discounts Dr.	Sales Cr.	Accounts Receivable Cr.		Other Accounts			
						✔	Amount	Account Title	F	Debit	Credit
1969											
Nov.	1	Issued 5,000 shares of capital stock at par value to Anthony Shaw.	315,000					Land		20,000	
								Building		180,000	
								Mortgages Payable			15,000
								Capital Stock			500,000

Note that a separate check mark column is set up for postings to the accounts receivable ledger. Otherwise, the posting rules and sequence for this cash receipts journal are identical to those for the simpler journal illustrated in Figure 6-5.

Figure 6-11.
Cash Receipts Journal with Other Accounts Debit and Credit Columns

ADAPTING THE CASH DISBURSEMENTS JOURNAL. The cash disbursements journal may also be expanded for transactions requiring multiple debits and credits. For example, if on November 2, 1969, the Bell Corporation purchases additional land costing $40,000, paying $10,000 in cash and giving a mortgage payable for the balance, the entire transaction could be recorded in a cash disbursements journal with Other Accounts Debit and Credit columns. This is shown in Figure 6-12.

CASH DISBURSEMENTS JOURNAL
Page 11

Date		Description	Accounts Payable Dr.		Purchases Discounts Cr.	Cash Cr.	Other Accounts			
			✔	Amount			Account Title	F	Debit	Credit
1969										
Nov.	2	Purchased land for cash and issued mortgage payable.				10,000	Land		40,000	
							Mortgages Payable			30,000

The posting rules and sequence for the expanded cash disbursements journal are the same as for the simpler journal shown in Figure 6-7.

Figure 6-12.
Cash Disbursements Journal with Other Accounts Debit and Credit Columns

Entries in the General Journal

Although special journals provide for recording frequently recurring transactions, a need for recording (1) unusual current transactions, (2) correcting entries, and (3) adjusting and closing entries remains. For these purposes, a simple two-column general journal is used in conjunction with the special journals.

UNUSUAL CURRENT TRANSACTIONS. All the transactions that cannot be entered in the special journals are recorded in the general journal. Sales returns and allowances and purchases returns and allowances, for example, are entered in the general journal if special journals for these transactions are not maintained. Other typical current transactions recorded in the general journal include (1) purchases on account of assets other than merchandise inventory, such as plant and equipment or supplies, and the incurrence of liabilities for services; (2) notes received from customers to apply toward accounts receivable; and (3) notes issued to creditors to apply toward accounts payable. The recording of a typical general journal entry is shown:

GENERAL JOURNAL   Page 35

1969					
July	7	Notes Receivable	115	350	
		Accounts Receivable–A. Small	111/✔		350
		To record receipt of 30-day note in full			
		settlement of account.			

The amount, $350, is posted to the general ledger as a debit to Notes Receivable and a credit to Accounts Receivable. The other posting is to the subsidiary ledger to support the corresponding credit to the Accounts Receivable controlling account. A dual credit posting is necessary because the simple two-column general journal—unlike the special journals—does not have classified columns allowing end-of-period posting of column totals.

Note that the detailed explanation of the transaction, which is omitted from special journals (the type of special journal and a reference to an invoice date or number generally suffice to explain a special journal entry), is retained in the general journal because of the unusual nature of the transactions recorded there.

CORRECTING ENTRIES. If it is discovered that an error has been made in the process of journalizing and posting, it may be corrected by a general journal entry. Erasures should be avoided because they may create doubt in the minds of persons who examine the records regarding the reason for the erasure. This becomes particularly important when the records are audited, and in cases of litigation when the records may be offered as evidence.

Assume that the following entry, recording the payment of an invoice for repairs to machinery, has been posted (actually recorded in the cash disbursements journal but for simplicity is shown here in general journal form):

1969
July 19   Machinery and Equipment   15
                    Cash   15

The debit should have been to an expense account; the error may be corrected by the following entry in the general journal:

GENERAL JOURNAL

1969					
July	26	Maintenance and Repairs Expense		15	
		Machinery and Equipment			15
		To correct entry of July 19 in			
		cash disbursements journal.			

If an error in a journal entry is discovered before it is posted, it may be corrected by drawing a line through the incorrect account or amount and entering the correction immediately above it.

ADJUSTING AND CLOSING ENTRIES. Adjusting and closing entries are always recorded in the general journal. These entries were discussed and illustrated in Chapter 4.

Forwarding Totals in the Special Journals

When the monthly transactions exceed the available space on a single journal sheet, it is necessary to carry forward the column totals. The column totals are entered on the last line of the completed page and brought forward to the top line of the next page, as shown in Figure 6-13.

CASH DISBURSEMENTS JOURNAL   Page 8

Date		Check No.	Account Debited	F	Other Accounts Dr.	Accounts Payable Dr.	Purchases Discounts Cr.	Cash Cr.
1969								
Aug.	2	56	Rent Expense		200			200
	4	57	Post Co.			400	8	392
	6	58	Allen's, Inc.			500	5	495
	24	84	Purchases		650			650
		85	West Co.			100	2	98
	24		Carried forward	✔	2,520	1,340	18	3,842

CASH DISBURSEMENTS JOURNAL   Page 9

Date		Check No.	Account Debited	F	Other Accounts Dr.	Accounts Payable Dr.	Purchases Discounts Cr.	Cash Cr.
1969								
Aug.	24		Brought forward	✔	2,520	1,340	18	3,842

Figure 6-13.
Totals Carried Forward

The equality of debits and credits should be proved before the column totals are brought forward. Forwarding column totals in the two-column general journal is not necessary because the entries are posted one by one. Some accountants, however, total the two columns on each page to prove their equality.

Direct Posting from Business Documents

In many business firms, data can be processed more efficiently and rapidly by posting from the original documents—sales invoices, sales slips, purchase invoices, and so on—directly to the subsidiary ledgers instead of first copying the information in special journals and then posting to the accounts. For example, if sales slips are serially numbered, a binder file of duplicate slips arranged in numerical order could take the place of a more formal sales journal. Amounts from the individual slips could be posted daily to the accounts receivable ledger; at the end of a designated period—a week or a month—the sales slips in the binder file are totaled and the following general journal entry is made:

GENERAL JOURNAL				Page 8
1969 Aug.	31	Accounts Receivable Sales To record charge sales for the month of August, 1969.	120,000	120,000

A similar procedure may be used to record purchases on account.

If the postings are made from sales slips to the accounts receivable ledger, and if for any reason a special sales journal is still desired, a streamlined journal can be constructed by simply eliminating the Account Debited, Terms, and folio (F) columns, as shown:

SALES JOURNAL

Date	Sales Slip No.	Amount

Accounting Concept:
Design of Accounting
System ▶

These changes in procedure and the increasing use of direct posting from original documents are discussed here to add emphasis to a statement made earlier in this chapter: ▶ Accounting records and procedures should be designed to meet the needs of the particular business firm. ◀

AUTOMATIC DATA PROCESSING

As businesses grow, handwritten record systems become too slow and cumbersome to meet management's need for prompt information. When this happens, *automatic data processing* (ADP) is usually installed. With ADP methods, information is recorded and processed by mechanical, electrical, or electronic means. In its broadest sense, the term embraces the use of any data-manipulating machine, including cash registers, rotary calculators, adding machines, comptometers, posting machines, desk calculators, punched-card equipment, and the various electronic data processing systems called *computers*.

The Flow of Information

Figure 6-14 shows in abbreviated form the flow of information for all data processing systems. The flow of information is the same in all these systems; the primary difference is in the methods used.

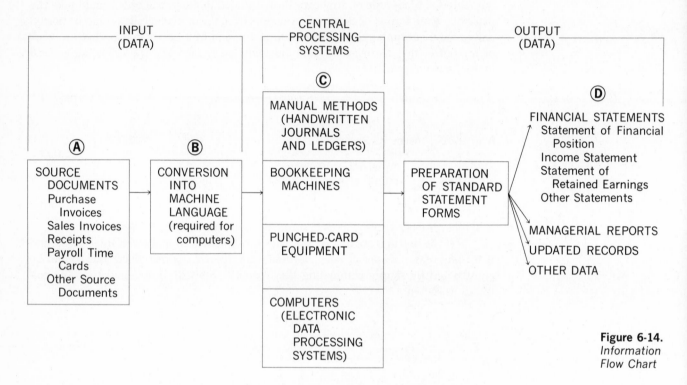

Figure 6-14.
*Information
Flow Chart*

Before data processing by any system can begin, some evidence that a transaction has occurred must exist. Source documents (Item A) such as purchase invoices, sales invoices and receipts indicate the occurrence of transactions. The data then must be introduced into the system; that is, they are *captured*. In a manual system, the data are captured immediately. For example, as indicated earlier in this chapter, information from a purchase invoice may be entered immediately into the purchases journal and posted to the accounts payable ledger. If a computer is used, the information must be converted into a form acceptable to the particular equipment (Item B). Item C includes the various central processing systems discussed in this text. Finally, the output data are prepared in the form of traditional statements and reports (Item D). The electronic data processing systems require that the information be reconverted for it to be usable.

Bookkeeping Machines

The simple *posting machine* and similar electromechanical equipment can perform the two basic operations involved in the distribution of business transaction information to appropriate accounts: (1) *listing*—that is, writing such information as cross-reference, date, and amount, and (2) *adding* or *subtracting* amounts. Depending upon the complexity of the machine—whether it has one or more *registers*, which allow it to accumulate amounts for further computation, and whether it has a built-in *program* (set of instructions for performing manipulations of data)—it may perform many additional tasks.

In a growing business, as the number of customers and charge transactions increases, the cost of hand posting to the accounts receivable ledger becomes excessive. It may be economical for such a company to buy or rent a simple posting machine that has a *horizontal register* (cross-footer) that can compute the difference between debits and credits on a single line. This type of machine can be used to post debits from sales slips or invoices and credits from receipts to each customer's account in the subsidiary ledger. The operator punches into the machine both debits and credits, if applicable, to the account. The machine records this information and prints out a new balance automatically.

The typical ledger account used in machine accounting is the balance-form card shown in Figure 6-15.

Figure 6-15.
Typical Machine Ledger Card

Date	Explanation	F or Code	Debit	Credit	Balance

A similar procedure is followed to post entries to the accounts payable ledger.

Many firms have ADP systems that permit posting by machine to all ledgers, including the general ledger. Economies can be achieved by machine accounting when the volume of similar accounting routines is large enough to enable the bookkeeper to gain speed through repetitive motions that can eventually become habitual. Accuracy and legibility of accounting records are attained by the use of electromechanical machines. These machines facilitate proofs of the accuracy of journalizing and posting. The more complex machines perform several stages of accounting—the preparation of source documents, journal entries, and ledger posting—in one operation.

Punched-Card Equipment

As a business engages in a larger number of transactions of similar nature, it may be economical to acquire punched-card equipment. This equipment rapidly, accurately, and automatically completes the three basic stages of distributing the details of accounting transactions to the appropriate accounts and reports: (1) recording information on a source document; (2) classifying the information according to the accounts affected; and (3) summarizing the resulting account balances. This kind of equipment is also useful for recording, classifying, and summarizing nonfinancial statistical data that help management to make decisions.

RECORDING TRANSACTIONS. Punched cards are used to record transaction information. The accounting and statistical information is recorded on the card by the means of punched holes. There are from 80 to 90 columns on each card in which information can be punched. One or more columns may be designated for recording each class of information. For example, in a sales analysis card, Column 1 may be used for a cross-reference code; Columns 2 through 6, the client number; Columns 7 through 12, the invoice number; Columns 13 through 18, the date; and so on. A single punch in a column indicates that a number has been recorded; two punches indicate a letter.

The punched card may be the original source document of a business transaction, or the information can be transferred to punched cards from sales invoices, purchase invoices, or receipts. Several punched cards may be used to record the information contained on a single original source document; for example, a separate card may be required for each debit to the accounts receivable ledger and another card for the total credit to Sales.

The *key-punch machine* used to punch the cards is operated by a keyboard similar to that of a typewriter. With more complex machinery, cards can be punched automatically from other cards or paper tape, or as a by-product of other machine operations.

CLASSIFYING INFORMATION. A *sorter* is used to classify the information contained on the punched cards according to the accounts affected. The machine senses the holes punched in the cards electrically and causes them to drop into appropriate slots. Since the machine can only sort for one vertical column of information at a time, it is necessary to run the cards through the sorter several times to accomplish a complete classification.

SUMMARIZING INFORMATION. A *tabulator,* by means of an electrically wired control panel, can list items, select items of a given type, add, and subtract. Thus, the information contained on the punched cards, now classified according to the accounts affected, can be summarized by running the cards through a tabulator.

All the typical accounting records and reports can be prepared by the tabulator. For example, many of the journals can be printed by passing all the punched cards for a given class of transactions through the tabulator, which lists the items and obtains totals. Posting to the accounts receivable ledger and the general ledger, and even the preparation of a trial balance and financial statements, can be accomplished by the use of punched cards and the tabulator.

One distinct advantage of punched cards is that the information contained in a single set of cards can be used to accumulate several different types of reports and records. In addition to the typical accounting records that can be prepared by successive runs of the punched cards through the sorting and tabulating equipment, other financial and statistical analyses can be prepared, such as an analysis of sales by product or by territory.

Electronic Data Processing

Electronic data processing (EDP) systems, which offer the greatest speed, volume, and reliability, consist of combinations of several pieces of electronic equipment centered around *digital computers.* These machines are designed to receive a large mass of input data, store them for future use, perform the four basic arithmetic operations on the data (addition, subtraction, multiplication, and division), make comparison-type decisions regarding the data, and almost instantly supply the information, or *output,* that results from these operations. Of course, EDP equipment is very expensive, and the businesses that use it must have a volume of transactions sufficiently large to justify the cost of the equipment and the specially trained personnel required for its operation.

In accounting, computers are used for repetitive types of volume operations, such as payroll preparation, accounts receivable and payable processing, and inventory control.

Many certified public accounting firms throughout the country are installing computer systems as a part of their management services departments. These systems perform a total accounting operation for the clients, including the billing of customers; the preparation of monthly, quarterly, and annual financial statements; and the preparation of a multitude of managerial analyses and reports.

Banks are beginning to use *on-line real-time* computer systems. An on-line real-time computer is designed to capture data immediately from an operational center, such as a teller's window. When a deposit is made, the teller punches the information into a machine that transmits it immediately to the main computer center for processing. In this kind of system, the delay in recording information and making it available is substantially reduced by combining data processing, decentralized input and output, and communications. In one bank, for example, all its operations are included in the system—savings and checking accounts, mortgages, Christmas club and school accounts, payroll, payroll savings, general ledger posting, cost accounting, and trust operations.

Another example of the trend in computer usage is that of a gas company that acquired a computer capable of adding 16,000 five-digit figures in a second for processing meter readings into completed bills and making up-to-the-minute statistics available to management. This computer also handles inventory accounting for 20,000 items—from gas jets to 36-inch pipeline—that the company uses, payroll accounting for about 4,000 employees, accounting for the appliances sold by the company, and the preparation of dividend checks and proxy notices.

The main advantage of electronic data processing is the computer's ability to compute at high rates of speed and to store details for later use. These abilities allow results of recent operations to be made available in time to help management make decisions. The information derived from a manual system is often received so late that it is of little or no use. With on-line real-time computers, reports can be prepared daily. Such timely reporting enables managers to keep their fingers on the pulse of the business at all times. Also, the lower cost of clerical analyses and reanalyses makes it possible to provide decision-making information for more levels of management. The computer assists in the maintenance of inventory, helps to facilitate control over costs and revenue, and speeds up the preparation of operating budgets and other forecasts.

Use of EDP systems does not eliminate all difficulties. Often there is a communication failure between managerial personnel engaged in the analysis of certain computer problems. If the specific problem or the various aspects of the problem are not correctly identified, the problem cannot be solved even with the aid of a computer.

Also, if the input to the system is uncontrolled—not audited in any way—the output may prove to be worthless. Computer centers established to process data from many clients must devise some means of auditing the input to assure a reliable output. The output of computers must be controlled in such a way that it permits an independent review and facilitates the internal control of assets. This may mean that the print-out of typical journals and ledgers is mandatory. Similarly, the use of traditional accounting records may help to implement the internal control of assets.

As businesses grow more complex, the accounting function will tend to utilize the computer installations more efficiently and work more closely with computer manufactures, assisting them in developing business orientated electronic equipment. This improved equipment will make possible the preparation of more meaningful information for management as well as for interested outsiders.

SUMMARY

With the growth of large businesses and the increased volume of business documents, more efficient and time-saving methods of processing business transactions have developed. Special journals are used to record like transactions that occur frequently, enabling a business to process data more rapidly and efficiently. Among the most frequently used are the sales journal, the purchases journal, the cash receipts journal, and the cash disbursements journal.

The sales journal is used to record all sales on account. The total of the Amount column in the sales journal is posted as a debit to the Accounts Receivable account and as a credit to the Sales account in the general ledger. The individual items are posted to the appropriate accounts in the accounts receivable ledger.

All purchases of merchandise on account are recorded in the purchases journal. The total of the Amount column in the purchases journal is posted as a debit to Purchases and as a credit to Accounts Payable. The individual items are posted to the appropriate accounts in the accounts payable ledger.

A cash receipts journal is used to record all transactions involving the receipt of cash. The totals of the Sales Discounts and Cash columns in this journal are debited to the appropriate general ledger accounts and the totals of the Sales and Accounts Receivable columns are credited to general ledger accounts. Items in the Other Accounts and Accounts Receivable columns are posted to the proper accounts in the general ledger or the accounts receivable ledger.

All transactions involving the payment of cash are entered in the cash disbursements journal. The total of the Accounts Payable column in the cash disbursements journal is debited to the Accounts Payable account in the general ledger, and the totals of the Purchases Discounts and Cash columns are credited to the proper accounts in the general ledger. The individual items in the Other Accounts and Accounts Payable columns are debited to the appropriate accounts in the general ledger or accounts payable ledger.

Other special journals, such as the sales returns and allowances journal, the purchases returns and allowances journal, the notes receivable register, the notes payable register, and the voucher register are frequently employed. They should be set up when the potential clerical labor saving and the addition of an element of flexibility to the accounting system indicate the need for a specific journal.

Even though the majority of the transactions of a business recur frequently and are recorded in special journals, a general journal remains necessary for recording (1) current transactions of a more unusual nature, (2) correcting entries, and (3) adjusting and closing entries.

An alternate method of processing data, which is more efficient and rapid for some firms, is the posting of transactions to subsidiary accounts directly from the original business documents.

Recently, increased attention has been given to automatic data processing (ADP), in which data are captured and manipulated by mechanical, electric, or electronic means to produce information useful for many purposes. ADP includes machines ranging from the simple posting machine to complex computers. The posting machine can list—write descriptive information such as cross-reference source, date, and amount—and add and subtract amounts. This type of equipment is easily adaptable to the maintenance of accounts receivable and accounts payable ledgers. More complex posting machines are capable of performing more difficult tasks; for example, the source document, journal entry, and ledger posting may be prepared simultaneously.

The functions of recording information on a source document, classifying the information according to the accounts affected, and summarizing the resulting account balances can be performed with the use of punched-card equipment. Another application of this type of equipment is the recording, classifying, and summarizing of nonfinancial statistical data that are beneficial to management in making decisions.

The most frequent application of computers is for repetitive volume operations such as payroll preparation and inventory accounting. Other less frequent uses are in the area of research problems of an engineering or scientific nature and advanced business data processing. The fundamental advantages of electronic data processing are (1) the computer's ability to compute at high rates of speed and to store details for later use, (2) the provision of decision-making information to more levels of managements because of the lower costs of clerical analysis and reanalysis, (3) fuller utilization of the management by exception principle, and (4) fuller utilization of the managerial tools of simulation and model-building. Potential causes of problems in the use of electronic data processing systems are communication failures between personnel engaged in the analysis of specific computer problems, lack of sufficient time for the conception, development, application, and testing of techniques, and the quality of the input—if the input is uncontrolled the output may be worthless, and the output of computers must be controlled in a way that permits an independent audit and facilitates internal control of assets.

☐ QUESTIONS

Q6-1. (a) What is the function of special journals? (b) What determines the types of special journals to be used? (c) Do the special journals entirely eliminate the need for a general journal? (d) How do special journals save time and labor? (e) Are there other advantages in using special journals?

Q6-2. Richard Walker makes approximately 400 charge sales each month to about 300 different customers. (a) What economies are effected by using a sales journal rather than a two-column general journal? (b) Would it be possible to keep the customers' accounts in the general ledger in order to eliminate the accounts receivable ledger? (c) If the customers' accounts were kept in the general ledger, what would be the effect on the trial balance? (d) What are the advantages of removing the customers' accounts from the general ledger?

Q6-3. The Mason Company does not use a sales journal. It makes out a sales slip for each charge sale and at the end of each month it makes a general journal entry for the total charge sales for that month. It made 500 sales totaling $3,500 during June. (a) What is the general journal entry made on June 30? (b) How may the information be recorded in the accounts receivable ledger? (c) Are there disadvantages to the Mason Company's system of recording sales?

Q6-4. (a) What two types of purchase are not entered in a purchases journal? (b) What types of purchases are recorded in a purchases journal? (c) Would the purchase of merchandise on account for the immediate use of the owner of the business be recorded in the purchases journal? (d) Is it possible to design a purchases journal to record all purchases? Explain.

Q6-5. (a) When are postings made from the purchases journal to (1) the general ledger and (2) the accounts payable ledger? (b) What is the relationship of the amounts posted? (c) How is it possible to trace postings from the journals to the ledgers? (d) What is the significance of the check mark in the folio (F) column of the purchases journal? (e) Would it be advisable to use code numbers as posting references for creditor's accounts rather than check marks?

Q6-6. The bookkeeper of the Kay Company complains to the accountant that the accounts receivable ledger, owing to the rapidly expanding number of customers, is bulky and unwieldy, that there are too many accounts in the subsidiary ledger to be controlled effectively by the Accounts Receivable controlling account, and that it is difficult to locate errors. Is there any way in which the accountant can improve the system?

Q6-7. The following questions relate to the simple cash receipts journal illustrated in this chapter: (a) What are the special columns? (b) What is the purpose of the Other Accounts Credit column? (c) Why is the journal cross-footed at the end of each month? (d) Explain the postings from this journal to (1) the general ledger and (2) the accounts receivable ledger.

Q6-8. The James Company uses sales, purchases, cash receipts, cash disbursements, and general journals. State the journal in which each of the following transactions should be recorded:

a. A sale of merchandise on account
b. A purchase of store supplies on account
c. A return of a cash sale
d. A purchase of delivery equipment on account
e. A payment to a creditor

 f. A sale of merchandise for cash

 g. Adjusting entries

 h. A purchase of merchandise on account

 i. A note receivable issued by a customer in full settlement of his account

 j. A return of a credit purchase

 k. A withdrawal of cash by owner for his own use

 l. Closing entries

 m. A payment of rent

 n. A purchase of merchandise for cash

 o. A note payable given to a creditor to apply on account

 p. A withdrawal of merchandise by the owner for his own use

Q6–9. The bookkeeper of the Hales Lumber Company made the following entry in the general journal:

1969

| Jan. 10 | Accounts Payable–Northern Mills, Inc. | 150 | |
| | Purchases Returns and Allowances | | 150 |

In posting this entry, he failed to debit the controlling account. How will this error be discovered?

Q6–10. To maintain a sound system of internal control, every business should adopt a book-keeping system which includes as a minimum requirement sales, purchases, cash receipts, cash disbursements, and general journals. Is this statement correct? Explain.

Q6–11. Since applications of automatic data processing equipment to accounting systems have increased in recent years, it has been charged that the increased usage of ADP will cause a decline in the demand for the services of accountants. Do you agree with this statement? Discuss.

☐ **EXERCISES**

E6–1. The Helyn Company made the following credit sales during March, 1969.

1969

Mar.	2	Sold merchandise on account to Frank Fail, $140.
	3	Sold merchandise on account to Nathan Nome, $100.
	4	Sold merchandise on account to Melvin Baker, $200.
	7	Sold merchandise on account to Sumner Carter, $350.
	7	Sold merchandise on account to Frank Fail, $160.
	12	Sold merchandise on account to Nathan Nome, $50.
	20	Sold merchandise on account to Melvin Baker, $70.
	31	Sold merchandise on account to Sumner Carter, $150.

 a. Record the transactions in a sales journal similar to the one illustrated in this chapter. The terms on credit sales are 1/10 EOM, n/30. Number the sales, starting with 101.

 b. Open the customers' accounts in the accounts receivable ledger.

 c. Open the following accounts in the general ledger: Accounts Receivable 111 and Sales 301.

 d. Post from the sales journal to the accounts receivable ledger and the general ledger.

E6–2. The Marley Barber Supply Company made the following credit purchases during December, 1969:

1969

Dec. 1   Purchased merchandise from the Hale Company on account, $400.

    2   Purchased merchandise from the Raymond Company on account, $160.

    5   Purchased merchandise from the Vatter Company on account, $325.

  13   Purchased merchandise from the Sanderson Supply Company on account, $400.

  17   Purchased merchandise from the Vatter Company on account, $210.

  19   Purchased merchandise from the Hale Company on account, $230.

  22   Purchased merchandise from the Raymond Company on account, $198.

  26   Purchased merchandise from the Hale Company on account, $175.

  30   Purchased merchandise from Sanderson Supply Company on account, $205.

a. Record the transactions in a purchases journal similar to the one illustrated in this chapter. The terms on all purchases of merchandise on account are 2/10, n/30.

b. Open the following accounts in the general ledger: Accounts Payable 201 and Purchases 351.

c. Open the creditors' accounts in the accounts payable ledger.

d. Post from the purchases journal to the accounts payable ledger and the general ledger.

E6–3. The Garter Company uses sales, purchases, cash receipts, cash disbursements, and general journals. On January 31, 1969, it had the following accounts in its general ledger after the books had been closed:

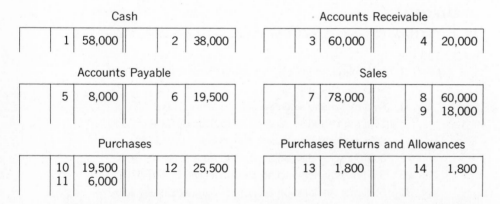

	Cash						Accounts Receivable				
	1	58,000			2	38,000		3	60,000		4	20,000

	Accounts Payable						Sales				
	5	8,000			6	19,500		7	78,000		8	60,000
											9	18,000

	Purchases						Purchases Returns and Allowances				
	10	19,500			12	25,500		13	1,800		14	1,800
	11	6,000										

On a sheet of paper opposite numbers 1 through 14 corresponding to the numbers that appear in the folio columns of the accounts, indicate the most probable journal source for each posting. Use the abbreviations J, S, P, CR, and CD to identify the journals, as shown in the following example:

Number	Journal Source
1	CR

E6–4. The Newton Company had the following two journals among its records as of May 31, 1969:

SALES JOURNAL   Page 1

Date	Sales Slip No.	Account Debited	Terms	F	Amount
1969 May 5	1	Henry Benrus	2/10, n/30		600
15	2	Robert Fungall	1/10, n/60		500
27	3	Edward Yaeger	n/30		800
		Total			1,900

CASH RECEIPTS JOURNAL   Page 1

Date	Account Credited	F	Other Accounts Cr.	Sales Cr.	Accounts Rec. Cr.	Sales Discounts Dr.	Cash Dr.
1969 May 1	Capital Stock		1,500				1,500
15	Henry Benrus				600	12	588
15	Sales			1,000			1,000
25	Robert Fungall				300	3	297
28	Notes Payable		1,000				1,000
29	Edward Yaeger				400		400
31	Sales			900			900
	Totals		2,500	1,900	1,300	15	5,685

Post from the journals to the proper ledger accounts and prepare a schedule of accounts receivable (provide account numbers).

E6–5. The Anderson Corporation received its charter on February 1, 1969. During the month of February, it completed the following cash receipt transactions:

1969

Feb. 1   Capital stock of $25,000 was issued at par for cash.

     8   Received a check for $98 from Norman Lang in settlement of a $100 sales invoice.

    15   Cash sales for February 1 through 15 were $1,200.

    17   Received $50 in cash from Robert Sampson (no discount).

    23   Borrowed $1,000 in cash from the State Street Bank and gave a note payable due March 24, 1969.

    25   Received a check for $194 from Richard Burroughs in settlement of a $200 sales invoice.

    28   Cash sales for February 16 through 28 were $1,500.

    28   Sold a parcel of land purchased on February 1 at its cost of $4,000.

a. Record the transactions in a cash receipts journal similar to the simple one illustrated in this chapter.

b. Open the following general ledger accounts:

> Cash 101
> Accounts Receivable 111
> Land 121
> Notes Payable 205
> Capital Stock 251
> Sales 301
> Sales Discounts 311

Post a debit of $600 to Accounts Receivable, dated February 28. This amount is from the sales journal.

c. Open the following accounts in the accounts receivable ledger and record the amounts given in the Debit and Balance columns (these are summary totals posted from the sales journal): Richard Burroughs, $300; Norman Lang, $200; Robert Sampson, $100.

d. Post from the cash receipts journal to the accounts receivable ledger and the general ledger.

e. Prepare a schedule of accounts receivable.

E6–**6.** The Reese Company had the following two journals among its records as of March 31, 1969:

PURCHASES JOURNAL   Page 1

Date		Account Credited	Terms	F	Amount
1969					
March	1	Robert Mather	2/10, n/30		700
	5	Peter Smithson	1/10, n/30		600
	7	Arthur Sesson	3/10, n/60		800
	20	Robert Mather	2/10, n/30		500
	25	Peter Smithson	1/10, n/30		300
		Total			2,900

CASH DISBURSEMENTS JOURNAL   Page 1

Date		Check No.	Account Debited	F	Other Accounts Dr.	Accounts Payable Dr.	Purchases Discounts Cr.	Cash Cr.
1969								
March	1	1	Rent Expense		400			400
	10	2	Robert Mather			700	14	686
	13	3	Purchases		800			800
	15	4	Peter Smithson			600	6	594
	16	5	Prepaid Insurance		150			150
	17	6	Arthur Sesson			800	24	776
	30	7	Robert Mather			200	4	196
			Totals		1,350	2,300	48	3,602

Post from the journals to the appropriate ledgers and prepare a schedule of accounts payable (provide account numbers).

E6–7. The Castle Company was organized on March 1, 1969. The following cash disbursements were made during the month:

1969

March   1   Purchased land and building for $30,000 in cash. Land is appraised at $5,000; building, $25,000.

      10   Paid the Matterhorn Company $490 in settlement of a purchase made on March 2; the invoice price was $500.

      15   Cash purchases for March 1 through 15 were $6,000.

      17   Paid the Nelson Company $1,000 on account (no discount).

      20   Purchased office equipment for $2,000 in cash.

      31   Paid the Peters Company $500 on account (no discount).

      31   Paid a 6%, 30-day note due this date. Face value of the note was $5,000; interest was $25.

      31   Cash purchases for March 16 through 31 were $10,000.

a. Record the transactions in a cash disbursements journal similar to the simple one illustrated in this chapter.

b. Open the following general ledger accounts:

> Cash 101
> Land 201
> Building 202
> Office Equipment 203
> Accounts Payable 301
> Notes Payable 302
> Purchases 401
> Purchases Discount 402
> Interest Expense 501

Enter the following account balances:

1. Debit balance in Cash, $100,000—posted from the cash receipts journal
2. Credit balance in Accounts Payable, $4,000—posted from the purchases journal
3. Credit balance in Notes Payable, $5,000—posted from the cash receipts journal

c. Open the following accounts in the accounts payable ledger and record the amounts given in the Credit and Balance columns (these are summary totals posted from the purchases journal); Matterhorn Company, $500; Nelson Company, $1,600; Peters Company, $1,900.

d. Post from the cash disbursements journal to the accounts payable ledger and the general ledger.

e. Prepare a schedule of accounts payable.

E6–8. The following transactions were among those of the Taussig Company during April, 1969:

1969

April 1   Issued an additional 800 shares of capital stock to John Ransom in exchange for the net assets of his single proprietorship:

Assets received:

Cash	$11,000
Accounts Receivable	19,000
Merchandise Inventory	10,000
Land	12,000
Building	38,000

Liabilities assumed:

| Mortgage Payable | 10,000 |

2 Sold marketable securities that had cost $10,000 for $12,000.

3 Purchased additional land for $50,000, paying $15,000 in cash and giving a mortgage payable for the balance.

4 Paid $960 in cash and issued $1,000 worth of capital stock in full settlement of a $2,000 account with the Allis Company. The remaining $40 represents an allowed cash discount.

Record the transactions in expanded cash receipts and cash disbursements journals as illustrated in this chapter.

E6–9. A bank uses an on-line real-time computer system. Information is punched into the system by tellers at their windows and by other bank officials in various departments. The central system processes the data directly, thus by-passing certain conventional recording steps. Identify the problems that may arise under such a system.

E6–10. A company has quadrupled in size over the past four years, but its return on investment has started to decline. A major problem is that financial statements and nonfinancial operating reports are presented to management too late for timely decisions; therefore, many unsound decisions were made during the preceding year. Would an EDP system help to alleviate this problem? Explain and identify the kinds of reports, other than the basic financial statements, that can be furnished to various levels of management through the use of an EDP system.

☐ DEMONSTRATION PROBLEMS

DP6–1. (*Special journals*) The Reardon Company has been in operation for five years, selling merchandise for cash only. Beginning in January, 1969, it plans to start making sales on account. The general ledger of the Company shows the following account balances on January 1, 1969:

101	Cash	$20,000
121	Accounts Receivable	–0–
131	Merchandise Inventory	30,000
141	Prepaid Insurance	–0–
201	Store Equipment	10,000
201A	Accumulated Depreciation–Store Equipment	4,000
301	Accounts Payable	–0–
401	Capital Stock	50,000
402	Retained Earnings	6,000
501	Sales	–0–
502	Sales Returns and Allowances	–0–
503	Sales Discounts	–0–
601	Purchases	–0–
602	Purchases Returns and Allowances	–0–
603	Purchases Discount	–0–
701	Salesmen's Salaries Expense	–0–

Transactions during the month of January were:

1969

Jan. 2 Sold merchandise to Aaron Johnson on account, $800; terms 2/10, n/30.

4 Sold merchandise to William Barker on account, $200; terms 2/10, n/30.

6 Sold merchandise to Walter Carson on account, $400; terms 2/10, n/30.

7 Sold merchandise to David Kirk on account, $900; terms 2/10, n/30.

8 Purchased merchandise from the Nelson Company on account, $1,000; terms 1/10, n/30.

9 Purchased merchandise from the Owen Company on account, $1,500; terms 1/10, n/30.

10 Purchased merchandise from the Parsons Company on account, $600; terms n/45.

11 Purchased merchandise from the Queens Company on account, $1,100; terms n/60.

12 Received a check from Aaron Johnson for the amount due from the sale of January 2.

13 Issued additional capital stock for $5,000 in cash.

15 Cash sales of $4,000 were made.

16 Received a check from William Barker for $50; Barker indicated that he would pay the balance by February 10.

17 Received a check for $196 from Walter Carson in partial settlement of his account—invoice price $200 less discount of $4. Since the check was mailed before the expiration of the discount period, it was allowed.

18 Cash sales of $2,000 were made.

18 Paid $240 for a comprehensive insurance policy for two years, dating from January 1, 1969.

18 Paid the amount due the Nelson Company for the purchase made on January 8.

19 Paid $990 in partial settlement of the amount due the Owen Company: invoice price of $1,000 less discount of $10.

20 Paid salesmen's salaries of $300.

20 Cash purchases for the month totaled $3,000.

28 Issued a 6%, 90-day note to the Owen Company in settlement of account.

30 Returned merchandise to the Parsons Company and received credit, $100.

31 Credited David Kirk for $75 for merchandise returned.

Required: 1. Set up general and subsidiary ledgers.

2. Journalize all the charge sales in a sales journal and post them to the accounts receivable ledger. Summarize the sales journal and make the January 31 postings to the general ledger.

3. Journalize all the charge purchases in a purchases journal and post them to the accounts payable ledger. Summarize the purchases journal and make January 31 postings to the general ledger.

4. Journalize all the cash receipts in a cash receipts journal and post them to the accounts receivable ledger. Summarize and cross-foot the journal and make January 31 postings to the general ledger.

5. Journalize all the cash disbursements in a cash disbursements journal and post them to the accounts payable ledger. Summarize and cross-foot the journal and make January 31 postings to the general ledger.

6. Journalize any other transactions in a two-column general journal.

7. Prove the balances of the Accounts Receivable and Accounts Payable accounts by preparing a schedule of accounts receivable and a schedule of accounts payable.

DP6–2. (*Expanded cash receipts and cash disbursement journals*) The following cash receipts and disbursements requiring multiple debits and/or credits took place at the Vance Corporation during May, 1969:

1969

May 1 Issued an additional 1,000 shares of capital stock to Ronald Frazer for the net assets of his single proprietorship:

Assets received:	
Cash	$50,500
Accounts Receivable	9,500
Merchandise Inventory	25,000
Land	20,000
Liability assumed:	
Mortgage Payable	5,000

2 Purchased office equipment for $4,000 and office supplies for $600; paid $3,200 in cash and issued a 6%, 90-day note for the balance.

3 Sold part of the land acquired on May 1 at a cost of $5,000 for $7,000. (Credit Gain on Sale of Land, $2,000.)

4 Paid $2,000 in cash and issued stock with a par value of $8,000 to Nelson, Inc., in settlement of a $10,000 account.

Required: Record the transactions in expanded cash receipts and cash disbursements journals as illustrated in this chapter.

☐ **PROBLEMS**

P6–1. The Fashion Shop made the following charge sales and purchases during January, 1969:

1969

Jan. 2 Sold merchandise to Adam Baker on account, $150.

3 Purchased merchandise from the Windsor Company on account, $500.

4 Sold merchandise to Brian Carter on account, $280.

5 Sold merchandise to Cass Dawson on account, $420.

8 Purchased merchandise from Olivia Peters on account, $725.

9 Purchased merchandise from Raymond, Inc., on account, $860.

10   Sold merchandise to David Easton on account, $610.

14   Purchased merchandise from the Thomas Company on account, $980.

18   Purchased merchandise from Uriah Stores on account, $1,000.

20   Sold merchandise to E. E. Fieldson on account, $740.

25   Purchased merchandise from the Washington Company on account, $985.

31   Sold merchandise to F. E. Gloss on account, $192.

Required: 1. Record the transactions in a sales journal and a purchases journal;
number the sales, starting with 1.

2. Post from the journals to proper ledgers. Assign appropriate numbers to ledger accounts.

The terms of all sales are 2/10 EOM, n/45; the terms of all purchases are 2/10, n/30.

P6-2. During June, 1969 the Builders' Hardware Supply Company completed the transactions listed below.

1969

June 1   Sold merchandise on account to Donald Baty, $2,300.

3   Sold merchandise on account to Robert Ludlow, $920.

7   Issued additional capital stock, $3,000.

10   Sold merchandise on account to Richard Mason, $560.

12   Sold merchandise on account to Donald Baty, $710.

13   Received a check from Robert Ludlow for the amount due.

15   Cash sales to date, $4,650.

18   Sold merchandise on account to Joseph Bateman, $380.

20   Borrowed $600 in cash from First State Bank and gave a 6%, 30-day note
for that amount.

23   Received a $200 check from Richard Mason to apply on account.

24   Received a check from Joseph Bateman for the amount due.

26   Sold merchandise on account to Robert Briant, $520.

27   Received a check from Donald Baty for the amount due.

28   Sold merchandise on account to Richard Mason, $200.

29   Received a check from Robert Briant for the amount due.

30   Cash sales from June 16 through 30 were $4,060.

30   Received $200 in rent on land for June.

Required: 1. Record the transactions in a sales journal and a cash receipts
journal similar to the ones illustrated in this chapter. Terms of
2/10, n/30 apply to all sales on account. Number the sales,
starting with 51.

2. Open the following accounts in the general ledger:

Cash 101	Sales 301
Accounts Receivable 111	Sales Discounts 311
Notes Payable 205	Rent Earned 803
Capital Stock 251	

3. Open the customers' accounts in the accounts receivable
ledger.

4. Post from the two journals to the accounts receivable ledger and general ledger.
5. Prepare a schedule of accounts receivable.

P6–**3.** The completed sales journal and cash receipts journal of the Cliff House, Inc., for October, 1969, are given:

SALES JOURNAL   Page 20

Date	Sales Slip No.	Account Debited	F	Amount
1969				
Oct. 1	71	Irving Camp		3,000
8	72	Henry Doucher & Son		1,500
16	73	B. Henderson, Inc.		1,600
20	74	Irving Camp		4,000
30	75	Pillcher's, Inc.		3,200
				13,300

CASH RECEIPTS JOURNAL   Page 23

Date	Account Credited	F	Other Accounts Cr.	Sales Cr.	Accounts Receivable Cr.	Sales Discount Dr.	Cash Dr.
1969							
Oct. 4	Capital Stock		6,000				6,000
9	Irving Camp				3,000	60	2,940
15	Sales			6,600			6,600
19	Henry Doucher & Son				1,000		1,000
25	B. Henderson, Inc.				1,600	80	1,520
27	Notes Payable		4,000				4,000
31	Sales			7,000			7,000
			10,000	13,600	5,600	140	29,060

Required: 1. Post from the two journals to the accounts receivable ledger and general ledger.
2. Prepare a schedule of accounts receivable (provide account numbers).

P6–**4.** The Sparrow Plumbing Supply Company completed the following transactions during July, 1969.

1969

July 1 Purchased merchandise from the Chase Supply House on account, $2,520; terms 2/10, n/30.

3 Paid $600 in cash for a five-year insurance policy.

4 Received credit for $60 for merchandise returned to the Chase Supply House.

5 Paid $475 in cash for merchandise.

8   Paid the Chase Supply House the amount due.

10 Purchased merchandise from the Jud Plumbing Store on account, $910; terms 1/10, n/30.

12 Purchased merchandise from Sally's Inc., on account, $620; terms 2/10, n/30.

14 Received credit for $75 for merchandise returned to the Jud Plumbing Store.

15 Paid $210 for freight charges to date.

16 Purchased merchandise from Fieldson Pipe Supply on account, $250; terms 1/10, n/30.

17 Received credit for $60 for merchandise returned to Sally's, Inc.

18 Paid the Jud Plumbing Store the amount due.

20 Paid $80 for advertising.

21 The owner, L. L. Sparrow, withdrew $400 for his personal use.

22 Purchased merchandise from the Chase Supply House on account, $925; terms 2/10, n/30.

24 Paid $200 to Sally's Inc., on account.

28 Paid $125 for telephone and telegraph invoices for the month.

30 Paid $90 additional freight charges on merchandise purchased.

30 Paid monthly office salaries of $400.

30 Paid $150 to Fieldson Pipe Supply on account.

Required: 1. Record the transactions in a cash disbursements journal, a purchases journal, and a two-column general journal.

2. Open the following accounts in the general ledger:

Cash 101
Prepaid Insurance 141
Accounts Payable 201
L. L. Sparrow, Drawing 252
Purchases 351
Transportation In 355
Purchases Returns and Allowances 361
Purchases Discounts 365
Advertising Expense 618
Telephone and Telegraph Expense 709
Office Salaries Expense 716

3. Open creditors' accounts in the accounts payable ledger.

4. Post from the journals to the appropriate ledgers.

5. Prepare a schedule of accounts payable.

P6-5. The general ledger of Pinta Company shows the following account balances on November 1, 1969:

101	Cash	$16,000
111	Accounts Receivable	2,200
115	Notes Receivable	225
125	Merchandise Inventory	32,000
141	Prepaid Insurance	-0-
162	Delivery Equipment	8,000

162A	Accumulated Deprecia-tion–Delivery Equipment	$ 800	
164	Store Equipment	14,000	
164A	Accumulated Deprecia-tion–Store Equip-ment	2,000	
201	Accounts Payable	1,800	
251	Capital Stock	60,000	
252	Retained Earnings	7,825	
301	Sales	–0–	
305	Sales Returns and Allowances	–0–	
311	Sales Discounts	–0–	
351	Purchases	–0–	
361	Purchases Returns and Allowances	–0–	
365	Purchases Discounts	–0–	
703	Rent Expense	–0–	
705	Heat and Light Expense	–0–	
714	Wages Expense	–0–	

The following information was taken from the subsidiary ledgers on October 31, 1969:

Accounts Receivable

Customer	Date of Sale	Terms	Amount
Applebee Company	October 24	2/10, n/30	$ 600
Hillory Company			–0–
Munsin Company	October 27	2/10, n/30	875
Zurback Company	October 31	2/10, n/30	725
Total			$2,200

Accounts Payable

Creditor	Date of Purchase	Terms	Amount
Danvers Company	October 15	1/10 EOM, n/60	$ 465
Jarvis Supply Company	October 6	n/30	835
Kelly Company	October 20	1/15, n/30	500
Total			$1,800

Transactions for November were:

1969

Nov. 1 Purchased merchandise from the Jarvis Supply Company on account, $800; terms n/30.

2 Issued Check 300 in the amount of $300 for a one-year insurance policy.

2 Issued a credit memorandum for $35 to the Zurback Company for the return of merchandise on the sale of October 31.

3 Received a check from the Applebee Company in payment for the sale made on October 24.

1969
Nov. 3   Paid the Kelly Company for the purchase of October 20.

      3   Purchased merchandise from the Danvers Company on account, $800; terms 1/10 EOM, n/60.

      4   Paid the Jarvis Supply Company for the purchase of October 6.

      4   Paid $180 for the November rent.

    10   Paid the Danvers Company for the purchase of October 15.

    10   Sold merchandise to the Hillory Company on account, $1,500; terms 2/10, n/30.

    11   Issued additional capital stock for $10,000 in cash.

    12   Received a check from the Munsin Company for the sale of October 27.

    12   Sold merchandise to the Applebee Company on account, $1,600; terms 2/10, n/30.

    13   Purchased merchandise from the Kelly Company on account, $1,200; terms 1/15, n/30.

    14   Paid semimonthly salaries totaling $360.

    15   Cash sales from November 1 through 15 were $2,750.

    17   Sold merchandise to the Munsin Company on account, $1,550; terms 2/10, n/30.

    18   Received a credit memorandum for $25 from the Kelly Company for the return of defective merchandise.

    19   Received a check from the Hillory Company for $400 on account; no discount was allowed.

    20   Purchased merchandise for $1,800 in cash.

    21   Received a check for $200 from the Applebee Company and a note for the balance due; no discount was allowed.

    27   Received a check from the Munsin Company for the sale of November 17.

    28   Paid the Kelly Company for the purchase made on November 13.

    30   Paid semimonthly salaries totaling $360.

    30   Paid $70 for heat and light for November.

    30   Cash sales from November 16 through 30 were $3,250.

    30   Purchased merchandise from the Kelly Company on account, $1,100; terms 1/15, n/30.

Required: 1. Record the transactions in a sales journal, a purchases journal, a general journal, a cash receipts journal, and a cash disbursements journal.

          2. Open the accounts listed in the general ledger. Using the date November 1, record the account balances.

          3. Open the listed accounts in an accounts receivable ledger and an accounts payable ledger. Record the appropriate dates and amounts.

          4. Post from the journals to the appropriate ledgers.

          5. Prepare a trial balance.

          6. Prepare a schedule of accounts receivable and a schedule of accounts payable.

P6-**6.** The journals of the Carbone Company are shown in skeleton form (Date and folio (F) columns are omitted):

SALES JOURNAL

Account	Amount
N. Ruggles	750
J. Janes	460
K. Goddard	600
	1,810

PURCHASES JOURNAL

Account	Amount
Coleman Co.	260
Betro, Inc.	500
Fettig Supply Co.	600
	1,360

SALES RETURNS AND
ALLOWANCES JOURNAL

Account	Amount
J. Janes	60
N. Ruggles	70
	130

PURCHASES RETURNS AND
ALLOWANCES JOURNAL

Account	Amount
Betro, Inc.	60
Coleman Co.	30
	90

GENERAL JOURNAL

Notes Receivable	300	
Accounts Receivable–J. Janes		300
Store Equipment	950	
Arnold Carbone, Capital		950

CASH RECEIPTS JOURNAL

Account Credited	Other Accounts Cr.	Sales Cr.	Accounts Receivable Cr.	Sales Discounts Dr.	Cash Dr.
Arnold Carbone, Capital	10,000				10,000
Rent Earned	100				100
Sales		750			750
J. Janes			100		100
N. Ruggles			300	6	294
K. Goddard			200	2	198
	10,100	750	600	8	11,442

CASH DISBURSEMENTS JOURNAL

Account Debited	Other Accounts Dr.	Accounts Payable Dr.	Purchases Discounts Cr.	Cash Cr.
Store Equipment	2,500			2,500
Coleman Co.		100	2	98
Prepaid Insurance	150			150
Fettig Supply Co.		300	9	291
	2,650	400	11	3,039

Required: 1. Open general and subsidiary ledger T accounts and post the transactions (provide account numbers).
2. Prepare a trial balance.
3. Prepare a schedule of accounts receivable and a schedule of accounts payable.

P6–7. The Carolina Company started operations on July 1, 1969. During July, the Company used the following accounts:

Cash 101
Accounts Receivable 111
Prepaid Insurance 117
Office Supplies 118
Land 131
Store Building 141
Store Fixtures 151
Office Equipment 154
Accounts Payable 201
Mortgage Payable 231
Capital Stock 401
Sales 501
Sales Discounts 521
Sales Returns and Allowances 531
Purchases 601
Purchases Discounts 611
Purchases Returns and Allowances 621
Transportation In 631
Salaries Expense 701
Delivery Expense 711
Office Expense 721
Utilities Expense 731

The following transactions took place during July:

1969

July 1 Issued capital stock worth $25,000 for cash.

1 Purchased a store building and site for $45,000, of which $11,000 is considered land cost. Paid $5,500 in cash and issued a mortgage of $39,500 for the balance.

1 Purchased store fixtures from the National Company for $6,500 on account; terms n/60.

1969

July 2 Purchased merchandise from Jones, Inc., on account, $6,000; invoice date, July 1; terms 2/10, n/60.

2 Purchased merchandise from Hill Baker on account, $7,000; invoice date, July 2; terms 2/10, n/60.

6 Purchased a six-year fire insurance policy for $840 in cash.

8 Purchased merchandise for $4,000 in cash.

9 Returned unsatisfactory merchandise to Jones, Inc., and received credit for $1,500.

13 Sold merchandise to David Evans on account, $7,700; Invoice 1; terms 1/10, n/30.

14 Paid Jones, Inc., and Hill Baker the amounts due.

15 Cash sales from July 1 through 15 were $1,400.

16 Sold merchandise to Kenneth Johnson on account, $6,000; Invoice 2; terms 1/10, n/30.

16 Sold merchandise to George Hooker on account, $5,500; Invoice 3; terms 1/10, n/30.

16 Paid salaries for July 1 through 15 totaling $1,800.

19 Sold merchandise to Stephen Gold on account, $6,000; Invoice 4; terms 1/10, n/30.

21 Purchased merchandise from the Sanders Company on account, $3,700; invoice date, July 21; terms 1/10, n/30.

21 Received a bill for $130 from the Office Supply Company for items chargeable to Office Expense; terms, n/30.

23 Received merchandise returned by Stephen Gold; issued Credit Memo 1 for $1,200.

23 Received cash from David Evans for Invoice 1, less discount.

26 Received cash from Kenneth Johnson for Invoice 2, less discount.

26 Purchased merchandise from Dumont, Inc., on account, $8,000; invoice date, July 24; terms 3/10, n/30. Paid transportation charges of $90.

28 Received $5,500 cash from George Hooker.

28 Sold merchandise to Mason Wills on account, $3,000; Invoice 5; terms 1/10, n/30.

29 Paid $140 in cash for electricity.

29 Paid the Sanders Company on the invoice of July 21, less discount.

29 Received cash from Stephen Gold for the balance of Invoice 4, less discount.

31 Cash sales from July 16 through 31 were $1,700.

31 Paid salaries for July 16 through 31 totaling $2,200.

31 Received a bill for $66 from the Canter Company for delivery service for the month. Purchased two filing cabinets and a typewriter at a cost of $600 and various office supplies at a cost of $200; paid $300 in cash and issued $500 par value capital stock for the balance.

Required: 1. Record the transactions in a general journal, an expanded cash receipts journal, an expanded cash disbursements journal, a sales journal, and a purchases journal.

2. Indicate how the postings would be made from the journals by entering the appropriate posting references.

P6–**8.** Fine Furniture, Inc., uses a single-column sales journal, a two-column general journal, and a cash receipts journal that includes an Accounts Receivable column. A monthly trial balance is prepared. The accounts receivable ledger is shown:

Rankin Stores

1969						
Jan.	1	Balance	✔			600
	10		S5	300		900
	19		CR3		600	300
	25		J8		50	250
	28		S5	400		650

Stonackers, Inc.

1969						
Jan.	1	Balance	✔			250
	5		CR3		250	—
	11		S5	310		310
	20		S5	450		760
	27		CR3		200	560
	30		J8		10	550

Thomas, Inc.

1969						
Jan.	1	Balance	✔			200
	12		J8		20	180
	15		S5	800		980
	31		CR3		180	800

Required: 1. Reconstruct the Accounts Receivable controlling account exactly as it appeared in the general ledger of Fine Furniture, Inc., after all postings from the journals had been completed, including dates and posting references.
2. Rule and balance the Accounts Receivable account.
3. Verify the ending account balance by preparing a schedule of accounts receivable.

CASE PROBLEM
Mallory College

The controller of Mallory College decided to revise the format of the journals used in the accounting department. He started by asking one of his assistants to prepare a summary of the types of transaction experienced by the college. Parts of this summary are given:

1. Students must pay a tuition deposit when their applications for admission are submitted. The deposit is returned only if the college rejects the application.

2. Students must pay additional tuition deposits when they register for specific classes. The deposit is returned only if the college cancels the student's registration during the first ten days of classes, which is extremely rare.

3. At least one-third of the balance of the tuition must be paid when the semester is one-quarter over; at least two-thirds of the balance must be fully paid when the semester is three-quarters over. Accelerated payments are, of course, permitted.

4. If registration is canceled by a student during the first ten days of classes, the student is not obligated to pay the remainder of the tuition. All payments already made are refunded. If the registration is canceled after the first ten days of classes, the student is obligated to pay the remainder of the tuition, as indicated, for that semester.

5. Students must pay room deposits when their applications for housing are submitted. The deposit is returned only if the college rejects the application of a student or if the student cancels a room application ten days or more before registration begins.

6. Students must pay additional room deposits when they receive their room keys. The deposit is returned only if the college cancels the registration of a student during the first ten days of classes, which is extremely rare.

7. At least one-third of the balance of the room rent must be paid when the semester is one-quarter over; at least two-thirds of the balance must be paid when the term is half over; and the balance must be fully paid when the semester is three-quarters over. Accelerated payments are permitted.

8. If registration is canceled by a student during the first ten days of classes, the student is not obligated to pay the remainder of the room rent. All payments already made are refunded. If the registration is canceled after the first ten days of classes, the student is obligated to pay the remainder of the room rent, as indicated, for that semester.

9. Books and school supplies are sold for cash only in the college book store. Discounts are not given. Returns are permitted only on rare occasions, such as when the wrong books are purchased or when early registration cancellations are made.

10. Books and supplies purchased for resale are subject to payment terms of 1/5, n/30. Transportation charges are paid by the college when the shipments are received. Unused books may be returned for full credit at any time.

11. The college regularly (at least monthly) makes payments for:
    a. Salaries of the faculty and clerical staff
    b. Maintenance and repairs for buildings, equipment, and grounds
    c. Supplies to be used by the faculty and staff
    d. Utilities (electricity, gas, heat, telephone, and water)
    e. Retirement of the mortgage and interest thereon
    f. Insurance coverage of several types

12. Depreciation of buildings and equipment is recorded monthly.

13. Interest on individual investments is received twice a year. Since the college has numerous investments, some interest is received every month.

Required: 1. What journals would be most useful to Mallory College?
2. Design the format of the journals that you have indicated as most useful.
3. Justify the inclusion of each column heading in your format.

4. Identify the advantages and disadvantages of these journals.
5. What factors govern the format of the journals to be used?
6. What types of changes will influence changes in format in the future?
7. Explain the connection between these journals and the subsidiary and the general ledgers.
8. Explain the role played by these journals in the whole accounting process.

PRACTICE SET—SPENCER WHOLESALE HARDWARE COMPANY

The practice set, containing transactions of the Spencer Wholesale Hardware Company, a single proprietorship, should be assigned after Chapter 6. This is a short set and can be solved in approximately ten hours. The list of transactions and working papers are in a separate package.

Part
Two

Income
Measurement
and Valuation
Problems
Related
to Sources
and Uses
of Invested
Capital

Chapter Seven
Short-Term Business Financing

Business firms often find it more economical to use some means of short-term financing rather than to pay cash for various purchases. An extremely popular form of short-term financing is the purchase of merchandise, supplies, and equipment on 30-, 60-, or 90-day open charge accounts. Cash terms—no carrying charges are assigned—are often extended for a period of 90 days or more. During this period, cash may be obtained from new sales and used to pay for merchandise obtained on the open charge accounts. This form of financing has already been discussed in Chapter 5. Several other short-term financing devices are considered in this chapter, as follows:

1. Issuance of notes to trade creditors
2. Borrowing from banks on a company's own notes
3. Discounting notes receivable from customers

Managers faced with the decision as to which method to choose must consider for each method both its current and expected future availability and its effective cost. In general, a financial manager should choose the method or methods that will produce and continue to produce the desired short-term funds at the lowest long-run cost. In applying this general rule to specific financial decisions, management must consider such related variables as the availability of collateral, financial institutional connections, and the attendant effect on long-term debt financing.

PROMISSORY NOTES

A *negotiable promissory note* may be defined as an unconditional written promise to pay a specified sum of money to the order of a designated person, or to bearer, at a fixed or determinable future time or on demand.

A typical note is illustrated in Figure 7-1. Richard Baldwin, the *maker*, gives Edward Fenn, the designated *payee*, a 6-percent, 60-day note for $2,000, dated April 19, 1969, in payment for a purchase of merchandise.

$ 2,000.00	Boston, Mass.	April 19, 1969
Sixty days	after date I	promise to pay
to the order of	Edward Fenn	
Two Thousand and no/100		Dollars
Payable at	First National Bank	100
Value received with interest at 6%		
No. 40 Due June 18, 1969	Richard Baldwin	

Figure 7-1.
A Promissory Note

The outstanding characteristics of a note are the following:

The instrument must be in writing, signed by the maker.
The instrument must contain an unconditional promise to pay a certain sum of money.
The instrument may be payable to the order of a designated person, the payee, or it may be payable to *bearer* (that is, anyone who holds the note).
The instrument must be payable either on *demand* or at a determinable time in the future.
The instrument may or may not be interest-bearing.

The ownership of a negotiable promissory note is transferred simply by delivery if it is payable to the bearer; otherwise, it is transferred by *endorsement* and delivery.

A *blank endorsement* consists of the signature of the owner, or the payee, on the back of the instrument. A *full endorsement* consists of the notation on the back of the document, "Pay to the order of the Blank Company," accompanied by the signature of the owner. If the *endorser*—the owner who is transferring the document —wishes to pass title to the instrument and at the same time to relieve himself of any further liability, he places his signature on the back of the note and adds the phrase "without recourse" (this is a *qualified endorsement*).

From the viewpoint of the maker, Richard Baldwin, the note illustrated in Figure 7-1 is a liability and is recorded by crediting Notes Payable. From the viewpoint of the payee, Edward Fenn, however, the same note is an asset and is recorded by debiting Notes Receivable. At the maturity date, Edward Fenn, or his *agent* the First National Bank, will expect to receive $2,020 in cash for the note and interest, and Richard Baldwin will expect to pay $2,020 in cash.

Maturity Dates and Their Determination

The *term* of a note may be expressed in years, months, or days. To determine the maturity of a note expressed in months or years, count the number of months or years from the issuance date. For example, a two-year note dated April 3, 1969, is due on April 3, 1971; and a two-month note dated April 3, 1969, is due on June 3, 1969. Occasionally, when time is expressed in months, there may be no corresponding date in the maturity month, in which case the last day of the month of maturity is used; a three-month note dated March 31 is due on June 30, and a one-month note dated January 29, 30, or 31 is due on the last day of February. If the term of the note is expressed in days, the maturity is found by counting forward the specified number of days after the date of the note, excluding the date of the note but including the maturity date. The note of Richard Baldwin in Figure 7-1 has an issuance date of April 19; the due date of June 18 is determined as follows:

Total days in April	30
Date of note in April	19
Number of days note runs in April (excluding April 19)	11
Total days in May	31
Total number of days note has run through May 31	42
Due date in June (60 days minus 42 days)	18
Term of the note	60

If the term of a note that is expressed in days includes an entire month, count the actual number of days in that month. The determination of the number of calendar days in a term expressed in months is the same as the calculation for a term expressed in days. Thus, a two-month note dated April 19 is due 61 days later on June 19. Interest may be computed for either 60 or 61 days. Though banks generally compute interest by using the exact number of days—61 days in the example—on their direct loans, the usual commercial practice is to calculate interest (as in the example) for two months of 30 days each, or 60 days rather than 61 days. The typical commercial practice is followed in this text; that is, the interest computation on a one-month note is based on 30 days; on a two-month note, 60 days; and so on.

Interest

Interest is the price of credit, a payment made (or collection received) for the use of money or the equivalent of money. Being similar to the price of merchandise, interest to the maker—the debtor—is an expense; to the payee—the creditor—interest is a revenue.

The interest specified on a note, unless otherwise indicated, is an annual rate on the *principal*, or face amount of the note. Thus, in Richard Baldwin's note, the price, or charge for the use of $2,000 for one year, is $120 ($2,000 × .06). Since the term of the note is less than one year, the interest must be computed by multiplying the interest amount for one year by a fraction—the numerator is the term of the note in days and the denominator, the number of days in a year. The formula is:

$$\text{Principal} \times \text{Rate} \times \text{Time} = \text{Interest}$$

This is usually stated as $P \times R \times T = I$. In Baldwin's note, the interest calculation for the 60-day period is:

$$\$2,000 \times .06 \times \frac{60}{360} = \$20$$

It is common commercial practice to assume that the year contains 360 days (or 12 months of 30 days each) in computing interest. This practice will be followed here, but it should be understood that the amount of bias in the final interest calculation is $\frac{1}{73}$, that is, $\frac{365 - 360}{365} = \frac{1}{73}$.

A considerable amount of time can be saved through various short-cut methods of computing interest. Two of these are referred to as the *6-percent, 60-day method* and the *6-percent, 6-day method*. Since the interest at 6-percent for 60 days on any principal is 1 percent ($60/360 \times 6\%$), interest at 6 percent for 60 days on any principal can be figured by moving the decimal point two places to the left in the principal, which is the same as multiplying the principal by 1 percent. Similarly, the interest at 6 percent for 6 days can be figured by moving the decimal point three places to the left in the principal. Either or both of these short methods may be used for note terms other than 6 or 60 days. The term of the note can be stated as a fraction or multiple of 6 or 60 days, and the interest may then be quickly computed.

Short methods can also be applied when the interest rate is other than 6 percent. The interest calculation is first made at 6 percent, then an adjustment is made for the difference between 6 percent and the particular rate.

The following two examples illustrate interest computation by the short methods:

1. Interest at 7 percent on $3,600 for 90 days:

Interest at 6% for 60 days	$36
Interest at 6% for 30 days (½ of $36)	18
Interest at 6% for 90 days	$54
Interest at 1% for 90 days (⅙ of $54)	9
Interest at 7% for 90 days	$63

2. Interest at 4½ percent on $4,800 for 30 days:

Interest at 6% for 60 days	$48
Interest at 6% for 30 days (½ of $48)	$24
Less interest at 1½% for 30 days (¼ of $24)	6
Interest at 4½% for 30 days	$18

An advantage of the short methods is that they require relatively simple arithmetical computations, thereby reducing the possibility of error. This is true when interest rates and terms are such that the mathematical manipulations are obvious, but if rates and terms require elaborate adjustments for the use of these methods (for example, 4.25 percent for 27 days) the calculation time will not be reduced, but increased. In such cases it is better to use the basic interest formula, $PRT = I$.

Recording Procedures

All notes payable may be recorded in a single Notes Payable account in the general ledger as shown:

GENERAL LEDGER

Notes Payable   Acct. No. 111

1969				1969			
Dec.	24	F. T. Anson (paid)	450	Nov.	15	B. B. Baker, 5%, 60 days	2,000
					24	F. T. Anson, 6%, 30 days	450
				Dec.	3	C. L. Jones, 6%, 90 days	800
					10	F. E. Merrick, 6%, 60 days	1,000
					18	P. O. Paulson, 6%, 90 days	950

The Notes Payable account may be used to record many of the supplementary details of the notes, including the name of the payee, the interest rate, the maturity date, and the term of the note. The credit entries in the account represent the issuance of notes payable, and the debit entry indicates the payment of a note. In addition to this record, carbon copies of the notes may be placed in a *tickler file* in order of maturity dates. When the maker pays the note and receives the cancelled original (either perforated or marked *Paid*), he may destroy the carbon copy and place the cancelled original in a *paid note file*. It is important that a record of paid notes be maintained in case of later disputes. The files of unpaid and paid notes can serve as subsidiary records of notes payable.

If the volume of notes payable becomes large, however, a special notes payable register may be created. This register can serve both as a special journal and as a subsidiary record of notes payable. In addition to Debit and Credit money columns, memorandum columns can be provided for supplementary information.

ISSUANCE OF NOTES FOR PLANT AND EQUIPMENT. The following examples illustrate the use of notes payable in the acquisition of plant and equipment.

Assume that on July 10, 1969, the Able Company buys a bookkeeping machine at a cost of $2,000 from the Bourrim Machine Company; the creditor agrees to take a 90-day, noninterest-bearing note for the purchase price. This transaction is recorded as follows:

```
1969
July 10   Office Equipment                               2000
               Notes Payable                                        2000
               To record the purchase of a bookkeeping machine
               and the issuance of a 90-day, noninterest-bearing
               note to the Bourrim Machine Company.
```

On the maturity date, 90 days later, the payment of the note is recorded as follows:

```
1969
Oct.  8   Notes Payable                                  2000
               Cash                                                 2000
               To record payment of a 90-day, noninterest-bearing
               note issued to the Bourrim Machine Company.
```

Although the transaction of October 8, 1969, should be entered in the Able Company's cash disbursements journal, a general journal entry is shown to illustrate the *effect* of the transaction. (With very few exceptions, the general journal form is used to show the effect of transactions throughout the remainder of the text.)

Few creditors accept noninterest-bearing notes. Therefore, in the second example, assume that the Able Company purchases the same bookkeeping machine, but gives the Bourrim Machine Company a 6-percent, 90-day note. The journal entry is similar to the previous one.

1969

July 10	Office Equipment	2000	
	Notes Payable		2000
	To record the purchase of a bookkeeping machine and the issuance of a 6%, 90-day note to the Bourrim Machine Company.		

On October 8, 1969, the payment of the note and interest to the Bourrim Machine Company is recorded as follows:

1969

Oct. 8	Notes Payable	2000	
	Interest Expense	30	
	Cash		2030
	To record payment of a 6%, 90-day note and interest to the Bourrim Machine Company.		

ISSUANCE OF NOTES FOR MERCHANDISE. A business may use notes as a means of postponing payment for merchandise purchased for resale. These transactions could be recorded as were those in the preceding section; but since the volume of business done with a particular supplier or customer must be known for managerial purposes, such as applying for quantity discounts, it is helpful to have a subsidiary ledger account showing the total history of all transactions with a particular firm. To supply management with this information, the accountant may wish to record all merchandise transactions involving notes through the Accounts Payable account and the individual creditors' accounts in the subsidiary ledger. For example, assume that on October 10, 1969, the Able Company purchases merchandise costing $1,800 from the Baldwin Company and issues a 6-percent, 45-day note to the creditor. The note and interest are paid on November 24, 1969. These transactions are recorded as follows:

1969

Oct. 10	Purchases	1800.00	
	Accounts Payable–Baldwin Company		1800.00
	To record merchandise purchased.		
10	Accounts Payable–Baldwin Company	1800.00	
	Notes Payable		1800.00
	To record the issuance of 6%, 45-day note to the Baldwin Company.		

Nov. 24	Notes Payable	1800.00	
	Interest Expense	13.50	
	Cash		1813.50
	To record payment of a note and interest to		
	the Baldwin Company.		

ISSUANCE OF NOTES IN SETTLEMENT OF OPEN ACCOUNTS. A firm may issue a note to an open account creditor as a means of postponing payment further, or a creditor may require a debtor to give a note if the account is past due. Legally, a note is no more binding or collectible than an open account. Businessmen, however, prefer to hold notes because they are better legal evidence of the existence of debts, they are negotiable, and most makers of notes have a strong aversion to defaulting. They fear that the default of a note indicates a weak financial position to the business world more than failure to pay an open account does, and therefore does more damage to their credit standing.

The entry for the issuance of a note in settlement of an open account payable is similar to the second entry dated October 10 in the previous section.

ISSUANCE OF NOTES TO BORROW FROM BANKS. A business faced with the possibility of losing cash discounts may find it advantageous to borrow money from a bank to pay the open accounts within the discount periods. A 2/10, n/30 cash discount, for example, represents an annual cost saving of 36 percent, as was illustrated in Chapter 5. It is a sound financial decision to borrow money at 6 percent, for example, to prevent the loss of a 36-percent cost saving.

There are two ways in which banks and other grantors of credit handle notes: (1) money may be borrowed on an interest-bearing note signed by the borrower, or (2) money may be advanced on a noninterest-bearing note *discounted* by the borrower. In the first case, the borrower receives the face value of the note and pays the face value plus the accumulated interest on the maturity date. In the second case, the note is noninterest-bearing because the interest, or *discount,* is deducted in advance, and the borrower receives only the discounted value. At the maturity date, the borrower pays the face value of the note. The element of interest is present in either case: the difference is primarily one of form. There may also be notes that are noninterest-bearing as far as both the maker and the payee are concerned.

Assume that on March 1, 1969, the Able Company borrows $5,000 from the First National Bank, giving a 6-percent, 60-day note, and that on April 30 it pays the bank for the note and interest. The issuance and payment of the note are recorded in the Able Company's books as follows:

1969

Mar. 1	Cash	5000	
	Notes Payable		5000
	To record a 6%, 60-day note issued to the First		
	National Bank.		
Apr. 30	Notes Payable	5000	
	Interest Expense	50	
	Cash		5050
	To record payment of a 6%, 60-day note to the		
	First National Bank.		

Assume that on May 1, 1969, the Able Company borrows money from the City National Bank, discounting its own $5,000, 60-day, noninterest-bearing note at the *discount rate* of 6 percent. The amount of cash received in this case is $4,950, or $5,000 less a discount of $50 computed by applying the discount rate to the face value for the discount period of 60 days. If the maturity date falls within the current accounting period—the calendar year is assumed—the following entries are made in the Able Company's books:

1969

May	1	Cash	4950	
		Interest Expense	50	
		Notes Payable		5000
		To record noninterest-bearing note issued to the City National Bank discounted at 6% for 60 days.		
June	30	Notes Payable	5000	
		Cash		5000
		To record payment of a noninterest-bearing note to the City National Bank.		

Assume that the Able Company had issued the note on December 16, 1969. Since the maturity date falls in the accounting year 1970, the following entry would be made:

1969

Dec.	16	Cash	4950	
		Discount on Notes Payable	50	
		Notes Payable		5000
		To record noninterest-bearing note discounted at 6% for 60 days.		

The $50 discount is not prepaid and should not be debited to Prepaid Interest, as is sometimes done. The interest is not paid until the note matures. At that time, the net amount borrowed of $4,950 plus total interest of $50 is paid; therefore, the balance of Discount on Notes Payable represents a potential interest expense. Accordingly, an adjusting entry is required at December 31, 1969, to transfer the expense portion of the balance of Discount on Notes Payable to the Interest Expense account; the entry is illustrated later in this chapter.

Discount on Notes Payable should be shown in the statement of financial position as a contra account to Notes Payable under current liabilities to indicate clearly the source of the net amount of funds received from creditors. Later, as adjustments are made to the Discount on Notes Payable account, the difference between the Notes Payable account and the balance of the Discount on Notes Payable account shows the net amount borrowed plus accrued interest on that amount.

In reference to the March 1 and May 1 bank loans, the amount paid at maturity was $50 more than the amount received from the bank by the borrower. However, the borrower had the use of $5,000, or the full face value of the interest-bearing note (March 1 bank loan), whereas only $4,950 was available from the noninterest-bearing discounted note. The *effective interest* (i) on a discounted note may be computed by the following formula:

$$\frac{D}{P} \times \frac{12}{T} = i$$

where D = the amount of the discount,
 P = the net proceeds,
 12 = months in the year, and
 T = the term of the note in months.

The effective interest in the example is not 6 percent; rather, it is:

$$\frac{\$50}{\$4,950} \times \frac{12}{2} = 1.01\% \times 6 = 6.06\%$$

The accountant should carefully determine the effective interest rate of a loan since this is relevant to making any short-term financial decision.

A discount may be defined as a deduction made from a gross future sum. The amount of the discount on a note is the difference between its value on the date of discount and its future value at maturity. Since discount and interest are similar in that each represents the charge for the use of money, the Interest Expense account is used in this text to record the incurred portion of expense for each of these items. The use of the Interest Expense account is further extended when a firm discounts customers' notes receivable, another short-term financing device discussed in this chapter.

End-of-Period Adjustments

Since interest is incurred continuously throughout the life of a note payable, it is necessary to make adjusting entries for the interest expense on those notes payable that mature in a later accounting period. Two kinds of adjustment are considered: the accrual of interest on an interest-bearing note payable and the expense apportionment on a discounted note payable.

Assume that the Boston Company has the following accounts in its general ledger as of December 31, 1969:

				Discount on Notes Payable			Acct. No. 131		
1969									
Dec.	16				72				

						Notes Payable			Acct. No. 205	
						1969				
						Dec.	1	Hamilton Co., 6%, 90 days		4650
							16	Bank of Orange, 120 days, discounted at 6%		3600

At December 31, 1969, the following two adjusting entries are made:

```
1969
Dec. 31   Interest Expense                              23.25
              Accrued Interest Payable                          23.25
                  To record accrued interest on the note issued to
                  the Hamilton Co.: Interest for 30 days at 6% on
                  $4,650 is $23.25.

       31   Interest Expense                               9.00
              Discount on Notes Payable                          9.00
                  To record the transfer of $9 interest from the
                  Discount on Notes Payable account to the
                  Interest Expense account on the note discounted
                  at the Bank of Orange.
```

Comments on these two entries are:

1. The amount of the accrued interest on a note issued to the Hamilton Company is figured at 6 percent for 30 days, the number of days after December 1, including December 31. Of course, no interest for the time period after December 31, 1969, should be recorded as an expense of 1969.
2. The second adjusting entry transfers interest from the Discount on Notes Payable account to the Interest Expense account. There are two methods by which the interest expense of $9 for 1969 can be determined. First, the amount of the discount may be multiplied by a fraction consisting of the age of the note as of the adjustment date divided by the term: in the example, $\frac{15}{120} \times \$72 = \$9$. Second, an ordinary interest computation may be made: interest at 6 percent on $3,600 for 15 days is $9.

On March 1, 1970, when the Boston Company pays the Hamilton Company for the note and interest, the following journal entry is made:

```
1970
Mar.  1   Notes Payable                               4650.00
              Accrued Interest Payable                    23.25
              Interest Expense                            46.50
                  Cash                                           4719.75
                      To record payment of a 6%, 90-day note
                      and interest to the Hamilton Co.
```

The credit to Cash of $4,719.75 represents the payment of two liabilities already on the books, Notes Payable and Accrued Interest Payable, and a payment of interest expense of $46.50 ($6\% \times \frac{60}{360} \times \$4,650$) entirely applicable to 1970.

The payment of the $3,600 on April 15, 1970, to the Bank of Orange is recorded in the following journal entry:

```
1970
Apr. 15   Notes Payable                               3600
              Cash                                              3600
                  To record payment of a note to the Bank of Orange.
```

Since the note is noninterest-bearing, no interest is recorded at the time of payment. However, there is a $63 balance in the Discount on Notes Payable account, which represents an expense of the year 1970. The following adjusting entry is made as of December 31, 1970, to transfer this amount to the Interest Expense account:

```
1970
Dec. 31   Interest Expense                                63
              Discount on Notes Payable                             63
                  To apportion the amount of interest expense
                  applicable to the year 1970.
```

NOTES RECEIVABLE FINANCING PROBLEM

Another financial device that is often employed to obtain short-term funds is discounting customers' notes receivable. Before this is discussed, however, it would be helpful to understand the accounting for notes received from customers.

In general, the accounting for notes receivable is similar to that for notes payable; however, some procedures warrant additional discussion.

Recording Procedures

Many businesses make use of promissory notes to establish a legal basis for their claims against a customer and to create a legal document that may be easily discounted at a bank should the need for funds arise. They include firms selling high-priced durable goods such as furniture, farm machinery, and automobiles. Notes receivable are also received by a financial institution when it loans money.

It is perhaps even more important to keep good accounting records for notes receivable than it is for notes payable. After all, the payee of a note payable will send a statement to the maker that a note is due, so there is little danger that the maker will overlook the due date. The holder of notes receivable must have his records arranged so that he can notify the debtor that the note is due. This requires that notes receivable be filed chronologically by maturity date in a tickler file.

All notes receivable are usually recorded in a single general ledger account. The tickler file of notes receivable, plus the general ledger account containing such information as the maker, the term, the interest rate, and any collateral pledged, make it unnecessary for a firm to maintain a subsidiary notes receivable ledger. The Notes Receivable account of the Carson Company is shown:

		Notes Receivable				Acct. No. 111	
1969				1969			
Nov.	1	C. Adams, 45 days, 6%	775	Dec.	16	C. Adams	775
	20	B. Baker, 90 days, 7%	425				
Dec.	20	L. Wilson, 60 days, 6%	500				

Each debit posting indicates that an asset, Notes Receivable, has been acquired from a customer; each credit entry indicates that a particular note has been settled by payment or renewal, or has been dishonored. In addition to the dollar amounts in the money columns, the Explanation columns give the maker's name, the term of the note, the interest rate, and any other relevant information.

If the volume of transactions warrants it, a special notes receivable register, like the notes payable register, could be created. Special Debit and Credit money columns could be inserted, along with memorandum columns for supplementary information. This register could serve as both a journal and a subsidiary record of notes receivable.

Receipt of a Note for a Sale

Assume that on March 5, 1969, the Dawson Company sells merchandise to John Roch and receives a 6-percent, 90-day note for $650. The following entries are made:

1969

Mar. 5	Accounts Receivable–John Roch	650	
	Sales		650
	To record sale of merchandise.		
5	Notes Receivable	650	
	Accounts Receivable–John Roch		650
	To record the receipt of a 6%, 90-day note from John Roch.		

The first entry is made so that the customer's account in the subsidiary ledger will contain a complete record of all credit sales transactions. This information is useful to management in making decisions as to collection efforts and further extension of credit.

On June 3, 1969, when the Dawson Company receives payment from John Roch, the following entry is made:

1969

June 3	Cash	659.75	
	Notes Receivable		650.00
	Interest Earned		9.75
	To record receipt of payment from John Roch for note and interest due today.		

The Interest Earned account is a revenue account. The balance of this account is closed at the end of the accounting period to the Revenue and Expense Summary account.

RECEIPT OF A NOTE IN SETTLEMENT OF AN OPEN ACCOUNT. Assume that Ralph Towne owes the Dawson Company $1,850, due on July 10, 1969. On August 1, the Dawson Company agrees to accept a 60-day, noninterest-bearing note with a face value of $1,868.50 (the amount receivable, $1,850, plus interest at 6% for 60 days) in settlement of the open account. This procedure is common among retailers who plan to discount their notes at banks. Banks prefer that most—if not all—of their notes be noninterest-bearing. Since the maturity date of this note falls within the current accounting period—the calendar year is assumed—the following entry is made:

1969

Aug. 1	Notes Receivable	1868.50	
	Accounts Receivable–Ralph Towne		1850.00
	Interest Earned		18.50

To record receipt of a 60-day, noninterest-bearing note, with interest of $18.50 included in the face value, from Ralph Towne.

The credit of the entire $18.50 to the revenue account, Interest Earned, is permissible since that amount will become revenue by the time the books are closed on December 31.

On September 30, when payment is received, the following entry is made:

1969

Sept. 30	Cash	1868.50	
	Notes Receivable		1868.50

To record collection of note from Ralph Towne.

If the note of August 1, 1969, had been received on December 1, 1969, all the interest would not be earned by December 31, 1969. The following entry is required:

1969

Dec. 1	Notes Receivable	1868.50	
	Accounts Receivable–Ralph Towne		1850.00
	Unearned Interest (included in face of notes receivable)		18.50

To record receipt of a 60-day, noninterest-bearing note, with interest of $18.50 included in the face value, from Ralph Towne.

The Unearned Interest account, credited for $18.50, represents the interest that will be partly earned in 1969 and partly earned in 1970. Since the interest is not received in the form of cash, it should not be classified as a current liability, as is sometimes done. Rather, it should be shown as a contra account to Notes Receivable, to reduce that account to an estimate of its present value—the amount that could be received by discounting the note at a bank. The Unearned Interest account will require an adjusting entry at December 31, 1969, to apportion the amount of revenue earned in 1969 to the operations of the period. This procedure is described later in this chapter.

RENEWAL OF A NOTE RECEIVABLE. A customer who has given a note to a business firm may not be able to pay at the maturity date, but may be willing to renew the old note by the issuance of a new note, thus extending the time of the payment of the debt. To illustrate, assume that Samuel Thompson gives a 6-percent, 60-day note for $1,540 to the Dawson Company on April 1, 1969. On May 31, Thompson agrees to pay the Dawson Company cash for the interest on the old note and to give a new

6-percent, 90-day note for the principal. The May 31 transaction is recorded on the Dawson Company's books as follows:

1969

May 31	Notes Receivable (new 90-day note)	1540.00	
	Cash	15.40	
	Notes Receivable (old 60-day note)		1540.00
	Interest Earned		15.40
	To record the collection of cash in interest on the old note and to record the receipt of a new 6%, 90-day note in renewal of the old note.		

Since there is an equal debit and credit to the same account, there might be some question as to the propriety of including Notes Receivable in the journal entry. However, the omission of the debit and the credit would fail to disclose the action taken and would leave a gap in the permanent records of the Dawson Company. For example, the new note would still carry an entry date of April 1, 1969, and would appear to be past due. The entry as shown is the only way that a permanent record of this transaction can be achieved and the only way to avoid possible confusion.

DISHONOR OF A NOTE RECEIVABLE BY THE MAKER. If a note cannot be collected at maturity, it is said to be *dishonored* by the maker. Another term that is often used is *defaulting* on a note. Once the maturity date of a note passes without the note being collected, an entry should be made transferring the face value of the note plus any uncollected accrued interest to the Accounts Receivable account.

Assume that Ronald Ronson issued a 6-percent, 90-day note for $2,000 to the Dawson Company on June 1, 1969. At the maturity date, August 30, 1969, Ronson fails to pay the amount of the note and interest, at which time the following entry is made on the books of the Dawson Company:

1969

Aug. 30	Accounts Receivable–Ronald Ronson	2030	
	Notes Receivable		2000
	Interest Earned		30
	To record the dishonor by Ronald Ronson of a 6%, 90-day note.		

Two questions arise in connection with this entry: (1) Why should $30 be recognized as revenue and credited to the Interest Earned account? and (2) why should the amount of the note and interest not be written off to Allowance for Doubtful Accounts?

Under the accrual concept, the interest has been earned. It represents a valid claim against the maker of the note; if the face of the note is collectible, so is the interest. This leads to the answer to the second question: The fact that a note is uncollectible at its maturity is not a definite indication that it will never be collected. Unless there is some evidence to the contrary, most business firms assume that notes will ultimately be collected. Certainly, if the amounts involved are material, all possible steps including legal action will be taken to collect both accounts and notes receivable, and only after such steps have failed will an account be written off to Allowance for Doubtful Accounts.

The transfer of dishonored notes and interest to Accounts Receivable accomplishes two things: (1) the Notes Receivable account is relieved of past due notes, reflects only the current notes, and therefore represents a highly liquid asset; and (2) use of the Accounts Receivable account emphasizes the legal fact of dishonor (legally, a past due note is the same as an open account claim against a customer) and presents a complete picture of all transactions with the customer.

End-of-Period Adjusting Entries

The adjusting entries for interest on notes receivable parallel the adjusting entries for interest on notes payable. The major problem is accurate measurement of the revenue Interest Earned and the asset Accrued Interest Receivable, or the contra account Unearned Interest. To illustrate the adjusting entries and the effect they have on the accounting for notes and interest in the next accounting period, assume that the Eason Company has the following accounts in its general ledger as of December 31, 1969:

		Notes Receivable			Acct. No. 111
1969 Nov.	1	John Phillips, 6%, 150 days	1720		
Dec.	1	George Archer, 90-day, non-interest-bearing note, but interest of $33 is in the face	2233		

	Unearned Interest			Acct. No. 111A
		1969 Dec.	1	Interest in face of George Archer note	33

At December 31, 1969, the accountant for the Eason Company makes the following adjusting entries:

```
1969
Dec. 31   Accrued Interest Receivable                        17.20
              Interest Earned                                         17.20
                  To record the accrued interest on the John
                  Phillips note at 6% for 60 days.

       31   Unearned Interest                                  11.00
              Interest Earned                                         11.00
                  To record the transfer of ⅓ of $33 interest on
                  the note from George Archer from the
                  Unearned Interest account to the revenue
                  account.
```

Comments about these adjustments follow:

1. The accrued interest receivable on the note from John Phillips is figured at 6 percent for 60 days, the number of days after November 1 including December 31. No interest for the period after December 31, 1969, should be recorded as revenue in the year 1969.
2. The second adjustment involves the apportionment of interest revenue earned in a given period, 1969, to that period.

On March 1, 1970, when the Eason Company collects the note, the following entry is made:

1970

Mar.	1	Cash	2233	
		Notes Receivable		2233
		To record collection of a note from George Archer.		

Since the note is noninterest-bearing, no interest is recorded at the time of collection. However, a balance of $22 remains in the Unearned Interest account, representing revenue earned in the year 1970. Thus, an adjusting entry is necessary as of December 31, 1970, to transfer this amount to the Interest Earned account:

1970

Dec. 31	Unearned Interest	22	
	Interest Earned		22
	To apportion the amount of interest revenue applicable to the year 1970.		

A slightly different problem is associated with the collection of the note from John Phillips. The following entry is made on March 31, 1970, when the note is collected:

1970

Mar. 31	Cash	1763.00	
	Notes Receivable		1720.00
	Accrued Interest Receivable		17.20
	Interest Earned		25.80
	To record collection of a 6%, 150-day note and interest from John Phillips.		

The debit to cash of $1,763 represents the collection of two receivables already on the books, Notes Receivable and Accrued Interest Receivable, and of a revenue, Interest Earned of $25.80, which was earned in and is entirely applicable to the year 1970.

DISCOUNTING CUSTOMERS' NOTES RECEIVABLE

For a business that receives a large number of notes from customers, it may be economically advantageous to obtain short-term funds by discounting these notes at a bank rather than holding them to maturity. If the credit rating of the firm is good, most banks will usually discount customers' notes receivable because they are secured loans. If the maker fails to pay the maturity value when it is due, the firm that has discounted the note—having previously endorsed it—must make payment to the bank. This obligation is referred to as a *contingent liability*.

Determining the Cash Proceeds

As far as the bank is concerned, it is making a loan to the borrower based on the maturity value of the note, including any interest, because that is the amount the bank will collect from the maker at the maturity date. The discount that the bank deducts is based on a stipulated rate of the maturity value for the period of time the note has to run.

The sequence for computing the proceeds of a discounted note is:

1. The maturity value, or the principal plus the total interest to maturity, is determined.
2. The discount period, or the number of days the note still has to run after the date of the discount, is found.
3. The discount is computed at the stipulated bank rate for the discount period.
4. The discount is deducted from the maturity value to find the cash proceeds.

This sequence may be stated as $MV - (MV \times D \times RL) = P$

where MV = the maturity value
D = the rate of discount
RL = the remaining life of the note
P = the cash proceeds

Assume that on April 19, 1969, the Faison Company receives a 6-percent, 60-day note for $2,000 from Edward Goodson in settlement of a past-due open account. This transaction is recorded as follows:

1969

Apr. 19	Notes Receivable	2000	
	Accounts Receivable–Edward Goodson		2000
	To record receipt of a 6%, 60-day note from Goodson in settlement of a past-due open account.		

On May 1, 1969, the Faison Company, needing short-term funds, decides to discount Goodson's note at the bank's rate of 5 percent. Calculation of the proceeds follows:

1. Maturity value of note (principal of $2,000 plus total interest of $20)		$2,020.00
2. Due date	June 18	
3. Period of discount:		
May 1–May 31 (not counting May 1)	30 days	
June 1–June 18 (including June 1)	18 days	
	48 days	
4. Discount at 5% for 48 days on the maturity value:		
Interest on $2,020 at 6% for 60 days	$20.20	
Less interest on $2,020 at 6% for 12 days ($\frac{1}{5} \times \$20.20$)	4.04	
Interest on $2,020 at 6% for 48 days	$16.16	
Less interest on $2,020 at 1% for 48 days ($\frac{1}{6} \times \$16.16$)	2.69	
Discount (or interest) on $2,020 at 5% for 48 days		13.47
Total cash proceeds		$2,006.53

Recording The Proceeds

The entry on the Faison Company's books is:

```
1969
May   1   Cash                                    2006.53
              Notes Receivable Discounted                      2000.00
              Interest Earned                                     6.53
                  To record the discounting of Edward
                  Goodson's 6%, 60-day note at the bank at 5%.
```

The Notes Receivable Discounted account is used to indicate that the Faison Company, having endorsed the note before turning it over to the bank, is now obligated to pay the bank if Goodson fails to do so. That is, the Faison Company would have to pay the $2,000 contingent liability plus the $20 interest at 6 percent for 60 days, plus any *protest fee* charged by the bank. The obligation assumed by the Faison Company is contingent on Goodson's payment, and the account is therefore referred to as a *contingent liability account*. This account brings to the attention of the reader of the statement of financial position the existence of the contingent liability. (In preparing financial statements, full disclosure of all essential facts is of paramount importance. The significance of *full disclosure* is discussed later in this chapter.) Goodson does not need to be informed that the note has been discounted, and no entry is required on his books; his obligation to pay the maturity value of the note upon its presentation by the legal holder in due course remains unchanged.

Presentation on the Statement of Financial Position

Assume that on May 31 the Notes Receivable account shows a balance of $3,500 (including the $2,000 note discounted on May 1). The statement of financial position prepared on that date may disclose the existence of the contingent liability as follows:

Assets

```
      Current Assets
          Notes Receivable                         $3,500
          Deduct Notes Receivable Discounted        2,000
              Net Notes Receivable                              $1,500
```

Disclosure of the contingent liability can also be made by a footnote or supplementary note to the statement of financial position:

Assets

```
      Current Assets
          Notes Receivable (see Note 1)         $1,500

          Note 1:  The Company is contingently liable for
          notes receivable discounted in the amount of
          $2,000.
```

Payment of a Discounted Note

If notification of dishonor is not received from the bank (the bank normally does not notify the borrower of payment by the maker), it is assumed that the maker has paid the note at the maturity date, and the borrower is released from his contingent liability. The entry on the Faison Company's books to eliminate the contingent liability is:

1969

June 18	Notes Receivable Discounted	2000	
	Notes Receivable		2000
	To eliminate the contingent liability on Goodson's note, which was discounted on May 1, 1969.		

The entry on Edward Goodson's books on the date of payment is:

1969

June 18	Notes Payable	2000	
	Interest Expense	20	
	Cash		2020
	To record payment to the bank for a 6%, 60-day note issued to the Faison Company on April 19, 1969.		

The debit to Interest Expense is for the full 60-day period. It is assumed that no adjusting entry has been made for any interest expense.

Nonpayment of a Discounted Note

If Edward Goodson dishonors the note at the maturity date, the bank must follow a certain formal procedure involving the preparation of notarized protest documents to establish the legal basis for the collection of the full amount from the Faison Company. Assuming that the bank charges a protest fee of $5, the following entries are made on the Faison Company's books when the Company pays the bank the face value of the note, the interest, and the protest fee.

1969

June 18	Accounts Receivable–Edward Goodson	2025	
	Cash		2025
	To record payment of Edward Goodson's note, which was discounted and is now dishonored by Goodson:		

	Face value	$2,000
	Interest	20
	Protest Fee	5
	Total	$2,025

18	Notes Receivable Discounted	2000	
	Notes Receivable		2000
	To record the elimination of the contingent liability and Goodson's discounted and dishonored note.		

Note that Accounts Receivable is debited in the entry recording the cash payment, instead of Notes Receivable Discounted. This procedure avoids the error of treating discounted notes as though they were actual liabilities; since payment is made as soon as the contingency is realized, no book liability need be recorded. The second journal entry is necessary to remove the contingent liability after the cash payment is made for the dishonored note.

The fact that a note is dishonored does not mean that it will be definitely uncollectible or that it should be written off to Allowance for Doubtful Accounts. Goodson, in this case, may pay at a later date, either voluntarily or on a court order. The account remains open in the accounts receivable ledger until it is settled or definitely determined to be uncollectible and written off.

DRAFTS

A *draft* is a written order to pay, such as a bank check, with the same negotiability as a note for which it is often used as a substitute. Commercial drafts, excluding checks, are used to enforce the collection of open accounts, to obtain the advantages of both a written acknowledgment and a negotiable instrument, and for C.O.D. (collect on delivery) shipments.

The person who issues the order and draws the draft is the *drawer;* the person to whom it is addressed and who is to make payment is the *drawee;* and the person to whom payment is to be made is the *payee.* If the drawer names himself as the payee—a common occurrence with commercial drafts—the draft becomes a two-party document similar to a note. The types of draft used in business are: (1) *ordinary checks,* (2) *certified checks,* (3) *cashier's or treasurer's checks,* (4) *sight drafts,* (5) *time drafts,* and (6) *trade acceptances.*

Ordinary Check

The most common form of the three-party draft is the ordinary check. It is used by most firms to make business payments. A check is a written order by a depositor for his bank to pay a specific sum of money to a designated person when the check is presented to the bank. The Cash account is credited when a check is written and debited when a check is received.

Certified Check

An ordinary bank check—personal or business—that has been stamped *Certified* and signed by an official of the bank is called a certified check. The bank official—having certified that the money is in the bank—immediately reduces the drawer's account and holds the amount in a special fund to pay the check on presentation. The check may be certified on the request of the drawer (to assure the payee of the availability of sufficient funds at the bank to pay the check) or of the holder (to insure prompt payment of the check when it is presented later by an ultimate *endorsee*). Certified checks often are used as a type of warranty deposit when a firm is bidding for a contract or ordering a special shipment of goods for the first time. As with the ordinary check, Cash is credited when a certified check is given and debited when a certified check is received.

Cashier's Check

A cashier's, or treasurer's, check is drawn by a bank against its own funds and may be purchased in the same manner as a money order or travelers' check. The treasurer of a state-chartered bank issues a treasurer's check, the cashier of a national bank issues a cashier's check—otherwise they are the same. The buyer pays the bank the full amount of the check plus a nominal fee and tells the bank to whom the check is to be made out—himself, a business firm, or another person. Since it is a bank check, it is signed by the bank; the name of the buyer of the check does not appear on it. Such checks are used either when a debtor does not have a checking account or when a personal check is not acceptable. Again, a cashier's check is treated from an accounting point of view as cash.

Sight Draft

A sight draft is a demand for payment drawn by the person to whom money is owed. Sight drafts may be used effectively when merchandise is shipped to another city to a new customer without an established credit rating. The sight draft, attached to the *order bill of lading* (the document authorizing the passage of title to the goods and a receipt given by the common carrier), is mailed to the customer's bank. Since the customer cannot get the merchandise without the bill of lading, the payment of the draft must precede receipt of the bill of lading and delivery of the goods by the warehouse or the transportation firm. To help account for the shipment of merchandise, a journal entry may be made at the time the sight draft is drawn, debiting Accounts Receivable and crediting Sales. No entry would be made for the draft itself at this time because the drawing of a draft is simply an intent until the draft is accepted. When the draft is honored by payment and the drawer is notified of the fact, Cash and any collection expense that may be charged by the bank are debited and Accounts Receivable is credited.

Time Draft

A time draft is due after the passage of a specified period of time. The drawer presents the instrument to the drawee, who indicates his agreement to pay the draft at maturity by writing "Accepted" across the face of the draft and signing it properly. The accounting entry is usually made on the drawee's book when the drawee accepts a time draft drawn by a creditor for an amount of a past-due open account is a debit to Accounts Payable and a credit to Notes Payable. When he receives the accepted draft from the debtor, the drawer debits Notes Receivable and credits Accounts Receivable. The accounting for any interest that the draft bears would be similar to that for notes. The interest may accrue from the date of the draft—*60 days from date*—or from the date the draft was accepted by drawee—*60 days from sight.*

Trade Acceptance

A trade acceptance is a special form of time draft used in connection with a specific sales transaction. The document is drawn by the seller of merchandise. Its acceptance by the buyer serves as an acknowledgment of the purchase, and it then assumes the same status as a note.

Trade acceptances may be used to insure prompt payment and to borrow money. Assume, for example, that the salesmen of the Sun Company (manufacturers of swimsuits) obtain orders from their customers during the months of November and December, 1968, for delivery in time for the 1969 summer season. Upon receipt of the orders, the Sun Company mails time drafts to the buyers for the total amount of each order, due in two equal installments on July 15, 1969, and August 15, 1969, less a 2-percent discount. The buyer signifies his acceptance of these terms by signing the time drafts, which then become trade acceptances. The Sun Company discounts the acceptances with its bank, thereby raising needed working capital for the manufacture of the product. The customers have also received extended credit terms and the 2% discount customarily granted by the Sun Company.

THE COST OF BORROWING MONEY

An essential factor in all short-term financial decisions is the effective cost of the particular means of financing. The rate of interest stated in loan documents often gives no indication of the effective annual cost of the loan. Loans arising out of the purchase of consumer goods on the installment plan, for example, frequently provide for a flat interest charge, often referred to as a *carrying charge,* on the full amount of the loan rather than on the unpaid balance remaining at the beginning of each period. Assume that an item may be purchased either for $600 in cash or for $6 down and $55 per month for 12 months. This is equivalent to borrowing $594 ($600 less $6 down payment). The cost of buying on the installment plan and the actual interest rate may be calculated by a laborious arithmetical sequence, as follows:

Down payment	$ 6
Monthly payment (12 × $55)	660
Total cost	$666
Cash price	600
Interest or carrying charge	$ 66

If it is assumed that each installment payment of $55 consists of a uniform monthly reduction of $5.50 in the carrying charge ($66 ÷ 12) and $49.50 on the principal ($594 ÷ 12), the balance of the loan outstanding at the end of each month is:

End of Month	Reduction of Principal	Balance of Principal
0	–0–	$ 594.00
1	$ 49.50	544.50
2	49.50	495.00
3	49.50	445.50
4	49.50	396.00
5	49.50	346.50
6	49.50	297.00
7	49.50	247.50
8	49.50	198.00
9	49.50	148.50
10	49.50	99.00
11	49.50	49.50
12	49.50	–0–
Totals	$594.00	$3,861.00

Monthly average balance outstanding ($3,861 ÷ 12)	$321.75
Annual interest rate for the 12-month period (interest of $66 ÷ $321.75)	20.51%

The computation in the example is for one year. If a different period of time is involved, a monthly rate of interest could be obtained and multiplied by 12 to obtain the annual interest rate.

Although the absolute interest sum ($66) is approximately 11 percent of the principal, the effective annual interest rate is in excess of 20 percent. The reason for the difference is that the principal amount is being decreased monthly by $49.50. For example, the borrower has the use of only $49.50 during the last month.

To avoid this laborious method, the following formula may be used:

$$\frac{2MC}{P(N + 1)} = i$$

where M = the number of payments that would be made if the term were one year
      C = the absolute amount of interest or carrying charge
      P = the principal sum (cash price less down payment)
      N = the total number of payments
      i = the effective annual rate of interest

Substituting the values in the example:

$$\frac{2 \times 12 \times \$66}{\$594(12 + 1)} = \frac{1584}{7722} = 20.51\%$$

The determination of the effective cost of borrowing money is especially important when the loan agreement does not state the effect of periodic loan repayments, carrying charges, insurance, clerical costs, legal fees, and so on. Management must have this information to make sound short-term financial decisions. The effective interest rate varies depending on the financial reputation of the customer, the size of the loan, the region, and cyclic fluctuations in interest rates. Although in a particular case the borrower may not be able to bargain for favorable terms, he should be fully aware of the effective cost involved and, whenever possible, choose the cheapest alternative means of short-term financing.

FULL DISCLOSURE

Accounting Concept: Full Disclosure ▶

Although financial statements are prepared primarily for the use of the owners, they are of increasing concern to government agencies, creditors, potential investors, employees, and others. ▶ The statements must provide the user with all the information he needs to make sound decisions regarding the business and its management. The CPA is bound by his code of ethics to disclose all the necessary facts known to him in order not to make the statements misleading; he must report any misstatements, omissions, or departures from generally accepted accounting principles. Disclosure of pertinent information may be made in the body of the statements, in footnotes appended to the statements, or in a covering report accompanying the statements. The principle of full disclosure extends to significant events occurring after the position statement date but before publication of the statements. ◀ The destruction of a vital part of the plant, for example, should be made known to the users of a position statement even if the event took place after the date of the statement.

Outstanding discounted notes typify the kind of information essential to the reader but sometimes omitted from the body of the statement. The fact that a contingent liability exists may affect the reader's decision concerning the company since it may ultimately turn into a liability. This information may be conveyed to the reader by offsetting Notes Receivable Discounted against the Notes Receivable account, or it may be shown in a footnote.

Significant information is hidden when the statements show only totals or net balances and when amounts are classified incorrectly. Essential data are being withheld, for example, if expenses are combined into one amount, if the book value of machinery is shown instead of the original cost less the accumulated depreciation, or if a loss on a lawsuit is charged to a miscellaneous expense account.

SUMMARY

Firms often find it more economical to obtain short-term financing rather than to pay cash for purchases. The particular type of short-term financing is dependent upon current and future availability and effective cost of the funds. The method or methods chosen should produce the desired short-term funds at the lowest long-run cost.

Perhaps the most common form of short-term financing is the purchase of goods on open account. The issuance of notes to creditors is another popular short-term financing device. A promissory note is a negotiable instrument that constitutes an unconditional written promise to pay a specified sum of money to the order of a designated person, or to bearer, at a fixed or determinable future time or on demand. On the books of the maker, the liability for a note is recorded by a credit to Notes Payable; on the books of the payee, the asset reflecting the right to receive a fixed sum of money at a future time is recorded by a debit to Notes Receivable. If the term of a note is expressed in months or years from the issuance date, the maturity date is determined by counting the months or years. If the term of the note is expressed in days, the maturity date is determined by counting forward the number of days—the issuance date is excluded and the maturity date included in the count.

Interest is the cost of obtaining money or credit—to the maker of a note, it is a cost for the use of money and thus an expense; to the payee of a note, it is compensation for lending the money and thus revenue. The amount of the interest payment on an interest-bearing note is computed by multiplying the three factors of (1) the face value of the note, (2) the specified interest rate, and (3) the term of the note stated as a fraction of an assumed commercial year of 360 days.

If a note is issued for the purchase of merchandise, it should first be recorded as a credit to the Accounts Payable account; then the amount is removed from this account by a debit and recorded as a credit in the Notes Payable account. If money is borrowed from a bank or other financial institution by the issuance of an interest-bearing note, then the borrower receives the face value of the note and at maturity must pay the face value plus the accrued interest. The accounting for a note of this type parallels the accounting for the issuance of a note for the settlement of an open account. If money is advanced from the bank, however, on a noninterest-bearing note discounted by the borrower, the borrower receives the face value of the note less the discount amount and at maturity must repay only the face value of the note. If the issuance and maturity dates are in the same accounting period, Interest Expense is debited for the discount amount. If the maturity date falls within a future accounting period, the discount amount is debited to Discount on Notes Payable, and at the end of the current accounting period an adjusting entry is made transferring the expense portion to Interest Expense. If a note payable is issued in the current accounting period but is not due until a future period, an adjusting entry recognizing the interest expense applicable to that period and the related liability is required on the maker's books at the end of the current period. On the books of the payee of the note, an adjusting entry recognizing the interest earned during the period and the related asset is required.

The accounting for notes receivable is typically the mirror-image of the accounting for notes payable. For emphasis, however, these points should be reiterated: (1) The receipt of a note for the sale of merchandise should first be recorded in the Accounts Receivable account for managerial purposes. (2) If a note receivable is renewed, an entry recognizing the issuance of the new note and the cancellation of the old is required. (3) If a note is dishonored at maturity, the face value of the note and any uncollected accrued interest—if the note is interest-bearing—should be transferred to the Accounts Receivable account.

Another short-term financing device is the discounting of customers' notes at a bank or other financial institution. The maker of the note, at maturity, pays the face value of the note and any interest accrued thereon to the bank. The discounter is liable for the amount due at maturity if the maker defaults. The cash obtained from the discounting of a note is the maturity value of the note less the discount amount, the bank charge for the loan. When a customer's note is discounted, the resultant contingent liability is recognized by a credit to Notes Receivable Discounted. This contingent liability may be reflected on the statement of financial position by deducting Notes Receivable Discounted from the total Notes Receivable thus deriving the net notes on hand in the Current Assets section, or by showing only the net notes on hand as a current asset and disclosing the contingent liability in a footnote.

A draft is a three-party instrument with the same negotiable characteristics of a note; some types of draft are often used as substitutes for promissory notes. Common forms include checks, certified checks, cashier's checks, sight drafts, time drafts, and trade acceptances.

Often, the interest rate stated in a loan document gives no indication of the effective cost of borrowing money. For example, installment contracts frequently provide for a carrying charge expressed as a percentage of the total contract price rather than as a percentage of the unpaid balance. Thus, in appraising the merits of various financing devices, one must look beyond the rates expressed in contracts and agreements and determine the effective rates to make valid comparisons.

☐ QUESTIONS

Q7-1. Explain the following terms or procedures: (a) negotiable instrument, (b) the 6-percent, 60-day method, (c) interest-bearing note, (d) the maker of a note, and (e) the payee of a note.

Q7-2. Explain the following terms or procedures: (a) discounting a note, (b) bank discount rate, (c) contingent liability, (d) proceeds, (e) maturity value, and (f) a dishonored note.

Q7–3. The accountant for the Nashua Company recorded the receipt of a note on a sale to John Lane as follows:

Notes Receivable	750	
Sales		750

State how you think the transaction should have been recorded and give your reason.

Q7–4. The Norman Company negotiated a 90-day loan (reference 1) with the Beacon Bank, which was paid on its due date (reference m). It arranged for another 90-day loan (reference x) with the Astor Bank, which was also paid when due (reference y).

Cash		Notes Payable to Bank		Interest Expense	
(1) 3,000	(m) 3,045	(m) 3,000	(1) 3,000	(m) 45	
(x) 2,955	(y) 3,000	(y) 3,000	(x) 3,000	(x) 45	

(a) Describe the type of negotiable instrument used by the Beacon Bank; (b) the Astor Bank. (c) Which loan is more favorable to the Norman Company? Why?

Q7–5. The following account balances appear in the general ledger of the Goodwin Company:

Notes Receivable		Notes Payable		Notes Receivable Discounted	
35,000			20,000		15,000

(a) What is the amount of customers' notes outstanding? (b) What amount of customer notes are in the Goodwin Company's possession? (c) What amount of customers' notes have been discounted? (d) What is the Goodwin Company's contingent liability on discounted notes? (e) Do the accounts furnish enough data to compute the Company's working capital position? (f) How would these accounts be shown in the position statement?

Q7–6. Six transactions related to a sale to a customer are recorded in the T accounts. Describe each transaction.

Cash		Accounts Receivable		Notes Receivable	
(c) 904	(d) 911	(a) 900	(b) 900	(b) 900	(e) 900
(f) 916		(d) 911	(f) 911		

Notes Receivable Discounted		Sales		Interest Earned	
(e) 900	(c) 900		(a) 900		(c) 4
					(f) 5

Q7-7. (a) What is a contingent liability? (b) May there be more than one person contingently liable on a particular note? Explain. (c) What amounts must a person who is contingently liable on an interest-bearing note pay if the maker dishonors the note on its due date?

Q7-8. (a) What is meant by the principle of full disclosure? (b) How is full disclosure effected in financial statements? (c) Should post-statement-date events be reported by the public accountant, assuming that the statements are still in the process of being prepared for publication?

Q7-9. (a) Does the rate of interest stated on a loan document necessarily reflect the actual cost of the loan? Explain. (b) What is meant by real annual interest? (c) How is the real annual interest rate computed?

Q7-10. Discuss the managerial factors that a company must consider in determining what method of short-term financing it should choose.

☐ **EXERCISES**

E7-1. Information regarding five notes is given:

Date of Note	Term of Note	Interest Rate	Principal
(1) March 1, 1969	60 days	4%	$1,250
(2) April 4, 1969	90 days	6%	1,500
(3) August 24, 1969	15 days	8%	3,965
(4) September 12, 1969	3 months	5%	1,560
(5) November 3, 1969	2 months	6%	675

Determine the maturity date and maturity value of each note.

E7-2. The following were among the transactions of the Boston Company for 1969 and 1970:

1969

Jan. 2 Purchased $4,400 worth of merchandise from the Ace Company, and issued a 6%, 45-day note.

Feb. 16 Paid note and interest due the Ace Company.

Mar. 15 Issued a 6%, 90-day note to the Persian Company in settlement of an open account of $5,000.

June 13 Paid the Persian Company $2,000 on principal and all the interest for the preceding 90 days; issued a new 7%, 60-day note for the balance of the principal.

Aug. 12 Paid the remaining amount due the Persian Company.

Nov. 25 Issued a 6%, 75-day note to the Melson Company in settlement of an open account of $6,600.

1970

Feb.   8   Paid the amount due the Melson Company.

Journalize the transactions, including any necessary adjusting entries on December 31, 1969.

E7-3. The following were among the transactions of the Drexel Company for 1969 and 1970:

1969

June 10   Discounted its own 90-day, noninterest-bearing note, made out to the Bank of Columbia in the principal amount of $4,000, at a discount rate of 4%.

Sept. 8   Paid the Bank of Columbia amount due.

Dec.   1   Discounted its own 90-day, noninterest-bearing note, made out to the National Bank in the principal amount of $3,900, at a discount rate of 6%. (Assume that the books are closed on December 31.)

1970

Mar.   1   Paid the amount due the National Bank.

Journalize the transactions, including any necessary adjusting entries on December 31, 1969 and 1970.

E7-4. The following were among the transactions of the Fetter Corporation for 1969 and 1970:

1969

Jan. 18   Sold merchandise worth $850 to H. Hiller and received a 6%, 70-day note.

Mar. 29   Collected the amount due from H. Hiller.

May 12   Received a 6%, 120-day note from B. Nottingham in settlement of an open account of $2,400.

Sept. 9   B. Nottingham dishonored his note.

Nov. 15   Received a 6%, 90-day note from R. Havelson in settlement of an open account of $3,000.

1970

Feb. 13   Collected the note and interest from R. Havelson.

Journalize the transactions, including any necessary adjusting entries as of December 31, 1969.

E7-5. The following were among the transactions of the Goodman Company for 1969 and 1970:

1969

Mar.   1   Received a 90-day, noninterest-bearing note from Albert Isaacs, the principal amount of which included a past due open account of $2,400 plus interest at 6% for 90 days. (The books are closed annually on December 31.)

May 30   Collected the amount due from Isaacs.

Dec.   1   Received a 120-day, noninterest-bearing note from Malcolm Salvan, the principal amount of which included a past due open account of $4,840 plus interest at 5% for 120 days.

1970

Mar. 31   Collected the amount due from Salvan.

Journalize the transactions, including any necessary adjusting entries on December 31, 1969 and 1970.

E7–**6.** Phillips, Inc., completed the following transactions in 1969:

1969

Aug.   1   Sold $600 worth of merchandise to the Range Company on account.

Oct.   8   Received a 90-day, 6% note in full settlement of account.

Dec.   5   Discounted the note at 5% at the Merchants Bank.

1970

Jan.   6   The note was paid at maturity.

Journalize the transactions on the books of Phillips, Inc., and the Range Company, including any necessary adjusting entries on December 31, 1969.

E7–**7.** On September 5, 1969, the A and D Television Company sold $1,800 worth of merchandise to Mitchell Company on account and received a 5-percent, 60-day note. This note was discounted at 6 percent on October 20, 1969, at the Foxboro Trust Company. At maturity date the note was dishonored by the Mitchell Company and the A and D Television Company paid the maturity value plus a $2.50 protest fee.

Journalize the transactions on the books of the A and D Television Company.

E7–**8.** Richard Evans received a 6-percent, 120-day note for $3,000 from Edward Larkin, dated March 3, 1969. Evans discounted Larkin's note 30 days later at 8 percent with William Reynolds. Larkin paid the note at maturity.

Journalize the transactions on the books of Evans and of Reynolds.

E7–**9.** Kenneth Secord owed the Frank Marston Company $850 for merchandise that he had purchased. Since the debt was past due, Marston drew a sight draft and sent it to Secord's bank for collection. Secord paid the sight draft. The bank charged $1.50 for its services.

Journalize the transactions on the books of Kenneth Secord and the Frank Marston Company.

E7–**10.** The Molurta Company accepts trade notes from its customers. As of December 31, 1969, it had accepted only one: a 5-percent, 90-day note on December 1, 1969. At the end of the year, the following adjusting entry was made:

1969

Dec. 31   Accrued Interest Receivable   10.25
         Interest Earned   10.25
               To record interest at 5% for 30 days on
               the note received from K. V. Barr on
               December 1 in settlement of an open
               account receivable.

Reconstruct the entry made on December 1 to record the receipt of the note from K. V. Barr. Show all your calculations.

☐ DEMONSTRATION PROBLEMS

DP7-1. (*Computing maturity dates*) The following notes were received by Allison, Inc.:

Date of Note	Term of Note
March 10, 1969	60 days
April 4, 1969	90 days
March 10, 1969	2 months
April 4, 1969	3 months
January 31, 1969	1 month

Required: Determine the maturity date of each note.

DP7-2. (*Computing interest by short-cut methods*) The following information pertains to five notes:

1. $3,200 at 6% for 60 days
2. $4,600 at 6% for 30 days
3. $2,400 at 6% for 72 days
4. $6,600 at 5% for 60 days
5. $9,000 at 7½% for 45 days

Required: Using the short-cut methods discussed in this chapter, compute the amount of interest on each note.

DP7-3. (*Journalizing notes payable transactions*) The Thompson Company completed the following transactions during 1969 and 1970:

1969

Jan. 2 Purchased $3,680 worth of merchandise from the Nolta Company; issued a 6%, 60-day note.

Mar. 3 Paid the Nolta Company the amount due for the note and interest.

       3 Issued a 6%, 45-day note for $4,000 to Owens, Inc., in settlement of an open account.

Apr. 17 Paid Owens, Inc., $3,000 on the March 3 note plus all the interest; issued a new 7%, 30-day note for the balance of the principal.

May 17 Paid Owens, Inc., for the April 17 note.

June 1 Discounted its own 30-day, noninterest-bearing note, made out to the First National Bank in the amount of $8,000, at a discount rate of 6%.

July 1 Paid the First National Bank the amount due.

Dec. 1 Issued a 6%, 90-day note for $5,680 to the Petersen Company in settlement of an open account.

Dec. 16 Discounted its own 60-day, noninterest-bearing note, made out to the Second National Bank in the amount of $10,000, at a discount rate of 6%.

1970

Feb. 14 Paid the Second National Bank the amount due.

Mar. 1 Paid amount due to Petersen Company for the note issued on December 1, 1969.

Journalize the transactions, including any necessary adjusting entries on December 31, 1969 and 1970.

DP7-**4.** (*Journalizing note receivable transactions*) The following were among the transactions of the Queens Company for 1969 and 1970:

1969
Jan. 6 Sold merchandise worth $1,860 to I. Rose and received a 6%, 45-day note.
Feb. 20 Collected the amount due from I. Rose.
Mar. 1 Received a 6%, 75-day note for $3,400 from N. Richards in settlement of an open account.
May 15 N. Richards dishonored his note.
June 1 Sold merchandise worth $2,000 to W. Walters and received a 90-day, noninterest-bearing note for the amount of the sale plus interest at 6%.
Aug. 30 Collected the amount due from W. Walters.
Nov. 16 Received a 6%, 120-day note for $4,860 from J. Aikens in settlement of an open account.
Dec. 1 Received a 90-day, noninterest-bearing note from H. Barrow in settlement of an open account of $4,400. The note had interest of $66 included in the face value.

1970
Mar. 1 Received the amount due from H. Barrow.
    16 Received the amount due from J. Aikens.

Journalize the transactions, including any necessary adjusting entries on December 31, 1969 and 1970.

DP7-**5.** (*Journalizing note discounted transactions*) Record in general journal form the following note transactions on the books of S. Young, the maker, and W. Highland, the payee:

a. On July 1, S. Young purchased $4,900 worth of merchandise on account from W. Highland.
b. S. Young gave a 6%, 90-day note, dated August 21, to W. Highland in settlement of his account.
c. On August 31, W. Highland discounted S. Young's note at the Second Street Bank at a discount rate of 6%.
d. On the maturity date, S. Young paid the bank the maturity value of the note.

DP7-**6.** (*Effective interest computation*) The following transactions took place at the Harrod Company:

a. Discounted its own 90-day, noninterest-bearing note for $5,000 at a bank at 6%.
b. Borrowed $4,800 in cash from a bank; interest at 5% on $4,800 is added to the note, making the principal amount of the note $5,040; the note is to be paid off in monthly installments over 12 months ($420 each month).

Compute the effective interest cost in each case.

☐ **PROBLEMS**

P7-**1.** The Samuel Marcus Company completed the following transactions with Gerald Lucas:

1969

Jan. 10 Sold $1,250 worth of merchandise to Lucas on account.

Mar. 1 Received a 6%, 60-day note in full settlement of the account.

17 Discounted the note at 4% at the Seamen's Bank.

May 5 Received a notice from the bank that Lucas failed to honor the note.

5 Paid the bank the maturity value of the note plus a protest fee of $2.50.

19 Received a check from Lucas for the full amount due, plus interest at 6% on the maturity value of the old note from the due date to the present.

Record the transactions in general journal form on the books of the Samuel Marcus Company.

P7–**2.** Mario Alves borrowed $3,500 from the Pilgrim Trust Company, giving his 6-percent, 60-day note. On the same day, Alves borrowed from the United Trust Company by discounting his $3,500 note for 60 days at 6 percent.

Required: 1. Give the entries in general journal form to: (a) record both bank loans, and (b) record the payments of the loans on the maturity date.

2. Explain which loan was more favorable to Alves.

P7–**3.** During 1969, the Walter Hersey Company completed the following transactions, among others:

1969

Jan. 5 Sold merchandise worth $2,800 to C. T. Perkins on account.

7 Received a 6%, 30-day note, dated January 7, from C. T. Perkins, payable at the National Shawmut Bank.

8 Purchased $3,400 worth of merchandise from the E. Beale Company, giving a 4%, 45-day note payable at the Second National Bank.

10 Purchased $2,000 worth of merchandise from the J. A. Nelson Company on account.

15 Gave the J. A. Nelson Company a 4½%, 60-day note in settlement of the account, payable at the Second National Bank.

17 Sold merchandise worth $900 to the A. F. Duling Company on account.

19 Sold merchandise worth $3,400 to Charles J. Collins on account.

21 Received a 3%, 20-day note, dated January 20, from the A. F. Duling Company, payable at the Merchants Trust Company.

22 Received a 4%, 50-day note from Charles J. Collins, payable at the First National Bank.

28 Purchased $5,500 worth of merchandise from the C. A. Gerden Company, giving a 6%, 75-day note, payable at the National Shawmut Bank, in full payment.

30 Discounted its own $6,000 note for 30 days at 6% with the Second Federal Bank.

31 Purchased $400 worth of merchandise from the D. W. Haley Company. A 1% cash discount was allowed upon signing two trade acceptances of equal amount due March 1 and April 1 and payable at the Guaranty Bank and Trust Company.

Feb. 1 Discounted Charles J. Collins' note of January 22 at the Acton National Bank at 6%.

Feb. 6   Received payment from C. T. Perkins for his note of January 7.

     10   The A. F. Duling Company dishonored its note of January 21.

     23   Paid the E. Beale Company for the note of January 8.

Mar. 1   Paid the Second Federal Bank for the loan made on January 30.

      1   Paid the D. W. Haley Company for the first trade acceptance.

     15   Charles J. Collins paid the bank for his note due on March 13.

Required: Record the transactions in general journal form.

P7–4. During 1969, the Indeck Manufacturing Company completed the following transactions, among others:

1969

Jan. 3   Purchased merchandise worth $4,500 from the A. L. Kalman Company
           giving a 6%, 30-day note, payable at the First National Bank.

      4   Sold $3,000 worth of merchandise to S. M. Friedberg on account.

      6   Sold $4,500 worth of merchandise to C. D. Burch on account.

      8   Purchased merchandise worth $500 from McDermott & Company on
           account.

     10   Gave McDermott & Company a 4%, 30-day note, payable at the Merchants
           Trust Company.

     12   C. D. Burch gave a 4%, 20-day note, payable at the First National Bank.

     15   S. M. Friedberg gave a 5%, 30-day note, payable at the National Shawmut
           Bank.

     16   Sold $3,200 worth of merchandise to E. Hazelwood, Inc., on account.

     24   Received a 6%, 20-day note, payable at the Worcester County Trust Com-
           pany, from E. Hazelwood, Inc.

     24   Sold $7,500 worth of merchandise to Fenn & Company and received a
           4%, 30-day note, payable at the Second National Bank.

Feb. 1   C. D. Burch's note of January 12 was dishonored.

      2   Paid the A. L. Kalman Company for the note due today.

      9   Paid the McDermott Company for the note due today.

     13   Received a check from E. Hazelwood, Inc., for $1,200 plus interest, and
           accepted a new 6%, 90-day note payable at the Worcester County Trust
           Company for the balance of the note of January 24.

     14   Received payment from S. M. Friedberg in payment of his note due today.

     23   Received a check from Fenn & Company for $3,500 plus interest, and
           accepted a new 4%, 30-day note payable at the Second National Bank for
           the balance of the note of January 24.

     28   Discounted Fenn & Company's note of February 23 at the Lynn Bank at
           6%.

Mar. 25   Received notice that Fenn & Company had dishonored its note of February
           23. Paid the bank the maturity value of the note plus a $3 protest fee.

Required: Record the transactions in general journal form.

P7–5. On November 1, 1969, the Evans Company adopted a policy of requesting customers
whose accounts have become past due to substitute interest-bearing notes for the
open account. In many cases, the Company discounts the notes receivable obtained
from customers. The bank charges a 6-percent discount on such transactions.

The following ledger accounts reflect the note transactions, interest expense, and interest earned during November and December. The Company closes its books at the end of the calendar year, December 31.

Notes Receivable   Acct. No. 111

1969					1969				
Nov.	6	J. Johns, 30-day	J2	700	Dec.	6	J. Johns	J4	700
	24	D. M. Bell, 60-day	CD1	1,500					
Dec.	12	A. G. Lee, 90-day	J6	4,000					
	18	K. Murray, 5%, 30-day	J7	1,200					

Notes Receivable Discounted   Acct. No. 111A

					1969				
					Dec.	9	D. M. Bell	CR1	1,500
						20	K. Murray	CR1	1,200

Notes Payable   Acct. No. 202

					1969				
					Nov.	18	B. E. Ray, 5%, 90-day (settle open account)	J3	2,100

Interest Earned   Acct. No. 311

					1969				
					Dec.	6	J. Johns	J4	3.50
						9	D. M. Bell	CR1	3.64
						31	Adjustment	J10	12.67

Interest Expense   Acct. No. 713

1969									
Dec.	20	K. Murray	CR1	.62					
	31	Adjustment	J10	12.54					

Required: 1. Prepare in general journal form all the entries made by the Evans Company to record the information in the ledger accounts. Assume that all the notes bear interest at the rate of 6 percent, unless otherwise indicated. Also assume that the accounts include the necessary adjustments for interest at December 31. For the two notes receivable discounted, determine whether the bank in fact charged interest at an annual rate of 6 percent (show your computation).

2. Show how the facts regarding all the notes should be disclosed in the statement of financial position.

P7–**6.** On June 30, the Malone Company's trial balance included the following accounts:

Notes Receivable	$12,600
Notes Receivable Discounted (credit)	5,000

The notes receivable register showed the following supporting details:

Note No.	Face Value	Date of Note	Term of Note	Interest Rate	Remarks
1	$3,000	May 29, 1969	60 days	5%	Discounted at bank on June 30, 1969. Bank discount rate, 4%.
2	2,000	May 1, 1969	120 days	6%	Discounted at bank on June 16, 1969. Bank discount rate, 4%.
3	4,000	June 16, 1969	30 days	4%	
4	3,600	June 21, 1969	90 days	6%	

The disposition of the four notes was:

Note 1: Paid at the bank by the maker on the maturity date.

Note 2: Dishonored by the maker. The Malone Company paid the bank the maturity value of the note plus a $3 protest fee.

Note 3: Paid by the maker on the maturity date.

Note 4: On July 10, 1969, the Malone Company had its own $3,000 noninterest-bearing note due at the bank. Malone Company paid its $3,000 note by discounting Note 4 (the bank discount rate was 4%) and received the balance due in cash. The maker of Note 4 paid the bank on the maturity date.

Required: Prepare dated general journal entries to record the disposition of each note.

P7–**7.** The Home Appliance Company sells a standard refrigerator for $240 in cash or on terms of $25 down and $40 a month for six months. In order to meet competition, the Company is considering changing its credit terms to a $25 down payment and $20 a month for 12 months.

Required: Compute the real annual interest rate under (a) the present plan and (b) the proposed plan. Carry your computations to two decimal places. Assume that each installment includes a uniform monthly reduction in the carrying charge.

P7–**8.** At December 31, 1969, the Reeson Appliance Company's ledger contained the following information in the Notes Receivable and Notes Payable accounts:

Analysis of Notes Receivable:

Maker	Date of Note	Principal	Term of Note	Interest Rate	Remarks
	1969				
A. Able	November 2	$ 2,380	90 days	6%	
W. Cutler	December 8	3,460	60 days	5%	
M. Bower	December 16	4,488	90 days		Interest of $88 included in face value.
Total		$10,328			

Analysis of Notes Payable:

Payee	Date of Note	Principal	Term of Note	Interest Rate	Remarks
Dawer Company	November 10, 1969	$3,670	120 days	4½%	
Evart Company	November 20, 1969	2,860	90 days	6%	
State Bank	December 1, 1969	3,600	120 days		Discounted at 6%.

Required: Prepare the adjusting journal entries. Show your calculations, properly labeled.

CASE PROBLEM
Albert's Home Products Company

Albert's Home Products Company is a large retail operation that specializes in household appliances such as refrigerators, ranges, water heaters, washing machines, dryers, and air conditioners. It has been in business for a number of years and has developed a good reputation. The firm maintains perpetual inventory records to account for appliances sold and on hand.

The firm uses a different method of financing purchases from each of four dealers, as follows:

1. Eastinghouse, Inc., forwards a *demand for payment* (sight draft) to the Company's bank, the Chatham Bank, when it ships merchandise. Upon receiving the demand, the bank pays Eastinghouse, Inc., thereby making Albert's Home Products Company liable to the bank for the amount. The Company is required to pay the bank immediately upon sale of the particular appliance. The bank charges interest at 5 percent.
2. Scorch-Point, Inc., accepts promissory notes from the Company in payment for its appliances. A separate note is prepared for each appliance, and is due immediately upon the sale of the appliance. Interest is charged at 4 percent.
3. The Sergeant Electric Company places its appliances in the showroom or warehouse of the Company. The Company does not actually buy any item from Sergeant until a customer buys the same item from the Company. In other words, there is a simultaneous purchase and sale by Albert's Home Products Company.
4. Servinator, Inc., ships products to the Company C. O. D. Therefore, when shipments are received, Albert's Home Products Company must make immediate payment. The Company issues a promissory note to the Chatham Bank, and the bank increases the checking account balance of the Company. The checking account balance includes a deposit that will later be equal to the check issued to Servinator, Inc. Albert's Home Products Company is required to pay the bank immediately upon sale of the appliance. The bank charges interest at 5 percent.

The firm also uses different financing methods when selling the appliances to its customers, as follows:

1. Some customers pay cash for an appliance at the time of the sale.
2. Some preferred customers are permitted to charge their purchases on open account, at terms of n/30 or n/60.
3. The remaining customers sign promissory notes, which will be paid according to agreed dates. These notes include interest and carrying charges in the face value. The Company computes interest at a 6-percent annual rate, and carrying charges are a standard amount of $10.

a. Some of these promissory notes are discounted at the local bank at a rate of 5 percent. Customers pay the bank directly for discounted notes. The Company remains contingently liable for the notes.

b. The notes that are not discounted at the bank are held by the Company, requiring the customer to make payments directly to Albert's Home Products Company.

During 1969, the following selected transactions took place:

Sept. 1   Placed an order with Eastinghouse, Inc., for a $125 water heater. On September 15, the heater was received and the sight draft was received and honored by the bank. On October 20, the heater was sold for $180 in cash; on the same day, the company fulfilled its commitment to the bank.

April 20   Ordered a range that cost $240 from Scorch-Point, Inc. On May 1, the range was received and the Company immediately issued a promissory note. On May 22, a preferred customer, William Rocke, purchased the range for $315 on open account; terms n/30. Both Albert's Home Products Company and Rocke paid their creditors on the due dates.

Mar. 20   Placed an order with the Sergeant Electric Company for an air conditioner costing $150. On April 7, the air conditioner was received. On June 1, the air conditioner was sold to Timothy Michaels for $260. Michaels chose to sign a promissory note for his purchase. Since he is expecting a Christmas bonus from his employer, he asked that the note mature on January 2. The face value of the note includes the cost of the appliance, the interest, and the standard carrying charge. The Company discounted the note at the bank on July 1. On the following January 2, Michaels paid the bank the amount of the note. Albert's Home Products Company and the Sergeant Electric Company handled the transactions between themselves in the customary way.

June 4   Placed an order with Servinator, Inc., for a refrigerator costing $265. On June 14, the appliance was received C.O.D. and a check was issued in payment; on the same day, a note was signed at the bank and the bank made a deposit to the Company's checking account. On July 10, the refrigerator was sold to Lawrence Davis for $350. Davis signed a promissory note for the purchase price plus interest to November 10 and the carrying charge. Both Albert's Home Products Company and Davis paid their creditors on the due dates.

Required: 1. Record the transactions in general journal form. Arrange the transactions by appliances in chronological order and indicate the dates. Pay close attention to the dates and the interest rates.

2. Indicate in a form similar to the following outline the net effect of each transaction on the accounts indicated. Use a plus sign (+) to indicate an increase, a minus sign (−) to indicate a decrease, and a zero (0) to indicate no effect. The transaction of September 15 is given as an example.

Transaction Date	Current Assets	Current Liabilities	Owners' Equity	Net Income
September 15	+	+	0	0

3. Describe the relationship of the full disclosure concept to these procedures. Justify the validity of the concept.

Chapter Eight

Controlling and Forecasting Cash

Cash includes any item that a bank customarily accepts for deposit. Coins, *currency* (paper money), bank drafts, cashier's checks, money orders, and bank balances are included in the Cash account. Postdated checks and I.O.U.'s are receivables, not cash; postage stamps are prepaid expenses.

Effective management and control of cash is of the greatest importance because cash represents instantly available purchasing power and because nearly every transaction ultimately involves the exchange of cash. The problems of good cash management are twofold: (1) a proper cash balance must be maintained at all times, and (2) adequate safeguards must be established to prevent the theft, or misappropriation, of cash. While emphasizing the control of cash, this chapter deals with *petty cash, bank reconciliation,* and *cash forecasting.*

INTERNAL CONTROL

One of the primary functions of management is to protect the assets of a business against avoidable loss. As a business grows in size and complexity, it becomes increasingly important to organize the supervision of the bookkeeping and accounting records to control the receipt of cash, to minimize or prevent the unauthorized disbursement of cash, and to eliminate errors. Employees must be carefully selected and trained, and their duties, responsibilities, and authority clearly defined. Adequate organization also requires the separation of duties, so that no one person is in complete charge of any business transaction. An error—whether intentional or not—is more likely to be discovered if a transaction is handled by two or more persons, so that, as far as possible, the work of each employee who records property is checked automatically by some other employee. It is customary business practice, for example, for one person to make the sale and prepare a sales slip and for another person to receive the cash or record the charge to the customer's account; one person may prepare the payroll and another person make the actual payments to employees; one employee may prepare the check for payment to a creditor, another employee or an officer may sign the check, and a third employee may post the debit to the creditor's account. Adequate organization also provides for a regular follow-up to see how well the accounting work is being done. This system of self-policing is referred to as *internal control.*

Cash Control

Cash is naturally vulnerable to theft or misuse. If cash is handled and controlled properly, both the employer and the employee benefit—the employer safeguards the asset and the employee avoids suspicion of inaccuracy or dishonesty. Embezzlers often begin their criminal careers by temporarily borrowing funds from the company, intending to replace the cash. The intention usually falters. It is to the advantage of both employer and employee to institute such safeguards as will deter employees from misappropriating funds. The safeguards must be designed to prevent the following:

1. Misappropriation of cash on receipt and failure to record the transaction in the cash receipts journal. For example, scrap and waste material may be sold by an employee to a scrap dealer for cash and not reported.
2. Delay in recording the receipt of cash (the cash being withheld during the interval), or recording false entries. For example, cash may be pocketed on receipt of a payment from a customer but his account may be credited with an offsetting debit to Sales Returns and Allowances.
3. The recording of fictitious charges to expense accounts or other accounts to cover fraudulent cash withdrawals. For example, a branch supervisor may carry a terminated employee's name on the payroll for several additional pay periods, forging the endorsement of the former employee and appropriating the cash.

Certain basic controls must be instituted to prevent the misuse of funds. The individual responsibility for the flow of cash must be clearly established. An entry to record the receipt of cash must be made promptly. All checks should be rubber-stamped *For deposit only* on receipt to prevent their misuse. All cash receipts should be deposited intact daily; payments should be made by company check and not out of receipts. Mechanical accounting control devices should be used wherever possible.

The protection of cash against losses through fraud, error, and carelessness requires certain fundamental steps, including:

1. A clear segregation of duties and responsibilities.
2. Provision of the necessary facilities, such as cash registers, and furnishing definite instructions with respect to authorization for the removal of property or the payment of cash.
3. Organization of the flow and recording of documents so that, whenever possible, the work of one employee is subject to automatic verification by

another employee. The handling and recording of cash should be so planned that no one person both receives or disburses cash and records it in the cash journals.

4. Periodic testing to see if internal controls are operating effectively. Recorded cash receipts, for example, should be compared at unannounced times with cash on hand and deposits made.

Petty Cash

For adequate internal control, all cash receipts should be deposited intact daily and all disbursements should be made by check. There are occasions, however, when payment by check is impractical, such as for postage, small contributions, express charges, carfare, and minor supplies. A special fund, called the *petty cash fund*, should be set up for these purposes. The fund is placed in the charge of one person, and payments should be supported by signed receipts, called *petty cash vouchers*, that show the purpose of the expenditures, the dates, and the amounts.

To set up the petty cash fund, a check is drawn and cashed for the amount to be placed in the fund. The journal entry is:

Petty Cash	50	
Cash		50

The money and the signed vouchers should be secured in the *petty cash box.* An analysis sheet is maintained to record disbursements from the fund, as illustrated in Figure 8-1.

Figure 8-1.
*Petty Cash
Analysis Sheet*

PETTY CASH ANALYSIS SHEET

Date	Explanation	Voucher Number	Amount Received	Petty Cash Paid	Postage Expense	Telephone and Telegraph Expense	Misc. Selling Expense	Misc. General Expense	Other Accounts Account Title	Other Accounts Amount
1969										
Apr. 1	Fund established (Check 75)		50.00							
3	Postage	1		4.00	4.00					
7	Windows cleaned	2		3.50				3.50		
9	Express–Williams Co.	3		4.25					Transportation In	4.25
12	Telegram–Wilson	4		1.75		1.75				
17	Envelopes–Allen Co.	5		4.50					Stationery & Printing	4.50
19	Entertainment–Maynard	6		8.50			8.50			
24	Tip to delivery boy	7		.25				.25		
27	Telegram–Holmes Co.	8		2.25		2.25				
28	Ad in *Weekly News*	9		6.00			6.00			
30	Postage	10		8.00	8.00					
30	Totals		50.00	43.00	12.00	4.00	14.50	3.75		8.75
30	Balance			7.00						
			50.00	50.00						
May 1	Balance		7.00							
1	Replenishment (Check 168)		43.00							

When the cash on hand approaches a stated minimum—or at the end of each month—the fund is replenished; the signed petty cash vouchers serve as evidence of the disbursements. The entry in the cash disbursements journal to record a check for $43 issued to replenish the petty cash fund is:

Postage Expense	12.00	
Telephone and Telegraph Expense	4.00	
Miscellaneous Selling Expense	14.50	
Miscellaneous General Expense	3.75	
Transportation In	4.25	
Stationery and Printing Expense	4.50	
Cash		43.00

The Petty Cash account in the general ledger remains at its original balance of $50. It does not change unless the amount of the fund itself is either increased or decreased. It is for this reason that the method described here is called the *imprest* (or fixed) petty cash system. The fund should be replenished at the end of each accounting period to record all the expenses incurred during the period and to bring the amount of cash on hand in the fund up to the balance of the Petty Cash account in the general ledger.

The Bank Statement

It is customary for banks to send depositors a monthly statement together with the canceled checks and notices of bank charges and credits. The statement shows the activities for the month; it should list:

1. The beginning balance
2. The deposits received
3. The checks paid
4. Other charges and credits to the account
5. The ending balance

Frederick Hall's bank statement for September, 1969, is shown in Figure 8-2.

The letter combinations listed in the lower section of the bank statement form identify certain entries on the statement.

CERTIFIED CHECK (CC). When the depositor requests a check to be certified, the bank immediately deducts the amount of the check from the depositor's balance.

TOTAL OF LISTED CHECKS (LS). A number of checks issued by the depositor may be presented to the bank for payment on the same day. To conserve space, the bank shows only one entry for the total and attaches a listing of the individual amounts to the checks themselves.

NOT SUFFICIENT FUNDS (NSF). Deposits generally include checks received from trade customers. A customer's check that has been deposited may not clear upon presentation for payment because the customer's bank balance is less than the amount of the check. If so, the check is deducted from the depositor's balance, the entry is identified by the letters NSF, and the check is returned to the depositor. The legal authority for this deduction by the bank is established when the depositor endorses the customer's check at the time of deposit.

SERVICE CHARGE (SC). A service charge is a charge by the bank for acting as a depository for funds. The charge is based on the activity of the account in terms of

STATEMENT OF ACCOUNT
WITH
UNITED STATES TRUST COMPANY
BOSTON, MASS.

Frederick Hall
14 Billings Street
Boston, Mass., 02115

Acct. No. 037-325079

Figure 8-2.
Bank Statement

Checks and Other Debits			Deposits	Date	Balance
Balance forward from last statement				Sept. 1, 1969	7,320.00
			450.00	Sept. 1	7,770.00
49.00	1,237.00			Sept. 2	6,484.00
			48.00	Sept. 3	6,532.00
175.00	1,300.00 CC			Sept. 6	5,057.00
14.00			1,650.00	Sept. 11	6,693.00
			762.00	Sept. 15	7,455.00
28.50	27.25	275.00	1,312.00	Sept. 18	8,436.25
2,000.00	367.00	2.00 DM	500.00 CM	Sept. 29	6,567.25
4.00 SC				Sept. 30	6,563.25

CC—Certified Check	DM—Debit Memo
LS—Total of Listed Checks	CM—Credit Memo
NSF—Not Sufficient Funds	OD—Overdraft
SC—Service Charge	

number of items deposited and checks presented for payment. Credit is generally allowed for interest on the average daily balance.

DEBIT MEMO (DM). A debit memo is a deduction from the depositor's account for additional services rendered (or an adjustment of an error); for example, the charge for collecting a note receivable is reported in a debit memo.

CREDIT MEMO (CM). A credit memo is a credit, usually shown in the Deposits column, for items collected (or an adjustment of an error); for example, the collection of a note receivable left at the bank by a depositor is reported in a credit memo.

OVERDRAFT (OD). An overdraft is the amount by which withdrawals exceed the depositor's available balance. The overdraft, if permitted, is usually entered in red in the Balance column. Because of automatic bank loan renewal arrangements or for other reasons, a bank may pay checks even when an overdraft results.

Depositor's Monthly Bank Reconciliation Procedure

The use of a checking account facilitates the control of cash. If all cash receipts are deposited intact and all cash payments are made by check, the records of the bank can be *reconciled* regularly with those of the depositor. The *bank reconciliation* underscores the reciprocal relationship between the bank's records and the depositor's. For each entry in the depositor's books, there should be a counterpart in the bank's books. All debits to Cash in the depositor's books should be matched by credit entries to the depositor's account in the bank's books; all credit entries to Cash in the depositor's books should be matched by debit entries to the depositor's account. For instance, cash received from a customer is recorded in the company's books by debiting Cash and crediting Accounts Receivable; the bank, upon receiving the cash, debits Cash and credits the depositor's account. The company records a payment to a creditor by debiting Accounts Payable and crediting Cash; the bank debits the depositor's account and credits Cash.

Assuming that every item was properly recognized, no errors were made, and the beginning balances were equal, the reciprocal accounts would show the following:

DEPOSITOR'S BOOKS
Cash (Name of Bank)   Acct. No. 101

Opening balance	Checks issued
Deposits made to bank	Bank debit memos
Bank credit memos	

BANK'S BOOKS
Frederick Hall   Acct. No. 037-325079

Checks cleared	Opening balance
Debit memos	Deposits received
	Credit memos

The records of the depositor and of the bank will not normally agree at the end of the month because of items that appear on one record but not on the other. It is necessary, therefore, to reconcile the two balances and to determine the *adjusted*, or true, cash balance. Discrepancies between the balances may be due to the time lag in recording debits and credits, special charges and credits of which either the depositor or the bank is unaware, or errors and irregularities.

The bank reconciliation is prepared as follows:

1. The deposits shown on the bank statement are compared with those entered in the cash receipts journal. Deposits made too late in the month to be credited by the bank on the current statement are referred to as *deposits in transit.* The bank reconciliation for the previous month should be inspected for any deposits in transit at the end of that period; they should appear as the initial deposits of the current period. Any items not on the statement should be reconciled.

2. Checks paid and returned by the bank (*canceled checks*) are arranged in numerical order and compared with the entries in the cash disbursements journal. Checks that have not yet been presented for payment are called *outstanding checks.* The previous bank reconciliation should be inspected for outstanding checks.

3. Special debits and credits made by the bank—usually reported in debit or credit memos—are compared with the depositor's books to see if they have already been recorded.

4. Any errors in the bank's or the depositor's records that become apparent during completion of the prior steps are listed.

A pro forma bank reconciliation is given in Figure 8-3. Errors and adjustments in the Per Books section require entries in the general journal to correct the books; adjustments in the Per Bank section do not require entries.

Figure 8-3.
Pro Forma
Bank
Reconciliation

NAME
Bank Reconciliation
Date

Per Books

Cash balance per ledger				$xxx
Add	(1)	Any proper increases in cash already recorded by the bank that have not been recorded as yet by the firm		
		Example: Collection of note by bank	$xx	
	(2)	Any error in the firm's books that failed to reveal a proper increase in cash or that improperly decreased cash		
		Example: Check from customer for $90 entered as $70	xx	xx
		Total		$xxx
Deduct	(1)	Any proper decreases in cash already recorded by the bank that have not been recorded as yet by the firm		
		Example: Bank service charges	$xx	
	(2)	Any error in the firm's books that failed to reveal a proper decrease in cash or that improperly increased cash		
		Example: Check issued in payment to a creditor for $462 entered as $426	xx	xx
Adjusted cash balance				$xxx

Per Bank

Cash balance per bank statement				$xxx
Add	(1)	Any proper increases in cash already recorded by the firm that have not been recorded as yet by the bank		
		Example: Deposits in transit	$xx	
	(2)	Any error by the bank that failed to reveal a proper increase in cash or that improperly decreased cash		
		Example: Another depositor's check incorrectly charged to this depositor's account	xx	xx
		Total		$xxx
Deduct	(1)	Any proper decreases in cash already recorded by the firm that have not been recorded as yet by the bank		
		Example: Outstanding checks	$xx	
	(2)	Any error by the bank that failed to reveal a proper decrease in cash or that improperly increased cash		
		Example: Firm's deposit of $679 entered by bank as $697	xx	xx
Adjusted cash balance				$xxx

Frederick Hall's August bank reconciliation is shown in Figure 8-4. Note that the ending cash balance per the bank is the same as the beginning balance of the September statement (Figure 8-2).

FREDERICK HALL
Bank Reconciliation
August 31, 1969

Cash balance per ledger, August 31, 1969		$6,400
Adjusted cash balance, August 31, 1969		$6,400
Cash balance per bank statement,		
August 31, 1969		$7,320
Add deposit in transit, August 31, 1969		450
Total		$7,770
Deduct outstanding checks		

Figure 8-4. *Bank Reconciliation*

Check	Amount	
680	$ 49	
694	1,237	
701	84	$1,370
Adjusted cash balance, August 31, 1969		$6,400

Hall's cash records for September show the following:

Cash deposits

1969	
Sept. 3	$ 48.00
10	1,650.00
14	762.00
18	1,312.00
30	1,050.00
	$4,822.00

Checks issued

1969		
Sept. 2	702	$ 175.00
5	703	1,300.00
8	704	14.00
15	705	82.50
15	706	312.25
18	707	27.25
26	708	2,000.00
26	709	367.00
30	710	103.00
		$4,381.00

The statement received from the bank (Figure 8-2) shows a balance of $6,563.25 as of September 30, 1969. The following items were received from the bank together with the bank statement:

Canceled checks:

Check	Amount
680	$ 49.00
694	1,237.00
702	175.00
703	1,300.00
704	14.00
705	28.50
707	27.25
708	2,000.00
709	367.00
Check of Frederick Hale	275.00

Memos:

Credit memo, $500, for a note receivable collected by the bank on September 29.

Debit memo, $2, dated September 29, for collection fee charged by bank.

Notification of a certified check for $1,300 deducted on September 6. (Even if the certified check, Check 703, had not been canceled by the bank during September it would not be listed as outstanding, because it has been entered on both Hall's and the bank's records and would therefore not need to be reconciled.)

Service charge notification, $4, dated September 30.

Following receipt of the bank statement, Hall prepares the bank reconciliation statement shown in Figure 8-5.

FREDERICK HALL
Bank Reconciliation
September 30, 1969

Per Books

Figure 8-5. *Bank Reconciliation*

Cash balance per ledger, September 30, 1969		$6,841.00
Add Customer's note collected by bank		500.00
Error in entering Check 705:		
Entered as	$82.50	
Correct amount	28.50	54.00
Total		$7,395.00
Deduct Bank service charge	$ 4.00	
Collection fee	2.00	6.00
Adjusted cash balance, September 30, 1969		$7,389.00

Per Bank

Cash balance per bank statement, September 30, 1969		$6,563.25
Add Deposit of Sept. 30 in transit to bank		1,050.00
Check of Frederick Hale deducted by bank in error		275.00
Total		$7,888.25
Deduct outstanding checks		

Check	Amount	
701	$ 84.00	
706	312.25	
710	103.00	499.25

Adjusted balance, September 30, 1969	$7,389.00

The following points should be emphasized:

1. The beginning balance in the Per Books section is taken from the general ledger Cash account; it was determined as follows:

Cash balance per ledger, August 31, 1969 (Figure 8-4)	$ 6,400
Add deposits	4,822
Total	$11,222
Deduct checks issued	4,381
Cash balance per ledger, September 30, 1969	$ 6,841

2. Check 705 was incorrectly recorded as $82.50 instead of $28.50 in Hall's books. The error overstated cash disbursements and therefore understated the ending cash balance by $54 ($82.50 − $28.50).

3. The beginning balance in the Per Bank section is the last amount in the Balance column of the bank statement for the month of September (Figure 8-2).

4. The deposit of $1,050 made on September 30 was not credited on the bank statement because it was in transit.

5. While determining the outstanding checks, Hall discovered that the bank had deducted in error a check for $275 signed by another depositor, Frederick Hale. This resulted in an understatement of the bank balance on the bank statement. The bank was notified about this error.

6. Check 701 was listed as an outstanding check on the bank reconciliation of August 31 (Figure 8-4). Since it has not yet been presented to the bank for payment, it continues to be listed as an outstanding check.

All the items that appear in the Per Bank section of the bank reconciliation for the previous month must be traced to the current month's bank statement. For example, a deposit not credited in the prior month should appear with the initial deposits for the current month; similarly, improper charges or credits of the preceding month should be adjusted on the current month's statement.

All additions to and deductions from the balance per books must be entered on Hall's books to bring the general ledger Cash account balance into agreement with the adjusted cash balance. The Cash account balance of $6,841 should be increased by $548 ($500 + $54 − $6) to show the actual cash balance of $7,389 as of September 30, 1969.

The required entries are:

Cash	498	
Bank Service and Collection Charges Expense	2	
Notes Receivable		500
To record collection of sight draft by bank and related charge.		
Cash	54	
Accounts Payable		54
To record correction for error in entering Check 705 as $82.50 instead of $28.50.		
Bank Service and Collection Charges Expense	4	
Cash		4
To record bank service charge for September.		

These entries may be made in the cash journals for September if the journals have not been footed and posted, or the following compound entry may be made in the general journal:

Cash	548	
Bank Service and Collection Charges Expense	6	
Notes Receivable		500
Accounts Payable		54
To adjust the Cash account per bank reconciliation for September.		

After the entry is posted, Hall's Cash account appears as shown. Note that the beginning balance for the new period (October) agrees with the adjusted cash balance in the bank reconciliation.

			Cash			Acct. No. 101	
1969				1969			
Sept.	1	(Beginning balance)	6,400	Sept. 30	(Checks issued)		4,381
	30	(Cash deposits)	4,822	30	Balance		7,389
	30	(Adjustment)	548				
			11,770				11,770
1969							
Oct.	1	Balance	7,389				

Only those items that either increase or decrease the balance per books need to be entered in the journal. Those items that increase or decrease the balance per bank already have been recorded on the depositor's books. If a running cash balance is maintained in the checkbook, the necessary adjustments must also be made there.

The form of bank reconciliation shown in Figure 8-5 is commonly used because the adjusted cash balance is a significant figure; it represents the true cash balance, the amount subject to withdrawal. The form also may be prepared in advance and the items entered directly into the appropriate sections as they are determined.

Cash Short or Over

The daily count of cash in the cash registers may differ from the cash register readings. If the records do not disclose a clerical error, it may be assumed that the shortage or overage was caused by an error in making change. The discrepancy may be entered temporarily in the books as a debit or credit to Cash Short or Over. To illustrate, assume that the cash register tape shows cash sales for the day of $100 but the count shows the cash on hand to be $101.50. The journal entry to record the cash sales and the cash overage is:

Cash	101.50	
Sales		100.00
Cash Short or Over		1.50

If the cash count showed $98.50, the entry would be:

Cash	98.50	
Cash Short or Over	1.50	
Sales		100.00

Cash Short or Over is classified on the income statement as General Expense if a debit or Other Revenue if a credit.

MANAGEMENT CONTROLS—CASH FORECASTS

The managers of a business must make certain that adequate cash funds are available at all times. Good management requires that sufficient cash be available for the timely payment of invoices, payrolls, and other costs and operating expenses. An adequate cash balance is also essential to maintain a good credit rating. But excessive cash balances, particularly during inflationary periods when cash suffers a loss of purchasing power, indicate ineffective management of cash resources.

The regular cash needs of the business should be anticipated to ensure that purchases and expenses can be met promptly; that bank loans can be paid at maturity; that taxes and dividend payments can be met; that funds will be available for additional machinery, equipment, and buildings; and that excess funds, if any, are appropriately invested. All this requires a projected plan, or *cash forecast,* for a number of months in advance. The period covered by the forecast may be one month, three months, six months, or a year, depending on how accurately a company is able to forecast its receipts and disbursements. Some companies make fairly accurate forecasts for the next three-month period and rougher approximations for the remaining nine months. If the cash balance is low and sales are erratic, weekly forecasts may be desirable.

A cash forecast is a projection based on a careful analysis of prior periods, with appropriate adjustments for anticipated changes. The forecast deals exclusively with estimates involving *cash*. Noncash items such as depreciation are excluded. The cash forecast is a summary of projected cash receipts, cash disbursements, and resulting cash balances for the budgeted periods. Cash receipts from customers are projected on the basis of estimated sales and collection patterns experienced in prior periods. Other cash collections are generally lesser in amount and can be readily identified as to period of collectibility. When cash disbursements are forecast, consideration must be given to the various goods and services to be purchased and the timing of the required payments. Detailed operating forecasts are prepared for such items as materials and supplies, utilities, rent, payrolls, and taxes, from which the required cash disbursements are determined. The forms and schedules used should provide for the comparison of actual results with estimates so that any *variances* may be analyzed. If the variances indicate significant errors in the original estimates, corresponding revisions should be made in future forecasts.

The cash forecast of the Sterns Company for the first quarter of 1970 (Figure 8-6) is prepared from the following estimates:

	January	February	March
Cash sales	$ 7,500	$ 8,750	$ 9,200
Credit sales	30,000	35,000	37,000
Purchases of merchandise on account	22,000	20,000	30,000
Selling expenses	5,000	7,000	7,500
General and administrative expenses	6,000	6,500	7,000
Interest earned on investments	300	300	300
Taxes	350	400	425
Miscellaneous expenses	1,000	1,100	1,300

Estimated cash balance, January 1, is $12,500

Estimated purchases of merchandise on account for December, total $25,000

Sales are billed on terms of 2/10, n/30, but collections are expected as follows:
    80% within the month of billing and also within the discount period
    10% in the month following billing and after discount period
     8% in the second month following billing
     2% generally prove to be uncollectible

Estimated credit sales for November are $26,000; and for December, $29,000

The company buys merchandise on terms of 1/15, n/30. It is expected that discounts will be taken on all payments, which are made as follows:
    60% in the month of purchase
    40% in the month following purchase

STERNS COMPANY
Cash Forecast
For Three Months Ending March 31, 1970

Figure 8-6.
Cash Forecast

	January	February	March
Cash balance at beginning of month	$12,500	$13,482	$19,700
Add: estimated cash receipts			
Cash sales	7,500	8,750	9,200
Collections on accounts receivable (Schedule A)	28,500	32,760	34,908
Interest earned on investments	300	300	300
Total available cash	$48,800	$55,292	$64,108
Deduct: estimated disbursements			
Payments on purchases of merchandise (Schedule B)	$22,968	$20,592	$25,740
Selling expenses	5,000	7,000	7,500
General and administrative expenses	6,000	6,500	7,000
Taxes	350	400	425
Miscellaneous expenses	1,000	1,100	1,300
Total disbursements	$35,318	$35,592	$41,965
Cash balance at end of month	$13,482	$19,700	$22,143

To compute the cash balance at the end of the month, the beginning balance is added to the estimated cash receipts for that month and the anticipated disbursements for the month are deducted. The ending cash balance of any month is the beginning cash balance of the next month.

STERNS COMPANY   Schedule A

Forecast of Collections on Accounts Receivable

For Three Months Ending March 31, 1970

Figure 8-7.
Forecast of Collections from Customers

	January	February	March
November credit sales:			
$26,000 × .08	$ 2,080		
December credit sales:			
$29,000 × .10	2,900		
$29,000 × .08		$ 2,320	
January credit sales:			
$30,000 × .80 $24,000			
Deduct discounts 480	23,520		
$30,000 × .10		3,000	
$30,000 × .08			$ 2,400
February credit sales:			
$35,000 × .80 $28,000			
Deduct discounts 560		27,440	
$35,000 × .10			3,500
March credit sales:			
$37,000 × .80 $29,600			
Deduct discounts 592			29,008
Total monthly collections	$28,500	$32,760	$34,908

STERNS COMPANY   Schedule B

Forecast of Payments of Purchases of Merchandise

For Three Months Ending March 31, 1970

Figure 8-8.
Forecast of Payments to Creditors

	January	February	March
December purchases:			
$25,000 × .40	$10,000		
January purchases:			
$22,000 × .60	13,200		
$22,000 × .40		$ 8,800	
February purchases:			
$20,000 × .60		12,000	
$20,000 × .40			$ 8,000
March purchases:			
$30,000 × .60			18,000
Totals	$23,200	$20,800	$26,000
Deduct discounts	232	208	260
Total monthly payments	$22,968	$20,592	$25,740

Management uses the cash forecast to determine whether sufficient cash will be available for tax payments, dividends, acquisition of equipment, or purchases of securities as investments. At the end of each month, the actual amount of each item is entered in an extra column headed Actual to provide a month-by-month comparison with the budgeted figures.

SUMMARY

Cash includes those items that a bank customarily accepts for deposit—coins, paper money, bank drafts, cashier's checks, money orders, and bank balances.

Basic controls must be instituted to prevent the misuse of funds. These controls include a clear segregation of duties and responsibilities, use of mechanical aids, the furnishing of definite authorization for cash payments, and organizing the flow and recording of documents so that the work of one employee is subject to automatic verification by another employee. No one person should both receive and disburse cash. All cash receipts should be deposited intact daily and all disbursements should be made by check. When payment by check is impractical, a petty cash fund should be set up.

Control of cash is further facilitated by the use of checking accounts. Since the records of the depositor and the bank will not normally agree at the end of the month, it is necessary to reconcile the two balances and to determine the adjusted, or true, cash balance. Differences between the balances may be due to the time lag in recording debits and credits, special charges and credits of which either the depositor or the bank is unaware, or possible errors or irregularities. A statement is prepared to reconcile the two balances. Amounts entered on one set of records only, and all errors and irregularities, constitute the items that will reconcile the two balances to the adjusted balance. All additions to and deductions from the balance per books must be recorded to bring the general ledger cash balance into agreement with the adjusted cash balance.

The regular cash needs of a business should be anticipated to ensure that funds will be available when needed and that excess funds are invested. This requires a cash forecast for a number of months in advance, based on a careful study and analysis of prior periods with appropriate adjustments for anticipated changes. The forecast is a summary of projected cash receipts and disbursements and the resulting cash balance for the budgeted periods.

☐ QUESTIONS

Q8–1. The Sloan Company employs an office manager, a cashier, an accounts receivable bookkeeper, two clerk-typists, and ten salesmen. The bookkeeper records all charge sales made to customers; she also opens the mail each day and credits the customers' accounts for remittances, turning the money over to the cashier. The monthly bank statement is received directly by the bookkeeper, who prepares the bank reconciliation.

Collections from cash sales are turned over by the salesmen to the cashier together with a cash sales invoice. The cashier compares these invoices daily with the cash register tapes. Disbursements for petty cash items are made by the cashier out of cash receipts. The cashier fills out a petty cash slip, which is signed by the person receiving the cash. All other disbursements are by check, signed by either the office manager or the owner of the company. Entries in the cash receipts journal and in the cash disbursements journal are generally made by the office manager. In his absence, the cashier handles the cash receipts journal and the accounts receivable bookkeeper handles the cash disbursements journal.

What is wrong with this system? What basic internal controls are lacking? Can the system be improved without increasing the present staff?

Q8-2. Why is it advantageous to deposit all cash receipts intact and to make all disbursements by check?

Q8-3. (a) What is a petty cash fund? (b) How does it operate? (c) Why should the petty cash fund always be replenished at the end of each accounting period?

Q8-4. Explain the reciprocal relationships between the cash records of the bank and of the depositor.

Q8-5. Explain the following:
a. certified check
b. total of listed checks
c. service charge
d. not sufficient funds
e. debit memorandum
f. credit memorandum
g. overdraft

Q8-6. Explain the effect, if any, on the bank statement balance of each of the following bank reconciliation items:
a. Outstanding checks total $323.
b. The bank recorded a $650 deposit as $560.
c. The service charge for the month was $7.
d. Deposits in transit total $800.
e. A note payable of $500 made to the bank by the depositor became due.

Q8-7. (a) What is the purpose of a cash forecast? (b) Describe the basic steps in the preparation of a cash forecast. (c) What are some of the problems that may be encountered in its preparation?

☐ **EXERCISES**

E8-1. On April 1, 1969, the Ahearn Company established a petty cash fund of $200. On April 30, 1969, the fund consisted of cash and other items as follows:

Coins and currency	$47.50
Postage stamps	22.00
Freight and express invoices	64.00
Salvation Army contribution receipt	25.00
Postdated check from an employee	41.50

Make the entries to (a) establish the fund; (b) replenish the fund; (c) increase the fund from $200 to $300 on April 30; (d) reduce the fund from $200 to $150 on April 30.

E8-2. The George Campbell Company has an imprest petty cash fund of $500. On December 31, 1969, the fund consisted of cash and other items as follows:

Coins and currency		$263.22
Vouchers for:		
Transportation In	$112.62	
Telephone	10.75	
Postage Expense	108.16	
Stationery	.50	232.03
Total		$495.25

Assuming that the petty cash fund was not replenished, make the necessary adjusting entry at December 31, 1969.

E8–3. The Allen Company's general ledger Cash account shows a balance of $6,989.49 as of April 30, 1969. The balance on the bank statement on that date is $7,828.09. Checks for $250, $177.82, and $42.18 are outstanding. There is a charge for a check made out by the Alton Company for $25. The bank statement shows a credit of $400 for a customer's note that had been left with the bank for collection. Service charges for the month were $6.40. What is the true cash balance as of April 30?

E8–4. Prepare a bank reconciliation and entries to adjust the books of the George Lowe Company as of January 31, 1969, from the following data:

Balance on bank statement	$4,833.46
Balance on books	4,487.71
Bank service charge	8.35
Credit for a customer's note collected by the bank	130.60
Deposit made on January 31, not credited by the bank	254.10
Check 786 for $261.54 was entered in the cash disbursements journal as $216.45.	
A customer's check for $12.90 was returned marked NSF on January 30.	
Outstanding checks were:	

Check	Amount
817	$ 50.00
818	75.05
825	410.54

E8–5. The bookkeeper for the Walsh Company prepared the following statement:

WALSH COMPANY
Bank Reconciliation
May 31, 1969

Cash balance per ledger, May 31, 1969		$4,341.10
Deduct bank service charges		4.12
Adjusted cash balance, May 31, 1969		$4,336.98
Cash balance per bank statement, May 31, 1969		$5,590.38
Add deposit in transit		1,314.15
Total		$6,904.53
Deduct outstanding checks:		

Check	Amount	
680	$ 476.10	
690	891.44	
695 Certified check for $500		
701	1,200.01	2,567.55
Adjusted cash balance, May 31, 1969		$4,336.98

a. How did the bookkeeper determine the amounts to be added or deducted?
b. Why is Check 695 excluded from the total of outstanding checks?
c. What journal entry is necessary to adjust the books at May 31, 1969?

E8-**6.** From the following data, prepare a cash forecast for the Burnham Company for January, February, and March, 1970. Actual balances as of December 31, 1969 are:

Cash	$20,000
Accounts Receivable	25,000
Accounts Payable	35,000

Estimates for the first quarter of 1970 are:

	January	February	March
Sales on account	$30,000	$20,000	$22,000
Cash sales	12,000	17,000	13,000
Purchases on account	39,000	23,000	27,000
Cash operating expenses	15,000	12,000	9,000
Depreciation expense	2,000	2,000	2,000

Terms of sales and purchases on account are n/30.

E8-**7.** Actual and projected sales data for the J. J. Jones Company follow:

	Cash Sales	Credit Sales
November, 1969–Actual		$20,000
December, 1969–Actual		24,000
January, 1970–Estimated	$12,000	22,000
February, 1970–Estimated	10,000	33,000
March, 1970–Estimated	21,000	54,000

The cash balance on January 1, 1970, was $18,000.

Experience indicates that 50 percent of the credit sales are collected in the month of the sale, 40 percent in the month following the sale, and 10 percent in the second month following the sale. Compute the cash collections by months for the first quarter of 1970.

E8-**8.** The bookkeeper of the Carlson Company, in need of money to pay off debts, "borrows" $500 by pocketing some cash and checks mailed in by customers. He enters appropriate credits to each customer's account for payment made. Can this misappropriation be concealed for a short period? Indefinitely? What measures should a company take to prevent the misappropriation of cash or other assets?

E8-**9.** Gross sales of the Gaynor Company for the year 1969 were $800,000. Accounts receivable were $75,000 at the beginning of the year and $59,000 at the end of the year. Accounts receivables written off during the year were $2,050 and the year's provision for uncollectible accounts was $1,650. Customers returned merchandise for $4,600 in credit and took cash discounts of $8,900. Compute the cash collections made from customers during 1969.

E8-**10.** The following statement was made by the treasurer of the Hurley Corporation: "As nearly as I can determine, 60 percent of our customers pay within the discount period. Our terms are 3/10, n/30. Eighty percent of the amount due is collected within the 30-day period; 5 percent of the delinquent receivables remains uncollected at the end of a 60-day period. As a matter of collection policy, at that point I consider such outstanding receivables as doubtful of collection."

Sales on account for March, April, May, June, and July were $14,000, $11,000, $10,000, $12,000, and $16,000 respectively. On the basis of the Company's collection experience, compute the monthly forecast of collections on accounts receivable for May, June, and July.

E8–11. The Electra Corporation has been formed to sell appliances on the installment plan. The following estimates are made for the first year of operations:

1.	Selling price per unit	$85
2.	Cost to produce per unit	$35
3.	Selling and administrative expenses per unit	$25
4.	Sales (units):	
	First month	50
	Second month	100
	Third month	150
	Monthly during rest of year	200
5.	Terms of sale:	
	Down payment	$20
	Monthly for 13 months	$ 5
6.	All costs and expenses are paid in the month of sale.	

Prepare a statement showing estimated monthly and cumulative cash requirements for the first twelve months.

☐ **DEMONSTRATION PROBLEMS**

DP8–1. (*Recording petty cash fund transactions*) The transactions of the petty cash fund at the Winston Company during the month of July, 1969, were:

1969

July   1   Established an imprest petty cash fund in the amount of $70.

      10   Replenished the fund and increased it to $150. The following items were in the petty cash box:

Coins and currency		$ 2.50
Vouchers for:		
Telephone and telegraph		24.86
Advances to employees		10.00
Postage stamps		20.00
Miscellaneous office supplies		12.64
Total		$70.00

      31   Replenished the fund again at the close of the Winston Company's fiscal year. The petty cash box contained the following items:

Coins and currency		$ 44.22
Vouchers for:		
Telephone and telegraph	$31.34	
Office supplies	21.00	
Postage	37.44	
Traveling expense	1.60	
Entertainment expense	11.20	
Repairs	.80	
Hardware supplies	2.40	105.78
Total		$150.00

Required: Journalize the transactions.

DP8-2. (*Bank reconciliation*) The cash account of the Iris Company showed a balance of $2,123.31 on March 31, 1969. The bank statement showed a balance of $2,302.94. Other differences between the information in the firm's Cash account and the bank's records were:

1. A deposit of $118.60 made on March 31 was not recorded by the bank before the bank statement was issued.

2. The following items were returned with the bank statement:
   a. A credit memo for $112.30, the proceeds of a draft for $115 drawn on the George Company and accepted by the drawee 60 days ago. The bank deducted $2.70 from the total collected for the cost of collection.
   b. A debit memo for $4.80 for annual rental of a safety deposit box.
   c. A customer's check for $7.50 received on account, which the firm had included in its deposit on March 27, was returned marked NSF.
   d. A canceled check in the amount of $205 drawn by the Ibis Company and charged by the bank against the account of the Iris Company by mistake. The check is being returned to the bank.

3. Check 298 was made out correctly for $17.67 in payment for office supplies, but was entered in the cash disbursements journal as $17.76.

4. Outstanding checks on March 31 totaled $403.14.

Required: 1. Prepare a bank reconciliation as of March 31, 1969.
          2. Prepare the journal entries to adjust the Cash account as of March 31, 1969.

DP8-3. (*Cash forecast*) The Eastern Electrical Company estimates the following sales, purchases, and operating expenses for the first four months of 1969:

	Operating Expenses	Purchases	Sales
January	$6,000	$ 50,000	$160,000
February	7,000	100,000	200,000
March	9,500	80,000	180,000
April	8,500	220,000	220,000

Balances on January 1, 1969 were:

Accounts Receivable	$30,000
Accounts Payable	20,000

Required: 1. Prepare a schedule of estimated monthly cash collections for the first four months of 1969. Approximately 25 percent of sales are for cash; sales on account are on terms of n/30 and are collected in the month following the sale.
          2. Prepare a schedule of estimated monthly cash disbursements for the period. Purchases are made on terms of n/15, so that half the purchases are paid for in the month of purchase and the remainder in the following month. Operating expenses are paid for in the month in which they are incurred.

☐ **PROBLEMS**

P8-1. The Wynn Company has an imprest petty cash fund of $500. On June 30, 1969, the end of the Company's fiscal year, the composition of the fund was as follows:

Currency and coins		$ 97.94
Vouchers for:		
Postage	$106.08	
Stationery	25.00	
Transportation out	153.62	
Telephone and telegraph	115.30	400.00
Total		$497.94
Cash shortage		2.06
Total		$500.00

Required: 1. Prepare the entry to replenish the fund on June 30.
2. Assuming that the fund was not replenished:
   a. What adjusting entry should be made on June 30?
   b. What amount will be reported in the June 30 position statement?
3. Should the custodian of the petty cash fund have the authority to withdraw cash from the bank whenever he needs to replenish the fund?

P8-2. According to the statement that John Madison received from his bank as of March 31, 1969, his balance was $2,700. He noted the following discrepancies between the bank statement and his records:

A deposit of $500 that was made on March 31 was credited by the bank on April 1.

Outstanding checks as of March 31 were: 652, $100; 689, $51; 701, $59; and 710, $86.

Check 655 for $350, issued on March 10 for advertising expense, was not recorded in the cash disbursements journal but was paid by the bank on March 16.

A 4-percent, 90-day note of Thomas Field for $400 maturing on March 31, was discounted by Madison on March 12, and dishonored at maturity. No entry has been made in Madison's records. The bank charged Madison's account for the note plus a $2.50 protest fee.

Bank service charges for March were $3.

Required: 1. Determine the cash balance on the books before adjustments and prepare a bank reconciliation showing the true cash balances as of March 31, 1969.
2. Prepare the journal entries necessary to adjust the books.

P8-3. The following data are taken from the records of Priem, Inc., and from the monthly bank statement furnished them by the Boston Trust Company:

1. Balance per bank statement, June 30, 1969	$74,159.86
2. Balance per books, June 30, 1969	44,673.40
3. Outstanding checks, June 30, 1969	32,108.42
4. Receipts of June 30, 1969, deposited July 2, 1969	5,317.20
5. Service charge for June, per debit memo	3.85
6. Proceeds of bank loan, June 15, 1969, discounted for 3 months at 5% per annum, omitted from the Company's books	9,875.00
7. Deposit of June 30, 1969, omitted from bank statement	2,892.41
8. Error on bank statement in entering deposit of June 25, 1969:	

Correct amount	$3,182.40	
.Entered as	3,181.40	1.00

9. Check of Prime Company, charged in error   2,690.00
10. Proceeds of a customer's note collected by bank on June 16, 1969; not entered in the company's books:

Principal	$2,000.00	
Interest	20.00	
Total	$2,020.00	
Less collection fee	5.00	2,015.00

11. Error on bank statement in entering deposit of June 10, 1969:

Entered as	$4,817.10	
Correct amount	4,807.10	10.00

12. Deposit of Preem Corporation, credited in error   1,800.00
13. Debit memo for noninterest-bearing note not recorded by the Company   5,000.00
14. A check from Brown, Inc., was returned marked NSF; no entry has been made on the Company's records   417.50

Required: 1. Prepare a bank reconciliation as of June 30, 1969.
2. Prepare the journal entries necessary to adjust the books of Priem, Inc., as of June 30, 1969. The books are closed annually on June 30.

P8–**4.** The Wale Company prepared the following bank reconciliation as of July 31, 1969:

WALE COMPANY
Bank Reconciliation
July 31, 1969

Balance per bank		$12,463.75
Less outstanding checks		

Check	Amount	
580	$2,025.50	
599	98.00	
600	3.40	2,126.90
Balance per books		$10,336.85

The bank statement for the month of August was as follows:

SECOND NATIONAL BANK
Statement of account with Wale Company

Checks			Deposits	Date	Balance
				1969	
				August 1	12,463.75
2,025.50				2	10,438.25
98.00	12.00	115.00	785.00	6	10,998.25
100.00			195.00	11	11,093.25
62.23	198.50	3.40		16	10,829.12
1,110.00	90.00 NSF			21	9,629.12
860.00	15.40		2,500.00	25	11,253.72
2.75 SC			760.80	29	12,011.77

Cash receipts for the month were:

Date		Amount
August	5	$ 785.00
	10	195.00
	23	2,500.00
	28	760.80
	31	500.00

Cash disbursements for the month were:

Check	Amount	Check	Amount
601	$ 12.00	607	$682.21
602	860.00	608	49.90
603	115.00	609	20.00
604	100.00	610	760.00
605	1,110.00	611	62.23
606	143.50	612	198.50

The canceled checks returned by the bank included a check for $15.40 made out by the Wail Company and charged to the Wale Company in error. The NSF check had been received from a customer on account.

Required: 1. Prepare the bank reconciliation as of August 31, 1969.
2. Make the necessary adjusting journal entries.

P8-5. The general ledger of the Boston Manufacturing Company included the following account balances as of January 1, 1969:

Cash	$20,000
Accounts Receivable	35,000
Accounts Payable	18,000

Projected sales, purchases, and cash operating expenses for the first three months of 1969 were:

	January	February	March
Sales	$30,000	$40,000	$45,000
Purchases	20,000	30,000	25,000
Cash operating expenses	8,000	10,000	7,500

All sales and purchases are on terms of n/30, so that remittances by customers are received in the month following the sale, and all payments for merchandise are made during the month following the purchase. Cash operating expenses are paid for during the month in which they are incurred.

Required: Prepare a schedule showing cash requirements by months for the first quarter of 1969.

P8-6. Estimates of the Flange Manufacturing Company for the first four months of 1969 are as follows:

	January	February	March	April
Sales	$50,000	$60,000	$70,000	$65,000
Purchases	36,000	40,000	40,000	45,000
Payrolls	10,000	12,000	14,000	9,500
Other expenses	5,000	6,000	7,000	6,500

The general ledger includes the following account balances at January 1, 1969:

Cash	$10,000
Accounts Receivable	45,000
Accounts Payable	30,000

All sales are on account on terms of n/30; 90 percent are collected in the month following the sale, 8 percent in the second month following the sale, and 2 percent are ultimately written off as bad debts. All payments on purchases and other expenses are made in the month following the month of purchase. Payrolls are paid during the month. The Accounts Receivable balance of January represents total sales for December of the prior year, and the Accounts Payable balance represents purchases for that month.

Required: 1. Prepare a cash forecast by months for the first four months of 1969.
2. Based on the forecast, what financial policies do you recommend?

P8–7. The Electro Company has two notes payable of $50,000 each with due dates of May 31 and June 30, 1969. The Company wishes to arrange in advance for any refinancing that may be needed (1) to pay the notes on their due dates and (2) to provide a minimum end-of-month cash balance of $15,000. You are furnished with the following projected data:

	Sales		Purchases
February	$60,000	March	$51,000
March	85,000	April	39,000
April	60,000	May	45,000
May	63,000	June	36,000
June	70,000		

The cash balance on April 1 was $16,000.

All sales are on terms of 2/10 E.O.M. (a 2-percent discount is allowed if the invoice is paid by the tenth of the month following the sale). Past experience indicates that 70 percent of the sales are collected within the first ten days of the first month following the sale, 20 percent during the remainder of the first month following the sale, and 8 percent in the second month following the sale. Bad debts losses are estimated at 2 percent of sales.

Terms of purchases are 2/10, n/30. Since all payments are made within the discount period, two-thirds of the invoices will be paid in the month of the purchase and one third in the month following the purchase.

Operating expenses are $6,000 per month and are paid for when they are incurred. The Electro Company receives $1,500 monthly from property rentals; $2,500 will be realized in June from the sale of obsolete equipment.

Required: Prepare a report, with supporting schedules, advising management of the amount of additional borrowing that will be necessary.

CASE PROBLEM
Carson Company

The Carson Company was formed a number of years ago to sell office equipment, furniture, and supplies at retail. The business was successful, and James Carson, the founder, con-

[Ch. 8]

verted his company to the corporate form to attract additional capital from local investors. The Company has continued to expand, but its cash position has become increasingly "tight." Carson, as president and treasurer of the Company, has approached you about helping to plan new cash policies. You begin by collecting the following data as of June 12, 1969:

CARSON COMPANY
Comparative Statement of Financial Position
May 31, 1969 and 1968

Assets

	1969	1968
Current Assets:		
Cash	$ 800	$ 1,100
Accounts Receivable	30,000	26,000
Merchandise Inventory	39,000	34,000
Prepaid Expenses	1,200	1,250
Total Current Assets	$ 71,000	$ 62,350
Plant and Equipment:		
Land	$ 20,000	$ 20,000
Depreciable Assets	80,000	80,000
Accumulated Depreciation	(27,500)	(25,000)
Total Plant and Equipment	$ 72,500	$ 75,000
Total Assets	$143,500	$137,350

Liabilities and Stockholders' Equity

	1969	1968
Current Liabilities:		
Accounts Payable–suppliers	$ 20,250	$ 20,600
Accrued Liabilities	450	400
Total Current Liabilities	$ 20,700	$ 21,000
Long-Term Liabilities:		
Mortgage Payable, 5%	40,100	41,000
Total Liabilities	$ 60,800	$ 62,000
Stockholders' Equity:		
Capital Stock	$ 50,000	$ 50,000
Retained Earnings	32,700	25,350
Total Stockholders' Equity	$ 82,700	$ 75,350
Total Liabilities and Stockholders' Equity	$143,500	$137,350

CARSON COMPANY
Comparative Statement of Net Income and Retained Earnings
For Years Ended May 31, 1969 and 1968

	1969	1968
Revenues:		
Charge sales (net)	$300,000	$280,000
Cash sales (net)	25,000	20,000
Total sales (net)	$325,000	$300,000
Cost of Goods Sold	243,750	225,000

Gross margin	$ 81,250	$ 75,000
Expenses:		
Depreciation Expense	$ 2,500	$ 2,500
Salaries and Wages	19,272	18,787
Interest Expense	2,028	2,073
Other Expense	33,000	32,800
Total Expenses	$ 56,800	$ 56,160
Net Income Before Income Taxes	$ 24,450	$ 18,840
Provision for Income Taxes	8,362	6,443
Net Income After Income Taxes	$ 16,088	$ 12,397
Retained Earnings, beginning of year	25,350	21,453
Total	$ 41,438	$ 33,850
Dividends	8,738	8,500
Retained Earnings, end of year	$ 32,700	$ 25,350

You make the following notes regarding expectations for the next year:

1. Charge sales are on terms of n/30 (charge sales of one month are generally collected the following month).
2. Prepaid expenses and accrued liabilities are expected to remain at present levels.
3. No purchases of land or depreciable assets are expected.
4. Purchases of merchandise are on terms of n/60.
5. Mortgage payable requires a monthly payment of $75 plus interest at annual rate of 5 percent on the unpaid balance.
6. Salaries and wages are expected to be $19,600 during the next year, evenly distributed throughout the year.
7. For the next year, other expenses are expected to be $20,000 plus 4 percent of net sales. (Apportion the $20,000 equally throughout the year but relate the 4 percent to each month's sales separately.)
8. State and federal income taxes are expected to be about 34.2 percent of operating income. (For this case, treat income taxes as being paid in full on the last day of the fiscal year.)
9. Dividends are expected to be about $9,000 during the next year, to be paid quarterly in equal amounts beginning in August.
10. Charge sales for the year beginning June 1 are expected to be $320,000, and, based on the company's experience, are expected to be distributed during the fiscal year beginning in June as follows: 7%, 7%, 8%, 8%, 9%, 10%, 11%, 10%, 9%, 8%, 7%, and 6%.
11. Cash sales are expected to total $30,000, equally distributed throughout the year.
12. Purchases are expected to lead sales by about 60 days.
13. Mr. Carson wishes to get the collection of receivables and the payment of payables "on schedule" as soon as possible. He also wishes, if possible, to avoid borrowing any money. However, he can borrow at a 6% rate at the local bank.

Required: 1. For the fiscal year beginning June 1, 1969, prepare a projected statement of net income and retained earnings for the year and a projected statement of net income (before deducting income taxes) for each month. Round all amounts to the nearest whole dollar.

2. Prepare a cash forecast by months for the fiscal year beginning June 1. Round all amounts to the nearest whole dollar.

3. Identify the usefulness and limitations of these projected statements in the conduct of the affairs of the Carson Company.

4. Explain how the Carson Company could make greater use of the projected statements.

5. Identify the assumptions that you applied if you felt that insufficient information was given. Give briefly your justification for making these assumptions.

6. Give some reasons why the cash balance declined during the year by $300, even though retained earnings increased by $7,350.

7. What suggestions would you offer to Carson for improving the cash position of the Carson Company?

Chapter Nine
The Measurement and Control of Receivables

Making sales and purchases on account has become standard practice in the modern American system. Individuals and businesses alike buy and sell merchandise, invest in stocks and bonds, and even acquire plant and equipment on credit. Consequently, the increasing trend toward the extension of credit terms for transactions involving all types of goods and services has led to a greater need for control and analysis of receivables by management.

SOURCES AND CLASSIFICATION OF RECEIVABLES

There are two classes of trade receivables: accounts receivable, which are claims against customers for sales made on open account, and notes receivable, which are claims against customers supported by written formal promises to pay. From a legal point of view, a note receivable is probably better security than an account receivable because it is a written acknowledgement of the debt; however, in this country, the unsecured open account form of credit is well established and will be widely used for a long time.

Receivables arise from a variety of sources and, in the interest of full disclosure and fairness of presentation, must be properly recorded in separate accounts for major classifications. Accounts receivable represent amounts due from others for goods sold, services rendered, money lent, deposits made, and so on. These claims should be shown under specific designations, such as:

1. Accounts Receivable–Trade. This account represents claims against customers for goods sold or for services rendered.
2. Accounts Receivable–Nontrade. This account represents claims arising from sources other than normal trade transactions, including:
   a. Loans to officers or employees

b. Deposits made on contract bids with public utilities or government agencies

c. Claims against common carriers for loss or damage to goods in shipment, loss claims against insurance companies, and claims against the U.S. Treasury for tax refunds

d. Amounts due from affiliated companies

e. Amounts due or accrued from rentals, interest, and royalties

Notes are similarly classified as trade or nontrade receivables. Nontrade notes receivable should be carried in accounts specifically designated as to source (officers, affiliated companies, rental property) and properly classified on the statement of financial position.

Receivables that are due and collectible within a year should be shown in the Current Assets section of the statement of financial position. The terms *Accounts Receivable* and *Notes Receivable*, if unqualified, should be understood to represent trade receivables collectible within one year or operating cycle. Nontrade receivables that are not due or are not collectible within a year should be shown under Long-Term Investments.

RECOGNITION OF LOSSES ON UNCOLLECTIBLE ACCOUNTS

▶ A basic principle in accounting is that the earned revenue of any accounting period and the actual expense incurred in realizing that revenue should be related. ◀ The cost of the goods sold and all other expenses incurred during the period should be related or deducted from the revenue of that period. Hence, the cost of a machine is spread over the period during which the machine is used to arrive at a fair measure of the net income for each period. It would be inaccurate to charge the entire cost at the time of purchase or disposal of the machine.

Similarly, since the balance in the Accounts Receivable account represents uncollected amounts included in revenue, losses that may arise through failure to collect any of the receivables should be recognized as an expense of doing business during the period when the sales were made. Thus, accounts receivable originating from sales made on credit in 1969 and determined to be uncollectible in 1970 represent a bad debts expense of the year 1969. It also follows that the Accounts Receivable account in the statement of financial position should be shown at the amount expected to be realized through actual cash collections from customers. If accounts receivable are shown at their gross amount without any accompanying adjustment for the estimated uncollectible portion, then the total assets and the total stockholders' equity would be overstated to the extent of the failure to recognize an expense that arises out of the sale of goods on account.

◀ *Accounting Concept: Matching Revenue and Expenses*

Recording the Bad Debts Adjustment

To illustrate the recording of a bad debts adjustment, assume that on December 31, 1969, the credit department of the Greene Corporation, having analyzed sales during 1969 and past due accounts, determines that out of the current year's sales, $550 will be uncollectible. This amount represents a bad debts expense to be shown in the General and Administrative Expense section of the income statement as a deduction from revenue. The estimated losses pertain to accounts receivable resulting from sales of the current period; therefore, in accordance with the principle of the periodic matching of expenses and revenues, estimated bad debts losses should be charged against revenue.

The adjusting general journal entry recorded on December 31, 1969, and the posting of the entry to the general ledger are shown:

```
        1969
   ┌─── Dec. 31  Bad Debts Expense                           550
   │             Allowance for Doubtful Accounts                        550 ───┐
   │               To record estimated loss on uncollectible               │
   │               accounts receivable.                                     │
   │                                                                        │
   │                                           Allowance for Doubtful Accounts │
   │         Bad Debts Expense (expense)           (asset valuation)          │
   │    ─────────────────────────────────    ───────────────────────────────  │
   │    1969                                  1969                            │
   │    Dec. 31        550                    Dec. 31        550 ◄───────────┘
   └──────────────────▲
```

It is assumed that there was no balance before adjustments in Allowance for Doubtful Accounts and that no account receivable had been written off during the year 1969. These complications are discussed in more detail later in this chapter.

Since the amount of $550 is an estimate and is not related to specific customers' accounts, the credit must be made to a contra (valuation) account. If the credit were to be made directly to Accounts Receivable without corresponding credits to subsidiary accounts, the equality of the controlling account and the subsidiary accounts would no longer exist. The use of the valuation account Allowance for Doubtful Accounts permits a reduction in the asset account without destroying this essential equality. Allowance for Doubtful Accounts is shown in the statement of financial position as a deduction from the related asset account, as shown:

Assets

Current Assets		
Cash		$1,210
Accounts Receivable	$6,945	
Deduct Allowance for Doubtful Accounts	550	6,395
Notes Receivable		1,000

The amount of $6,395 represents the anticipated net realizable value of the accounts receivable.

As actual accounts receivable are determined to be uncollectible during subsequent accounting periods, Allowance for Doubtful Accounts is debited instead of Bad Debts Expense, with offsetting credits to the controlling account and the specific customers' accounts involved. This procedure is required since the loss already has been recognized by the bad debts adjusting entry. A debit to Bad Debts Expense at the time of write-off would cause the loss to be recorded twice.

Assume that on May 1, 1970, the Greene Corporation decides that a claim of $75 against John Landry for a sale made on March 1, 1969, is uncollectible. The entry is:

```
1970
May   1   Allowance for Doubtful Accounts              75
               Accounts Receivable–John Landry                    75
                  To write off the uncollectible account.
```

Estimating the Amount of Bad Debts Expense

It is necessary for management to make a careful estimate, based on judgment and past experience, of the amount of its uncollectible accounts. Accurate records must be kept and overdue accounts must be carefully analyzed.

There are two alternative approaches commonly used in estimating bad debts. In this text, these methods are referred to as (1) *the income statement approach*, based on the volume of sales, and (2) *the statement of financial position approach*, based on the amount of receivables.

THE INCOME STATEMENT APPROACH. The income statement method associates the bad debts expense directly with sales volume. Typically the estimate is based on a percentage of sales less sales returns and allowances. The percentage is based on the company's past experience. It may be desirable to establish the percentage on the basis of charge sales only, excluding cash sales, particularly if the proportion of cash sales to total sales fluctuates from year to year. The method is simple to apply and furnishes an equitable basis for distributing bad debts losses. Any existing balance in Allowance for Doubtful Accounts is ignored. It should be noted, however, that even though the Bad Debts Expense item on the income statement may be quite close to reality, the Allowance for Doubtful Accounts on the statement of financial position may be greatly distorted. A small error in the same direction over the years will accumulate to a large amount in the Allowance for Doubtful Accounts since its balance is ignored in the adjustment process.

To illustrate the adjustment by this approach, assume that an examination of the accounts of a given company for the preceding five years show that approximately 1/2 of 1 percent of credit sales have proved to be uncollectible. Assume further that credit sales for a particular year are $100,000 and that there is a credit balance of $85 in Allowance for Doubtful Accounts before adjustments are made. The bad debts expense for the year is $500 (.005 × $100,000), and in recording the adjustment the $85 balance in the Allowance for Doubtful Accounts is ignored. The adjusting entry is:

```
Bad Debts Expense                       500
     Allowance for Doubtful Accounts            500
```

THE STATEMENT OF FINANCIAL POSITION APPROACH. The statement of financial position method requires an adjustment of the existing balance of Allowance for Doubtful Accounts to an amount that, when deducted from Accounts Receivable on the statement of financial position, will show accounts receivable at their net realizable value. In the statement of financial position approach, the amount of accounts receivable rather than sales volume is used as the base for the adjustment. The necessary adjustment for the balance of Allowance for Doubtful Accounts is determined by either of two procedures: (1) the balance necessary to maintain the Allowance for Doubtful Accounts is established by *aging* the accounts receivable (that is, analyzing them by the amount of time they have remained unpaid) and adjusting the existing balance of Allowance for Doubtful Accounts to the proper amount or (2) the balance of Allowance for Doubtful Accounts is adjusted to an amount equal to an estimated percentage of current accounts receivable. Aging the accounts receivable involves consideration of such factors as the date on which payment was due, the number of days that have elapsed since the due date, and any other available data of a financial nature that give some clue as to collectibility of the accounts. A columnar worksheet like the one shown in Figure 9-1 is often used to facilitate the analysis of the Accounts Receivable account. It is sometimes referred to as an *aging schedule*.

Figure 9-1.
Analysis of Accounts Receivable by Age

WALTER CARTER COMPANY
Analysis of Accounts Receivable by Age
December 31, 1969

Customer's Name	Total Balance	Not Yet Due	1–30 Days Past Due	31–60 Days Past Due	61–90 Days Past Due	Over 90 Days Past Due
Walter G. Arnold	$ 880	$ 800	$ 80			
Allan Conlon	1,800	1,000	500	$ 300		
Charles Peacock	50				$ 50	
Richard C. Smith	320	100	200	20		
Jerome Werther	960				900	$ 60
[Others]	51,990	27,220	15,460	5,280	730	3,300
Totals	$56,000	$29,120	$16,240	$5,600	$1,680	$3,360
Percent of total	100	52	29	10	3	6

All the accounts in the subsidiary accounts receivable ledger with their corresponding account balances are listed in the Customer's Name and Total Balance columns. The component charges that make up each balance in the Total Balance column are then extended to the appropriate columns. The aging method yields a more satisfactory Allowance for Doubtful Accounts than does any other method because the estimate is based on a study of individual customers' accounts rather than a blanket percentage of a single general ledger account balance. Only a detailed analysis will disclose those accounts that are not past due but that may be uncollectible and those long overdue accounts that may give indication of eventual collectibility. Yet, if recoveries of accounts receivable previously written off or the write-off in the current year of accounts receivable arising from prior years' sales are run through the Allowance for Doubtful Accounts without any designation of which of these items affect prior years' net income, the bad debts expense of the current year could be greatly distorted.

Management should also compare the current analysis of accounts receivable by age with those of earlier periods, especially the age-group percentages. Presently, 52 percent of the total accounts receivable are not yet due, 29 percent are past due from 1 to 30 days, and so on. When compared with earlier years, percentage increases in the lower age classifications with offsetting decreases in the older classes are favorable.

The analysis in Figure 9-1 may be used to determine the proper balance to be established in Allowance for Doubtful Accounts. To make this determination, companies may apply a sliding scale of percentages based on previous experience to the total amount shown in each column. The computation to determine expected losses for the Walter Carter Company is shown:

	Amount	Estimated Percentage Uncollectible	Allowance for Doubtful Accounts
Not yet due	$29,120	2	$ 582.40
1–30 days past due	16,240	4	649.60
31–60 days past due	5,600	10	560.00
61–90 days past due	1,680	20	336.00
Over 90 days past due	3,360	50	1,680.00
Totals	$56,000		$3,808.00

On the basis of this summary, $3,808 of the outstanding accounts receivable on December 31 may become uncollectible. Consequently, an Allowance for Doubtful Accounts with a balance of $3,808 should be established. Before the adjusting entry is made, the existing balance in the account must be considered. The Walter Carter Company has a present credit balance in Allowance for Doubtful Accounts of $200, a provision remaining from earlier periods. The adjusting entry amount will be for $3,608 ($3,808 − $200); when it is transferred to the allowance account it will bring that account up to $3,808, the estimated probable uncollectible accounts. The adjusting journal entry is:

```
1969
Dec. 31   Bad Debts Expense                    3,608
              Allowance for Doubtful Accounts          3,608
              To increase the asset valuation
              account to the estimated loss.
```

Assume, however, that the Allowance for Doubtful Accounts had a debit balance of $300 before adjustment, rather than a credit balance of $200. The adjusting entry would be for $4,108 ($3,808 + $300); after it is posted the allowance account will contain the desired credit balance of $3,808.

An analysis of accounts receivable by age is time-consuming; if there is a reliable pattern, the Allowance for Doubtful Accounts may be based on a single percentage of Accounts Receivable computed as follows:

End of Year	Balance of Accounts Receivable	Total Losses from Uncollectible Accounts
1966	$20,000	$ 800
1967	24,000	480
1968	22,000	700
Totals	$66,000	$1,980

The average loss of the past three years has been 3 percent ($1,980 ÷ $66,000). Assume that at the end of 1969, total accounts receivable are $25,000 and a credit balance of $150 is in the allowance account. Estimated uncollectible accounts at 3 percent of Accounts Receivable are $750 ($25,000 × .03). The following adjusting entry at the end of 1969 increases the Allowance for Doubtful Accounts to the desired amount of $750.

1969			
Dec. 31	Bad Debts Expense	600	
	Allowance for Doubtful Accounts		600
	To increase the asset valuation account to the estimated uncollectible account.		

A portion of the information for the following partial statement of financial position is taken from the preceding data.

WALTER CARTER COMPANY
Partial Statement of Financial Position
December 31, 1969

Assets

Current Assets		
Cash		$ 3,200
Accounts Receivable	$25,000	
Less Allowance for Doubtful Accounts	750	24,250
Notes Receivable		$18,000

Promissory notes receivable arising from the sale of merchandise may also prove to be uncollectible. The amount due from the customer on a dishonored note is removed from Notes Receivable and transferred to Accounts Receivable. The amount will remain in the Accounts Receivable account until it either is collected or is determined to be uncollectible and written off in the usual manner. When notes receivable specifically arise from the sale of merchandise, the current provision for estimated bad debts losses should be adequate to cover outstanding notes receivable and accounts receivable. The following partial statement of financial position presentation shows that the allowance covers Notes Receivable and Accounts Receivable jointly:

WALTER CARTER COMPANY
Partial Statement of Financial Position
December 31, 1969

Assets

Current Assets		
Cash		$ 3,200
Accounts Receivable	$25,000	
Notes Receivable	18,000	
Total	$43,000	
Deduct Allowance for Doubtful Accounts and Notes	750	42,250

Writing Off Uncollectible Accounts

When it is decided that a customer's account is definitely uncollectible, the amount due should be written off. Assuming that on February 15, 1970, the Walter Carter Company definitely determined that Charles Peacock's account (Figure 9-1) is uncollectible, the entry to record the write-off is:

1970			
Feb. 15	Allowance for Doubtful Accounts	50	
	Accounts Receivable–Charles Peacock		50

This entry has no effect on the net realizable value of the receivables; it only adjusts the balances of the two reciprocal accounts. The entry does not affect expenses because no expense was incurred on February 15, 1970; the expense was recorded by the adjusting entry of December 31, 1969. Assume that immediately before this entry was made, the books of the Walter Carter Company showed the following balances:

Accounts Receivable	$60,000
Allowance for Doubtful Accounts (credit)	2,110

When the entry to write off Peacock's account is posted, the result is:

	Balances Before Write-Off	Write-Off	Balances After Write-Off
Accounts Receivable	$60,000	$50	$59,950
Allowance for Doubtful Accounts	2,110	50	2,060
Estimated Realizable Value	$57,890		$57,890

This points up the fact that since the loss was recorded in the period when the sale was made, the subsequent write-off does not change assets, liabilities, or stockholders' equity.

Recovery of Bad Debts

An account that is written off as uncollectible may later be recovered in part or in full. In that event, the entry that was made to write off the account is reversed to the extent of the amount recovered or expected to be recovered. Assuming that Charles Peacock settles with his creditors for 50 cents on the dollar and that a check for $25 is received, the required journal entries are:

```
1970
Nov. 15   Accounts Receivable–Charles Peacock         25
              Allowance for Doubtful Accounts                    25
              To restore the collectible portion
              of the account previously written off.

          Cash                                         25
              Accounts Receivable–Charles Peacock              25
              To record payment received.
```

The debit and the credit to Accounts Receivable–Charles Peacock cancel each other, but they are necessary if a complete record of all transactions with the customer is to be maintained. Such a record may be of considerable aid if further extension of credit to Charles Peacock comes up for consideration at some future date.

The amount of Allowance for Doubtful Accounts should ideally be sufficient to absorb all write-offs of uncollectible accounts receivable; but since there may be a lag between uncollectibility and recognition of this fact or between the write-off of a receivable arising from the current year's sales and the adjusting entry for the bad debts expense, any debit or credit balance in the Allowance for Doubtful Accounts account before adjustments cannot be construed to be the result of an error.

Yet, because of changing economic conditions and the very fact that the percentage is based on past losses, errors can occur. Assume, for example, that the accountant of the Walter Carter Company, after analyzing Sales and Accounts Receivable, determines that the bad debts expense for 1969 is $4,000 and that the Allowance for Doubtful Accounts at December 31, 1969, should be $4,100; yet there is a debit balance of $1,000 in Allowance for Doubtful Accounts before adjustments. The appropriate adjusting entry is:

```
1969
Dec. 31   Walter Carter, Capital                     1,100
          Bad Debts Expense                           4,000
              Allowance for Doubtful Accounts                  5,100
              To correct a material underestimate
              of uncollectibles and to provide
              for an adequate allowance
              account.
```

Note in this case that if there had not been an error in prior years there would have been a $100 credit balance in Allowance for Doubtful Accounts before adjustments. If the Walter Carter Company had been a corporation, the debit of $1,100 would have been made to Retained Earnings.

Direct Write-Offs in Period of Discovery

A company that uses the direct write-off method postpones recognition of a bad debts expense until the receivable is definitely known to be uncollectible. In this case, an Allowance for Doubtful Accounts is not used, and no end-of-period adjusting entry for estimated losses is made. The February 15, 1970, entry on the books of the Walter Carter Company to remove Charles Peacock's account in full under the direct write-off method is:

```
1970
Feb. 15    Bad Debts Expense                              50
               Accounts Receivable–Charles Peacock                50
```

By this method, the loss is recognized in the period of write-off rather than in the period when the sale is made. The direct write-off method, as well as the methods previously illustrated, is acceptable for Federal income tax reporting purposes. This method, however, does not charge each accounting period with the losses arising out of sales made in that period and therefore violates the principle of matching expenses and revenue in each accounting period.

An account previously written off in the period of discovery may be subsequently collected in part or in full. Assume again that on November 15, 1970, Peacock makes a settlement of 50 cents on the dollar and issues a check for $25. The required journal entries are:

```
1970
Nov. 15    Accounts Receivable–Charles Peacock             25
               Bad Debts Recovered                                  25
                   To restore the collectible portion of
                   the account previously written off.

           Cash                                            25
               Accounts Receivable–Charles Peacock                 25
                   To record payment received.
```

Bad Debts Recovered is a revenue account; its balance may be reported in the Other Revenue section of the income statement.

Comparison of the Two Recording Procedures

The two methods of recording bad debts expense are shown in Figure 9-2, assuming the following data:

Allowance for Doubtful Accounts (credit balance, January 1)	$ 4,200
All sales on account	410,000
Cash collections on account	395,000
Sales returns and allowances	4,000
Accounts receivable written off as uncollectible	3,950
Bad debts recovered	250

The basis for estimating bad debt losses is
1 percent of Sales minus Sales Returns and
Allowances.

Allowance Accounts for Returns and Allowances and Cash Discounts

The net realizable amount of receivables on the statement of financial position indicates the amount of collections available to the firm after allowing for bad debts losses. For example, Accounts Receivable of $15,000 and a corresponding Allowance for Doubtful Accounts of $1,000 should result in a company's collecting approximately $14,000. In reality, other types of deductions may be made that will decrease

Transactions (Jan. 1–Dec. 31, 1969)	Estimating Bad Debts Expense		Direct Write-off	
All sales on account	Accounts Receivable 410,000		Accounts Receivable 410,000	
	Sales	410,000	Sales	410,000
Cash received on account	Cash 395,000		Cash 395,000	
	Accounts		Accounts	
	Receivable	395,000	Receivable	395,000
Sales returns and allowances	Sales Returns		Sales Returns	
	and Allowances 4,000		and Allowances 4,000	
	Accounts		Accounts	
	Receivable	4,000	Receivable	4,000
Accounts receivable determined to be uncollectible	Allowance for		Bad Debts Expense 3,950	
	Doubtful Accounts 3,950		Accounts	
	Accounts		Receivable	3,950
	Receivable	3,950		
Bad debts recovered	Accounts Receivable 250		Accounts Receivable 250	
	Allowance for		Bad Debts	
	Doubtful Accounts	250	Recovered	250
	Cash 250		Cash 250	
	Accounts		Accounts	
	Receivable	250	Receivable	250
Adjusting entry, December 31, 1969 ($410,000 − $4,000 = $406,000 × .01 = $4,060	Bad Debts Expense 4,060		(No entry is made)	
	Allowance for			
	Doubtful Accounts	4,060		
Closing Entry, December 31, 1969	Sales 410,000		Sales 410,000	
	Sales Returns		Bad Debts	
	and Allowances	4,000	Recovered 250	
	Bad Debts Expense	4,060	Bad Debts Expense	3,950
	Revenue and		Sales Returns	
	Expense Summary	401,940	and Allowances	4,000
			Revenue and	
			Expense Summary	402,300

Figure 9-2.
Two Methods of Accounting for Bad Debts Expense

this amount. Typical deductions are sales returns, sales allowances, cash discounts granted to customers for prompt payments, and collection expenses.

Ideally, all these additional deductions should have corresponding valuation accounts, so that Accounts Receivable in the statement of financial position will be stated at an amount closer to the net amount that will be collected. However, such valuation accounts as Allowance for Sales Returns and Allowances and Allowance for Sales Discounts are rarely used because, as a practical matter, the adjusting entry to debit the expense account will have no significant effect on net income. Also, these adjustments are not recognizable for income tax purposes.

Opposite Balances in Accounts Receivable and Accounts Payable

In the accounts receivable ledger, the customers' accounts normally have debit balances. Sometimes an overpayment, a sales return, a sales allowance, or an advance payment may convert the balance into a credit.

Assume that there is a net debit balance of $14,800 in an accounts receivable ledger consisting of 100 accounts, as follows:

98 accounts with a debit balance	$15,000
2 accounts with a credit balance	200
Net debit balance of 100 accounts receivable	$14,800

The debit amount of $15,000 and the credit amount of $200 should appear on the statement of financial position as follows:

Current Assets		Current Liabilities	
Accounts Receivable	$15,000	Credit Balances in	
		Customers' Accounts	$200

The controlling account balance of $14,800 should not be used in the statement of financial position because it would conceal the current liability of $200. Similarly, if the accounts payable ledger contains creditors' accounts with debit balances, the statement of financial position should show the total credit balances and the total debit balances of accounts payable. For example, if a company has a net balance in the Accounts Payable controlling account of $44,300 with certain subsidiary ledger accounts having debit balances that total $700, it should disclose this information in its statement of financial position as follows:

Current Assets		Current Liabilities	
Debit Balances in Creditors'		Accounts Payable	$45,000
Accounts	$700		

ACCOUNTS RECEIVABLE—MANAGERIAL ANALYSIS

The manager of a business that sells on credit must watch carefully for past-due accounts and guard against possible losses. A detailed analysis of the due date of each customer's account is desirable and should be secured periodically by preparing an aging statement similar to Figure 9-1. Two guides to the overall condition of the accounts receivable are the average collection period and the receivable turnover per year. If goods are sold on terms of 2/10, n/30, the amount of accounts receivable outstanding at any time should be less than the credit sales for the last 30 days because many of the sales will have been paid within the discount period. If allowance is made for slow-paying accounts, the receivables may represent 30 to 35 days' sales. If the receivables exceed this limitation, a careful analysis of all the accounts should be made.

To illustrate the computation of the average collection period, or number of days' sales uncollected, and the receivable turnover per year, the following data for the Morton Company are assumed:

	1970	1969	1968
Credit sales for year	$183,600	$165,600	$160,000
Trade accounts and notes receivable (net) at end of year	14,420	17,200	$15,000

Only receivables (accounts and notes) arising out of sales of merchandise on account are used. Discounted notes are included; the balance of Allowance for Doubtful Accounts is deducted in computing the average trade receivables balance.

		1970	1969
	1. Net credit sales	$183,600	$165,600
	2. Days in year (assuming commercial practice)	360	360
	3. Net credit sales per day (Line 1 ÷ Line 2)	$510	$460
	4. Average trade receivables (balance at beginning of year + balance at end of year ÷ 2)	15,810	16,100
	Average collection period (Line 4 ÷ Line 3)	31 days	35 days
	Receivable turnover per year (Line 1 ÷ Line 4)	11.6 times	10.3 times

Figure 9-3.
*Managerial Analysis
of Receivables*

If Line 1 covered sales for a period of less than one year, then Line 2 would be changed accordingly. Thus, if the sales were for a three-month period, Line 2 would show 90 days (1/4 of 360 days).

Average collection periods vary with the line of business. Wholesalers of shoes may average 45 days, compared with grocery wholesalers whose average is approximately 15 days. In the illustration in Figure 9-3, assuming that sales are on terms of 2/10, n/30, both years show a healthy situation, with 1970 particularly good.

The receivables turnover per year or the ratio of credit sales to receivables, is calculated by dividing net credit sales by the average balance of trade receivables. In Figure 9-3, the receivables for the year 1969 have been collected at a rate of approximately 10.3 times per year. For a standard of comparison, the preceding year's rate or the industry rate may be used. An increasing turnover of receivables as exhibited in Figure 9-3 indicates an improvement and reflects a decreasing relative amount of investment of working capital in receivables.

INTERNAL CONTROL—ACCOUNTS RECEIVABLE

As in the case of cash, adequate safeguards must be established for accounts receivable. It is important that persons who maintain the accounts receivable records should not have access to cash. Returns and allowances, discounts, and bad debt write-offs should be authorized by an officer and should be separated from the cash receipt and disbursement functions. Statements of account should be checked and mailed to customers by someone other than the accounts receivable bookkeeper. An independent check should be established to see that the statements sent to customers are in agreement with the accounts receivable records. Delinquent accounts should be reviewed periodically by a responsible official. Adequate control over receivables begins with the approved sales order and continues through the remaining stages in the credit sales process: approval of credit terms, recording of shipment, customer billing, recording the receivable and its collection, and approval of subsequent adjustments.

SUMMARY

Receivables represent amounts due from others for goods sold, services rendered, money lent, and deposits made. Those due within the year or the operating cycle, whichever is longer, should be classified as current assets; those not due within this period of time should be disclosed as long-term investments on the statement of financial position. Receivables should be segregated into Accounts Receivable–Trade, which are claims against customers for goods sold or services rendered, and Accounts Receivable–Nontrade, which are claims arising from sources other than normal sales of its regular product or service. These nontrade receivables include loans to officers or employees, deposits made on contract bids or with public utilities and public agencies, claims against common carriers for loss or damage to goods in shipment, loss claims against insurance companies, claims against the U.S. Treasury for tax refunds, amounts due from affiliated companies, and amounts due or accrued from rentals, interest, and royalties.

The balance of the Accounts Receivable–Trade account represents uncollected sales that have previously been recognized as revenue. Thus, to properly match revenues and expenses, any amounts that are expected to be uncollectible should be recognized as an expense in the period in which the related sales were realized as revenue. On the statement of financial position, Accounts Receivable–Trade should be valued at their net realizable value, or the amount that is ultimately expected to be collected. To accomplish this, an adjusting entry debiting Bad Debts Expense and crediting Allowance for Doubtful Accounts is made at the end of each accounting period. Bad Debts Expense is classified as a general and administrative expense in the income statement and Allowance for Doubtful Accounts is a contra account to Accounts Receivable in the statement of financial position. Two methods of estimating the amount of the bad debts adjustment are: (1) Income Statement Approach— the estimate of the bad debts expense is based on a specific percentage of sales or charge sales during the year; (2) Statement of Financial Position Approach—the estimate of the uncollectible accounts is determined by aging the accounts receivable or by taking a specific percentage of the total balance of Accounts Receivable. Regardless of the method of estimating the bad debts adjustment employed, the percentages should be based on previous years' experience amended for any developments expected to change the relationship. If the income statement approach is used, the adjusting entry is made for the amount of the estimated bad debts expense without reference to the balance of the Allowance for Doubtful Accounts. If the statement of financial position approach is followed, Allowance for Doubtful Accounts is adjusted to the balance determined in the analysis of the accounts receivable. The income statement approach yields a better estimate of the bad debts expense and thus a better measurement of net income; whereas the statement of financial position approach yields a better valuation of Accounts Receivable.

When a specific account proves to be uncollectible, it is written off by a debit to Allowance for Doubtful Accounts and a credit to Accounts Receivable. No expense is recognized at this time since the expense was previously recorded by the bad debts adjustment. If an account previously written off as uncollectible is collected, Accounts Receivable is debited with an accompanying credit to Allowance for Doubtful Accounts. The collection of the account is then recorded in the normal manner. Any material error in estimating the bad debts adjustment that results in a material over or understatement in Bad Debts Expense or Allowance for Doubtful Accounts should be corrected.

An alternative method of accounting for losses from uncollectible accounts is the direct write-off method. Under this procedure, no allowance account is utilized and losses are recognized in the period in which the accounts prove uncollectible. This method violates the matching principle since the expenses relating to the uncollectible accounts are not recorded in the period in which the related revenue is recognized.

Other possible valuation accounts to Accounts Receivable–Trade include deductions for sales returns and allowances, cash discounts, and collection expenses. In practice these adjustments are very rarely used since the amount involved is generally immaterial and none of these adjustments is allowed for Federal income tax purposes.

Any credit balances in customers' accounts in the accounts receivable ledger should be disclosed as current liabilities and not as offsets against the debit balances in the Accounts Receivable account.

Two devices that aid management in determining the effectiveness of internal control over Accounts Receivable are the receivables turnover and the average collection period (number of days' sales outstanding).

Internal control over receivables requires the segregation of the maintenance of accounts receivable and related records, handling of cash, and sending of statements to customers; the proper authorization of returns and allowances, discounts, and bad debts written off; reviews of delinquent accounts; and an independent check to determine that statements mailed to customers are in agreement with the customers' accounts.

☐ **QUESTIONS**

Q9–1. List eight different categories of receivables and state the probable financial position statement classification of each. The following format is suggested:

	Probable Financial Position
Receivable Item	Statement Classification

Q9–2. Discuss the general principle of the valuation of trade receivables.

Q9–3. a. Explain the function of the Allowance for Doubtful Accounts account.
      b. What methods may be used to estimate the Allowance for Doubtful Accounts?
      c. How is Allowance for Doubtful Accounts shown on the position statement?

Q9–4. Distinguish between the income statement approach and the statement of financial position approach in estimating the bad debts expense.

Q9–5. A company attempting to state its accounts receivable at their net realizable value may have to establish accounts other than the Allowance for Doubtful Accounts. Name three other valuation accounts for Accounts Receivable.

Q9–6. How would you interpret each entry in the following account?

ALLOWANCE FOR DOUBTFUL ACCOUNTS

1969						1968					
Mar.	10			J58	1,260	Dec.	31			J50	3,650
1970						1969					
Jan.	5			J68	750	Dec.	31			J65	3,420
						1970					
						Apr.	6			J70	555

Q9-**7.** The following entry was made to record the recovery of a bad debt:

Cash	365	
Allowance for Doubtful Accounts		365

Discuss the validity of this method of recording the recovery.

Q9-**8.** a. Discuss the reasons for credit balances occurring in Accounts Receivable accounts.

b. How are such balances presented in the statement of financial position?

Q9-**9.** a. Why is management concerned with the average collection period of Accounts Receivable?

b. Describe its computation.

Q9-**10.** The Slavon Company, which had Accounts Receivable of $56,850 and an Allowance for Doubtful Accounts of $2,610 on January 1, 1969, wrote off in 1969 a past due account of N. Healy for $575.

a. What effect will the write-off have on the total current assets of the Company immediately before and after the write-off?

b. On net income for 1969? Explain.

☐ EXERCISES

E9-**1.** The Jewel Company maintains a controlling account entitled Receivables, the balance of which at December 31, 1969, was $47,650. Subsidiary ledger and other information reveal the following:

304 trade accounts (debit balances)	$35,000
4 trade accounts (credit balances)	650
5 trade notes	8,000
2 loans to the president and vice president	5,300
Allowance for Doubtful Accounts	3,000

Show how this information should be reported on the statement of financial position.

E9-**2.** The Adjuster Company, which uses an Allowance for Doubtful Accounts, had the following transactions involving worthless accounts in 1969 and 1970:

1969

Dec. 31   Recorded bad debts expense of $2,000.

1970

Mar. 5   Wrote off N. O. Girard's account of $420 as uncollectible.
Apr. 10   Wrote off A. M. Stanley's account of $560 as uncollectible.
Sept. 6   Recovered $560 from A. M. Stanley.

Journalize the transactions.

E9-**3.** The Cashbas Company uses the direct write-off method of accounting for bad debts. It had the following transactions involving worthless accounts in 1969:

1969

Feb. 13   Wrote off Joseph White's account of $275 as uncollectible. The merchandise had been sold in 1968.

Aug. 13   Wrote off Alfred Green's account of $513 as uncollectible.

Dec. 10   Recovered $275 from Joseph White.

Journalize the transactions.

E9-4. The Benson Trading Company had charge sales of $550,000 during 1969 and Accounts Receivable of $52,500 and a credit balance of $150 in Allowance for Doubtful Accounts at the end of the year. Record the bad debts expense for the year, using each of the following methods for the estimate: (a) The Allowance for Doubtful Accounts is to be increased to 5 percent of Accounts Receivable. (b) Bad debts expense is estimated to be .5 percent of charge sales. (c) The Allowance for Doubtful Accounts is to be increased to $3,000, as indicated by an aging schedule. (d) Which method would you choose and why?

E9-5. The trial balance of the Halsey Company included the following accounts on August 31, 1969, the end of its fiscal year:

Accounts Receivable	$ 53,000
Allowance for Doubtful Accounts (credit)	250
Sales	383,000

Uncollectible accounts are estimated at 5 percent of Accounts Receivable. (a) Make the adjusting entry to record the bad debts expense. (b) State the bad debts expense for the year. (c) Show the presentation of Accounts Receivable and Allowance for Doubtful Accounts in the August 31, 1969, position statement. (d) Give the entry to write off the account of an insolvent customer, James Whitney, for $660.

E9-6. The accounts receivable ledger of the Valley Distributing Company shows the following data on December 31, 1969. The general ledger showed a $200 credit balance in Allowance for Doubtful Accounts before adjustments.

Name of Customer	Invoice Date	Amount
Modesto Fruit Company	May 2, 1969	$ 600.00
Neri Brothers	August 15, 1969	335.50
Paley Fruitrees, Inc.	October 2, 1969	719.85
	December 8, 1969	275.00
Temple Grapefruit Company	March 3, 1969	445.00
Royal Fruit Company	November 11, 1969	822.50
Yosemite Produce Company	November 20, 1969	250.00
	September 4, 1969	465.75
	July 10, 1969	922.00
[Others]	December 5, 1969	20,000.00

Terms of sale are n/30.

(a) Prepare an analysis of accounts receivable by age.

(b) Compute the estimated loss based on the following fixed percentages:

		Estimated Percentage Uncollectible
Accounts not due		0.5
Accounts past due:	1–30 days	1.0
	31–60 days	3.0
	61–90 days	10.0
	91–120 days	25.0
	121–365 days	50.0

(c) Record the bad debts expense.

E9-7. The Cash account page in the general ledger of the Winslow Corporation has been temporarily misplaced. The following data are available:

| | December 31 | | Year |
	1969	1968	1969
Accounts Receivable, Trade	$73,000	$59,000	
Allowance for Doubtful Accounts	5,200	3,100	
Sales			$605,000
Sales Discounts			10,350

During 1969, accounts receivable of $4,350 were written off as uncollectible and one account of $600, written off in 1967, was collected and recorded in the following manner:

Accounts Receivable	600	
Allowance for Doubtful Accounts		600
Cash	600	
Accounts Receivable		600

Compute the cash received from customers during 1969.

E9–**8.** The following transactions of the Spring Company occurred during 1969:

1969

Jan.   2   Sold merchandise with a list price of $6,500 subject to a trade discount of 20%, 10%, and 10%, terms 2/10, n/30, to John Olesum on credit.

     10   Received a check from John Olesum in settlement of his account.

     20   Sold merchandise worth $6,000 to Arthur Samuelson on account; terms n/10.

Feb.   1   Received a 6-percent, 120-day note from Samuelson in settlement of account.

     19   Discounted Samuelson's note at the Bank of Chapel Hill at 4 percent. Endorsed the note in blank and followed the practice of recording the contingent liability.

June 2   Samuelson dishonored his note. The bank charged for the note and interest plus a protest fee of $2.50.

a. Journalize the transactions. Use the gross methods of recording receivables and handling cash discounts.

b. What is the equivalent lump-sum trade discount to a 20%, 10%, and 10% chain trade discount? Show computations.

E9–**9.** The records of the General Appliance Company show that amounts due from customers were $200,000 and $260,000 at the beginning and the end of the year 1969, respectively, and that sales for that period were $2,000,000. What conclusions can be drawn regarding the collection of accounts receivable, assuming that:

a. Terms of sale are 2/10, n/30
b. Terms of sale are 2/10, n/40
c. Terms of sale are 2/10, n/40, and 25 percent of the sales are for cash?

E9–**10.** The Pacific Appliance Company sells on terms of 2/10, 1/20, n/60. Approximately 40 percent of its sales are for cash. The Accounts Receivable account shows a balance of $31,384 as of December 31, 1969. Total sales for the year were $365,200.

What is the average collection period?

☐ . **DEMONSTRATION PROBLEMS**

DP9–1. (*Use of Allowance for Doubtful Accounts*) The following transactions of the Elvond Company occurred in 1968, 1969, and 1970. The company uses the estimating procedure in accounting for bad debts.

1968
Dec. 31   Recorded bad debts expense of $4,650 for 1968.

1969
Mar. 10   Wrote off O. N. Collier's account of $650 as uncollectible.
Nov. 10   Wrote off various other accounts of $3,150 as uncollectible.
Dec. 31   Recorded bad debts expense of $4,265 for 1969.

1970
Feb.   6   O. N. Collier remitted $450 of the amount he owed the firm and agreed to pay the remainder in 30 days.

Required: Journalize the transactions.

DP9–2. (*Direct write-off method*) The following transactions of the Darwin Company occurred in 1969 and 1970. The company uses the direct write-off method of accounting for bad debts.

1969
Jan. 13   Wrote off B. E. Goodson's account of $313 as uncollectible.
Nov. 13   Wrote off O. N. Fair's account of $213 as uncollectible.
      20   Recovered the $313 from B. E. Goodson.
Dec. 13   Wrote off S. P. Santee's account of $613 as uncollectible.

1970
Mar. 10   Recovered the $213 from O. N. Fair.

Required: Journalize the transactions.

DP9–3. (*Adjusting entries for bad debts*) The partial trial balance of the Dellur Company at December 31, 1969, before any adjustments are made, is given:

DELLUR COMPANY
Partial Trial Balance
December 31, 1969

	Debit	Credit
Accounts Receivable	$80,000	
Notes Receivable	30,000	
Allowance for Doubtful Accounts and Notes	600	
Sales		$112,500
Sales Returns and Allowances	2,500	

Required: Prepare the adjusting entries for the bad debts expense under the following assumptions:
  a. Allowance for Doubtful Accounts and Notes is to be increased to 4 percent of trade receivables.
  b. The bad debts expense is estimated to be 1.8 percent of net sales.

☐ **PROBLEMS**

P9-1. The balance of Allowance for Doubtful Accounts of the Richfield Company on January 1, 1969, was $3,200. During 1969, uncollectible accounts totaling $2,900 were written off. The Company collected $200 on one of these accounts after it had been written off. The balance of the Accounts Receivable account on December 31, 1969, was $82,000.

Required: Make the journal entries to (a) charge off the worthless accounts during 1969, (b) record the collection of the $200, and (c) make the adjusting entry on December 31, 1969, for the bad debts expense. Assume that uncollectible accounts average 4 percent of the uncollected accounts.

P9-2. The Newman Company uses a cash receipts journal, a cash disbursements journal, a single-column purchases journal, a single-column sales journal, and a two-column general journal. The Accounts Receivable account in the general ledger at May 1, 1969, is given (posting references have been omitted):

Accounts Receivable

1969				1969		
May	1	Balance	22,500	May	5	1,500
	25		1,502		10	125
	31		26,200		28	1,502
					31	19,750

During the month, the general journal was used to record transactions with only two customers. The subsidiary ledger accounts of these two customers are shown:

William Donald

1969						
May	1	Balance	✔			(300) cr.
	6		S2	700		400
	10		J4		125	275

Allen Young

1969						
May	1	Balance	✔			1,500
	5	(20-day note)	J4		1,500	–0–
	25		CD6	1,502		1,502
	28		J4		1,502	–0–

Required: 1. Explain the $300 credit balance on May 1 in William Donald's account.
2. What would the posting references for the May 31 entries in the Accounts Receivable controlling account be?
3. What should be the total of the schedule of accounts receivable on May 31?
4. Explain the transaction that resulted in the debit of $1,502 on May 25 in Allen Young's account.
5. State in narrative form the transactions that resulted in each of the following credits to the Accounts Receivable controlling account: May 5, $1,500; May 10, $125; May 28, $1,502.

P9-3. The Allowance for Doubtful Accounts of the Bay State Company showed a credit balance of $200 on December 31, 1969, before adjustments were made. The bad debts expense for 1969 is estimated at 2 percent of the charge sales of $90,000 for the year.

The following transactions occurred during the next two years:

1970

May   1   Wrote off George Shaw's $900 account as uncollectible.

Oct. 15   Wrote off John Foley's $1,200 account as uncollectible.

Nov. 30   Received a check from George Shaw for $100 in final settlement of the account written off on May 1. He had been adjudged bankrupt by the courts.

Dec. 31   An analysis of accounts receivable by age indicated that accounts doubtful of collection totaled $1,900.

1971

Aug. 21   Wrote off Joseph Sack's $1,800 account as uncollectible.

Dec. 31   Estimated that uncollectible accounts receivable totaled $2,400.

Required: 1. Record transactions in general journal form.
2. Post to a T account for Allowance for Doubtful Accounts. Rule and balance the account at the end of each year.

P9-4. The balance of the Accounts Receivable account of the Rangeley Company at December 31, 1969, was $72,360. Two customers' accounts in the subsidiary ledger show credit balances of $3,160 and $1,200.

Required: 1. What is the amount that would be shown on the position statement as Accounts Receivable under Current Assets?
2. How would the credit balances in the customers' accounts be disclosed?

P9-5. The Accounts Receivable controlling account of the Wine Corporation shows a balance of $345,000 on June 30, 1969. A summary of the analysis of accounts receivable by age shows accounts outstanding from the date of the invoice as follows:

1–30 days	$260,000
31–60 days	40,000
61–90 days	25,000
91–180 days	15,000
Over 180 days	5,000
Total	$345,000

Allowance for Doubtful Accounts has a debit balance of $210 on June 30, before adjustments. The adjustment of the allowance account is to be based on the following schedule of percentages estimated uncollectible:

1–30 days	½ of 1%
31–60 days	3%
61–90 days	6%
91–180 days	20%
Over 180 days	50%

Required: 1. Prepare the necessary adjusting entry.
2. Prepare a partial position statement, showing Accounts Receivable and Allowance for Doubtful Accounts.

P9-**6.** The accounts receivable ledger of the Lowe Company showed the following information on March 31, 1970:

Franklin Davis

1969						
Aug.	12		S27	4,250 00		4,250 00
Sept.	10		S33	743 00		4,993 00
	30		CR15		4,250 00	743 00
Oct.	12		S45	1,407 00		2,150 00
Nov.	4		S52	415 00		2,565 00
Dec.	10		CR27		415 00	2,150 00
1970						
Jan.	12		S6	500 00		2,650 00
	13		CR4		1,407 00	1,243 00
	15		S7	783 00		2,026 00
	17	Allowance on 1/15 invoice	J2		93 00	1,933 00

M. Kaditch

1969						
Nov.	12		S51	1,000 00		1,000 00
Dec.	12		CR28		500 00	500 00
1970						
Jan.	29		S9	761 00		1,261 00
Mar.	10		S17	550 00		1,811 00
	31		CR11		550 00	1,261 00

Peter Wallace

1969						
Dec.	12		S56	5,401 00		5,401 00
1970						
Jan.	12	Note	J2		3,000 00	2,401 00
Feb.	26		S14	1,800 00		4,201 00
Mar.	26		S22	2,000 00		6,201 00

Paul Winik

1969									
Aug.	1			S24	973	00		973	00
Oct.	12			S45	76	00		1,049	00
1970									
Jan.	2	Return		J2			700 00	349	00
Feb.	3			S10	699	00		1,048	00
	12			S13	200	00		1,248	00
Mar.	30			CR11			899 00	349	00

Required: 1. Prepare an analysis of accounts receivable by age as of March 31, 1970. Assume that the terms of sale are n/30.

2. Make the adjusting entry for the bad debts expense on the basis of the age of the account as follows:

1–30 days	½%
31–60 days	2%
61–90 days	5%
91–120 days	10%
Over 120 days	33⅓%

There is a debit balance of $123 in Allowance for Doubtful Accounts on March 31, 1970, before adjustments.

P9–7. On December 31, 1969, John Delaney's trial balance showed the following:

Accounts Receivable	$72,000
Allowance for Doubtful Accounts (credit)	300

After making an analysis of the accounts receivable, Delaney estimates the accounts doubtful of collection at $3,000.

During the year 1970, the following transactions occurred:

1. Sales on account were $320,000.
2. Accounts written off as uncollectible totaled $3,300.
3. Collections from customers on account were $308,900. This includes a receipt of $100 that had been written off during the year as uncollectible.

On December 31, 1970, the accounts doubtful of collection were estimated at $3,400.

Required: 1. Set up T accounts for Accounts Receivable and Allowance for Doubtful Accounts, post the balances as of December 31, 1969, and make the entries for 1969 and 1970 directly into the T accounts.

2. Compute the bad debts expense deduction in the income statement for the year 1970, using: (a) the direct write-off method; (b) the Allowance for Doubtful Accounts method.

P9–8. During November and early December, 1969, the Chapel Hill Sales Company had the following sales and receivables transactions. All sales were made on account and carried terms of 2/10, n/30.

1969

Nov. 1 Sold merchandise to Jay Swan for $390 on Invoice 1001.

2 Sold merchandise to Ray Faulk for $2,150 on Invoice 1002.

7 Credited Ray Faulk for returned merchandise with an invoice price of $350.

9 Received a check for the amount due from Jay Swan on Invoice 1001.

10 Sold merchandise to the Scuppernong Company for $460 on Invoice 1003.

13 Received $205.80 in cash from the Scuppernong Company in partial payment of Invoice 1003. Discounts are allowed on partial payments.

14 Received a check for the amount due from Ray Faulk.

15 Sold merchandise to the Albermarle Company for $3,000 on Invoice 1004.

23 Received a check for the amount due from the Albermarle Company on Invoice 1004.

30 Sold merchandise to the Paris Company for $2,850 on Invoice 1005.

30 Sold merchandise to the Ronson Company for $3,250 on Invoice 1006.

30 Estimated the bad debts expense for November to be 2.5 percent of charge sales less sales returns and allowances.

Dec. 8 Received notice that the Scuppernong Company had been adjudged bankrupt. The balance of its account is therefore regarded as uncollectible.

Required: 1. Journalize the transactions.
2. Post all entries to the Accounts Receivable controlling and subsidiary accounts.
3. Prepare a schedule of accounts receivable at November 30, 1969.

CASE PROBLEM
Northwest Loan Company

The Northwest Loan Company has been in operation for five years, having started business on July 1, 1964. During this period, the Company has followed a policy of writing off potentially uncollectible loans receivable directly to the expense account. On the recommendation of an outside accountant, the management has decided to begin using the allowance method.

The maximum period of a loan is one year. The Company's credit manager reviews the loan accounts that are past due every day, and whenever he deems it advisable, he instructs the bookkeeper to write off particular accounts. Even after accounts are written off, the manager continues his efforts to collect. Collections of accounts previously written off are recorded by debiting Cash and crediting Miscellaneous Revenue. A memorandum notation is made on the subsidiary loans receivable record.

The following data have been accumulated, some of which will be useful in the development of a revised loan policy for the fiscal year ending June 30, 1969.

	1969	1968	1967	1966	1965
Total debits to Loans Receivable for loans extended during the fiscal year	$860,000	$500,000	$200,000	$80,000	$40,000
Total debits to expense for accounts written off during the fiscal year	25,730	28,650	8,300	5,600	1,560
Total amounts collected during the fiscal year on loans previously written off	3,740	2,550	1,560	630	–0–
Total loans receivable (after deducting loans written off) as of the end of the fiscal year	573,280	314,200	127,800	49,610	25,630
Total loans written off that originated during the fiscal year	22,900*	30,140	10,750	3,900	2,150
Total amounts collected on loans originating during the fiscal year and previously written off	1,100*	5,140	1,350	380	510
Total credits to Loans Receivable for collections received during the fiscal year (excluding collections for loans previously written off)	575,190	284,950	113,510	50,420	12,810
Total amounts collected on loans originating during the fiscal year (excluding collections for loans previously written off)	263,820	469,860	189,250	76,100	37,850

* These are not conclusive data, since all loans receivable on June 30, 1969, originated during 1969, some of which may later be considered uncollectible and may afterwards be collected.

Required: 1. Explain why the outside accountant recommended the substitution of the allowance method for the direct write-off method.
2. What is the objective of the allowance method?
3. What effect does this method have on each of the financial statements? Are these effects justified?
4. Reconstruct the Loans Receivable controlling account of the Northwest Loan Company.
5. Construct a separate Loans Receivable account for each of the five years in which the postings are based on events that are specifically identified (or matched) with each separate year in which the loans originated instead of being based on the timing of the transaction entries.
6. What basis would you recommend for determining the amount that will be debited annually to Bad Debts Expense and credited to Allowance for Doubtful Accounts? Show your computations.
7. Prepare a series of journal entries (or a compound summarizing entry) to adjust Bad Debts Expense for the year ended June 30, 1969, and Allowance for Doubtful Accounts to the recommended amount.
8. Describe to the management the procedures that should be followed in writing off bad loans receivable and the procedures that should be followed if one of these written-off loans is later collected.
9. Prepare a partial statement of financial position illustrating how Loans Receivable and Allowance for Doubtful Accounts are to be reported.

Chapter
Ten
The
Measurement
and
Control
of
Inventory

Inventory in a wholesale or retail business—that is, a nonmanufacturing business—is generally understood to mean goods owned by the business for sale to customers. Alternative terms are *merchandise* and *merchandise inventory*. Up to this point in the text, the amount of the merchandise inventory was specified and, therefore, assumed to be correct. The factors involved in arriving at the value of the inventory—classification of items, determination of physical quantities on hand, and techniques of assigning costs—were not stated. These factors, however, are indispensable in valuing the merchandise inventory for the preparation of financial statements.

THE IMPORTANCE OF INVENTORY VALUATION

The proper valuation, or *costing*, of the merchandise inventory is of considerable importance. The inventory is often large in proportion to the other items in the financial statements; a misstatement of the inventory will cause a misstatement in the period when the error occurs of the cost of goods sold, gross margin on sales, and net income, and will misstate current assets, and stockholders' equity as of the end of that period. Furthermore, since the ending inventory of one accounting period is the beginning inventory of the next period, any over or understatement will also misstate the cost of goods sold, gross margin on sales, and net income of the next period.

The following information is taken from the income statements of a retail store at December 31, 1968 and 1969:

	1969		1968	
Sales		$300,000		$250,000
Cost of Goods Sold				
Beginning Inventory	$ 90,000		$ 80,000	
Purchases	150,000		120,000	
Total	$240,000		$200,000	
Deduct Ending Inventory	105,000	135,000	90,000	110,000
Gross Margin on Sales		$165,000		$140,000
Expenses		130,000		120,000
Net Income		$ 35,000		$ 20,000

If it is assumed that the ending inventory for 1968 should have been valued at $85,000 rather than $90,000, the effect of the error on the income statements is evident from the corrected statements:

	1969		1968	
Sales		$300,000		$250,000
Cost of Goods Sold				
Beginning Inventory	$ 85,000		$ 80,000	
Purchases	150,000		120,000	
Total	$235,000		$200,000	
Deduct Ending Inventory	105,000	130,000	85,000	115,000
Gross Margin on Sales		$170,000		$135,000
Expenses		130,000		120,000
Net Income		$ 40,000		$ 15,000

The $5,000 overstatement of the ending inventory in 1968 resulted in the following errors in the two income statements:

	1969	1968
Cost of Goods Sold	Overstated	Understated
Gross Margin	Understated	Overstated
Net Income	Understated	Overstated

Since the misstatements cancel each other, the error has no overall effect on the two-year span covered by the statements. That fact, however, does not diminish the seriousness of an inventory valuation error. The interpretation and analysis of the income statement for each period may influence some basic management decisions. Since both income statements are in error, their reciprocal canceling effect does not cancel management errors caused by reliance on two incorrect statements.

THE BASIS OF INVENTORY VALUATION

Inventories are recorded at cost. The term *cost*, as defined in Accounting Research Bulletin No. 43, includes all expenditures "incurred in bringing the inventory to its existing condition and location."[1] Cost consists of the invoice price of the merchandise

---

[1] *Accounting Research and Terminology Bulletins*, 1961. New York: American Institute of Certified Public Accountants, *Accounting* Research Bulletin No. 43., p. 28.

(less purchase discounts) plus transportation in, insurance while in transit, and any other expenditures made by the buyer to get the merchandise to his place of business. In the interest of simplifying the clerical task of prorating these other costs to the various items of inventory purchased, they are frequently carried in separate accounts and the Purchases account shows only the invoice price. If these amounts are significant in relation to the invoice price of the merchandise, a proportionate part should be added to the cost of the goods on hand at the end of the period. The cost of the inventory may be determined in several different ways. Accounting Research Bulletin No. 43 specifies that the method used to determine cost should be the one that "most clearly reflects periodic income."[2]

Accounting Concept: Valuation of Assets at Cost ▶

The term *value* is defined as "the amount at which an item is stated, in accordance with the accounting principles related to that item."[3] "Since accounting is predominantly based on cost, the proper uses of the word *value* in accounting are largely restricted to the statement of items at cost, or at modifications of cost."[4] ▶ The accountant, therefore, usually expresses *value* in terms of *cost*. ◀ There are, of course, other concepts of value; the accountant's valuation is *historical*, or prior, cost which is objective, being subject to measurement. It is this objectivity that accounts for the predominance of historical cost as a valuation basis. The economist, on the other hand, relates value to current and anticipated prices, which, in the absence of available bases of measurement, are subjective. The distinction between these two concepts is especially important during periods of rapidly rising prices with their concomitant effect on financial statement valuations. Many persons in and out of the profession question the usefulness of cost as a valuation concept when prices are unstable. Nevertheless, the cost concept is thoroughly established in accounting.

Periodic and Perpetual Inventory Methods

There are two methods used for determining inventory quantities on hand: periodic (physical count) and perpetual (continuous record).

PERIODIC INVENTORY. With the periodic inventory method, the value of the inventory for statement of financial position presentation and for the determination of the cost of goods sold is determined at the end of each accounting period by a complete physical count and pricing of all inventory items. Acquired goods not on hand are assumed to have been sold. Possible merchandise losses through misappropriation, breakage, or other causes are reflected in the cost of goods sold as a deduction from revenue, although these goods do not actually create revenue. Small retail businesses often use the periodic method as a matter of expedience since it does not require a continuous record of inventory balances.

---

[2] *Ibid.*, p. 29.

[3] *Accounting Research and Terminology Bulletins*, 1961. New York: American Institute of Certified Public Accountants, *Accounting Terminology Bulletin No. 1*, p. 17.

[4] *Ibid.*, p. 16.

PERPETUAL INVENTORY. The perpetual inventory method provides for a continuous book inventory of items on hand; it is a method of recordkeeping. A card or sheet may be kept for each inventory item acquired; when units are purchased or sold, the inventory record for the item must be adjusted accordingly to show the quantity on hand at any time. The maintenance of continuous inventory records does not preclude the need for a complete annual physical inventory. Some companies that use the perpetual inventory method take physical counts of portions of the inventory during the course of the year to test whether the records are in agreement with quantities actually on hand. This practice may be followed instead of taking a complete annual physical inventory.

A perpetual inventory may be costly to maintain, especially when the inventory includes numerous items of small value. A company may, therefore, maintain continuous records for only certain classifications of its inventory. A hardware supply company, for example, may find it feasible to use the perpetual inventory method only for items with a high unit selling price and the periodic inventory method for all other items.

Assigning the Cost of the Merchandise

The total cost of goods available for sale must be allocated between the cost of goods sold and the cost of goods on hand. With the periodic inventory method, this allocation takes place at the end of each accounting period; with the perpetual inventory method, it takes place after each sale and each acquisition.

The process of assigning costs would be relatively simple—and ideal—if each item acquired could be marked and identified with a specific invoice cost. Such a procedure is possible in certain businesses where the items are large or otherwise readily traceable. In most instances, however, specific identification of each inventory item is neither feasible nor practical, particularly when successive acquisitions are commingled in common storage facilities. The problem is complicated further by the fact that acquisitions of like items are usually made at fluctuating prices. Consequently, a method of assigning costs to merchandise items—with either a perpetual or periodic inventory method—based on an assumed flow of goods must be adopted and followed consistently. (The principle of consistency is discussed later in this chapter.) The most commonly used methods of assigning costs to inventory items are:

Perpetual Inventory Method
1. First-in, first-out (FIFO)
2. Last-in, first-out (LIFO)
3. Moving average
4. Specific identification

Periodic Inventory Method
1. First-in, first-out (FIFO)
2. Last-in, first-out (LIFO)
3. Weighted average
4. Specific identification

When costs are determined by either the FIFO or the LIFO procedure, it is essential that the inventory method used—periodic or perpetual—be clearly stated.

This is especially significant with LIFO costing because the resulting cost assignments may be different.

To illustrate the various methods of assigning costs to inventories, the following information pertaining to a single inventory item is given. Prior to April 1, 1969, the specific identification method of inventory valuation was in use.

1969
April 1   Inventory on hand consisted of 20 units, purchased at $2.20 each.
     5   Purchased 60 units at $2.60 each.
   10   Purchased 35 units at $2.80 each.
   11   Sold 30 units.
   15   Purchased 40 units at $3.50 each.
   19   Sold 50 units.
   22   Purchased 100 units at $3.20 each.
   30   Sold 60 units.

For convenience, the data are rearranged as follows:

	Units	Unit Cost		Total Cost
Inventory, April 1	20	$2.20		$ 44
Purchases				
April 5	60	2.60	$156	
10	35	2.80	98	
15	40	3.50	140	
22	100	3.20	320	714
Totals	255			$758
Sales				
April 11	30			
19	50			
30	60			
Total	140			
On hand, April 30	115	(255 − 140)		

FIRST-IN, FIRST-OUT (FIFO) COSTING. The FIFO method of determining the cost of goods on hand and the cost of goods sold is based on the assumption that the units are sold in the order in which they were acquired; that is, the oldest units on hand are sold first, the units acquired next are the next to be sold, and so on. This assumption relates only to the method of accounting and not to the actual physical movement of the goods. The unsold units on hand at the date of the inventory are assumed to be the units acquired most recently.

Perpetual Inventory Method—FIFO Costing. A detailed perpetual inventory card illustrating the FIFO procedure for assigning costs is shown in Figure 10-1.

Date	Ref.	Received (or Purchased)			Issued (or Sold)			Balance		
		Quantity	Unit Cost	Total Cost	Quantity	Unit Cost	Total Cost	Quantity	Unit Cost	Total Cost
1969 April 1	Balance							20	2.20	44.00
5	P.O. 673	60	2.60	156.00				20 60	2.20 2.60	44.00 156.00
10	P.O. 678	35	2.80	98.00				20 60 35	2.20 2.60 2.80	44.00 156.00 98.00
11	S.R. 401				20 10	2.20 2.60	44.00 26.00	50 35	2.60 2.80	130.00 98.00
15	P.O. 690	40	3.50	140.00				50 35 40	2.60 2.80 3.50	130.00 98.00 140.00
19	S.R. 407				50	2.60	130.00	35 40	2.80 3.50	98.00 140.00
22	P.O. 701	100	3.20	320.00				35 40 100	2.80 3.50 3.20	98.00 140.00 320.00
30	S.R. 409				35 25	2.80 3.50	98.00 87.50	15 100	3.50 3.20	52.50 320.00

Figure 10-1.
Perpetual Inventory Card (FIFO)

As each shipment of goods is received, the quantity, unit cost, and total cost are recorded in the appropriate columns. When goods are issued, the unit cost of the oldest goods on hand is recorded in the Unit Cost column; this cost is then multiplied by the number of units, and the total is written in the Total Cost column. For instance, 30 units were issued on April 11 on Stock Requisition 401; 20 units are recorded at the cost of the 20 units on hand at April 1, and the rest at the cost of the shipment received on April 5 on Purchase Order 673. The balance on hand, unit cost, and total cost for each shipment from which units are assumed to remain are recorded in the Balance column.

The inventory on April 30 is assumed to consist of:

$$
\begin{array}{llr}
\text{15 units @ \$3.50} & = & \$\ 52.50 \\
\underline{\text{100}} \text{ units @ \$3.20} & = & \underline{\ 320.00} \\
\underline{\underline{\text{115}}} \text{ units} & = & \underline{\underline{\$372.50}}
\end{array}
$$

Periodic Inventory Method—FIFO Costing. When FIFO costing is used with the periodic inventory method, a continuous record of balances on hand is not kept. Rather, a physical count of the units is taken on April 30; they are valued on the assumption that they consist of the most recent acquisitions as follows:

Date Acquired	Quantity	Unit Price	Total Price
April 22	100	$3.20	$320.00
15	15	3.50	52.50
Total	115		$372.50

The cost of the units sold is decided on the assumption that the sales of April 11 (30 units) and April 19 (50 units) came from the 20 units on hand on April 1 and the 60 units purchased on April 5. The 60 units sold on April 30 are assumed to be the 35 units acquired on April 10 and 25 units of those acquired on April 15. Therefore, the 115 units on hand on April 30 are assumed to consist of the 15 unsold units from the April 15 purchase and the 100 units acquired on April 22. The cost of the units sold may be summarized as follows:

Cost of beginning inventory plus purchases			$758.00
Cost of April 30 ending inventory			
	15 units at $3.50	$ 52.50	
	100 units at $3.20	320.00	
Total	115 units		372.50
Cost of goods sold			$385.50

When FIFO costing is used, the amount of the ending inventory as well as the amount of the cost of goods sold is identical with either the periodic or the perpetual inventory method because in each instance the goods on hand are assumed to consist of the most recently acquired units.

LAST-IN, FIRST-OUT (LIFO) COSTING. LIFO costing is based on the assumption that the cost of goods sold should be based on prices paid for the most recently acquired units and that the inventory consists of the oldest units on hand. The major advantage claimed for this procedure is that during periods of continuously rising prices, the higher prices of the most recent purchases are included in the cost of goods sold, thereby reducing the gross margin on sales and the taxable income. It is further claimed that the cost of goods sold is more realistic because LIFO costs most nearly approximate current replacement costs.

Perpetual Inventory Method—LIFO Costing. The application of LIFO costing to the perpetual inventory method is illustrated in Figure 10-2.

Issued goods are listed at the unit cost of the latest acquisition, up to the amount assumed to be still on hand. For instance, of the 50 units sold on April 19, 40 are recorded at the cost of the 40 units received on April 15, 5 at the cost of the 5 units remaining of those received on April 10, and 5 at the cost of the units received on April 5. The balance on hand, unit cost, and total cost for each shipment from which units are assumed to remain are recorded in the Balance column.

Date	Ref.	Received (or Purchased)			Issued (or Sold)			Balance		
		Quantity	Unit Cost	Total Cost	Quantity	Unit Cost	Total Cost	Quantity	Unit Cost	Total Cost
1969										
April 1	Balance							20	2.20	44.00
5	P.O. 673	60	2.60	156.00				20	2.20	44.00
								60	2.60	156.00
10	P.O. 678	35	2.80	98.00				20	2.20	44.00
								60	2.60	156.00
								35	2.80	98.00
11	S.R. 401				30	2.80	84.00	20	2.20	44.00
								60	2.60	156.00
								5	2.80	14.00
15	P.O. 690	40	3.50	140.00				20	2.20	44.00
								60	2.60	156.00
								5	2.80	14.00
								40	3.50	140.00
19	S.R. 407				40	3.50	140.00	20	2.20	44.00
					5	2.80	14.00	55	2.60	143.00
					5	2.60	13.00			
22	P.O. 701	100	3.20	320.00				20	2.20	44.00
								55	2.60	143.00
								100	3.20	320.00
30	S.R. 409				60	3.20	192.00	20	2.20	44.00
								55	2.60	143.00
								40	3.20	128.00

The inventory on April 30 is assumed to consist of:

Figure 10-2.
Perpetual Inventory Card (LIFO)

20 units @ $2.20	$ 44
55 units @ 2.60	143
40 units @ 3.20	128
115 units	$315

The cost of goods sold is $443 (goods available for sale, $758, less ending inventory, $315).

Periodic Inventory Method—LIFO Costing. Under the periodic inventory method, the 115 units in the ending inventory on April 30 are assumed to consist of the beginning inventory of 20 units and, following the chronological sequence of purchases, the receipts of April 5, 60 units, and April 10, 35 units, for a total cost of $298. The cost of the units sold may be summarized as follows:

Cost of beginning inventory plus purchases			$758
Cost of April 30 inventory	20 units at $2.20	$ 44	
	60 units at $2.60	156	
	35 units at $2.80	98	
Total	115 units		298
Cost of goods sold			$460

Note that, unlike FIFO costing, the valuations of the cost of goods sold and ending inventory under LIFO costing may be different, depending on whether the perpetual or the periodic inventory method is used. When LIFO costing is used with the perpetual inventory method, prices at the beginning of the period that would be reflected in the ending valuation with the periodic inventory method may be dropped from the running balance as goods are issued. When the inventory is taken only at the end of the period, the various dates of sales are ignored. The LIFO procedure may be used appropriately with either periodic inventories or perpetual inventories even though the results may be different; the method selected, however, should be followed consistently. The following tabulation illustrates the different results of LIFO costing with the perpetual and the periodic inventory methods:

	Perpetual Inventory	Periodic Inventory
Inventory, April 1	$ 44	$ 44
Purchases	714	714
Total	$758	$758
Inventory, April 30	315	298
Cost of goods sold	$443	$460

Perpetual Inventory Method—Moving Average Costing. Under moving average costing, the cost of each purchase is added to the cost of units on hand, and the total cost is divided by the total quantity on hand to find the average price. Units issued are priced at the average price until additional units are purchased; then a new average price is computed. This method tends to level off price fluctuations. The application of moving average costing is shown in Figure 10-3.

Periodic Inventory Method—Weighted Average Costing. Under weighted average costing—not to be confused with moving average costing—the ending inventory is priced at the end of each accounting period at a unit cost computed by dividing the total cost of goods available for sale by the physical units available for sale. Similarly, all quantities sold are stated at a uniform price—the computed average price for the period. The assignment of costs to goods sold during the month must be delayed until the end of the month so that the weighted average cost computation can be made.

The average cost for the period, the inventory valuation, and the cost of goods sold is computed as follows:

Date			Units	Unit Cost	Total
1969					
April	1	Beginning inventory	20	$2.20	$ 44
	5	Purchase	60	2.60	156
	10	Purchase	35	2.80	98
	15	Purchase	40	3.50	140
	22	Purchase	100	3.20	320
		Totals	255		$758

Average unit cost ($758 ÷ 255)	$ 2.9725
Units on hand, April 30	115
Inventory valuation (115 × $2.9725)	$341.85
Units sold	140
Cost of goods sold (140 × $2.9725)	$416.15

Date	Ref.	Received (or Purchased)			Issued (or Sold)			Balance		
		Quantity	Unit Cost	Total Cost	Quantity	Unit Cost	Total Cost	Quantity	Unit Cost	Total Cost
1969										
April 1	Balance							20	2.20	44.00
5	P.O. 673	60	2.60	156.00				80	2.50	200.00(a)
10	P.O. 678	35	2.80	98.00				115	2.5913	298.00(b)
11	S.R. 401				30	2.5913	77.74	85	2.5913	220.26
15	P.O. 690	40	3.50	140.00				125	2.882	360.26(c)
19	S.R. 407				50	2.882	144.10	75	2.882	216.16
22	P.O. 701	100	3.20	320.00				175	3.06377	536.16(d)
30	S.R. 409				60	3.06377	183.83	115	3.06377	352.33

Computations

(a)	(b)	(c)	(d)
20 @ $2.20 = $ 44	80 @ $2.50 = $200	85 @ $2.5913 = $220.26	75 @ $2.882 = $216.16
60 @ 2.60 = 156	35 @ 2.80 = 98	40 @ 3.50 = 140.00	100 @ 3.20 = 320.00
80 $200	115 $298	125 $360.26	175 $536.16
Average $2.50	Average $2.5913	Average $2.882	Average $3.06377

The inventory valuation as of the end of the month is $352.33

Figure 10-3.
Perpetual Inventory Card (Moving Average Costing)

SPECIFIC IDENTIFICATION COSTING

The specific identification method of inventory valuation may be used if the goods purchased can be identified specifically with the related underlying documents. Some businesses mark the specific cost in code on every unit so that each item of inventory as well as each unit sold may be valued. Valuation by specific identification can be used with either the perpetual or the periodic inventory method. In either case, the cost of units sold as well as the cost of units remaining on hand is determined by reference to the related specific invoices.

Assume that the 115 units in the ending inventory consisted of 25 units purchased at $3.50 and 90 units purchased at $3.20, identified by the invoice numbers as being from the acquisitions of April 15 and April 22. The inventory valuation is computed as follows:

$$
\begin{array}{lll}
25 \text{ units @ } \$3.50 & = & \$ 87.50 \\
90 \text{ units @ } 3.20 & = & 288.00 \\
\hline
115 \text{ units} & & \$375.50
\end{array}
$$

The valuation of the units sold is computed as follows:

$$
\begin{array}{lll}
20 \text{ units @ } \$2.20 & = & \$ 44.00 \\
60 \text{ units @ } 2.60 & = & 156.00 \\
35 \text{ units @ } 2.80 & = & 98.00 \\
15 \text{ units @ } 3.50 & = & 52.50 \\
10 \text{ units @ } 3.20 & = & 32.00 \\
\hline
140 \text{ units} & & \$382.50
\end{array}
$$

In many instances, whether due to the volume of items involved or because the items are of a kind that make individual coding impossible, the method of specific identification is impracticable. Similar items acquired on different dates and at different prices may be commingled, or *fungible* (interchangeable) items—wheat in bins, coal in piles—might be matched with unrelated invoices, thereby misstating net income.

PERPETUAL AND PERIODIC INVENTORY METHODS COMPARED

With the periodic inventory method assumed in the preceding chapters, the beginning inventory is shown in a Merchandise Inventory account, and all purchases are entered in a Purchases account. The cost of goods sold does not appear as an account balance in the general ledger, but is determined only after the physical inventory is taken at the end of the period. With the perpetual inventory method, however, the beginning inventory and all purchases are shown as debits in a Merchandise Inventory (asset) account. The cost of all goods sold is debited to a Cost of Goods Sold Account and credited to the Merchandise Inventory account. The balance of the Merchandise Inventory account is the cost of the goods remaining in the inventory, provided there have been no shrinkages or other losses. The Merchandise Inventory account is a controlling account supported by a subsidiary inventory ledger made up of inventory record cards for all items.

The entries in summary journal form for both methods, based on the data in Figure 10-1, are:

Periodic Inventory

(1)

Purchases	714	
Accounts Payable		714
To record April purchases.		

(2)

Accounts Receivable	770	
Sales		770
To record April sales of		
140 units at $5.50 each.		

Perpetual Inventory

(1)

Merchandise Inventory	714	
Accounts Payable		714
To record April purchases.		

(2)

Accounts Receivable	770	
Sales		770
To record April sales		
of 140 units at $5.50 each.		

(3)

Cost of Goods Sold	385.50	
Merchandise Inventory		385.50
To record the cost of		
140 units sold (amounts from		
Issued column, Figure 10-1).		

After Entries 1 and 3 under the perpetual inventory method are posted, the affected accounts in the general ledger appear as shown:

Cost of Goods Sold			
April 30	385.50		

Merchandise Inventory			
April 1 Balance	44.00	April 30 Cost of goods sold	385.50
30 Purchases	714.00		

The Merchandise Inventory account shows a balance of $372.50, which is the cost of goods on hand to be reported in the statement of financial position for April 30.

The perpetual inventory cards (Figures 10-1, 10-2, and 10-3) combine a system of control of inventory quantities with a method of assigning costs. Some companies employ the perpetual inventory card form only for controlling quantities: receipts, issues, and running balances are recorded, but the procedure for determining the cost of the inventory is the same as with the periodic method. One advantage of using perpetual inventory cards is that financial statements may be prepared without taking a physical inventory; this is an important advantage to businesses that require frequent—usually monthly—statements.

INVENTORY VALUATION METHODS COMPARED AND ANALYZED

The primary basis for the valuation of inventories is cost. The most common methods of inventory valuation have been discussed in this chapter; others may be used in special circumstances. In a particular business, the method selected should be the one that will best measure net income.

If there are no significant price changes in the merchandise handled during a given period, and the quantity held does not change, FIFO, LIFO, and moving average costing will produce approximately the same results. If the prices of the goods acquired fluctuate significantly during the period, however, the method of inventory valuation used will have a direct effect on the financial statements. In Figure 10-1, the price of the item fluctuated from $2.20 to $3.50 during the month. To illustrate the comparative effect of rising prices on the financial statements under perpetual FIFO, moving average, and LIFO costing, the basic data (page 343) for the preceding discussions are used again. Two additional assumptions are made: (1) the selling price of each unit is $5.50, and (2) the operating expenses for the month are $100. These computations of income are for a single inventory item. The effect of the different methods on net income would be proportionately increased with increasing volume and number of items. The effect of the three methods of allocating inventory cost and cost of goods sold under the stated assumptions is further highlighted in Figure 10-4, which is abstracted from the preceding income computations:

	Perpetual FIFO		Perpetual Moving Average		Perpetual LIFO	
Sales (140 units × $5.50)		$770.00		$770.00		$770.00
Cost of Goods Sold						
Beginning Inventory	$ 44.00		$ 44.00		$ 44.00	
Purchases	714.00		714.00		714.00	
Total	$758.00		$758.00		$758.00	
Ending Inventory	372.50	385.50	352.33	405.67	315.00	443.00
Gross Margin on Sales		$384.50		$364.33		$327.00
Deduct Operating Expenses		100.00		100.00		100.00
Net Income		$284.50		$264.33		$227.00

Figure 10-4.
Summary Tabulation

	FIFO	Moving Average	LIFO
Ending inventory	$372.50	$352.33	$315.00
Cost of goods sold	385.50	405.67	443.00
Gross margin on sales	384.50	364.33	327.00
Net income	284.50	264.33	227.00

During a period of rising prices, FIFO costing results in the highest ending inventory valuation, gross margin on sales, and net income and the lowest cost of goods sold. Given the same rising market conditions, the LIFO inventory method gives the opposite results: lowest ending inventory valuation, gross margin on sales, and net income and highest cost of goods sold. During a period of falling prices, FIFO results in the lowest ending inventory valuation, gross margin on sales, and net income and the highest cost of goods sold; LIFO gives the opposite results.

The major advantage of LIFO costing is that during a prolonged period of generally rising prices lower year-to-year earnings are reported, with a concomitant income tax advantage. A major disadvantage is that during inflationary periods LIFO costing results in a significant understatement of current assets. Its purpose is to match revenue with current cost, rather than with earliest cost, as is done under FIFO costing.

Figure 10-4 shows that the amounts for the four income statement items listed under moving average costing fall between the corresponding amounts for FIFO and LIFO costing. The same position would be maintained in a falling market. Moving average costing minimizes the effect of widely fluctuating prices on inventory valuations.

The position statement classifies the ending inventory as a current asset; consequently, this statement as well as the income statement is affected by the method of inventory valuation used. The ending inventory is often the largest single item in the Current Assets section and has, therefore, a decided effect on the current ratio, the reported amount of working capital, the merchandise inventory turnover, the total stockholders' equity, and related ratios.

Some accountants recommend the use of replacement cost for inventory valuation. This may be defined as the current cost of replacing the inventory items at the inventory date, in the ordinary course of business, assuming access to the usual sources of supply and at volumes in which the goods are usually purchased.

A committee of the American Accounting Association, in a report on inventory measurement, criticized the historical cost method of inventory measurement for its "failure to recognize significant happenings during the holding or converting period,"[5] and said that "neither Fifo nor Lifo spotlights price gains or losses . . . when prices rise, Fifo buries price gains in the regular income figure; Lifo excludes the effects of price changes from the income statement. . . . ."[6] The majority of the members maintained that "replacement cost is the best of the several available inventory measurements" and that "both historical and replacement cost of inventories should be disclosed in an integrated set of financial statements."

> Other members of the committee find the problems of inventory and income measurement too complex for solution by selection of any one inventory pricing method. Hence, they recommend that disclosure be given to alternative inventory measures on a comparative basis. This is a multiple statement approach with complementary income statements and balance sheets prepared on different bases and presented together so a reader is made aware of the influence of alternative measurement methods. They favor the simultaneous presentation of statements based on historical (acquisition) cost and the best available estimate of "current value" in order to disclose adequately the status and progress of the enterprise.[7]

The Committee stressed the importance of reporting gains or losses from price changes in the periods in which they occur and observed that "when meaningful measurement can be made, it seems evident that the segregation of price or holding gains or losses (from inventory planning and control decisions) and trading or transaction gains or losses (from exchange of goods and services at replacement price levels) will be more helpful than their usual combination into one gross margin measure."[8]

LOWER OF COST OR MARKET (LCM)

The various methods of inventory valuation discussed thus far in this chapter are methods of arriving at the cost of the inventory. ► However, a long-standing convention in accounting holds that inventories may be valued at the *lower of cost or market.* ◄ The position of the American Institute of Certified Public Accountants is that:

Accounting Concept:
◄ *Lower of Cost or Market*

> A departure from the cost basis of pricing the inventory is required when the utility of the goods is no longer as great as its cost. Where there is evidence that the utility of goods, in their disposal in the ordinary course of business, will be less than cost, whether due to

---

[5] Supplementary Statement No. 2 to Accounting and Reporting Standards for Corporate Financial Statements—1957 Revision, American Accounting Association, Committee on Concepts and Standards—Inventory Measurement, "A Discussion of Various Approaches to Inventory Measurement," as reported in the Accounting Review, July, 1964, p. 703.

[6] *Ibid.,* p. 705.

[7] *Ibid.,* p. 700.

[8] *Ibid.,* p. 705.

physical deterioration, obsolescence, changes in price levels, or other causes, the difference should be recognized as a loss of the current period. This is generally accomplished by stating such goods at a lower level commonly designated as *market*.[9]

The term *market* generally means the cost of replacing the goods as of the position statement date. For Federal income tax purposes, market means the current bid price (current replacement cost) prevailing on the inventory date for the particular items for the volume usually purchased by the taxpayer.

Application of Lower of Cost or Market

The process of valuing the inventory at LCM takes place at the end of the accounting period, when financial statements are prepared. It may be done in any one of three ways:

1. By pricing each item individually at the lower of cost or market
2. By comparing the total cost with the total market price of the entire inventory and using the lower figure
3. By comparing the total cost with the total market price of each major inventory category and using the lower figure.

Based on the inventory tabulations in Figures 10-5 and 10-6 (FIFO costing is assumed), the valuation under each procedure is as follows (Items A and B are assumed to constitute Category X and the remaining items constitute Category Y):

1. If each item is valued individually, the inventory is reported as $5,725.
2. If the inventory is valued in total, it is reported as $6,225.
3. If the inventory is valued by major categories, it is reported as $5,925 (Figure 10-6).

Figure 10-5.
*Application of LCM—
Item and Total
Inventory Bases*

Item	Quantity	Unit Cost	Unit Market Price	Total Cost	Total Market	Lower of Cost or Market
A	100	$10	$9.00	$1,000	$ 900	$ 900
B	200	4	6.00	800	1,200	800
C	400	1	1.25	400	500	400
D	600	6	5.00	3,600	3,000	3,000
E	250	3	2.50	750	625	625
Totals				$6,550	$6,225	$5,725

Evaluation of LCM

The reason for LCM inventory valuation is to avoid the anticipation of profits and to provide for all foreseeable losses. This principle was developed when the influence of the grantor of credit was paramount and when primary emphasis was on the state-

---

[9] *Accounting Research and Terminology Bulletins*, 1961. New York: American Institute of Certified Public Accountants, *Accounting Research Bulletin No. 43*, p. 30.

ment of financial position and on conservative asset valuations. It is based on the assumption that a drop in the purchase price of goods will be followed by a corresponding drop in the selling price of those goods, thereby reducing or eliminating the normal profit margin.

Item	Quantity	Unit Cost	Unit Market Price	Total Cost	Total Market	Lower of Cost or Market
Category X						
Item A	100	$10	$9.00	$1,000	$ 900	
Item B	200	4	6.00	800	1,200	
Total				$1,800	$2,100	$1,800
Category Y						
Item C	400	1	1.25	$ 400	$ 500	
Item D	600	6	5.00	3,600	3,000	
Item E	250	3	2.50	750	625	
Total				$4,750	$4,125	4,125
Total at LCM						$5,925

Figure 10-6.
Application of LCM Major Categories Basis

The arguments against LCM are: (1) it is a departure from the cost concept; (2) it is inconsistent because presumed losses are anticipated but potential gains from an increase in the purchase price of goods are ignored, and some goods may be priced at cost and others at market when LCM is applied to individual items or categories; (3) the expectation of lower selling prices may not materialize, thereby distorting the income of several periods. This is not to say that a serious decline in inventory valuation should be ignored, but rather to challenge the arbitrariness of the LCM rule and its reliance on the dubious assumption of a normal profit margin.

A partial statement of the position of the American Accounting Association on inventory pricing follows:

> The residual cost should be carried forward in the balance sheet for assignment in future periods except when it is evident that the cost of an item of inventory cannot be recovered, whether from damage, deterioration, obsolescence, style change, over-supply, reduction in price-levels, or other cause. In such event the inventory item should be stated at the estimated amount of sales proceeds less direct expense of completion and disposal.[10]

The rule of lower of cost or market is generally applied to individual items—the required procedure for Federal income tax reporting—rather than to the whole inventory. Pricing each item individually results in a lower inventory valuation of those items for which the market value is below cost. The loss is typically absorbed in the cost of goods sold. The application of LCM to the total inventory, however, may be more useful for accounting purposes, either because (1) the value of

---

[10] *Accounting and Reporting Standards for Corporate Financial Statements and Preceding Statements and Supplements, Supplementary Statement No. 6,* "Inventory Pricing and Changes in Price Levels," 1953. Columbus: American Accounting Association, p. 36.

Accounting Concept:
Consistency of Reporting
for Tax Determination ▶ the entire inventory is of greater significance than the value of the parts or (2) goods in inventory with a market value less than cost are counterbalanced by equal quantities whose market value exceeds cost. A consistent procedure must be followed from year to year. ▶For Federal income tax purposes, greater emphasis is placed on *consistency of method* than on the particular method. ◀ Either cost or the lower of cost or market is acceptable for tax purposes, except for goods valued under LIFO costing. The Federal income tax regulations state that upon adoption of LIFO costing no other method of inventory valuation may be used in annual statements, including reports to stockholders or creditors. The use of LCM is not permitted in conjunction with LIFO costing, although this does not preclude the disclosure, by footnote or parenthesis, of the excess of the FIFO valuation of the inventory over the LIFO valuation.

POSITION STATEMENT DISCLOSURE—INVENTORY

Studies of financial reports prepared by leading corporations show that LCM is the most commonly used basis of valuation for inventories, the only other common basis being cost. Cost, of course, includes LIFO, FIFO, and weighted average valuations, by either the perpetual or the periodic inventory method. LIFO costing is the method most frequently used.

Some typical examples of how inventories are reported in statements of financial position from the published annual reports of business corporations are shown:

(1)

Current Assets
    Merchandise Inventories— at lower of cost or market $2,500,000

Note: Inventories are reported at the lower of FIFO cost or estimated market on the basis of specific items and classes of merchandise. Obsolete stock is carried at estimated salvage value.

(2)

Current Assets
    Merchandise Inventories $3,250,549

Note: Inventories are stated at cost, certain inventories at average cost and others at FIFO cost. These costs are not in excess of market value.

(3)

Current Assets
    Merchandise Inventories $ 552,100

Note: Inventories are stated at the lower of cost or market. During 1969, the Company adopted LIFO costing for a portion of its inventories. The effect of this change was to reduce net income by $27,000, and Federal income taxes by $12,000. FIFO costing is used for the balance of the inventories.

THE GROSS MARGIN METHOD OF ESTIMATING INVENTORIES

Taking a physical inventory or maintaining perpetual inventory records is often costly and time-consuming. For some purposes—preparing monthly financial statements; checking the accuracy of a physical inventory; or estimating inventory value when an accurate valuation cannot be made, as in the case of a fire loss—the *gross margin* method of estimating the inventory is used.

Assume that during the previous three years the Needham Company has averaged a gross margin rate on sales of 30 percent, as shown:

	Prior Years			
	1	2	3	Totals
Sales	$124,000	$142,000	$154,000	$420,000
Cost of Goods Sold	87,420	97,980	108,600	294,000
Gross Margin	$ 36,580	$ 44,020	$ 45,400	$126,000
Gross Margin Rate	29.5%	31%	29.5%	30%

For the current year, the following data are available from the records of the Company:

Inventory–January 1, 1969	$ 20,000
Purchases during 1969	110,000
Sales during 1969	160,000

Under the gross margin method, the estimated inventory on December 31, 1969, would be computed as follows:

Inventory–January 1, 1969		$ 20,000
Purchases		110,000
Total goods available		$130,000
Deduct estimated cost of goods sold		
Sales	$160,000	
Deduct gross margin (30% of $160,000)	48,000	112,000
Estimated inventory, December 31, 1969		$ 18,000

An alternative procedure is to arrange the data for the current year in conventional income statement form, and then to fill in the missing items as follows:

			Percent of Sales
Sales		$160,000	100
Cost of Goods Sold			
Inventory–January 1, 1969	$ 20,000		
Purchases	110,000		
Total	$130,000		
Estimated Inventory, December 31, 1969	? (d)	? (c)	? (a)
Gross Margin		? (b)	30

a) If the gross margin is 30 percent of sales, the cost of goods sold must be 70 percent.

b) If the gross margin is 30 percent of sales, then the gross margin is 30 percent of $160,000, or $48,000.

c) If the gross margin is $48,000, then the cost of goods sold must be $160,000 − $48,000, or $112,000.

d) If cost of goods sold is $112,000, then the ending inventory must be:

Total goods available	$130,000
Cost of goods sold	112,000
Ending inventory	$ 18,000

This method is based on the assumption that the rate of gross margin on sales is substantially the same in every period. It is accurate, therefore, only to the extent that the assumed gross margin rate reflects the experience of the current period. It is essential that a careful study be made of possible differences between the past data from which the assumed rate is derived and the corresponding current data. Appropriate adjustments should be made for significant differences. The inventory on hand at the end of the current period computed by this method is the amount that would result in a gross margin rate equal to the assumed rate.

RETAIL METHOD OF ESTIMATING INVENTORIES

Another method of estimating the ending inventory, commonly used by chain and department stores, is the *retail inventory* method. Its value is twofold: It serves as a means of computing the ending inventory without a physical count and also provides a method of centrally controlling inventories that consist of a variety of items dispersed over several departments or several branch stores. Goods are charged to the departments or branches at their selling price, records of both cost and selling price are kept centrally, and records of sales are kept in the usual manner. From these records, the inventory valuation may be prepared at any time as shown in Figure 10-7.

Figure 10-7.
Retail Inventory Method

	Cost	Retail
Inventory at beginning of period	$ 20,000	$ 30,000
Purchases during period	180,000	270,000
Total goods available	$200,000	$300,000

Cost percentage (ratio of cost to retail)

$$\frac{\$200,000}{\$300,000} = 66\tfrac{2}{3}\%$$

	Cost	Retail
Sales during period		258,000
Estimated inventory at retail		$ 42,000
Estimated inventory at cost (66⅔% of $42,000)	$ 28,000	

A company may find it necessary to increase or decrease previously established retail prices. Increases—called *markups*—are added in arriving at the total goods available for sale. Decreases—called *markdowns*—are excluded in arriving at the cost percentage but are combined with sales for the period. This results in a lower cost percentage and, therefore, a lower inventory when that percentage is applied to the retail figure. It is also a logical procedure because it assumes that goods that have been marked down have been sold, given away, or reduced to nominal value. It is also consistent with the principle that inventories should be valued at the lower of cost or market. Markups and markdowns are included in the computation as shown:

	Cost	Retail
Inventory at beginning of period	$ 20,000	$ 30,000
Purchases during period	179,000	270,000
Transportation in during period	1,000	
Markups during period		10,000
Total goods available	$200,000	$310,000

Cost percentage (ratio of cost to retail)

$$\frac{\$200,000}{\$310,000} = 64.516\%$$

Sales during period	$258,000	
Markdowns during period	8,000	
Total sales (at intended retail)		266,000
Estimated inventory at retail		$ 44,000
Estimated inventory at cost (64.516% of $44,000)	$ 28,387.04	

Both the gross margin method and the retail inventory method are based on a calculation of the gross margin rate: the gross margin method uses past experience as a basis; the retail inventory method uses current experience.

A physical inventory should be taken periodically. This inventory is first computed at the retail selling prices marked on the goods, reduced to cost by using the cost percentage, and then compared with the inventory value computed in the manner shown in Figure 10-7. If there have been losses due to thefts or shrinkage, the valuation based on the physical inventory will be less than that shown by the records, and an adjustment is made for the decrease.

The retail inventory method offers a means of determining a company's inventory at frequent intervals without taking a physical count—a valuable tool for purposes of preparing financial statements or other reports that require an inventory valuation. Its reliability rests on the assumption that the percentage of cost to retail is fairly uniform within the several departments of the company and for all the various items sold. If that is not the case, separate records should be maintained for the different departments and for the different items handled. Use of the retail inventory method is permissible for Federal income tax purposes.

MARKON COMPUTATIONS

Pricing goods held for sale requires an addition to the cost of the merchandise of a *markon* to cover operating expenses and profit. In most industries, percentage comparisons of markon, costs, and expenses are expressed in terms of net sales, but in some industries the comparisons are in terms of cost. It is essential, therefore, that the basis used—cost or sales—be clearly understood, particularly in quoting prices and in making internal and external income statement comparisons.

Assume, for example, that $25 is marked on an item costing $100, so that the item sells for $125. Using cost as the base (100 percent), the percentage of markon is computed as follows:

	Amount	Percent
Sales	$125	125
Cost	100	100 (base)
Gross margin (markon)	$ 25	25

$$\frac{\$125}{\$100} = 1.25 \text{ or } 125\% \qquad \frac{\$25}{\$100} = .25 \text{ or } 25\%$$

The use of the selling price as the base (100 percent) gives the following percentages of markon:

	Amount	Percent
Sales	$125	100 (base)
Cost	100	80
Gross margin (markon)	$ 25	20

$$\frac{\$100}{\$125} = .80 \text{ or } 80\% \qquad \frac{\$25}{\$125} = .20 \text{ or } 20\%$$

Accounting Concept:
Consistency ▶

CONSISTENCY IN THE APPLICATION OF PROCEDURES

Different procedures may be used in different areas of accounting. ▶ It is of paramount importance, therefore, that the selected method should be followed consistently from year to year. ◀ Lack of consistency in inventory pricing, cost allocations, and financial statement presentation would make year-to-year comparisons of operating results and financial position meaningless. Since such comparisons often serve as the basis for managerial decisions, the importance of consistency becomes evident.

The concept consistency may be applied at several levels. Consistency is important not only in the matter of valuation procedures followed but also with respect to the classification of items in financial statements. Consistency in classification applies to the grouping of items within each statement as well as to year-to-year consistency. The principle of consistency does not preclude required changes properly made and fully disclosed. A change from FIFO to LIFO inventory costing, for example, requires an explanation accompanying the financial statements of the year of change, giving the nature of the change and its effect.

INVENTORY CONTROL

Lack of control over inventories can be a serious detriment to the successful management of a business. An excessive inventory is expensive to carry. Studies made indicate that the costs of carrying an inventory—taxes, insurance, warehousing, handling, and inventory-taking—may be as high as 25 percent of the original purchase price. This is exclusive of lost potential earnings (interest) on the funds tied up in inventories.

On the other hand, sufficient items and quantities must be stocked to provide customers with good service.

Maintaining a proper balance, to avoid both shortages and excesses of inventory, requires organization and planning. Control plans must provide for day-to-day comparisons of projected inventory acquisitions with current sales volume. A reduction in sales volume will result in excess inventories unless adjustments are made.

Inventory Turnover

The cost of goods sold divided by the average inventory gives the *inventory turnover,* a useful guide in inventory control (see page 174). The turnover rate may be computed for individual items or for major categories in order to establish item-by-item control.

Ratio of Inventory to Working Capital

The ratio of inventory to working capital is an indication of the amount of working capital invested in inventory and the amount of currently maturing obligations that will have to be met with proceeds from the sale of the inventory. If, for example, a firm's ending inventory is $330,000 and its working capital is $300,000, the ratio is

$$\frac{\text{Ending Inventory}}{\text{Working Capital}} = \frac{\$330,000}{\$300,000} = 110\%$$

This ratio, being greater than 100 percent, indicates that the current debt cannot be paid in full from cash on hand and proceeds from receivables, but will require, in addition, part of the proceeds from the sale of inventory.

Maximum and Minimum Levels

It is customary to establish maximum and minimum stock levels for inventory items, so that the purchasing agent is automatically notified when the balance on hand is at the minimum quantity and the item must be replenished. Minimum levels should be set to allow for anticipated sales requirements during the time required for placing the replenishment order and receiving the goods, with a margin for unforeseen delay. Maximum balances should be set, based on sales requirements, minimum stock point, and the most economical buying quantities.

Economical Buying Quantities

Deciding the quantity to purchase involves considering the cost of acquisition and the cost of carrying the items. Ordering large quantities often results in a lower unit purchase price and lower transportation costs per unit, but the saving is offset by the increased cost of carrying the inventory. Carrying cost includes taxes, insurance, storage, losses due to obsolescence and deterioration, interest on the investment, and so on. The point at which the aggregate of all the cost elements—cost to order, carrying cost, and purchase cost—is lowest indicates the most economical quantity to order or the number of orders to place each year.

Assume, for example, that a quantity of steel pins is to be purchased; the company normally uses 12,000 of these pins each year. The seller has submitted three alternative lot sizes for consideration, with price reductions for the larger lots, as follows:

Lot Size	Unit Price	Number of Orders per Year
1,000	$1.00	12
2,000	.90	6
12,000	.87	1

Assume further that clerical and other costs of placing one order is $5, and that inventory carrying costs are 15 percent of the cost of the average inventory on hand. Normal usage is 1,000 pins each month. Assuming a reasonably consistent pattern of usage, the average inventory may be figured at one-half the lot size ordered. The computation of the most economical buying quantity is shown in Figure 10-8.

1 Annual Usage (Given)	2 Orders per Year (Col. 1 ÷ Col. 3)	3 Quantity Considered (Given)	4 Unit Price (Given)	5 Purchase Cost per Order (Col. 3 × Col. 4)	6 Total Purchase Cost (Col. 2 × Col. 5)	7 Order Cost (Col. 2 × $5)	8 Carrying Cost (½ of Col. 5 × 15%)	9 Total Annual Cost (Col. 6 + 7 + 8)
12,000	12	1,000	$1.00	$ 1,000	$12,000	$60	$ 75	$12,135
12,000	6	2,000	.90	1,800	10,800	30	135	10,965
12,000	1	12,000	.87	10,440	10,440	5	783	11,228

Figure 10-8.
Schedule for Determining Most Economical Buying Quantity

The most economical buying quantity is the 2,000 lot size, purchased six times yearly for a total annual cost of $10,965.[11]

PERIODIC PHYSICAL INVENTORIES—SPECIAL CONSIDERATIONS

A periodic physical count of the entire inventory is an essential element of inventory control. A physical count (that is, a count by weight or measure) and valuation serves to confirm perpetual inventory records. If perpetual records are not maintained, an annual physical inventory is an absolute necessity for the preparation of financial statements. A physical count also aids in reviewing the condition of the goods on hand and detecting errors or laxity in the system of accounting for, storing, and handling merchandise.

The taking of a physical inventory requires careful planning—setting the date, selecting and instructing the inventory takers, and establishing controls and procedures. It is advantageous to select a business year that ends when quantities are low and when the inventory taking will interfere least with the regular operations of the business. When necessary, technically trained personnel must be available to assist in identifying items; others must be available to move bulky items or to reach items not easily accessible.

---

[11] This example is taken from K. W. Bennett, "Special Report," *Iron Age*, September, 1957, V. 180, p. 83.

It is common practice to attach consecutively numbered tags to all inventory items for recording the counts as they are made. Upon completion of the count, the filled-in tags are removed and checked to ensure that they have all been returned. The inventory items and quantities are then accumulated on inventory sheets showing descriptions, quantities, unit costs, and total costs. If tags are not used, the inventory count is entered directly on the inventory sheets. The unit costs to be shown on the inventory sheets depend on the costing method employed—LIFO, FIFO, and so on. If there is a discrepancy between the records and the count, the inventory records are brought into agreement with the physical count. The cause of the discrepancy should be traced so that steps may be taken to prevent a recurrence.

Item descriptions on the inventory tags must be complete and accurate. To eliminate confusion resulting from incorrect or inadequate item descriptions, the tags may be prepared in advance from the stock records.

Some inventory items cannot be counted, measured, or weighed conveniently, such as piles of coal, large quantities of nails dumped in bins, and partially used tanks or containers of materials. Other appropriate means must be devised to estimate the quantities of such items on hand. Obsolete or damaged merchandise must be identified clearly and excluded from the inventory if it is unsalable. If such goods are salable at a reduced price, they should be valued at the reduced price less any selling costs.

Since the inventory is taken as of a specific date, a careful record must be kept of acquisitions, withdrawals, and goods in transit during the inventory period. Goods on hand for which the liability has been recorded are included in the inventory; goods held for shipment and charged to the customer must be excluded. Goods owned but physically elsewhere—at a branch warehouse or under *consignment*—must be included in the inventory.

SUMMARY

The proper valuation and costing of merchandise inventory is of considerable importance. Inventory includes goods owned by the business held for sale to customers. Cost includes the invoice price of the merchandise less purchase discounts plus transportation in, insurance while in transit, and any other costs paid by the buyer to get the merchandise to his place of business.

There are two methods for inventory and cost of goods sold valuations: periodic, based on a complete physical count and pricing of all inventory items, and perpetual, based on a continuous book inventory of items on hand.

Since specific identification of each inventory item is usually neither feasible nor practical, and since similar items are normally acquired at fluctuating prices, a method of assigning costs to merchandise items—under either a perpetual or periodic inventory system—based on an assumed flow of goods must be adopted and consistently followed. The commonly used methods based on actual cost include FIFO, LIFO, moving average, weighted average, and specific identification.

The FIFO method is based on the assumption that units are sold in the order in which they were acquired. The assumption relates only to the method of accounting and not to the actual physical movement of the goods. The LIFO method is based on the assumption that the cost of goods sold should reflect the prices paid for the most recently acquired units and that the inventory consists of the oldest units on hand.

Under the moving average method, the cost of each purchase is added to the cost of the units on hand, and their total cost is then divided by the total quantity on hand for a new average price. Units issued are priced at the newest average price until additional units are purchased and another new average price is computed. Under the weighted average method, the ending inventory is priced at a unit cost computed by dividing the total cost of goods available for sale by the physical units available for sale. Units issued are stated at a uniform price—the computed average price for the period.

The primary basis for the valuation of inventories is cost. In a particular business, the method that will best measure net income should be used.

Inventories may be valued at the lower of cost or market—cost as computed by any of the methods discussed and market meaning the cost of replacing the goods as of the position statement date. Lower of cost or market may be applied to each item individually, to the total inventory, or to each major inventory category.

Two methods are available for estimating the ending inventories, the gross margin method and the retail method. The gross margin method is based on the assumption that the rate of gross margin on sales is substantially the same during each period. It is accurate only to the extent that the assumed gross margin rate reflects the experience of the current period. The inventory is computed by deducting the estimated cost of goods sold (sales minus estimated gross margin on sales) from sales.

The retail method is also based on a calculation of the gross margin rate but, whereas the gross margin method is based on past experience, the retail method uses current experience for its gross margin relationship. The inventory is computed first at the retail selling prices of the goods, and then reduced to cost by using the cost-to-retail percentage.

Whatever the method used, a periodic physical count of the entire inventory is an essential element of inventory control.

☐ QUESTIONS

Q10-**1.** Distinguish between the terms *cost* and *value* when used in connection with inventory valuations. Is this distinction imperative during periods of price stability? during periods of rising prices? during periods of falling prices?

Q10-**2.** Why are accountants reluctant to abandon the assumption that the dollar is a stable unit of valuation?

Q10-**3.** Why is it important that the selected method of inventory valuation be applied consistently from year to year? Does strict compliance with the principle of consistency preclude a change from FIFO to LIFO?

Q10-**4.** Distinguish between the perpetual and periodic inventory methods. Does the perpetual inventory method eliminate the need for a physical inventory count?

Q10-**5.** How do over or understatements of inventory affect net income in the period when the error is made? in the following period?

Q10-**6.** What effect do the different methods of inventory valuation have on the financial statements?

Q10-**7.** Compare the gross margin method with the retail inventory method.

Q10-**8.** An audit of the records of the Lebanon Corporation showed that the ending inventory on December 31, 1968, was overstated by $5,200 and that on December 31, 1969, the inventory was understated by $8,400. What was the effect of the errors on the income statement for each year? What was the overall effect for the two-year period?

Q10-**9.** The Kraft Company maintains perpetual inventory cards for all merchandise items. An inventory is taken annually. Serially numbered perforated tags are placed on or alongside the various items. The inventory is taken by teams of two employees: one fills in the description and quantity of the item on each section of the tag; the second checks both the description and the count and removes the second half of the tag. The removed portions of the tags are then sent to the office, where the information is entered on inventory sheets and priced on the basis of lower of cost or market. Explain the purpose of each step of this procedure. Criticize the procedure followed. State what precautionary steps must be taken prior to the actual inventory count, during the count, and immediately following the completion of the count.

Q10-**10.** Explain the effect on the statement of financial position valuation and on the income determination of the use of LIFO as compared with FIFO (a) if prices have risen during the year; (b) if prices have fallen during the year.

Q10-**11.** (a) Define the term *market* as used in lower of cost or market inventory valuation. (b) What is the rationale for LCM? (c) Does LCM always produce conservative financial statements?

Q10-**12.** Explain the means by which a company can protect itself against errors, theft, or the improper use of inventory items.

☐ **EXERCISES**

E10-**1.** The inventory of the Lister Company on January 1 and December 31, 1969, consisted of 17,000 and 25,000 units, respectively, of Commodity X-1. The beginning inventory was priced at $1,360. The following purchases were made during the year:

Date		Quantity	Cost
January	10	9,000	$ 810
April	15	17,000	1,445
July	5	24,000	2,280
October	2	6,000	600
December	15	16,000	1,280

Determine the cost of the December 31, 1969, inventory by each of the following methods: (a) LIFO; (b) FIFO; (c) weighted average. Assume that the periodic inventory method is used.

E10-**2.** The beginning inventory, purchases, and sales of the West Company for the month of August, 1969, were:

1969
August 1 Inventory on hand consisted of 40 units at $1.05 each.
      12 Sold 25 units.

1969

August 15   Purchased 20 units at $1.00 each.

      17   Purchased 30 units at $.90 each.

      19   Sold 15 units.

      25   Purchased 25 units at $1.15 each.

      29   Sold 20 units.

What was the value of the units on hand on August 31 under (a) the perpetual inventory moving average method, and (b) the periodic inventory weighted average method?

E10–**3.** The following information was taken from the books of the Lowell Corporation:

1969

January	1	On hand	4,000 units @ $8.00
February	14	Purchase	6,000 units @ 8.60
June	12	Purchase	7,000 units @ 8.40
November	12	Purchase	5,000 units @ 8.50
December	31	On hand	6,000 units

The periodic inventory method is used. Compute the value of the inventory on December 31, 1969, under (a) FIFO and (b) LIFO.

E10–**4.** The O'Brien Company calculates its inventory by the gross margin method for interim statement purposes. The inventory on January 1 was $35,000, net purchases during January were $105,000, and net sales for the month were $150,000. The gross margin rate is estimated at 32 percent of net sales. What was the estimated inventory on January 31?

E10–**5.** The entire stock of the Ace Appliance Company was destroyed by fire on August 22, 1969. The books of the company (kept in a fireproof vault) showed the value of goods on hand on August 1 to be $83,400. Transactions for the period August 1 through August 22 resulted in the following amounts:

Sales	$197,560
Sales Returns	4,210
Purchases	159,600
Purchases Returns	3,625
Transportation In	2,950

The rate of gross margin on sales for the previous three years averaged 40 percent. Determine the cost of the inventory destroyed by the fire.

E10–**6.** The books of Jay's Department Store show the following data for the leather goods department for the year 1969, its first year of operations:

Purchases (at cost)	$19,612
Purchases (at original selling price)	34,580
Markups	2,250
Markdowns	1,110
Sales	31,673

Compute the inventory on December 31, 1969, by the retail method.

E10–7. (a) From the following data, compute the cost of the ending inventory:

Sales	10,000
Beginning inventory (cost)	5,000
Beginning inventory (retail)	7,000
Purchases (cost)	7,000
Purchases (retail)	9,000

(b) Recompute the ending inventory, assuming the following additional items:

Transportation In	$300
Purchases Returns (cost)	200
Purchases Returns (retail)	300
Sales Returns	400
Markups	350
Markdowns	250

E10–8. The year-end inventory of the Kahn Company consisted of the following groups of items, priced at cost and at market:

Item	Cost	Market
A	45,000	53,000
B	37,000	37,000
C	86,000	78,000
D	42,000	35,000

What inventory amount should be used in the financial statements?

E10–9. The records of the Snow Company show the following data as of December 31, 1969:

a. Cost of merchandise on hand, based on a physical count $45,000

b. Merchandise sold to a customer, but held for him pending receipt of shipping instructions (included in Item a)   1,000

c. Merchandise shipped out on December 30, F.O.B. destination; expected delivery time is 8 days   2,500

d. Merchandise purchased on December 28, F.O.B. shipping point, delivered to a carrier on December 29; expected delivery date is January 5   500

e. Cost of spoiled merchandise (to be given away); not included in Item a   250

What is the value of the inventory on December 31, 1969, for financial statement reporting purposes?

E10–10. The following items were included in the income statements of the Jefferson Company for the years ending December 31, 1969 and 1968:

	December 31	
	1969	1968
Cost of goods sold	$ 65,000	$ 70,000
Gross margin	130,000	120,000
Net income	40,000	32,000

An audit of the records revealed that the merchandise inventory at December 31, 1968, was understated by $4,000. What was the effect of the error on the amounts given?

☐ DEMONSTRATION PROBLEMS

DP10-1. (*Inventory valuation*) On January 1, 1969, the Francis Company had an inventory of 50 units of a product that cost $25 each. January receipts and issues were as follows:

	Received			Issued	
January 2	20 units @ $26	$ 520	January 1	10 units	
January 10	30 units @ 30	900	January 8	20 units	
January 23	10 units @ 27	270	January 17	30 units	
			January 25	20 units	
Total	60	$1,690	Total	80	

Required: 1. Compute the January 31 inventory using (a) FIFO based on a periodic inventory, (b) LIFO based on a perpetual inventory, and (c) weighted average.
2. Prepare summary journal entries for the transactions, assuming the use of LIFO and the perpetual inventory method, and post to the following T accounts: Merchandise Inventory, Accounts Receivable, Accounts Payable, Cost of Goods Sold, and Sales. The unit selling price was $40.
3. Does the use of a perpetual inventory system eliminate the need for taking periodic physical inventories?
4. What factors should be considered in choosing a method of inventory valuation?

DP10-2. (*Inventory valuation: gross profit method*) A fire destroyed the entire inventory of the Bolt Corporation on December 23, 1969. The following information is available for the years 1968 and 1969 (to the date of the fire):

	1969	1968
Merchandise Inventory, January 1	$ 27,850	$ 26,500
Sales	109,862	105,100
Sales Returns and Allowances	2,105	2,360
Purchases	92,308	79,460
Purchases Returns and Allowances	4,873	5,610
Transportation In	3,672	4,201

Required: 1. Estimate the amount of the inventory destroyed by the fire.
2. How reliable is the estimate?
3. Should this method be used for financial reporting purposes to eliminate the need for physical inventory taking?

DP10-3. (*Inventory valuation: retail inventory method*) The records of the Haverhill Shoe Company show the following information on January 31, 1969:

	Cost	Sales Price
Merchandise Inventory–January 1, 1969	$ 6,700	$ 9,500
Purchases during January	62,000	92,600
Transportation In	850	
Purchases Returns and Allowances	2,345	3,500
Markups		9,150
Markdowns		950
Sales		95,000

Required: 1. Find the lower of cost or market value of the January 31 inventory, using the retail inventory method.

2. Why are markdowns excluded in arriving at the cost-to-retail ratio? How would you describe the valuation if markdowns are not excluded? If both markups and markdowns are excluded?

☐ **PROBLEMS**

P10-1. The Dunn Machine Company buys and sells planers. Purchases and sales during April, 1969, were:

	Purchases	Sales
1969		
April 2	44 units @ $200	
3		80 units
9	42 units @ 250	
15	46 units @ 225	
20		30 units
25	44 units @ 240	
30		86 units

The inventory on April 1 consisted of 40 units at $300 each.

Required: 1. Compute the cost of goods sold during April, using LIFO and the periodic inventory method.

2. Compute the cost of goods sold during April, using FIFO and the perpetual inventory method.

P10-2. In January, 1969, the David Johnson Company began buying and selling a recently patented stamping machine. Transactions for the month were:

1969

January   2   Purchased a machine at $3,000.

7   Purchased a machine at $3,500.

15   Sold a machine at $7,000.

20   Purchased a machine at $4,000.

28   Sold a machine at $7,000.

Operating expenses for January were $4,000.

Required: 1. Record the information on perpetual inventory records, using each of the following methods: (a) FIFO, (b) moving average, and (c) LIFO.

2. Prepare an income statement based on each of the three methods of inventory valuation.
3. Give reasons for the variations in the cost of goods sold and the net income in the three statements.

P10–**3.** Purchases and sales data for the first three years of operation of the Grott Company were as follows. (Purchases are listed in order of acquisition.)

	1967	1968	1969
Sales	13,000 units @ $50	15,000 units @ $60	18,000 units @ $65
Purchases	4,000 units @ $22	5,500 units @ $32	7,000 units @ $40
	6,000 units @ 25	6,000 units @ 34	4,500 units @ 43
	5,000 units @ 30	4,000 units @ 37	5,000 units @ 45

Required: 1. Prepare a schedule showing the number of units on hand at the end of each year.
2. Compute the year-end inventories under the periodic inventory method for each of the three years, using (a) FIFO and (b) LIFO.
3. Prepare income statements for each of the three years through Gross Margin on Sales based on (a) FIFO, (b) LIFO, and (c) weighted average.
4. Which method of inventory valuation do you think is the most logical? Why?

P10–**4.** The inventory of the Floyd Upholstering Company on December 31, 1969, consisted of the following items:

		Unit	
	Quantity	Cost	Market
Frames			
Type F-1	220	$28.50	$31.00
Type F-12	150	52.00	45.00
Type F-15	120	43.00	42.00
Springs (sets)			
Type S-1	1520	14.50	17.00
Type S-12	1250	21.00	23.00
Type S-15	680	17.25	15.00

Required: 1. Compute the ending inventory at the lower of cost or market, applied to (a) each item, (b) each category, and (c) the entire inventory.
2. What is the effect of each application of LCM on the gross margin in the current year? in the following year?
3. It is maintained by some that LCM pricing is founded on invalid assumptions and that its application may result in income distortions. Discuss.

P10–**5.** The following data are taken from the books of the Jacinto Company:

	Units	Unit Cost
Beginning balance	50	$1.00
First purchase	100	1.00
Second purchase	200	1.10
First sale	175	
Third purchase	250	1.20
Second sale	275	
Fourth purchase	100	1.25
Third sale	50	

Required: Compute the cost value of the ending inventory under each of the following methods: (a) Weighted average—periodic, (b) FIFO—perpetual, (c) LIFO—perpetual, (d) FIFO—periodic, and (e) LIFO—periodic.

P10–**6.** On November 1, 1969, Joseph Sloan established the Sloan Company with an investment of $20,000 in cash. Purchases and sales during the month were:

1969
Nov. 1 Purchased 3,600 units at $24.
   10 Sold 2,100 units at $40.
   13 Purchased 3,000 units at $25.50.
   17 Sold 3,300 units at $40.
   22 Purchased 4,500 units at $26.50.
   30 Sold 2,400 units at $40.

Operating expenses were $28,000. Cash settlements on all transactions were completed by the end of the month.

Required: 1. Prepare perpetual inventory schedules, using (a) FIFO, (b) LIFO, and (c) moving average.
2. Prepare income statements and statements of financial position based on each method of inventory valuation.

P10–**7.** Assume the same facts as in Problem P10-6, except that the units purchased on November 13 cost $22 each and those purchased on November 22 cost $21 each.

Required: The same as for Problem P10-6.

P10–**8.** Assume the same facts as in Problem P10-6.

Required: 1. Discuss the effect of the three methods of inventory valuation on the ending inventory, the cost of goods sold, the gross margin on sales, the net income, and the total current assets during a period of (a) rising prices and (b) falling prices.
2. What other factors should Sloan consider in his choice of a method of inventory valuation?

P10–**9.** The records of the Federated Clothing Company show the following information for the month of July, 1969:

Sales	$75,000
Markups	6,000
Markdowns	10,500
Transportation In	1,200
Purchases at cost	57,000
Purchases at retail	84,000
Inventory–July 1, at cost	21,000
Inventory–July 1, at retail	30,000

Required: Compute the July 31 inventory at the lower of cost or market, using the retail inventory method.

P10–10. The Richards Company estimates its merchandise inventory when preparing monthly financial statements. The following information is available on June 30:

	Cost	Retail
Merchandise Inventory, June 1	$ 84,000	$ 130,000
Purchases during June (net)	650,000	1,100,000
Transportation In during June	4,000	
Sales during June (net)		640,000

Required: 1. Compute the estimated inventory on June 30, using the gross margin method. Based on past experience, the Richards Company estimates a rate of gross margin of 38 percent for the current year.
2. Compute the estimated inventory on June 30, using the retail inventory method.
3. (a) Give the reason for the difference in the ending inventory under the two methods. (b) Which method is more reliable? Why?

P10–11. The Witt Company closes its books annually on December 31, at which time the merchandise inventory is determined by a physical count. For its monthly interim statements, however, inventory estimates based on the gross margin method are used. Condensed partial income statements for the years 1966, 1967, and 1968 are given:

	1966	1967	1968
Sales	$175,000	$200,000	$220,000
Cost of Goods Sold	105,000	118,000	127,600
Gross Margin	$ 70,000	$ 82,000	$ 92,400

The merchandise inventory on December 31, 1968, was $35,000. During January, 1969, sales were $22,000 and purchases were $15,000.

Required: 1. Compute the inventory on January 31, 1969, based on (a) the gross margin rate for the prior three years and (b) the average annual gross margin rate.
2. Which gross margin rate should be used? Why?

P10–12. John Finch, the owner of a retail store, has always carried fire insurance on his inventory. Under the terms of the policy, he is to collect from the insurance company 80 percent of any loss of merchandise inventory from fire.

On the morning of July 16, 1969, Finch's store was destroyed by fire. The fixtures and inventory were a total loss. The records, which were kept in a fireproof safe, were not destroyed.

Operations for the period January 1 through July 15 resulted in the following balances:

Sales	$81,800
Heat, Light, and Water Expense	255
Inventory–January 1, 1969	12,000
Transportation In	1,500
Salaries and Wages	18,200
Purchases	59,500
Sales Returns and Allowances	280
Salesmen's Commissions	5,200
Purchases Returns and Allowances	1,150
Sales Discounts	1,520
Purchases Discounts	1,850

His records also include an Income Statement for the year ended December 31, 1968, which is condensed as follows:

Sales		$172,000
Cost of Goods Sold		120,400
Gross Margin		$ 51,600
Expenses		
Selling	$15,000	
General	19,400	34,400
Net Income		$ 17,200

Required: Compute the amount of merchandise inventory lost in the fire and the amount that Finch may expect to collect from the insurance company.

CASE PROBLEM
Kiser Distributing Company

The Kiser Distributing Company is a distributor of gasoline to service stations within its franchise area (assume that only one brand of gasoline is sold). The Company is preparing to adjust and close its books at March 31, 1969, the end of its third full year of business.

Herbert Kiser, the owner of the Company, is confused by the meaning and application of the terms FIFO, LIFO, weighted average, and moving average. He asks you to aid him in solving his inventory problem. He informs you that on March 31, 1967, and March 31, 1968, he determined the value of the ending inventory by multiplying the number of gallons of gasoline on hand by the last invoice price per gallon. He has since been told by a friend that this method is incorrect (even though sometimes it might yield the correct results).

After obtaining information about the firm and its operations, you recommend that inventory and cost of goods sold valuations be made annually on March 31 (except when Kiser needs interim statements) and that perpetual records of quantities on hand be maintained to help in planning purchases.

You begin by preparing condensed income statements for each of the earlier years, as shown:

KISER DISTRIBUTING COMPANY
Comparative Condensed Income Statement
For Years Ended March 31, 1967 and 1968

	March 31, 1968		March 31, 1967	
Sales		$153,150		$91,800
Cost of Goods Sold				
Beginning Inventory	$ 20,400		$ –0–	
Purchases	172,800		99,600	
Total Available for Sale	$193,200		$99,600	
Ending Inventory	47,250	145,950	20,400	79,200
Gross Margin		$ 7,200		$12,600
Expenses		10,530		9,900
Net Income (Loss)		$ (3,330)		$ 2,700

You next review invoices of purchases from the refineries, from which you prepare the following:

Period	Quantity (Gallons)	Cost per Gallon (Cents)	Total Cost
April–September, 1966	200,000	19.2	$ 38,400
October, 1966–March, 1967	300,000	20.4	61,200
April–September, 1967	600,000	22.5	135,000
October, 1967–March, 1968	200,000	18.9	37,800
April–September, 1968	400,000	22.5	90,000
October, 1968–March, 1969	900,000	24.3	218,700

From other records in the Company office, you note that the unsold quantity of gasoline and Kiser's cost computations at the end of each fiscal year were:

Date	Quantity (Gallons)	Cost per Gallon (Cents)	Total Cost
March 31, 1967	100,000	20.4	$20,400
March 31, 1968	250,000	18.9	47,250
March 31, 1969	90,000	24.3	21,870

Last, from a review of the delivery tickets covering sales to service stations, you note the following:

Period	Quantity (gallons)
April–September, 1966	150,000
October, 1966–March, 1967	250,000
April–September, 1967	300,000
October, 1967–March, 1968	350,000
April–September, 1968	500,000
October, 1968–March, 1969	960,000

Sales for the third year were $389,580; expenses were $12,890.

Required: Prepare a report for Kiser, covering the following points:

1. Explain the purpose of inventory valuations.
2. Explain the meaning of FIFO, LIFO, weighted average, and moving average, as applied to the determination of inventory value and the cost of goods sold; identify which of these methods may be used by the Kiser Distributing Company.
3. Prepare schedules of inventory and cost of goods sold valuations, using FIFO, LIFO, and weighted average, for each of the three years.
4. Prepare income statements in the form illustrated for each of the three years, using each of the three available methods (nine statements).
5. Explain why the different methods yield different operating results.
6. Answer Kiser's question as to "Which method is correct?"
7. Which method would you recommend? Why?

Chapter Eleven

Plant and Equipment— Acquisition, Depreciation, and Disposal

Industrial expansion often requires large expenditures for land, buildings, machinery, and equipment. When such expenditures must be made in an economic environment marked by sweeping technological changes, inflation, and high levels of taxation, the accounting problems become both more complicated and more controversial. This chapter deals with the determination of and accounting for the cost of plant assets, the allocation of asset costs to the appropriate accounting periods, the disposal or retirement of plant assets, and related problems of management planning and control.

The term *plant and equipment* denotes all types of land, structures, and equipment of a tangible and relatively permanent nature, acquired for use in the regular operations of the business—not for resale—and whose use or consumption will cover more than one accounting period. This classification includes land, buildings, machinery, trucks, fixtures, tools, office machines, furniture and furnishings, patterns, and dies. The terms *plant assets, capital assets, fixed assets, tangible assets,* and *noncurrent assets* are often used as synonyms for plant and equipment.

COST OF PLANT AND EQUIPMENT

The cost of plant and equipment includes the purchase price (less any discount) plus all other expenditures required to secure title and to get the asset ready for operating use. Hence the cost of land includes brokers' fees, legal fees, and transfer taxes. The cost of buildings includes permit fees, engineering fees, and remodeling costs. The cost of machinery includes transportation, installation, and all other costs incurred in preparing the machinery for operations.

Assume that a company purchases a machine for $5,000 at terms of 2/10, n/60, with freight to be paid by the buyer. Installation of the machine requires spe-

cialized electrical wiring and the construction of a cement foundation. All these expenditures are charged to the asset account. The total asset cost includes the
following:

Purchase price	$5,000
Deduct 2% cash discount	100
Net purchase price	$4,900
Transportation	125
Cost of wiring	75
Construction of a special foundation	110
Total asset cost	$5,210

If cash is paid immediately, the entry for the purchase of the machine is:

Machinery	4,900	
Cash		4,900

The entry for the freight payment is:

Machinery	125	
Cash		125

The entry to record the payment for installation of the machine is:

Machinery	185	
Cash		185

When these entries are posted, the Machinery account shows a total cost for the
machine of $5,210. If the discount of $100 is not taken, it should still be deducted
from the purchase price of $5,000 and charged to Discounts Lost—Nonmerchandise
Items. An asset acquired in some manner other than by cash payment—for example,
by gift or issuance of securities—is valued on the basis of the amount of cash that
would be required for its acquisition (*fair market value*). When a used plant asset is
acquired, all expenditures incurred in getting the asset ready for use—paint, replacement parts, and so on—are charged to the asset account.

DEPRECIATION OF PLANT AND EQUIPMENT

Depreciation is not necessarily a measure of the decline in the value of an asset, but
rather a recognition of the fact that depreciable assets used in the business have a
predictable and limited service life, over which asset costs should be allocated. ▶
Since most plant and equipment assets have a limited useful life, their cost is properly
allocable as an expense to the accounting periods in which the assets are used. ◀
Although the serviceable life of the asset cannot be definitely known at the time of
its acquisition, the cost of the asset cannot be considered as an expense chargeable
entirely either to the period of acquisition or the period of disposal. It is better to
make an estimation of the useful life of the asset for purposes of making the periodic
charge to expense than to omit the charge on the grounds that there is no strictly
scientific way of making such an estimation.

     Depreciation should be distinguished from *depletion*. Depletion (discussed
later in this chapter) refers to the process of estimating and recording the periodic

Accounting Concept:
◀ *Allocation of Costs*

charges to operations due to the exhaustion of a natural resource, such as coal, oil, or standing timber. *Amortization* is often used as a general term to cover depreciation, depletion, and write-downs of certain other assets.

There are several factors that limit the serviceability of plant assets, chiefly wear and tear through ordinary use, accidental damage, inadequacy, level of repairs of maintenance, and obsolescence. Inadequacy may be due to changes in the nature of the business—method of manufacture, location, or type or design of product— that necessitate the disposition or replacement of plant assets. Obsolescence is due to technological advances that necessitate replacement of an existing asset with a new model.

Estimated Useful Life (EUL)

It is often difficult to predict the useful service life of an asset. The estimate is important because the amount of cost assigned to each period (depreciation for a period) is deducted from current revenue, thereby affecting net income for the period. Past experience or standard operating policies may be used in estimating the period during which the asset can or will be used by the business. A machine may be able to withstand wear and tear for perhaps twenty years, but it may be used for only ten years because it has become too slow or too small for current requirements; or it may have to be replaced because the particular model becomes obsolete. In any case, the cost is allocated over *estimated useful life* (EUL) of the asset.

The Internal Revenue Service provides guidelines to the acceptable estimation of useful lives of about 75 broad classes of assets. In most cases, a single industry guideline class covers all the production machinery and equipment typically used in the industry. For example, the aerospace industry, which includes manufacturers of aircraft, spacecraft, rockets, missiles, and component parts, has for its plant assets a guideline life of eight years.

Estimated Salvage Value

The cost of the asset to be depreciated is its acquisition cost minus the amount that is expected to be recovered when the asset is ultimately scrapped, sold, or traded in. If an expenditure will be required in dismantling or removing the asset, the estimated gross salvage value is reduced by the anticipated removal cost. It is frequently assumed that the salvage value will be offset by the removal cost; in this case, depreciation is computed on the total cost of the asset. Also, total cost may be depreciated when the salvage value is known to be negligible. A company may trade in any assets that have a market value. For example, some businesses trade in cars, trucks, and office equipment for new models after a period of use. In such instances, the estimated cash market value at the date of trade-in should be deducted in arriving at the depreciable amount. Experience will enable the company to arrive at a salvage value factor.

Methods of Computing Depreciation

A number of methods are used to calculate periodic depreciation charges; they may give significantly different results. The method selected in any specific instance should be based on a careful evaluation of all the factors involved. Procedures for allocating the cost of the asset to each accounting period within its service life are based on either uniform or varying charges. By the use of certain methods, the amounts charged to each period may be irregular, or they may follow a regularly increasing or decreasing pattern.

STRAIGHT-LINE METHOD. Under the straight-line method, depreciation is considered a function of time, and a uniform portion of the cost is allocated to each accounting period. Degrees of use or age, or efficiency factors, are not considered in determining the amount of depreciation to be assigned to each period. The straight-line method may be expressed as follows:

$$\frac{\text{Cost less salvage value}}{\text{Number of accounting periods in the estimated useful life of the asset}} = \text{Depreciation for each accounting period}$$

Assume that a machine costing $5,210, with an estimated service life of five years and an estimated net salvage value of $210, is purchased on January 2, 1969. The annual depreciation charge is:

$$\frac{\$5,210 - \$210}{5} = \$1,000$$

The straight-line method is popular primarily because it is simple to use.

PRODUCTION METHODS. Production methods relate depreciation to usage or to results, recognizing either working hours or units of output.

The *working-hours method* requires an estimate of service hours in the life of the asset. The charge to depreciation for an accounting period is determined as follows:

1) $$\frac{\text{Cost less salvage value}}{\text{Total estimated working hours}} = \frac{\text{Depreciation expense}}{\text{per hour}}$$

2) $$\frac{\text{Depreciation expense}}{\text{per hour}} \times \frac{\text{Working hours for}}{\text{the period}} = \frac{\text{Depreciation expense}}{\text{for the period}}$$

Assume, for example, that a machine costing $21,000 with a salvage value of $1,000 is expected to render 40,000 hours of service. If it is used for 5,000 hours during an accounting period, the computation for that period would be:

1) $$\frac{\$21,000 - \$1,000}{40,000 \text{ hrs.}} = \$.50 \text{ per service hour}$$

2) $.50 \times 5,000$ hrs. $= \$2,500$ depreciation expense for the period

Under the *production-unit method,* depreciation is computed on units of output, and therefore an estimate of total units of output is required. If the machine in the previous example had an estimated productive life of 10,000 units and 1,500 units were processed during the current period, the charge to depreciation for the period would be:

1. $$\frac{\$21{,}000 - \$1{,}000}{10{,}000 \text{ units}} = \$2 \text{ per unit produced}$$

2. $\$2 \times 1{,}500 \text{ units} = \$3{,}000$ depreciation expense for the period

The production methods allocate cost in proportion to the use that is made of the asset. The straight-line method ignores use, emphasizing the fact that the asset is available; depreciation expense is regarded as a measure of such availability, irrespective of the extent of use.

DECLINING-AMOUNT METHODS. The use of a declining-amount method results in larger depreciation charges during the early years with gradually decreasing charges in later years. Some commonly used forms are the *declining-balance method* and the *sum of the years-digits method*.

Under the declining-balance method, a uniform depreciation rate is applied in each period to the remaining *carrying value* (cost less accumulated depreciation). For Federal income tax purposes, the rate may not exceed twice the straight-line rate (*double-rate* declining balance). The computation is made without an adjustment for salvage, even though the asset cannot be depreciated below a reasonable salvage value, presumably because the arithmetic of this formula is such that it will never reduce the asset balance to zero. At the end of the EUL, therefore, the remaining balance (less salvage) may be depreciated under the straight-line method over a period determined at that time or by an adjustment in the amount of the depreciation for the final period, or it may continue to be reduced at the fixed percentage of the carrying value until it is retired from use.

Assume that a $10,000 machine is purchased on January 2, 1969, with an estimated life of ten years and an estimated net salvage value of $500. A 20-percent depreciation rate—twice the straight-line rate of 10-percent—applied to the remaining carrying value gives the following results for the first three years:

Year	Computation	Annual Depreciation	Accumulated Depreciation	Carrying Value
1969	20% × $10,000	$2,000	$2,000	$8,000
1970	20% × 8,000	1,600	3,600	6,400
1971	20% × 6,400	1,280	4,880	5,120

The entry to record the depreciation charge for 1971 and the position statement presentation of the machine at the end of that year are as follows:

Depreciation Expense–Machinery and Equipment	1,280	
Accumulated Depreciation–Machinery and Equipment		1,280

Plant and Equipment		
Machinery and Equipment	$10,000	
Deduct Accumulated Depreciation	4,880	$5,120

Under the sum of years-digits method, depreciation for any year is determined by multiplying the cost less salvage of the asset by a fraction, the denominator of which is the sum of the numbers of the years or months of estimated useful life of the asset and the numerator of which is the number of the specific period applied in reverse order.

Assume that a machine costing $15,300 is purchased on January 2, 1969; the EUL is five years and the estimated salvage value is $300. The denominator of the fraction used is 15 (1 + 2 + 3 + 4 + 5). The annual depreciation is computed as follows:

Year	Years Digits	Fraction	Annual Depreciation
1969	5	$5/15 \times $15,000$	$ 5,000
1970	4	$4/15 \times$ 15,000	4,000
1971	3	$3/15 \times$ 15,000	3,000
1972	2	$2/15 \times$ 15,000	2,000
1973	1	$1/15 \times$ 15,000	1,000
Total	15		

Total depreciation for five years $15,000

The denominators of the fraction used in the sum of the years-digits method can be computed by multiplying the number of years of estimated useful life by the midpoint of the series. The midpoint is found by adding the first and the last years and dividing by two. In the previous example, the computation would be:

$$\text{Number of years in series} = 5\left(\frac{\text{First year} + \text{Last year}}{2}\right) = 5\left(\frac{1 + 5}{2}\right) = 15$$

Based on the same facts, the results under the double-rate declining-balance method (20% $\times$ 2) are as follows (amounts are rounded to nearest dollar):

Year	Computation	Annual Depreciation	Accumulated Depreciation	Carrying Value
1969	40% of $15,300	$6,120	$ 6,120	$9,180
1970	40% of 9,180	3,672	9,792	5,508
1971	40% of 5,508	2,203	11,995	3,305
1972	40% of 3,305	1,322	13,317	1,983
1973	40% of 1,983	793	14,110	1,190

A comparison of the three methods shows the following depreciation under each.

Year	Straight-Line	Double-Rate Declining Balance (40%)	Sum of Years Digits
1969	$ 3,000	$ 6,120	$ 5,000
1970	3,000	3,672	4,000
1971	3,000	2,203	3,000
1972	3,000	1,322	2,000
1973	3,000	793	1,000
Totals	$15,000	$14,110	$15,000

The double-rate declining-balance method results in a higher depreciation in the first year due to the higher rate and the higher base ($15,300 as compared with $15,000). However, an undepreciated balance of $1,190 ($15,300 − $14,110) remains at the end of the fifth year.

Group Rates and Composite Rates

To simplify the computation of depreciation and to charge depreciation uniformly to all service years including the final one, some companies use a *blanket group* or *composite* rate, applied either to all the assets owned or to each major asset category. The term *group* refers to a number of homogeneous assets. When a group rate is applied to a number of nonhomogeneous assets, it is called a composite rate; it is a special application of the group rate. The group rate is especially useful if there are a large number of individual units with similar service lives and relatively low costs (for example, railroad tracks and ties, telephone poles and cables, and restaurant and hotel furniture). The use of a group rate eliminates the clerical work necessary to compute individual periodic depreciation and the need for detailed records of accumulated amounts. Its use is satisfactory if the assets are kept for relatively long periods and if variations in individual rates, either over or under the group rate, tend to cancel out.

Several methods may be used to develop a composite rate; one is illustrated:

Asset	Cost	Estimated Salvage Value	Depreciable Cost	EUL (Years)	Annual Depreciation (Straight-Line)
A	$20,000	$2,000	$18,000	6	$3,000
B	15,000	–0–	15,000	10	1,500
C	10,200	600	9,600	12	800
	$45,200	$2,600	$42,600		$5,300

The *composite life* for this group of assets is 8.04 years, computed as follows:

$$\frac{\text{Depreciable cost}}{\text{Annual depreciation}} = \frac{\$42,600}{\$5,300} = 8.04 \text{ years of average life}$$

A group rate may be used with either straight-line depreciation or a declining-amount method. Assuming that the straight-line method is used, the annual rate to be applied is:

$$\frac{\text{Annual depreciation}}{\text{Total cost}} = \frac{\$5,300}{\$45,200} = 11.72\%$$

Total depreciation at a mean rate of 11.72 percent, applied each year for 8.04 years to the total cost of $45,000, will be $42,600 ($45,200 × 11.72 × 8.04, adjusted for rounding), the amount to be depreciated. The annual depreciation charge is $5,297.44 ($45,200 × 11.72%).

When any unit in the group is disposed of, it is assumed that it has been fully depreciated and no gain or loss on disposal is recognized. Underdepreciation on items in the group that are used for less than their estimated useful lives is assumed to be offset by overdepreciation on items used longer than their EUL's. Although accumulated depreciation records on the individual units in the group are not kept, a record of original costs is kept.

Assume that Asset A is retired at zero salvage value after four years of service. The entry to record the retirement is:

Accumulated Depreciation	20,000	
Asset Account		20,000
To record retirement of Asset A; salvage value is zero.		

If $4,000 in salvage value were realized, the entry would be:

Accumulated Depreciation	16,000	
Cash	4,000	
Asset Account		20,000
To record sale of Asset A for $4,000.		

The debit to Accumulated Depreciation is the cost of the asset less proceeds from the sale.

Given accurate estimates of EUL and salvage values, the carrying value of the group is zero when the last item in the group is retired and there is indeed no gain or loss on disposal. But, since errors in forecasting are likely, and since an error made on one item affects the rate used on all the items in that group, it is essential that the rate be revised whenever acquisitions or disposals change the composition of the group with respect to types of assets, estimated useful lives, and so on.

Depreciation for Partial Accounting Periods

A consistent method should be followed for recording depreciation on assets acquired or retired during the accounting period. A variety of procedures, such as the following, are used:

1. Depreciation is charged on a plant asset from the date it is acquired to the date it is retired.
2. Depreciation is charged for one-half year during the year a plant asset is acquired and also during the year it is retired. Of course, a full year's depreciation is taken during each of the remaining years of EUL.
3. Depreciation is charged for a full year on a plant asset during the year it is acquired; but no depreciation is charged on this same asset during the year it is retired, with, of course, a full year's depreciation being taken during each year the asset is used for a full 12 months.
4. Depreciation is charged for a full year on a plant asset in the year of retirement; but no depreciation is charged on this asset during the year it is acquired, with, of course, a full year's depreciation being taken during each year the asset is used for a full 12 months.

A method that is popular because of its simplicity is to consider that a plant asset is purchased as of the beginning of the month of acquisition if it is purchased on or before the fifteenth of the month and to consider that it is purchased on the first day of the following month if the asset is purchased on or after the sixteenth of the month, with depreciation being determined, then, by method 1 described above.

Assume that a machine costing $6,500 with an estimated life of ten years and salvage value of $500 was purchased on November 10, 1969. Depreciation on the machine for the calendar year 1969 is:

$$\frac{\$6,500 - \$500}{10} \times \frac{2}{12} = \$100$$

The year-end entry to record depreciation on the machine for two months is:

Depreciation Expense–Machinery and Equipment	100	
Accumulated Depreciation–Machinery and Equipment		100

If the machine had been acquired on or after November 16, the amount in the entry would be $50. Depreciation may have to be recorded for a partial accounting period when an asset is sold, discarded, or exchanged for another asset. In these situations, depreciation must be recorded to the date of the event, assuming that the asset has not already been fully depreciated. The amount of depreciation to be charged for the month of disposal is based on the method followed for acquisitions. The rules must be applied consistently.

DEPRECIATION METHODS COMPARED—MANAGEMENT CONSIDERATIONS

Accounting Concept:
Purpose of Depreciation ▶

▶ The process of recording depreciation gives recognition to the expiration of asset costs through use. Depreciation is not a process of valuation; that is, its purpose is not to report the asset at the amount for which it could be sold at the time since the asset was not acquired for resale. ◀ The method that is most practical and meaningful for the user should be selected. Since the amount of the depreciation deduction has a direct effect on net income and since the alternative methods of calculating depreciation result in different amounts, the choice of method may significantly affect the income tax liability. The declining-amount methods, in contrast to the straight-line method, reduce the tax liability and conserve working capital during the early life of the asset.

The straight-line method is simple to apply and is satisfactory under conditions of fairly uniform usage. Two objections to the method are:

1. The straight-line depreciation charge results in a uniform deduction from revenue without adjustment for variation in sales volume or rate of output during the period.
2. If expenditures for repairs increase gradually with continued use of the asset, the deduction from revenue for the combined expenses of repairs and depreciation will increase annually, thus distorting the reported income.

The production methods allocate depreciation in proportion to usage or output. This is important if usage is the dominant cause of loss in value of the asset. It should be emphasized that the estimate of useful life is based on anticipated total usage before disposal of the asset for whatever reason—wear and tear, obsolescence, or inadequacy.

The declining-amount methods are based on the hypothesis that the service rendered by a plant asset is greatest in the early years of use; hence, that depreciation charged under these methods results in a more accurate matching of expense and revenue. The rapidity of the decline in service value varies with the demand for the product and the rate of technological progress. If revenues drop significantly during the early years of use, and if rapid changes in technology shorten the economic life of the asset, then the deduction of larger amounts of depreciation in early years are matched with the relatively larger revenues and the concomitant diminishing depreciation deductions in later years are matched against the diminishing revenues of those years.

Another reason for using the declining-amount methods is that as an asset gets older, it requires more maintenance. The increasing maintenance expenses in later years are offset by the diminishing depreciation expense, thus equalizing, to some extent, the total expenses of the asset and thereby achieving a better matching of expense with revenue. ▶ A more recent argument is that declining-amount methods more closely reflect the economic fact that an investment in an asset is made for the purpose of realizing a desired annual rate of return on the unrecovered portion of the investment. "Entrepreneurs . . . buy the asset to make a profit; hence, conceptually, they discount the bundles of future net services which they purchase. Therefore, by inference, an *ideal depreciation* method is one which allocates cost in such a way as to produce a uniform return on remaining unamortized investment in all periods at the rate of return implicit in the original transaction by which the asset was acquired."[1] ◀

Accounting Concept:
Depreciation and
Investment

When a plant and equipment item is depreciated, the depreciable cost of the asset is written off over its useful life. Depreciation expense is included in the income statement as a deduction from revenue. The process of recording depreciation does not provide or segregate funds for the replacement of the property at the end of its EUL; an asset should be depreciated even if there is no intention of replacing it. The acquisition of a new asset creates a new series of depreciation charges. Of course, depreciation deductions reduce income taxes, but the amount by which the tax liability is reduced does not necessarily remain in the business as cash available for the replacement of equipment. It may be employed for a multitude of other purposes—inventory expansion, dividends and so on. It is possible for a business to segregate an amount of cash equal to the periodic depreciation charges but such funds, if available, probably would result in a greater return when used in the regular operations of the business.

CAPITAL AND REVENUE EXPENDITURES

The term *expenditure* refers to a payment or a promise to make a future payment for benefits received; that is, for assets or services. Expenditures made on plant and equipment assets during the period of ownership may be classified as *capital* expenditures or *revenue* expenditures. A capital expenditure results in an addition to an asset account; a revenue expenditure results in an addition to an expense account.

---

[1] Isaac N. Reynolds, "Selecting the Proper Depreciation Method," *Accounting Review,* April, 1961, pp. 243–44.

Capital expenditures are payments for asset alterations, additions, and replacements that are significant in amount and that benefit future accounting periods. They prolong the useful life of the asset, making it more valuable or more adaptable, and are recorded as increases in plant and equipment; the expenditure is said to have been *capitalized*. Purchases of land, buildings, machinery, and office equipment are also capital expenditures.

Expenditures for extraordinary repairs made to equipment during its life are also classified as capital expenditures if they extend the useful life or capacity of the asset or otherwise make the asset more serviceable (for example, replacing a manually operated elevator with a fully automated one). Some accountants view an extraordinary repair as a restorative process; they record the increase in the asset by debiting Accumulated Depreciation, thereby cancelling past depreciation charges.

Revenue expenditures benefit a current period and are made for the purpose of maintaining the asset in satisfactory operating condition. A routine repair or the replacement of a minor part that has worn out is an expense of the current accounting period, to be deducted from the revenue for the period. These expenditures do not increase the serviceability of the asset beyond the original estimate, but rather represent normal maintenance costs.

Careful distinction between capital and revenue expenditures is one of the fundamental problems of accounting—it is essential for the matching of expenses and revenue and, therefore, for the proper measurement of net income. A capital expenditure that is recorded as a revenue expenditure, as, for example, a purchase of office equipment charged to Office Expense, causes an understatement of net income in that year. If the error is not corrected, net income for the following years will be overstated by the amount of depreciation expense that would otherwise have been recognized. Conversely, a revenue expenditure that is recorded as a capital expenditure, as, for example, an office expense charged to Office Equipment, overstates net income for that year. If the error is not corrected, net income for the following years will be understated by the depreciation charge on the overstated portion of the Office Equipment account.

DISPOSAL OF PLANT AND EQUIPMENT

An asset may be disposed of by sale, by being *traded in* as part of the purchase price of a replacement, or by simply being discarded. The accounting treatment of sales and of discards is similar; the treatment of *trade-ins* is somewhat different.

An asset may still be in use after it is fully depreciated; that is, when the balance of the Accumulated Depreciation account—assuming that salvage value is zero —is equal to the cost of the asset. In this case, no further depreciation is taken and no further entries are required until the asset is disposed of. In the statement of financial position, the Accumulated Depreciation or Plant and Equipment account may be followed by a notation of the portion of the account that represents fully depreciated assets still in use.

Sale or Discard of Plant and Equipment

When an asset is sold or discarded, the entry for the transaction must remove the appropriate amounts from the asset and the accumulated depreciation accounts. Assume, for example, that a company acquires a truck on January 2, 1969, at a cost of $5,000. Depreciation is recorded on a straight-line basis at the rate of $1,000 annually (salvage value is assumed to be zero). Five possible situations, together with the methods of accounting for the disposal of the truck are illustrated:

Example 1—*Discard of fully depreciated asset:* The truck is discarded on March 1, 1974 (in the sixth year).

Accumulated Depreciation–Trucks	5,000	
Trucks		5,000

The purpose of this entry is to eliminate the accumulated charges from the Accumulated Depreciation account and to reduce the asset account by the original cost of the truck. No depreciation expense would be recorded for the truck for the time it was in use during 1974 because the truck has been completely depreciated by December 31, 1973, the end of its fifth year of use.

Example 2—*Sale of fully depreciated asset:* The truck is sold on March 1, 1974, for $50.

Cash	50	
Accumulated Depreciation–Trucks	5,000	
Trucks		5,000
Gain on Disposal of Equipment		50

Gains and losses on disposal of plant assets are measured by the difference between the carrying value of an asset and the proceeds from its disposal: a gain results when the proceeds are greater than the carrying value; a loss results when the proceeds are less than the carrying value. If the asset is fully depreciated, as in the example, the carrying value is zero and the gain is the full amount realized from the sale. A gain or a loss may be indicative of errors in estimating the asset's useful life, salvage value, or both, in which case the gain or loss is, in fact, a correction of prior years' earnings. The Gain on Disposal of Equipment is shown in the income statement under Other Revenue. A loss would be shown under Other Expenses.

Example 3—*Sale of asset at a price equal to carrying value:* The truck is sold on July 1, 1973, for $500. The first entry is to record the depreciation for the current year, up to the date of the sale.

Depreciation Expense–Trucks	500	
Accumulated Depreciation–Trucks		500
To record depreciation on trucks for the six-month period 1/1/73 to 7/1/73.		

The Accumulated Depreciation account now has a credit balance of $4,500, as shown:

Accumulated Depreciation–Trucks	
12/31/69	1,000
12/31/70	1,000
12/31/71	1,000
12/31/72	1,000
7/1/73	500

The entry to record the sale is:

Cash	500	
Accumulated Depreciation–Trucks	4,500	
Trucks		5,000

Example 4—*Sale of asset at a price above carrying value:* The truck is sold on July 1, 1973, for $600. The entry to record the depreciation for the current year, up to the date of the sale, is the same as in Example 3 and is assumed to have been made. The following entry is made to record the sale:

Cash	600	
Accumulated Depreciation–Trucks	4,500	
Trucks		5,000
Gain on Disposal of Equipment		100

The gain of $100 is computed as follows:

Cost of truck	$5,000
Deduct accumulated depreciation	4,500
Carrying value of truck	$ 500
Amount received	600
Gain on disposal	$ 100

Example 5—*Sale of asset at a price below carrying value:* The truck is sold on July 1, 1973, for $400 in cash. Again, the entry to record the depreciation applicable to the year of sale is the same as in Example 3 and is assumed to have been made. The entry to record the disposal is:

Loss on Disposal of Equipment	100	
Cash	400	
Accumulated Depreciation–Trucks	4,500	
Trucks		5,000

The loss of $100 is computed as follows:

Cost of truck	$5,000
Less accumulated depreciation	4,500
Carrying value of truck	$ 500
Amount received	400
Loss on disposal	$ 100

Loss on Disposal of Equipment is shown in the income statement under Other Expenses.

Trade-in of Plant and Equipment—Recognition of Gain or Loss

It is common practice to exchange, or trade in, used property when new property is acquired. If the trade-in allowance is not arbitrarily excessive (as a partial offset to an unrealistic list price of the new asset), it may be considered the proper selling price of the old asset, and the new asset is recorded at its list price. After the accumulated depreciation up to the date of the trade-in is recorded, the carrying value of the old asset is compared with its trade-in allowance. A gain is recognized if the trade-in allowance is greater than the carrying value, and a loss is recognized if the trade-in allowance is less than the carrying value. When the carrying value and the trade-in allowance are equal, there is no recognized gain or loss. If the list price or trade-in allowance is not realistic, the new asset should be recorded at its *cash market price,* or the cash payment plus the fair market value of the asset traded in. The gain or loss then may be measured by the difference between the cash market price of the new equipment and the total of the cash outlay and the carrying value of the old equipment.

Example 1—*Trade-in allowance greater than fair market value:* A truck with a cost of $5,000 and accumulated depreciation up to the date of the trade-in of $4,500 is exchanged for a new truck listed at $6,000. A trade-in allowance of $1,000 is granted on the old truck. The fair market value of the old truck, however, is only $600. The entry to record the trade-in is:

Truck (new)	5,600	
Accumulated Depreciation–Trucks	4,500	
Truck (old)		5,000
Cash		5,000
Gain on Disposal of Equipment		100

The new truck is recorded at its cash market price—the cash payment ($5,000) plus the fair market value ($600) of the old truck. The inflated list price is reduced by the excess ($400) of the trade-in allowance ($1,000) over the fair market value ($600) of the old truck, as shown:

List price	$6,000
Deduct trade-in allowance	1,000
Cash payment	$5,000
Fair market value of old truck	600
Fair market price of new truck	$5,600

The gain on the trade-in is computed in either of the following ways:

1. Cost of old truck		$5,000
Accumulated depreciation to date of trade-in		4,500
Carrying value		$ 500
Fair market value		600
Gain on trade-in		$ 100
2. Cash market price of new truck		$5,600
Cash outlay for new truck	$5,000	
Carrying value of old truck	500	5,500
Gain on trade-in		$ 100

The following three examples illustrate the possibilities involved in trade-ins when the trade-in allowance is *equal* to the fair market value of the truck traded in.

Example 2—*Trade-in allowance greater than carrying value:* A truck that cost $5,000 with accumulated depreciation up to the date of the trade-in of $4,500 is exchanged for a new one listed at $4,000; the trade-in allowance is $800. The fair market value of the old truck is $800. Again, the new truck is recorded at its cash market price—the cash payment plus the fair market value of the old truck. The transaction is recorded as follows:

Truck (new)	4,000	
Accumulated Depreciation–Trucks	4,500	
Cash		3,200
Truck (old)		5,000
Gain on Disposal of Equipment		300

The gain on disposal of the truck is computed as follows:

Cost of old truck	$5,000
Accumulated depreciation to date of trade-in	4,500
Carrying value—unrecovered cost	$ 500
Trade-in allowance	800
Gain on trade-in	$ 300

Example 3—*Trade-in allowance less than carrying value:* The old truck in Example 2 is traded in for an allowance of $400.

Truck (new)	4,000	
Accumulated Depreciation–Trucks	4,500	
Loss on Disposal of Equipment	100	
Cash		3,600
Truck (old)		5,000

The loss on disposal of the truck is computed as follows:

Cost of old truck	$5,000
Accumulated depreciation to date of trade-in	4,500
Carrying value—unrecovered cost	$ 500
Trade-in allowance	400
Loss on trade-in	$ 100

Example 4—*Trade-in allowance the same as carrying value:* The old truck in Example 2 is traded in for an allowance of $500.

Truck (new)	4,000	
Accumulated Depreciation–Trucks	4,500	
Cash		3,500
Truck (old)		5,000

There is no gain or loss in this case because the trade-in allowance is the same as the carrying value.

Trade-in of Plant and Equipment—Nonrecognition of Gain or Loss

An alternative procedure for recording exchanges of assets is required by the Internal Revenue Service. The cost of the new asset for income tax purposes must consist of the carrying value of the old asset plus the required additional expenditure (cash paid or its equivalent), or:

$$\text{Cost of new asset} = \text{Carrying value of old asset} + \text{Expenditure}$$

The excess of trade-in allowance over carrying value is viewed not as a gain but as a reduction from an inflated list price, whereas the excess of carrying value over trade-in value is viewed not as a loss but as an addition to the cost of the new asset. List prices and trade-in values are not recognized in the accounts. They only enter into the computation of the required cash outlay. Under this rule, the unrecognized gain or loss on the exchange is absorbed in the cost valuation of the new asset. An objective of the Internal Revenue Service's rule of nonrecognition of gain or loss on the trade-in of assets is to prevent the shifting of income for income tax purposes from one year to the next. A company with a large gain on a trade-in could defer trading the asset until the following tax year, thereby shifting the gain to that year. ▶ The income tax method of recording asset exchanges violates the accounting principle that plant and equipment, like inventories, should be recorded at actual cash (or equivalent) cost. Future periodic charges for depreciation should be based on cost rather than on a conglomerate figure that may reflect a sales price adjustment of the new asset as well as the unrecovered cost of the old asset. A gain or loss on an asset exchange is an integral part of the complete transaction cycle and should, therefore, be recognized. ◀ The income tax method is frequently used to account for exchanges so that further analysis and adjustment may be avoided when income tax returns are prepared, but this tendency to adjust accounting principles to conform with tax rules for the sake of expediency should not be condoned.

Accounting Concept: Recording of Assets at ◀ *Cost*

CHANGING DEPRECIATION CHARGES

The periodic depreciation charge may require revision as the result (1) of a capital expenditure that does not prolong the useful life of the original asset and (2) of errors in the original EUL. In either case, the new depreciable cost is typically allocated over the remaining life of the property on which the expenditure was made. Assume, for example, that an additional wing costing $8,000 is added to a five-year-old factory building. The original cost of the building was $33,000, the estimated salvage value was $3,000, and the estimated useful life was 25 years. The straight-line method of depreciation has been used. The calculation of the revised annual depreciation charge is:

Original cost	$33,000
Deduct five years' accumulated depreciation ($30,000 × 0.04 = $1,200 per year × 5 years)	6,000
Carrying value	$27,000
Additional cost	8,000
New carrying value	$35,000
Deduct estimated salvage value	3,000
New depreciable cost	$32,000
New annual depreciation charge, based on a remaining useful life of 20 years	$ 1,600

If the improvement prolongs the life of the asset or increases its salvage value, the calculations must be altered to give effect to such changes. For example, if after the addition of the wing the remaining useful life was estimated to be 24 years and the estimated salvage value was $3,800, the revised annual depreciation charge would be determined as follows:

New carrying value	$35,000
Deduct estimated salvage value	3,800
New depreciable cost	$31,200
New annual depreciation charge, based on a remaining useful life of 24 years	$ 1,300

DEPLETION OF NATURAL RESOURCES

Natural resources, or wasting assets, such as oil wells, mines, or timber tracts, should be recorded in the asset account at cost. As the resource is extracted, its asset value is reduced. This reduction in value, or expiration of the cost, of the asset resulting from production is called *depletion* and is recorded on the books by a debit to the Depletion Cost account and a credit to the Accumulated Depletion account. Theoretically, the depletion cost item becomes a part of the cost of the merchandise inventory and ultimately becomes an expense chargeable against revenue on the income statement when the goods are sold. In the statement of financial position, accumulated depletion is deducted from the cost of the resource.

The periodic depletion charge is usually calculated on an output basis similar to the production-unit method of recording depreciation. The cost of the wasting asset is divided by the estimated available units of output to arrive at a per-unit depletion charge. The number of units removed during the accounting period multiplied by the per-unit depletion charge represents depletion for that period. The computation is:

$$\frac{\text{Cost} - \text{Salvage}}{\text{Estimated tons to be mined}} = \text{Depletion}$$

Assume that a mine costs $180,000 and contains an estimated 400,000 tons of ore. It is estimated that the net salvage value will be $20,000. The per-unit depletion charge is:

$$\frac{\$180,000 - \$20,000}{400,000} = \$.40 \text{ per ton}$$

If 10,000 tons are mined during an accounting period, the depletion charge is 10,000 × $.40, or $4,000, and the entry to record the depletion for that period is:

Depletion Cost–Mine	4,000	
Accumulated Depletion–Mine		4,000

The amount of the recorded depletion cost to be transferred to the Inventory account is the number of units on hand multiplied by the per-unit depletion charge. Assume that 2,000 tons remain unsold at the end of the period. The required entry is:

Ore Inventory	800	
Depletion Cost–Mine		800

The balance of the Depletion Cost account, $3,200 ($4,000 − $800), is deducted in the income statement from the revenue realized from the sale of 8,000 tons of ore. The balance of the Ore Inventory account includes not only the allocated portion of mine depletion cost but also labor and other costs of extracting the ore (*overhead*). This is illustrated in the following T-account flow chart:

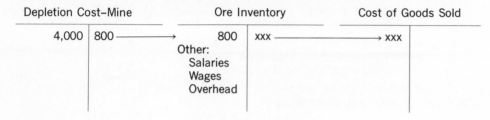

Depletion Cost–Mine	Ore Inventory	Cost of Goods Sold
4,000	800 ⟶ 800	xxx ⟶ xxx
	Other: Salaries Wages Overhead	

INTANGIBLE ASSETS

Intangible assets are nonmaterial rights that are of value to the business, such as patents, copyrights, franchises, leaseholds, and goodwill. Intangibles should be recorded at cost. Some intangibles have a limited useful life and are therefore subject to *amortization*. Others may not be subject to amortization because their useful life is unlimited. Intangible assets are shown on the statement of financial position as the final items on the asset side.

The procedure for the amortization, or periodic write-off of a portion of the cost, of an intangible asset is the same as for computing and recording depreciation on a plant and equipment item by the straight-line method. The amount to be amortized annually is computed by dividing the asset cost by the legal life or the estimated useful life, whichever is shorter. The entry is a debit to an amortization account and a credit to the asset account.

Patents

The U.S. Patent Office grants *patents,* or exclusive rights to the owners to produce and sell their inventions or discoveries, for a period of 17 years. All the costs involved in developing and acquiring a patent are included in the intangible asset Patents account. The cost of a patent may be large and should be capitalized and amortized over the life of the asset or 17 years, whichever is shorter. The Patents account may be credited directly for the amortized portion; the account debited is called Amortization of Patent Cost.

Copyrights

A *copyright* is an exclusive right to publish a literary or artistic work, granted by the government. The copyright is recorded at cost and is subject to amortization either over its legal life—28 years—or its useful economic life. If the copyright is obtained directly, the cost is small and is usually written off entirely in the first year. If it is purchased, the cost may be large enough to warrant periodic amortization. In practice, however, since revenues from copyrighted material are uncertain and are often limited to a relatively brief period, the cost of a copyright is added to the other costs of the first printing and enters into the inventory cost of the books or other printed materials.

Franchises

A *franchise* is a monopolistic right granted by a government to render a service. A right to operate a bus line or railroad or the exclusive use of a television transmitting channel are valuable assets to the owner. The cost of obtaining the franchise is amortized over its life. If the term of the franchise is indefinite, it need not be amortized.

Leaseholds and Leasehold Improvements

Leaseholds are rights to the use of land, buildings, or other property. They are frequently paid for in advance and should be classified as a capital expenditure. Leasehold improvements, such as buildings, are sometimes constructed on leased property. Leaseholds and leasehold improvements should be amortized over the life of the lease or over the estimated useful life of the asset, whichever is shorter.

Goodwill

Goodwill is a general term embodying a variety of intangible factors relating to the reputation of a firm and its ability to realize above-normal net income returns on an investment. Such factors as favorable customer relations, loyal and competent employees, possession of valuable patents, franchises, or copyrights, a high-quality product, and efficient management all aid in the development of goodwill. Self-developed goodwill is not recorded on the books. However, if the assets and goodwill of one company are purchased by another, the purchased goodwill should be recorded as an asset at cost.

The amount to be paid for goodwill is usually a product of a bargaining process between the buyer and the seller. The debit to Goodwill is the excess of the purchase price over the amounts allocable to the other assets.

Organization Costs

This is an intangible asset resulting from expenditures made incidental to incorporation and is discussed further in Chapter 13.

PLANT AND EQUIPMENT—MANAGERIAL ANALYSIS

The investment by a company in plant and equipment assets may vary considerably, depending on the nature of the business. Manufacturing concerns require a greater investment in machinery and equipment than do retail or wholesale firms. The relationship of the plant and equipment to total assets and to sales should be in proper proportion for the industry. If the amount invested in plant and equipment is too high, fewer funds are available for working capital purposes. Depreciation charges will also be high, resulting in either higher sales prices or lower profits. Finally, the long-term liabilities will be greater, resulting in greater interest costs and the need for funds to pay off debts as they mature.

The following ratios are used to determine whether there has been an over-investment in plant and equipment:

1. Plant and equipment to long-term liabilities
2. Plant and equipment to stockholders' equity
3. Net sales to plant and equipment

The condensed comparative position statement of the Hassett Corporation (Figure 11-1) is used to illustrate these ratios.

The ratio of plant and equipment to long-term liabilities is obtained by dividing the total carrying value of the plant and equipment by the long-term liabilities (Line 2 ÷ Line 5). The ratios for the Hassett Corporation, given in percentages, are:

December 31	Percent
1968	170
1969	182
1970	178
1971	150

This comparison is of particular significance to the long-term creditors if any of the plant and equipment has been mortgaged as security for loans. On December 31,

Figure 11-1.
Comparative Statement of Financial Position

HASSETT CORPORATION
Comparative Statement of Financial Position
December 31, 1968–1971
(In Thousands of Dollars)

	Line No.	1968		1969		1970		1971	
		Amount	%	Amount	%	Amount	%	Amount	%
Assets									
Current Assets	1	$240	74	$260	72	$295	65	$300	59
Plant and Equipment (net)	2	85	26	100	28	160	35	210	41
Total Assets	3	$325	100	$360	100	$455	100	$510	100
Liabilities and Stockholders' Equity									
Liabilities									
Current Liabilities	4	$120	37	$130	37	$145	32	$170	33
Long-Term Liabilities	5	50	15	55	15	90	20	140	27
Total Liabilities	6	$170	52	$185	52	$235	52	$310	60
Stockholders' Equity									
Capital Stock	7	$ 80	25	$ 80	22	$ 80	18	$ 80	16
Retained Earnings	8	75	23	95	26	140	30	120	24
Total Stockholders' Equity	9	$155	48	$175	48	$220	48	$200	40
Total Liabilities and Stockholders' Equity	10	$325	100	$360	100	$455	100	$510	100
Net Sales	11	$255		$325		$400		$420	

1968, the Corporation owned $1.70 in plant and equipment assets for every $1 of long-term debt; on December 31, 1971, there was only $1.50. The reduced ratio reflects an increased dependence on long-term borrowing to finance plant and equipment acquisitions. It is apparent, for example, that the additional plant and equipment assets acquired in 1971 were paid for by long-term borrowing.

The ratio of plant and equipment to stockholders' equity is obtained by dividing the total carrying value of the plant and equipment by the stockholders' equity (Line 2 ÷ Line 9). The ratios for the Hassett Corporation are:

December 31	Percent
1968	55
1969	57
1970	73
1971	105

On December 31, 1971, investment in plant and equipment exceeded the stockholders' equity in the Corporation. This indicates a possible overinvestment in plant and equipment, resulting in higher interest, taxes, maintenance expenses, and depreciation charges and lower working capital. A heavy investment in land, buildings, and machinery greatly restricts the mobility of a company if a change in plant location or type of product manufactured is desirable.

The ratio of net sales to plant and equipment—or *plant and equipment turnover*—is found by dividing net sales by the total carrying value of the plant and equipment (Line 11 ÷ Line 2). The ratios for the Hassett Corporation are:

Year	Percent
1968	300
1969	325
1970	250
1971	200

In 1968, sales were 300 percent of plant and equipment; that is, for every $1 of plant and equipment there were sales of $3; in 1971, there were only $2 in sales for every $1 of plant and equipment. This, too, underscores a possible overinvestment in plant and equipment, especially during 1970 and 1971. Although sales have increased each year, the investment in plant and equipment has increased at a greater rate. The following comparison shows that a 147 percent increase in plant and equipment resulted in only a 65 percent increase in sales.

	Line	Sales	Plant and Equipment
1971	1	$420	$210
1968	2	255	85
Net change	3	$165	$125
Percent of change (Line 3 ÷ Line 2)		65	147

PLANT AND EQUIPMENT REPLACEMENT—MANAGEMENT CONSIDERATIONS

The decision to replace plant and equipment items and the timing of the replacement is often a complex matter requiring careful analysis by management. The decision is particularly difficult when it involves not merely the replacement of a worn-out or obsolete unit, but the acquisition of a machine with a different purchase price, capacity, or operating cost. The problem of asset replacement involves a careful study of the expense of doing the given task with the present unit as compared with the expense of using the new unit. Generally, a replacement is advisable if the larger profits resulting from the use of the new equipment will justify the additional investment required. This consideration is discussed in detail in Chapter 23.

SUMMARY

The term plant and equipment includes land, natural resources, structures, and equipment of a tangible and relatively permanent nature acquired for use in the regular operations of the business. Intangible assets include copyrights, franchises, leaseholds, goodwill, and organization costs.

   The cost of plant and equipment includes the purchase price less any discounts plus all other expenditures required to secure title and to get the asset ready for use. Plant and equipment—except land—is subject to depreciation in recognition of the predictable limited service life over which the cost of the asset should be allocated as an expense of each period in which the asset is used. Depreciation should be distinguished from depletion, which relates to natural resources, and from amortization, which relates to intangible assets.

   There are several depreciation methods; they may give significantly different results. The straight-line method considers depreciation to be a function of time and allocates a uniform portion of the cost to each accounting period. The production methods relate depreciation to usage or results. The declining-amount methods—double-rate declining-balance and sum of the years digits—result in larger depreciation charges during the early years with gradually decreasing charges in later years. These methods are based on the assumption that the service received from the asset is greatest in the early years of use. Some companies use a blanket group or composite rate applied either to all assets owned or to each major category of assets.

   Expenditures made on plant and equipment during the period of ownership may be classified as (1) capital expenditures or (2) revenue expenditures. Capital expenditures are recorded as increases of the asset account because they benefit future accounting periods by prolonging the useful life of the asset or by making it more valuable or more serviceable. Revenue expenditures benefit only the current period and are made to maintain the asset in satisfactory operating condition.

   A gain or loss on the disposal of a plant asset is measured by the difference between the carrying value of the asset and the proceeds from the sale. A new asset acquired by trade-in of an existing asset is recorded at (1) list price if the trade-in allowance is not arbitrarily excessive, (2) cash market price of the new asset if the list price or trade-in allowance is not realistic, or (3) the carrying value of the old asset plus the cash paid. Method 3—the income tax method—assumes that list prices and trade-in allowances are inflated—essentially, disguised trade discounts—and does not, therefore, recognize the difference between the trade-in value and the carrying value as either gain or loss.

   The periodic depreciation charge may require revision due to additional capital expenditures made subsequent to acquisition. The additional expenditure is allocated over the remaining life of the asset.

Natural resources are recorded at cost; periodic depletion is calculated on an output basis similar to the production method. Copyrights are recorded at cost and amortized over either the legal life or the useful economic life. A franchise is recorded at cost and—if limited—is amortized over its life. Leaseholds are amortized over the life of the lease or over the useful life of the property, whichever is shorter. Goodwill—the ability of a firm to realize above average normal earnings on the investment—is recorded at cost if it was purchased. Self-developed goodwill is not recorded on the books.

☐ QUESTIONS

Q11–1. What does the term *plant and equipment* encompass?

Q11–2. (a) List some expenditures other than the purchase price that make up the cost of plant and equipment. (b) Why are cash discounts excluded from the cost of plant and equipment? (c) What problems in cost determination arise when used plant assets are acquired?

Q11–3. (a) What distinguishes a capital expenditure from a revenue expenditure? (b) What is the effect on the financial statements if this distinction is not properly drawn?

Q11–4. Student A maintains that if a plant asset has a fair market value greater than its cost after one year of use, no depreciation need be recorded for the year. Student B insists that the fair market value is irrelevant in this context. Indicate which position you support and give your reasons.

Q11–5. (a) What are some of the factors that must be considered when the depreciation method to be used is chosen? (b) When depreciation is recorded?

Q11–6. The basis for depreciation is generally original (historical) cost. Is there any other basis that could logically be used?

Q11–7. Since the total amount to be depreciated cannot exceed the cost of the asset, does it make any difference which method is used in calculating the periodic depreciation charges?

Q11–8. Describe the conditions that might require the use of each of the following methods of depreciation: (a) Straight-line, (b) Production, (c) Declining-amount.

Q11–9. (a) Distinguish between the composite rate and the group rate of depreciation. (b) Give reasons to support the use of these procedures and state their underlying assumptions.

Q11–10. What procedures may be followed in recording depreciation on assets acquired during the accounting period?

Q11–11. What is the relationship, if any, between the amount of the annual depreciation charges on plant assets and the amount of money available for the new plant assets?

Q11–12. (a) What are the accounting problems resulting from the trade-in of one like plant asset for another? from the sale of a plant asset?

Q11–13. (a) Distinguish between the terms depreciation, depletion, and amortization. (b) How is the periodic depletion charge determined?

Q11–14. (a) What are intangible assets? (b) What factors must be considered when the acquisition of intangibles is recorded? (c) When intangibles are amortized?

Q11–15. What ratios are useful in evaluating the level of investment in plant assets?

□ **EXERCISES**

E11–1. The Forrest Manufacturing Company acquired an old building for $35,000 and spent $20,000 to put it into usable condition. One year later, an additional expenditure of $1,150 was made for painting, plumbing, and electrical repair work. Record all the expenditures.

E11–2. The Wilson-Sloan Corporation purchased a machine for $10,000; terms 1/10, n/60. Record (a) the acquisition of the machine and (b) payment of the invoice within the discount period.

E11–3. The Johnson Corporation solicited bids for a new wing for its factory building. The lowest bid received was $20,000. The Corporation decided to do the work with its own staff, and the wing was completed for a total cost of $17,500. Record the expenditure.

E11–4. The Alomax Corporation purchased a truck on January 2, 1969, for $3,600. It had an estimated useful life of four years and a trade-in value of $400. Compute the depreciation charge for the year 1969 under the following methods: (a) straight-line, (b) sum of the years-digits, (c) double-rate declining-balance, and (d) production, assuming an operating life of 50,000 miles and 12,000 miles of actual use the first year.

E11–5. On January 2, 1969, the Birrell Company purchased land and an old building for $125,000. The land is appraised at $20,000; the building is estimated to have a useful life of ten years and a salvage value of $5,000. After three year's use, the building was remodeled at a cost of $55,000. At this time, it was estimated that the remaining useful life of the building would be 20 years with a salvage value of $10,000. Using the straight-line method of depreciation, give the entries for (a) the purchase of the land and building, (b) depreciation for 1969, (c) remodeling costs, and (d) depreciation for 1972.

E11–6. On August 1, 1969, the Marchant Corporation acquired a truck costing $7,500 with an estimated useful life of five years and a salvage value of $500. On August 1, 1972, the truck was traded in for a new one with a cash market price of $9,000. The dealer allowed $2,100 on the old truck, and the balance was paid in cash. Record the trade-in on the books of the Marchant Corporation, based on (a) recognition of gain or loss and (b) nonrecognition of gain or loss. (c) Contrast the entries in (a) and (b) and state how the nonrecognition of the gain or loss in (b) is compensated for.

E11–7. The Standard Corporation acquired a building for $60,000 with an estimated useful life of 20 years and an estimated salvage value of $5,000. Four years later, an addition to the building was constructed at a cost of $15,000. Using straight-line depreciation, compute the annual depreciation charges before and after the construction of the addition to the building.

E11–8. The Phillips Company acquired three machines as follows:

| | Machine | | |
	A	B	C
Cost	$40,000	$35,000	$47,000
Estimated salvage value	4,000	3,000	5,000
Estimated life (years)	9	8	6

Assuming that the straight-line method is used, compute (a) the composite life for the three machines and (b) the annual depreciation rate.

E11-9. The Abel Company made the following expenditures on the acquisition of a new machine:

Invoice cost ($10,000) less 2% cash discount	$9,800
Transportation charges	200
Installation charges	500
Property insurance—premiums for three years	300
Materials and labor used during test runs	150

What is the cost of the machine?

E11-10. The condensed income statement of the Star Company for the year ended June 30, 1969, was as follows:

Sales	$100,000
Cost of Goods Sold	60,000
Gross Margin	$40,000
Operating Expenses	
(includes depreciation expense of $3,500)	25,000
Net Income	$ 15,000

(a) Assuming that beginning and ending Accounts Receivable, Accounts Payable, and Merchandise Inventory balances were approximately the same, how much cash was generated by operations? (b) Did the depreciation expense deduction result in a direct cash increase of $3,500? Explain.

E11-11. The Delta Mining Company purchased a mine for $210,000. It was estimated that the land contained 800,000 tons of a recoverable mineral deposit, and that after recovery of the deposits the land would have a salvage value of $10,000. During the first year, 60,000 tons were recovered and 50,000 tons were sold. Labor and overhead costs were $100,000. Determine (a) the cost of goods sold and (b) the ending inventory valuation.

E11-12. The comparative financial statements of the Bailey Corporation show the following information:

	Plant and Equipment	Long-Term Liabilities	Stockholders' Equity
December 31, 1969	$110,000	$ 50,000	$125,000
1968	100,000	48,000	115,000
1967	85,000	42,500	105,000
1966	90,000	45,000	100,000

Sales: 1969	$250,000
1968	220,000
1967	200,000
1966	180,000

(a) Compute the appropriate ratios and (b) evaluate the significance of the ratios.

E11-13. The unadjusted trial balance of the Colt Company at December 31, 1969, includes the following accounts:

Patents (granted January 2, 1969)	$12,000
Copyrights (acquired July 1, 1969)	3,125
Goodwill	2,700
Research and Development (new products)	5,000
Organization Costs	1,500

(a) What is the basis of valuation of each of these accounts? (b) What adjustments should be made on December 31, 1969? (c) What additional information is needed to complete Requirement (b)?

E11–14. For each of the following items, indicate the account to be debited:

1. Expenditure for installing machinery

2. Expenditure for trial run of new machinery

3. Expenditure for conveyor system for machinery

4. Payment of delinquent taxes on land (taxes were delinquent at the date of purchase of the land)

5. Expenditure for extensive plumbing repairs on a building just purchased

6. Sales tax paid on new machinery just purchased

7. Payment of incorporation fees to the state

8. Expenditure for a major overhaul that restores a piece of machinery to its original condition and extends its useful life

9. Expenditure for an addition to a building leased for 20 years

10. Amount paid for a purchased business in excess of the appraised value of the net assets

E11–15. On April 1, 1969, a calculating machine used in the office of the Donne Company was sold for $250. The sale was recorded by a debit to Cash and a credit to Office Equipment for $250. The machine had been purchased on October 1, 1965, for $750 and had been depreciated at the rate of 10 percent annually (no salvage value) through December 31, 1968. The Donne Company closes its books annually on June 30. Make an entry to correct the accounts as a result of the transaction.

E11–16. The Capital Glass Corporation reported a net income of $50,000 for the year 1969. The president of the Corporation noted that the beginning and ending inventories were $200,000 and $250,000, respectively, although the physical quantities on hand were relatively stable. He also noted that deductions for depreciation averaged 10 percent on plant and equipment costing $450,000, although the current dollar value of the assets is estimated at $600,000. The president suggests that the reported net income is erroneous. Comment.

☐ **DEMONSTRATION PROBLEMS**

DP11–1. (*Computing depreciation expense*) The Childs Company began business on January 2, 1969, with three new machines. Data for the machines are given:

Machine	Cost	Estimated Salvage Value	EUL (Years)
A	$66,000	$ 6,000	10
B	90,000	10,000	8
C	24,000	4,000	5

Required: Compute the depreciation expense for the first two years by each of the following methods: (a) straight-line, (b) sum of the years-digits, (c) double-rate declining-balance, and (d) composite rate based on straight-line depreciation.

DP11–2. (*Capital and revenue expenditures*) On January 2, 1969, the Volpone Construction Company purchased a machine for $20,000. Its estimated useful life was ten years with no salvage value. Additional expenditures were made for transportation, $300, and installation costs, $600. On June 30, 1975, repairs costing $5,000 were made, increasing the efficiency of the machine and extending its useful life to two years beyond the original estimate. On December 1, 1977, some minor worn-out parts were replaced for $200. On October 1, 1979, the machine was sold for $2,500.

Required: Give the journal entries to record (a) the purchase, (b) annual depreciation for 1969, (c) the extraordinary repair on June 30, 1975, (d) annual depreciation for 1975, (e) the ordinary repair on December 1, 1977, and (f) the disposal on October 1, 1979.

DP11–3. (*Asset sale; trade-in*) On January 2, 1969, the Dwight Corporation purchased a machine costing $12,000 with a useful life of ten years and salvage value of $800. Assume that the sum of the years-digits method is used to record depreciation.

Required: Give the journal entries to record the sale or trade-in of the machine, based on each of the following assumptions:

1. Sale of the machine for $2,000 at the end of the sixth year.
2. Sale of the machine for $3,000 at the end of the fourth year.
3. Trade-in of the machine at the end of the sixth year for a new machine listed at $14,000. The Corporation paid $8,400 in cash to acquire the new machine. (Recognize the gain or loss on the exchange.)
4. Assuming the same facts as in (3), record the trade-in under the income tax method.

DP11–4. (*Managerial considerations*) The board of directors of the Artex Corporation, after reviewing the following data taken from the firm's records, is concerned about a possible overinvestment in plant and equipment.

	1967	1968	1969
Current Assets	$65,000	$ 73,750	$ 75,000
Plant and Equipment	25,000	40,000	55,000
Current Liabilities	32,500	36,250	42,500
Long-Term Liabilities	13,750	22,500	24,000
Capital Stock	20,000	20,000	33,500
Retained Earnings	23,750	35,000	30,000
Net Sales	81,250	100,000	105,000

Required: You have been asked to prepare a report on this matter to the board of directors. Include appropriate analyses and computations to support your conclusions.

☐ **PROBLEMS**

P11–1. On January 2, 1969, the Mart Company purchased a new machine for $64,000 with an estimated salvage value of $4,000 and an estimated useful life of five years, or 6,000 machine hours. The plant manager expects to use the machine for 1,500 hours during 1969 and 1,300 hours during 1970.

Required: 1. Compute the depreciation expense for each of the first two years by the following methods: (a) straight-line, (b) production, (c) sum of the years-digits, and (d) double-rate declining-balance.
2. What factors determine useful life?
3. Does the method of depreciation affect the Company's working capital?

P11–2. A piece of machinery was acquired by Fredericks, Inc., for $6,000 on January 2, 1969. It was estimated to have a five-year life and a salvage value at the end of that time of $300.

Required: Prepare tables showing periodic depreciation over the five-year period, for each assumption listed:

1. Depreciation is to be calculated by the straight-line method.
2. Depreciation is to be calculated by the sum of years-digits method.
3. Depreciation is to be calculated by the double-rate declining-balance method.
4. Repair charges are estimated at $100 for the first year and are estimated to increase by $100 in each succeeding year; depreciation charges are to be made on a diminishing scale so that the sum of depreciation and estimated repairs is the same over the life of the asset.

P11–3. The Nett Corporation purchased a machine on January 3, 1969, at a cost of $40,000. In addition, the Corporation paid $400 to have the machine delivered and $1,600 to have it installed. The estimated useful life of the machine is six years with a trade-in value of $3,000 at the end of that time.

Required: Prepare four separate schedules, showing the annual depreciation charge for the six-year period under each of the following methods: (a) straight-line. (b) production, assuming a total operating life of 30,000 hours with actual annual hours of use as follows: 4,000; 5,000; 6,000; 5,700; 4,600; 4,700. (c) double-rate declining-balance. (d) sum of the years-digits.

P11–4. The Bates Corporation purchased land and buildings for $200,000: the buildings were demolished at a cost of $8,500, salvaged materials were sold for $2,000, and a new building was constructed on the site for $2,000,000. The following additional expenditures were incurred during construction:

Fees for permits and licenses	$ 500
Interest on money borrowed for payment of construction costs	750
Architectural fees	10,000
Insurance	650
Real estate taxes	850
Land grading and leveling	4,000
Promotional literature describing the new facility	500
Trees, shrubs, and other landscaping costs	2,500

Required: Open T accounts for (a) Land, (b) Buildings, and (c) Operating Expenses. Post the transactions to the accounts.

P11–5. The following information was taken from the books of the Green Corporation.

	Machine A	Machine B	Machine C
Date acquired	January 2, 1969	January 2, 1970	January 2, 1971
Cash payment	$15,400	$4,400	$19,200
Estimated salvage value	1,000	1,200	1,600
Estimated useful life in years	4	5	6
Method of depreciation	Sum of the years-digits	Straight-line	Double-rate declining-balance

On January 2, 1970, Machine A, with a value of $9,400, was traded for Machine B which listed for $14,000.

Required: 1. Give all the necessary entries to record the transactions through December 31, 1971. The books are closed annually on December 31.

2. What is the entry for the trade-in of Machine A for Machine B when the income tax method is used?

P11-**6.** The Whyte Corporation acquired two factory buildings. Subsequently, major improvements were made to roofs and foundations, extending the useful life of each building. The following information was taken from the records:

	Building A	Building B
Date acquired	1/2/69	7/1/69
Original cost	$92,000	$160,000
Estimated salvage value	$ 4,000	$ 10,000
Estimated useful life	20 years	25 years
Date improvements completed	7/1/70	7/1/70
Improvement costs	$10,000	$26,000
Revised estimated salvage value	$ 3,000	$ 7,000
Revised estimated useful life	25 years	25 years
Method of depreciation	Straight-line	Straight-line

Required: Give the journal entries to record the transactions, including year-end adjustments through December 31, 1971. The books are closed annually on December 31.

P11-**7.** The general ledger of the Metro Company includes the following accounts:

Machinery and Equipment

1965 Jan. 2	A	5,000	
1966 Apr. 1	B	5,500	
1968 June 1	C	7,500	

Accumulated Depreciation–Machinery and Equipment

1965	
Dec. 31	833.33
1966	
Dec. 31	1,245.83
1967	
Dec. 31	1,383.33
1968	
Dec. 31	1,820.83

The straight-line method is used, the machines have no salvage value and gains and losses on trade-ins are recognized. Details regarding the computation of depreciation expense are summarized:

Machine No.	Date Acquired	Cost	EUL (Years)	Accumulated Depreciation (12/31/1968)
A	1/2/1965	$5,000	6	$3,333.32
B	4/1/1966	5,500	10	1,512.50
C	6/1/1968	7,500	10	437.50

On January 2, 1969, Machine A was traded in for Machine D, with a cash outlay of $4,500. The cash value of the new machine is $6,500. Its estimated useful life is ten years.

On August 1, 1969, Machine B was traded in for Machine E. The new machine lists for $8,000 and its estimated useful life is six years. A trade-in allowance of $4,000 is received on the old machine; the fair market value of the old machine is $3,500.

Required: 1. Record all the necessary entries for the year 1969 through December 31.
2. Record the trade-in of Machine B, assuming that it had been depreciated under the sum of the years-digits method instead of the straight-line method.
Note: Computations for depreciation for Machine B for the years 1966 and 1967, using the sum of the years-digits method, would be as follows:

	Year 1966	Year 1967
April 1, 1966 through March 31, 1967:		
$^{10}\!/_{55} \times \$5,500 = \$1,000$, allocable to:		
1966: $\frac{3}{4} \times \$1,000$	$750	
1967: $\frac{1}{4} \times \$1,000$		$250
April 1, 1967 through March 31, 1968:		
$^{9}\!/_{55} \times \$5,500 = \$900$, allocable to:		
1967: $\frac{3}{4} \times \$900$		675
Totals	$750	$925

P11–**8.** On January 2, 1969, the Neale Corporation purchased a group of machines for $120,000 for the manufacture of a new product. The machines have an estimated useful life of 10 years, during which time management plans to produce 440,000 units of the new product. The estimated salvage value of the machines is $10,000.

The following projections were prepared for use in selecting the depreciation method to be followed:

Year	Units of Output	Equipment Maintenance and Repairs	Net Taxable Income Before Depreciation
1969	36,000	$ 6,000	$24,500
1970	40,000	7,000	24,900
1971	44,000	9,000	25,200
1972	48,000	12,000	26,000
1973	52,000	16,000	30,000

All operating expenses have been deducted including equipment maintenance and repairs but excluding depreciation expense on the machine, to arrive at net taxable income.

Required: 1. Prepare separate depreciation schedules for the five-year period based on the following methods of depreciation: (a) straight-line, (b) production, based on units of output, (c) double-rate declining-balance, (d) sum of the years-digits. Use the following headings for each schedule.

Year Ending December 31	Annual Depreciation Expense	Accumulated Depreciation	Carrying Value at End of Year

2. Write a report to management, stating the advantages and disadvantages of each method of depreciation and giving your recommendations as to choice of method. Support your conclusions with schedules showing the total annual cost of operating the machines. Compute the net income before and after income taxes and evaluate the tax consequences of the different methods of depreciation. (Assume a corporate income tax rate of 30 percent.)

3. Write a supplement to your report, based on any pertinent assumptions you wish to make. For example: (a) the machines can be leased for an annual rental of $25,000; (b) a favorable statement of financial position is essential in connection with an anticipated bank loan.

CASE PROBLEM
Charcoal Briquet Company

The Charcoal Briquet Company recently began operations as a manufacturer and wholesaler of charcoal briquets. Management has been holding regular meetings at which decisions are made regarding various Company policies. One of the items on the agenda for the next scheduled meeting is the depreciation policy of the Company. Kenneth Willis, the Company treasurer and controller, is responsible for developing relevant supporting data. As a staff assistant to Willis, you are responsible for gathering the information that he requests.

You select from the Plant and Equipment section of the general ledger the following data:

Land	$ 10,000
Buildings	100,000
Furniture, fixtures, machinery, and equipment	150,000
Transportation equipment	8,000
Kilns	14,000

Based on information that has been obtained from reliable sources, you suggest to Willis the following useful lives and salvage values for the assets:

Buildings	45 years and $15,000
Furniture, fixtures, machinery, and equipment	10 years and $10,000
Transportation equipment	6 years and $ 1,200
Kilns	6 years and no salvage value

Based on comprehensive forecasts of sales and expenses, management estimates net income before depreciation and income taxes as follows:

First year of operations	$45,000
Second year of operations	60,000
Third year of operations	90,000

The Company is subject to a Federal corporate income tax rate of 22 percent on the first $25,000 of taxable income and 48 percent on all taxable income in excess of $25,000. Also, management plans to use the same depreciation amounts on both the corporate financial statements and the corporate tax returns.

Required: As preparation for Willis's presentation at the forthcoming meeting, you are instructed to do the following:

a. Using the straight-line, sum of the years-digits, and double-rate declining-balance methods, prepare depreciation schedules for the first three years of operations.

b. Calculate the net income under each method.

c. Describe the effect of each method on the Company's cash balance during the first three years of operations.

d. Describe the effect of each depreciation method on the cash balance after the first three years.

e. Identify the difficulties of estimating useful lives and salvage values.

f. List the criteria for determining the Company's depreciation policy.

g. Explain briefly what depreciation expense is and why it is included in the measurement of net income.

h. Explain briefly what accumulated depreciation is and why it is included in the preparation of statements of financial position.

Chapter Twelve
Control of Cash Disbursements and Payroll

Two separate but related issues are considered in this chapter: (1) Control of cash disbursements through the use of a *voucher system* and (2) payroll. These two areas have a high degree of practical significance. Some system of authorizing and verifying cash disbursements—the basic elements of a voucher system—is used by nearly all businesses. Also, virtually all businesses are required by law to withhold specified amounts from their employees' earnings. Businesses in turn are subject to various tax levies based on the payroll.

THE VOUCHER SYSTEM

The accounting system must be designed not only to enable the recording of transactions and the preparation of financial statements but also to achieve other managerial objectives: to furnish analyses and reports of past, current, and projected events; and to establish internal controls to protect the assets of the business against loss through errors or fraud. The achievement of these objectives goes hand in hand with the achievement of maximum operating efficiency and maximum earnings. A properly functioning voucher system plays a key role in establishing and maintaining effective internal control.

The voucher system is a method of accumulating, verifying, recording, and disbursing all the expenditures of a business. The system covers any transaction that will require the payment of cash, including the purchase of merchandise, services, supplies, and plant and equipment, and the payment of expenses. Expenditures are verified, classified, and recorded when they are incurred. All expenditures must be properly authorized and, except for petty cash transactions, are paid by check.

Reference was made in Chapter 8 to the importance of having a built-in system to protect the assets of a business against loss through fraud or error. The voucher system is designed to achieve this internal control by assigning the duties of authorizing the expenditure, reporting the receipt of goods or services, and signing the check in settlement of the liability to different persons or different departments. This division of duties prevents cash being disbursed from the business without the knowledge and approval of several members of the organization.

The Voucher

The *voucher* is a serially numbered form that is the written authorization for each expenditure. It is prepared from the seller's invoice or group of invoices or from other documents that serve as evidence of the expenditure. The voucher form is tailored to meet the needs of the particular business.

The voucher—not the invoice—is the basis for the accounting entry. The invoice, together with acknowledgments or approvals of the receipt of goods or services and other supporting papers, are the underlying documents for the voucher. Some of these documents are discussed in detail later in this chapter. The voucher form provides space for:

1. A summary of the invoice data
2. The accounts to be debited
3. The details of payment
4. The signature of the person who authorizes the payment
5. The signature of the person who records the voucher.

The Voucher Jacket

The *voucher jacket* is a folded voucher form or envelope that serves both as a voucher and as a cover for the invoice—or group of invoices from a particular vendor—and related documents. Space is provided on the outside of the jacket form for the details needed for the accounting entry.

Assume that, during January, 1969, the Ajax Company received ten invoices from a creditor, the Silver Company, with terms of 2/10 EOM, n/30. Upon receipt, the invoices are verified for quantities, prices, and extensions and are filed in a voucher jacket. The total price of the invoices, shown on the voucher jacket, is entered in the journal to record the liability and to classify the expenditures. The unpaid vouchers then are filed according to their due date so that payment will be made within the discount period. Another advantage of filing unpaid vouchers according to due date is that the amount of cash needed daily to pay vouchers due may be readily determined. Paid vouchers are filed alphabetically.

The Voucher Register

The *voucher register* is an elaboration of the purchases journal. It is a journal for recording all liabilities approved for payment. The register is ruled in columns for the frequently used accounts to be charged or credited. The precise form of the register and the number and arrangement of the column headings vary with the needs of the particular business. The voucher register of the Deacon Company is shown in Figure 12-1 (pp. 410–411).

The function of the Vouchers Payable account is the same as that of the Accounts Payable account. It is a controlling account: its balance represents the total of the unpaid vouchers recorded in the voucher register. Unpaid vouchers may, therefore, be readily determined to be those without entries on the corresponding line of the Paid column or those in the *unpaid voucher* file. At the end of the period, a list of the unpaid vouchers should be prepared for reconciliation with the balance of the Vouchers Payable account in the general ledger.

The voucher register illustrated in Figure 12-1 is used for recording all transactions—of whatever category—requiring a cash payment. Each transaction is entered in the voucher register first, followed by an entry in the check register when payment is made. The check register is a book of original entry for all cash disbursements. The vouchers are entered in the voucher register in numerical order. Transactions involving liabilities that are not initially credited to Vouchers Payable—notes payable and accrued expenses, for example—are usually not entered in the voucher register until payment is due. Vouchers are not prepared for accrued expenses; rather, a voucher is prepared for the full amount when the invoice is received or when payment is to be made. (The entries for payroll are discussed on page 426, following the general discussion of payrolls.)

An entry is made in the Credit Vouchers Payable column for the amount due on each voucher. The account or accounts to be debited are indicated on the voucher, and entries are made in one of the special debit columns or in the Other General Ledger Accounts column if no special column is available. The Debit Other General Ledger Accounts column provides space for the name of the account to be debited, a ledger folio (F) column, and an Amount column. Entries in the Other General Ledger Accounts column may be posted daily; all the other columns are posted in total only at the end of the month to the general ledger account indicated in the column heading. Ledger folio references are shown beneath the double ruling for the special columns and in the folio (F) column for the other general ledger accounts items. The posting procedure is the same as for other special journals.

The supporting details for the control accounts—Selling Expense Control 600 and General and Administrative Expense Control 700—are kept on subsidiary *expense analysis sheets* like the one shown:

Selling Expense Analysis Sheet

Date	Reference	608	609	612	618	619	Summary

Each column represents a certain type of selling expense; the column headed 608 may represent Advertising Expense, the column headed 609, Printing Expense, and so on.

The Check Register

No payment is made until a specific voucher has been prepared, recorded, and approved. Hence, each entry is a debit to Vouchers Payable, a credit to Cash, and a credit to Purchases Discounts, if any. No other columns are needed because the trans-

VOUCHER

| Date | Voucher No. | Name | Paid | | Credit |
			Date	Check No.	Vouchers Payable 201
1969					
Jan. 2	314	Wheaton Company	1/11	710	3,500
2	315	Palmer Company	Cancelled by note. See J12.		1,200
4	316	Johnson and Son	Cancelled by Voucher 322.		350
7	317	Petty Cash	1/7	708	100
8	318	Davis Brothers			65
8	319	Dover Furniture Company	1/10	709	800
14	320	Able Company	Cancelled by Vouchers 329, 330.		4,000
15	321	Payroll	1/15	713	1,575
15	322	Johnson and Son	1/15	711	305
15	323	King Company	1/15	712	25
16	324	Bent and Company	Cancelled by Voucher 334.		750
20	325	L. Kett	1/31	719	90
22	326	Palmer Company	1/22	714	1,204
25	327	Daniel Lynch	1/31	718	300
27	328	R. Lincoln Company			75
28	329	Able Company	1/31	715	2,000
28	330	Able Company			2,000
29	331	John Bates, Inc.	1/31	720	60
31	332	Payroll	1/31	716	1,650
31	333	Petty Cash	1/31	717	80
31	334	Bent and Company			730
31	335	Internal Revenue Service	1/31	721	850
31	336	State Division of Employment Security	1/31	722	297
31	337	Internal Revenue Service	1/31	723	126
31	338	First National Bank	Deducted on bank statement.		3
		Totals			22,135
					(201)

action already has been classified under an appropriate heading in the voucher register. Checks are entered in the check register in numerical sequence, one line to each check. The check register of the Deacon Company is illustrated in Figure 12-2. At the time that the check is entered in the check register, a notation must also be made in the Paid column of the voucher register showing the date of payment and the check number.

REGISTER

Purchases 351	Selling Expense Control 600 Account No.	F	Amount	General and Administrative Expense Control 700 Account No.	F	Amount	Account	F	Amount Debit	Credit
3,500										
1,200										
	618	✔	350							
				702	✔	65	Petty Cash	105	100	
							Office Equipment	163	800	
4,000										
							Accrued Wages and Salaries Payable	211	1,575	
							Vouchers Payable (Voucher 316)	201	350	
							Selling Expense Control	600/ 618		45
	619	✔	25							
750										
				708	✔	90				
							Notes Payable	203	1,200	
							Interest Expense	851	4	
300										
	618	✔	75							
							Vouchers Payable (Voucher 320)	201	4,000	
				707	✔	60				
							Accrued Wages and Salaries Payable	211	1,650	
30	609	✔	5	720	✔	10				
	608	✔	15	719	✔	8				
	612	✔	5	712	✔	7				
							Vouchers Payable (Voucher 324)	201	750	
							Purchases Returns and Allowances	360		20
							F.I.C.A. Taxes Payable	212	240	
							Income Tax Withholdings Payable	215	610	
							State Unemployment Taxes Payable	213	297	
							Federal Unemployment Taxes Payable	214	126	
				721	✔	3				
9,780			475			243			11,702	65
(351)			(600)			(700)			(X)	(X)

Figure 12-1.
Voucher Register

CHECK REGISTER   Page 6

Date	Voucher Number	Name	Check Number	Debit Vouchers Payable 201	Credits Purchases Discounts 365	Cash 101
1969						
Jan. 7	317	Petty Cash	708	100		100
10	319	Dover Furniture Company	709	800		800
11	314	Wheaton Company	710	3,500	70	3,430
15	322	Johnson and Son	711	305		305
15	323	King Company	712	25		25
15	321	Payroll	713	1,575		1,575
22	326	Palmer Company	714	1,204		1,204
31	329	Able Company	715	2,000	40	1,960
31	332	Payroll	716	1,650		1,650
31	333	Petty Cash	717	80		80
31	327	Daniel Lynch	718	300	3	297
31	325	L. Kett	719	90		90
31	331	John Bates, Inc.	720	60		60
31	335	Internal Revenue Service	721	850		850
31	336	State Division of Employment Security	722	297		297
31	337	Internal Revenue Service	723	126		126
31	338	First National Bank	✔	3		3
		Totals		12,965	113	12,852
				(201)	(365)	(101)

Figure 12-2.
Check Register

The check register is posted at the end of each month, in total only, to the accounts named in the column headings. The insertion of folio references under the double rulings is the same as for the other special journals.

Use of the Voucher Register and the Check Register

The voucher register form must be tailored to meet the needs of the particular enterprise. The voucher register in Figure 12-1 is designed for a company that keeps subsidiary ledgers for selling and general expenses. These subsidiary ledgers are controlled in the general ledger by the Selling Expense Control account and the General and Administrative Expense Control account. The register provides columns for each general class of expenditure, with space to the left of each general column for the account number of the specific detail account to be debited. This gives the advantage of virtually unlimited flexibility combined with economy of space.

The check register in Figure 12-2 has a Purchases Discounts column because vouchers are recorded in the voucher register at gross amounts. This register shows not only the serial number of the check but also the number of the voucher being paid.

Some companies prepare each voucher for the net amount due. This means that if payment is not made within the discount period an additional voucher will be required, underscoring the expense for lost discounts. The entry in the voucher register for the additional voucher is (the amount is assumed):

Purchases Discounts Lost	5	
Vouchers Payable		5

One check is made out for the full amount due as shown by the two vouchers.

The illustrated voucher register and check register show the recording of some ordinary transactions under a voucher system. A number of special transactions have also been included for illustration purposes.

ORDINARY VOUCHER TRANSACTIONS. *Recording and Paying a Voucher.* The first entry in the voucher register is for approved voucher 314, payable to the Wheaton Company for $3,500 worth of merchandise received; terms 2/10, n/30. On January 11, Check 710 is issued to the Wheaton Company for $3,430. An entry is made in the check register, dated that day, debiting Vouchers Payable for $3,500 and crediting Purchases Discounts and Cash for $70 and $3,430, respectively. The number 314 entered in the Voucher No. column cross-references the check with the paid voucher. After this entry is made, the date of the entry and the check number are entered in the Paid column of the voucher register on the line for Voucher 314. The voucher with its supporting documents is removed from the unpaid voucher file and filed in the *vendors' file.*

Recording the Petty Cash Fund. To establish a petty cash fund, a voucher is made out and a check is issued, payable to Petty Cash. The entries are shown in the voucher register (Voucher 317) and check register (Check 708). To replenish the fund, petty cash payments are classified and totaled to determine the accounts to be debited, the voucher for the replenishment of the fund is recorded, and the check is issued. When the check is cashed, the petty cash fund is restored to its original amount. These entries are illustrated by Voucher 333 and Check 717.

Recording the Payroll. The payroll entries are discussed on page 426.

Recording and Paying Bank Charges. The bank service charge in the illustration is $3. The bank has already deducted this amount on the monthly statement. An entry is made in the check register to reduce the cash balance correspondingly but since a check is not actually issued, a check mark is placed in the Check No. column. Under the voucher system, an entry is made in the check register only to cancel a voucher. It is necessary, therefore, to prepare Voucher 338 for $3 to record the bank charge. The notation "Deducted on bank statement" is entered in the Paid column of the voucher register.

SPECIAL VOUCHER TRANSACTIONS. Certain transactions do not fall into the routine pattern that characterizes the voucher system. That is, for effective internal control the voucher system requires that the amount of the voucher be exactly the same as the amount of the check to be issued when payment is due, except for purchases. It will not operate efficiently when adjustments and corrections are frequent. Provision must be made, however, for errors, purchases returns and allowances, payments by note, and partial payments.

Errors. An error in the amount of a voucher may be discovered after the liability has been entered in the voucher register. In this case, it is generally desirable to cancel the old voucher and issue a new one for the corrected amount. This procedure maintains the established internal controls for authorization and approval of all vouchers.

The procedure for correcting an error is illustrated by the entries for Vouchers 316 and 322. The original charge of $350 was found to be in error, and Johnson and Son sent a corrected invoice for $305. Voucher 322 for the adjusted amount is recorded in the voucher register as follows:

Vouchers Payable (Voucher 316)	350	
Vouchers Payable (Voucher 322)		305
Selling Expense Control (600/618)		45

The credit of $45 to Selling Expense Control is an offset to the original debit of $350 and is entered in the Other General Ledger Accounts Credit column. A notation is made in the Paid column alongside the entry for Voucher 316 to show its cancellation and the number of the new voucher. Voucher 316 is removed from the unpaid voucher file, and Voucher 322 is filed in its proper sequence.

Purchases Returns and Allowances. The procedure for recording purchases returns and allowances is similar to that followed for the adjustment for errors. The problem is essentially the same: the amount to be paid is changed after the liability has been entered in the voucher register. If a credit memorandum is received before the voucher for the corresponding invoice has been prepared, the allowance is deducted from the invoice and no adjusting entry is necessary. If the credit memorandum is received after the voucher has been entered in the voucher register, the old voucher is canceled, and a new voucher is prepared for the reduced amount. The entry in the voucher register to record the allowance received from Bent and Company is:

Vouchers Payable (Voucher 324)	750	
Vouchers Payable (Voucher 334)		730
Purchases Returns and Allowances		20

The debit to Vouchers Payable is for the amount of the old voucher and is entered in the Other General Ledger Accounts Debit column. The credit to Purchases Returns and Allowances is for the amount of the credit memorandum and is entered in the Other General Ledger Accounts Credit column. A notation is made in the Paid column alongside the entry for Voucher 324 to show its cancellation and the new voucher number.

Notes Payable. When a voucher is entered in the voucher register, the credit in the Vouchers Payable column represents an amount due on a current account payable. If a note is issued later in settlement of the account, the voucher is canceled by a general journal entry.

Assume that Voucher 315 is canceled by the issuance of a 20-day, 6-percent note dated January 2. The following entry is made on page 12 in the general journal:

Vouchers Payable (Voucher 315)	1,200	
Notes Payable		1,200

A notation is made in the Paid column of the voucher register and on the old voucher indicating that the account has been settled by the issuance of a note payable. When the note becomes due, a new voucher is prepared for the maturity value of the note and entered in the voucher register. In the illustration, Voucher 326 was issued to authorize payment of the liability to the Palmer Company. Two lines are required for the accounts debited in the Other General Ledger Accounts column: Notes Payable ($1,200) and Interest Expense ($4). The payment of the voucher then is recorded in the check register in the usual manner.

Partial Payments. If partial or installment payments are anticipated, an individual voucher is prepared for each installment and no adjustments are needed. If a voucher is prepared with the assumption that it will be paid in full when due, but is later paid in several installments, the original voucher is canceled and a new voucher is issued for each installment. The entry in the voucher register is:

Vouchers Payable (Voucher 320)	4,000	
Vouchers Payable (Voucher 329)		2,000
Vouchers Payable (Voucher 330)		2,000

The debit to Vouchers Payable is for the amount of the original voucher and is entered in the Other General Ledger Accounts Debit column. The credits to Vouchers Payable are entered on two lines and numbered consecutively. A notation is made in the Paid column opposite the entry for the original voucher, indicating its cancellation and referring to the new voucher numbers.

POSTING FROM THE VOUCHER REGISTER. The voucher register money columns are footed at the end of the month, and the totals of the debit columns are compared with the totals of the credit columns to determine that they are equal. The totals of all the special columns are posted to the proper accounts in the general ledger; the amounts in the Other General Ledger Accounts Debit and Credit columns have been posted individually. The posting symbol reference VR8 is entered in the ledger account folio (F) columns to cross-reference postings from the voucher register.

The individual amounts in the Selling Expense and General and Administrative Expense Control columns are posted to the subsidiary ledger accounts during the month. The specific accounts to be debited in the subsidiary ledgers are indicated by the account numbers in the Account column to the left of the Amount columns. For example, Account 618 in the Selling Expense Control Account No. column is the code number for the Advertising Expense account. After the amount of $350 is posted to Account 618 in the subsidiary ledger, a check mark is placed in the Selling Expense Control folio (F) column to indicate that the amount has been posted.

POSTING FROM THE CHECK REGISTER. The check register columns are footed at the end of the month. The total of the Vouchers Payable Debit column should equal the totals of the two credit columns, Purchases Discounts and Cash. Postings are made at the end of the month to the three general ledger accounts. The symbol ChR with the page number is used in the ledgers to cross-reference postings from the check register.

The Control of Unpaid Vouchers

The unpaid vouchers can be determined readily: They are the ones that have not been marked either "Paid" or "Canceled" in the Paid column. A schedule of unpaid vouchers is prepared at the end of the month; the total should correspond with the balance of the Vouchers Payable account in the general ledger and should equal the total of the vouchers in the unpaid file. A schedule of the unpaid vouchers from Figure 12-1 follows:

DEACON COMPANY
Schedule of Vouchers Payable
January 31, 1969

Voucher No.	Name	Amount
318	Davis Brothers	$ 65
328	R. Lincoln Company	75
330	Able Company	2,000
334	Bent & Company	730
	Total	$2,870

This total agrees with the credit balance of $2,870 in the Vouchers Payable account in the general ledger, as shown:

			Vouchers Payable				Acct. No. 201
1969				1969			
Jan.	2	J12	1,200	Jan. 31	VR8	2,870	22,135
	15	VR8	350				
	28	VR8	4,000				
	31	VR8	750				
	31	ChR6	12,965				
			19,265				

Elimination of the Accounts Payable Ledger

When the voucher system is used, the subsidiary accounts payable ledger can be eliminated. Each numbered voucher is entered on a separate line in the voucher register and may be considered as a credit to a separate account. When the liability is settled and a notation is made in the Paid column, it is equivalent to a debit to that account. The file of unpaid vouchers replaces the accounts payable ledger. The total of the unpaid vouchers must agree with the total of the Vouchers Payable controlling account.

Paying the Voucher—the Voucher Check

If a company pays all its invoices within the discount period, it may use the voucher check system. This system involves the use of a two-part form in triplicate prepared on the vouchering date. One part is the check; the other part, separated by a perforation, is in the form of a remittance letter ruled to indicate the invoices being paid, the discounts taken, and the amount of the check. The first copy—an exact copy of the original but not perforated—may serve as the voucher jacket; invoices and other related documents are attached to it. This voucher copy is filed alphabetically and provides a complete credit file. The second copy may be filed either numerically or chronologically and provides a record of all authorized paid vouchers. This copy may be modified to provide additional columns for the accounts and amounts debited and credited.

Advantages of the Voucher System

In a properly functioning voucher system, all invoices must be verified and approved for payment. As a result, responsibility is fixed and the possibility of error or fraud is reduced. The recording of all vouchers in a single journal (the voucher register) provides for prompt recognition and proper distribution of assets, liabilities, costs, and expenses. Economy in recording is effected by the elimination of the accounts payable ledger and by grouping invoices under a single voucher. The maintenance of a chronological unpaid voucher file facilitates the payment of invoices when they are due. This file also enables management to determine its future cash needs for the settlement of liabilities without loss of discounts. The systematic filing of paid vouchers provides a ready reference source for data and underlying documents in support of all disbursements.

On the other hand, the voucher system has certain limitations. The difficulties in handling special transactions and the need for the preparation of separate vouchers or voucher jackets involve extra clerical and accounting work. The elimination of the accounts payable ledger results in a loss of valuable reference data although this may be overcome by maintaining an alphabetical file by vendor of copies of all vouchers.

THE ROLE OF SUPPORTING DOCUMENTS IN THE ACCOUNTING SYSTEM

Supporting business forms are basic to any accounting system. Much time and effort is devoted by the employees of the enterprise in preparing, using, and filing these forms which vary widely in shape, size, color, and content. These forms—sales slips, invoices, vouchers, cash register tapes, bank statements, insurance policies, contracts, leases, pension plans, labor agreements, negotiable instruments, mortgages—constitute the starting point as well as the evidence for the recording of accounting transactions in the journals. If the entry is cross-referenced to the supporting documents, the need for a detailed explanation accompanying each entry in the journals is eliminated.

The forms are not only evidence of the accounting transaction but are also a means of transmitting information and a basis for analyses, studies, and special reports. The sales slip, for example, authorizes the withdrawal of merchandise from stock, serves as the basis for recording the sales and the inventory reduction, and also may be used as a source of data for a special study of sales by type and quantity of product sold.

Three supporting documents commonly used in the voucher system are:

1. The purchase order
2. The receiving report
3. The vendor's invoice

Purchase Order

The purchase order originates in the purchasing department. It is the written authorization to the vendor to supply goods, setting forth the descriptions and quantities, delivery dates, shipping and billing instructions, and specific terms and conditions: in effect, it is the legal contract between buyer and seller. Multiple copies of the order are prepared and distributed to several departments to inform them of what is on order. The original and one copy are sent to the vendor, the copy to be signed as an acknowledgment of receipt of the purchase order and returned to the buyer. Other copies may be distributed to the receiving department, the accounting department, the department or person who requested that the purchase be made, and others, depending on the existing conditions.

Receiving Report

The receiving report is prepared in the receiving department and is a record of the quantity, quality, condition, and description of the goods received. The receiving report may consist simply of notations on a copy of the purchase order or the *packing slip* sent by the vendor with the shipment. Larger companies prepare multiple copies of receiving reports for distribution to the purchasing department, accounting department, and any other departments or persons involved.

Invoice

The invoice is the form sent by the seller to the buyer and is the charge, or *bill,* for the materials or services supplied. The invoice shows the quantity, description, and price of the merchandise shipped; the buyer's name and address; the date and the invoice number; and the terms of payment. It is held until the goods are received, at which time it is compared with the purchase order and the receiving report for the quantity and quality of goods received, the charges, and the terms. Upon approval of the invoice, a voucher is prepared and the purchase is recorded.

Figure 12-3 illustrates the role of documents in the accounting system.

MANAGERIAL CONTROL OF PAYROLL

The payroll of a firm is a significant part of total expense, making continuous management control essential. The availability of machines and high-speed electronic equipment has facilitated the processing of payroll data and the establishment of effective controls at a reasonable cost.

Effective managerial control of payroll requires that

1. Management has properly authorized the payroll payment.
2. Wages paid are correct and have been received by authorized employees; that is, for example, that no fictitious names or names of persons no longer employed have been listed on the payroll.
3. The numerous reports based on payroll information that are made to governmental agencies, union organizations, and employees are reliable.

Payroll Deductions

It is unusual for an employee to receive the full (*gross*) amount of his salary or wages.

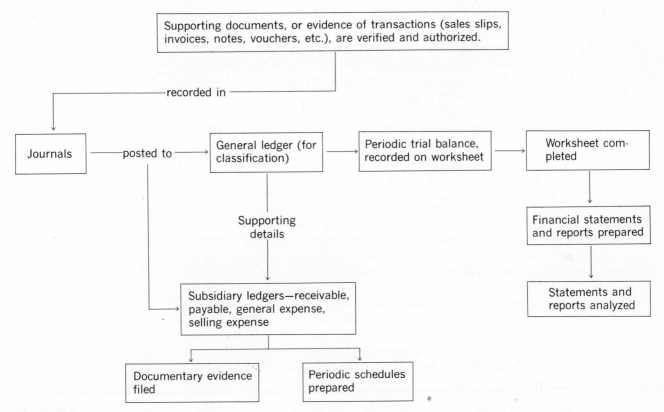

Figure 12-3.
An Accounting Flow

Some deductions are required by law and must be *withheld* by the employer from the employee's regular pay. These include the following:

1. Federal income taxes of the employee.
2. Old-Age, Survivors and Disability Insurance (OASDI) and Hospital Insurance Tax (both often referred to as *F.I.C.A.*, for Federal Insurance Contributions Act).
3. State unemployment tax (in some states).

Other deductions are optional with the employee, such as the purchase of U.S. savings bonds or corporate stock; group, life, accident, and hospitalization insurance; and savings clubs. Deductions may also be required under union agreements or to settle other claims. The deductions are paid to the Federal and state governments and other designated agencies. Adequate records must be maintained to account for the deductions and their related liabilities and to prepare the required reports to the agencies involved.

Fair Labor Standards Act

The Fair Labor Standards Act—popularly known as the Federal Wage and Hour Law—relates to industries engaged directly in the production of goods for interstate commerce. It currently requires that workers not specifically exempted be paid a minimum hourly rate and an overtime wage of *time and one-half*, or one and one-half times the hourly rate, for time worked over 40 hours a week. If no more than 40 hours are worked in a week, no overtime compensation need be paid regardless of the number of hours worked in any one day. Employers and employees may, of course, agree to more favorable terms, such as time and one-half for all work over eight hours in any day and double time for Sunday or holiday work. The act does not place a limitation on total working time; it fixes the 40-hour workweek as the basis for overtime pay.

The Social Security Act and Payroll Deductions

The Social Security Act (approved on August 14, 1935) is a Federal law, operated in part by the states with assistance from the Federal government. The Act includes programs to provide funds for payments to employees who have lost their jobs and for the payment of benefits to retired workers, their families, and their survivors. Funds for the payment of unemployment benefits are currently provided by a tax on the employer of 3.1 percent applied to the first $3,000 paid to each employee. Funds for the payment of benefits to retired workers are provided by a tax imposed on both employers and employees, at the same rate, applied to the first $6,600 of wages paid to each employee. These programs are commonly referred to as the Federal Unemployment Tax Act (F.U.T.A.) and the Federal Insurance Contributions Act (F.I.C.A.). Since all the states have their own state unemployment compensation laws, there is a tie-in between the Federal and the state unemployment compensation systems.

THE FEDERAL INSURANCE CONTRIBUTIONS TAX. Under the provisions of the Federal Insurance Contributions Act, the employer is required to deduct currently 4.9% (1969–1972) of each employee's gross pay, up to a maximum of $6,600 of wages paid by an employer to each employee in each calendar year. An employee who works for more than one employer during the year may, as a result, pay more than the annual maximum of $323.40 (4.9% of $6,600). Refund of any excess is secured when the employee files his Federal income tax return (Form 1040). Some groups are exempt from the F.I.C.A. withholding requirement, including student nurses and interns in hospitals; employees subject to the Railroad Retirement Act; and students working for the school, college, or university. The reader should keep informed of all recent amendments or provisions that may have altered rates, amounts, eligible groups, and so on. Some groups who are exempted from the Federal income tax withholding requirements are subject to F.I.C.A. tax withholding (for example, agricultural workers). Current tables of F.I.C.A. tax withholding rates are available in Circular E, *Employer's Withholding Tax Guide*, published by the Internal Revenue Service.

Since the F.I.C.A. tax rate and the applicable maximum earnings base may be changed by Congress at any time, and to simplify the computations, a rate of 5 percent applicable to the first $6,600 paid to an employee during a calendar year is used in all illustrations and problems in this textbook. The accounting principles and recording procedures are the same irrespective of the rates used. The proposed rates applicable to the first $6,600 paid to an employee during a calendar year as of the time of this writing are shown in Figure 12-4.

Figure 12-4.
Schedule of
F.I.C.A. Tax
Rates

Year	OASDI Tax Rate (%)	Hospital Tax Rate (%)	Total F.I.C.A. Tax (%)	Maximum Amount of Tax
1966	3.85	.35	4.20	$277.20
1967–1968	3.90	.50	4.40	290.40
1969–1972	4.40	.50	4.90	323.40
1973–1975	4.85	.55	5.40	356.40
1976–1979	4.85	.60	5.45	359.70
1980–1986	4.85	.70	5.55	366.30
1987 and after	4.85	.80	5.65	372.90

FEDERAL INCOME TAX WITHHOLDING. Employers are required by the Federal Revenue Act to make deductions from each employee's earnings for Federal income taxes. The amount that the employer is required to withhold (certain classes of wage payments are exempt) depends on the total number of exemptions that the employee claims, the employee's earnings, and the frequency of the payroll period. Upon being hired, the employee fills out an Employee's Withholding Exemption Certificate, Form W-4, indicating the number of exemptions claimed. A new form is filed when there is a change in the number of exemptions. The employee may claim exemptions for (1) himself, (2) his wife (unless she is employed and claims her own exemption), and (3) each qualified dependent. Additional exemptions may be claimed for old age (sixty-five years or older) and blindness of the claimant or his wife.

The Internal Revenue Service furnishes withholding tables for different payroll periods in Circular E. A section of an income tax withholding table is shown:

Figure 12-5.
Weekly Payroll
Period—Withholding
(Married)

If the wages are—		And the number of withholding exemptions claimed is—						
At least	But less than	0	1	2	3	4	5	6
		The amount of income tax to be withheld shall be—						
100	105	15.00	12.70	10.60	8.50	6.50	4.50	2.50
105	110	15.80	13.50	11.30	9.30	7.30	5.30	3.20
110	115	16.70	14.40	12.10	10.00	8.00	6.00	4.00
115	120	17.50	15.20	12.90	10.80	8.80	6.80	4.70
120	125	18.40	16.10	13.80	11.50	9.50	7.50	5.50

The table shows that if an employee earns $110 weekly, for example, and claims three withholding exemptions—for himself, his wife, and one child—the amount of income tax to be withheld is $10.00. (Since tax rates are subject to change, persons responsible for payrolls should be acquainted with the latest tax rates and regulations, both Federal and state, and in some cases, municipal.)

OTHER DEDUCTIONS. In some states, employees as well as employers are taxed under the state unemployment insurance programs. A number of states and some cities levy income taxes on the gross earnings of the employee. In some states, employees are taxed to provide funds for the cost of disability benefits. Such additional tax assessments are generally deducted from gross earnings by the employer and forwarded to the designated agencies.

Recording and Paying the Payroll

Accurate payroll records are necessary to determine operating expenses and to report earnings information to employees and to Federal, state, and other agencies. The records must show the names, earnings, and payroll deductions of all employees for each pay period. An individual record for each employee, showing his earnings and deductions must also be kept. A general journal entry is made to record the payroll for the pay period. Assume that the Burns Company payroll entry for the week ended January 28, 1969, was as follows:

Salesmen's Salaries Expense	1,018.00	
Executive Salaries Expense	750.00	
Office Salaries Expense	320.00	
F.I.C.A. Taxes Payable (assumed rate of 5%)		104.40
Income Tax Withholding Payable		218.80
Bond Deductions Payable		47.50
Accrued Salaries and Wages Payable		1,717.30
To record the payroll for the week ended January 28.		

The debits are to a selling expense account for $1,018 and to two general and administrative expense accounts for $1,070, or a total payroll of $2,088, of which the employees' *take-home* pay is $1,717.30. The entries under a voucher system are explained later in this chapter.

Employer's Payroll Taxes

In addition to the amounts that he must withhold from employees' pay, payroll taxes are levied on the employer. The rates and maximum amounts are indicated in the following paragraphs.

F.I.C.A. TAX. The Federal Insurance Contributions Act levies a tax on employers to help finance the social security program. The rates and maximum amounts are applicable equally to employer and employee.

FEDERAL UNEMPLOYMENT COMPENSATION TAX. The Federal Unemployment Compensation Tax Act currently provides for an additional tax on the employer of 3.1 percent on the first $3,000 paid to each covered employee during a calendar year. The tax is split into two portions—2.7 percent is payable to the state and the remaining 0.4 percent is payable to the Federal government. The Federal portion of the tax applies only to employers who have had four or more employees on at least one day of each of twenty calendar weeks in a calendar year.

STATE UNEMPLOYMENT COMPENSATION TAX. All the states have laws requiring the payment of an unemployment compensation tax. Funds are provided by a payroll tax levy on the employer and, in several states, on both the employer and the employees. Unemployed persons who qualify for benefits are paid by a state agency from funds acquired through the tax.

State unemployment tax laws vary in their detail and application. The maximum tax rate is generally 2.7 percent of the first $3,000 of remuneration paid to each employee during a calendar year, but it may be reduced on a *merit basis* if the employer's annual contributions are sufficiently in excess of withdrawals for unemployment payments made to discharged employees. The *merit-rating plan* provides an incentive to employers to maintain steady employment.

Recording the Employer's Payroll Tax Expense

The employer's payroll tax expense may be recorded at the end of each payroll period or at the end of each month. Assuming that the Burns Company records the payroll tax expense for each payroll and that, due to its merit-rating record, it is subject to a state unemployment tax rate of only 2 percent, the accrued payroll tax liability for the week ended January 28 is computed as follows:

F.I.C.A. tax ($2,088 × .05)	$104.40
State unemployment compensation tax ($2,088 × .02)	41.76
Federal unemployment compensation tax ($2,088 × .004)	8.35
Total	$154.51

The general journal entry to record the expense is:

Payroll Tax Expense	154.51	
F.I.C.A. Taxes Payable		104.40
State Unemployment Taxes Payable		41.76
Federal Unemployment Taxes Payable		8.35
To record accrued payroll taxes		
for week ended January 28.		

The debit is to the Payroll Tax Expense account; the three credits are the accrued liabilities to the Federal and state agencies. The liability for F.I.C.A. taxes ($104.40) matches the amount deducted from the employees' wages. In this entry, payroll taxes were based on $2,088, assuming that all the earnings were subject to payroll taxes. But, as of this writing, the maximum from which F.I.C.A. taxes are deducted is the first $6,600 of gross earnings by each employee in each calendar year, and the maximum subject to the unemployment tax is $3,000. Therefore, any earnings of any employee in excess of these maximums are not subject to payroll taxes. Assume, for example, that the Burns Company payroll for the week ended October 27 was $3,050, including $1,200 of nontaxable F.I.C.A. earnings and $2,000 of nontaxable unemployment compensation earnings. The accrued payroll tax liability is computed as follows:

	F.I.C.A. Tax	Unemployment Taxes
Total payroll	$3,050	$3,050
Payroll (in excess of $6,600 per employee) not subject to F.I.C.A. tax	1,200	
Payroll (in excess of $3,000 per employee) not subject to unemployment taxes		2,000
Payroll subject to taxes	$1,850	$1,050

Payroll taxes
F.I.C.A. tax ($1,850 × 0.05) $ 92.50
State unemployment compensation
  tax ($1,050 × 0.02)   21.00
Federal unemployment compensation
  tax ($1,050 × 0.004)   4.20
Total tax liability $117.70

The entry to record the payroll taxes and the accrued liability is:

Payroll Tax Expense   117.70
  F.I.C.A. Taxes Payable   92.50
  State Unemployment Taxes Payable   21.00
  Federal Unemployment Taxes Payable   4.20
    To record accrued payroll taxes
    for week ended October 27.

Reporting and Payment of Payroll Taxes

The reporting and payment requirements for the employer's payroll taxes and the amounts withheld from employees' earnings are discussed in the following sections.

INCOME TAXES WITHHELD AND F.I.C.A. TAXES. The Federal income taxes withheld and F.I.C.A. taxes withheld from the employees' earnings and the employer's F.I.C.A. taxes are reported quarterly. The tax report form is filed during the month following the close of each calendar quarter; for the months of October, November, and December, for example, the form must be filed by January 31. The amounts required to be paid are the amounts accumulated in the Income Taxes Withholdings Payable account and in the F.I.C.A. Taxes Payable account. If the sum of Income Tax Withholdings Payable and F.I.C.A. Taxes Payable exceeds $100 in either the first or the second month of each quarter, the employer is required to deposit the amount due for that month in a Federal depositary bank. The deposit must be made by the fifteenth day of the following month. The card form (Form 450, the Federal Depositary Receipt) used for this purpose is receipted and returned for submittal with the quarterly tax report (Form 941). Assume that the accounts of the Burns Company show the following tax liabilities on October 31:

Income Tax Withholdings Payable (October) $910.70
F.I.C.A. Taxes Payable (October)   295.50

Payment of these tax liabilities must be made to a Federal Reserve Bank or an authorized commercial bank before November 15. The entry to record the deposit is:

Income Tax Withholdings Payable   910.70
F.I.C.A. Taxes Payable   295.50
  Cash   1,206.20
    To record payment of tax liabilities.

The amount due for the third month of each quarter may either be deposited or be sent in with the quarterly tax report. If the Burns Company remits the December liability with the quarterly return, two depositary receipts covering the taxes for

October and November and a check for the taxes for December must accompany the return. Monthly deposits are not required for the first or second month of any quarter if the sum of the income taxes withheld from employees' earnings and the total F.I.C.A. taxes on the employer and the employees does not exceed $100. Payment for these months accompanies the quarterly return.

By January 31 of each year, the employer is required to give each employee a Withholding Statement, Form W-2, showing his gross earnings and the amounts withheld during the previous calendar year. The employee, in turn, is required to submit a copy of this statement with his Federal income tax return.

STATE UNEMPLOYMENT COMPENSATION TAX. The employer's state unemployment compensation tax liability is accumulated in the State Unemployment Taxes Payable account. The employer files a tax report form—the form varies with the states—and pays the required tax. Timing of the payments—monthly or quarterly—varies with the states. Assume that the balance of the State Unemployment Taxes Payable account of the Burns Company was $84.50 on December 31, for the fourth quarter (October through December), and that the tax report form must be filed and payment must be made to the proper collecting agency by January 31. The entry to record the payment of the accrued liability is:

State Unemployment Taxes Payable	84.50	
Cash		84.50
To record payment of tax liability.		

FEDERAL UNEMPLOYMENT COMPENSATION TAX. The employer must pay the Federal unemployment compensation tax annually. The tax liability is accumulated during the year in the Federal Unemployment Taxes Payable account. Assume that the Federal Unemployment Taxes Payable account for 1969 (January through December) on the books of the Burns Company shows an accumulated tax liability of $319.50. The tax report form must be filed and payment must be made to the proper Federal agency by January 31, 1970. The entry to record payment of the accrued liability is:

Federal Unemployment Taxes Payable	319.50	
Cash		319.50
To record payment of tax liability.		

Accrual of Salaries and Wages

If the end of the payroll period does not coincide with the end of the accounting period, an adjusting entry is made for salaries and wages earned but not paid. Assume that the Burns Company closes its books on October 31, and that the last payroll period in October ended on the 27th (Friday). The entry to accrue the salaries for the partial pay period is:

Salesmen's Salaries Expenses	406	
Executive Salaries Expenses	300	
Office Salaries Expenses	128	
Accrued Salaries and Wages Payable		834
To record salaries and wages accrued from October 28 to 31.		

The entire credit for the accrued payroll is made to a single liability account rather than to separate liability accounts for the government and the employees. Amounts to be withheld from employees' earnings for income taxes and for F.I.C.A. taxes are based on the earnings for an entire payroll period. Insofar as the employer is concerned, the total liability is $834; its breakdown into the several liability accounts does not provide additional useful information and may, therefore, be deferred until the date of payment. Although the employer's payroll taxes are levied only on amounts actually paid, the employer's payroll tax expense on the accrued payroll for the partial pay period should be recognized. The entry for the Burns Company is:

Payroll Taxes   61.72
  Accrued Payroll Taxes Payable   61.72
    To record the employer's payroll tax liability on the accrued payroll from October 28 to 31:

F.I.C.A. ($834 × 0.05)	$41.70
State unemployment insurance ($834 × 0.02)	16.68
Federal unemployment tax ($834 × 0.004)	3.34
Total	$61.72

Payroll under the Voucher System

Under the voucher system, the payroll for the period is recorded as usual in the payroll records. The liability is entered in the general journal by debiting the payroll expense accounts and crediting Accrued Salaries and Wages Payable and the accounts for the deductions. A voucher is prepared for the amount of the net payroll, and a check is issued to the *paymaster*. In Figure 12-1, the payroll of January 15 is covered by Voucher 321 and paid with Check 713.

At the end of the month, payment of the tax liabilities is recorded in the voucher register. Assuming that the total taxable December payroll of the Deacon Company was $2,400 and that income taxes of $610 were withheld from employees' earnings, Voucher 335 and Check 721 (Figure 12-2) are made payable to the Internal Revenue Service for $850 ($610 + $240 in F.I.C.A. taxes). The check and the depositary receipts for October and November accompany the report form.

January 31 is also the last day for filing the state unemployment tax form for the last quarter (October through December). Assuming that wages subject to the tax were $14,850, Voucher 336 and Check 722 are made payable to the State Division of Unemployment Security for $297 ($14,850 × 0.02).

Assuming that the total payroll subject to the Federal unemployment compensation tax was $31,500 in 1969, Voucher 337 records the liability for $126 ($31,500 × 0.004). Check 723 for that amount is attached to the Federal tax return.

SUMMARY

The voucher system is a method of accumulating, verifying, recording, and disbursing all the expenditures of a business. It covers any transaction that requires a cash payment. The voucher is a serially numbered form that serves both as the written authorization for each expenditure and as the basis for the accounting entry. Invoices, receiving reports, and other forms serve as supporting documents for vouchers.

The voucher register is a journal for recording all liabilities approved for payment. It is ruled in columns headed by the proper accounts to be charged. Each appropriate transaction is entered in the voucher register first, followed by an entry in the check register when payment is made. The check register is the book of original entry for all cash disbursements. At the same time that the check is entered in the check register, a notation is made in the Paid column of the voucher register, showing the date of payment and the check number. The posting procedure is the same as for other special journals.

The total of unpaid vouchers—those that have not been marked either paid or canceled in the Paid column of the voucher register—should equal the balance of the Vouchers Payable account in the general ledger and, correspondingly, the total of the vouchers in the unpaid vouchers file. This file replaces the accounts payable ledger.

Both employer and employees are subject to certain taxes on wages. The employer must deduct from each employee's pay amounts for income, F.I.C.A., and state unemployment insurance taxes (in some states). Deductions may also be required under union agreements or to meet other claims. The employer, in turn, is subject to the following payroll taxes:

1. F.I.C.A. at 4.9 percent of the first $6,600 of each employee's annual earnings.
2. A state unemployment tax of 2.7 percent (this may be reduced on a merit basis, subject to the level of employee turnover) of the first $3,000 of each employee's annual earnings.
3. A Federal unemployment tax of 0.4 percent of the first $3,000 of each employee's annual earnings.

   Withheld income taxes and F.I.C.A. taxes are deposited monthly in a Federal depositary bank and reported quarterly to the Internal Revenue Service on Form 941. State unemployment taxes are reported and paid quarterly to the appropriate state agency. Federal unemployment taxes are reported on Form 940 and paid annually to the Internal Revenue Service.

□ **QUESTIONS**

Q12–1. (a) What is the voucher system? (b) What is a voucher? (c) What is a voucher jacket? (d) What is a voucher register? (e) What is a check register? (f) What are the advantages of the voucher system? (g) The disadvantages?

Q12–2. What is the function of the various business forms in an accounting system?

Q12–3. (a) What two types of Federal taxes are most employers required to withhold from their employees' wages? (b) When do taxes withheld become liabilities to the employer? (c) When and in what manner is the employer required to pay to the responsible Federal agency the amounts withheld?

Q12–4. (a) What are three common payroll taxes levied on an employer? (b) What is the rate of each tax? (c) When and in what manner does the employer pay the tax?

Q12–**5.** (a) What are the main purposes of the Federal Wage and Hour Law? (b) Does it limit the number of hours an employee may work? (c) Are all businesses subject to the provisions of this law?

Q12–**6.** (a) What classes of employees are subject to the Federal unemployment compensation tax? (b) What is the tax rate? (c) When is a Federal unemployment tax liability incurred? (d) When is the liability paid to the proper governmental agency?

Q12–**7.** (a) What is a state unemployment merit-rating plan? (b) Why are merit ratings assigned by the several states? (c) What are the maximum state unemployment tax rates? (d) How was the maximum rate initially established in the Federal Unemployment Compensation Act? (e) When does the employer become subject to a state unemployment tax liability? (f) When and to whom is the liability paid?

Q12–**8.** A company may pay its employees in: (a) cash, (b) checks drawn on the regular checking account, or (c) checks drawn on a special payroll bank account. Discuss the advantages and disadvantages of each form of payment.

☐ **EXERCISES**

E12–**1.** Foley, Inc. completed the following transactions, among others, during October, 1969:

Oct. 1 Issued Voucher 45 payable to the McGill Company for $700 worth of merchandise; terms 2/10, n/30.

6 Received a credit memorandum for $75 from the McGill Company for unsatisfactory merchandise returned. Canceled Voucher 45 and issued Voucher 61 for the proper amount.

10 Issued Check 25 in payment of Voucher 61, less a 2 percent discount.

Record the transactions in general journal form, indicating the journal in which each transaction would be properly recorded.

E12–**2.** The Jason Company records all vouchers at the net amount. Record the following transactions in general journal form, indicating the proper book of original entry.

1969

Oct. 2 Issued a voucher payable to the Snow Company for $1,000 worth of merchandise; terms 2/10, n/30.

5 Issued a voucher payable to White's, Inc., for $1,500 worth of merchandise; terms 3/10, n/30.

12 Issued a check to the Snow Company in payment of the October 2 voucher.

Nov. 4 Issued a voucher payable to White's, Inc., for the discount not taken on the transaction of October 5.

4 Issued a check payable to White's, Inc., for the amount due.

E12–**3.** Calculate the total wages of the following employees; all are covered by the Fair Labor Standards Act:

1. Philip Baker: Regular rate, $2.50 an hour; worked 45 hours in a particular week.

2. George Campat: Regular rate, $100 for a 40-hour week; worked 46 hours in a particular week.

3. Alfred Finn: Regular monthly rate, $650 based on a 40-hour week; worked 52 hours in a particular week and 48 hours in another week. Did not work over 40 hours in any of the remaining weeks of that month.

4. George Wilson: Regular piece rate, $.03; worked 60 hours and completed 5,000 pieces during a given week.

E12-4. The payroll records of the Williams Company for the week ended January 20 showed the following:

Total wages earned		$2,000
Deductions		
F.I.C.A. tax	$100	
Federal income tax	220	
Accounts receivable	100	420
Net amount paid		$1,580

Assuming that a voucher system is used, record in general journal form: (a) the total payroll, (b) the payment of the payroll, (c) the employer's payroll tax expense, using rates of 5 percent, 2.7 percent, and 0.4 percent. Indicate the journal in which each entry would be properly reported.

E12-5. All the thirty employees of the Gerry Company earned over $3,000 during the calendar year 1969. The Gerry Company is subject to a state unemployment tax rate of 2.7 percent.

(a) What was the state unemployment tax expense for 1969? (b) Compute the tax expense based on a tax reduced by a merit rating to 0.5 percent. (c) Compute the Federal unemployment tax expense for 1969.

E12-6. From the payroll records of Lee Cordar for the week ended September 10 the following information is obtained:

Total Earnings	$2,050
Earnings subject to unemployment compensation tax	750
Earnings subject to F.I.C.A. tax	1,200
Deductions	
F.I.C.A. tax	60
Federal income tax	215
Accounts receivable	50

Record (a) the payroll and (b) the employer's payroll tax liability, using the following rates: F.I.C.A., 5 percent; state unemployment, 1.5 percent; Federal unemployment, 0.4 percent.

E12-7. The Hallows Company had ten employees who worked during an entire calendar year. One of them, Martin Dorfman, earned $9,500. What was the employer's total expenditure for Dorfman's services for the year? Assume a state unemployment tax rate of 2.7 percent.

E12-8. The following payroll data for the year 1969 were taken from the records of the Rebello Company:

Total wages expense	$90,000
Wages to employees with earnings in excess of $3,000	35,000
Wages to employees with earnings in excess of $6,600	15,000

Calculate the employer's payroll tax expense for the year, using the following rates: F.I.C.A., 5 percent; state unemployment, 2.2 percent; Federal unemployment, 0.4 percent.

E12–**9.** John Hynes pays his ten employees weekly. The payroll summary for the week ended January 15 is given:

Total earnings		$1,050.00
Deductions		
F.I.C.A. tax	$ 52.50	
Federal income tax	210.00	
Union dues	20.00	
Total deductions		282.50
Net amount paid		$ 767.50

Journalize (a) the payment of the payroll and (b) the employers' liability for payroll taxes, using the following rates: F.I.C.A., 5 percent; state unemployment, 2.7 percent; Federal unemployment, 0.4 percent.

E12–**10.** The Mattson Company uses a voucher system. During May, 1969, the following selected transactions were completed:

1969

May   1   Issued Voucher 171 payable to the Hanscom Company for $2,500 worth of merchandise; terms n/10.

     11   Gave the Hanscom Company a 20-day, 4-percent note in payment of Voucher 171.

     31   Issued Voucher 189 payable to the Hanscom Company for the maturity value of the note of May 11.

     31   Issued Check 97 in payment of Voucher 189.

Record the transactions in general journal form, indicating the journal in which each transaction would be properly recorded.

☐ DEMONSTRATION PROBLEMS

DP12–**1.** (*Voucher register*) A portion of a voucher register, showing the unpaid vouchers as of April 30, 1969, is given:

Date		Vou. No.	Name	Paid		Credit Vou. Pay.	Debit Purch.	Other General Ledger Accounts		
				Date	Ck. No.			Account	Debit	Credit
1969										
April	5	270	Gilbert Spack			900				
	10	272	William Murphy			800				
	21	291	Baldwin Company			1,000				
	30	305	Norman Geller			600				

The following transactions, among others, occurred during May:

1969

May   1   Issued Check 651 in payment of Voucher 270, less 2 percent.

     1   Issued Voucher 309 to Herbert Sedlin for $1,500 worth of merchandise, terms n/15.

1969

May 5   Received a credit memorandum from the Baldwin Company for $300 for unsatisfactory merchandise returned. Canceled Voucher 291 and issued Voucher 310 for the proper amount.

     8   Issued Check 652 in payment of Voucher 305, less 1 percent.

     15 Issued Check 653 in payment of Voucher 310, less 1 percent.

     16 By special agreement with Herbert Sedlin, the purchase of May 1 is to be paid for in installments; $500 immediately and the balance by June 16. Canceled Voucher 309 and issued Vouchers 311 and 312. Check 654 was issued in payment of Voucher 311.

Required: 1. Enter the unpaid vouchers in a voucher register similar to the one shown (draw double rules under the last entry to exclude these amounts from the May totals); record the May transactions in the voucher register and a check register.

2. Enter the total of unpaid vouchers as of April 30, $3,300, as a credit in the Vouchers Payable general ledger account; post to Vouchers Payable from the voucher register and check register.

3. Prepare a schedule of unpaid vouchers.

DP12–2. (*Recording transactions in special journals*). The Adams Company uses a voucher system. During June, 1969, the following selected transactions were completed:

1969

June 1 Purchased $2,000 worth of merchandise from the Roche Company; terms 2/10, n/30.

     10 Made a partial payment on the June 1 purchase. The check is made out for $837.90, representing a partial payment on which a discount is allowed.

     15 Paid a 45-day, 6-percent note for $4,000 due today (the Company closed its books on May 31).

     20 Returned merchandise with an invoice price of $200 to the Roche Company and received credit.

     25 Paid $500 in rent for June.

     30 Accrued, vouchered, and paid the following payroll:

	Gross Wages	F.I.C.A. Tax	Employees' Income Tax Withheld
Sales staff	$2,000	$100	$155.00
Office staff	1,000	50	77.50

     30 Recorded the employer's total payroll tax expense, based on the payroll given. The total payroll is subject to a state unemployment tax rate of 2 percent.

Required: Record the transactions in general journal form and indicate the journal in which each transaction would be properly recorded.

DP12–3. (*Recording payroll*). The partially completed payroll register of the Black Company for the week ended July 12 is given:

Payroll Register

Name	Earnings		Deductions		Net Amount	Distribution		
	Week Ending July 12	Cumu-lative Through July 5	F.I.C.A. Tax	Federal Income Tax		Sales-men's Salaries	Exec-utive Salaries	Office Salaries
Bates, John	85	3,035		6.10		85		
Hanlon, Robert	110	3,050		11.00		110		
Perry, John	250	6,550		21.00			250	
Silver, Clifford	90	2,995		4.80				90
Totals								

Required: 1. Prepare a payroll register similar to the one shown, filling in all the blank columns.
2. Record the Black Company's payroll for the week.
3. Record the Black Company's payroll tax expense, assuming the following rates: F.I.C.A., 5 percent; state unemployment, 2.1 percent; Federal unemployment, 0.4 percent.

☐ **PROBLEMS**

P12–1. The Allen Company prepares its vouchers for the net amount due. A portion of the voucher register, showing the unpaid vouchers as of June 30, is given:

Date	Vou. No.	Name	Paid		Credit Vou. Pay.	Debit Purch.	Debit Purch. Disc. Lost	Other General Ledger Accounts		
			Date	Ck. No.				Account	Debit	Credit
1969 June 1	78	Robert Doyle			49					
3	81	Bennett Co.			980					
5	82	Gates & Son			196					

1969
July 1 Issued Check 110 in payment of Voucher 78.

5 Issued Voucher 83 payable to Gates & Son for $4 discount lost on the purchase of June 5.

6 Issued Check 111 in payment of Vouchers 82 and 83.

10 Issued Voucher 84 to the Giles Company for $500 worth of merchandise; terms 2/10, n/30.

14 Issued Voucher 85 to Warren's, Inc., for $750 worth of merchandise; terms 1½/10, n/30.

16 By special arrangement with the Bennett Company the purchase of June 3 (invoice $1,000; terms 2/10 EOM, n/30) is to be paid for in installments; $400 immediately and the balance on August 16. Issued

Voucher 86 for the purchase discount lost. Canceled Vouchers 81 and 86 and issued Vouchers 87 and 88. Check 112 was issued in payment of Voucher 87.

20 Issued Check 113 in payment of Voucher 84.

Required: 1. Enter the unpaid vouchers as of July 1 in a voucher register similar to the one shown; record the July transactions in the voucher register and a single-column check register.
2. Enter the total amount of unpaid vouchers as of July 1 ($1,225) as a credit to the Vouchers Payable general ledger account; post to a Vouchers Payable T account from the voucher register and the check register.
3. Prepare a schedule of unpaid vouchers.

P12–2. The Guilmet Company uses the voucher system. The unpaid vouchers on April 1 were:

Vou. No.	Payee	Invoice Date	Terms	Amount
340	Emerson Company	March 7	n/30	$ 200
348	S. Furry Company	March 14	1/10 EOM, n/60	500
352	L. Scotch Company	March 19	2/10, n/30	200
358	J. Waitt Company	March 28	2/10, n/30	100
	Total			$1,000

During April, 1969, the following transactions were completed:

1969

April 1 Established a petty cash fund of $50 by the issuance of Voucher 362; issued Check 357 in payment of this voucher.

1 Purchased a one-year insurance policy from the Liberty Insurance Company for $600 (charge Prepaid Insurance). Issued Voucher 363 and Check 358 in payment of the voucher.

2 Issued Voucher 364 payable to the Clemson Realty Company for $200 for the April rent (charge to Rent Expense); issued Check 359 in payment of the voucher.

3 Issued Voucher 365 payable to R. Kelly, Inc., for $925 worth of merchandise; terms 1/10, n/30.

4 Gave the Emerson Company a 20-day, 6-percent note in settlement of Voucher 340.

7 Issued Check 360 in payment of Voucher 358, less 2 percent.

7 Issued Voucher 366 payable to L. Scotch Company for $1,200 worth of merchandise; terms n/10.

8 Issued Voucher 367 payable to Danvers Supply Company for $200 worth of office supplies (charge Office Supplies Expense); issued Check 361 in payment of the voucher.

10 Issued Check 362 in payment of Voucher 348, less 1 percent.

11 Issued Check 363 in payment of Voucher 352.

14 Issued Voucher 368 payable to J. Waitt Company for $1,025 worth of merchandise; terms 2/10, n/30.

15 Recorded the following payroll data in the general journal:

Earnings		
Salesmen's salaries	$ 750	
Office salaries	450	
Executive salaries	1,000	$2,200
Deductions		
F.I.C.A. tax	$ 110	
Federal income tax	300	
U.S. bonds	75	
Accounts receivable	20	
United fund	10	515
Net amount due		$1,685

15 Issued Voucher 369 payable to Payroll for the net amount due to employees. Issued Check 364 in payment of the voucher.

16 Returned defective merchandise worth $25 to R. Kelly, Inc.; credit was received. Canceled Voucher 365 and issued Voucher 370 for the correct amount.

17 The L. Scotch Company agreed to an extension of time on its invoice due today, as follows: $600 payment due in 20 days and another $600 payment due in 30 days. Canceled Voucher 366 and issued Vouchers 371 and 372.

20 Purchased three electric typewriters from the Atlas Office Company for $1,500. Issued Voucher 373 for $500 and Check 365 in payment. Issued Voucher 374 for $1,000 for the balance, payable in 30 days.

21 Made an adjustment with the J. Waitt Company because of an error in billing on the purchase of April 14. The correct amount is $1,250. Issued Voucher 375 and canceled Voucher 368. (Debit Purchases for the amount of the adjustment.)

22 Issued Voucher 376 payable to the S. Furry Company for $800 worth of merchandise; terms 1/10 EOM, n/60.

23 Issued Check 366 in payment of Voucher 370.

24 Issued Check 367 in payment of Voucher 375, less 2 percent.

24 Issued Voucher 377 payable to the Emerson Company for the maturity value of the note on April 4. Issued Check 368 in payment of the voucher.

25 Returned defective merchandise worth $20 to the S. Furry Company, and received credit. Canceled Voucher 376 and issued Voucher 378 for the correct amount.

28 Issued Voucher 379 to the *Salem Sun* for $75 worth of advertising. Issued Check 369 in payment of the voucher.

30 Recorded in the general journal the following payroll data from the payroll records:

Earnings		
Salesmen's salaries	$ 820.00	
Office salaries	450.00	
Executive salaries	1,000.00	$2,270
Deductions		
F.I.C.A. tax	$ 113.50	
Federal income tax	315.50	
U.S. bonds	75.00	
Accounts receivable	35.00	
United fund	12.00	551
Net amount due		$1,719

30 Issued Voucher 380 payable to Payroll for the net amount due to employees. Issued Check 370 in payment of the voucher.

30 Issued Voucher 381 payable to Petty Cash to replenish the petty cash fund. Petty cash slips indicate that payments were made as follows: Transportation In, $10; Travel Expense, $7; Miscellaneous Selling Expense, $6; Stationery and Printing, $3; Postage Expense, $4. Check 371 was issued in payment of the voucher. (Transportation In is in the general ledger.)

30 Issued the following vouchers: Voucher 382 payable to Internal Revenue Service for (March) F.I.C.A. Taxes Payable, $440, and Income Tax Withholdings Payable, $610; Voucher 383 payable to the State Division of Employment Security for (January to March) State Unemployment Taxes Payable, $286.20; Voucher 384 payable to the First National Bank for (April) Bank Services and Collection Charges, $3.25.

30 Issued the following checks: Check 372 in payment of Voucher 382; Check 373 in payment of Voucher 383.

30 Recorded the bank service and collection charges in the check register. Payment of Voucher 384 was indicated in the voucher register.

Required: 1. Prepare a voucher register and a check register similar to the illustrations in the text. A two-column general journal is also required.

2. Enter the four unpaid vouchers as of April 1 in the voucher register and insert the amounts in the Credit Vouchers Payable column only. These amounts are for memorandum purposes, so that upon payment the proper notations may be made in the Paid column. Draw double rules under the last amount because these vouchers were already recorded in March and are not to be included in the April total.

3. Journalize the April transactions. Refer to Requirements 5, 6, and 7 for account titles and identifying numbers.

4. Foot and rule the voucher register and check register.

5. Open the following T accounts in the general ledger: Vouchers Payable 201, Purchases Returns and Allowances 360, Selling Expense Control 600, and General Expense Control 700.

6. Open a selling expense analysis sheet with the following columns: Travel Expense 610, Miscellaneous Selling Expense 612, Salesmen's Salaries 615, and Advertising Expense 618.

7. Open a general expense analysis sheet with the following columns: Rent Expense 703, Office Supplies Expense 708, Executive Salaries 715, Office Salaries 716, Stationery and Printing 719, Postage Expense 720, and Bank Service and Collection Charges 721.

8. Post to the two subsidiary ledgers.

9. Enter the April 1 credit balance of $1,000 in the Vouchers Payable account and complete all postings to the general ledger accounts (Requirement 5).

10. Prove the April 30 balances of the controlling accounts by preparing: (a) a schedule of selling expense, (b) a schedule of general expense, (c) a schedule of unpaid vouchers.

P12-**3.** The following information regarding the payroll of the Winter Corporation for the week ended July 27, 1969, is given:

Employee	Type of Work	Cumulative Gross Wages to July 20, 1969	Gross Wages for Week ended July 27
James P. Morris	Salesman	$5,000	$400
Frederick M. Phillips	Salesman	6,550	350
Jane Dolittle	Office Clerk	2,460	100
Thomas O. Waters	Office Clerk	2,950	150

Deductions Other Than F.I.C.A.

	Federal Income Taxes Withheld	State Income Taxes Withheld	Group Life Insurance Premiums Withheld
James P. Morris	$50	$10	$10
Frederick M. Phillips	30	6	5
Jane Dolittle	12	2	5
Thomas O. Waters	20	5	8

Required: 1. Prepare a journal entry on July 27, 1969, to record and classify the payroll expense.
2. Prepare a journal entry on July 27, 1969, to record the employer's payroll taxes, using rates of 5 percent, 2.7 percent, and 0.4 percent.
3. Prepare a journal entry on July 29, 1969, to record the payment of the payroll.

P12-**4.** The Anderson Company had five employees (all married) during the week ended September 25, 1969. The payroll records show the following:

No.	Name	Amount Earned	Cumulative Earnings for Year to Date	Exemptions Claimed
1	Anson, J.	$100	$6,625	3
2	Cohen, F.	115	2,200	5
3	Mann, E.	124	3,024	4
4	Stow, C.	105	3,050	1
5	Vicks, R.	118	7,000	2

Anderson Company's tax rates are: F.I.C.A., 5 percent; state unemployment, 2.7 percent; Federal unemployment, 0.4 percent. Use the payroll tax table on page 421.

Required: 1. Prepare a payroll register for the week, similar in form to the one given with Demonstration Problem DP12-3.
2. Record the payroll.
3. Record the employer's payroll tax expense.

P12-**5.** The Mattson Sales Company pays its salesmen monthly. On November 30, the following information was available:

F.I.C.A. Taxes Payable		Income Tax Withholdings Payable	

State Unemployment Taxes Payable		Federal Unemployment Taxes Payable	
	1968 (Oct.–Nov.) 200		1968 (Jan.–Nov.) 360

The December payroll was:

Total earnings		$9,500
Deductions		
F.I.C.A. taxes	$230	
Federal Income taxes	990	1,220
Net amount due		$8,280

Required: Copy the T accounts with the November 30 balances and enter the following:

1. The December payroll.
2. The December employer's payroll tax expense. The taxable portion of the December payroll for state and Federal unemployment taxes is $2,500; the applicable rates are 2.0 percent and 0.4 percent, respectively.
3. Checks and appropriate report forms mailed on January 31, 1969, as follows:
   a. To the Internal Revenue Service: a check for December and depositary receipts for October and November.
   b. To the Internal Revenue Service: a check for the Federal unemployment tax liability for 1968.
   c. To the State Division of Employment Security: a check for the state unemployment tax liability for the fourth quarter of 1968.

P12–**6.** The general ledger of the Marsh Company showed the following on November 30, 1969:

Name of Account	Period Covered	Amount
Accrued Salaries and Wages Payable		None
F.I.C.A. Taxes Payable	November	$ 180.00
State Unemployment Taxes Payable	October–November	98.20
Federal Unemployment Taxes Payable	January-November	201.72
Income Tax Withholdings Payable	November	150.20
Bond Deductions Payable		320.00
United Fund Payable		125.00
Salaries and Wages Expense	January–November	97,800.00
Payroll Tax Expense	January–November	3,010.00

Following is the payroll summary for December. The last pay period ended December 27.

Total earnings		$8,900.00
Deductions		
F.I.C.A. taxes	$182.50	
Federal income taxes	860.00	
U.S. bonds	150.00	
United fund	75.00	
Total deductions		1,267.50
Net amount paid		$7,632.50

Additional information taken from the records follows:

1. December earnings (through the last pay period) of $2,050.75 were subject to a state unemployment tax rate of 2 percent.

2. On December 5 a check was issued to Merchants National Bank for the purchase of four U.S. savings bonds at $37.50 and two at $18.75.

3. On December 29, a check was mailed to the United Fund for contributions withheld from employees' earnings through December 27.

4. Wages accrued on December 31 were $1,010.50; the taxable portion for state and Federal unemployment taxes is $350, with rates of 2.0 percent and 0.4 percent, respectively; the taxable portion for F.I.C.A. tax is $500.

Required: 1. Record the transactions relating to payroll, payroll deductions, and payroll tax expense for December. Checks are mailed on due date to the proper agencies.

2. List the affected ledger accounts and their balances as of December 31, after all entries have been posted.

CASE PROBLEM
Baines Company

The Baines Company, a men's and ladies' clothing store, has been in business for a number of years. You have purchased merchandise there on a number of occasions and have become familiar with the owner, Alfred Baines. He has now (early in January, 1969) engaged you, a local Certified Public Accountant, to examine the Company records and to make appropriate adjustments.

You begin by examining the payroll data, making note of the employees' names and their weekly salaries as follows:

Miss Booth	$ 70
Mr. Bowen	80
Mr. Everette	130
Mr. Jordan	60
Mrs. Malone	50

Each of these employees has worked for the Company throughout the calendar year ended December 31, 1968. Also, each has taken the allowed two weeks paid vacation. Along with her sales duties, Mrs. Malone keeps the accounting records, but she readily admits that her knowledge of accounting is small. However, you do verify that she has kept dependable records of each employee's salary and deductions, which you summarize as follows:

	Gross Salary	F.I.C.A. Deductions	Federal Income Taxes Withheld	State Income Taxes Withheld	Deductions to Repay Loans	Net Amount Paid
Miss Booth	$ 3,640	$ 182	$ 475.80	$ 72.80		$ 2,909.40
Mr. Bowen	4,160	208	317.20	44.72	$150	3,440.08
Mr. Everette	6,760	338	374.40	69.16	250	5,728.44
Mr. Jordan	3,120	156	382.20	55.64		2,526.16
Mrs. Malone	2,600	130	293.80	41.08		2,135.12
Totals	$20,280	$1,014	$1,843.40	$283.40	$400	$16,739.20

You detect an error for the deductions from Mr. Everette's salary: $338.00 (5% of $6,760.00) was withheld as the F.I.C.A. tax although the maximum amount should be $330 (5% of $6,600).

Upon examining copies of the payroll tax returns, you verify that correct amounts of taxes were paid early in the following quarter. You summarize these reports and amounts as follows:

Period	Employees' F.I.C.A. Tax Deductions	Employees' Federal Income Taxes Withheld	Employees' State Income Taxes Withheld	Employer's F.I.C.A. Tax Payments	Employer's Federal Unemployment Taxes	Employer's State Unemployment Taxes	Totals
Jan. 1–Mar. 31	$ 253.50	$ 460.85	$ 70.85	$ 253.50		$136.89	$1,175.59
Apr. 1–Jun. 30	253.50	460.85	70.85	253.50		126.36	1,165.06
Jul. 1–Sep. 30	253.50	460.85	70.85	253.50		70.20	1,108.90
Subtotal	$ 760.50	$1,382.55	$212.55	$ 760.50		$333.45	$3,449.55
Oct. 1–Dec. 31	245.50	460.85	70.85	245.50	$58.40	60.75	1,141.85
Totals	$1,006.00	$1,843.40	$283.40	$1,006.00	$58.40	$394.20	$4,591.40

At this point, you are optimistic since only one error has been discovered. But your optimism wanes when you examine the general ledger and find the following account balances as of December 31:

Loans Receivable from Employees	$ 400.00
Salaries Expense	16,739.20
Payroll Taxes Expense	3,449.55

Postings were not made to the Loans Receivable from Employees account during the past year.

Since salaries are paid each Saturday for the work week ending that day and since December 31 is a Tuesday, you accrue two sixths of the weekly payroll plus the appropriate taxes thereon.

Required: 1. After deciding that an adjusting entry is necessary as of December 31 *to correct* the existing errors, you insert the proper amounts in an entry in the following form:

	Debit	Credit
Salaries Expense	?	
Loans Receivable from Employees		?
Account Payable to Mr. Everette		?
Employees' F.I.C.A. Tax Deductions Payable		?
Employees' Federal Income Tax Deductions Payable		?
Employees' State Income Tax Deductions Payable		?
Employer's F.I.C.A. Tax Payments Payable		?
Employer's F.U.T. Payments Payable		?
Employer's S.U.T. Payments Payable		?
Payroll Taxes Expense		?

2. Prepare an adjusting entry to accrue the proper portion of the weekly payroll and the appropriate taxes thereon as of December 31.

3. What journal entries have been prepared by Mrs. Malone throughout the year when the weekly payroll is paid and when the quarterly payments for taxes are remitted?
4. Prepare sample entries, using amounts taken from the data given, for Mrs. Malone's guidance when she records the transactions during the next year.
5. How often and to whom should the Company make payments of employee's and employer's F.I.C.A. taxes, and employees' Federal income taxes withheld? Does it appear to be fulfilling this requirement? How do you know?
6. How often and to whom should the Company make payments of unemployment taxes? Does it appear to be fulfilling this requirement? How do you know?
7. Present calculations to verify the following:

F.I.C.A. deductions (from the payroll summary)	$1,014.00
Employees' F.I.C.A. tax deductions (from the payroll tax summary)	1,006.00
Employer's F.I.C.A. tax payments (from the payroll tax summary)	1,006.00
Employer's Federal Unemployment tax payments (from the payroll tax summary)	58.40
Employer's State Unemployment tax payments (from the payroll tax summary)	394.20

8. How is each of the other payroll deductions determined?

Chapter Thirteen

Contributed Capital— Single Proprietorships, Partnerships, and Corporations

The owner's, partners', or stockholders' equity of a business results from assets contributed by the proprietor, partners, or stockholders and from earnings reinvested in the business. The characteristics of single proprietorships, partnerships, and corporations and the accounting for single proprietorship, partnership, and corporate capital contributions are presented in this chapter. The entries for the regular operating transactions are the same for all forms of business organization; only the entries for the formation of the business, the withdrawal of funds, and the closing process are different. The accounts used for recording the contributed capital in a single proprietorship, a partnership, and a corporation are shown in Figure 13-1.

SINGLE PROPRIETORSHIPS

The accounting procedures applicable to the capital accounts of single proprietorships were discussed and illustrated in the introductory chapters of this text. A brief review follows.

To illustrate the accounts used for recording the contributed capital in a single proprietorship, assume that on January 1, 1969, James Leary formed the Leary Appliance Company with a cash investment of $20,000. On June 15, he withdrew $6,000 in anticipation of earnings; a summary of the accounts on December 31 showed the net income for the year to be $10,000. The entries to record these events are:

1969				
Jan.	1	Cash	20,000	
		James Leary, Capital		20,000
		To record investment by proprietor to form a retail appliance business to be called the Leary Appliance Company.		

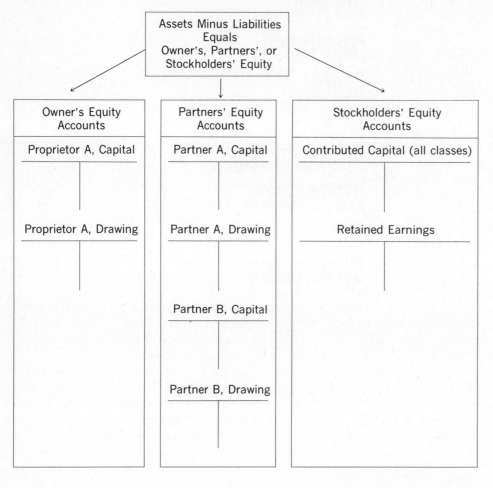

Figure 13-1.
Accounts for Recording Capital

June 15	James Leary, Drawing	6,000	
	Cash		6,000
	To record withdrawal by proprietor in anticipation of earned income.		
Dec. 31	Revenue and Expense Summary	10,000	
	James Leary, Drawing		10,000
	To close net income to the Drawing account.		
31	James Leary, Drawing	4,000	
	James Leary, Capital		4,000
	To close the balance of the Drawing account.		

The James Leary, Drawing account is debited for all withdrawals in anticipation of earned income and is credited at the end of the period with the actual net income. It is then closed by transferring its balance to the Capital account.

The Owner's Equity section of the statement of financial position as of December 31, 1969, would appear as follows:

Owner's Equity
James Leary, Capital $24,000

The statement of owner's equity for 1969 would appear as shown:

LEARY APPLIANCE COMPANY
Statement of Owner's Equity
For Year Ended December 31, 1969

James Leary, Capital (Investment, January 1, 1969)	$20,000
Add Net Income for the Year	10,000
Total	$30,000
Deduct Withdrawals	6,000
James Leary, Capital, December 31, 1969	$24,000

PARTNERSHIPS

A partnership, according to The Uniform Partnership Act, is "an association of two or more persons to carry on, as co-owners, a business for profit." It is a contractual association whereby the partners pool their financial resources, services, skill, and knowledge and as a result hope to accomplish together what any one of them could not achieve individually. This association of two or more persons should be effected by a written contract called the *articles of copartnership*. The law, however, does not require any written agreement and, in the absence of any evidence to the contrary, considers the partners to share equally in profits or losses. Any other method of distributing profits or losses must be clearly agreed upon by all the partners.

The partnership form of business organization is the least common of the three principal forms. It is most often found in the professional fields, primarily medicine, accounting, and law, where there exists a personal responsibility. State laws generally do not permit incorporation in these professions because of this intimate personal responsibility.

Types of Partnerships

Most trading partnerships are *general partnerships*. In this type of association, the members are called *general partners*. They take an active part in the business, and each one is subject to unlimited liability. If the partnership is unable to meet its obligations, the creditors may look to the personal assets of any of the partners for the full payment of the partnership debts.

The Limited Partnership Act allows some partners, but not all, a limited personal liability equal to the amounts that they have agreed to contribute to the business. Once they have made the agreed contributions, neither the partnership nor the creditors can expect to receive any further financial aid from them. *Limited partners* cannot have their names appear as a part of the firm name, cannot act as agents for the firm, and cannot withdraw any part of their agreed investment. Not all states permit this form of partnership organization. *Silent partners* do not participate in the firm management and are not known to be members. They do have a financial interest in the partnership. *Secret partners* do participate in the management of the firm and have a financial interest but their association with the firm is not revealed to persons outside the partnership. *Nominal partners* differ from general partners in that they have made no financial contributions. They take an active part in management and do not conceal their association with the firm. As a result of open participation in the affairs of the firm they incur the same liability status as general partners. *Special partnerships* are formed to accomplish a single objective. The partnership is liquidated upon completion of the objective.

Advantages of Partnerships

The advantages of the partnership form of business are:

1. The money, skill, and knowledge of two or more persons can be combined.
2. Partnerships can be formed easily and quickly.
3. Government regulations do not limit the sphere of activity of a partnership. Partnerships may change from one type of business to another at will or may expand without limitation, whereas a corporation is limited to the sphere of activity stated in its charter.
4. A partnership can act promptly as a business enterprise in all matters (withdrawal of funds, for example). A corporation may be restricted in its actions on certain matters by its charter or bylaws.
5. Many of the formal governmental reports required of the corporation are not required of the partnership.
6. Federal income taxes are not levied against partnerships, although they are required to file information returns. The partners, however, report their distributive shares of partnership income, as shown on the partnership information return, on their individual tax returns. The partnership itself is not a taxable entity.

Disadvantages of Partnerships

The disadvantages of the partnership form are:

1. The liability of general partners is unlimited. Each member is jointly and individually liable for all the debts of the partnership.
2. The life of the partnership is limited. Death, withdrawal, or admission of a partner; agreement to terminate; bankruptcy; and incapacity are major causes for the termination of a partnership relationship. By amending the existing partnership agreement, a new partnership can be brought into existence without cessation of the actual business carried on by the enterprise.
3. The general partnership is a mutual agency; that is, each partner may act in business matters as the agent of the partnership, and the remaining partners

will be bound by his actions. If a partner purchases, in the name of the firm, merchandise used in the course of business, the other partners are also liable, although they may not have consented to or even been aware of the purchase.

4. The partners may find it difficult to cooperate, thus leading to dissolution of the partnership.
5. Partial or entire partnership interests may be difficult to transfer to another individual.
6. The ability of a partnership to raise funds is limited.

Nature of Partnership Accounting

The partnership type of business organization presents no new problems in accounting for assets, liabilities, expense, and revenue. The primary difference between a single proprietorship and a partnership is that the accounts of the partnership must show the equities of the individual members of the partnership.

Each partner's share of ownership is recorded in an equity account, and its balance is in turn reported on the statement of financial position. Upon formation of a partnership, the contribution of each partner is also recorded in an equity account. To illustrate, assume that Robert Walsh and John Snow form a partnership, each investing $8,000 in cash. The opening entry is shown:

Cash	16,000	
Robert Walsh, Capital		8,000
John Snow, Capital		8,000
To record the investments of the partners		
in the Walsh and Snow Company.		

It is not necessary that each partner invest the same amount of cash. If it is assumed that Walsh contributed $5,000 and Snow $10,000, the following entry is required:

Cash	15,000	
Robert Walsh, Capital		5,000
John Snow, Capital		10,000

Neither is it necessary that the original contributions be limited to cash. Assume that Walsh contributed land worth $3,000, a building worth $20,000, and merchandise costing $6,200, and that the partnership assumed a mortgage payable of $10,000 and $200 in interest accrued on the mortgage. Snow invested $15,000 in cash. The opening entry is shown:

Cash	15,000	
Merchandise Inventory (or Purchases)	6,200	
Land	3,000	
Building	20,000	
Mortgage Payable		10,000
Accrued Mortgage Interest Payable		200
Robert Walsh, Capital		19,000
John Snow, Capital		15,000

THE FUNCTION OF PARTNERSHIP EQUITY ACCOUNTS. It is possible to record all equity changes in the partnership Capital accounts. Since several individuals are involved, it is generally desirable to detail the reasons for equity changes in *capital subdivision* accounts, referred to as *personal, current,* or *drawing* accounts. The functions of partnership equity accounts are explained in the following paragraphs.

The following T account shows the recording of transactions in the Capital accounts:

Name of Partner, Capital
(separate account for each partner)

1. Permanent withdrawals of capital are recorded as debits.	1. The original investment is recorded as a credit.
2. A Drawing account debit balance is closed into this account at end of the period.	2. Additional permanent investments are also credited to this account.
	3. A Drawing account credit balance is closed into this account at end of the period.

After the closing entries have been posted, the Capital account normally has a credit balance showing the partner's equity in the net assets of the firm. A debit balance indicates the minimum additional investment that must be made by the partner to provide for the cumulative excess of his withdrawals and losses over his investments and profits.

The following types of transactions are recorded in the Drawing account:

Name of Partner, Drawing
(separate account for each partner)

1. Withdrawals made during the period are debited to this account.	Each partner's share of net income for the period is recorded as credits.
2. Each partner's share of any net loss for the period is recorded as a debit to his Drawing account.	

The balance of the Drawing account is transferred periodically to the partner's Capital account. A partner's Drawing account is similar to the Drawing account of a single proprietor. Debit item 1 includes periodic withdrawals made in anticipation of earned income and not as partial capital distribution.

SHARING OF PROFITS AND LOSSES. The allocation of profits and losses to the partners is based on mutual agreement. If no articles or other evidence of agreement exist, the law assumes that profits and losses are to be divided equally even when the factors of investment, ability, or time are unequal. Since allocation is based on mutual agreement, there are many ways to distribute profits and losses. The more common are:

1. Earnings are divided in an agreed ratio.
2. Interest is allowed on the capital investments and the balance is distributed in an agreed ratio.
3. Salaries are allowed to the partners and the balance is distributed in an agreed ratio.
4. Salaries are allowed to the partners, interest is allowed on capital investments, and the balance is distributed in an agreed ratio.

To illustrate these methods of sharing profits and losses, assume the following figures:

Robert Walsh, Capital		John Snow, Capital	
	1969		1969
	Jan. 1 19,000		Jan. 1 15,000
	July 1 6,000		July 1 5,000

Revenue and Expense Summary	
	1969
	Dec. 31 12,000

1. **Agreed Ratio.** The partners may agree to divide the net income in any ratio. If, for example, Walsh contributed twice as much time to the business as Snow, and if earnings are distributed accordingly, the entry to distribute the net income is:

Revenue and Expense Summary	12,000	
Robert Walsh, Drawing		8,000
John Snow, Drawing		4,000
To distribute the net income		
for the year in 2 to 1 ratio.		

2. **Interest and Agreed Ratio.** The partners may agree to allow for differences in capital investments as well as for differences in services rendered by allowing interest on capital balances and distributing the remainder in an agreed ratio. Interest, as it is used here, is not an expense but rather a mechanism for dividing a portion of the earnings in the ratio of contributed capitals, with the remainder divided in some other ratio. If 6 per cent interest is allowed on opening capital balances, the division is as follows:

	Walsh	Snow	Total
Interest on opening capital			
6% of $19,000	$1,140		
6% of $15,000		$ 900	
Total interest			$2,040
Remainder: 2/3 and 1/3	6,640	3,320	9,960
Totals	$7,780	$4,220	$12,000

The entry to record this distribution of net income is:

Revenue and Expense Summary	12,000	
Robert Walsh, Drawing		7,780
John Snow, Drawing		4,220
To distribute the net income		
for the year divided 2:1		
after allowing for 6% in-		
terest on opening capital		
balances.		

3. **Salaries and Agreed Ratio.** A part of the net earnings may be divided in the form of salaries to recognize differences in the quality or quantity of the services rendered with the remainder divided in an agreed ratio. The salaries are not an expense but a mechanism for dividing a part of the net income. Assuming salaries of $4,000 to Walsh and $2,000 to Snow with the remainder divided equally, the distribution is:

	Walsh	Snow	Total
Salaries	$4,000	$2,000	$ 6,000
Remainder divided equally	3,000	3,000	6,000
Totals	$7,000	$5,000	$12,000

The entry to record this distribution of net income for the year is:

Revenue and Expense Summary	12,000	
Robert Walsh, Drawing		7,000
John Snow, Drawing		5,000
To distribute the net income		
for the year equally after		
allowing for salaries of		
$4,000 to Walsh and		
$2,000 to Snow.		

4. **Salaries, Interest, and Agreed Ratio.** A part of the net income may be divided to recognize differences in capital balances, another part to recognize differences in the value of services rendered, and the remainder in an agreed ratio. Such a computation follows:

	Walsh	Snow	Total
Salaries	$4,000	$2,000	$ 6,000
Interest on opening capital			
6% on $19,000	1,140		
6% on $15,000		900	
Total			2,040
Remainder divided equally	1,980	1,980	3,960
Totals	$7,120	$4,880	$12,000

The entry to record the distribution is:

Revenue and Expense Summary	12,000	
Robert Walsh, Drawing		7,120
John Snow, Drawing		4,880

To distribute the net income
for the year equally after
allowing for salaries and
interest on capital balances.

In the absence of an agreement to the contrary, the salary and interest distributions must be made even though the net income is less than the total of such distributions. The excess is divided in the same ratio used for dividing an excess of net income over total salaries and interest. To illustrate, assume the same facts as in the previous example except that the net income for the year is $7,000. The computation is:

		Walsh	Snow	Total
Salaries		$4,000	$2,000	$6,000
Interest on opening capital				
6% on $19,000		1,140		
6% on 15,000			900	2,040
Totals		$5,140	$2,900	$8,040
Deduct excess of salary and interest				
allowances over net income				
Net income	$7,000			
Deduct allowances	8,040			
Excess divided equally		520	520	1,040
Distribution of net income		$4,620	$2,380	$7,000

The entry to record the distribution is:

Revenue and Expense Summary	7,000	
Robert Walsh, Drawing		4,620
John Snow, Drawing		2,380

To distribute the net income for the year.

PARTNERSHIP FINANCIAL STATEMENTS. The changes in partners' equity accounts during the year are shown in a statement of partners' equities. Its form is similar to the statement of owner's equity for a single proprietorship and the statement of retained earnings for a corporation. It is a supporting statement for the total partners' equities reported in the statement of financial position. Assume that Walsh and Snow each withdrew $3,000 during the year. The statement of partners' equities for the Walsh and Snow Company is shown:

WALSH AND SNOW COMPANY
Statement of Partners' Equities
For Year Ended December 31, 1969

	Walsh	Snow	Total
Balances, January 1, 1969	$19,000	$15,000	$34,000
Add additional investments	6,000	5,000	11,000
Net income	4,620	2,380	7,000
Totals	$29,620	$22,380	$52,000
Deduct withdrawals	3,000	3,000	6,000
Balances, December 31, 1969	$26,620	$19,380	$46,000

The entries to close the partners' Drawing accounts are as follows:

Robert Walsh, Drawing	1,620	
Robert Walsh, Capital		1,620
To close the partner's drawing account (net income credit, $4,620, minus withdrawals debit, $3,000).		

John Snow, Capital	620	
John Snow, Drawing		620
To close partner's drawing account (withdrawal debit, $3,000, minus net income credit, $2,380).		

The financial statements of a partnership are similar to those of a single proprietorship. The allocations of net income to the partners may be shown below the Net Income line of the income statement or, if they are too numerous, in a supplementary statement. The statement of financial position shows the individual Capital account balances as of the end of the period and their total; or, if they are too numerous, the individual balances are shown in the supplementary statement of partners' equities.

THE CHARACTERISTICS OF A CORPORATION

John Marshall, Chief Justice of the United States, gave this classic definition of a corporation in a famous 1819 decision: "A corporation is an artificial being, invisible, intangible, and existing only in contemplation of law." The corporation is, from both the legal and the accounting point of view, a special and separate being, or separate *legal entity,* created by law. That is the characteristic that makes it almost ideally suited to doing business. The weaknesses inherent in single proprietorships and partnerships do not generally exist with the corporate form. The death or retirement of a single proprietor or of a partner may terminate the business, whereas the corporate form continues indefinitely irrespective of changes in stockholders.

A stockholder may sell his stock whenever he chooses without the prior consent of other stockholders, with the corporation simply recording the change in ownership; whereas a partner wishing to sell his interest must first get the consent of all the other partners. The purchase and sale of stock is a relatively simple matter because of the existence of stock exchanges (the New York Stock Exchange, for example). The sale and transfer of a block of stock from one holder to another is a private matter between the buyer and the seller. The transfer does not affect the issuing corporation.

Single proprietors and partners are fully liable to the firm's creditors. Their personal fortunes—in addition to their investments in the business—may have to be used. A stockholder, on the contrary, having paid for his stock in full, is not further liable either to the corporation or to satisfy the creditors' claims. For example, the possible losses of an investor who pays $500 to a corporation for ten shares of $50 par value stock is limited to $500. This is a distinct advantage to the investor in a corporation. It may also be a disadvantage, especially to the smaller corporation seeking credit. Since satisfaction of creditor claims is limited to the assets of the corporation, the extent of credit tends to be limited to the level of corporate assets.

Because the corporation is treated as a legal person, separate and distinct from the stockholders who own it, it enjoys the same legal rights and privileges as do single proprietorships and partnerships, and may therefore engage in almost any type of business activity, provided it is authorized by the charter. The corporate form of business organization is of great advantage for a large business because it may sell its stock to anyone willing to invest his money and is therefore able to raise large sums of capital. Although most large-scale businesses are incorporated and do a much larger volume of business than all other forms of business organization, there are many small businesses that are also incorporated—frequently with only a few stockholders—because of the advantages that the corporate form offers.

The corporate form also has its disadvantages. Because it is an artificial legal being created by the state, it must file reports with the state in which it was organized; it may engage in only that type of business for which it was chartered; it cannot distribute profits arbitrarily as do partnerships but must treat all shares of stock of the same class alike; and it is subject to special taxes and fees. Corporate laws vary from state to state and are often complex and undefined. The rights and obligations of corporations, directors, and stockholders are therefore often difficult to determine. The corporation is taxed as a business entity, and its prorata distributions of earnings to stockholders in the form of dividends are taxed as personal income. The earnings of single proprietorships and partnerships, on the other hand, are taxed only once, as the personal income of the owners.

Ownership of Corporations

Ownership in a corporation is represented by shares of stock, which may be owned by individuals or by other corporations or estates and trusts. Each share of stock represents a fractional part of the ownership. Ownership of a corporation may be vested in a single individual who owns all the stock, in a family whose members own all the stock (this was the case, until recently, of the Ford Motor Company), or by hundreds of thousands of stockholders. The holders of stock in a corporation are entitled to certain rights, including the right to participate in the distribution of earnings and the right to vote at elections of members of the board of directors, thereby participating, albeit indirectly, in the management of the corporation.

Organizing a Corporation

A corporation may be organized for a number of reasons. The purpose may be to start a new business or to buy a previously existing single proprietorship or partnership. It should be emphasized that the work of organizing a corporation must be done by competent attorneys since it involves legal matters.

To form a corporation it is first necessary for at least three incorporators to file a form known as the Articles of Incorporation with the Secretary of State or Corporation Commissioner (or other designated official), setting forth the name and address of the proposed corporation, the nature of the business it is to operate, a description of the stock and the amount to be authorized, and any other information required by the state in which incorporation takes place. Upon approval of the application, a charter is issued by the state.

The incorporators then hold the initial stockholders' meeting. Capital stock certificates are issued, the stockholders elect a board of directors, and a set of rules and regulations (known as *bylaws*) governing the internal activities of the corporation is approved. The directors in turn elect the officers of the corporation, who execute the policies approved by the board of directors for the operation of the business.

State laws pertaining to incorporation vary widely among the several states. Approximately one-third of the corporations whose stock is listed on the New York Stock Exchange are incorporated in the State of Delaware since its laws are more liberal than most other states with respect to the taxation of corporations, the classes of shares a corporation may issue, the valuation of property or services exchanged for stock, the establishment of stated values, and the bases for dividend declarations.

ORGANIZATION COSTS. The formation of a corporation makes certain expenditures necessary, including legal fees, fees and commissions paid to promoters, and statutory fees and taxes. Since these expenditures are made to bring the corporation into existence, they may be regarded as of benefit during the entire life of the corporation and may therefore be charged to Organization Costs, which is classified as an intangible asset in the position statement. Since the life of a corporation is indefinite, there is theoretical justification for retaining the account on the books indefinitely. In practice, however, organization costs are often amortized over the early years of the corporation, the charge being to a nonoperating expense account, Amortization of Organization Costs. Under the 1954 Internal Revenue Code, organization costs may be written off over a period of not less than five years. The entry to record the periodic amortization of organization costs is:

Amortization of Organization Costs	xxx	
Organization Costs		xxx

THE STOCKHOLDERS. The stockholders occupy the top position in the corporate organization chart. The stockholders may attend annual and special meetings and participate in the management of the company by voting on matters presented for their consideration. If a stockholder is unable to attend the meeting, he may designate someone else—often the Secretary of the corporation—to cast his vote by *proxy*. A stockholder is entitled to one vote for each share of voting stock he holds. The meeting of stockholders need not be a routine affair, particularly if conflicting groups are attempting to gain control. On such occasions, each group seeks to obtain the largest number of proxy votes to assist it in acquiring control.

THE BOARD OF DIRECTORS AND OFFICERS. The stockholders elect the board of directors, who are then primarily responsible for the affairs of the corporation. All decisions reached by the board as a unit are recorded in a *minute book;* the recorded decisions are referred to as *minutes of meetings of the board of directors*. The accountant makes frequent reference to these minutes as the underlying authority for transactions affecting the accounts, particularly the capital stock accounts.

The board of directors selects the officers—president, vice presidents, treasurer, auditor, and so on—who carry on the daily activities of the corporation. But the responsibility of the board of directors does not end with the selection of officers. Directors are in effect trustees with responsibility to stockholders and creditors alike; they are legally liable for any acts they may perform that are not authorized by the corporate charter or bylaws. Only the board of directors may declare dividends.

Capital Stock

Ownership in a corporation is represented by its stock, which is divided into shares representing fractional ownership. There may be more than one type of stock, each in turn divided into shares. Each share in a class of stock must be treated like every other share in that class with respect to whatever rights and privileges attach to it.

Whenever there is more than one class of stock, one of the classes may enjoy the right, for example, to receive dividends before the other classes of stock. By the same token, certain restrictions, such as not having the right to vote, may be placed on a particular class of stock. If only one class of stock is issued, it is referred to as *common stock;* if two classes of stock are issued, they are usually referred to as common stock and *preferred stock*. There may be subclasses of stock within each major class, also with specific rights, privileges, and restrictive provisions.

The rights and privileges attached to common stock are:

1. The stockholder's right to sell his stock or to dispose of it in any way he sees fit
2. The stockholder's so-called *pre-emptive right* to participate in any additional issues of stock in proportion to his holdings in the class of stock being issued
3. The right to vote
4. The right to participate in dividend distributions

STOCK CERTIFICATE. A *stock certificate* is a printed or engraved serially numbered document issued to the stock purchaser as evidence of his ownership of the stated number of shares of capital stock of the issuing corporation. Transfer of the shares from one person to another is accomplished by filling in the assignment section on the reverse of the stock certificate. The buyer sends the assigned stock certificate to the corporation or to its transfer agent, who records the transfer on the corporation's capital stock records, cancels the old certificate, and issues a new one. Stock certificates are often bound with attached stubs in the same manner as checkbooks. The perforated stock certificate is removed, and the stub is filled in and retained as a permanent record.

STOCKHOLDERS' LEDGER. The *stockholders' ledger* furnishes the detail for the Capital Stock controlling accounts in the general ledger. An account is opened for each stockholder to show the certificates issued or canceled and the number of shares held. This record is used for purposes of establishing the voting and dividend rights of each stockholder. Only those persons whose names appear in the stockholders' ledger are recognized as share owners.

STOCK TRANSFER JOURNAL. The purpose of the *stock transfer journal* is to record transfers or exchanges of stock from one person to another. The date, certificate numbers (old and new), and number of shares exchanged are recorded in it. This work is often done by independent *transfer agents*—banks or trust companies—who handle the recording of the sale and transfer of stock. The stock transfer journal may be used for posting to the subsidiary stockholders' ledger. The function of recording all certificates issued and canceled is often done by a *registrar*—also usually a bank or trust company.

Sources of Capital

Operating transactions of corporations are recorded in the same manner as those of single proprietorships and partnerships. Care must be taken, however, to distinguish between the primary sources of corporate capital. These sources are from (1) investments by stockholders and (2) retained earnings from operations. This distinction is essential because state laws provide that earnings may be distributed to the stockholders but that the investments must not be distributed, both for the protection of corporate creditors and for the continued operation of the business. Hence, separate accounts should be kept for capital contributed by stockholders for:

1. Each class of stock
2. Contributions in excess of par or stated value for each class or source
3. The discount—by class—on stock issued below par value
4. Retained earnings (explained in Chapter 14)

These separate accounts must be clearly set forth in the Stockholders' Equity section of the corporate statement of financial position.

Authorized and Unissued Capital Stock

The charter granted by the state of incorporation authorizes the newly formed corporation to issue a designated number of shares of capital stock. The corporation usually secures authorization to issue more shares than it anticipates issuing at the outset. This allows for additional sales in the future without further authorization by the state. The total number of shares issued, however, cannot exceed the number of shares authorized.

General ledger accounts for authorized but unissued stock need not be opened. Detail with respect to the number of shares authorized is customarily included as a part of the description in the Stockholders' Equity section of the position statement. The position statement presentation may be as shown:

```
Stockholders' Equity
  Contributed Capital
    Common Stock, $100 par value, authorized 1,000 shares,
      issued 500 shares                                          $50,000
```

Classes of Stock

Stock is usually issued in two classes, *common* and *preferred.*

PREFERRED STOCK. One of the reasons for issuing two or more classes of stock is to endow one class with certain features that will make it more salable. The attractive feature of preferred stock is that, when a dividend declaration is made by the board of directors, the preferred stockholders must be paid at the stated rate and amount for the class of stock before payments are made to other stockholders. The same preference applies when a corporation is dissolved: assets remaining for distribution to stockholders are used first to redeem the claims of preferred stockholders; the remainder, if any, is paid to the other stockholders. Preferred stockholders, on the other hand, are often restricted to a specific dividend rate and do not, therefore, benefit from extra earnings. A preferred stockholder is usually denied the right to vote.

COMMON STOCK. If a corporation issues only one class of stock, then all shares are treated alike, and, there being no preferences, that class of stock is called common stock. If there is more than one class, the class that does not have preferences and that shares only in the remainder of earnings or assets distribution is known as common stock. This class of stock does have voting privileges.

Par Value

The term *par value* refers to a specific dollar amount per share, which is printed on the stock certificate, representing the minimum amount that must be paid to the issuing corporation by the purchaser of the stock; otherwise the purchaser may be held liable for the *discount,* or difference, in case of future claims by the corporate creditors. This contingent liability for the discount passes from the original buyer to successive buyers, provided each buyer in the chain is made aware of the fact that the particular stock had been acquired in the first instance at a discount. The par value may be any amount set forth in the corporation's charter and is not necessarily an indication of what the stock is actually worth. Par value is used as the basis for recording the stock on the corporate books; beyond that, it may have little or no significance.

The use of par value stock was, at first, considered to be advantageous to the stockholder and creditor, since it requires payment in full or the assumption of a liability for the discount. The value of stock, however, is determined not by its par value but rather by the value of the corporation's net assets and by its earnings. Furthermore, in some cases, evasive schemes were evolved to bypass the par value rule, and creditors also found it difficult to recover the stock discount from stockholders in a bankrupt company. The evasive schemes usually involved the issuance of *watered stock;* that is, the transfer of property or the rendering of services to the corporation for its capital stock at highly inflated values, thereby overstating the stockholders' equity in the position statement. Sometimes this stock would then be given back to the corporation for sale at whatever price it would bring without any liability for the discount because the stock had already been fully paid for. The Securities and Exchange Commission of the Federal government may and does interfere when obviously inflated values are assigned to assets being turned over in payment for capital stock, so that the flagrant abuses of past periods have been checked. The investor and the creditor, therefore, enjoy a high degree of protection against unprincipled promoters.

No-Par Value

Par value was often misleading. *No-par value* stock began to be used widely in order to overcome some of the abuses and disadvantages of par value stock. The use of no-par value stock made it unnecessary to resort to evasive schemes for bypassing the contingent liability arising from a sale of par value stock at a discount. The attempted evasion of the par value rule through overvaluation of assets or services would no longer be necessary. Differences of opinion can and do exist, however, with regard to the proper value to be placed on an asset in exchange for stock, and resort to the use of no-par value stock has not eliminated this problem.

When no-par value stock is issued, the directors often assign a *stated,* or uniform value to each share. This value becomes the basis for recording the stock on the corporate books, and the accounting is the same as for par value stock. Since, in most cases, the directors may change the stated value—unlike the par value—at will, there is usually no occasion for recording a discount on the sale of no-par value stock.

To illustrate the entries for the sale of stock, assume that the King Corporation issues 1,000 shares of common stock for $110,000.

1. Assuming that the par value of the stock is $100:

Cash	110,000	
Common Stock		100,000
Premium on Common Stock		10,000

2. Assuming that the stock is no-par value with a $75 stated value:

Cash	110,000	
Common Stock		75,000
Contributed Capital—Excess over Stated Value of Common Stock		35,000

3. Assuming that the stock is no-par value and has no stated value:

Cash	110,000	
Common Stock		110,000

There are several other terms denoting the concept of value, which give a more direct indication of the worth of the stock. The term *book value* is used to indicate the value per share based on net assets (assets minus liabilities), or stockholders' equity. The book value of a share of stock is derived by dividing the total stockholders' equity by the number of shares of stock issued and outstanding. If the market value of the assets is either above or below their recorded cost values, then the book value per share computed in the above manner is not a fair indication of its value. The term *market value* is used to indicate the amount that a share will bring the seller if the stock is offered for sale. Such prices can be determined readily for many stocks by reference to the stock market quotations carried in daily newspapers or to a financial magazine or financial service publication.

Legal or Stated Capital

The term *legal capital,* or *stated capital,* is incorporated in the laws of a number of states for the purpose of placing a restriction on the return of capital to the stockholders. The purpose of this restriction is to protect the creditors because it prevents the stockholders from withdrawing their investment—either as dividends or by the reacquisition of capital stock—to the point where there may be insufficient funds left to satisfy creditors' claims. The creditors of a corporation do not have access to the personal resources of the stockholders; their only protection is in the corporate assets. Stated capital is the minimum amount of capital that must be left in the corporation and that cannot be withdrawn by the stockholders. Since there is a legal limit on stockholder withdrawals, creditors are assured that in the event of corporate losses the investors as a group will absorb the losses up to the amount of the stated capital.

There is considerable variation in the several state laws as to the method of determining and applying such provisions; the accountant may require the assistance of an attorney on questions involving legal capital. In some states, for example, legal capital is considered to be the total proceeds from the sale of stock. In other states, the directors of a corporation that has issued no-par value stock may, by resolution, designate a portion of the contributed capital as the stated capital, or the state may designate a minimum amount. On par value stock, the stated capital is the par value of all the shares issued. When, as is often the case, the par value is low in relation to the issue price, the stated capital will be much less than the total contributed by shareholders.

Recording Stock Transactions

Great care needs to be taken to record stock transactions in strict compliance with the corporate laws of the state of incorporation, keeping in mind the interests of the stockholders and creditors. The entries should show clearly the sources of capital invested in the corporation. Enough accounts should be created so that the Stockholders' Equity section shows in adequate detail the sources of the corporate capital.

THE AUTHORIZATION AND ISSUANCE OF STOCK. The initial entry on a corporate set of books may be a simple narrative statement setting forth certain basic data taken from the corporate charter, including the name and date of incorporation, the nature of the business, and the number and classes of shares authorized to be issued. Assume that the following three transactions took place at the Crown Corporation, which is organized as a wholesale hardware supply business with an authorized capital of $200,000 consisting of 2,000 shares at $100 par value.

1. One-half the stock is issued at par value for cash.

Cash	100,000	
Common Stock		100,000

2. A total of 900 shares are issued for $40,000 in cash plus land and buildings having a fair cash value of $10,000 and $40,000, respectively.

Cash	40,000	
Land	10,000	
Buildings	40,000	
Common Stock		90,000

3. A total of 100 shares are issued to the organizers of the corporation in payment for their services:

Organization Costs	10,000	
Common Stock		10,000

The Stockholders' Equity section of the Crown Corporation statement of financial position after the foregoing transactions shows the following:

Stockholders' Equity
  Contributed Capital
    Common Stock, $100 par value; authorized and issued
    2,000 shares $200,000

Issuance of Stock at a Premium. Assume that a corporation is organized with an authorized capital of $100,000 consisting of 1,000 shares of $100 par value stock, which are issued for $108,000. The entry is:

Cash	108,000	
Common Stock		100,000
Premium on Common Stock		8,000

When capital stock is offered for sale, the price it will bring depends not only on the condition and reputation of the corporation, but also on the availability of funds for investment and other external factors. When stock is issued above its par value, the difference is credited to Premium on Common Stock or to Excess over Par Value of Common Stock. The account represents the excess of the issue price per share over the par value per share. Although the premium appears in a separate account it is part of the total capital contributed by investors. By using a separate account for the excess over par value paid in on the stock, the par value may be shown readily in the statement of financial position. Premium on Common Stock should be kept separate from the account showing corporate earnings. If more than one class of stock has been issued at a premium, separate premium accounts should be kept.

The Stockholders' Equity section immediately following the issue of the 1,000 shares for $108,000 appears as shown:

```
Stockholders' Equity
   Contributed Capital
      Common Stock, $100 par value; authorized
         and issued 1,000 shares                    $100,000
      Premium on Common Stock                           8,000
         Total Contributed Capital                               $108,000
```

Issuance of Stock at a Discount. Assume that a corporation is organized with an authorized capital of $100,000 consisting of 1,000 shares of $100 par value stock which are issued for $90,000. The entry is:

```
Cash                                  90,000
Discount on Common Stock              10,000
   Common Stock                                 100,000
```

When the issue is for less than par value, that is, the stock has been issued at a discount, the difference between the par value and the issue price of the stock is charged to Discount on Common Stock. Purchasers of stock at a discount are contingently liable to the corporation's creditors for the amount of the discount. When such stock is transferred, the discount liability is noted on the stock certificate as foreknowledge that the liability passes to the new owner. In most states par value stock may not be issued at a discount. The account appears as a deduction in the stockholders' equity section of the position statement and designates the existence and amount of the contingency as shown below:

```
Stockholders' Equity
   Contributed Capital
      Common Stock, $100 par value; authorized
         and issued 1,000 shares                    $100,000
      Discount on Common Stock                         10,000*
         Total Contributed Capital                               $ 90,000
```
* Deduction.

The use of premium and discount accounts makes it possible to show in the position statement the par value or stated value as well as the amount actually contributed. Premiums and discounts should not be offset. If, for example, a corporation that is authorized to issue 1,000 shares of $100 par value common stock issues 500 shares at $105 a share and later issues 250 shares at $98 a share, separate premium and discount accounts should be set up. The position statement presentation would be as shown:

```
Stockholders' Equity
   Contributed Capital
      Common Stock, $100 par value; authorized 1,000
         shares; issued 750 shares                  $75,000
      Premium on Common Stock                          2,500
      Discount on Common Stock                           500*
         Total Contributed Capital                               $77,000
```
* Deduction.

If only the net excess of $2,000 ($2,500 premium less $500 discount) is reported, the existence of the discount liability is concealed from readers of the statement.

Stock Subscriptions

The descriptions of stock issuance transactions in the previous sections were based on the assumption that full payment for the stock was received and the stock certificates issued at once. This condition normally exists for small or closely held corporations. In the following transactions, *subscriptions,* or pledges to buy the stock, are taken first, and payment is made later in single lump sums or in installments. The purchaser signs a formal, legally enforceable *subscription contract* in which he agrees to buy a certain number of shares of stock and to make certain specified payments. The stock certificates are issued upon completion of the payment.

The Subscriptions Receivable account is similar in nature and function to the Accounts Receivable account. It is a current asset and shows the amount due on stock that has been subscribed but has not been fully paid for. It is debited for the issue price—not necessarily the par or stated value—of the stock and is credited for collections as they are received. Like the Accounts Receivable account, it is a controlling account with supporting detail kept in a subsidiary *subscribers' ledger,* which contains the accounts of the individual subscribers. When more than one class of stock is issued, separate Subscriptions Receivable accounts should be kept for each class.

The Capital Stock Subscribed account is a temporary capital stock account. It shows the amount of stock that has been subscribed, but the stock certificates for the amount in the account have not been issued pending receipt of the balance still due on the stock as shown in the Subscriptions Receivable account. The account is credited for the par or stated value of the subscribed stock and is debited for the par or stated value when the stock is issued, with the permanent Capital Stock account being credited. If no-par value shares without a stated value are issued, the Capital Stock Subscribed account is debited or credited for the full subscription price.

The subscriber to stock normally acquires the full status of a stockholder with all rights and privileges even though he is not in possession of the stock certificate. The stock subscription agreement, however, may restrict such rights until full payment is received.

ISSUANCE BY SUBSCRIPTION AT PAR VALUE. The Reed Corporation is authorized to issue 6,000 shares of $100 par value common stock. On July 1, 5,000 shares are issued at par value for cash and subscriptions are received for 1,000 shares. A 60-percent down payment is received; the remaining 40 percent is payable in two installments of $20,000 each on August 1 and September 1. The journal entries are:

```
1969
July   1   Cash                                      500,000
               Common Stock                                     500,000
                   To record the issuance of
                   5,000 shares for
                   cash at par value.
```

1969				
July	1	Subscriptions Receivable–Common Stock	100,000	
		Common Stock Subscribed		100,000
		To record the receipt of subscriptions for 1,000 shares of $100 par value stock at $100 per share.		
	1	Cash	60,000	
		Subscriptions Receivable–Common Stock		60,000
		To record the receipt of a 60% down payment on subscriptions to stock.		
Aug.	1	Cash	20,000	
		Subscriptions Receivable–Common Stock		20,000
		To record the receipt of the first 20% installment on the stock subscription of July 1.		
Sept.	1	Cash	20,000	
		Subscriptions Receivable–Common Stock		20,000
		To record the receipt of the second and final installment on the stock subscription of July 1.		
	1	Common Stock Subscribed	100,000	
		Common Stock		100,000
		To record the issuance of stock certificates for 1,000 shares of stock.		

Partial statements of financial position as of July 1 and September 1 are shown:

July 1, 1969

Assets

Current Assets
    Subscriptions Receivable–Common Stock $ 40,000

Stockholders' Equity

Contributed Capital
    Common Stock, $100 par value; authorized 6,000 shares;
        issued 5,000 shares $500,000
    Common Stock, subscribed but not issued, 1,000 shares   100,000

September 1, 1969

Stockholders' Equity

Contributed Capital
    Common Stock, $100 par value; authorized and issued
        6,000 shares $600,000

ISSUANCE BY SUBSCRIPTION AT A PREMIUM. Assume the same facts as in the previous example, except that the Reed Corporation issued the stock at a price of $105 per share.

1969

July	1	Cash	525,000	
		Common Stock		500,000
		Premium on Common Stock		25,000
		To record the issuance of 5,000 shares of $100 par value stock for cash at $105 per share.		
	1	Subscriptions Receivable–Common Stock	105,000	
		Common Stock Subscribed		100,000
		Premium on Common Stock		5,000
		To record the receipt of subscriptions for 1,000 shares of $100 par value stock at $105 per share.		
	1	Cash	63,000	
		Subscriptions Receivable–Common Stock		63,000
		To record the receipt of a 60% down payment on the stock subscription of July 1.		
Aug.	1	Cash	21,000	
		Subscriptions Receivable–Common Stock		21,000
		To record the receipt of the first 20% installment on the stock subscription of July 1.		
Sept.	1	Cash	21,000	
		Subscriptions Receivable–Common Stock		21,000
		To record the receipt of the second and final installment on the stock subscription of July 1.		
	1	Common Stock Subscribed	100,000	
		Common Stock		100,000
		To record the issuance of stock certificates for 1,000 shares of stock.		

When stock is issued at a premium, the entire excess over par or stated value is credited to the Premium on Stock account at the time the stock is subscribed (see the entry of July 1). The premium is considered to be fully realized at the time of subscription—not proportionately as installments are collected. The amount of the entry for the issuance of the stock certificates is the par or stated value of the stock; the existence of a premium or discount does not affect the amount recorded.

Partial statements of financial position as of July 1 and September 1 are shown:

July 1, 1969

Assets

Current Assets	
Subscriptions Receivable–Common Stock	$ 42,000

Stockholders' Equity

Contributed Capital	
Common Stock, $100 par value; authorized 6,000 shares, issued 5,000 shares	$500,000
Common Stock, subscribed but not issued, 1,000 shares	100,000
Premium on Common Stock	30,000

September 1, 1969

Stockholders' Equity

Contributed Capital	
Common Stock, $100 par value; authorized and issued 6,000 shares	$600,000
Premium on Common Stock	30,000

ISSUE BY SUBSCRIPTION AT A DISCOUNT. Assume the same facts as in the previous example, except that the Reed Corporation issued the stock at $95 a share.

1969				
July	1	Cash	475,000	
		Discount on Common Stock	25,000	
		Common Stock		500,000
		To record the issuance of 5,000 shares of $100 par value stock for cash at $95 per share.		
	1	Subscriptions Receivable–Common Stock	95,000	
		Discount on Common Stock	5,000	
		Common Stock Subscribed		100,000
		To record the receipt of subscriptions for 1,000 shares of $100 par value stock at $95 per share.		

All the remaining entries are the same as in the previous example, except that the amount of the down payment is $57,000 (60% of $95,000) and the amount of each installment is $19,000 (20% of $95,000). The amount of the entry to record the issuance of the stock remains the same; $100,000. The discount, like the premium, is recorded in full on July 1 when the subscription is received and is not involved when the payments are made. The Stockholders' Equity section of the statement of financial position as of July 1 is shown:

July 1, 1969

Assets

Current Assets
    Subscriptions Receivable–Common Stock $ 38,000

Stockholders' Equity

Contributed Capital
    Common Stock, $100 par value, authorized 6,000 shares,
        issued 5,000 shares $500,000
    Common Stock, subscribed but not issued, 1,000 shares   100,000
    Discount on Common Stock   30,000*

    * Deduction.

If preferred stock is issued in addition to common stock, special accounts would be opened up as required for Subscriptions Receivable–Preferred Stock, Preferred Stock Subscribed, Discount on Preferred Stock, and Premiun on Preferred Stock.

SUMMARY

The capital contributions of single proprietors and partners are credited to their Capital accounts; profits, losses, and withdrawals are entered in Drawing accounts; the balances in the Drawing accounts are closed to the Capital accounts at the end of the period. The Owner's Equity section of the statement of financial position shows only the owners' Capital accounts. These figures are supported by a statement of owner's equity for a single proprietorship or by a statement of partners' equity for a partnership, showing the changes in the equity accounts during the period because of additional investments, withdrawals, and earnings or losses.

Partnerships can be formed easily and quickly and permit combining the money, skill, and knowledge of two or more persons. Each partner may act as agent for the partnership and is jointly and individually liable for its debts. The partnership should be effected by a written agreement called the articles of copartnership. Partners share equally in profits and losses unless the partnership agreement provides otherwise.

There are many ways to distribute profits and losses; provision for salaries and interest on capital are common. Such provisions are not to be considered as deductions from revenue but rather as mechanisms for dividing a part of the net income. The remainder can be distributed in any manner agreed upon.

The corporation is, from both the legal and accounting points of view, a legal entity. The corporation continues indefinitely, irrespective of changes in stockholders; a stockholder may sell all or a part of his holdings without the prior consent of the other stockholders; and the stockholder, having paid for his stock in full, is not further liable either to the corporation or to its creditors.

A corporation is formed when at least three incorporators file articles of incorporation with the appropriate state office, receive the charter, hold a stockholders' meeting, issue stock, elect a board of directors, prepare bylaws, and elect corporate officers. Legal fees and other expenditures necessary to organize the corporation are charged to Organization Costs, which is classified as an intangible asset in the statement of financial position.

The stockholder's rights and privileges include selling his stock, participating in additional issues, voting, and participating in dividend distributions.

Separate capital accounts should be kept for (1) each class of stock, (2) contributions in excess of par or stated value for each class or source, (3) the discount—by class—on stock issued below par value, and (4) retained earnings.

More than one class of stock may be issued, endowing one class with certain preferences over another. The term par value refers to a specific dollar amount per share, printed on the stock certificate, representing the minimum that must be paid by the purchaser. When no-par value stock is issued, the directors often assign a stated value to each share.

When stock is issued for cash or other assets, the Capital Stock account is credited. If the issuing price is above par value, the excess is credited to a Premium on Capital Stock account; if the issuing price is less than par value, the deficiency is charged to a Discount on Capital Stock account. When payment is not received in full at once, issuance of the stock certificates is deferred until completion of the payments. The amount due is debited to a Subscriptions Receivable account, a current asset; the par or stated value is credited to a Capital Stock Subscribed account, a temporary capital stock account that is closed to Capital Stock when the certificates are issued.

☐ **QUESTIONS**

Q13-**1.** (a) What are some of the distinct features of the partnership form of business organization? (b) What are its advantages? (c) What are its disadvantages?

Q13-**2.** Describe each of the following: (a) general partner, (b) limited partner, (c) secret partner, (d) nominal partner.

Q13-**3.** Compare the partnership form of business organization with the single proprietorship and corporate forms.

Q13-**4.** Why should agreements reached in forming a partnership be in writing? What are some of the matters that should be specifically covered in a partnership agreement?

Q13-**5.** Can a partnership business continue after the death or retirement of one of the partners? Explain.

Q13-**6.** James Brown and Cedric Lee formed a partnership. Brown invested $10,000 in cash; Lee invested land and a building with a cash market value of $25,000. Five years later they agree to terminate the partnership, and Lee demands the return to him of the land and building. Is he justified in his demand?

Q13-**7.** D. Myers and S. Sacks agreed orally to form a partnership as of January 10, 1969. They postponed formalization of their agreement pending the return of their attorney, who was out of town. D. Myers invested $40,000 in cash; S. Sacks invested land and buildings worth $20,000 and $80,000 respectively. On January 11, the building was completely destroyed by an accidental explosion, and they terminated their partnership. Sacks claims that both the land and the $40,000 belong to him. Is he right? Explain.

Q13-**8.** Frank Fish and Homer Little are partners with capital account balances of $40,000 each. They share profits one-third and two-thirds, respectively. (a) Is this an equitable arrangement? (b) Assume that 5-percent interest on capital balances is agreed upon. How will profits of $12,000 be distributed? (c) What account should be charged for the interest on the capital balances?

Q13-**9.** Douglas Evans and Stanley Byrd form a partnership by oral agreement. The matter of profit distribution was not discussed. Evans invests $15,000 and Byrd, $10,000. At the end of the first year, Evans contends that he should be credited with 60 percent of the profits of $10,000. Byrd disagrees. (a) Is Evans right? (b) How could this disagreement have been avoided?

Q13-**10.** What books and records do corporations have that are not necessary for single proprietorships or partnerships? What is meant by the following terms: authorized capital stock, stock certificate, share of stock, par value stock, no-par value stock?

Q13-**11.** What is meant by preferred stock? common stock? stockholders' equity? retained earnings?

Q13-**12.** What is the purpose and function of the following corporate records: subscription ledger, stockholders' ledger, stock transfer journal, minute book?

Q13-**13.** Distinguish between authorized and unissued stock and issued and outstanding stock.

Q13-**14.** Student A says that if he were buying stock, he would purchase only stock having a par value. Student B takes the opposite viewpoint. Discuss.

Q13-**15.** What is legal capital? How is it determined? How does it differ from contributed capital? retained earnings? stockholders' equity? Why should the state of incorporation regulate the amount that may be distributed to stockholders in the form of dividends?

Q13-**16.** Student A says that Subscriptions Receivable is a current asset; Student B argues that the account belongs in the Stockholders' Equity section. Discuss.

Q13-**17.** Define and give the significance of each of the following terms: (a) par value of stock; (b) pre-emptive right; (c) market value of stock; (d) preferred stock; (e) corporation.

☐ **EXERCISES**

E13-**1.** Carl Fox, owner of the Clarion Diner, asks you to determine his equity in the business at December 31, 1969. You determine his net income for the year from the diner to be $11,000. In addition, the following transactions occurred during the year:

Original investment	$15,000
Additional investment	2,000
Personal withdrawals	8,000

(a) Post the transactions to appropriate T accounts, and (b) prepare a statement of owner's equity.

E13-**2.** Frank King and Ralph Thompson formed a partnership on June 8, 1969. King contributed $5,000 in cash, land worth $3,000, a building appraised at $20,000 (the land and the building are encumbered by a mortgage of $4,000, which is assumed by the partnership), and a truck valued at $1,000. Ralph Thompson contributed $5,000 in cash.

(a) Make the entries to record the formation of the partnership. (b) Why may Frank King be willing to enter into a partnership in which he contributes five times as much as his partner?

E13-**3.** Enter the following transactions in appropriate T accounts:

a. Thomas Finos and James Lacey form a partnership with cash investments of $14,000 and $11,000, respectively.

b. Finos and Lacey withdrew $3,000 and $5,000, respectively, in anticipation of earnings.

c. Finos made an additional cash investment of $2,000, and Lacey turned over to the partnership the title to a parcel of land with a fair market value of $6,000.

d. The net income for the period was $13,000 (profits and losses are shared equally).

E13-**4.** In their partnership agreement, Richard Barker and Ernest Jones agreed to divide profits and losses as follows: (a) 5-percent interest on average capital balances, (b) salaries of $6,000 each, and (c) the remainder shared equally. Prepare a schedule showing the distribution of net income of $19,500, assuming average capital balances of $10,000 and $20,000 for Barker and Jones, respectively.

E13-**5.** The following information relates to the partnership of Boris and Milton:

Average capital balances for 1969	
Boris	$60,000
Milton	70,000
Net income for 1969	6,500

The partnership agreement states that profits shall be divided as follows:

Salary allowances:	
Boris	$8,000
Milton	6,000
Interest allowance: 6% on average capital balances	
Remainder:	
Boris ¾	
Milton ¼	

Prepare the closing journal entries (make three separate entries) to distribute the net income in accordance with the partnership agreement.

E13-**6.** The Cameo Corporation, organized on September 30, 1969, was authorized to issue 12,000 shares of $15 par value common stock.

1969

Oct. 1 Issued 120 shares to an attorney for services, valued at $1,800, in organizing the corporation.

15 Received subscriptions for 4,000 shares at $20 a share with a down payment of 50 percent, the balance due on December 15.

25 Issued for cash 2,000 shares at $21 a share.

Nov. 10 Issued for cash 1,000 shares at $19.50 a share.

Dec. 15 Received amounts due from subscribers and issued the stock certificates.

Record the transactions.

E13-**7.** The Lynn Corporation is authorized to issue 10,000 shares of $100 par value common stock. The following transactions occurred:

1. Issued for cash 2,000 shares at par value.
2. Issued 100 shares to the promoters for services valued at $10,000.
3. Issued 50 shares to attorneys for services, valued at $5,000, in organizing the corporation and securing the corporate charter.
4. Issued 900 shares in exchange for a factory building and land valued at $80,000 and $10,000, respectively.
5. Issued for cash 1,000 shares at $95 per share.
6. Issued for cash 2,000 shares at $105 per share.

Record the transactions.

E13-**8.** The Andrea Corporation was authorized to issue 10,000 shares of common stock. Record the issue of 8,000 shares at 14½, assuming that (a) the shares have a $10 par value; (b) the shares have no-par and no stated value; (c) the shares have a stated value of $7.50.

E13-**9.** The Gilfax Corporation was authorized to issue 10,000 shares of no-par value common stock and 10,000 shares of $10 par value preferred stock. Organizers of the Corporation received 1,500 shares of the no-par value common stock for services valued at $7,500. A total of 2,000 shares of the preferred stock were issued for cash at $9 a share, and 1,500 shares of common stock were issued for cash at $6 a share. A total of 2,000 shares of preferred stock were subscribed at $12 a share. One-half of the subscribers paid in full. (a) Record the transactions in T accounts; (b) prepare a statement of financial position.

E13-**10.** The Stockholders' Equity section of the Troy Corporation's position statement as of December 31, 1969, shows the following:

Common Stock, $100 par value; authorized 1,000 shares; subscribed but not issued 800 shares	$80,000
Discount on Common Stock	3,000
Premium on Common Stock	8,000

The Current Assets section shows:

Subscriptions Receivable	$40,000

How much cash has been collected from the stock subscribers?

E13-**11.** The Hood Corporation was authorized to issue 30,000 shares of no-par value common stock with a $10 stated value and 5,000 shares of 5% preferred stock, $100 par value. At the end of one year of operations, the Hood Corporation's trial balance included the following account balances: Preferred Stock, $300,000; Common Stock, $200,000; Subscriptions Receivable–Common, $48,000; Subscriptions Receivable–Preferred, $125,000; Preferred Stock Subscribed, $150,000; Common Stock Subscribed, $75,000; Premium on Common Stock, $30,000; Discount on Preferred Stock, $20,000.

How much cash has been collected from the stock transactions?

E13-**12.** The W. E. Stone Corporation acquired the plant and equipment of the J. Leibfried Company in exchange for 15,000 shares of its $20 par value common stock. Record the acquisition, assuming that if the assets had been acquired for cash, the purchase price would have been (a) $310,000; (b) $275,000.

☐ **DEMONSTRATION PROBLEMS**

DP13–**1.** (*Recording partnership transactions*) The following selected transactions took place in the partnership of Jergens and Small:

1969

Jan. 1   John Jergens and Samuel Small formed a partnership on this date, making the following investments:
Jergens invested $50,000 in cash. Small contributed his equity in a building and lot. The partners agreed that the building was worth $60,000 and the land, $10,000; there was, however, a mortgage on the land and building with a face value of $18,000; the mortgage carried an interest rate of 6%, and the interest was last paid on October 1, 1968. The partnership assumed all liabilities relative to the investment.

Mar. 1   Jergens withdrew $500 cash in anticipation of income to be earned.

Apr. 1   Small withdrew merchandise from the business. The merchandise cost $450 and had a selling price of $600. The firm uses the periodic inventory system.

Oct. 1   Jergens was allowed to withdraw $10,000 in cash to pay a personal debt. This amount far exceeds any anticipated income to be earned.

Required: Record the transactions.

DP13–**2.** (*Distribution of partnership profits and losses*) Edward Herson and Maurice Slight formed a partnership on January 1, 1969, with investments of $20,000 and $35,000, respectively. On July 1, 1969, Slight invested an additional $10,000. On October 1, 1969, Herson and Slight withdrew $5,000 and $5,500, respectively, in anticipation of earnings.

Required: Make the appropriate journal entries to record the distribution of profits and losses based on each of the following assumptions:

1. Net income is $10,000; profits and losses are shared equally.

2. Net loss is $4,500; the partnership agreement provides that profits are to be distributed 60 percent to Herson and 40 percent to Slight; the method of distributing losses was not specified.

3. Net income is $8,000; to be distributed in the ratio of capital balances as of December 31, 1969.

4. Net income is $15,000; to be distributed as follows: salaries of $8,000 to Herson and $9,000 to Slight; interest of 5 percent on ending capital balances; remainder to be distributed equally.

DP13–**3.** (*Recording capital stock issuance; stockholders' equity*) The Reston Company was organized on July 1, 1969, with authority to issue 25,000 shares of $100 par value preferred stock and 15,000 shares of no-par value, $30 stated value common stock. The following transactions occurred during the year:

1969

July 1   Issued for cash 12,000 shares of preferred stock at $101 a share.

10   Issued for cash 8,000 shares of common stock at $40 a share.

15   Issued for cash 2,000 shares of preferred stock at $99 a share.

20   Received subscriptions for 4,000 shares of common stock at $35 a share with a down payment of 50 percent and the balance due on September 30.

1969

July 31   Received subscriptions for 6,000 shares of preferred stock at $102 a
           share; one half the price was received upon subscription, with the re-
           mainder due on September 30.

Aug. 22   Issued 50 shares of preferred stock to an attorney in payment for serv-
           ices rendered in organizing the corporation.

Sept. 15   Issued 1,000 shares of common stock in exchange for land and a
           building appraised at $10,000 and $30,000, respectively.

     30   Collected the installment due on the subscriptions of July 20 and
           July 31.

     30   Net income from operations, after income taxes for the period July 1
           to September 30, was $35,000 (close the Revenue and Expense Sum-
           mary account).

           Required: 1. Record the transactions in appropriate T accounts.
                      2. Prepare the Stockholders' Equity section of the statement
                          of financial position as of September 30, 1969.

☐ **PROBLEMS**

P13–1. James Berger and Walter Kell form a partnership to operate a food brokerage
        business.

            Required: Record their initial investments, based on each of the following
        assumptions:

        1. Berger and Kell each invest $6,500 in cash.

        2. Berger and Kell invest $3,000 and $2,000 in cash, respectively.

        3. Berger invests $3,000 in cash, merchandise worth $5,000, a building worth
            $20,000, and land worth $6,000. Kell invests $8,000 in cash, office equipment
            worth $5,000, and store equipment worth $7,000.

        4. Berger and Kell transfer the following assets and liabilities to the partnership
            as their initial investments:

	Berger	Kell
Cash	$ 4,500	$ 2,000
Accounts Receivable	8,000	10,000
Merchandise Inventory	16,500	14,200
Delivery Equipment (net)	8,500	–0–
Store Equipment (net)	–0–	10,000
Accounts Payable	12,000	10,000
Notes Payable to Bank	10,000	15,000

P13–2. Walter King, Raymond O'Connel, and John Stewart formed a partnership on May 1,
        1968, with investments of $12,000, $8,000, and $10,000, respectively. Profits and
        losses were to be shared equally. During the next twelve months, King and O'Connel
        made additional investments of $3,000 each; Stewart invested an additional $4,000
        and withdrew $1,500. Net income for the period was $21,000.

            Required: Prepare (a) a statement of partners' equities for the year ended
        April 30, 1969, and (b) entries to close the partners' Drawing accounts.

P13–3. Michael Peters and Raymond Stone formed a partnership on January 1, 1969. Cer-
        tain relevant accounts are given as of December 31, 1969:

Michael Peters, Capital			
1969	1969		
Aug. 1 5,000	Jan. 1	40,000	
	July 1	10,000	

Raymond Stone, Capital		
1969		
Jan. 1	50,000	
Dec. 1	6,000	

Michael Peters, Drawing	
1969	
Dec. 31 3,000	

Raymond Stone, Drawing	
1969	
Dec. 31 4,000	

The net income for 1969 was $5,000. The following provisions appeared in the articles of copartnership:

> Net income shall be divided as follows:
> Salary allowances: Peters $3,000; Stone, $4,000
> Interest allowances: 6% on beginning-of-year capital balances
> Remainder: divided 60% to Peters and 40% to Stone

Required: Prepare the journal entries to distribute the net income to the partners' accounts and to complete the closing process.

P13–**4.** Donald Ames and Sheldon Rich form a partnership.

Required: Journalize their investments, based on each of the following assumptions:

1. Each partner invests $3,000 in cash.

2. Ames invests $4,000 in cash, and Rich invests $6,000 in cash.

3. Ames invests $1,000 in cash, land worth $5,000, a building worth $15,000, and merchandise worth $2,000. Rich invests $20,000 in cash.

4. Ames invests $2,000 in cash, land worth $3,000, and a building worth $10,000. The partnership agrees to assume a mortgage payable of $6,000 on the land and building. Rich invests $2,000 in cash, store equipment worth $4,000, and merchandise worth $1,500.

5. Before the formation of the partnership, Ames and Rich were competitors. They decide to form the partnership for their mutual advantage; the partnership assumes their existing assets and liabilities at book values as follows:

	Ames	Rich
Cash	$ 3,000	$ 3,500
Accounts Receivable	6,500	8,000
Merchandise Inventory	15,200	11,100
Delivery Equipment (net)	3,500	5,200
Store Equipment (net)	6,000	10,000
Totals	$34,200	$37,800
Accounts Payable	$13,400	$12,200
Notes Payable	5,000	6,000
Ames, Capital	15,800	
Rich, Capital		19,600
Totals	$34,200	$37,800

6. Assume the same facts as in Assumption 5, except that the merchandise and equipment are to be recorded at their fair market valuations as follows:

	Ames	Rich
Merchandise Inventory	$14,000	$11,000
Delivery Equipment (net)	4,000	5,000
Store Equipment (net)	5,000	7,000

P13–5. John Dwight, an investor, and Richard England, an inventor, decided to form Rentron, Inc., to manufacture and sell a product developed by England. The corporation is chartered by the state, with 5,000 shares of $100 par value common stock authorized.

1. Dwight invests $150,000 and England invests $100,000 in cash for stock at par value. England is issued an additional $50,000 in stock at par value in payment for his patent on the product to be manufactured.

2. The Corporation issues 100 shares of common stock at par value to each promoter as payment for promotion and incorporation fees.

3. Rentron, Inc., sells stock on a subscription basis to five investors. Each investor subscribes to 100 shares of the common stock at $110 per share, making a down payment of 40 percent of the subscription price. The remainder is to be paid at a later date.

4. Four of the five subscribers pay the remaining installment.

Required: Journalize the transactions.

P13–6. The following selected transactions took place at the newly formed King Corporation:

1969

July 1 Received a charter authorizing the issuance of 10,000 shares of $100 par value preferred stock and 100,000 shares of no-par value common stock with a stated value of $10 per share.

2 Issued 50,000 shares of common stock at $25 per share for cash.

2 Issued 1,000 shares of common stock to an incorporator for a patent that he had perfected.

3 Received subscriptions from four investors for 500 shares each of preferred stock at $105.

5 Received 60 percent down payments on the subscriptions from all four subscribers.

20 Received payment in full from three of the preferred subscribers, and issued the stock.

31 Received payment in full from the fourth preferred subscriber, and issued the stock.

Aug. 10 Received a subscription from Richard Ring for 1,000 shares of the preferred stock at $98 per share.

12 Collected 70 percent of Richard Ring's subscription total. The balance is due on September 1, 1969.

Required: Record the transactions.

P13–7. The Hyde Corporation was organized on January 2, 1969, with authority to issue

5,000 shares of $100 par value common stock. The following transactions occurred during the year:

1969

Jan. 10   Issued for cash 100 shares at $101 per share.

Feb. 15   Issued for cash 100 shares at $99.50 per share.

Mar. 1   Issued 1,000 shares for land and a building with a fair market value of $100,000. One tenth the total valuation was allocable to the land.

June 1   Received subscriptions for 500 shares at $102 per share, payable 40 percent down and the balance in two equal installments due on August 1 and October 1.

     10   Paid $1,500 for legal fees incurred in organizing the corporation.

July 5   Purchased equipment for $50,000 in cash.

Aug. 1   Received the installment due on the subscription of June 1.

Oct. 1   Received the installment due on the subscription of June 1.

Dec. 15   Received subscriptions for 500 shares at $98 per share payable 40 percent down and the balance in two equal installments due on February 15, 1970, and April 15, 1970.

     31   Recorded the following entry, summarizing the results of operations before income taxes for the year:

Cash	27,000	
Accumulated Depreciation–Building		4,500
Accumulated Depreciation–Equipment		2,500
Revenue and Expense Summary		20,000

     31   Recorded the income tax liability of $4,500.

     31   Closed the Revenue and Expense Summary account.

   Required: 1. Record the transactions in appropriate T accounts.
              2. Prepare a statement of financial position as of December 31, 1969.

P13-8. On December 31, 1969, the ledger of the Eon Company included the following accounts:

Notes Receivable	$10,000
Merchandise Inventory	50,000
Marketable Securities–U.S. Government Bonds	5,000
Common Stock ($100 par value)	200,000
Retained Earnings	65,000
Subscriptions Receivable–Common Stock	25,000
Preferred Stock ($10 par value)	100,000
Goodwill	20,000
Common Stock Subscribed	100,000
Organization Costs	15,000
Premium on Preferred Stock	8,000
Building	150,000
Premium on Common Stock	21,000
Notes Receivable Discounted	5,000
Cash	60,000
Research and Development Costs	75,000

Required: Prepare the Stockholders' Equity section of the statement of financial position as of December 31, 1969.

CASE PROBLEM
Tumble Products, Inc.

Until twelve years ago, William Hoyle was employed as production manager for a large manufacturer of metal furniture; at that time he decided to begin his own firm, which he named the Tumble Products Company. The main activity of his company was the fabrication of baby furniture, sold directly to retailers.

After managing all phases of the business for six years, Hoyle decided to admit as partners, Thomas Smith and John Draper, in whom he had a lot of confidence. Hoyle retained a 52-percent equity in the firm. Each of the other partners was allowed a 24-percent equity in exchange for investments of cash. With the admission of the partners, Hoyle was relieved of some of his responsibilities. Smith was designated as the sales manager, and Draper was the production manager. Hoyle's title was general manager.

The partners now wish to expand the production facilities. They wish to add metal lawn furniture, dinette sets, wrought iron furniture, and metal office furniture to their line of products. Preliminary to expanding the facilities, the partners applied for and received a corporate charter. They plan to dissolve the partnership and to transfer all partnership assets and liabilities to the Corporation. The charter authorizes the Corporation, to be known as Tumble Products, Inc., to issue 1,000,000 shares of $1 par value voting common stock and 10,000 shares of $100 par value, 6%, nonvoting preferred stock. Amounts received in excess of the par value of shares issued are to be credited to appropriately titled accounts. According to the laws of the state of incorporation, these amounts do not become a part of the legal capital.

The new Corporation has engaged in the following transactions:

1. Three separate notes payable for $1,200 each were issued to the incorporators for cash they had loaned to the Corporation.
2. Incorporation fees of $75 were paid.
3. Fees of $150 for legal services were paid.
4. Stock certificate printing costs of $400 were paid.
5. The assets and liabilities of the partnership were transferred to the Corporation. The trial balance of the partnership at that time was:

	Debit	Credit
Cash	$ 5,400	
Accounts Receivable	12,000	
Allowance for Doubtful Accounts		$ 360
Inventories	19,000	
Prepaid Expenses	400	
Land	12,000	
Building	60,000	
Accumulated Depreciation		10,000
Equipment	40,000	
Accumulated Depreciation		10,000
Accounts Payable		15,000
Accrued Liabilities		700
William Hoyle, Capital		58,625
Thomas Smith, Capital		27,057
John Draper, Capital		27,058
Totals	$148,800	$148,800

It was agreed that the amounts were to be recorded as shown, except that the depreciable assets were to be recorded at their carrying values and that the Corporation should begin with zero balances in the Accumulated Depreciation accounts. Each partner was to be issued common stock at par value in an amount equivalent to his equity in the partnership.

6. A local investor subscribed to 400 shares of preferred stock at $102 per share.

7. A number of local citizens subscribed to 12,000 shares of common stock at $1.25 per share.

8. The local investor paid for one-half of his subscribed shares, and a certificate was issued.

9. The local citizens remitted $6,500 in cash in payment of their subscriptions, consisting of payment in full for 2,500 shares and partial payment on the remaining 9,500 shares. Certificates were issued for the fully paid shares.

10. The three incorporators agreed to accept at par value common stock certificates for the notes that they hold (see Transaction 1), and the certificates were issued.

The new management, consisting of Hoyle as president-secretary-treasurer, Smith as vice-president in charge of sales, and Draper as vice-president in charge of production, plans to raise more funds by issuing additional stock. However, before proceeding further, they wish to know how they stand.

Required: 1. Record the transactions in general journal form.

2. Prepare a statement of financial position for the Corporation upon completion of the transactions.

3. This entity has changed from a single proprietorship to a partnership and then to a corporation. What are the characteristics—advantages and disadvantages—of each form of organization so far as Tumble Products, Inc., is concerned?

4. Describe the legal relationships between the stockholders, the board of directors, and the company officers of Tumble Products, Inc.

5. What portion of the total stockholders' equity belongs to each of the three officers?

6. What portion of the voting power belongs to each of the three officers?

7. If all the voting common stock were issued, how many additional shares must be obtained collectively by the three officers for them to retain control of the organization?

8. What is the significance of the term legal capital?

9. What is the preferred accounting treatment of the organization costs? Why?

Chapter Fourteen

Dividends, Retained Earnings, and Treasury Stock

The stockholders' equity in a corporation arises from a number of sources. It is of the utmost importance that these sources be clearly distinguished and stated. It is equally important that the terminology used to designate them be precise and meaningful.

The various sources of the stockholders' equity discussed in this chapter and in Chapter 13 are outlined in Figure 14-1.

CONTRIBUTED CAPITAL

As implied in the previous chapter, contributed capital, also referred to as *paid-in capital,* may include items other than the par or stated value of stock. Among these, in addition to premiums on common or preferred stock, may be donations and amounts transferred from the Common Stock account if the board of directors revises the stated value of no-par value stock.

Excess over Par or Stated Value

The premium on stock, or excess over par or stated value, is that part of the capital contributed by stockholders that is not credited to the capital stock accounts. Some accountants refer to it as *capital surplus,* but this term may be confusing, as other accountants use it to designate retained earnings. Separate contributed capital accounts are kept so that the position statement shows the specific sources of capital. Such precise source accounts are also desirable to establish the availability of source of funds for dividends or other distributions to stockholders, in states that permit such distributions.

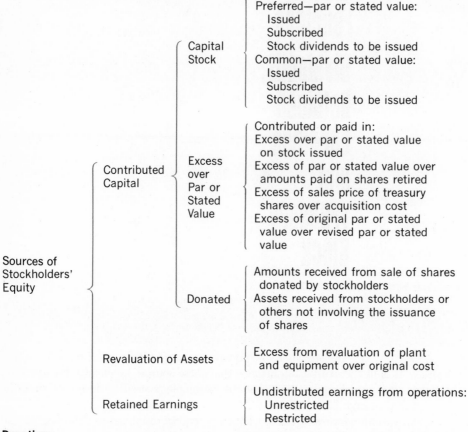

Figure 14-1.
*Sources of
Stockholders' Equity*

Donations

A gift or donation to a corporation increases the assets and the stockholders' equity and is credited to Contributed Capital–Donations. Gifts of land, buildings, or other facilities are sometimes made by a local organization to encourage a corporation to do business in the area. Sometimes donations of assets or stock are made by the stockholders to a company in financial difficulties to enable it to raise funds.

A contribution of land and buildings by a town to a newly established firm is recorded by the receiving corporation at the fair market value of the assets contributed as shown (the fair market values are assumed):

Land	80,000	
Buildings	20,000	
Contributed Capital–Donations		100,000

To assist a corporation in raising needed working capital, its stockholders, instead of investing additional funds, may donate a portion of their fully paid stock to the corporation. Such stock is known as *treasury stock*, explained later in this chapter. Sales of the donated stock for cash are recorded by a debit to Cash and a credit to Contributed Capital–Donations.

Revaluations

The upward revaluation of corporate assets, generally following a continuing increase in price levels, results in an increase in the stockholders' equity. The practice of revaluing assets to reflect current market values is not common. There is a natural reluctance to replace historical (cost) data, which are readily verifiable, with amounts based on individual judgments requiring continuing and complex adjustments. There are, however, circumstances when market or reproduction values are more significant than original cost, particularly when there is a wide disparity between these values. A financial statement prepared, for example, pursuant to a proposed sale of a business, as a basis for establishing insurance coverages, or for certain credit purposes, may be more informative to the user if it is based on replacement—rather than depreciated cost—values. When assets are revalued, the increase should be debited to a special Buildings–Appreciation in Value account and credited to a specifically designated Revaluation Capital account. Increases in the stockholders' equity from asset revaluations are not a result of earnings and, in most states, may not properly be used as a basis for cash dividends.

RETAINED EARNINGS

Nondistributed earnings from regular operating transactions, gains from the sale of plant and equipment assets and investments are classified as *retained earnings*. These are sources of stockholders' equity other than from transactions involving the company's own stock and from revaluations. Such terms as *earned surplus, retained income, accumulated earnings,* and *earnings retained for use in the business* are also used to designate the earnings that have not been distributed to the stockholders as dividends. If losses and dividend distributions exceed earnings, the Retained Earnings account will have a debit balance and will be shown in the position statement under the caption *Deficit*.

The creation of special Restricted Retained Earnings accounts indicates that a portion of the earnings of the corporation is not available for dividend distribution. This does not mean that a special cash fund has been set up, nor does the restriction provide cash funds. The restrictions do not alter in any way the total retained earnings or the stockholders' equity. The segregation of retained earnings is a bookkeeping device by which a corporation, following a resolution of the board of directors, intentionally reduces the amount of earnings available for dividend distributions, thus indicating its intention to conserve corporate assets for other purposes. The restriction of retained earnings does not reduce the overall retained earnings but merely *earmarks*, or sets aside, a portion of the earnings in an account specifically designated to indicate its purpose.

Each restricted account, although separated from the parent Retained Earnings account, is nevertheless a part of retained earnings and is so classified in the Stockholders' Equity section of the position statement. When the special account has served its purpose and the requirement for which it was set up no longer exists, the amount in the restricted account is returned to the Retained Earnings account. Following are some examples of Restricted Retained Earnings accounts:

Retained Earnings—Restricted for Plant Expansion
Retained Earnings—Restricted for Contingencies
Retained Earnings—Restricted for Retirement of Preferred Stock
Retained Earnings—Restricted for Treasury Stock Acquisition
Retained Earnings—Restricted for Bond Redemption

Alternative titles using the term *reserve* (as in Reserve for Plant Expansion, Reserve for Contingencies, and so on) are often found in practice. The term is appropriately used only in account titles designating restrictions of retained earnings.

Restriction for Plant Expansion

A restriction for plant expansion is set up by voluntary action of the board of directors. The purpose of this restriction is to show management's intention to retain cash or other assets for use in connection with a projected plant expansion program rather than to distribute them in the form of dividends. When cash dividends are paid, the assets of the corporation are depleted. To the degree, then, that dividend declarations are restricted, assets are retained for other business purposes such as plant expansion.

Assume, for example, that a company plans to erect an additional building and equip it at an estimated cost of $250,000. Aware of the need to conserve working capital to meet the requirements of the expansion program, the board of directors passes a resolution to restrict $250,000 of retained earnings to indicate that this amount is not available for dividends. The journal entry is:

Retained Earnings	250,000	
Retained Earnings–Restricted for Plant Expansion		250,000

When the purpose for which the restriction was set up is accomplished, the restriction is removed by the following entry:

Retained Earnings–Restricted for Plant Expansion	250,000	
Retained Earnings		250,000

Restriction for Contingencies

A restriction of retained earnings for contingencies may be set up by voluntary resolution of the directors of a corporation for losses that may occur but whose nature or amount cannot be predicted with absolute certainty. Assume, for example, that a company is faced with a damage suit resulting from the accidental death of an employee on its premises. It is estimated that the amount of the damage settlement may exceed the normal insurance coverage by $50,000. The journal entry would be as follows:

Retained Earnings	50,000	
Retained Earnings–Restricted for Contingencies		50,000

The following entry would be made upon determination of the actual judgment liability of $35,000.

Loss from Damage Suit	35,000	
Cash		35,000

Loss from Damage Suit, when classified as an income statement account following the all-inclusive concept (see p. 576), is transferred to Retained Earnings indirectly in the closing process by an entry debiting Revenue and Expense Summary and crediting Loss from Damage Suit. The alternative procedure, following the current operating concept (see p. 575), is to debit Retained Earnings directly—not Loss from Damage Suit—bypassing the income statement entirely.

Retained Earnings	35,000	
Loss from Damage Suit		35,000

The Retained Earnings–Restricted for Contingencies account, having served its purpose, may now be closed out:

Retained Earnings–Restricted for Contingencies	50,000	
Retained Earnings		50,000

The restriction of retained earnings did not, of course, automatically ensure the availability of cash. It did, however, restrict dividends to the extent of $50,000, thereby making it more likely that the required cash would be available when needed. In the last analysis, however, a dividend distribution is made possible only by profitable operations, available cash, and a vote of the board of directors.

Restriction for Retirement of Preferred Stock

A restriction of retained earnings for the retirement of preferred stock is set up for the purpose of restricting earnings in connection with a planned reduction by retirement in the outstanding preferred stock. The journal entries are similar to those already illustrated.

Legal Restrictions—Contractual

Voluntary types of restrictions of retained earnings have been discussed thus far. Involuntary restrictions may be required either by state statute, covered later in this chapter, or by contract. When a corporation enters into an agreement for a long-term loan, the terms of the contract may require periodic restrictions of retained earnings, accumulating over the term of the loan to an amount equal to the loan. The purpose of the restriction is to reduce the amount of earnings that might otherwise be distributed to the stockholders as dividends, thereby improving the corporation's ability to make periodic interest payments and any other payments required under the terms of the loan. The restriction does not ensure the availability of working capital; it does, however, limit the use of working capital for dividend distributions. The journal entry to record this type of restriction is a debit to Retained Earnings and a credit to Retained Earnings–Restricted for Long-Term Loan Retirement.

DIVIDENDS

The term *dividend* refers to the distribution by a corporation of cash, stock, or other corporate property to the stockholders. A dividend must be declared formally by the board of directors, and entered in the minute book; the entry should indicate the date the dividend was declared, the *record date* to determine the eligibility of *stock-*

holders of record on that date, and the date of the payment. For a dividend distribution to be made, there must be accumulated unrestricted earnings and there must be assets available for distribution. If there are no earnings, the dividend becomes a reduction in contributed capital, which is normally illegal. There may be adequate earnings but insufficient cash or other readily distributable type of assets. A corporation may have a good earnings record but no cash available for dividends because the cash may have been used to acquire other assets (land, buildings, machinery, or inventory), or funds are being accumulated for an anticipated expansion program or other corporate needs. Only the board of directors has the authority to determine whether a dividend distribution is to take place, to which classes of stock it is to be paid, and the time, manner, and form of payment. This applies to all classes of stockholders, preferred and common.

The board of directors is the ultimate authority in regard to dividend declaration. There have been court cases in which stockholders have attempted to force a dividend declaration that they felt was being deliberately withheld by the board of directors. Except in rare instances, courts have been reluctant to interpose and order dividend payments. Once formal action has been taken by the board, however, the declaration immediately becomes a current liability of the corporation. The state corporation laws contain dividend provisions that must be observed by the board of directors. It is customary, for example, particularly for larger corporations with numerous stockholders, to make a public announcement of the dividend declaration in newspapers or magazines.

The term *dividend* is most often used to designate a cash distribution out of corporate earnings. A dividend may be paid in property other than cash; a company may, for example, distribute marketable securities or merchandise. A well-known distillery once declared a dividend and made a pro rata distribution of whiskey late in December. The term *stock dividend* is used to designate the distribution of additional shares of stock to existing stockholders. The term *liquidating dividend* refers to a distribution of assets by a company being liquidated, or a distribution whose effect is to reduce the stockholders' equity from contributed or revaluation capital. Thus, a liquidating dividend is a distribution of contributed capital when there are no accumulated retained earnings, or when a deficit exists.

Declaration of a Dividend

The dividend may be stated as a percentage of par value or as a specified amount per share if the stock has no par value. Following are typical dividend notices:

UNIVERSAL TOBACCO COMPANY, INC.

Cash Dividend on Preferred Stock

The regular quarterly dividend of 2 percent on the preferred stock of the Universal Tobacco Company, Inc., has been declared, payable April 1, 1969, to preferred stockholders of record at the close of business on March 13, 1969.

Cash Dividend on Common Stock

The regular quarterly dividend of 50¢ per share on the common stock of the Universal Tobacco Company, Inc., has been declared, payable May 1, 1969, to common stockholders of record at the close of business on April 10, 1969.

Curtis M. Duncan, Jr., Secretary

The holder of 100 shares of common stock of the Universal Tobacco Company, Inc., will receive $50 on May 1. An investor who purchases common stock of this company prior to April 10, the record date, will receive the dividend. An investor who buys stock of this company after April 10 is said to buy the stock *ex-dividend;* that is, without the right to receive the latest declared dividend. Stock traded on the stock exchanges are quoted ex-dividend two or three days prior to the record date to allow time for the recording and delivery of the securities. During the interval between April 10 and May 1, the Company prepares the list of eligible stockholders and performs all other tasks incident to the mailing of the dividend checks.

Recording Cash Dividends

To illustrate the recording of a cash dividend, assume that on August 2, 1969, the board of directors of Magnetics, Inc., declared a quarterly dividend of $3,000 on 2,000 shares of $100 par value 6% preferred stock, and a $2,000 dividend on 10,000 shares of $10 par value common stock. The dividends are payable on September 1, 1969, to stockholders of record at the close of business on August 15, 1969. The entries to record the dividend declaration and the payment are:

```
1969
Aug.   2   Dividends–Common Stock                      2,000
           Dividends–Preferred Stock                   3,000
               Dividends Payable–Common Stock                    2,000
               Dividends Payable–Preferred Stock                 3,000
                   To record the declaration of a dividend on the
                   outstanding preferred and common
                   stock, payable September 1, 1969, to
                   stockholders of record on August 15,
                   1969: 1.5% on $200,000 preferred,
                   and 2% on $100,000 common.

Sept.  1   Dividends Payable–Common Stock              2,000
           Dividends Payable–Preferred Stock           3,000
               Cash                                              5,000
                   To record payment of dividends
                   to stockholders of record on
                   August 15, 1969.
```

The Dividends accounts are closed out at the end of the accounting year to Retained Earnings. The use of a Dividends account has the advantage of segregating dividends declared during the year; it also keeps Retained Earnings clear of charges that would require analysis at the end of the year. The Dividends account is a temporary stockholders' equity account; it has a debit balance and represents a reduction in the stockholders' equity. It is shown on the statement of retained earnings as a deduction from the total of the beginning balance of Retained Earnings plus net income and other credits to Retained Earnings. Dividends Payable, on either common or preferred stock, is a current liability.

Dividends on Preferred Stock

As mentioned in the previous chapter, preferred stock enjoys certain dividend preferences. The right to a dividend of a preferred stockholder must await a formal declaration by the board of directors. Upon declaration, the preferred stockholders are entitled to a stated amount per share before any dividend distribution is made to holders of common stock.

If the preferred stock is *cumulative*, undeclared dividends are accumulated and must be paid together with the current dividend before any dividend payment is made on common stock. If the preferred stock is *noncumulative*, a dividend bypassed in any one year is lost forever. Preferred stock may be either *participating* or *nonparticipating*. If the preferred stock is participating, it receives its specified dividend rate and a share of any additional dividends declared. The manner of determining the amount of the additional dividend depends on the terms of the stock contract. If the preferred stock is fully participating, it participates on a pro rata basis with the common stock in dividend distributions after the common stock has received an amount equal to the stipulated preference rate on the preferred stock. The participation may be limited in the stock contract to a specified rate or amount per share. If the preferred stock is nonparticipating, it receives the stipulated rate only, and the balance of the dividend distribution, irrespective of amount, is paid to the common stockholders. Most preferred stock issues are cumulative and nonparticipating.

The extent to which preferred stockholders participate in distributions above the regular rates depends on the specific provisions of the corporate charter. The following examples illustrate the application of the dividend preference of preferred stock.

1. *Cumulative and Nonparticipating.* A corporation has outstanding 1,000 shares of 5% cumulative preferred stock and 2,000 shares of common stock, each with a par value of $100. Undistributed earnings are $75,000, there are no dividends in arrears, and a $27,000 dividend is declared. Assuming that the preferred stock is nonparticipating, the required journal entry for the dividend declaration is shown:

Dividends–Preferred Stock	5,000	
Dividends–Common Stock	22,000	
Dividends Payable–Preferred Stock		5,000
Dividends Payable–Common Stock		22,000

2. *Cumulative and Fully Participating.* Assume the same facts as in Illustration 1, except that the preferred stock is cumulative and fully participating; that is, the preferred stock shares at an equal rate with the common stock in the amount distributed in excess of the 5-percent preferred dividend and a comparable dividend on the common stock. The required journal entry is shown:

Dividends–Preferred Stock	9,000	
Dividends–Common Stock	18,000	
Dividends Payable–Preferred Stock		9,000
Dividends Payable–Common Stock		18,000

The allocation is computed as follows:

		To Preferred	To Common
Current rate at 5%, or $5 per share:			
To preferred stock:	1,000 shares × $5	$5,000	
To common stock:	2,000 shares × $5		$10,000
Participation at 4%, or $4 per share:			
To preferred stock:	1,000 shares × $4	4,000	
To common stock:	2,000 shares × $4		8,000
Total distribution		$9,000	$18,000

Note that each stockholder receives $9 per share because the preferred stock is fully participating, and the common stock receives a current rate equal to the preference rate on preferred stock.

3. *Cumulative and Partly Participating.* Assume the same facts as in Illustration 2, except that the preferred stock participates to a maximum of 2 percent, or $2 per share, above its preference rate; the allocation of the $27,000 is computed as follows:

		To Preferred	To Common
Current rate		$5,000	$10,000
Participation:			
Preferred stock:	1,000 shares × $2	2,000	
Common stock:	remainder		10,000
Total distribution		$7,000	$20,000

Preferred stock participates at the stated maximum only if the proportionate distribution to the common stock—at a rate on the par value, or in an amount per share on no-par value stock—equals or exceeds the distribution to the preferred stock. In this illustration, the preferred rate per share is $7 and the common rate is $10. The amount actually received on participation may be less than $2 a share, as shown in the following illustration.

4. *Dividend Arrearage.* This illustration is based on the same facts as in Illustration 3, except that there is a dividend *arrearage* (amounts owed from previous periods) on the preferred stock of $9,000. The dividend distribution is computed as follows:

To preferred stock:	
Arrearage	$ 9,000
Current year's preference dividend	5,000
Participation	1,000
Total to preferred	$15,000
To common stock:	
Remainder	12,000
Total distribution	$27,000

The distribution to the preferred stock due to the participation provision is computed as follows:

Total dividend		$27,000
Deduct: Arrearage payment	$ 9,000	
Current year's preference–preferred stock	5,000	
Current year's rate–common stock	10,000	24,000
Available for participation		$ 3,000
Number of shares outstanding		3,000
Rate per share on participation		1
To preferred stock: 1,000 × $1		$ 1,000

Preferred stock may also be preferred in distributing assets; this means that if the corporation is liquidated, the preferred stockholders must be paid before any liquidating payments are made to the common stockholders. The manner of the preference application depends on the wording in the stock contract. The preference may be for the par value of the preferred stock, the par value and accumulated dividends, or some other stipulated amount. If the preferred stock is not preferred as to assets, then the assets are usually distributed to all classes of stockholders on an equal basis proportionate to the respective par values.

Stock Dividends

The term *stock dividend* refers to the issuance by a corporation of additional shares of its authorized stock without additional payment of any kind by the stockholders. There are various occasions for the declaration of a stock dividend, such as:

1. A large unappropriated retained earnings balance
2. A desire by the directors to reduce the market price of the stock
3. A desire to increase the permanent capitalization of the company by converting a portion of the retained earnings into capital stock
4. A need to conserve available cash

A stock dividend does not change the total stockholders' equity in the corporation because an equal amount of retained earnings is transferred to a Capital Stock account. A cash dividend, on the other hand, decreases both the assets and the stockholders' equity. A stock dividend has no effect on either total assets or total stockholders' equity; the change is entirely within the Stockholders' Equity section (Retained Earnings decreases and Capital Stock increases). To illustrate, assume that the Truro Corporation, with $500,000 common stock, $100 par value, outstanding and retained earnings of $80,000 declares a $50,000 stock dividend. The effect of the declaration on the stockholders' equity is shown below:

	Stockholders' Equity		
	Immediately Before Declaration	Immediately After Declaration	Immediately After Stock Issuance
Stockholders' equity:			
Common stock, $100 par value	$500,000	$500,000	$550,000
Stock dividends to be issued		50,000	
Retained earnings	80,000	30,000	30,000
Total stockholders' equity	$580,000	$580,000	$580,000

The Stock Dividends to be Issued account is part of the stockholders' equity. It is not a liability because its reduction will result not in a reduction of a current asset but rather in an increase in capital stock. The account should therefore be shown under Capital Stock in the Stockholders' Equity section of the position statement.

The following journal entries are made to record the declaration and issuance of the stock dividend (assuming that the amount of retained earnings to be transferred to the capital stock accounts as a legal minimum must be at least equal to the par value of the shares and the ratio of the shares issued is less than 20 or 25 percent of the number previously outstanding):

Retained Earnings	50,000	
Stock Dividends to be Issued		50,000
To record the declaration of a 10% stock dividend payable on (date) to stockholders of record on (date).		
Stock Dividends to be Issued	50,000	
Common Stock		50,000
To record the issuance of 500 shares of additional common stock as a stock dividend—voted by the board of directors on (date).		

Accounting Concept: Treatment of Stock Dividends ▶

▶ The effect of a stock dividend is to transfer a portion of the retained earnings to the capital stock accounts, which is tantamount to an increase in the stated capital. The amount to be transferred is within the discretion of the board of directors, except for any minimum amounts that may be specified in the laws of the state of incorporation. The Committee on Accounting Procedure of the AICPA has stated that the corporation should transfer "from earned surplus to the category of permanent capitalization (represented by the capital stock and capital surplus accounts) an amount equal to the fair value of the additional shares issued."[1] ◀ To illustrate, assume that the market value of the shares issued by the Truro Corporation was $60,000 (500 shares at $120 a share) and that the board of directors, in authorizing the stock dividend, directed that the dividend be recorded at market value. The entries to record the declaration and stock issuance are:

Retained Earnings	60,000	
Stock Dividends to be Issued		50,000
Contributed Capital–Excess Over		
Par or Stated Value on Stock Dividends		10,000
Stock Dividends to be Issued	50,000	
Capital Stock		50,000

It is evident that a stock dividend has no effect on the total stockholders' equity; the relative interest of each stockholder is, therefore, unchanged. For example, John Green, a stockholder with 100 shares before the stock dividend, will have 110 shares after the stock dividend. His proportionate holdings remain unchanged

---

[1] *Accounting Research and Terminology Bulletins*, 1961, New York: American Institute of Certified Public Accountants, *Accounting Research Bulletin No. 43*, p. 51.

at 2 percent of the total stock outstanding. Hence, all his rights and privileges are unaltered, as shown:

	Line	Before Declaration	After Declaration
Total stockholders' equity	1	$580,000	$580,000.00
Number of shares outstanding	2	5,000	5,500.00
Stockholders' equity per share (Line 1 ÷ Line 2)	3	$ 116	$ 105.45
Shares owned by John Green	4	100	110.00
Green's equity (Line 4 × Line 3)	5	$ 11,600	$ 11,600.00

A stock dividend, nevertheless, is significant to the stockholder. The dividend does not alter the recipients' equity in the company and is not, therefore, considered income. There is no income tax on a stock dividend. If the stock dividend does not cause a significant decline in the price of stock, the stockholder's gain is equal to the market value of the new shares received. If, in addition, the corporation continues to pay its customary cash dividends per share, the stockholder gains the dividends on the additional shares. It is this aspect—the expectation of greater dividends as well as the availability of more shares for possible ultimate profitable resale—that creates a favorable reception for a stock dividend.

A stock dividend provides certain advantages to the corporation. Its earnings are capitalized (that is, earnings are transferred to capital stock accounts); there is no reduction in working capital; and the corporation may plow back its earnings for expansion or other purposes. The corporation also may wish to reduce the market price of its shares in order to attract more buyers; by issuing more shares, the price per share will decrease. At the same time, it makes possible larger total dividend distributions without a change in the regular dividend rate.

When there are two classes of stockholders, the stock dividend normally applies only to the common stockholders. Payment, however, may be in either preferred or common stock. The various court rulings are not consistent with respect to the rights of preferred stockholders to participate in a stock dividend, although generally no such rights inhere in preferred stock.

Stock Split-Ups

A corporation may wish to reduce the par value of its stock, or it may desire to reduce the price at which the stock is being issued to make it more salable. This is accomplished by a stock split-up whereby the shares outstanding are increased and the par or stated value per share is reduced; there is no change, however, in the total par or stated value of the outstanding shares. No journal entries are required, and there is no change in retained earnings. The capital stock ledger account headings are changed to show the new par or stated value per share and the subsidiary stockholders' ledger is revised to show the new distribution of shares.

Assume, for example, that a corporation has outstanding 100,000 shares of $50 par value common stock. The current market price of the stock is $175 per share. The corporation, wishing to reduce this high market price to create a broader market for a forthcoming additional stock issue, reduces the par value from $50 to $25 and increases the number of shares from 100,000 to 200,000. This is called a 2-for-1 split-up because the number of shares owned by each shareholder is doubled. The split in shares may be accomplished by calling in all the old shares and issuing certificates for new shares on a 2 for 1 basis or by issuing an additional share for each old share previously owned. This action is recorded either by a memorandum notation in the capital stock account or by the following journal entry:

Common Stock, $50 par value	5,000,000	
Common Stock, $25 par value		5,000,000
To record a 2 for 1 split-up, increasing the number of outstanding shares from 100,000 to 200,000 and reducing par value from $50 to $25.		

It may be assumed that the market price of the shares will now be reduced sufficiently to enhance the marketability of the new issue.

TREASURY STOCK

A corporation may reacquire some of its own stock—preferred or common—either by purchase or gift, or in settlement of a debt. Such stock is known as *treasury stock*. Treasury stock, if it has been fully paid for originally, may be issued at a price below par or stated value without the assumption of the usual contingent discount liability by the purchaser of discount stock, to the corporation's creditors for the amount of the discount. Another feature of treasury stock is that it need not first be offered to present stockholders in compliance with their pre-emptive rights to participate in any additional issues. Treasury stock does not fall into the category of new issues; it is the corporation's own stock that has been issued and later reacquired. It is issued but not outstanding stock and therefore does not have voting or dividend rights.

A corporation may purchase some of its own stock to bolster a sagging market, or to meet the needs under a plan whereby the company's own stock is distributed to its employees in lieu of other compensation, at or below the market price. Sometimes the stock is purchased because it is available at a favorable price. Acquisition of treasury stock has the effect of reducing the assets and the stockholders' equity. The Treasury Stock account, therefore, should appear in the Stockholders' Equity section as a deduction from the total contributed capital. Since the acquisition of treasury stock results in a distribution of corporate assets to stockholders, some states have enacted restrictive provisions pertaining to this kind of stock to protect the corporate creditors. If a corporation faces financial difficulties, certain influential stockholders could have the corporation buy back their shares, thereby reducing the amount available for the creditors and other stockholders. The restrictive provisions vary widely among the states. Some states require a restriction of retained earnings to the extent of the disbursement for the treasury stock.

Recording the Purchase of Treasury Stock

When a corporation reacquires shares of its own stock, the Treasury Stock account is debited for the cost of the shares acquired. To illustrate, assume that the Lee Corporation reacquires 10 shares of its own stock at $55 per share. The entry is as shown:

| Treasury Stock–Common | 550 | |
| Cash | | 550 |

The Stockholders' Equity section of the Lee Corporation's position statement after this transaction is shown in Figure 14-2 (other amounts are assumed).

Figure 14-2.
*Treasury Stock and
the Position Statement*

Stockholders' Equity
  Contributed Capital
    Common Stock, $50 par value; authorized and issued
      1,000 shares of which 10 shares are held

in treasury	$50,000
Premium on Common Stock	2,500
Total Contributed Capital	$52,500
Retained Earnings	20,000
Total Contributed Capital and Retained Earnings	$72,500
Deduct Cost of Treasury Stock–Common	550
Total Stockholders' Equity	$71,950

The purchase of the 10 shares of stock reduces cash by $550 and the stockholders' equity by $550 (from $72,500 to $71,950). It also reduces the number of shares outstanding. It does not reduce the amount of issued stock. Common Stock remains at $50,000 because the purchase of the shares is recorded not by a debit to Common Stock but by a debit to a special Treasury Stock account.

Issuance of Treasury Stock—Above Cost

The reissuance of treasury stock is recorded by a credit to Treasury Stock for the cost of the shares. The difference between the cost and the issue price of treasury stock when it is issued above cost is credited to Contributed Capital from Treasury Stock Transactions. To illustrate, assume that the Lee Corporation reissues five shares for $65 per share. The entry is as shown:

Cash	325	
Treasury Stock–Common		275
Contributed Capital from Treasury Stock		
Transactions–Common		50

The Stockholders' Equity section of the Lee Corporation's position statement after the reissuance of the five shares is shown in Figure 14-3.

Figure 14-3.
*Treasury Stock
After Reissue*

Stockholders' Equity
  Contributed Capital
    Common Stock, $50 par value; authorized and issued
      1,000 shares of which 5 shares are held

in treasury	$50,000
Premium on Common Stock	2,500
From Treasury Stock Transactions	50
Total Contributed Capital	$52,550
Retained Earnings	20,000
Total Contributed Capital and Retained Earnings	$72,550
Deduct Cost of Treasury Stock–Common	275
Total Stockholders' Equity	$72,275

Issuance of Treasury Stock—Below Cost

The entry to record the issuance of treasury stock below cost depends on the existence of capital accounts that are not considered to be a part of the stated capital. To illustrate, assume that the Lee Corporation issues the five remaining shares of treasury stock (which cost $275) for $225. The "loss" of $50 is charged to Contributed Capital from Treasury Stock Transactions, as follows:

Cash	225	
Contributed Capital from Treasury Stock Transactions	50	
Treasury Stock–Common		275

If the "loss" on the issue of the shares exceeds the amount in Contributed Capital from Treasury Stock Transactions–Common, the excess is charged to any other contributed capital account arising from the original issuance of the same class of stock and not a part of the stated capital (Excess over Par or Stated Value, for example). In the absence of such accounts, the difference between the cost and the selling price of the treasury stock is charged to Retained Earnings. Assume, for example, that the Lee Corporation issues the five shares for $200 and that Premium on Common Stock is considered to be a part of the legal capital. The entry to record the issue is as shown:

Cash	200	
Contributed Capital from Treasury Stock Transactions	50	
Retained Earnings	25	
Treasury Stock–Common		275

A part ($25) of the "loss" on the sale of the treasury stock is charged to Retained Earnings because the balance in Contributed Capital from Treasury Stock Transactions–Common ($50) is inadequate to absorb the $75 difference, and Premium on Common Stock cannot be charged because it is considered to be a part of the legal capital.

Treasury Stock Donated

One or more shareholders may donate a portion of their shares to the corporation for reissuance to raise needed cash. Shares acquired by donation do not affect the position statement, as there is no change in the assets, liabilities, or stockholders' equity. On acquisition, a memorandum is made in the Treasury Stock account indicating the date and the number of shares donated. When the shares are reissued, the proceeds are credited to Contributed Capital–Donations. Assume that 100 shares are donated to the Lee Corporation by its principal stockholder on May 1. The shares are reissued on June 15 at $45 per share. Upon receipt of the shares, the following memorandum is made in the Treasury Stock account:

Treasury Stock

May 1	100 shares donated	

The journal entry to record the reissuance is as shown:

```
Cash                                        4,500
    Contributed Capital-Donations                       4,500
    To record the reissuance
    for cash of 100 shares of
    donated treasury stock.
```

Legal Restrictions–Treasury Stock Acquisitions

Some states limit the amount of treasury stock that a corporation may acquire to the amount of unrestricted retained earnings available for dividend distribution. If so, the corporation must reduce the amount of retained earnings available for dividends by the cost of the shares acquired. Treasury stock is issued stock and a part of the legal capital. The purchase of treasury stock temporarily impairs this legal capital; the restriction on retained earnings is intended to make good this impairment. Assume, for example, that the Shell Corporation acquired 100 shares of its own common stock at $10 a share. The entries to record the purchase of the treasury stock and the restriction of retained earnings are as shown:

```
Treasury Stock-Common                                   1,000
    Cash                                                        1,000

Retained Earnings                                       1,000
    Retained Earnings-Restricted for Treasury Stock Acquisition  1,000
```

The amount of restricted retained earnings must always be equal to the cost of the treasury stock on hand. Entries to record the subsequent issue by the Shell Corporation of 50 shares of its treasury stock at $12 a share are as shown:

```
Cash                                                    600
    Treasury Stock-Common                                        500
    Contributed Capital from Treasury Stock Transactions          100

Retained Earnings-Restricted for Treasury Stock Acquisition  500
    Retained Earnings                                            500
```

Book Value of Capital Stock

The value of a share of stock may be expressed in terms of par, market, or book value. The book value of a share of stock, or the stockholders' equity per share—assuming that there is only one class of stock outstanding—is computed as follows:

	Line	Amount
Total stockholders' equity	1	$750,000
Number of shares outstanding	2	6,000
Book value per share (Line 1 ÷ Line 2)	3	$ 125

When there is more than one class of stock outstanding, it becomes necessary to determine the claims of each class in the net assets of the corporation (assets minus liabilities). If, for example, the preferred stock is cumulative and nonparticipating and there are dividends in arrears, the stockholders' equity is divided between the two classes based on the preferences accorded to the preferred stock. Assume that a corporation has the following capital structure:

Common stock, $100 par value; issued 1,000 shares	$100,000
Preferred stock (6%), $100 par value; cumulative, nonparticipating; issued 1,000 shares	100,000
Retained earnings	45,000
Retained earnings–restricted for plant addition	10,000
Excess over stated value of no-par common stock	5,000
Total stockholders' equity	$260,000

Dividends are in arrears for the prior and the current year. The book value of a share of preferred stock at the end of the year is computed as follows:

Preferred stock, $100 par value; issued 1,000 shares	$100,000
Dividends in arrears (2 years × $6,000)	12,000
Total equity of preferred stockholders	$112,000
Number of shares outstanding	1,000
Book value per share	$ 112

The book value of a share of common stock is computed as shown:

Total stockholders' equity	$260,000
Deduct equity of preferred stockholders	112,000
Total equity of common stockholders	$148,000
Number of shares outstanding	1,000
Book value per share	$ 148

If the preferred stock is participating, an additional portion of the retained earnings is allocated to the preferred stockholders' equity based on the participation provisions. Hence, in computing the book value of preferred stock its preference rights—dividends in arrears, dividend participation rights, and preference in dividing the assets on dissolution—must be known.

The book value and the market value of a share of stock may be and usually are different in amount. The market value of a share of stock—the price that a share of stock commands on the stock exchange—reflects price level changes, the amount of available investment funds, economic, political, and psychological factors; and so on. Since these factors are not reflected in the accounts, there is often a disparity between book and market values. The book value per share is what each stockholder would receive for each share held in the theoretical event of liquidation after the assets are sold without gain or loss. Since the valuations on the books—especially for inventories and plant and equipment—do not necessarily reflect market conditions, the book value of a share of stock may be of little significance as an indicator of the resale value of the stock.

CONTRIBUTED CAPITAL IN THE STATEMENT OF FINANCIAL POSITION

The Stockholders' Equity section of the Dwight Corporation's statement of financial position as of December 31, 1969, is shown in Figure 14-4. Each item in the statement is numbered and is discussed in the following paragraphs. Duplicate numbers are used for related items. Brief technical account titles may be used, for convenience, in journal and ledgers because these records are for internal use only and the functions of the accounts are understood by the users. However, for external financial reporting these account titles should either be replaced or be supplemented by descriptive language to minimize possible misunderstanding by nontechnical readers of the statement. The nature and significance of the items should not be obscured by the use of jargon or the lack of supporting detail.

DWIGHT CORPORATION
Partial Statement of Financial Position
December 31, 1969

Figure 14-4.
Partial Statement of Financial Position—Stockholders' Equity

	Stockholders' Equity		
	Contributed Capital		
	Capital Stock		
①	Preferred Stock, 5% cumulative, nonparticipating, $100 par value, authorized 2,500 shares, issued 2,000 shares	$200,000	
②	Common Stock, no-par value, $40 stated value, authorized 7,000 shares, issued 5,000 shares of which 500 shares are held in treasury	200,000	$400,000
	Contributed Capital in Excess of Par or Stated Value		
①	Premium on Preferred Stock	$ 10,000	
②	Excess over Stated Value on Common Stock	50,000	
③	From Treasury Stock Transactions—Common	2,500	
②	Excess from Reduction of Stated Value of 5,000 Shares of Common Stock from $50 to $40 Per Share	50,000	112,500
⑦	Donated Capital (land site donated by the Town of Needham)		50,000
	Total Contributed Capital		$562,500
⑧	Excess of Appraised Value of Land over Cost		10,000
	Retained Earnings		
⑤	Restricted For Plant Expansion	$ 45,000	
⑤	For Contingencies	5,000	
④	For Treasury Stock Acquisition	27,500	
	Total Restricted Retained Earnings	$ 77,500	
⑥	Unrestricted	122,500	
	Total Retained Earnings		200,000
	Total		$772,500
④	Deduct Cost of Treasury Stock–Common		27,500
	Total Stockholders' Equity		$745,000

DWIGHT CORPORATION
Statement of Retained Earnings
For Year Ended December 31, 1969

Figure 14-5.
Statement of Retained Earnings

⑥	Net Income for 1969	$250,000
⑥	Deduct Dividends	50,000
	Retained Earnings, December 31, 1969	$200,000

① On January 2, 1969, the date of its organization, the Dwight Corporation issued 2,000 shares of preferred stock at $105 per share. The total par value of these shares (2,000 × $100 = $200,000) is labeled Preferred Stock. This amount represents part of the legal, or stated, capital. The excess ($5 × 2,000) over the par value of the preferred stock is reported separately as Premium on Preferred Stock.

② The Dwight Corporation also issued 5,000 shares of no-par value common stock at $60 per share. The stated value of the shares—originally $50 per share but reduced to $40 per share on December 31—multiplied by the number of shares issued ($40 × 5,000) is shown as Common Stock. The excess of the issue price ($60) over the original stated value ($50) multiplied by the number of shares issued ($10 × 5,000), not being a part of the stated capital, is shown separately as Excess over Stated Value on Common Stock. The excess of the original stated value ($50) over the revised stated value ($40), multiplied by the number of shares issued ($10 × 5,000), is also entered separately, for the same reason; it is labeled Excess from Reduction of Stated Value of 5,000 Shares of Common Stock from $50 to $40 Per Share.

③ On July 10, the Dwight Corporation acquired 1,000 shares of its own common stock for $55 per share. On August 2, it sold 500 shares for $60 per share. The excess of the issue price over the cost is shown as Contributed Capital from Treasury Stock Transactions.

④ On July 10, the Dwight Corporation reacquired 1,000 shares of its own common stock for $55,000. The laws of the state in which it is incorporated limit the payment of dividends to the extent of the amount in the unrestricted Retained Earnings account. Since the effect of a purchase of treasury stock is the same as a cash dividend—a reduction in corporate assets and in the stockholders' equity—the limitation applies equally to dividend payments and to treasury stock acquisitions. A company with free retained earnings of $25,000, for example, may either reacquire treasury stock or declare cash dividends, or do both, provided the total disbursement is not over $25,000. Such a restriction prevents a corporation from bypassing restrictions on dividend distributions and improves the protection of the corporate creditors. The amount of $27,500 ($55,000 from the transaction of July 10 less $27,500 from the transaction of August 2) appears twice in the Stockholders' Equity section: (1) as a part of restricted retained earnings equal to the cost of treasury stock still on hand and (2) as a reduction in the stockholders' equity resulting from a distribution of $27,500 in cash to the stockholders from whom the stock was acquired.

⑤ To conserve working capital for anticipated needs for an extension of the factory building ($45,000) and for certain contingencies ($5,000), separate Retained Earnings accounts were established to restrict earnings otherwise available for dividends.

⑥ Dwight Corporation earned $250,000 from operations for the year, of which $50,000 was to be distributed to the stockholders on January 15,

1970; $77,500 was restricted for specific purposes; and the remainder, $122,500 is unrestricted.

⑦ A building site with an estimated cash market value of $50,000 was donated by the town of Needham as an inducement to the Dwight Corporation to establish itself there. This gift increased the assets and the contributed capital.

⑧ The $10,000 increase in the Land account following an appraisal of the current market value of the land increased the assets and the stockholders' equity.

SUMMARY

The sources of the stockholders' equity are contributed capital, retained earnings, and asset revaluations. The sources of contributed capital are (1) the par or stated value of capital stock issued or subscribed, or a stock dividend to be issued, (2) the excess over the par or stated value of capital stock, and (3) donations.

Donated assets are recorded at the fair market value of the assets received. When assets are revalued to reflect current market values—not a common practice—the increase should be credited to a special stockholders' equity account. Earnings from regular operating transactions—that is, increases in the stockholders' equity other than from transactions involving the company's own stock and from revaluations—are classified as retained earnings. A portion of the retained earnings may be segregated from the parent Retained Earnings account to indicate the intention of the board of directors to conserve corporate assets for purposes other than dividend distributions. Such restrictions may be voluntary or they may be required by state statute or by contract.

The term dividend refers to the distribution of cash, stock, or other corporate property to the stockholders. The charge is to accumulated unrestricted Retained Earnings. Preferred stockholders are entitled to a stated amount per share before any distribution is made to common stockholders. If the preferred stock is cumulative, undeclared dividends accumulate and must be paid together with the stated preference rate before any dividend payment is made on common stock. If the stock is participating, it receives its specified dividend rate and a share of any additional dividends declared. If the stock is preferred as to assets on liquidation of the firm, preferred stockholders must be paid before any liquidating payments are made to the common stockholders.

The term stock dividend refers to the issuance by a corporation of additional shares of its authorized stock without payment of any kind by the stockholders. The charge is to Retained Earnings. Hence, a stock dividend, unlike a cash dividend, has no effect on assets or the total stockholders' equity. Its effect is to transfer from Retained Earnings to the capital stock accounts an amount equal to the fair value of the additional shares issued. If the additional shares are issued to reduce substantially the price at which the stock is being traded, or to reduce the par value, the action is termed a stock split-up. There is no charge to retained earnings, and only a memorandum notation is made in the stock accounts.

Treasury stock is a corporation's own stock that has been issued and later reacquired. It is issued but not outstanding stock. Its acquisition reduces the assets and the stockholders' equity, and is reported in the position statement as a deduction from total contributed capital.

When treasury stock is reissued, the difference between the cost and the reissue price is recorded in a Contributed Capital from Treasury Stock Transactions account. In the absence of such an account, an excess of cost over selling price is debited to Retained Earnings. Shares acquired through donation are recorded by memorandum only; upon reissue, the proceeds are credited to Contributed Capital–Donations. In some states, a corporation must reduce the amount of retained earnings available for dividends by the cost of the shares issued.

The book value of a share of stock, when there is only one class of stock outstanding, is the total stockholders' equity divided by the number of shares outstanding. When there is more than one class outstanding, it is necessary to determine the claims of each class in the net assets of the corporation, taking into consideration preference rights—dividends in arrears, dividend participation rights, and preference as to assets on liquidation.

☐ QUESTIONS

Q14-1. (a) What are the major subdivisions of the Stockholders' Equity section of the statement of financial position? (b) Why must particular care be taken in subdividing the Stockholders' Equity section?

Q14-2. (a) What is the purpose of restricting retained earnings? (b) Is the restriction of retained earnings tantamount to the establishment of a special cash fund?

Q14-3. The following quotation is adapted from the notes to the financial statements of a large company: "Retained earnings of $28,500,000 are restricted from payment of cash dividends on common stock because of a promissory note agreement. Further restrictions of $1,700,000 are made to cover the cost of the Company's own common stock reacquired." What is the significance of this note to (a) a short-term creditor, (b) a long-term creditor, (c) a stockholder?

Q14-4. What is meant by the term *book value*? How is book value computed? Has it any real significance as a financial measure of the worth of stock?

Q14-5. The unclassified statement of financial position of the Quaker Corporation is shown:

QUAKER CORPORATION
Statement of Financial Position
December 31, 1969

Assets

Cash	$ 15,000
Accounts Receivable	35,000
Merchandise Inventory	40,000
Other Assets	10,000
Total Assets	$100,000

Liabilities and Stockholders' Equity

Liabilities		
Accounts Payable		$ 15,000
Notes Payable		5,000
Total Liabilities		$ 20,000
Stockholders' Equity		
Common Stock, $100 par value	$50,000	
Retained Earnings	30,000	80,000
Total Liabilities and Stockholders' Equity		$100,000

The members of the board of directors are considering several dividend distribution plans. They seek your advice with respect to these alternatives: (a) a cash dividend of 20 percent, (b) a stock dividend of 50 percent, (c) no dividend distribution. Discuss.

Q14–**6.** Preferred stock enjoys certain preferences. (a) What are these preferences? (b) How do they affect dividend distributions?

Q14–**7.** (a) What is a stock dividend? (b) What conditions prompt the declaration of a stock dividend? (c) How does a stock dividend affect (1) the total stockholders' equity, (2) the total assets, (3) the book value per share, (4) the taxable income of the recipient, (5) the market price per share?

Q14–**8.** (a) What is accomplished by a stock split-up? (b) How is it recorded? (c) How does it affect (1) the total stockholders' equity, (2) the book value per share, (3) the market price per share?

Q14–**9.** (a) What is treasury stock? (b) Why do corporations buy back their own shares? (c) How does the reacquisition of its own shares affect a company's financial position? (d) Why do some states place certain restrictions on treasury stock acquisitions? (e) How is the purchase of treasury stock recorded? (f) The issuance of treasury stock? (g) How does the issuance of treasury stock affect the financial statements?

Q14–**10.** *Limited liability* is one of the distinguishing characteristics of the corporate form of organization. In state corporation law it is recognized in a number of the provisions relating to financial aspects of the corporation. Indicate three such provisions that are relevant to the financial and accounting aspects of the stockholders' equity.

☐ **EXERCISES**

E14–**1.** The outstanding capital stock of the St. John Corporation consisted of the following:

5% Preferred Stock, par value $100 (3,000 shares)	$300,000
Common Stock, par value $50 (9,000 shares)	450,000

Earnings from operations for the year 1969 were $78,000. Compute the earnings per share on the preferred and common stock.

E14–**2.** The Stockholders' Equity section of the Civitas Metals Company's statement of financial position shows the following:

Common Stock, no-par value, issued 10,000 shares	$230,000
Retained Earnings	70,000
Total	$300,000

What is the cumulative effect on stockholders' equity of each of the following events, occurring in sequence: (a) the declaration of a 10-percent stock dividend; (b) the distribution of the dividend; (c) the acquisition of 100 shares of the Company's own stock for $20 per share; (d) the issuance of these shares for $22 per share; (e) the declaration of a $2-per-share cash dividend; (f) the payment of the dividend.

E14–3. The Tri-Zone Corporation, having 100,000 shares of $15 par value common stock authorized and issued, finds itself in need of working capital. The stockholders agree to donate 10 percent of their holdings to the Corporation. The shares are then reissued at $12 per share. Record the transactions.

E14–4. The City Gas Company restricted retained earnings of $25,000 to cover a lawsuit by a customer. The lawsuit was ultimately settled for $18,750. Make all the necessary journal entries.

E14–5. The Holden Corporation has issued and outstanding 2,000 shares of $100 par value common stock and 1,000 shares of $100 par value 6% cumulative and non-participating preferred stock. Jerome Frank owns 10 shares of the common stock, which he purchased at $55 per share; Leon Curtiss owns 10 shares of preferred stock, which he acquired for $110 per share. (a) What basic rights and privileges does Frank have? (b) Curtiss? (c) How are these shares reported on the Holden Corporation's statement of financial position? (d) How much will Frank and Curtiss each receive if over a three-year period the Corporation distributes earnings of $5,000, $12,000, and $30,000? (e) How much would Curtiss receive if the preferred stock were cumulative and participating?

E14–6. The Sloan Corporation entered into an agreement with the town of Sunbury to build a plant there. The town donated land and buildings valued at $25,000 and $75,000, respectively. Record the transaction.

E14–7. The Crystal Corporation was authorized to issue 100,000 shares of $2 par value common stock, all of which was issued to the principal incorporator in payment for machinery and equipment he sold to the corporation. Shortly thereafter, the incorporator donated 50,000 shares to the Corporation. The shares then were reissued for cash at an average price of $1.75 per share.
   a. Make all the necessary journal entries.
   b. Prepare statements of financial position immediately before and immediately after the reissuance of the donated shares.

E14–8. The capital stock of the Heilbronner Corporation consists of no-par value common stock with a $10 stated value. Record: (a) the issuance of 500 shares at $15 per share, (b) the reacquisition of 100 shares at $12 per share (restriction of retained earnings is not required), (c) the reissuance of the treasury stock at $14 per share, (d) a reduction in the stated value to $5 per share, (e) a 3 for 1 stock split-up.

E14–9. The Dryatt Corporation has issued and outstanding 2,000 shares of common stock and 1,000 shares of 4% preferred stock, each with a par value of $100. Retained earnings are $50,000, and the directors declare a $25,000 cash dividend. Record the dividend declaration, assuming that (a) the preferred stock is cumulative and nonparticipating and there are no dividends in arrears; (b) the preferred stock is cumulative and participates up to $3 per share above the regular 4-percent rate; (c) the preferred stock is cumulative and fully participating, and there was no dividend declaration during the previous year.

E14–10. The Excelsior Mining Company's statement of financial position shows the following:

Common Stock, par value $100; 6,000 shares	$600,000
Retained Earnings	200,000

Give the effect on these accounts of each of the following situations: (a) All the stock is called in and 12,000 shares of no-par value stock is issued, the entire proceeds constituting legal capital; (b) the old shares are replaced by 12,000 shares of no-par value, $50 stated value common stock; (c) each stockholder receives a stock dividend of one additional share for every three shares he now holds.

E14–11. Indicate the effect, if any, of each of the following transactions on total retained earnings of the Beaumont Company.

1. The board of directors declared a stock dividend to be issued one month from the current date.
2. Issued the stock dividend declared in Transaction 1.
3. Wrote off accounts receivable against the Allowance for Doubtful Accounts.
4. Paid accounts payable.
5. Collected accounts receivable.
6. Issued $100 par value common stock at $97 per share.
7. Restricted retained earnings for contingencies.
8. Issued $100 par value preferred stock at $103 per share.
9. Purchased machinery on open account.
10. Issued long-term notes and received cash in return.

E14–12. On July 31, 1969, the directors of the Bridge Bar Dough Corporation, after a successful year with its new products, declared $60,000 in dividends on all classes of stock. There are outstanding 4,000 shares of $50 par value, 6% cumulative preferred stock participating to 9 percent, and 20,000 shares of no par common stock. Dividends are in arrears for the preceding two years on the preferred stock. Common stock also has not received any dividends for the preceding two years. The same number of shares of preferred stock was outstanding on July 31, 1968; however, on July 31, 1967, only 3,000 shares of preferred stock were outstanding. The Common Stock account has remained unchanged for more than three years. Compute the amount of dividends each class will receive as a result of the dividend declaration.

☐ .DEMONSTRATION PROBLEMS

DP14–1. (Recording corporate transactions; stockholders' equity) Following is the Stockholders' Equity section of the statement of financial position of the Stenn Corporation as of December 31, 1968:

Common Stock, no-par value; issued and		
outstanding 25,000 shares		$300,000
Retained Earnings		
Restricted		
For Lawsuit Damages	$ 25,000	
For Plant Expansion	125,000	
Unrestricted	75,000	225,000
Total Stockholders' Equity		$525,000

The following transactions occurred during the year 1969 (restriction of retained earnings is required).

1. Acquired 5,000 shares of its own common stock at $10 per share.
2. Paid $5,000 in settlement of the lawsuit for injuries.
3. Issued 2,500 shares of treasury stock at $15 per share.
4. One of the stockholders donated land and a building worth $20,000 and $80,000, respectively.
5. Paid a cash dividend of $1 per share.
6. Reduced the retained earnings restriction for plant expansion by $100,000.
7. Wrote off organization costs of $10,000.
8. Net income for the year after income taxes was $50,000 (make the closing entry).

Required: 1. Enter the December 31, 1968, balances in T accounts.
2. Journalize the transactions and post to the appropriate accounts.
3. Prepare the Stockholders' Equity section of the statement of financial position as of December 31, 1969.

DP14–2. (*Effect of cash and stock dividends*) The Stockholders' Equity section of the Dixon Corporation's statement of financial position consists of the following accounts:

Common Stock, $100 par value; issued 1,000 shares	$100,000
Retained Earnings	25,000
Total Stockholders' Equity	$125,000

Required: 1. a. Prepare the journal entries to record the declaration and the payment of a $10-per-share cash dividend.
   b. Compute the book value per share of the common stock immediately before the declaration of the dividend and immediately after the payment of the dividend.
2. Assume that the corporation declares a stock dividend instead of a cash dividend, each stockholder to receive one dividend share for each ten shares he now holds. Complete Requirements 1a and 1b based on this assumption.
3. John Fellner owns 20 shares of Dixon Corporation stock. What was his equity (a) before the stock dividend and (b) after the stock dividend?
4. Discuss the purpose, advantages, and disadvantages of a stock dividend from the viewpoint of (a) the stockholder and (b) the issuing corporation.

DP14–3. (*Computing dividend distributions*) The Majestic Corporation has outstanding 5,000 shares of $100 par value common stock and 5,000 shares of $100 par value 5% preferred stock. The board of directors declared a cash dividend of $100,000.

Required: Journalize the declaration of the cash dividend based on each of the following assumptions:

1. The preferred stock is cumulative and nonparticipating.
2. The preferred stock is cumulative and fully participating.
3. The preferred stock is cumulative and nonparticipating, and dividends have not been declared for the current year or for the two years preceding the current year.

4. The preferred stock is cumulative and fully participating, and dividends have not been declared for the current year or the preceding year.

5. Assume the same facts as in Requirement 4 except that the board of directors declared a cash dividend of $65,000.

☐ **PROBLEMS**

P14-1. The following account balances were taken from the ledger of the Spark Company as of December 31, 1969:

Excess from Revaluation of Building	$ 30,000
Premium on Preferred Stock	25,000
Contributed Capital–Donated	60,000
Contributed Capital from Treasury Stock Transactions–Common	5,000
Preferred Stock, 6%, $100 par value; issued 4,000 shares	400,000
Retained Earnings–Restricted for Plant Additions	80,000
Retained Earnings–Restricted for Contingencies	10,000
Contributed Capital–Excess of Original Stated Value over Revised Stated Value of Common Stock	75,000
Common Stock, no-par value; stated value $20; issued 10,000 shares	200,000
Retained Earnings	165,000
Treasury Stock–Common	40,000
Contributed Capital–Excess over Stated Value of Common Stock	20,000
Estimated Income Taxes Payable	48,000
Organization Costs	10,000

Required: 1. Prepare the Stockholders' Equity section of the statement of financial position as of December 31, 1969.

2. Give a brief statement of the origin and function of each account.

P14-2. The following information is taken from the Stockholders' Equity section of the Lenox Corporation's statement of financial position as of December 31, 1969:

Preferred Stock, 6%, cumulative and nonparticipating, $100 par value; authorized and issued 1,500 shares	$150,000
Common Stock, no-par value; stated value $20; authorized 20,000 shares; issued 10,000 shares	200,000
Excess over Stated Value of Common Stock	420,000
Retained Earnings–Restricted for Plant Expansion	40,000
Retained Earnings–Restricted for Bond Redemption	30,000
Retained Earnings–Unrestricted	140,000
Total Stockholders' Equity	$980,000

Dividends on the preferred stock are in arrears for 1968 and 1969.
Required: Compute the book value per share of the common stock.

P14-3. The condensed statement of financial position of the Crystal Corporation as of December 31, 1969, was as follows:

Total Assets	$725,000
Liabilities	$200,000
Preferred Stock, 7%, $100 par value; cumulative	100,000
Common Stock, no-par value; stated value $10	300,000
Retained Earnings	50,000
Premium on Preferred Stock	10,000
Excess over Stated Value of Common Stock	25,000
Retained Earnings–Restricted for Plant Expansion	40,000
Total Liabilities and Stockholders' Equity	$725,000

Required: 1. Find the book value per share of common stock, assuming that there are no dividend arrearages. The liquidating value of the preferred stock is equal to the par value.
2. Find the book value per share of common stock, assuming that dividends on the preferred stock are in arrears for the years 1968 and 1969.
3. What is the significance of the book value per share?

P14-**4.** On February 1, 1969, the Moore Corporation was authorized to issue 20,000 shares of $20 par value common stock and 1,000 shares of 6% preferred stock, $100 par value. The following transactions occurred between February 1 and December 31, 1969:

1. Received subscriptions for 5,000 shares of common stock at $20 per share and 1,000 shares of preferred stock at $101 per share.

2. Purchased the assets of the Heinch Company at their fair cash value; the assets consisted of land worth $15,000, buildings worth $125,000, and plant and equipment worth $175,000. Issued 15,000 shares of common stock in payment.

3. Collected in full for the stock subscribed in Transaction 1.

4. Purchased 500 shares of its own common stock at $18.75 per share. (The laws of the state of incorporation require a restriction of retained earnings equal to the cost of treasury stock.)

5. Established a restriction on retained earnings for contingencies of $10,000.

6. Issued 200 shares of treasury stock for $19 per share.

7. Earnings through December 31 after Federal income taxes were $62,000 (make the closing entry).

8. Declared a $.50-per-share dividend on the common stock and a $3 dividend on the preferred stock.

Required: 1. Record the transactions in appropriate T accounts.
2. Prepare the Stockholders' Equity section of the statement of financial position as of December 31, 1969.

P14-**5.** The Stockholders' Equity section of the Lund Corporation's statement of financial position as of June 30, 1968, is shown:

Stockholders' Equity	
Common Stock, $100 par value; issued 1,000 shares	$100,000
Retained Earnings	50,000
Total Stockholders' Equity	$150,000

The following transactions occurred during the next 12 months:

1. Established a retained earnings restriction of $8,000 for a pending lawsuit.
2. Received, as a donation from the town of Lee, land and a building worth $10,000 and $90,000, respectively.
3. Received 100 shares of stock as a gift from one of the stockholders of the Corporation.
4. Declared a 2 percent stock dividend. The shares to be issued are currently quoted at $110 per share.
5. Purchased 50 shares of its own stock for $108 per share.
6. Issued the stock certificates for the stock dividend.
7. Issued 50 of the donated shares for $5,500.
8. Issued 25 shares of treasury stock for $3,000.
9. Net income for the year after income taxes was $20,000 (make the closing entry).

> Required: 1. Enter the balances as of June 30, 1968, in T accounts.
> 2. Record the transactions directly into the T accounts.
> 3. Prepare the Stockholders' Equity section of the statement of financial position as of June 30, 1969.

P14–6. The Stockholders' Equity section of the Jackson Corporation's statement of financial position as of December 31, 1968, was as follows:

Stockholders' Equity
  Capital Stock
    Preferred Stock, 5%, $100 par value; authorized and
      issued 2,000 shares $200,000
    Common Stock, $40 par value; authorized and issued
      10,000 shares 400,000
    Premium on Common Stock 50,000
  Retained Earnings 200,000
    Total Stockholders' Equity $850,000

Transactions for the year 1969 were:

1. Declared a $60,000 cash dividend for 1969. (The preferred stock is cumulative and nonparticipating; there are no dividends in arrears).
2. Paid the dividend declared in Transaction 1.
3. Purchased 500 shares of its own preferred stock for $100 per share (a restriction of retained earnings is not required).
4. Established a restriction on retained earnings of $10,000 for contingencies.
5. Issued 300 shares of treasury stock for $105 per share.
6. Earnings from operations for the year after income taxes were $200,000 (make the closing entry).
7. Issued 200 shares of treasury stock for $90 per share.
8. The principal stockholder donated a warehouse valued at $35,000 to the Corporation.

> Required: 1. Prepare journal entries to record the transactions.
> 2. Post to T accounts.

3. Prepare the Stockholders' Equity section of the statement of financial position as of December 31, 1969.

P14-**7**. The following information was taken from the ledger of Scout, Inc., as of June 30, 1969:

Cash	$ 50,000
Accounts Receivable	200,000
Cash Dividends Payable	40,000
Organization Costs	1,500
Common Stock Subscribed	100,000
Preferred Stock Subscribed	200,000
Common Stock, $5 par value	300,000
Preferred Stock, $10 par value	500,000
Subscriptions Receivable–Common Stock	20,000
Subscriptions Receivable–Preferred Stock	50,000
Premium on Preferred Stock	45,000
Premium on Common Stock	25,000
Retained Earnings	100,000
Retained Earnings–Restricted for Contingencies	15,000
Contributed Capital–Donated	20,000
Contributed Capital from Treasury Stock Transactions—Common	9,000
Retained Earnings–Restricted for Retirement of Preferred Stock	35,000
Discount on Common Stock	15,000
Allowance for Doubtful Accounts	11,000
Retained Earnings–Restricted for Plant Addition	45,000
Estimated Income Taxes Payable	23,000
Accumulated Depreciation–Building	18,000

Required: Prepare the Stockholders' Equity section of the statement of financial position as of June 30, 1969.

P14-**8**. A listing of the balances of all the Stockholders' Equity accounts, taken from the statement of financial position of Zeide, Inc., at December 31, 1969, is given:

Preferred stock, $100 par value; 6%, cumulative; entitled to $105 per share plus cumulative dividends in arrears in liquidation; authorized 10,000 shares, issued 8,000 shares of which 500 are held in treasury	$800,000
Paid-In capital in excess of par value of preferred stock	24,000
Paid-In capital from treasury stock transactions–preferred	2,000
Common stock, no-par value; stated value $40; authorized 20,000 shares, issued 16,000 shares	640,000
Stock dividend, to be issued at stated value 4,000 common shares	160,000
Paid-In capital in excess of stated value of common stock	56,000
Paid-In capital from stock dividend–common stock	16,000
Discount on common stock	1,000
Land donated by Suffolk County	15,000
Retained earnings	
Restricted in the amount of treasury stock purchased at cost	51,500
Unrestricted	90,300
Treasury stock, preferred—at cost	51,500

Required: 1. Prepare a properly classified Stockholders' Equity section.

2. Compute (a) the amount contributed by the preferred

stockholders, (b) the amount contributed by the common stockholders, (c) the book value per share of common stock, (d) the book value per share of preferred stock, assuming that one year's preferred dividends are in arrears.

P14–**9.** The Bye Corporation was organized on January 2, 1969, with authority to issue 10,000 shares of no-par value common stock and 5,000 shares of 6% preferred stock, $100 par value. During 1969, the following transactions occurred:

1. Received subscriptions to 500 shares of preferred stock at $103 per share. Collected down payments of $10,000.

2. Issued 4,000 shares of common stock for cash at $13 per share. A stated value of $10 per share is set by the board of directors for the common stock.

3. Issued 100 shares of common stock, in lieu of a $1,000 fee, to the Corporation's attorneys for their services in drafting the articles of incorporation and a set of by-laws.

4. Received additional payments of $33,000 from subscribers to preferred stock; 310 shares are issued to the subscribers who paid in full.

5. Acquired 200 shares of common stock for $2,500 from the estate of a deceased stockholder.

6. Received the balance of subscriptions due and issued the shares.

7. Reissued the 100 shares of the treasury stock acquired in Transaction 5 at $16 per share.

8. Declared a 6% dividend on preferred stock and a $.30 per share dividend on common stock. The dividends are payable on January 15, 1970, to stockholders of records on December 31, 1969. The board also authorized the restriction of retained earnings of $8,000 for plant expansion.

Required: Prepare the journal entries to record the transactions.

P14–**10.** An analysis of the Treasury Stock account of Gordon, Inc., shows the following debit entries during 1969:

Date	Lot No.	Description	No. of Shares	Class of Stock	Amount
1969					
Jan. 10	1	Purchase	120	Common	$4,800
Feb. 15	2	Purchase	80	Preferred	1,600
Apr. 20	3	Purchase	50	Common	2,100
May 2	4	Gift	25	Preferred	625
2	5	Gift	25	Common	800

The following credit entries were made:

Date	Lot No.	Description	No. of Shares	Class of Stock	Amount
1969					
Feb. 5	1	Sale	50	Common	$2,200
11	1	Sale	20	Common	860
16	1	Sale	20	Common	780
29	2	Sale	70	Preferred	1,750
Apr. 20	3	Sale	40	Common	1,840
22	1	Sale	20	Common	700
July 20	4	Sale	25	Preferred	500
26	5	Sale	20	Common	400

The bookkeeper has followed the policy of debiting the account at cost for purchases and at the prevailing market price for gifts; all credits to the account are for the net proceeds from sales. The common stock was originally issued at a substantial premium; the preferred stock was originally issued at par value.

Required: 1. Give the journal entries to correct the Treasury Stock account (compute costs by specific identification).
2. Give the journal entry to restrict an amount of retained earnings equal to the cost of the shares on hand.

CASE PROBLEM
Martin Development Corporation

The Martin Development Corporation was formed ten years ago to acquire real estate for the development of suburban housing and shopping areas. It was originally organized as a closed Corporation, financed by the investments of five businessmen. During the first years of operations, the board of directors, which consisted of the five original stockholders, voted to restrict the payment of dividends and to reinvest all earnings, if any, in the expanding projects of the Corporation. This policy was favored by all the members of the board of directors, although one of them, Peter Holt, was reluctant. To placate him, the other members did agree on different occasions to issue two stock dividends and a stock split-up.

After another year of operations, the board of directors agreed, except for Holt, to issue some preferred stock to a number of individuals who had indicated an interest in the organization. Holt, being suspicious of the motivations of the new investors, offered his stock to the Corporation. The other members of the board of directors voted to buy all his shares at 10 percent more than their book value. Holt accepted the offer. Shortly thereafter, preferred stock was issued to the new investors.

A review of the sequence of events affecting the Stockholders' Equity section of the Corporation's statement of financial position is given:

1. The corporate charter was received, authorizing the issuance of 20,000 shares of $100 par value voting common stock and 40,000 shares of $50 par value cumulative, 5%, participating to 6% (for the latest year only), nonvoting preferred stock. The preferred stock can become fully voting on a per-share basis when preferred dividends are in arrears, beginning with the third year of arrearage.

2. Each of the five original stockholders purchased 500 shares of common stock at par value.

3. The Corporation reported a net loss of $8,500 for the first year of operations.

4. The Corporation reported a net income of $17,500 for the second year of operations.

5. The directors voted to restrict all retained earnings for the expansion of operations.

6. The Corporation reported a net income of $40,000 for the third year of operations.

7. The directors voted to restrict all retained earnings for the expansion of operations.

8. The directors voted to issue a 10-percent stock dividend and to release the appropriate amount of restricted retained earnings.

9. The Corporation reported a net income of $55,000 for the fourth year of operations.

10. The directors voted to issue a 20-percent stock dividend.
11. The Corporation reported a net income of $65,000 for the fifth year of operations.
12. The corporate charter was changed, authorizing the issuance of 50,000 shares of $50 par value voting common stock (the preferred stock authorization was not changed).
13. The directors voted a 2 for 1 common stock split-up.
14. The Corporation reported a net income of $75,000 for the sixth year of operations.
15. Holt sold all his shares of common stock to the Corporation for 110 percent of book value. The directors voted to restrict an equal amount of retained earnings.
16. New investors purchased 5,000 shares of preferred stock at par value.
17. The Corporation reported a net income of $90,000 for the seventh year of operations.
18. At the end of the first two full years since the preferred stock was issued, the directors declared a $65,000 cash dividend.
19. The directors voted to sell one-fourth of the treasury stock to another local investor for 5 percent more than its cost. An equal amount of retained earnings was released. The other three-fourths of the treasury stock was canceled.
20. The Corporation reported a net income of $80,000 for the eighth year of operations.

Required: Answer the following questions in terms of the Martin Development Corporation.

1. Record the events in the Corporation's general journal.
2. Describe the meaning of the following terms relating to capital stock:
   a. Capital stock authorized
   b. Capital stock issued
   c. Par value
   d. Voting and nonvoting
   e. Cumulative
   f. Participating to 6%
   g. Outstanding
3. What purpose is served by restricting the retained earnings?
4. What is a stock dividend; what function does it normally serve?
5. What is a stock split-up; what function does it normally serve?
6. What is the book value? How is it determined?
7. Based upon the information given, why did the directors decide to pay a cash dividend? What was the cash dividend amount per share? Show your calculations.
8. What was the amount of treasury stock? Is it an asset, a liability, part of the stockholders' equity, or a contra to one of these classifications? Why?
9. What are retained earnings? What is the source of retained earnings? Why is the amount of retained earnings not equal to the amount of cash on hand?
10. Prepare a partial statement of financial position that will disclose the stockholders' equity after all twenty events have been completed.

Chapter Fifteen

Managerial Financial Decisions— Debt

The financial managers of modern corporations are constantly faced with the problem of how and where to get corporate capital for both short-term and long-term needs. The various alternative sources are outlined as follows:

1. Investments of the owners, discussed in Chapter 13.
2. Retention of earnings, discussed in Chapter 14.
3. Financing by creditors, which may create current or long-term liabilities discussed in this chapter.

Only summary consideration is given to current liabilities in this chapter, since they have been discussed in various other parts of this text. More detailed attention is paid to various long-term liabilities, such as Bonds Payable, Mortgage Payable, and Liabilities Under Pension Contracts.

CURRENT LIABILITIES

As previously defined, current liabilities represent obligations, the liquidation of which requires the use of current assets or the creation of other current liabilities within a year or an operating cycle, whichever is the longer period of time. Various kinds of current liabilities have been discussed elsewhere in this text, including:

Bank overdrafts
Accounts payable, trade; or vouchers payable
Notes payable, trade
Notes payable, bank
Maturing bonds payable
Current installments of serial bonds payable
Credit balances in customers' accounts

Accrued interest payable
Sales taxes payable
F.I.C.A. taxes payable
State unemployment compensation taxes payable
Federal unemployment compensation taxes payable
Federal income taxes payable
Employees' income tax withholdings payable
Unearned subscriptions

Bonds Payable, though they may have been originally issued with lives as long as 50 years or more, are classified as a current liability on the statement of financial position prepared at the end of the fiscal year immediately preceding the date of retirement. Unearned Subscriptions are not liquidated by the use of current assets but are earned within the next year or cycle; current assets are consumed in the earning process. Current liabilities are generally presented on the statement of financial position at their full maturity value.

All these current liabilities provide cash or some other asset, such as merchandise. They are significant to a financial manager since payment or refunding must be accomplished; but the management of current liabilities may also influence decisions made in regard to long-term debt financing. For example, if there is a large amount of unsecured accounts payable outstanding, these short-term creditors may bring pressure to bear to prevent the issuance of long-term secured bonds payable.

BONDS PAYABLE

One of the means used by businesses to acquire funds that will not be repaid for many years is the issuance of bonds. A *bond,* or *bond certificate,* is a written promise under the corporate seal to pay a specific sum of money on a specified or determinable future date to the order of a person named in the certificate or to the order of the bearer. An example of a corporate bond is the 2⅞% First Mortgage Callable Bond Payable, Series A, due 1996, issued by the Bessemer and Lake Erie Railroad Company, a subsidiary of the United States Steel Corporation. Most industrial bonds are issued in denominations of $1,000 each; this enables the issuing company to obtain funds from many different classes of investors. Denominations other than $1,000 are also used; bonds with a face value of $50, $100, or $500 are not uncommon. These smaller denominations, for example, are used by the United States Government in its Series E Savings Bond issues. On the other hand, municipal bond issues in $5,000 denominations are also common.

Bonds may be issued directly by the borrowing corporation or they may be transferred to banks, brokers, or other underwriting syndicates who, in turn, market the bonds through their own channels. *Bondholders* are creditors of the corporation; with the exception noted above, the Bonds Payable account is a long-term liability. Bonds contain provisions for interest to be paid at regularly stated intervals. Interest is usually paid semiannually on industrial bonds.

A bond, like a promissory note, represents a corporate debt to the lender, which must be satisfied from the assets of the corporation in preference to stockholders' equity claims. The main functional difference between bonds and promissory notes is that bonds are used in long-term financing, whereas promissory notes are used in short-term financing.

Bonds Compared with Capital Stock

A better understanding of bonds may be obtained if they and related concepts are compared with capital stock. The following parallel listing should help the reader to get firmly fixed in his mind the nature of bonds.

Bonds	Capital Stock
Bondholders are creditors.	Stockholders are owners.
Bonds Payable is a long-term liability account.	Capital Stock is a stockholders' equity account.
Bondholders, along with other creditors, have primary claims on assets in liquidation.	Stockholders have residual claims on assets in liquidation.
The interest rate on bonds is frequently lower than the dividend rate that would be necessary to raise the same amount of funds through the issuance of some type of capital stock.	The dividend rate on capital stock issued to raise funds is frequently higher than the interest rate on bonds.
Interest is typically a fixed charge; it must be paid or the creditors can institute bankruptcy proceedings against the debtor corporation.	Dividends are not fixed charges; even preferred dividends are at best only *contingent charges.*
Interest is a valid expense.	Dividends are not expenses; they are distributions of net income.
Interest is deductible in arriving at both taxable and business income.	Dividends are not deductible in arriving at taxable and business income.
Bonds do not carry voting rights.	All stock carries voting rights unless they are expressly denied by contract, as is usually the case with preferred stock.

Classifications of Bonds

There are many types of bonds, each tailored to meet the particular financial needs of the issuing corporation. Some common classifications of bonds are described in the following paragraphs.

REGISTERED BONDS. *Registered* bonds are issued in the name of the bondholder. They require proper endorsement on the bond certificate to effect a transfer from one owner to another. The debtor corporation or its transfer agent—usually a bank or trust company appointed by the corporation—maintains complete ownership records. Bonds may be registered both as to principal and interest, in which case interest checks are issued only to bondholders of record. It is possible, however, to register the principal only (*coupon bonds*); the owner detaches *interest coupons* from the bond certificate and deposits them at the stated interest dates at his bank, or at a designated bank.

BEARER BONDS. Bonds may be issued without being registered in the name of the buyer; title to them is vested in the *bearer*. The procedure for making interest payments is the same as with coupon bonds. This method is least burdensome to the issuing corporation, but the owner must take particular care against loss or theft of the certificates.

SECURED BONDS. A *secured* bond is one that pledges some part of the corporate property as security for the bond. The property pledged may consist of land and buildings (*real-estate mortgage* bonds), machinery (*chattel mortgage* bonds), negotiable securities (*collateral trust* bonds), or other corporate property. Several loans may use the same property for collateral; this gives rise to *first mortgage* bonds, *second mortgage* bonds, and so on. The numbers indicate the order to be followed in satisfying the mortgageholders' claims if the corporation fails to meet its obligations under the *bond indenture*—the contract between the corporation and the bondholder. In the event of default *foreclosure* and sale of the property follow. Second and third mortgage bonds necessarily carry a higher interest rate than first mortgage bonds because of the order of priority of payment in the event of a default; thus, they are not as marketable as first mortgage bonds and are more costly to the borrowing company. It is, therefore, desirable for the borrower to raise the required funds through a single, large first mortgage bond issue.

UNSECURED DEBENTURE BONDS. Unsecured bondholders rank as general, or ordinary, creditors of the corporation and rely upon the corporations' general credit. Such bonds are commonly referred to as *debenture* bonds. Sometimes debenture bonds are issued with a provision that interest payments will depend on earnings; such bonds are called *income* bonds.

Bonds may have other special features; for instance, the bonds may mature serially (*serial* bonds), which means that specified portions of the outstanding bonds will mature in installments and be paid at stated intervals. Sometimes the issuing corporation retains an option to call in the bonds before maturity (*callable* bonds); or, in other cases, the bondholder may be given an option to exchange his bonds for capital stock (*convertible* bonds). The bond indenture may require the issuing corporation to deposit funds—often to a trustee for the bondholders—at regular intervals to insure the availability of adequate funds for the redemption of the bonds at maturity (*sinking fund* bonds).

Managerial Reasons for Issuing Bonds Instead of Capital Stock

Among the many factors that influence management in regard to the issuance of bonds instead of capital stock is that management may be enabled to tap another market source of creditor funds that it would not be able to tap by the issuance of stock. For example, many banks and other financial institutions are not permitted by law or regulation to buy stocks, but they are allowed to buy bonds.

A second factor is *leverage,* or *trading on the bondholders' equity.* This practice can be described very simply: if funds can be borrowed at an interest rate of 4 percent and utilized in the business to earn 10 percent after taxes, then the additional earnings of 6 percent (10% − 4%) accrue to the common stockholders. However, there is always the possibility of the opposite reaction taking place; in other words, the borrowed funds may earn less than the cost of borrowing—an instance of unfavorable leverage.

A third reason why corporations decide to issue bonds rather than capital stock is that there is a high income tax rate on corporate net income. If a corporation pays out at least half its net income in Federal and state income taxes, it naturally considers the issuance of bonds as a means of effecting a considerable tax saving.

To illustrate the way that leverage and heavy income taxes affect financial decision-making involving the choice of alternative methods of fund-raising, assume that the Hunt Corporation, which has $100 par value common stock outstanding in the amount of $1,000,000, needs $500,000 to purchase additional plant and equipment. Three plans are under consideration: Plan 1 is to issue additional common stock at $100 par value; Plan 2 is to issue 6% preferred stock at $100 par value, cumulative and nonparticipating; Plan 3 is to issue 5% bonds.

	Plan 1	Plan 2	Plan 3
Common stock	$1,000,000	$1,000,000	$1,000,000
Additional funds	500,000	500,000	500,000
Total	$1,500,000	$1,500,000	$1,500,000
Net income before bond interest and income taxes	$ 300,000	$ 300,000	$ 300,000
Deduct bond interest expense	–0–	–0–	25,000
Net income after bond interest expense	$ 300,000	$ 300,000	$ 275,000
Deduct income taxes (assumed rate of 50%)	150,000	150,000	137,500
Net income after income taxes	$ 150,000	$ 150,000	$ 137,500
Deduct dividends on preferred stock	–0–	30,000	–0–
Available for common stock dividends	$ 150,000	$ 120,000	$ 137,500
Earnings per share on common stock (15,000 shares outstanding under Plan 1; 10,000 shares under Plans 2 and 3)	$10	$12	$13.75

All the plans assume that the securities will be issued at par value, that earnings of $300,000 annually before the bond interest expense is deducted will be maintained, and that an income tax rate of 50 percent will prevail.

Assuming that earnings per share on common stock is an accepted decision-making criterion, Plan 3 appears to be the most promising for the common stockholders, particularly if the annual earnings exceed $300,000, because the bond interest rate is fixed. If the annual earnings fall below $300,000, one of the other plans may become more advantageous. Since the securities market and corporate net earnings remain uncertain, there is no exact mathematical formula to solve this financial problem. The decision requires sound judgment based on past experience and projected future needs.

A fourth reason for the issuance of bonds instead of common stock is the fact that bonds—and to a lesser extent preferred stock—aid in offsetting losses due to shrinkage in the purchasing power of the funds invested in assets. Bonds, for example, carry fixed contract maturity values in terms of the monetary unit at the maturity date. If the value of the dollar decreases before the bonds are paid, a gain resulting from the use of the more valuable money received at the time of borrowing accrues to the owners of the business.

A fifth factor is control. The issuance of additional common stock may result in a loss of management control because the ownership of the corporation is distributed over a larger number of stockholders. Bondholders, on the other hand, are creditors and do not participate in managerial decisions, except in the rare instances when this is a specific provision of the bond indenture.

Other reasons may influence the decision of management to issue bonds; but these five factors indicate the scope of the problem.

Authorizing the Bond Issue

Even after management decides that bonds should be issued, it is faced with months of preliminary work before the bonds can actually be *floated*, or sold. For example, the exact amount to be borrowed, the *contract* or *nominal interest rate* (the rate on the bond certificate that applies to the face value), the maturity date, and the assets, if any, to be pledged must be determined. The provisions of the bond indenture must be chosen with extreme care: For instance, should the bonds be callable; and should they be convertible into some other form of security? Careful long-range financial planning helps to reduce the cost of securing the long-term funds. For example, if there is any chance that the company will need additional funds in the near future, management should not close the door on the possibility of marketing additional bonds by pledging the company's total mortgageable assets. In this case, management probably should seek authority for a bond issue large enough to meet all foreseeable needs.

The financial vice president, working with other corporate officers, is responsible for finding answers to these and other questions. He prepares a written report for the board of directors, summarizing the proposed features of the bond financing and stating why the funds are needed, how they are to be used, and the means of ultimately retiring the bond issue. Various alternative methods of raising funds, such as those shown in the example of the Hunt Corporation, no doubt, are presented to point up the financial advantage of issuing the bonds.

The board of directors studies this written report, along with the laws of the state of incorporation, the corporate charter, and the corporate bylaws, before passing a resolution recommending to the stockholders that bonds be issued; a record of the resolution is entered in the minute book of the corporation. Next, the proposal is presented to the stockholders for their approval. Once this approval has been gained, the board of directors prepares a resolution instructing the proper corporate officers to issue the bonds and sign the necessary documents. The final step is the issuance of a formal certified statement that the approval of the board of directors and the stockholders has been obtained. Approval by the stockholders is required since the bondholders have a preferred position; as creditors, they have a prior claim to the assets of the corporation in the event of liquidation.

Accounting for the Issuance of Bonds

No formal journal entry is required to record the authorization of the bond issue by the stockholders, but a memorandum should be made in the Bonds Payable account indicating the total amount authorized. This information is needed when the statement of financial position is prepared since it should disclose the total authorization as well as the amount issued.

The issue price—usually stated as a percentage of the face value—is affected primarily by the prevailing market interest rate on bonds of the same grade. Bonds are graded by various financial institutions; the grade depends on the financial condition of the issuing corporation. The highest grade is AAA; the next, AA; and so on in descending order: A, BBB, BB, B. If, on the issue date, the stated interest rate applicable to the face value of the bonds—also called *contract,* or *nominal,* rate—is established at the prevailing market interest rate for the particular grade of bonds, the authorized bonds will sell at face value. On the other hand, if there is a disparity between the contract bond interest rate and the prevailing market rate for that grade of bonds, the bonds will sell at a price above or below face value; that is, at a *premium* or a *discount.*

BONDS ISSUED AT FACE VALUE. The first example involves the simple situation in which a corporation issues bonds at face value on an interest date. The same sequence is followed in each of the first three illustrations: First, an entry is made to record the issuance of the bonds; next, any peculiarity of financial statement presentation is discussed; after this, the accounting procedure for interest payments is described; and finally, the recording of the *retirement* of the bonds at the maturity date is shown.

Assume that on July 1, 1969, the Grogan Corporation is authorized to issue 5% debenture bonds with a face value of $200,000 and a maturity date of June 30, 1989. Interest is paid semiannually on June 30 and December 31. All the bonds are issued on July 1, 1969, at 100, or face value, and the following entry is made:

```
1969
July  1   Cash                                      200,000
              Debenture Bonds Payable                          200,000
                  To record the issuance of all the authorized
                  5% bonds due on June 30, 1989.
```

The similarity between this entry and that for the issuance of notes, discussed in Chapter 7, is clear.

A statement of financial position prepared after this transaction would report the bond issue as follows:

```
Long-Term Liabilities
    5% Debenture Bonds Payable, due June 30, 1989        $200,000
```

The following entry records the payment of interest on December 31, 1969 (the bond issue and interest payment entries are normally made in the cash receipts and cash disbursements journals):

1969

Dec. 31   Bond Interest Expense   5,000
        Cash   5,000
            To record the payment of the semiannual
            interest on the 5% bonds payable.

A similar entry is made each June 30 and December 31 until the bonds are retired. It is possible for all the interest paid by the Corporation to be recorded in a single Interest Expense account; however, in the present case, the interest on bonds payable is considered to be material enough to warrant a separate general ledger account.

On June 30, 1989, the bonds are retired by the payment of cash to the bond-holders. The following compound entry is made on that date to record the last interest payment and the retirement of the bonds:

1989

June 30   Debenture Bonds Payable   200,000
        Bond Interest Expense   5,000
        Cash   205,000
            To record the final interest payment and
            retirement of the 5% bonds payable
            due today.

ISSUING BONDS AT A DISCOUNT OR A PREMIUM. If the average effective market interest rate on bonds of any particular grade exceeds the contract interest rate of bonds of the same grade being issued, investors will offer less than the face value of the bonds in order to make up the difference between the rates. The difference between the issue price and the face value, which the investors will receive at maturity, plus receipts of the semiannual interest, will give them a return on their investments approximating the yield of similar amounts invested at the prevailing market interest rate. By the same token, if the stated interest rate is more favorable than the current market rate, investors will tend to offer more than the face value because they know that the premium paid will, in effect, be returned to them to the extent that the periodic interest payments exceed the amount that they would otherwise receive on investments made at the current market rate.

Two examples are presented to emphasize the reasons for bonds selling at a premium or discount. First, assume that the Strong Company has an AAA financial rating and is planning to issue debenture bonds. Assume also that all the AAA debenture bonds on the market have an effective average market interest rate of 4 percent. If the Strong Company issues debenture bonds with a 4-percent contract interest rate, it will receive the face value of the bonds; if it issues bonds with a 5-percent contract interest rate, it will receive an amount in excess of the face value; but even with its excellent credit rating, if it issues bonds with a 3 percent contract rate, it will receive an amount less than the face value.

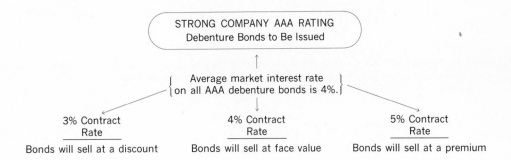

The second example will help to show that the financial condition of a company is not the only determinant of the issue price of the company's bonds. Assume that the Weak Company, with a BB financial rating, intends to issue first mortgage bonds. Further assume that the average effective market interest rate on BB first mortgage bonds is 6 percent. If the Weak Company issues its bonds with a 6 percent contract interest rate, it will receive the face value of the bonds. Even with its relatively poor credit rating, if it issues bonds with a 7 percent contract interest rate, it will receive an amount in excess of the face value; but if it issues bonds with a 5 percent contract interest rate, it will receive an amount less than the face value.

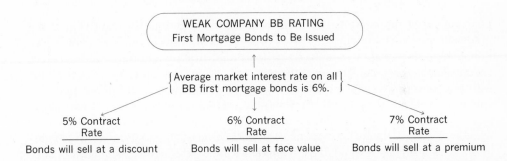

The exact price that an investor must pay for the bonds to yield a given effective rate can be determined by a compound interest computation, or by reference to a *bond yield table*. To illustrate the compound interest computation, assume that a 10-year (20 semiannual periods), 6%, $1,000 bond with interest paid semiannually is to yield 4 percent (or 2% every six months). The issue price is calculated as shown:

Present value of $1,000 for 20 periods at 2%:	
$1,000 × 0.672971	$ 672.97
Add present value of 20 interest payments of $30 each at 2%:	
$30 × 16.351433	490.54
Total price to yield 4%	$1,163.51

For a discussion of the principles of compound interest used in this example, see Chapter 23.

ACCOUNTING FOR BONDS ISSUED AT A PREMIUM. Assume that on July 1, 1969, the Hunt Corporation is authorized to issue 5% first mortgage bonds with a face value of $300,000 and a maturity date of June 30, 1984. Interest is paid semiannually on June 30 and December 31. All the bonds are issued on July 1, 1969, at 103; that is, at 103 percent of their face value; and the following entry is made:

```
1969
July  1   Cash                                       309,000
              First Mortgage Bonds Payable                        300,000
              Premium on Bonds Payable                              9,000
                  To record the issuance of 5% first mortgage
                  bonds due June 30, 1984.
```

A statement of financial position prepared on July 1, 1969, would show Bonds Payable and Premium on Bonds Payable as follows:

```
Long-Term Liabilities
  5% First Mortgage Bonds Payable, due June 30, 1984     $300,000
  Premium on Bonds Payable                                  9,000
     Total Long-Term Liabilities                                     $309,000
```

The assets pledged as security for the bonds payable would be disclosed in the following footnote:

> Land and buildings costing $600,000 are pledged as security for the bonds payable.

This method of disclosure is consistent with the concept that the right side of the statement of financial position describes the sources of business funds. Of course, the Premium account will be reduced by periodic amortization and thus will be smaller and smaller on each subsequent statement; but, again, this procedure is consistent with the concept that when bonds are issued at a premium, each interest payment contains, in effect, a payment of the interest earned on the investment and also a partial return of the amount borrowed from the investor. If part of the $309,000 borrowed is repaid, a statement of financial position prepared at a later date would naturally show a smaller amount. The footnote describing the assets pledged as security for the long-term debt is a disclosure of important information that may influence the decision of an investor to buy the company's bonds or not.

The amount received from the issuance of the bonds is $9,000 greater than the amount that must be repaid at maturity. This amount is not a gain, for it is illogical to assume that revenue can result directly from the borrowing process. The premium arose because the contract rate of interest on the bonds issued was higher than the prevailing market rate on similar grade bonds; therefore, it is sound accounting practice to allocate part of the Premium on Bonds Payable to each period as a reduction of the periodic bond interest expense. The straight-line method of allocation is most commonly used. In summary, the total bond interest expense over the life of a bond issue is equal to the total amount of cash paid in interest minus the amount of the premium.

The bond interest expense of the Hunt Corporation is recorded on December 31, 1969, as follows:

1969			
Dec. 31	Bond Interest Expense	7,200	
	Premium on Bonds Payable	300	
	Cash		7,500
	To record the semiannual bond interest payment and amortization; the amount of the amortization is: $\frac{1}{2} \times \frac{1}{15} \times \$9,000 = \$300$		

If the \$9,000 premium on the bonds payable represents a reduction in interest over the entire 15-year life of the bonds, it is evident that the reduction in interest for the six months ended December 31, 1969, is \$9,000 divided by 30 semiannual periods (calculated as $\frac{1}{2} \times \frac{1}{15} \times \$9,000$ in the journal entry), or \$300.

This compound entry emphasizes that the \$7,500 constitutes the payment of effective bond interest expense of \$7,200 and a partial return of the amount borrowed, the \$300 amortized. (It is suggested for the problems in this text that premiums or discounts on bonds payable be amortized each time the bond interest expense is recorded to emphasize that this amortization is an adjustment of the bond interest expense.)

Even though the compound entry is acceptable, two separate entries are generally made to record the payment of the semiannual bond interest and the semiannual amortization of the premium, as shown:

1969			
Dec. 31	Bond Interest Expense	7,500	
	Cash		7,500
	To record the semiannual bond interest payment.		
31	Premium on Bonds Payable	300	
	Bond Interest Expense		300
	To record the semiannual amortization of the premium on bonds payable: $\frac{1}{2} \times \frac{1}{15} \times \$9,000 = \$300$		

When the debit of \$7,500 and the credit of \$300 to Bond Interest Expense are combined, the net expense is \$7,200, the amount of the effective interest for six months. The validity of the \$7,200 semiannual bond interest figure can be established as follows:

Cash payments	
Face value of bonds at maturity	\$300,000
Total interest—5% × 15 yrs. × \$300,000	225,000
Total cash payments	\$525,000
Cash receipts	
Bonds with face value of \$300,000 issued at 103	309,000
Net interest expense for 15 years	\$216,000
Net semiannual interest expense	
$\dfrac{\$216,000}{30 \text{ semiannual periods}}$	\$ 7,200

A formula for the approximation of effective interest rate (i) on bonds issued at a premium can be stated as follows:

$$i = 1 \div \left(F + \frac{P}{2} \right), \text{ where}$$

1 = Annual absolute interest, adjusted for amortization of premium
F = Face value of bonds
P = Total premium

The effective interest rate on the Hunt Corporation bonds is approximately 4.73 percent $\left[\$14{,}400 \div \left(\$300{,}000 + \frac{\$9{,}000}{2} \right) \right]$; that is, the absolute effective amount of annual interest divided by the average carrying value (face value plus unamortized premium) of the bonds issued. Exact effective rates may be determined readily from bond yield tables. The effective interest rate computation emphasizes the fact that the premium on the bonds results in a downward adjustment of the 5 percent contract rate to the effective rate.

Assume that the 5-percent first mortgage bonds payable are retired on June 30, 1984. After the first two of the following entries—the last semiannual interest payment and last semiannual amortization of the Premium on Bonds Payable account— are made, the Premium on Bonds Payable account has a zero balance. The third entry, recording the retirement of the bonds at maturity, is similar to the one that records the retirement of the Grogan Company bonds in the first bond example, as shown:

1984			
June 30	Bond Interest Expense	7,500	
	Cash		7,500
	To record the last semiannual interest payment on the 5% bonds payable.		
30	Premium on Bonds Payable	300	
	Bond Interest Expense		300
	To record the semiannual amortization of bond premium.		
30	First Mortgage Bonds Payable	300,000	
	Cash		300,000
	To record the retirement of the 5% bonds payable at maturity.		

ACCOUNTING FOR BONDS ISSUED AT A DISCOUNT. Assume that on July 1, 1969, the Ironson Company is authorized to issue 4% debenture bonds with a face value of $400,000 and a maturity date of June 30, 1979. Again, assume that interest is paid semiannually on June 30 and December 31. All the bonds are issued on July 1, 1969, at 97. The discount is due to the influence of the prevailing market interest rate on similar grades of debenture bonds. In the case of the Ironson Company's debenture bonds, their contract interest rate is lower than the prevailing market rate on a similar grade of securities. The issuance of these bonds may be recorded as follows:

```
1969
July  1  Cash                                              388,000
         Discount on Bonds Payable                          12,000
             Debenture Bonds Payable                                    400,000
                 To record the issuance of 4% debenture
                 bonds due June 30, 1979.
```

A statement of financial position prepared on July 1, 1969, would disclose the Bonds Payable and Discount on Bonds Payable as follows:

```
Long-Term Liabilities:
  4% Debenture Bonds Payable, due June 30, 1979          $400,000
  Deduct Discount on Bonds Payable                         12,000
      Total Long-Term Liabilities                                     $388,000
```

Note the similarity of this method to the disclosure of a premium on bonds payable.

The following compound entry records the first semiannual interest payment by the Ironson Company and semiannual amortization of the Discount on Bonds Payable account.

```
1969
Dec. 31  Bond Interest Expense                              8,600
             Cash                                                        8,000
             Discount on Bonds Payable                                    600
                 To record semiannual bond interest payment and
                 amortization; the amount of amortization is:
                 ½ × ⅒ × $12,000 = $600
```

This entry indicates that the effective semiannual interest expense is $8,600, not $8,000. Assuming that the straight-line method of amortization is used, the effective interest is equal to the cash interest payment plus a pro rata share of the discount, which is, in effect, a part of the total interest cost over the entire life of the bonds. This accounting procedure, therefore, recognizes the reason for the discount on the bonds: that the contract rate of interest was lower than the prevailing market interest rate on similar grades of securities.

Instead of a compound entry, *two* journal entries may be made as follows:

```
1969
Dec. 31  Bond Interest Expense                              8,000
             Cash                                                        8,000
                 To record the semiannual bond interest
                 payment on the 4% bonds.

     31  Bond Interest Expense                               600
             Discount on Bonds Payable                                    600
                 To record the semiannual amortization
                 of discount on bonds payable.
```

The two debits to Bond Interest Expense total $8,600, the amount of the effective interest expense for the six months ended December 31, 1969. The proof of this semiannual bond interest expense can be established as follows:

Cash payments
  Face value of bonds at maturity $400,000
  Total interest—4% × 10 yrs. × $400,000   160,000
    Total cash payments $560,000

Cash receipts
  Bonds with face value of $400,000 issued at 97 $388,000
  Net interest expense for 10 years $172,000

Net semiannual interest expense
$$\frac{\$172,000}{20 \text{ semiannual periods}}$$ $ 8,600

A formula for the approximation of effective interest rate (i) on bonds issued at a discount can be stated as follows:

$$i = I \div \left(F - \frac{D}{2}\right), \text{ where}$$

I = annual absolute interest, adjusted for amortization of discount
F = face value of bonds
D = total discount

The effective interest rate is approximately 4.37 percent $\left[\$17,200 \div \left(\$400,000 - \frac{\$12,000}{2}\right)\right]$. The bond discount results in an upward adjustment of the 4-percent contract rate to its effective yield rate of 4.37 percent.

On June 30, 1979, the 4% debenture bonds payable are retired. After the first two of the following entries—the last semiannual interest payment and the last semiannual amortization of the Discount on Bonds Payable account—are made, the Discount on Bonds Payable account has a zero balance. The third entry records the retirement of the bonds at maturity.

1979
June 30 Bond Interest Expense   8,000
           Cash   8,000
             To record the last semiannual interest
             payment on the 4% bonds payable.

      30 Bond Interest Expense   600
           Discount on Bonds Payable   600
             To record the final amortization of
             bond discount.

      30 Debenture Bonds Payable   400,000
           Cash   400,000
             To record the retirement of the 4%
             bonds payable at maturity.

AMORTIZATION AND END-OF-PERIOD ADJUSTMENTS. The preceding examples emphasized the basic accounting procedures and the reasons for amortizing bond premiums and discounts. A more complex problem involving the issuance of bonds between interest dates, bond premium amortization, and end-of-year adjustments is presented in the following paragraphs.

Bonds may be authorized by the stockholders but not issued for several months or even years because market conditions are not favorable. Some of the bonds may be issued and the rest held until a specific need for the additional funds arises. Often the time needed for clerical work delays issuance past an interest date. The interest on bonds issued between interest dates will have accrued from the last interest date to the date of issuance. Since the bonds carry an inherent promise to pay not only the face value at maturity but six months' interest at each interest date, it is customary in these cases for the investor to pay the issue price of the bonds plus an amount equal to the accrued interest. In turn, the first interest payment will be for one full interest period—six months' interest—thereby returning to the purchaser the accrued interest that he paid plus the interest earned from the date of purchase to the current interest date.

Assume that on October 1, 1967, the Johnson Company is authorized to issue 6% debenture bonds with a face value of $1,000,000 and a maturity date of October 1, 1977. The semiannual interest dates are April 1 and October 1. The bonds are held until June 1, 1969, when bonds with a face value of $400,000 are floated at 105 plus accrued interest. The amount of cash that the Johnson Company receives is $424,000: $420,000 for the bonds plus $4,000 for accrued interest. Note that the promise to pay six months' interest is not retroactive beyond April 1, 1969, the interest date preceding the date of issuance. On October 1, 1969, the purchaser of the bonds receives an interest payment of $12,000, although the interest on $400,000 at 6 percent from June 1 to October 1 is only $8,000. The payment includes a return of the $4,000 that the investor paid for accrued interest on June 1, as illustrated in Figure 15-1.

Figure 15-1.
Accumulation of Interest

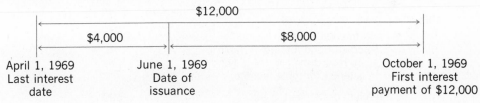

The Johnson Company records the bond issuance as shown:

```
1969
June   1   Cash                                    424,000
               Debenture Bonds Payable                      400,000
               Premium on Bonds Payable                      20,000
               Accrued Bond Interest Payable                  4,000
                   To record the issuance of bonds
                   at 105 plus accrued interest.
```

The accrued interest is credited to a current liability account since it must be repaid on the next interest date.

The entries to record the payment of semiannual interest and the amortization of bond premium are shown:

```
1969
Oct.  1   Bond Interest Expense                        8,000
          Accrued Bond Interest Payable                4,000
              Cash                                                    12,000
                  To record the payment of semiannual
                  interest on 6% bonds payable.

      1   Premium on Bonds Payable                       800
              Bond Interest Expense                                     800
                  To record the amortization of the bond
                  premium for 4 months:
                      $20,000 ÷ 100 mos. × 4 = $800
```

The entry for the interest payment reflects the figures shown in Figure 15-1; that is, the semiannual cash payment includes a return of $4,000 for the accrued interest that was sold to the investor plus $8,000 for interest actually earned by the investor for the four months' use of his money.

The amortization covers only the period from the date of issuance to the maturity date. The date of authorization and even the preceding interest date are not relevant to the start of the amortization period. For the bonds of the Johnson Company, the amortization periods begin on June 1, 1969, and end on October 1, 1977, a total of 100 months. The amount of bond premium to be amortized each month is $200 ($20,000 ÷ 100 mos.); the amount for four months is $800 ($200 × 4).

Assuming that the Johnson Company closes its books on a calendar-year basis, the following adjusting entries are made on December 31, 1969:

```
1969
Dec. 31   Bond Interest Expense                        6,000
              Accrued Bond Interest Payable                          6,000
                  To record the accrual of bond
                  interest for three months.

      31  Premium on Bonds Payable                       600
              Bond Interest Expense                                    600
                  To record the amortization of bond
                  premium for three months:
                      3 × $200 = $600
```

The effect of the end-of-year adjustments is that the Bond Interest Expense account reflects the correct interest expense ($12,600) incurred for the seven months during which the bonds were outstanding (June 1 to December 31). The Bond Interest Expense account is closed to Revenue and Expense Summary. The Accrued Bond Interest Payable account is shown as a current liability on the statement of financial position and remains on the books until the next regular interest date.

On April 1, 1970, the next regular interest date, the following entries are made to record the payment of interest and the amortization of the bond premium:

1970			
Apr. 1	Bond Interest Expense	6,000	
	Accrued Bond Interest Payable	6,000	
	Cash		12,000
	To record the payment of semiannual bond interest.		
1	Premium on Bonds Payable	600	
	Bond Interest Expense		600
	To record the amortization of bond premium for three months.		

Note that only three months' amortization of the bond premium is recorded. This coincides with the three months' bond interest expense incurred and recorded up to April 1, 1970.

Underwriting Bond Issues

Brokers, banks, or investment syndicates often *underwrite* the flotation of a bond issue, just as in the issuance of capital stock. The entire authorized bond issue of a corporation may be turned over to the *underwriter* at a specified price, say 103; the underwriter then offers the bonds to the public at a slightly higher market price, say 104. This arrangement ensures that the issuing corporation will receive the full specified amount of funds on a given date. The amount of premium or discount is based on the net amount that the issuing corporation receives from the underwriter, not on the market price paid by the investors for the bonds.

Consider, for example, the case of a company that plans to issue 6% bonds with a face value of $1,000,000. The company turns the bonds over to the underwriter at 103, for a total price of $1,030,000. The underwriter, according to the underwriting agreement, plans to sell the bonds at 104. Even though the investors pay $1,040,000 for the bonds, the issuing company receives only $1,030,000 and hence considers that the bonds are issued at a premium of $30,000.

Retirement and Refunding of Bonds Payable

The borrowing company may retire its outstanding bonds at the maturity date by paying the contract face value in cash. Even if the bonds were originally issued at a premium or discount, the entry to record the retirement is a debit to Bonds Payable and a credit to Cash for the face value. Serial bonds are retired in serial installments. Assume, for example, a $500,000, 10-year serial bond issue, $50,000 to be retired at face value at the end of each year. The annual retirement entry is again a debit to Bonds Payable and a credit to Cash for $50,000. The retirement schedule is established by the issuing corporation and may provide for several retirement dates beginning a fixed number of years after the date of issue.

Other methods of retiring bonds include (1) the retirement of all or part of a bond issue by call, or purchase on the open market before the bonds are actually due, (2) the retirement of bonds by *refunding*, or refinancing by issuing new bonds on new terms, (3) the conversion of bonds payable into capital stock, and (4) the retirement of bonds with sinking fund assets and the attendant problem of accumulating the sinking fund.

RETIREMENT OF BONDS BEFORE MATURITY. A corporation that has issued bonds may find itself with more cash than it expects to need for operations, permitting it to retire all or part of its outstanding bonded indebtedness prior to maturity date. Management may decide to retire the bonds immediately if the cash is available, if there appears to be no better alternative use now or in the future for the excess cash, and if they wish to decrease the fixed charges for the bond interest. For bonds to be retired by a corporation before maturity, they must contain a *call provision*, permitting the issuing corporation to redeem the bonds by paying a specified price, usually slightly above face value; or if the bonds are not callable, the issuing company may redeem them before the maturity date by purchasing them on the open market. Retirement of bonds below the carrying value results in a gain; a loss is incurred if the purchase price exceeds the carrying value.

For example, assume that the Marion Company has bonds outstanding with a face value of $500,000, callable at 102 on any interest date. Interest is payable on January 1 and July 1. Assume that after the July 1, 1969 entries for the bond interest payment and the amortization of the bond premium have been made, there is an unamortized premium balance of $4,200. The Company exercises the call provision and records the retirement of all the bonds as shown:

1969				
July	1	Bonds Payable	500,000	
		Premium on Bonds Payable	4,200	
		Loss on Retirement of Bonds Payable	5,800	
		Cash		510,000
		To record the retirement of the entire bond issue by call at 102.		

To illustrate a gain on a retirement by purchase on the open market, assume that the Nelson Company has a 5% bond issue outstanding with a face value of $1,000,000. Interest is paid semiannually on April 1 and October 1. The bonds had been issued on April 1, 1959, at 98 and had a maturity date of April 1, 1979. The unamortized Discount on Bonds Payable account balance at April 1, 1969, after the bond discount amortization entry is made, is $10,000. On September 1, 1969, the Company retires bonds with a face value of $600,000 by purchase on the open market at 97 plus accrued interest. The following sequence of entries is suggested to record the retirement. To insure that only the bond discount applicable to the bonds being retired is amortized, the accrued bond interest and the accompanying bond discount amortization should be placed on the books first. The retirement of the bonds is recorded in a separate entry. The amount of accrued interest payable on 5% bonds with a face value of $600,000 for five months is $12,500. The amount of the applicable bond discount amortization is $250, computed as follows:

Annual amortization on all bonds
$$\frac{\$20,000 \text{ (original discount)}}{20 \text{ (life in years)}} \qquad \underline{\underline{\$1,000}}$$

Annual amortization on $600,000 of bonds
$$60\% \times \$1,000 \qquad \underline{\underline{\$\ \ 600}}$$

Five months' amortization on $600,000 of bonds
$600 × ⁵/₁₂ $ 250

The entries to record the accrued bond interest payable of $12,500 and the amortization of bond discount of $250 are shown:

1969
Sept. 1 Bond Interest Expense   12,500
            Accrued Bond Interest Payable   12,500
               To record the accrued interest applicable to
               bonds with a face value of $600,000 being
               retired.

      1 Bond Interest Expense   250
            Discount on Bonds Payable   250
               To record the amortization of bond discount
               on bonds being retired.

Before the bond retirement entry can be made, it is necessary to compute the carrying value of the bonds being retired—the face value less the applicable unamortized bond discount—and to determine any gain or loss on the retirement. The carrying value on April 1, 1969, is found as shown:

Total bonds outstanding	$1,000,000
Deduct unamortized discount	10,000
Carrying value of all bonds	$ 990,000
Carrying value of $600,000 of bonds (60% × $990,000)	$ 594,000

This figure can be determined by a different computation:

Face value of bonds on April 1, 1969	$600,000
Deduct unamortized discount (60% × $10,000)	6,000
Carrying value of bonds at April 1, 1969	$594,000

The carrying value of the bonds as of September 1, 1969, is calculated next:

Face value	$600,000
Deduct unamortized discount ($6,000 − $250)	5,750
Carrying value at September 1, 1969	$594,250

The following calculation shows the gain on the retirement of the bonds:

Carrying value at September 1, 1969	$594,250
Deduct retirement price (97% × $600,000)	582,000
Gain on retirement of bonds payable	$ 12,250

The total cash paid out in the retirement transaction is:

Bonds at 97	$582,000
Accrued interest for five months	12,500
Total cash paid out	$594,500

The entry to record this information is as follows:

1969

Sept.	1	Bonds Payable	600,000	
		Accrued Bond Interest Payable	12,500	
		Cash		594,500
		Discount on Bonds Payable		5,750
		Gain on Retirement of Bonds Payable		12,250
		To record the retirement of bonds		
		by purchase on the open market		
		at 97 plus accrued interest.		

Gains and losses on the retirement of bonds payable are classified in the income statement under Other Revenue or Other Expense.

REFUNDING. Bonds also may be retired by refunding, or refinancing by issuing new bonds on new terms. The proceeds from the new issue are specifically designated for the retirement of the old bond issue. The old bondholders may be given the option of exchanging their bonds for the new bonds at the call price. This procedure helps reduce the refinancing costs of the issuing corporation. A refunding decision may be warranted if it is possible to redeem bonds with a relatively high interest rate and substitute bonds with a lower interest rate. Other reasons for refunding are to replace an issue about to mature with a new issue, thus extending the maturity date, or to retire outstanding bonds containing such stringent restrictive provisions as a closed mortgage lien or a requirement that funds be accumulated to retire the bonds.

From a theoretical standpoint, there is nothing new in the accounting procedure for refunding. The retirement should be recorded in entries similar to those described in the preceding section. Accounting for the new issue is the same as described earlier in this chapter.

CONVERSION OF BONDS INTO COMMON STOCK. To make certain bonds more attractive to investors, and thus to increase their marketability, the bond agreement may give investors the option of exchanging bonds on a given interest date, or dates, for a certain number of shares of stock, usually common, of the issuing company. These securities, referred to as convertible bonds, have the advantage of offering the investor an initial fixed return on his investment combined with an opportunity to share in profitable operations of the issuing company by later conversion of the bonds to stock. The terms and conditions for conversion are designated in the bond indenture. Conversion is at the option of the bondholder, so that if earnings are unfavorable he does not need to exercise the conversion privilege and may retain the fixed return and greater security of the bonds. The conversion of bonds into stock changes the legal and accounting status of the security holder from creditor to owner.

Assume, for example, that the Avon Corporation has bonds outstanding on July 1, 1969, of $300,000, with an unamortized discount of $6,000. Interest dates are January 1 and July 1, and the bonds are convertible at the rate of a $1,000 bond for nine shares of the Avon Corporation's $100 par value common stock on any interest date after January 1, 1969. After the July 1, 1969, interest payment had been made and the discount amortization had been recorded, bonds with a face value of $100,000 are surrendered for conversion by bondholders because, let us assume, the market price of the common stock that would be received in exchange is higher than the market price of the bonds held. The entry to record these facts is shown:

```
1969
July  1   Bonds Payable                              100,000
              Discount on Bonds Payable                          2,000
              Common Stock                                      90,000
              Premium on Common Stock                            8,000
              To record the conversion
              of 100 bonds into 900
              shares of common stock.
                Face value of bonds
                  converted               $100,000
                Unamortized discount—
                  ⅓ × $6,000                 2,000
                Carrying value at July 1   $ 98,000
                Par value of common
                  stock issued:
                  900 shares × $100         90,000
                Premium on common
                  stock                    $  8,000
```

In this illustration, the carrying value identified with the converted bonds ($98,000) is transferred to contributed capital, which includes Common Stock and Premium on Common Stock. It is as if the Avon Corporation had sold 900 shares of common stock for $98,000 and used the proceeds to redeem the bonds.

BOND SINKING FUND. The borrowing corporation may agree in the bond indenture to accumulate funds to retire the bonds at maturity. Periodic cash payments are made to a sinking fund trustee, usually a bank or a trust company. These payments are ordinarily invested in revenue-producing securities. When the bonds mature, the sinking fund trustee sells the securities, and the proceeds are used to pay the bondholders. In some instances the corporation itself may act as trustee, thereby retaining control over the activities of the sinking fund.

To illustrate the operation of a simple sinking fund managed by a trustee, assume that on the authorization date, January 1, 1969, Wells, Inc., issues 10-year sinking fund bonds with a face value of $500,000. The bond indenture provides that at the end of each year a deposit of $50,000—reduced by any net earnings of the funds from its investments—be made to the trustee. The entry to record the initial deposit with the trustee is shown:

```
1969
Dec. 31   Bond Sinking Fund                          50,000
              Cash                                              50,000
              To record the initial sinking fund
              deposit with the trustee.
```

The bond sinking fund account is a controlling account. The trustee must invest all the available cash in the fund in revenue-producing securities. As a practical matter, it would not always be possible for the trustee to invest odd amounts of cash or to purchase securities immediately upon the receipt of cash. Hence, the bond sinking fund is composed of a number of individual items, such as cash, securities, and accrued interest receivable. It is unnecessary for Wells, Inc., to maintain a separate general ledger account for each asset contained in the bond sinking fund.

If, at the end of the second year, the trustee reports net earnings of $1,500 from investments in bonds, the following entries record the second deposit:

1970

Dec. 31	Bond Sinking Fund	1,500	
	Interest Earned		1,500
	To record net earnings of the bond sinking		
	fund per report of the trustee.		
31	Bond Sinking Fund	48,500	
	Cash		48,500
	To record the second sinking fund deposit		
	with the trustee; the amount is $50,000		
	less earnings of $1,500, or $48,500.		

The following entry is made to record the retirement of the bonds at maturity by the payment of assets in the bond sinking fund:

1979

Jan. 1	Sinking Fund Bonds Payable	500,000	
	Bond Sinking Fund		500,000
	To record the retirement of bonds		
	by the trustee.		

The Bond Sinking Fund account is classified in the Assets section as a long-term investment on each statement of financial position except the one prepared at the end of the year preceding the date of the retirement of the bonds. On this statement, the amount in the bond sinking fund should be shown as a current asset and Sinking Fund Bonds Payable should be disclosed as a current liability.

Another method of accumulating a sinking fund provides for a fixed amount to be deposited periodically with the trustee. It is assumed that these deposits, accumulating at compound interest, will equal the principal sum needed to retire the debt at maturity. If, at the retirement date, the accumulated funds exceed the required amount, the excess is returned by the trustee to the corporation; a shortage, on the other hand, requires an additional deficiency payment from the corporation.

RESTRICTION ON RETAINED EARNINGS FOR BOND REDEMPTION. In addition to the requirement for sinking fund deposits, the bond indenture may require a restriction on retained earnings up to the amount in the sinking fund. The bondholders thus are provided with twofold protection: the sinking fund ensures the availability of adequate cash for the redemption of the bonds, and the restriction on retained earnings for bond redemption reduces the amount available for distribution of dividends to the stockholders. This restriction enhances the company's working capital position and its ability to meet its regular needs as well as its requirements for bond interest and bond sinking fund payments. An improved working capital position also is advantageous in enabling the company to meet its regular operational cash requirements and to maintain a favorable credit standing.

To illustrate, assume that the bond indenture of Wells, Inc., provides for a restriction of retained earnings. The entry at the end of each year is:

Dec. 31	Retained Earnings	50,000	
	Retained Earnings–Restricted for Bond Redemption		50,000
	To record the restriction of retained earnings equal to the annual increase in the bond sinking fund.		

Retained Earnings–Restricted for Bond Redemption is shown in the Stockholders' Equity section of the statement of financial position under Retained Earnings. The restriction reduces the amount of retained earnings available for dividends. Earnings in excess of the annual restriction are, of course, available for dividends. There is not necessarily a direct relationship between the bond sinking fund and the restriction on retained earnings for bond redemption. The provisions of the bond indenture may require the creation of: (1) a bond sinking fund, (2) a restriction on retained earnings until the bonds are redeemed, or (3) both a bond sinking fund and a restriction on retained earnings. When the bonds are redeemed at maturity, the contractual restriction on retained earnings is removed. The journal entry to record the removal of the restriction is:

1979			
Jan. 1	Retained Earnings–Restricted for Bond Redemption	500,000	
	Retained Earnings		500,000
	To remove the restriction on retained earnings on retirement of the bonds.		

The unrestricted Retained Earnings account now has been increased by an amount equal to the maturity value of the bonds. The equivalent amount in funds may not be available for distribution to the stockholders because it has been permanently committed to the operations of the business in the form of plant expansion or debt retirement. In essence, the stockholders have been contributing capital to the corporation through earnings retained in the business that might otherwise have been distributed as dividends. Formal recognition of this fact is often made in the form of a stock dividend. That is, the increase in retained earnings resulting from the removal of the bond redemption restriction is capitalized permanently by issuing additional shares of stock to the stockholders.

The entry to record the stock dividend is:

1979			
Jan. 1	Retained Earnings	500,000	
	Common Stock		500,000
	To record the declaration and issuance of a stock dividend equal in amount to retained earnings previously restricted for bond redemption.		

OTHER LONG-TERM LIABILITIES

Among long-term liabilities found on the statement of financial position are those arising from the use of long-term financing devices such as secured or unsecured long-term notes and continuing obligations incurred under employee profit-sharing and pension plans and similar forms. Brief comments are made about each of these.

Instead of issuing bonds, a corporation may borrow from financial institutions, such as banks or insurance companies. A group of banks or insurance companies may jointly finance the transaction. By this arrangement, the corporation eliminates the need for dealing with many bondholders. The corporation issues long-term notes to the lending institutions. Such notes may also provide for a sinking fund and for a restriction on retained earnings. Notes are usually issued at face value; hence the accounting for these items is similar to that for short-term notes. They may be for a short period with optional renewal provisions. Renewable notes are often used when the bond interest rate is unfavorable.

Long-term financing may involve the pledging of specific assets. A corporation may, for example, acquire funds for plant expansion or other purposes by placing a mortgage on its plant and equipment. This creates a long-term liability—Mortgage Payable. Sometimes the lending institution advances funds for the construction of the plant and upon completion takes a mortgage on the newly constructed plant. This is known as a Construction Mortgage Payable. The title of the liability account should clearly indicate the nature and type of instrument used.

Accounting for liabilities under pension contracts and similar forms is rather complex and specialized; therefore, only very brief comments are made in this text. The accounting for employees' pension costs and the related liability depends upon whether the employees' rights in such plans are forfeitable or nonforfeitable. Under the forfeitable plans, a separate trust must be established; hence the company's long-term liability is limited to the cumulative amount of each year's contribution to the pension or profit-sharing trust. Under the nonforfeitable plan, the company simply accrues the liability on the books and records the offsetting expense. The amounts involved are usually determined by the use of compound actuarial tables.

SUMMARY

Sources of capital for a corporation include investments by owners, retention of corporate earnings, and investments by creditors. One of the primary sources of long-term capital from creditors arises through the issuance of bonds.

A bond is a written promise under the corporate seal to pay a specific sum of money on a specified or determinable future date to the order of a person named in the certificate or to the bearer. Registered bonds are registered in the name of the owner and thus require endorsement of the certificate to transfer ownership. If bonds are registered as to principal and interest, interest checks are mailed only to bondholders of record; however, if bonds are registered as to principal only (coupon bonds), interest coupons are detached from the certificate and presented by the holder to a designated bank for payment. Bearer bonds are not registered as to principal or interest and title is passed by delivery only. If specific corporate property is pledged as security for bonds, the bonds are said to be secured. Bonds that are backed by only the general credit of the corporation are referred to as unsecured bonds or debentures.

Although the decision whether to raise needed funds through the issuance of capital stock or bonds is a difficult one in which many factors must be considered, often the issuance of bonds is desirable for the following reasons: (1) bonds offer sources of funds that cannot be obtained through the issuance of capital stock because of regulations and legal restrictions; (2) if the funds resulting from the issuance of bonds can be used to yield a return that is higher than the interest rate on the bonds, the marginal earnings will accrue to the stockholders; (3) income taxes are one of the primary costs of operating a business, and bond interest, unlike dividends, may be deducted as an expense for income tax purposes; (4) bonds aid in offsetting a loss due to shrinkage in the purchasing power of funds invested in assets; and (5) the issuance of stock is more likely to result in a loss of present control over the corporation's affairs.

The issue price of bonds is primarily determined by the stated interest rate and the prevailing interest rate on bonds of the same grade. If the stated interest rate is higher than the market rate, the bonds will sell at a premium; if it is lower, the bonds will sell at a discount. The issuance of bonds requires a credit to Bonds Payable for the face value of the bonds. If bonds are issued for an amount higher than the face value, the excess is credited to Premium on Bonds Payable; if they are issued for an amount less than the face value, the deficiency is debited to Discount on Bonds Payable. If the bonds are issued at face value and one of the semiannual interest payments falls on the last day of the accounting period, the entire interest payment is debited to Bond Interest Expense. The normal rules for accruing interest apply if the end of the accounting period does not coincide with an interest date. If bonds are issued at a premium or a discount, the charge to Bond Interest Expense is based on the effective interest cost of the bonds; that is, the total interest cost of the bonds over their life is the total of the cash interest payments minus the amount of the premium or plus the amount of the discount. Therefore, the semiannual interest expense is the cash payment minus a proportion of the premium or plus a proportion of the discount. The proportion of premium or discount entering into the bond interest expense of a period is determined by amortizing the premium or discount over the period, beginning with the date of issuance of the bonds and ending with the date of retirement. If interest expense is accrued at the end of an accounting period, the amortization of the premium or discount element for a similar time period must also be recorded. If bonds are issued between interest dates, the purchaser pays the interest accrued to the date of issuance and the company pays interest at the stated rate to the purchaser on the next interest date, thereby returning to the purchaser the accumulated interest that he paid to the corporation. If bonds are issued through an underwriter or other financial agency, the amount of premium or discount is based on the net amount that the issuing corporation receives from the underwriter and not on the market price paid by the investors.

If bonds are retired at maturity, the retirement is recorded by a debit to Bonds Payable and a credit to Cash. If bonds are retired before maturity on a date other than an interest date, the bond interest applicable to the bonds being retired must be accrued to the date of retirement. The difference between the carrying value and the retirement price of the bonds is recognized as a gain or a loss and the balances of the Accrued Bond Interest Payable, Bonds Payable, and Premium or Discount on Bonds Payable accounts applicable to the bonds being retired are eliminated from the books in the retirement entry.

Convertible bonds contain a provision allowing the investor to exchange his bonds on a specific interest date or dates for a predetermined number of shares of stock, usually common, of the issuing company. To record the conversion of bonds to par value common stock, the amounts of the Bonds Payable and Premium or Discount accounts applicable to the bonds being converted are eliminated; the Common Stock account is credited for the par value of the shares issued, and the excess of the carrying value of the bonds over the par value of the stock is credited to Premium on Common Stock.

The bond indenture may require the corporation to accumulate a sinking fund over the life of the bonds to provide for the retirement of the bonds at maturity. Periodic payments are made to a sinking fund trustee, who invests the assets in securities. Bond Sinking Fund is disclosed as a long-term investment on the statement of financial position. The corporation may also agree to a restriction of retained earnings for the bond redemption, which reduces the amount of retained earnings available for dividend distribution. Although the restriction does not automatically provide money for the retirement of the bonds, it may increase the company's working capital position, thus making it more likely that there will be funds available for the retirement of the bonds. When the bonds are retired, the restriction is eliminated.

☐ **QUESTIONS**

Q15-1. In light of the definition of a current liability stated in this chapter, justify the classification of Unearned Magazine Subscriptions as a current liability.

Q15-2. (a) What is the difference between a stock certificate and a bond? (b) A bond and a promissory note?

Q15-3. Identify the following terms: (a) registered bonds; (b) bearer bonds; (c) secured bonds; (d) unsecured bonds; (e) serial bonds; (f) convertible bonds; (g) coupon bonds; (h) income bonds.

Q15-4. A corporation needs cash for the acquisition of plant and equipment. It is considering three alternative sources: additional common stock, 6% preferred stock, and 4% bonds. (a) What are some of the factors involved in this decision? (b) Will the decision affect the present common stockholders? Discuss.

Q15-5. (a) What are the general requirements for the approval of a bond issue? (b) Should the stockholders always approve a bond issue? Why?

Q15-6. (a) Why does the buyer of a bond purchased between interest dates pay the seller for accrued interest on the bond? (b) Is the accrued interest included in the stated purchase price of the bond?

Q15-7. (a) What is the difference to the issuing corporation between common stock issued at a premium and bonds issued at a premium? (b) Does revenue result from either?

Q15-8. Before its bonds mature, a corporation may retire them by: (a) paying cash; (b) refunding; or (c) conversion. Explain each of these methods.

Q15-**9.** On December 31, 1969, a corporation has serial bonds with a face value of $500,000 outstanding. These bonds mature annually in $100,000 amounts, beginning June 30, 1970. How will this be shown on the position statement as of (a) December 31, 1969, (b) December 31, 1970, and (c) December 31, 1971?

Q15-**10.** Why are bonds not always issued at the prevailing interest rate, thereby eliminating bond discount or bond premium?

☐ **EXERCISES**

E15-**1.** On the date of authorization, January 1, 1969, the White Corporation issued 10-year, 5% bonds with a face value of $600,000 at 100. Interest is payable each January 1 and July 1.

1. Record the issuance of the bonds.
2. Record the first interest payment.
3. Record the accrued interest expense on December 31, 1969.
4. Record the retirement of the bonds on January 1, 1979, by the payment of cash.

E15-**2.** On the date of authorization, January 1, 1969, the Jensen Corporation issued 20-year, 6% bonds with a face value of $500,000 at 102. Interest is payable each January 1 and July 1.

1. Record the issuance of the bonds.
2. Record the first interest payment and amortization of the premium.
3. Record the accrued interest expense and amortization of the premium on December 31, 1969.
4. Open a Bond Interest Expense account and post the transactions.
5. Prepare a schedule proving the interest cost for 1969.
6. Compute the approximate effective interest rate.

E15-**3.** On the date of authorization, January 1, 1969, the Dastor Corporation issued 10-year, 4% bonds with a face value of $200,000 at 97. Interest is payable each January 1 and July 1.

1. Record the issuance of the bonds.
2. Record the first interest payment and amortization of the discount.
3. Record the accrued interest expense and amortization of the discount on December 31, 1969.
4. Open a Bond Interest Expense account and post the transactions.
5. Prepare a schedule proving the interest cost for 1969.
6. Compute the approximate effective interest rate.

E15-**4.** On October 1, 1969, the Western Corporation issued 6% bonds with a face value of $800,000 at 103 plus accrued interest. The bonds mature on June 1, 1977, and interest is paid each June 1 and December 1. The amortization of premium is recorded each time Bond Interest Expense is recorded.

Prepare all the entries relating to the bond issue during 1969.

E15-**5.** On June 1, 1971, the Western Corporation (see Exercise E15-4) purchased its own bonds with a face value of $200,000 at 101 on the open market.

Assuming that the proper entries have been made on June 1, 1971, to record the payment of interest and related information, record the purchase and retirement of the bonds.

E15-**6.** On June 1, 1971, investors holding Western Corporation bonds (see Exercise E15-4) with a face value of $400,000 converted them into common stock, $100 par value, at a conversion rate of nine shares of common stock for each $1,000 bond.

Record the conversion on the books of the Western Corporation.

E15-**7.** On the authorization date, January 1, 1969, the Windham Corporation issued 10-year bonds with a face value of $500,000. Under the terms of the bond inden- ture, a sinking fund is to be maintained to provide for the retirement of the bonds at maturity. Deposits are to be made with a trustee at the end of each year in amounts that, when added to the sinking fund earnings, will total $50,000.

Record (a) the deposit with the trustee on December 31, 1969; (b) earnings of $2,180 during the second year; (c) the deposit with the trustee on December 31, 1970; and (d) the retirement of the bonds at maturity by the trustee.

E15-**8.** Assume that the bond indenture (see Exercise E15-7) requires a restriction on retained earnings equal to the amount of the sinking fund.

Record (a) the restriction at the end of 1969 and 1970 and (b) the removal of the restriction at the maturity date.

E15-**9.** In addition to 6% bonds with a face value of $400,000 outstanding, the total capi- talization of the Edwards Corporation at December 31, 1969, is:

6% Preferred Stock, Nonparticipating	$600,000
Common Stock	800,000
Retained Earnings	200,000

1. Prepare a schedule showing the distribution of net income of $140,000 before bond interest expense but after income taxes, and compute the rate of return on the investment of each of the equity groups—bondholders, preferred stock- holders, and common stockholders.
2. Prepare a similar schedule, assuming a distribution of $80,000.
3. Which rate of return reflects a favorable leverage position?

E15-**10.** On the date of authorization, January 1, 1969, the Fuller Company issued 20-year, 4% bonds. Interest is paid semiannually on January 1 and July 1. On July 1, 1969, the accountant for the Fuller Company prepared the following journal entry to record the payment of bond interest and the amortization of the discount:

1969

July 1	Bond Interest Expense	3,780	
	Cash		3,600
	Discount on Bonds Payable		180
	To record the bond interest expense for the preceding six months.		

From this information, reconstruct the journal entry that was made to record the issuance of the bonds. Show all your calculations.

☐ **DEMONSTRATION PROBLEMS**

DP15-**1.** (*Accounting for the issuance of bonds*) In each of the following cases, assume: (a) 6-percent bonds with a face value of $400,000; (b) date of authorization, Jan- uary 1, 1969; (c) interest payable each January 1 and July 1; (d) maturity date of bonds, January 1, 1979; and (e) year ends December 31.

	Case A	Case B	Case C	Case D
Date of issuance	Jan. 1, 1969	Jan. 1, 1969	Jan. 1, 1969	March 1, 1969
Issue price	100	102	97	101 plus accrued interest

Required: 1. Prepare all the journal entries for 1969 relating to each case.
2. For Cases B and C, prepare a schedule proving the interest cost for 1969.
3. For Cases B and C, calculate the approximate effective interest rate.

DP15–2. (*Retirement of bonds before maturity*) On April 1, 1969, the Rintab Company issued 6% bonds with a face value of $300,000 at 106 plus accrued interest. The bonds have a maturity date of August 1, 1977, and interest is paid each February 1 and August 1.

On December 1, 1970, the Rintab Company purchased its own bonds with a face value of $100,000 on the open market at 102 plus accrued interest.

Required: Assuming that the books of the Rintab Company are closed each December 31, prepare all the entries relevant to the bonds for the years 1969 and 1970.

DP15–3. (*Accounting for bond sinking fund*) On the date of authorization, January 1, 1969, the Funder Corporation issued four-year sinking fund bonds with a face value of $200,000 at 100. The sinking fund indenture requires an annual contribution at the end of each of the four years to provide for the retirement of the bonds at maturity. As an added protection, the terms of the bond indenture required that retained earnings be restricted in an annual amount equal to the total addition to the sinking fund. The Funder Corporation is to make a deposit to the Rex Bank, which has been named trustee of the sinking fund, of amounts that when added to the sinking fund earnings will total $50,000 each year. The Rex Bank guaranteed the Funder Corporation a return of 4 percent annually. The bank will credit the sinking fund account with this return each December 31.

Required: 1. Record the issuance of the sinking fund bonds.
2. Give all the entries for the four years to record the deposits to the sinking fund and the related restrictions on retained earnings.
3. Record the retirement of the sinking fund bonds by the trustee on the maturity date and the removal of the retained earnings restriction.

☐ **PROBLEMS**

P15–1. On the date of authorization, January 1, 1969, the Berry Corporation issued 6 percent, 20-year bonds with a face value of $1,000,000 at 100. Interest is payable each January 1 and July 1.

Required: 1. Record the issuance of the bonds.
2. Record the first interest payment.
3. Record the accrued interest payable on December 31, 1969.

4. State how the bonds payable should be shown on the statement of financial position, assuming that (a) the bonds are unsecured debenture bonds and (b) the bonds are secured by a first mortgage on land and buildings.

P15–2. On the date of authorization, March 1, 1969, the Powell Corporation issued 20-year, 6% bonds with a face value of $200,000 at 103. Interest is payable each March 1 and September 1.

Required: 1. Record the following transactions during 1969:
  a. The issuance of the bonds.
  b. The first interest payment and amortization of the premium.
  c. The accrual of interest on December 31, 1969, and amortization of the premium.
2. Calculate the approximate effective interest rate paid.
3. State how Bonds Payable and Premium on Bonds Payable should be shown on the statement of financial position prepared as of December 31, 1969, assuming that the bonds are unsecured debenture bonds.

P15–3. On the date of authorization, April 1, 1969, the Potter Company issued 10-year, 4½% bonds with a face value of $400,000 at 97. Interest is payable each April 1 and October 1.

Required: 1. Record the following transactions during 1969:
  a. The issuance of the bonds.
  b. The first interest payment and amortization of the discount.
  c. The accrual of interest on December 31, 1969, and amortization of the discount.
2. Calculate the approximate effective interest rate paid.
3. State how the bonds payable and discount on bonds payable should be shown on the statement of financial position as of December 31, 1969, assuming that the bonds are first mortgage bonds with land and buildings pledged as security.

P15–4. On April 1, 1969, the stockholders of the Natulus Corporation authorized the issuance of 10-year, 4% first mortgage bonds with a face value of $600,000. The bonds mature on April 1, 1979, and interest is payable each April 1 and October 1.

Required: Make journal entries to record the following transactions:

1969

June 1   Issued the bonds at 104 plus accrued interest.

Oct. 1   Paid the semiannual interest. (Assume that Premium on Bonds Payable is amortized each time Bond Interest Expense is recorded.)

Dec. 31   Accrued the bond interest.

31   Closed the Bond Interest Expense account.

1970

Apr. 1   Paid the semiannual interest.

Oct. 1   Paid the semiannual interest.

Dec. 31   Accrued the bond interest.

P15–**5.** On March 1, 1969, the authorization date, the Milkin Company issued 10-year, 3% convertible bonds with a face value of $500,000 at 101½. Interest is payable each March 1 and September 1. The Company closes its books on December 31. Bondholders are permitted to convert their bonds on any interest date after the fourth year from the date of issuance on the basis of a $1,000 bond for nine shares of $100 par value common stock. The following selected transactions and adjustments were made:

1969

Mar.   1   Issued all the bonds for cash.

Sept. 1   Paid the semiannual interest.

Dec. 31   Accrued the bond interest.

1970

Mar.   1   Paid the semiannual interest.

Sept. 1   Paid the semiannual interest.

Dec. 31   Accrued the bond interest.

1974

Mar.   1   Paid the semiannual interest.

Sept. 1   Paid the semiannual interest.

       1   Converted into common stock bonds with a face value of $200,000.

Dec. 31   Accrued the bond interest.

1975

Mar.   1   Paid the semiannual interest.

June   1   Purchased for retirement bonds with a face value of $50,000 on the open market at 100 plus accrued interest.

Sept. 1   Paid the semiannual interest.

Dec. 31   Accrued the bond interest.

1979

Mar.   1   Paid the semiannual interest.

       1   Paid the bonds outstanding at maturity.

Required: 1. Record the transactions. (Assume that the premium is amortized each time the bond interest expense is recorded.)
           2. Set up a Premium on Bonds Payable T account and post all entries to that account for the entire ten-year period.

P15–**6.** On January 1, 1969, the Haskell Corporation authorized and issued 10-year, 4% sinking fund bonds with a face value of $1,000,000. The bond indenture provided for (a) an annual deposit with a trustee at the end of each year of $100,000 less sinking fund earnings since the previous deposit and (b) an annual restriction on retained earnings.

Required: Record the following selected transactions relating to the bond issue:

1969

Dec. 31   Made the initial deposit with the sinking fund trustee.

      31   Made the restriction on retained earnings.

1970

Dec. 31   Received a report of sinking fund earnings of $3,900.

31   Made the deposit with the sinking fund trustee.

31   Made the restriction on retained earnings.

1978

Dec. 31   Paid the bonds at maturity.

31   Removed the contractual restriction on retained earnings.

P15–7. The Fenn Corporation, with 10,000 shares of $100 par value common stock outstanding, needs an additional $1,000,000 for plant expansion. Three plans for raising the funds have been proposed to the board of directors: (a) the issuance of additional common stock at $100 par value; (b) the issuance of 6% nonparticipating preferred stock; and (c) the issuance of 20-year, 5% bonds. It is estimated that the Corporation will earn $400,000 annually before bond interest and income taxes of 50 percent.

Required: Determine the earnings per share of common stock under each plan. Assume that the securities will be issued at par or face value.

P15–8. Selected accounts from three trial balances of the Leder Corporation are presented:

	Adjusted		Unadjusted
	12/31/67	12/31/68	12/31/69
Debits			
Bond Interest Expense	$ 900	$ 5,400	$ 3,600
Loss on Retirement of Bonds Payable	–0–	–0–	630
Credits			
Accrued Bond Interest Payable	2,000	2,000	–0–
6% Bonds Payable—issued 11/1/67	100,000	100,000	90,000
Premium on Bonds Payable	8,800	8,200	7,800

The data from the adjusted trial balances are correct. The bonds were issued between interest-payment dates. On September 1, 1969, the Corporation retired bonds with a face value of $10,000 by a disbursement of $10,630.

Required: 1. Compute the following:
   a. Original issue price as of November 1, 1967
   b. Maturity date
   c. Semiannual interest payment dates
2. Reconstruct the journal entry to record the issuance of the bonds on November 1, 1967.
3. Prepare any required adjusting or correcting entries as of December 31, 1969.

P15–9. The Bridgeman Company issued 4% bonds on September 1, 1969, at a certain price plus accrued interest. The bonds mature on June 1, 1979. Interest is paid each June 1 and December 1. The accountant for the Company recorded the first semiannual bond interest payment as follows:

1969
Dec. 1   Bond Interest Expense   2,897
           Accrued Bond Interest Payable   2,657
             Discount on Bonds Payable   240
             Cash   5,314
               To record the payment of semiannual
               bond interest and amortization of
               the discount for three months.

Required: 1. Compute the following:
               a. Face value of bonds issued
               b. Original issue price and discount
           2. Reconstruct the journal entry to record the issuance of the
              bonds on September 1, 1969.

CASE PROBLEM
Radford Corporation

The board of directors of the Radford Corporation has approved the recommendation of the management to expand the production facilities. The firm currently manufactures only heavy machinery, but plans are being developed for diversifying the Corporation's activities through the production of smaller and more versatile equipment.

The directors have concluded that, while a number of factors should influence their choice as to the method of financing to be used in obtaining the $1,500,000 needed, prime attention should be devoted to observing the expected income effect on the corporate equity of the common stockholders. They are considering the following methods of providing the necessary funds:

1. They can issue 25,000 shares of $50 par value common stock at a net price of $60 per share.
2. They can issue 15,000 shares of $100 par value, 5½%, cumulative, nonpartici-pating preferred stock at a net price of $100 per share.
3. They can issue $1,500,000 face value of 20-year, 5% bonds at a net price of 102.50.
4. They can issue $1,500,000 face value of 20-year, 4¾% bonds at a net price of 97.50.

The Corporation's current equity structure is:

Current liabilities	$ 120,000
4% bonds payable due in ten years	180,000
5½% preferred stock, cumulative and nonparticipating, $100 par value; authorized 50,000 shares; issued 8,000 shares	800,000
Common stock, $50 par value; authorized 100,000 shares; issued 20,000 shares	1,000,000
Excess over par value received–common stock	100,000
Retained earnings	400,000

Management expects that the investment of $1,500,000 will yield a return of 12 per-cent before income taxes, which will be computed at a 48-percent rate. The Corporation is currently realizing a return of 10 percent on all long-term capital before income taxes.

Required: 1. Using a form like the following, compare the expected effect of each proposed financing method on the corporate equity of the common stockholders.

	Currently (before expansion)	After Issuing Common Stock	After Issuing Preferred Stock	After Issuing 5% Bonds	After Issuing 4¾% Bonds
Cash proceeds available for investment					
Net income before bond interest and income taxes					
Less: Bond interest expense					
Net income before income taxes					
Less: Income tax expense					
Net income					
Less: Full dividend to preferred stockholders					
Portion of net income applicable to common stockholders					
Net income applicable to each share of outstanding common stock					
Portion of net income applicable to common stockholders as a percentage of common stockholders' equity					

2. Applying the single expressed criterion established by the directors, what method of financing should be employed? Why?
3. Discuss other factors that must influence a decision of this type.
4. Assuming that the directors decide to issue the 5% bonds, prepare the general journal entries:

     a. To record the issuance of the bonds

     b. To record the periodic interest payment six months after the issuance of the bonds

     c. To record the adjusting entry immediately prior to closing the books four months after entry b

     d. To record the periodic interest payment two months after entry c

     e. To record the periodic interest payment and the retirement of the bonds at maturity

5. A decrease in the tax rate will tend to favor which method of financing? An increase will tend to favor which method? Explain why.

Chapter Sixteen

Managerial Financial Decisions— Investments

Management may wish to invest excess funds not needed for current operations because of temporary reductions in inventory and accounts receivable. Available temporary excess cash is often invested in the securities of other companies for a favorable return in the form of interest or dividends; the investments should be made in securities for which a ready market exists so that they can be sold when cash is required. Such investments are classified as current assets because they can be and will be converted into cash in a relatively short period of time, when there is a seasonal shortage of cash. If the securities are to be held until they mature, or if they are not readily salable, the investments are classified as long-term investments on the statement of financial position. Investments are often also made for the purpose of obtaining control of another company, whose productive or other facilities are needed by the investing company. Such investments must always be shown on the statement of financial position as long-term investments.

MARKETABLE SECURITIES

A firm should give serious consideration to the investment of any seasonal excess of cash as it becomes available. In this way, it tends to maximize its income by putting idle, nonrevenue-producing funds to work when they are not needed in the operations of the business. If it is expected that the funds will be needed in the near future, they must be invested in readily marketable securities; they should be high-grade, *blue-chip* stocks or bonds that will not fluctuate widely in price and hence will yield, upon future sales, approximately the amount that was originally invested in the securities, or better, a larger amount. Of course, this kind of security yields a relatively low rate of return, a common characteristic of readily marketable, high-grade securities. Only a few securities qualify as marketable; these are United States Government bonds,

AAA industrial bonds, and certain blue-chip stocks that are listed on the various stock exchanges. The accounting examples that follow illustrate the recording of the purchase of bonds accompanied by the receipt of interest and the purchase of stock accompanied by the receipt of dividends.

Temporary Investment in Bonds

For example, consider the financial decision of the Owens Company on March 1, 1969, to purchase as temporary investments 4% bonds of Peters Company with a face value of $30,000 at 102 plus accrued interest. Interest is paid on January 1 and July 1. The brokerage fee and other costs incident to the purchase are $60. This information is recorded as follows:

```
1969
Mar.  1   Marketable Securities–Bonds of Peters Company        30,660
          Accrued Bond Interest Receivable                        200
              Cash                                                          30,860
                  To record the purchase of bonds of Peters
                  Company as temporary investments.
```

1. ▶ In accordance with the generally accepted principle of recording all assets at cost, Marketable Securities are recorded at full cost, including the brokerage fee and other incidental costs. ◀

   ◀ *Accounting Concept: Cost of Securities*

2. The account title, Marketable Securities–Bonds of Peters Company, includes the general ledger control account, Marketable Securities, and the name of the individual bond for posting to a subsidiary record, typically in the form of an *investment register.*
3. The transaction involves the purchase of two different assets: the bonds and the accrued bond interest. The amount of the accrued interest should be set up in a separate account (and not merged with Marketable Securities) since it has a maturity date different from the marketable securities.

The receipt of semiannual interest on July 1, 1969, is recorded as follows:

```
1969
July  1   Cash                                                  600
              Accrued Bond Interest Receivable                       200
              Bond Interest Earned                                   400
                  To record the receipt of semiannual bond
                  interest on bonds of the Peters Company.
```

1. The six months' interest represents a collection of the receivable that was purchased on March 1 and the amount of interest that was earned for the four-month period from March 1 to July 1.
2. Note that the premium element of the cost of the bonds is not amortized. Neither the premium element nor the discount element of the cost of bonds purchased as *temporary investments* is amortized because the purchasing firm is uncertain as to how long it will hold the temporary investments. On

the other hand, the premium or discount on bonds purchased as long-term investments is amortized.

To complete the cycle, assume that on August 1, 1969, the Owens Company found that it had a shortage of cash and decided to sell the bonds of Peters Company. They were sold at 101¾ plus accrued interest; the transaction is recorded as follows:

```
1969
Aug.  1   Cash                                           30,625
            Loss on Disposal of Marketable Securities      135
              Marketable Securities–Bonds of Peters Company        30,660
              Bond Interest Earned                                    100
                To record the sale of marketable securities.
```

1. The computation of the Loss on Disposal of Marketable Securities is:

Original full cost of bonds	$30,660
Selling price of bonds ($30,000 × 101.75%)	30,525
Loss on disposal of marketable securities	$ 135

2. The cash received comes from two sources: the sale of the bonds, $30,525, and the sale of the accrued interest, $100.

3. A mistake often made by beginners in accounting is to credit the Marketable Securities account with the selling price and thus not to recognize any gain or loss on the disposal. Note that this account must be credited with the same amount, the cost, for which it was originally debited.

Loss on Disposal of Marketable Securities is shown in the income statement under Other Expenses. Management must consider this loss along with the Bond Interest Earned in evaluating the success of its decision to invest in the bonds of Peters Company.

Temporary Investment in Stocks

To illustrate the recording of a purchase of stock as a temporary investment, assume that on April 1, 1969, the Arlex Company purchases 200 shares of Hurley Corporation $100 par value preferred stock at $105 per share. Brokerage fees are $108. The entry to record the purchase is:

```
1969
Apr.  1   Marketable Securities–Preferred Stock of
            Hurley Corporation                            21,108
              Cash                                                21,108
                To record the purchase of
                200 shares of Hurley
                Corporation $100 par
                value preferred stock at $105 per share.
```

1. The amount of the debit to the asset is the full cost. The par value is of no significance to the investor except as a possible base to measure the amount of dividends to be received when the dividend rate is stated as a percentage of par value.

2. Dividends do not legally accrue; therefore, no recognition is given to this

feature even for preferred stock until the dividend is actually declared. If the Hurley Corporation had declared a dividend on its preferred stock, and the Arlex Company had purchased the 200 shares between the declaration date and the dividend record date, then the Arlex Company should divide the purchase price between Marketable Securities and Dividends Receivable. One important facet of stock market behavior should be mentioned. The market price of both common and preferred stock reflects investors' anticipation of the ultimate declaration of dividends. In other words, if all other variables were constant, the market price of stock on which dividends are regularly declared would go up gradually from one dividend date to the next in approximately the same manner that interest accrues on bonds. On the dividend record date, the market price per share would drop by the amount of the dividend per share.

Assume that on July 1, 1969, a quarterly dividend of $1.50 per share is received on the Hurley Corporation stock. The entry to record the dividend is:

```
1969
July   1   Cash                                          300
                Dividends Earned                                300
                    To record the receipt of a quarterly dividend
                    from the Hurley Corporation.
```

Dividends Earned is classified under Other Revenue on the income statement.

Again, to meet a seasonal cash shortage, on September 15, 1969, the preferred stock of the Hurley Corporation is sold for $106.50 per share (net of brokerage fees and other costs). The sale is recorded as follows:

```
1969
Sept. 15   Cash                                        21,300
                Marketable Securities–Preferred Stock of
                Hurley Corporation                              21,108
                Gain on Disposal of Marketable Securities          192
                    To record the sale of preferred stock of
                    Hurley Corporation at $106.50
                    per share.
```

Gain on Disposal of Marketable Securities is determined as follows:

Selling price of preferred stock (200 × $106.50)	$21,300
Original full cost	21,108
Gain on disposal of marketable securities	$ 192

Gain on Disposal of Marketable Securities is shown on the income statement under Other Revenue. Management must consider this amount along with Dividends Earned in evaluating the success of its decision to buy the preferred stock as a temporary investment, for often in reality it represents the sale of nonrecognized accumulated dividends.

Valuation of Marketable Securities

Ideally, all current assets should be shown at net realizable value on the statement of financial position. However, this represents a departure from another generally accepted accounting principle, the cost principle. Only rarely do firms use the current market price in the valuation of marketable securities, mainly because in a rising market writing up the marketable securities would mean recording an unrealized gain. Specific attention is given here to (1) the cost and (2) the lower of cost or market methods of valuation, the two methods most often used.

Temporary investments are recorded at cost and may be presented on the statement of financial position at the same figure. Even if they are carried at cost, the current market value of the securities, obtainable from the financial page of any daily newspaper, should be disclosed in the statement of financial position by a parenthetical notation as shown to enable the reader to evaluate the item for purposes of financial position analysis:

Assets

Current Assets		
Cash		$562,000
Marketable Securities (shown at cost; current market price, $175,000)		158,000
Accounts Receivable	$200,000	
Deduct Allowance for Doubtful Accounts	8,000	192,000
Merchandise Inventory		300,000
Prepaid Insurance		2,000
Total Current Assets		$1,214,000

Note that even though the current market value is disclosed parenthetically, the securities are valued at cost; that is, only the original cost is added into the figures that are totaled. The cost method is consistent with the fundamental principle of matching expired costs (or expenses) and revenues as well as with income tax requirements.

Accounting Concept:
Conservatism ▶

Many firms value their marketable securities at the lower of cost or market. In effect, these firms value their securities at cost or *realizable cost*, whichever is the lower. The objective of this valuation method is to recognize the effect of market price declines without recognizing market price increases. ▶ Thus, it adheres to the concept of conservatism, the recognition of all anticipated losses without the recognition of unrealized gains. ◀ Although there are two possible methods of applying the lower of cost or market method to marketable securities (the *unit* method and the *total securities* method), the unit method—taking the lower of cost or market for each security owned—is the most conservative and the only method discussed in this text. To illustrate, assume that the lower of cost or market unit method is applied to the securities owned by the Duncan Company as of December 31, 1969, as shown:

Marketable Securities	Cost (at time securities were acquired)	Market (December 31, 1969)	Lower of Cost or Market
Preferred Stock of Anison Company	$12,550	$12,000	$12,000
Common Stock of Bassom Company	16,470	16,200	16,200
Bonds of Connors Company	20,000	20,500	20,000
Totals	$49,020	$48,700	$48,200

If the lower of cost or market unit method is applied to these three securities, the amount to appear in the statement of financial position for Marketable Securities is $48,200, which represents the December 31, 1969, market price of the stocks of Anison and Bassom Company plus the cost of the bonds of Connors Company. The adjusting entry necessary to give recognition to the valuation may take one of two forms: (1) direct asset reduction or (2) creation of a valuation account. Since cost must be retained for income tax requirements and other managerial evaluations, it is suggested that the second method is desirable and that the following valuation adjusting entry is proper:

1969

Dec. 31	Recognized Decline in Value of Marketable Securities	820	
	Allowance for Decline in Value of Marketable Securities		820
	To give recognition to the lower of cost or market unit method of valuation.		

The statement of financial position then shows the following:

Assets

Current Assets		
Marketable Securities (at cost)	$49,020	
Deduct Allowance for Decline in Value of Marketable Securities	820	
Marketable Securities at Lower of Cost or Market		$48,200

The $820 loss is reported on the income statement under Other Expenses.

To complete the cycle, suppose that on January 15, 1970, the Duncan Company sells the preferred stock of Anison Company for $12,060. This transaction is recorded as follows:

1970

Jan. 15	Cash	12,060	
	Allowance for Decline in Value of Marketable Securities	550	
	Marketable Securities–Preferred Stock of Anison Company		12,550
	Gain on Sale of Marketable Securities		60
	To record the sale of preferred stock of Anison Company.		

Observe that the gain or loss on the sale must be determined by comparing the selling price with the lower of cost or market figure used for the statement of financial position valuation. For the Anison Company stock, the gain is computed by comparing the $12,060 received with the $12,000 carrying value. It should be understood that the $60 gain is not recognized for tax purposes; instead a $490 loss is reported on the tax return for 1970 since securities that had cost $12,550 were sold for $12,060.

LONG-TERM INVESTMENTS

In addition to its primary operational activities, a firm may make investments in stock, bonds, and other securities that are expected to contribute to the success of the business largely by making independent contributions to business revenue. These investments may be temporary or long term. As suggested in the preceding section, investments are called Marketable Securities and classified as current assets only when they are readily marketable and it is the intention of management to convert them into cash when there is a seasonal need for such action. Investments that do not qualify as Marketable Securities are classified as long-term investments on the statement of financial position.

Investment in Stocks

A company may buy stock in another company for the dividend revenue, or it may acquire control of another company—a *subsidiary*—thereby expanding its operations and gaining a more prominent competitive position, possibly accompanied by a steady supply of merchandise or the creation of sales outlets.

Stock may be acquired directly from the issuing company, but it is more likely to be purchased through a broker on the New York Stock Exchange, the American Stock Exchange, or other exchanges in this or other countries. If shares of stocks are not listed on an exchange, they are said to be sold *over the counter.*

Long-term investment in stocks, as well as temporary investments, are recorded at full cost including brokerage fees and postage. If cash is paid for the purchase of stock, there is no problem in establishing cost. In other cases, problems of valuation may arise. A sound accounting rule is to record the investment in stock at the most objective measurement of the cash equivalent cost of the securities. Since dividends do not legally accrue, no recognition is given to the purchase of Dividends Receivable unless the issuing corporation has officially declared a dividend and the investing corporation purchases the stock between the dividend declaration date and the record date. To illustrate both cases, assume, first, that on July 1, 1969, the Satterfield Company purchases 1,000 shares of $100 par value common stock of James Corporation at 105 with a broker's fee of $440. The investor's total cost is $105,440, and the following entry is made:

```
1969

July   1   Investment in Stocks–Common Stock of James
               Corporation                                    105,440
                 Cash                                                    105,440
                   To record the purchase of 1000 shares of
                   $100 par value common stock of James
                   Corporation.
```

Observe that the asset, Investment in Stocks, is debited for the cost, not the par value, of the stock. The account title shows the general ledger controlling account, Investment in Stocks, and the subsidiary account title, Common Stock of James Corporation. The information about the specific stock is transferred to an investment register, which serves in place of a more formal subsidiary ledger.

To illustrate the handling of declared dividends, consider the purchase on July 20, 1969, by the Satterfield Company of 100 shares of common stock of Iser Company at 102½ plus a brokerage fee of $42. On July 10, 1969, the board of directors of the Iser Company had declared a $1 per share dividend, payable on August 10,

1969, to stockholders of record on July 25, 1969. The purchase price of $102.50 per share includes the cost of all rights. An analysis of this price, therefore, reveals that $101.50 is the cost of each share of stock, excluding the brokerage fees, and $1 per share is the cost of the Dividends Receivable purchased. This transaction is recorded in the journal as follows:

1969			
July 20	Investment in Stocks–Common Stock of Iser Company	10,192	
	Dividends Receivable	100	
	Cash		10,292
	To record the purchase of 100 shares of common stock of Iser Company with a $1 per share dividend receivable.		

When the dividend is received on August 10, an entry is made debiting Cash and crediting Dividends Receivable for the $100. Similarly, if a firm sells its stock in a company that has declared a cash dividend before the dividend record date, it should give recognition to a dividend revenue.

Normally, for convenience, a cash dividend is not recorded until the cash is actually received. For example, if the Satterfield Company receives a $.60 per share quarterly dividend on the stock of James Corporation on November 10, 1969, it records this information as follows:

1969			
Nov. 10	Cash	600	
	Dividends Earned		600
	To record the receipt of a $.60 per share dividend from the James Corporation.		

A necessary exception to the foregoing rule is the case of a dividend declared in one year and payable in another year. ◀ Sound accrual accounting theory dictates that the dividend revenue be recognized in the year in which the dividend is declared, not in the year in which it is paid. ◀ In this case, an entry is made on or before the last day of the fiscal year in which the dividend is declared, debiting Dividends Receivable and crediting Dividends Earned. Then, when the dividend is actually received in the subsequent accounting period, an entry is made debiting Cash and crediting Dividends Receivable.

◀ Accounting Concept: Recognizing Declared Dividends

Today, frequent use is made of stock dividends and stock split-ups to reduce the market price per share and thus to put the stock in a more favorable price range. The additional shares received by an investing company are not revenue to the stockholder. Only a memorandum entry is necessary to record the increase in the number of shares owned. The unit cost is decreased, however, because of the larger number of shares held after the stock dividend is issued. For example, assume that the James Corporation declares a 100-percent stock dividend (a two-for-one-split-up would be treated in the same way). The receipt of the additional 1,000 shares on December 12, 1969, by the Satterfield Company is noted in the journal as follows (the original 1,000 shares had cost $105,440):

1969

Dec. 12   Memorandum Entry—Today there was received 1,000 shares of stock of James Corporation, representing a 100% stock dividend. The cost per share of the stock is recomputed as follows:

Old number of shares	New number of shares
1,000	2,000
Total cost	New cost per share
$105,440	$52.72

The gain or loss per share on any subsequent sale of James Corporation stock is determined by comparing the selling price with the new cost of $52.72 per share.

The Dividends Earned balance is disclosed in the income statement under Other Revenue; whereas the Investment in Stock account is reported in the statement of financial position under Long-Term Investments, a noncurrent caption appearing between Current Assets and Plant and Equipment. The most commonly used method of valuation for long-term investments is cost. When, however, there is a material and presumably permanent decline in the market value of the investment, an adjustment may be made crediting the investment account and debiting the Loss from Decline in Market Value of Investment in Stocks account.

Investment in Bonds

A number of institutional investors are prohibited by law from buying common stock. These organizations, such as banks, insurance companies, some trusts, and pension funds, acquire bonds as sound investments. Industrial companies, either for the interest revenue to be received or for reasons of business connection, also frequently buy bonds.

Accounting for the purchase of long-term bonds is practically the mirror image of accounting for the issuance of bonds, with one exception: no premium or discount accounts are used when the bonds are purchased above or below face value. To measure the bond interest revenue properly, the amount of the discount or premium is amortized, however, with offsetting debits or credits to the Bond Interest Earned account. Two examples are presented to illustrate the accounting for investment in bonds; the second example involves more complex issues than the first.

In the first example, assume that on May 1, 1969, the Aman Company places a 4%, $300,000 bond issue with the Boston Finance Company at 98. The interest is payable on May 1 and November 1 and the bonds mature on May 1, 1979. The entries on both the issuing company's and the investing company's books for the year 1969 are shown in Figure 16-1.

Observe that the discount accumulation (comparable to the discount amortization for the issuer) results in a debit to the asset account and a credit to the Bond Interest Earned account. For better measurement of periodic revenue from the securities on the investor's books, the discount on long-term investments is accumulated over the outstanding life of the bonds, starting with the date of purchase and ending with the maturity date. Otherwise, the amount of the discount would have to be recognized as a gain in the accounting period during which the bonds mature. Such a

Transaction	Books of Aman Company (Issuer)			Books of Boston Finance Company (Investor)		
1969	**1969**			**1969**		

May 1 Aman Company issued the bonds to Boston Finance Company at 98.	May 1 Cash
	Discount on Bonds Payable
	  Bonds Payable
	    To record the issuance
	    of bonds at 98.
		294,000
		6,000
			
			300,000
				May 1 Investment in Bonds–
				  Aman Company Bonds
				  Cash
				    To record the
				    purchase of
				    bonds at 98.
					294,000	
						
						294,000

Nov. 1 Aman Company paid semiannual interest to Boston Finance Company.	Nov. 1 Bond Interest Expense
	  Cash
	    To record payment of
	    semiannual interest.
		6,000	
			6,000
				Nov. 1 Cash
				  Bond Interest Earned
				    To record the receipt of
				    semiannual interest.
					6,000	
						6,000

1 Amortized discount for six months.	1 Bond Interest Expense
	  Discount on Bonds Payable
	    To record the amortization
	    of bond discount for 6
	    months:
	      6/120 × $6000 = $300
		300	
			300
				1 Investment in Bonds–
				  Aman Company Bonds
				  Bond Interest Earned
				    To record the discount
				    accumulated for
				    six months.
					300	
						300

Dec. 31 Accrued interest for two months.	Dec. 31 Bond Interest Expense
	  Accrued Bond Interest Payable
	    To record the accrual of
	    interest for two months.
		2,000	
			2,000
				Dec. 31 Accrued Bond Interest
				  Receivable
				  Bond Interest Earned
				    To record the accrual of
				    interest earned for
				    two months.
					2,000	
						2,000

31 Amortized discount for two months.	31 Bond Interest Expense
	  Discount on Bonds Payable
	    To record the amortization
	    of bond discount for
	    two months:
	      2/120 × $6,000 = $100
		100	
			100
				31 Investment in Bonds–
				  Aman Company Bonds
				  Bond Interest Earned
				    To record the discount
				    accumulated for
				    two months.
					100	
						100

Figure 16-1.
Entries for Bonds on Books of Issuer and Investor

gain would reflect only the failure to adjust the Bond Interest Earned account in prior accounting periods.

The income statement of the Boston Finance Company for the year ended December 31, 1969, includes Bond Interest Earned of $8,400 ($8,000 + $400). Accrued Bond Interest Receivable of $2,000 is shown in the December 31, 1969, statement of financial position under Current Assets. The Investment in Bonds is shown under Long-Term Investments on the statement of financial position at $294,400 ($294,000 + $400). At maturity, the investment account will have a balance of $300,000. It will have been increased by periodic discount accumulation entries to this figure.

Only the investor's entries are shown in the more complex example: Assume that on March 1, 1969, the Western Company purchases 6% bonds of the Malcolm Company with a face value of $200,000 at 104 plus accrued interest. Interest is paid on May 1 and November 1. The bonds mature on November 1, 1985. The Western Company holds the bonds until August 1, 1973, at which time it sells them at 103½ plus accrued interest. The 1969 entries for the purchase of the bonds, receipt of interest, amortization of premium element of cost and accrual of bond interest, and the 1973 entries to record the sale are presented:

1969

Mar. 1	Investment in Bonds–Malcolm Company Bonds
	Accrued Bond Interest Receivable
	  Cash
	    To record the purchase of 6% bonds at 104
	    plus accrued interest.
		208,000
		4,000
			
			212,000

May	1	Cash	6,000	
		Bond Interest Earned		2,000
		Accrued Bond Interest Receivable		4,000
		To record the receipt of semiannual interest from the Malcolm Company.		
	1	Bond Interest Earned	80	
		Investment in Bonds–Malcolm Company Bonds		80
		To record the premium amortization for two months: $2/200 \times \$8000 = \$80$		
Nov.	1	Cash	6,000	
		Bond Interest Earned		6,000
		To record the receipt of semiannual interest from the Malcolm Company.		
	1	Bond Interest Earned	240	
		Investment in Bonds–Malcolm Company Bonds		240
		To record the premium amortization for six months: $6/200 \times \$8000 = \$240$		
Dec.	31	Accrued Bond Interest Receivable	2,000	
		Bond Interest Earned		2,000
		To record the accrual of two months' interest on the Malcolm Company Bonds		
	31	Bond Interest Earned	80	
		Investment in Bonds–Malcolm Company Bonds		80
		To record the premium amortization for two months: $2/200 \times \$8000 = \$80$		
1973				
Aug.	1	Accrued Bond Interest Receivable	3,000	
		Bond Interest Earned		3,000
		To accrue the interest for three months on the bonds to be sold.		
	1	Bond Interest Earned	120	
		Investment in Bonds–Malcolm Company Bonds		120
		To record the premium amortization for three months: $3/200 \times \$8000 = \$120$		
	1	Cash	210,000	
		Investment in Bonds–Malcolm Company Bonds		205,880
		Accrued Bond Interest Receivable		3,000
		Gain on Sale of Bonds		1,120
		To record the sale of bonds of Malcolm Company at 103½ plus accrued interest.		

1. On March 1, 1969, two assets are purchased; separate accounts are maintained for each asset, particularly since Accrued Bond Interest Receivable is a current asset and Investments in Bonds is a noncurrent asset.

2. For better measurement of periodic bond interest revenue, the premium element of the cost of the bonds is amortized over the outstanding life of the bonds. The amortization credit is made to the Investment in Bonds account.
3. The gain on the sale of bonds is determined as follows:

Selling price of bonds ($200,000 @ 103.50%)		$207,000
Deduct: Book value at date of sale		
Original cost	$208,000	
Total amortization to August 1, 1973		
(53 mos. × $40 per month)	2,120	
Book value at date of sale		205,880
Gain on sale of bonds		$ 1,120

Long-Term Investment in Secured and Unsecured Notes

Other types of long-term investments may be made, particularly by financial institutions. Notes secured by mortgages or deeds of trust and unsecured notes are typical. The accounting principles and procedures applicable to these investments are similar to those for investment in bonds. For example, mortgage notes are often acquired at a discount, in which case accounting theory dictates that the mortgage note be recorded at cost and the amount of the discount be accumulated (amortized) over the remaining outstanding life of the note. After the entry is made to record the periodic cash interest, the discount accumulation entry is made, debiting Investment in Mortgages and crediting Interest Earned.

MANAGERIAL ANALYSIS

In addition to the effective interest yield computations discussed in Chapter 15, there is another very important ratio used by investors in bonds: the *number of times bond interest expense is earned*. This ratio is of special interest to bond investors as a measure of the safety of their investment; it is an indication of a firm's ability to meet its annual bond interest requirement. To illustrate, assume that the Analee Corporation has bonds outstanding with a face value of $1,000,000, and that in 1969 it reports bond interest expense of $40,000, income taxes of $60,000, and net income (after income taxes) of $80,000. Since bond interest expense is deductible in determining taxable income, the following formula is appropriate:

Number of Times Bond Interest Expense Is Earned

$$= \frac{\text{Net Income} + \text{Income Tax} + \text{Annual Bond Interest Expense}}{\text{Annual Bond Interest Expense}}$$

Substituting the amounts given for the Analee Corporation:

$$\text{Number of Times Bond Interest Expense Is Earned} = \frac{\$80,000 + \$60,000 + \$40,000}{\$40,000}$$

$$= 4.5 \text{ times}$$

A ratio of 4.5 times appears to be relatively safe for the investors holding bonds of Analee Corporation, although there are no established universal standards of safety.

The safety margin depends in part upon the type of collateral used, the type of business in which the firm is engaged, and the liquidity of the firm. Investors in a private utility with mortgageable plant assets, for example, may feel secure with a ratio of 2.5 times; whereas investors in other businesses without mortgageable assets may feel insecure with a ratio smaller than 5 times.

SUMMARY

Marketable securities are temporary investments in high-quality securities that are readily marketable at approximately the amount that was originally invested. Marketable securities are often purchased when there is a seasonal excess of cash and subsequently liquidated when there is a cash shortage. Investments that do not qualify as marketable securities are classified as long-term investments. Such long-term investments may be made to increase earnings by gaining a more competitive market position or through the dividends or interest earned on the investments.

The purchase of marketable securities and long-term investments is recorded by debiting the appropriate asset accounts for the total cost to the company, exclusive of any accrued interest or declared dividends purchased. No discount or premium account is maintained for an investment in bonds; the discount or premium element is recorded in the asset account.

If a temporary investment is made in bonds, neither the premium nor the discount element is amortized since the purchasing firm is uncertain as to the length of time the investments will be held. The premium or discount element included in the total cost of a long-term investment in bonds, however, is amortized by an offsetting debit or credit to the investment account.

On the statement of financial position, marketable securities may be valued at cost or the lower of cost or market, and long-term investments are generally valued at cost. If marketable securities are valued at the lower of cost or market, the adjusting entry to effect this valuation is a debit to an expense account and a credit to a valuation account that is subtracted from the cost of marketable securities on the statement of financial position.

☐ QUESTIONS

Q16–1. What are marketable securities? How are they classified on the statement of financial position?

Q16–2. List four types of investments that may qualify as marketable securities.

Q16–3. Name and discuss the methods of valuation of marketable securities.

Q16–4. Discuss the accounting involved in the lower of cost or market method of valuation of marketable securities; give journal entries to illustrate your discussion.

Q16–5. Why do firms acquire stock as a long-term investment?

Q16–6. Do dividends legally accrue? Can a firm buy dividends receivable? Explain.

Q16–7. What is a stock split-up? Discuss the accounting for a stock split-up from point of view of the investor. Would there be any difference in the accounting for a stock dividend as compared to the accounting for a stock split-up from the point of view of the investor?

Q16-**8**. Name the various groups of investors who typically buy bonds as a long-term investment.

Q16-**9**. State the financial position statement classifications of (a) Bond Sinking Fund; (b) Bonds Payable; (c) Accrued Bond Interest Receivable; (d) Discount on Bonds Payable; (e) Premium on Bonds Payable; (f) Accrued Bond Interest Payable; (g) Retained Earnings–Restricted for Bond Redemption.

☐ **EXERCISES**

E16-**1**. The Investum Company had the following transactions in temporary investments during 1969:

1969

March 1 Purchased 4% bonds of Able Company with a face value of $100,000 at 103 plus accrued interest. Interest is paid on January 1 and July 1. Brokerage fees and other costs incident to the purchase were $75. The bonds have a maturity date of July 1, 1989.

April 10 Purchased 300 shares of $100 par value, 6% preferred stock of Baker Company at $108 per share. Dividends are paid semiannually on January 1 and July 1. Brokerage fees and other costs incident to the purchase were $60.

July 1 Received the semiannual interest from the Able Company.

     5 Received the semiannual dividends from the Baker Company.

Aug. 1 Sold the bonds of Able Company at 103½ plus accrued interest.

Journalize the transactions.

E16-**2**. The Valum Company had the following temporary investments as of December 31, 1969:

	Cost	Market Price at December 31, 1969
Bonds of Carson Company	$10,000	$ 9,600
Preferred Stock of Dawson Company	20,000	20,200

On February 1, 1970, immediately after receiving and recording the semiannual interest, the Valum Company sold the bonds of Carson Company for $9,500.

Assuming the use of a valuation offset account, record the necessary adjusting entry under the lower of cost or market unit method as of December 31, 1969, and the sale on February 1, 1970.

E16-**3**. The Parento Company had the following transactions in long-term investment in stocks during 1969:

1969

Jan. 5 Purchased 1,000 shares of $100 par value common stock of Sunno Company at 108. The Sunno Company had declared a $1 per share dividend on January 1, 1969, payable on January 20, 1969.

     20 Received the cash dividend from the Sunno Company.

Mar. 10 Purchased 2,000 shares of $100 par value common stock of Sunno Company at 112.

July 1 Received a $1.10 per share cash dividend from the Sunno Company.

Dec. 1   The Sunno Company split up its stock two for one. The Parento Company exchanged 3,000 shares of $100 par value stock for 6,000 shares of no-par value stock.

      31   The Sunno Company declared a $1 per share cash dividend payable January 18, 1970, to stockholders of record on December 31, 1969.

Journalize the transactions.

E16–4. On January 1, 1969, the Eiderdee Corporation purchased as a long-term investment 6% bonds of Charles Corporation with a face value of $300,000 at 102½. The bonds have a maturity date of January 1, 1979. Interest is payable each January 1 and July 1.

Record (a) the purchase of the bonds by the Eiderdee Corporation, and (b) all the necessary remaining entries for 1969.

E16–5. Assume that the Eiderdee Corporation (see Exercise E16-4) purchased the Charles Corporation bonds at 98 instead of 102½.

Prepare all the required entries for 1969.

E16–6. On May 1, 1969, the Gudderson Company purchased as a long-term investment 6% bonds of Celler Company. Interest is paid semiannually on May 1 and November 1. The bonds mature on May 1, 1981. On November 1, 1969, the accountant for the Gudderson Company prepared the following entry to record the receipt of bond interest and the amortization of the premium:

1969
Nov. 1	Cash	3,765	
	Investment in Bonds–Celler Company Bonds		90
	Bond Interest Earned		3,675
	To record the receipt of bond interest from the Celler Company and to amortize the premium for six months.		

From this information, reconstruct the journal entry that was made to record the purchase of the bonds. Show all your calculations.

□   **DEMONSTRATION PROBLEMS**

DP16–1. (*Accounting for marketable securities*) The Markat Company had the following transactions in temporary investments during 1969:

1969
Feb. 1   Purchased 6% bonds of Zebulon Company with a face value of $200,000 at 120 plus accrued interest. Interest is paid each May 1 and November 1. Brokerage fees and other costs incident to the purchase were $150. The bonds have a maturity date of November 1, 1989.

Mar. 15   Purchased 400 shares of $100 par value, 5% preferred stock of Yardley Corporation at $110 per share. Dividends are paid semiannually on March 15 and September 15. The Yardley Corporation had declared the regular semiannual cash dividend on their preferred stock on March 10, 1969, payable on March 20, 1969. Brokerage fees and other costs incident to the purchase were $80.

      20   Received the semiannual dividend from the Yardley Corporation.

May 1 Received the semiannual interest on the bonds of Zebulon Company.

Sept. 20 Received the semiannual dividends on the preferred stock of Yardley Corporation.

Oct. 1 Sold bonds of Zebulon Company with a face value of $100,000 at 118 plus accrued interest.

Nov. 1 Received semiannual interest on the remaining bonds of Zebulon Company.

Dec. 31 Accrued the interest on the bonds of Zebulon Company.

Required: Journalize the transactions.

DP16–2. (*Valuation of marketable securities*) The Lowerum Company had the following temporary investments as of December 31, 1969:

	Cost	Market Price at December 31, 1969
Bonds of Meeson Company	$15,740	$15,890
Preferred Stock of Newton Company	7,500	7,400
Preferred Stock of Owers Company	16,710	16,560

On February 1, 1970, the Lowerum Company sold the preferred stock of Newton Company for $7,280. On March 1, 1970, the Company sold the preferred stock of Owers Company for $16,600.

Required: 1. Assuming that a valuation offset account is used, record the necessary adjusting entry under the lower of cost or market unit method.
2. Show how the investments should be shown on the end-of-period financial statement.
3. Record the sales of marketable securities in 1970.

DP16–3. (*Accounting for long-term investment in stocks*) The Pater Company had the following transactions involving long-term investment in stocks in 1969:

1969

Jan. 6 Purchased 2,000 shares of $100 par value common stock of Sun Company at 120.

May 1 Received a $2 per share cash dividend from the Sun Company.

June 1 Purchased 1,000 shares of $100 par value common stock of Sun Company at 128.

Sept. 1 The Sun Company split up its stock four for one. The Pater Company exchanged 3,000 shares of $100 par value stock for 12,000 shares of no-par value stock.

Oct. 10 The Pater Company sold 1,000 shares of the stock of Sun Company for $40 per share. The Sun Company had declared a $1 per share cash dividend payable on October 25 to stockholders of record on October 20.

25 Received the cash dividend on the remaining shares of stock of Sun Company.

Required: 1. Journalize the transactions.
2. Show how the long-term investment in stocks should be

shown on the statement of financial position at December 31, 1969.

DP16-**4.** (*Accounting for the purchase of bonds as a long-term investment*) Assume that Adams, Inc., purchased 6% bonds of Pearl Corporation under each of the following conditions (the authorization date is January 1, 1969).

	Case A	Case B	Case C
Face value of each bond	$500	$1,000	$10,000
Term of bond issue (years)	10	20	20
Interest payable	Jan. 1 and July 1	Jan. 1 and July 1	Jan. 1 and July 1
Date of purchase	Jan. 1, 1969	Jan. 1, 1969	Mar. 1, 1969
Number of bonds purchased	20	10	10
Purchase price	100	98½	102 (plus accrued interest)

Required: For each case, record (a) the purchase of the bonds; (b) the receipt of the first interest payment, accompanied by the entry to record proper amortization, and (c) the adjusting entry for interest accrual on December 31, 1969, accompanied by the entry to record proper amortization.

☐ PROBLEMS

P16-**1.** The Tarex Company had the following transactions involving temporary investments during 1969:

1969

Jan. 1   Purchased 4% bonds of Zanrim Company with a face value of $180,000 at 102 plus accrued interest. Interest is paid each March 1 and September 1. Brokerage fees and other costs incident to the purchase were $160. The bonds have a maturity date of September 1, 1978.

Mar. 1   Received semiannual interest on bonds of Zanrim Company.

15   Purchased 600 shares of $50 par value, 6% preferred stock of Suskin Company at $40 per share. Dividends are paid semiannually on February 15 and August 15. Brokerage fees and other costs incident to the purchase were $60.

Aug. 15   Sold 200 shares of preferred stock of Suskin Company at $52 per share. The board of directors of the Suskin Company had declared the regular semiannual dividend on this stock payable on August 25 to stockholders of record on August 20.

25   Received the dividend on the remaining preferred stock of Suskin Company.

Sept. 1   Received semiannual interest on the bonds of Zanrim Company.

Oct. 1   Sold the bonds of Zanrim Company at 103 plus accrued interest.

Required: Journalize the transactions.

P16-**2.** The Rouser Company had the following temporary investments as of December 31, 1969:

	Cost	Market Price at December 31, 1969
Bonds of Sampson Company	$42,500	$43,000
Preferred Stock of Thompson Company	37,500	37,400
Preferred Stock of Uriah Company	53,650	53,575

The following transactions involving the investments took place in 1970:

1970

Jan. 15   Sold the preferred stock of Thompson Company for $37,480.

Feb. 15   Sold the preferred stock of Uriah Company for $53,520.

Required: 1. Assuming the use of a valuation offset account, record the necessary adjusting entry under the lower of cost or market unit method.
2. Show how the temporary investments should be shown on the end-of-period financial statement.
3. Record the sales of the temporary investments in 1970.

P16–3. The Patterson Company had the following transactions involving long-term investment in stocks in 1969:

1969

Jan. 4   Purchased 1,000 shares of $50 par value common stock of Sunner Company at 60.

Feb. 10   Purchased 3,000 shares of $50 par value common stock of Sunner Company at 67. The Sunner Company had declared a $1 per share cash dividend payable February 26 to stockholders of record on February 21.

26   Received the cash dividend on the stock of Sunner Company.

Mar. 2   Purchased 2,000 shares of $50 par value common stock of Sunner Company at 68.

Sept. 10   The Sunner Company declared a 100-percent stock dividend. The Patterson Company received 6,000 additional shares of $50 par value common stock from the Sunner Company.

Nov. 1   Sold 2,500 shares of the common stock of Sunner Company at 35.

Dec. 31   The Sunner Company declared a 75¢ per share cash dividend payable January 16, 1970 to stockholders of record on December 31, 1969.

Required: 1. Journalize the transactions.
2. Show how the long-term investment in stock should be shown on the statement of financial position of the Patterson Company as of December 31, 1969.

P16–4. On May 1, 1969, the Investure Company purchased 6% bonds of Barley Company with a face value of $160,000 at 103. The bonds mature on May 1, 1979, and interest is paid each May 1 and November 1. The books are closed each December 31.

Required: Journalize all necessary entries on the books of the Investure Company for 1969 and 1970, assuming that proper amortization is recorded each time bond interest is recorded.

P16–5. On April 1, 1969, the Riggsbee Company purchased 4½% bonds of Sparrow Company with a face value of $400,000 at 98 plus accrued interest. The bonds mature on August 1, 1977, and interest is paid each February 1 and August 1. On July 1,

1973, the Riggsbee Company sold bonds with a face value of $100,000 at 99 plus accrued interest. The books are closed each December 31.

Required: 1. Journalize all necessary entries on the books of the Riggsbee Company for 1969, assuming that proper amortization is recorded each time bond interest is recorded.

2. Assuming that the proper accounting is carried out in the years 1970 through 1972, prepare all the entries for the year 1973, including the receipt of interest on February 1 and August 1, the proper discount accumulation, the sale of the bonds on July 1, and the accrual of interest and other necessary adjusting and closing entries at December 31.

P16–**6.** On June 1, 1969, the Edens Company purchased as a long-term investment 6% bonds of Hanchrow Company at a certain price plus accrued interest. Interest is payable semiannually on April 1 and October 1. The bonds mature on October 1, 1988. On October 1, 1969, the accountant for the Edens Company prepared the following entry to record the receipt of bond interest and the amortization of the premium:

1969

Oct. 1	Cash	5,550	
	Investment in Bonds–Hanchrow Company		60
	Accrued Bond Interest Receivable		1,850
	Bond Interest Earned		3,640
	To record the receipt of semiannual bond interest from the Hanchrow Company and to amortize the premium for four months.		

Required: 1. Compute and state separately the following:
   a. Face value of bonds
   b. Original purchase price of bonds
2. From the information given, reconstruct the journal entry to record the purchase of the bonds by the Edens Company.

CASE PROBLEM
Goodeal Corporation

The Goodeal Corporation has three stockholders who own the following common shares (the Corporation has only common shares outstanding):

R. A. Goode	3000 shares
B. E. Deale	3000 shares
I. M. Inman	4000 shares

Inman has agreed to sell his shares at book value (based on generally accepted accounting principles) to the Nucorp Corporation, provided past profits have been recorded with reasonable accuracy. A review of past records of the Goodeal Corporation indicates the following:

The bad debts expense of the Corporation has been estimated to be 1 percent of credit sales. The Allowance for Doubtful Accounts appears as follows since the Corporation was formed:

Allowance for Doubtful Accounts

1966				1965			
July 10	Write-off	760		Dec. 31	Adjustment	1,500	
1967				1966			
Nov. 18	Write-off	1,000		Dec. 31	Adjustment	1,800	
1968				1967			
Sept. 2	Write-off	1,400		Dec. 31	Adjustment	2,400	
1969				1968			
Aug. 8	Write-off	1,360		Dec. 31	Adjustment	2,300	
				1969			
				Dec. 31	Adjustment	2,600	

In addition, the Goodeal Corporation made an investment in Renug Corporation bonds with a face value of $20,000 five years ago. The bonds cost $16,400 and had 18 years of life remaining at the time of purchase. The discount was never amortized because the Corporation had always intended to sell the bonds in the following year, but for one reason or another had not done so.

The Corporation had also made an investment in the stock of Rumson Corporation four years before, and it appears on the books at its original cost of $47,400. The stock has increased in market value steadily each year and is presently worth approximately $64,000.

The Goodeal Corporation's net income has averaged $80,000 during the past five years, and average stockholder's equity has been $400,000. Goodwill of $12,000 appears on the Corporation's books.

Required: 1. As an accounting consultant for the Nucorp Corporation, would you feel that the determination of past net income has been reasonably accurate?

2. If you were adjusting the assets of the Goodeal Corporation preparatory to the sale of Inman's stock, how much would the adjustment be? Discuss.

3. If you believe that the income has been incorrectly computed, state how you would change the Corporation's accounting policies.

**Part
Three**

**Financial
Reporting:
Analysis
and
Interpretive
Problems**

Chapter Seventeen
Corporate Financial Reporting

The accounting department of a business organization is responsible for preparing a number of different kinds of reports, which may be classified as follows:

1. Primarily for use by outside groups:
   a. Annual (or periodic) financial reports
   b. Prospectuses
   c. Special reports to grantors of credit
2. Primarily for use by management—various managerial reports and analyses.

These reports are discussed in this chapter in terms of their history and functions.

DEVELOPMENT OF FINANCIAL REPORTING TO OUTSIDE GROUPS

The importance of financial reporting to outside groups has paralleled the growth of the corporate type of enterprise. Early American corporations revealed very little financial information to anyone outside of internal management. Annual financial reports to stockholders were meager and consisted usually of condensed and unaudited financial statements.

With the growth of corporations, the New York Stock Exchange became interested in the type of information that was being furnished to stockholders. In 1898, for example, the Exchange, in reviewing the application of a particular company for a listing of its stock, requested that the applicant present detailed statements to the stockholders prior to each annual meeting. This was the genesis of the detailed annual corporate reports that are made available today to the stockholders. These reports, in addition to a summary letter from the President or the Chairman of the board of directors, contain detailed audited comparative statements of financial position and income and other descriptive and analytical information about the present and future outlook for the corporation.

The Securities and Exchange Commission (SEC), an independent quasijudicial agency of the United States Government, created by the Securities Act of 1933 and strengthened by the Securities Exchange Act of 1934 and the Securities Acts Amendments of 1964, requires prior registration with the SEC of all securities to be sold on a public exchange and unlisted securities that are sold over the counter of companies with total assets of over $1,000,000 and 500 or more stockholders. The SEC may exempt from the registration requirements certain offerings, particularly those of governmental agencies and certain common carriers such as interstate railroads.

The registration of securities with the SEC requires the filing of a registration statement and a *prospectus*, including detailed financial statements with a report and opinion of an independent public accounting firm. These data must be kept current by the filing of annual financial reports prepared in accordance with the rules and regulations of the SEC. The agency does not appraise the registered securities; it attempts to safeguard the investing public by requiring that all material facts be presented properly and that no important information be withheld. The SEC may require that any speculative features of a particular offering be made clearly evident. It has made a signal contribution to the improvement in financial reporting procedures of corporations and to the scope and nature of the data available to investors. Its influence has been far-reaching and salutary; the reporting requirements have been carried over into the annual reports to stockholders and thus have contributed to a degree of standardization in financial reporting.

Corporate financial reports may take a slightly different form when a corporation requests a loan from a bank or establishes a line of credit. The grantor of credit under these circumstances will dictate the type and form of reports. Often, only a statement of financial position will be required. In other cases, in addition to the statement of financial position, an income statement, a statement of sources and uses of funds (discussed in Chapter 18), and other narrative-type statistical and financial reports may be required.

MANAGEMENT NEEDS FOR FINANCIAL DATA

If business executives are to make intelligent decisions based on accounting data, they must understand these data. A major function of the accounting department of a corporation, therefore, is to supply the necessary financial reports to management in meaningful form. The accounting department records the data, prepares the financial statements, and also may prepare ratio, trend, and percentage analyses. The financial data are used by the corporate executives, who are responsible for the stewardship of the business, to measure past performance in terms of costs and revenue, to determine the efficiency and effectiveness of the various departments, to determine future business policies, and to report to the stockholders.

The format of managerial reports often cannot be predetermined. The particular form depends upon the decision that is to be made. If these reports are to be most beneficial, however, they should (1) be current, (2) contain sufficient details regarding the particular problem to be solved, and (3) present acceptable alternatives.

There is a constantly increasing reliance by business executives on financial reports. Large-scale production, wide geographical distribution, the increasing trend toward corporate business expansion with a concomitant delegation of authority, complex income tax legislation, and increasing governmental regulation of business are some of the factors requiring management reliance on corporate financial reports.

THE PURPOSE OF FINANCIAL STATEMENTS

Financial statements, whether in an annual report to stockholders, a prospectus for investors, or a report to grantors of credits or to management, should be prepared carefully. They should furnish the reader with interesting and attractive details about the company.

The purpose of financial statements appearing in annual corporate reports has been stated as follows:

> Financial statements are prepared for the purpose of presenting a periodical review or report on progress by the management and deal with the status of the investment in the business and the results achieved during the period under review. They reflect a combination of recorded facts, accounting conventions, and personal judgments; and the judgments and conventions applied affect them materially. The soundness of the judgments necessarily depends on the competence and integrity of those who make them and on their adherence to generally accepted accounting principles and conventions.[1]

Recorded facts refers to the data in financial statements as taken from the accounting records. The amounts of Cash, Accounts Receivable, and Plant and Equipment, for example, represent recorded facts. *Accounting conventions* are basic assumptions or conditions accepted by common consent. These conventions are concerned with the problems of asset valuation, allocation of expenditures between asset and expense classifications in the accounting period, and the proper measurement of

Accounting Concept: Basis of Reports ▶ income. ▶ Accounting statements are prepared on the assumption that each enterprise is a separate entity, that all business transactions can be expressed in dollars, that the enterprise will continue in business indefinitely, and that reports will be pre-

Accounting Concept: Importance of Personal Judgment ▶ pared at regular intervals. ◀

▶ Accounting is ultimately an art and not an exact science, and therefore financial statements must reflect the opinion and judgment of the accountant and of management. ◀ For example, the estimated life and the method of depreciation to be used in the valuation of plant and equipment, the method of inventory valuation, the valuation of intangibles (patents, goodwill, and so on) are some areas that require

Accounting Concept: Basic Purpose of Financial Statements ▶ opinion and judgment. Equally competent accountants, given the same set of facts, may arrive at different results. Thus, the element of personal judgment and preference affects the financial statements.

▶ In short, the basic purpose of financial statements is to transmit reliable and useful information to interested groups, both external and internal. Proper use of the information by these groups should result in their making sound decisions. ◀

---

[1] Examination of Financial Statements by Independent Public Accountants, *Bulletin of American Institute of Certified Public Accountants*, Jan., 1936, p. 1.

INTERPRETIVE FINANCIAL STATEMENT PRESENTATION

If the purpose of financial statements, as stated in the previous section, is to be achieved, these statements must be constructed in a manner that makes them as understandable and useful as possible to the reader. In preparing financial statements, the accountant should do his best to obtain an interpretative presentation of the information included therein. The following four basic devices are commonly utilized to achieve the desired interpretative statement presentation:

1. *Classification.* Items are presented together in classes to emphasize the similarity of the items within each class and to arrive at meaningful class totals.
2. *Arrangement.* Individual items, classes, totals, and other information are arranged within a statement to indicate important relationships in the data. The disclosure of total current assets and total current liabilities in juxta-position helps in evaluating the ability of a business to meet its current obligations.
3. *Order.* The order in which figures are shown directs attention to the most important data and reinforces the arrangement. For instance, the final figure on a typical income statement is the net income—the most important amount.
4. *Description.* Accountants have been accused of using out-dated, stereo-typed account titles in statements. This has been true in the past, but modern financial reports do not necessarily carry titles taken verbatim from the general ledger. Rather, serious consideration is given to the selection of words to ensure that descriptions of dollar amounts are both accurate and understandable.

The Statement of Financial Position

The statement of financial position, or balance sheet, often called the *statement of resources, liabilities, and owner's equity,* shows the financial position—the cost (or cost less accumulated amortization) of assets, the liabilities, and the equity of the owner or owners—as of a specific point in time. As previously explained, the statement may be prepared in one of two forms, account or report. A skeleton of the account form of position statement is shown:

Heading

Assets	Liabilities and Stockholders' Equity
Current Assets	Current Liabilities
Long-Term Investments	Long-Term Liabilities
Plant and Equipment	Deferred Credits
Intangible Assets	Total Liabilities
Deferred Charges	Stockholders' Equity
Total Assets	Total Liabilities and Stockholder's Equity

The chief advantage of this form of the statement of financial position is that the juxtaposition of subgroups helps to show the relationship of certain data and therefore facilitates statement analysis and interpretation.

An outline of a typical report form of position statement follows:

Heading

Assets

Current Assets
Long-Term Investments
Plant and Equipment
Intangible Assets
Deferred Charges
   Total Assets

Liabilities and Stockholders' Equity

Current Liabilities
Long-Term Liabilities
Deferred Credits
   Total Liabilities
Stockholders' Equity
   Total Liabilities and Stockholders' Equity

The advantages of this form include (1) ease of preparation and (2) expansibility. Since the totals do not have to be placed on the same line, this form of the statement is easier to prepare. In addition, a large number of items may be presented in an orderly manner.

The lists of class headings include several new terms. These are defined and illustrated on the following pages. The traditional class headings also are re-examined in light of the large number of items that have been introduced since classified statements were first discussed in Chapter 1.

CURRENT ASSETS. The term *current assets* is used to designate cash and other assets or resources commonly identified as those which are reasonably expected to be realized in cash or sold or consumed during the normal operating cycle of the business or one year, whichever is the longer period of time.[2] A normal operating cycle is the length of time it takes a business to purchase an entire stock of goods, convert them to accounts receivable, and collect the accounts receivable. One business may complete a single operating cycle in two years, whereas another business may have four cycles within a single year. In the latter case, the year is normally chosen as the length of time for determining the currency of assets; in the former case it would be two years.

Included in Current Assets are Cash, Marketable Securities, Accounts Receivable, Accrued Interest Receivable, Notes Receivable, Merchandise Inventory, and Prepaid Insurance and other prepaid expenses that will be consumed within a year or operating cycle, whichever is the longer period of time. Even though short-term prepaid expenses are not converted into cash as such, it is logical to include them among the current assets since in a break-even or profit-making operation their total cost will be recovered through revenue within the year or operating cycle.

---

[2] This definition is based on *Accounting Research and Terminology Bulletins,* Final Edition, 1961, New York: American Institute of Certified Public Accountants, *Accounting Research Bulletin No. 43,* p. 20.

Current assets are often subdivided into *quick current assets* and *trading current assets*. The quick current assets include Cash and the items that will normally be converted into cash rather rapidly, such as Marketable Securities and the receivables. The trading current assets include the inventories and prepaid expenses. This method of subdividing Current Assets is useful in financial statement analysis; for example, the acid-test ratio (Chapter 1) is determined by dividing quick current assets by total current liabilities.

LONG-TERM INVESTMENTS. The second asset caption is generally Long-Term Investments; it includes stocks and bonds purchased from other companies, long-term funds, long-term receivables, the cash surrender value of life insurance policies owned by the company, and land held for future use. To restrict the name long-term investments to this particular group of assets is somewhat misleading, since all assets represent investments. Nevertheless, it is a commonly accepted practice to include only the nonoperating, long-term assets under this caption.

PLANT AND EQUIPMENT. This group of assets includes those tangible, long-lived assets that are used in the operations of the business rather than being held for resale. Among these assets are land, buildings, machinery and equipment, and delivery equipment. Often called *fixed assets* or *fixed tangible assets*, these assets usually are disclosed on the statement of financial position in order of decreasing permanence, beginning with land and buildings.

A word of caution should be injected at this point. A generally accepted principle is that plant and equipment should be carried at original cost in the case of land and original cost less accumulated depreciation in the case of depreciable assets. Since this brief discussion is preparatory to the discussion of financial statement analysis, it should be kept in mind that most plant and equipment accounts contain a commingling of dollars with different purchasing powers. Sound financial statement analysis must take into account this fact, or perhaps even require that necessary price-level adjustments be made to the data that are being used in analysis relationships.

INTANGIBLE ASSETS. This group includes the long-term assets that have no form or substance but make a significant contribution to the production of revenue, typically by legally sheltering the company from competition. There are many intangible assets owned by entities. Some of them are current, such as Accounts Receivable; others are noncurrent, such as investments in bonds and stocks. The only items generally listed under Intangible Assets are goodwill, trademarks, copyrights, organization costs, patents, leaseholds, and leasehold improvements. Since only fixed assets appear under the caption Intangible Assets, it seems that the more descriptive caption Intangible Fixed Assets should be used.

DEFERRED CHARGES. Long-term unallocated debits against future operations commonly are referred to as *deferred charges*. This title to some extent describes all assets. Buildings depreciate and are allocated to future operations; merchandise is sold and its cost is allocated against future revenue; and even cash is held to acquire the assets that in turn become expenses, thus being allocated against future operations. Despite this fact, only a few items are generally shown under Deferred Charges; for instance, Research and Development Costs, Long-Term Prepaid Expenses, and Discount on Bonds Payable. Each of these items would be better disclosed under other statement of financial position captions. The first two are intangible fixed assets; the third should be offset against Bonds Payable under Long-Term Liabilities. There is little in accounting theory to justify the use of the classification Deferred Charges.

CURRENT LIABILITIES. Current liabilities represent obligations the liquidation of which requires the use of current assets or the creation of other current liabilities within a year or operating cycle, whichever is longer. Accounts Payable, Notes Payable, Accrued Expenses Payable, Sales Taxes Payable, and Unearned Revenue are typically carried under this caption, as well as currently maturing installments of long-term debts, such as the installment of serial bonds that is due within the coming year or operating cycle.

In much financial statement analysis, current liabilities are related either to current assets or to some subdivision of current assets. Thus it is important that any obligation that does not require the use of a current asset to liquidate it should not be classified as a current liability or else the resulting analyses will be misleading.

LONG-TERM LIABILITIES. Obligations that will not be liquidated until after the current year or operating cycle are referred to as Long-Term Liabilities, or Long-Term Debt. Shown under this caption are Bonds Payable, Mortgage Payable, Long-Term Contracts Payable, Liability Under Pension Contracts, and Long-Term Leases Payable. Proper disclosure dictates that maturity dates and other relevant information concerning these liabilities be clearly shown on the statement of financial position.

DEFERRED CREDITS. Appearing on many statements of financial position is the caption *Deferred Credits,* or *Deferred Revenue,* which represents long-term unallocated credits to future operations. As with the term Deferred Charges, Deferred Credits does not properly describe the items generally appearing under it, which are long-term unearned revenues such as Unrealized Gross Profit on Installment Sales, Premium on Bonds Payable, and similar items. Typically, this kind of caption becomes a catch-all classification for amounts that do not precisely fit under another caption. In attempting to analyze financial statements, it is extremely important to recognize this fact. Often a statement may have to be recast before it can be analyzed properly. As with Deferred Charges, there is little in financial reporting theory to justify this statement of financial position category.

STOCKHOLDERS' EQUITY. The Stockholders' Equity section of a statement of financial position for a corporation should not only disclose the major sources of capital, but should also show certain legal restrictions that are imposed on capital withdrawals. The following two outlines emphasize slightly different points of view:

Sources of Capital Approach

Stockholders' Equity
  Contributed Capital
    Preferred Stock
    Add Premium on Preferred Stock
      Total Capital Contributed by Preferred Stockholders
    Common Stock
    Deduct Discount on Common Stock
      Total Capital Contributed by Common Stockholders
    Other Contributed Capital
      Donation of Land by City of X
        Total Contributed Capital
  Retained Earnings
    Restricted for
      Contingencies
      Purchase of Treasury Stock
    Unrestricted
      Total Retained Earnings
    Deduct Treasury Stock–Common (at cost)
  Total Stockholders' Equity

Legal Capital Approach

Stockholders' Equity
  Capital Stock (legal capital)
    Preferred Stock
    Common Stock
      Total Legal Capital
  Other Contributed Capital (not legal capital)
    Premium on Preferred Stock
    Donation of Land by City of X
      Total
      Deduct Discount on Common Stock
        Total Other Contributed Capital
  Retained Earnings
    Restricted
      Contingencies
      Purchase of Treasury Stock
    Unrestricted
      Total Retained Earnings
    Deduct Treasury Stock–Common (at cost)
  Total Stockholders' Equity

Footnotes to Statements

Footnotes are used quite liberally to disclose methods of inventory pricing, depreciation methods, contingent liabilities, long-term lease provisions, and many other items. Some accounting theoreticians prefer to disclose contingent liabilities short, as shown:

Liabilities

Current Liabilities		
Accounts Payable		$ 50,000
Long-Term Liabilities		
Bonds Payable, due July 1, 1996		$100,000
Contingent Liabilities		
Pending Damage Lawsuits	$10,000	
Total Liabilities		$150,000

Since the amount of the contingent liabilities is not included in the total liabilities, this method of presentation is similar to a footnote; it is a memorandum included in the body of the statement of financial position. A criticism of this method of disclosure is that some readers will interpret these items to be actual liabilities.

The Income Statement and the Statement of Retained Earnings

Two other financial statements that appear in annual reports are the income statement and the statement of retained earnings. Opinion is divided concerning which of these two statements should be used to report extraordinary items such as losses from fires or natural hazards, nonrecurring gains or losses on the retirement of bonds payable or the disposal of assets, and corrections of errors in the income statements of prior periods. The two different theories that underlie the preparation of these statements are known as the *current operating performance concept* and the *all-inclusive concept.*

THE CURRENT OPERATING PERFORMANCE CONCEPT. There is as yet no precise and universally accepted definition of the term *net income;* for instance, there is disagreement as to the classification of an uninsured flood loss, and no single general method of reporting the discovery of a material error in computing depreciation in the preceding accounting period. Assume, for example, that the Baxter Company earns an ordinary income of $50,000 for each of the three years 1969 through 1971; in addition, in the first year it sells a patent that it developed but did not use for a gain of $100,000; in the second year it sells other plant assets for a gain of $70,000; and in the third year it experiences an uninsured fire loss in the plant of $50,000. Under the *current operating performance concept,* the Baxter Company's net income would be reported as *$50,000 each year.* However, under the all-inclusive concept, the net income would be reported as shown:

	1969	1970	1971
Ordinary income	$ 50,000	$ 50,000	$50,000
Extraordinary gain(loss)	100,000	70,000	(50,000)
Net income before income taxes	$150,000	$120,000	$ –0–

Those favoring the current operating performance concept would include in the income statement all recurring items only and exclude any nonrecurring or extraordinary items of material amount that are not related to the operations of the period.

Such nonrecurring items would be shown in the statement of retained earnings. Advocates maintain that under this concept the income statement shows what took place under normal business conditions and that statement comparability is thereby enhanced.

The statement of retained earnings in Figure 17-1 supports an income statement prepared in accordance with the current operating performance concept.

EVANS COMPANY
Statement of Retained Earnings
For the Year Ended December 31, 1969

Retained Earnings, December 31, 1968		$220,000
Corrections Applicable to Prior Periods		
Add Cost of Machinery Charged to Equipment Repairs	$10,000	
Deduct Understatement of Depreciation	1,000	9,000
Corrected Balance, December 31, 1968		$229,000
Net Income per Income Statement		65,000
Total		$294,000
Deduct Dividends Declared and Paid	$15,000	
Loss from Flood	5,000	
Loss from Sale of Land	10,000	30,000
Retained Earnings, December 31, 1969		$264,000

Figure 17-1.
Statement of Retained Earnings Under the Current Operating Performance Concept

THE ALL-INCLUSIVE CONCEPT. Advocates of the all-inclusive concept maintain that all items of revenue, expense, gain, and loss should be included in the income statement and that the statement of retained earnings should be used only for reporting dividends, retained income, and restrictions and releases of restrictions on retained earnings. They further maintain that the periodic income statements should record the total income history of the company; that allowing the omission of extraordinary

EVANS COMPANY
Condensed Income Statement
For the Year Ended December 31, 1969

Net Sales Revenue		$390,000
Cost of Goods Sold		200,000
Gross Margin on Sales		$190,000
Deduct Operating and General Expenses		60,000
Net Income Before Income Taxes		$130,000
Income Taxes		65,000
Net Income Before Extraordinary Items		$ 65,000
Add Adjustment of Cost of Machinery Charged to Equipment Repairs		10,000
Total		$ 75,000
Deduct: Understatement of Depreciation	$ 1,000	
Loss from Flood	5,000	
Loss from Sale of Land	10,000	16,000
Net Income After Extraordinary Items		$ 59,000

Figure 17-2.
Income Statement Under the All-Inclusive Concept

items from the income statement furnishes an opportunity of concealing pertinent information; and that the omission or inclusion of certain items in borderline cases may make possible the manipulation of reported net earnings. The income statement in Figure 17-2 and the supporting statement of retained earnings in Figure 17-3 are prepared in accordance with the all-inclusive concept.

Figure 17-3.
Statement of Retained Earnings Under the All-Inclusive Concept

EVANS COMPANY
Statement of Retained Earnings
For the Year Ended December 31, 1969

Retained Earnings, December 31, 1968	$220,000
Net Income After Extraordinary Items per Income Statement	59,000
Total	$279,000
Deduct Dividends Declared and Paid	15,000
Retained Earnings, December 31, 1969	$264,000

The proponents of the current operating performance concept state that all-inclusive income statements contain the following basic flaws: (1) Lay readers of the income statement make mental adjustments for the nonrecurring items and may therefore draw distorted conclusions regarding the earning power of the business. (2) Financial reporting services or newspapers are likely to publish the reported net income figures and may thereby mislead even knowledgeable readers who have not seen the original statements.

COMBINED STATEMENT OF INCOME AND RETAINED EARNINGS. Many accountants favor combining the statements of income and retained earnings to show within one statement both the recurring and the nonrecurring items. By placing the nonrecurring items in a separate section of the income statement, operating income as

Figure 17-4.
Combined Statement of Income and Retained Earnings Under the Current Operating Performance Concept

EVANS COMPANY
Statement of Income and Retained Earnings
For the Year Ended December 31, 1969

Net Sales Revenue		$390,000
Net Income After Income Taxes		$ 65,000
Add Retained Earnings, December 31, 1968		220,000
Total		$285,000
Correction Applicable to Prior Periods		
Add Cost of Machinery Charged to Equipment Repairs	$10,000	
Deduct Understatement of Depreciation	1,000	9,000
Total		$294,000
Deduct Dividends Declared and Paid	$15,000	
Loss from Flood	5,000	
Loss from Sale of Land	10,000	30,000
Retained Earnings, December 31, 1969		$264,000

well as net income may be shown. A disadvantage of the combined statement is that it does not end with the amount of Net Income. If care is exercised in distinguishing between recurring and nonrecurring charges and credits, the combined statement is convenient and useful. The combined statement of income and retained earnings for the Evans Company, prepared in accordance with the current operating concept, is illustrated in Figure 17-4. Figure 17-5 illustrates the combined statement of income and retained earnings under the all-inclusive concept. Some figures are omitted to avoid duplication of material in the previous statements.

EVANS COMPANY
Statement of Income and Retained Earnings
For the Year Ended December 31, 1969

Net Sales Revenue	$390,000
Net Income After Extraordinary Items (see Figure 17-2)	$ 59,000
Add Retained Earnings, December 31, 1968	220,000
Total	$279,000
Deduct Dividends Declared and Paid	15,000
Retained Earnings, December 31, 1969	$264,000

Figure 17-5.
Combined Statement of Income and Retained Earnings Under the All-Inclusive Concept

ALL-INCLUSIVE SINGLE-STEP INCOME STATEMENT. The all-inclusive single-step income statement shows all the revenue items and the amount of total revenues, followed by a listing of all costs and expenses whose total is deducted from total revenue to determine net income. This type of statement has the advantage of easy readability. There are no intermediate additions and deductions, with accompanying labeled subtotals that may confuse the untrained reader. It is primarily for this reason that this form has become increasingly popular in recent years. The single-step statement is best adapted for annual reports to stockholders since they are not vitally interested in operating details.

Certain intermediate figures that are important for management purposes, such as the cost of goods sold, the gross margin on sales, and the net income before income taxes, are not shown. Furthermore, only a skilled reader is able to determine operating income because nonrecurring items are intermingled with recurring items. The single-step statement does not furnish management with sufficient data for decision making. The income statement of the Evans Company is illustrated in single-step form in Figure 17-6.

ALL-INCLUSIVE MULTIPLE-STEP INCOME STATEMENT. The all-inclusive multiple-step income statement is illustrated in Figure 17-2. The groupings in this statement furnish the following essential data: gross margin on sales, operating income, net income before income taxes, and extraordinary items. These figures are valuable in making statistical analyses, in comparing current data with prior periods of the company and with data of the industry, and in financial planning. The usefulness of this form of statement to management justifies its popularity.

EVANS COMPANY

Income Statement

For the Year Ended December 31, 1969

Figure 17-6.
All-Inclusive
Single-Step
Income Statement

Revenue		
Net Sales Revenue	$390,000	
Purchase of Machinery Charged to Equipment		
Maintenance and Repairs	10,000	$400,000
Revenue Deductions		
Cost of Goods Sold	$200,000	
Selling and General Expenses	60,000	
Income Taxes	65,000	
Understatement of Depreciation	1,000	
Loss from Flood	5,000	
Loss from Sale of Land	10,000	341,000
Net Income		$ 59,000

THE INTERPRETATION AND ANALYSIS OF FINANCIAL DATA

Before an individual can adequately understand and evaluate financial statement data, he must (1) understand the nature and limitations of accounting, (2) understand the terminology of accounting and business, (3) have some knowledge of business, and (4) be acquainted with the nature and tools of financial statement analysis. The major problem for current consideration is a further look at Item 4, the tools of financial statement analysis.

The Tools of Financial Statement Analyses

The figures in financial statements may be said to have significance in at least three different respects. First, in themselves they are measures of absolute quantity. When an analyst sees that a company has $50,000 in cash, he understands that figure in terms of current purchasing power. However, the absolute amount does not tell him whether it is adequate for the current needs of the particular company. Some other means of determining its significance is required. Second, a degree of significance is indicated when figures are compared with similar amounts for other years and other companies. If $50,000 in cash was shown on the statement of financial position at the end of the previous year, if that amount was sufficient at that time, and if no changes in needs are foreseen, then it may be assumed that a Cash balance of $50,000 is adequate now. A third determinant of significance is the consideration of financial data in conjunction with related figures. When current assets are compared with current liabilities, the margin of safety—the dollars of current assets behind each dollar of current liabilities —can be determined.

The various tools of financial statement analysis are related to the ways in which financial data have significance. These tools are (1) comparative statements, (2) percentage analyses, (3) ratio analyses, and (4) a combination of the three. Percentage and ratio analyses have been illustrated throughout this text, but little has been said about comparative statements as such. In the following discussion, emphasis is placed on comparative statements; then a summary chart of the major ratios that have been discussed is presented.

Comparative Financial Statements

A study of the financial position of a company and the results of its operations for a period is more meaningful if the analyst has available the statements of financial position and income statements for several periods. Trends can be better ascertained when two or more financial statements are compared. It is not uncommon to find comparative statements for at least three years in annual reports. One large corporation in its recent annual report showed comparative financial statements covering a period of fifteen years.

▶ For effective analysis, the statements being compared must be based on the consistent application of generally accepted accounting principles over the period of time covered by the comparison. If there is an absence of comparability, it should be made known in the accountant's report. ◀ The effect on net income, for example, of a changeover from FIFO to LIFO in valuing inventories must be clearly disclosed in the report.

◀ *Accounting Concept: Comparability of Data on Statements*

The American Institute of Certified Public Accountants makes the following recommendations regarding comparative financial statements:

> The presentation of comparative financial statements in annual and other reports enhances the usefulness of such reports and brings out more clearly the nature and trends of current changes affecting the enterprise. Such presentation emphasizes the fact that statements for a series of periods are far more significant than those for a single period and that the accounts for one period are but an installment of what is essentially a continuous history.
>
> In any one year it is ordinarily desirable that the balance sheet (statement of financial position), the income statement, and the surplus statement (statement of retained earnings) be given for one or more preceding years as well as for the current year. Footnotes, explanations, and accountant's qualifications which appeared on the statements for the preceding years should be repeated, or at least referred to, in the comparative statements to the extent that they continue to be of significance . . . . This procedure is in conformity with the well-recognized principle that any change in practice which affects comparability should be disclosed.[3]

The use of comparative information in annual corporate reports to stockholders is nearly universal. Other devices are also used to present the entire financial story as clearly and attractively as possible. Although there is no uniformity in the type of visual and statistical aids used, some of the more common are comparative statements with accompanying *trend percentages; common-size* statements, which present individual figures as percentages of a base total or some other established norm; pictorial statements using bar or line graphs to emphasize particular trends, ratios, or relationships; and pie-charts showing the allocation of each company sales dollar. Any of these methods of presentation can make an interesting and informative report, aimed at perhaps the largest audience in the history of corporate reporting. Some of these devices are illustrated in this chapter.

---

[3] *Accounting Research and Terminology Bulletins,* Final Edition, 1961, New York: American Institute of Certified Public Accountants *Accounting Research Bulletin No. 43*, p. 15.

THE COMPARATIVE STATEMENT OF FINANCIAL POSITION. Successive statements of financial position of a company may be given side by side, showing only the dollar amounts. These statements can be made more meaningful if the dollar amount of increase or decrease and the percentage of increase and decrease are also shown. This is illustrated in Figure 17-7, the comparative position statement of the Melvin Company. In this illustration, the year 1968 is the base year and represents 100 percent. Accounts Receivable increased by 30.8 percent ($8,000 ÷ $26,000) during 1969; Notes Payable decreased by 5 percent ($1,000 ÷ $20,000); and Cash increased by $16,000, or 100 percent. The December 31, 1969, cash balance is twice the December 31, 1968, balance; Retained Earnings as of December 31, 1969, are almost twice the amount shown on December 31, 1968. No additional plant and equipment assets were acquired; the decreases reflect the annual depreciation deductions.

Figure 17-7.
*Comparative Statement
of Financial Position*

MELVIN COMPANY
Comparative Statement of Financial Position
December 31, 1969 and 1968

	December 31 1969	December 31 1968	Amount of Increase or (Decrease) During 1969	Percent of Increase or (Decrease) During 1969
Assets				
Current Assets				
Cash	$ 32,000	$ 16,000	$16,000	100.0
Accounts Receivable (net)	34,000	26,000	8,000	30.8
Inventories	45,000	36,000	9,000	25.0
Total Current Assets	$111,000	$ 78,000	$33,000	42.3
Plant and Equipment				
Store Equipment (net)	$ 23,000	$ 25,000	$ (2,000)	(8.0)
Building (net)	116,000	119,000	(3,000)	(2.5)
Land	7,000	7,000	—	—
Total Plant and Equipment	$146,000	$151,000	$ (5,000)	(3.3)
Total Assets	$257,000	$229,000	$28,000	12.2
Liabilities and Stockholders' Equity				
Current Liabilities				
Accounts Payable	$ 34,000	$ 26,000	$ 8,000	30.8
Notes Payable	19,000	20,000	(1,000)	(5.0)
Accrued Payables	11,000	8,000	3,000	37.5
Total Current Liabilities	$ 64,000	$ 54,000	$10,000	18.5
Long-Term Liabilities				
Mortgage Payable	55,000	60,000	(5,000)	(8.3)
Total Liabilities	$119,000	$114,000	$ 5,000	4.4
Stockholders' Equity				
Capital Stock	$109,000	$100,000	$ 9,000	9.0
Retained Earnings	29,000	15,000	14,000	93.3
Total Stockholders' Equity	$138,000	$115,000	$23,000	20.0
Total Liabilities and Stockholders' Equity	$257,000	$229,000	$28,000	12.2

MELVIN COMPANY

Comparative Statement of Income and Retained Earnings

For the Years Ended December 31, 1969 and 1968

	Years Ended December 31		Amount of Increase or (Decrease) During 1969	Percent of Increase or (Decrease) During 1969
	1969	1968		
Sales (net)	$197,000	$151,000	$46,000	30.5
Cost of Goods Sold	123,000	92,000	31,000	33.7
Gross Margin on Sales	$ 74,000	$ 59,000	$15,000	25.4
Operating Expenses				
Selling Expenses				
Advertising	$ 1,200	$ 1,100	$ 100	9.1
Sales Salaries	18,300	17,900	400	2.2
Depreciation Expense–Store Equipment	2,000	2,000	–0–	–0–
Total Selling Expenses	$ 21,500	$ 21,000	$ 500	2.4
General Expenses				
Depreciation Expense–Building	$ 3,000	$ 3,000		
Insurance Expense	675	650	$ 25	3.8
Miscellaneous General Expenses	425	350	75	21.4
General Salaries	7,200	8,000	(800)	(10.0)
Total General Expenses	$ 11,300	$ 12,000	$ (700)	(5.8)
Total Operating Expenses	$ 32,800	$ 33,000	$ (200)	(0.6)
Operating Income	$ 41,200	$ 26,000	$15,200	58.5
Other Expenses				
Interest Expense	2,750	3,000	(250)	(8.3)
Net Income Before Income Taxes	$ 38,450	$ 23,000	$15,450	67.2
Income Taxes	14,450	7,000	7,450	106.4
Net Income After Income Taxes	$ 24,000	$ 16,000	$ 8,000	50.0
Retained Earnings, January 1	15,000	9,000	6,000	66.7
Total	$ 39,000	$ 25,000	$14,000	56.0
Dividends Paid	10,000	10,000	–0–	–0–
Retained Earnings, December 31	$ 29,000	$ 15,000	$14,000	93.3

Figure 17-8.
Comparative Statement of Income and Retained Earnings

The trend for Melvin Company is apparently favorable. Current assets have increased by 42.3 percent, whereas current liabilities have increased by only 18.5 percent. The total stockholders' equity has increased by 20 percent; this is reflected by an increase in all the current assets. The favorable position of Retained Earnings, accompanied by an increase in working capital, was accomplished without resort to long-term borrowing because Mortgage Payable and Notes Payable have decreased during the period. Additional working capital was acquired by the sale of stock.

THE COMPARATIVE INCOME STATEMENT. A single income statement is just one link in a continuous chain reporting the operating results of the business. Comparative income statements are required for an analysis of trends and for making decisions regarding possible future developments. An income statement showing the results of operations for a single year is inadequate for purposes of analyzing the significance of the changes that have occurred.

The comparative statement of income and retained earnings of the Melvin Company is shown in Figure 17-8. The year 1968 is again used as the base year. Gross Margin on Sales increased by 25.4 percent, Net Income Before Income Taxes increased by 67.2 percent; and Total Operating Expenses decreased by 0.6 percent. These favorable changes resulted primarily from an increase in sales. The provision for income taxes increased by 106.4 percent due to the sharp change in the Federal corporate tax rate on earnings in excess of $25,000. In 1968, it was assumed that the entire net taxable income of $23,000 was subject to only the normal corporate tax rate; whereas, in 1969, $13,450 ($38,450 − $25,000) was assumed to be subject to both the normal and the surtax rates.

There is a close relationship between the cost of goods sold, the volume of sales, and net income before income taxes. In periods of exceptionally high sales volume, net income before income taxes tends to rise (percentage of increase, 67.2) at a faster rate than do sales (percentage of increase, 30.5). In periods of declining sales volume, earnings fall more sharply than sales. This is because a significant part of the operating expenses are constant—they are not affected by the current sales volume. Such fluctuations in net income can be eliminated if unit sales prices are increased in periods of low sales volume and reduced in periods of high sales volume. Such a pricing policy, however, would be undesirable from the customers' viewpoint and impracticable from the company's viewpoint. It becomes important, therefore, that management knows the volume at which profits begin. This figure, the *break-even point,* is that volume of sales at which the business will neither make a profit nor incur a loss. Break-even analysis is discussed and illustrated in Chapter 22.

Percentage increases or decreases are calculated only when the base figure is positive. When there is no figure for the base year or when base year amounts are negative, there is no extension into the Percent of Increase or (Decrease) column. When there is a positive amount in the base year and none in the following year, the percent of decrease is 100, as shown:

	1969	1968 (Base Year)	Amount of Increase or (Decrease)	Percent of Increase or (Decrease)
Notes Receivable	$3,000	–0–	$3,000	—
Notes Payable	–0–	$2,000	(2,000)	(100)
Net Income or (Loss)	4,000	(1,000)	5,000	—

Trend Percentages

Comparative financial statements for several years may be expressed in terms of trend percentages. Management can more readily study changes in financial statements between periods by establishing a base year and expressing the other years in terms of the base year. The base year may be any typical year in the comparison—the first, the last, or any of the others. To illustrate, a partial comparative income statement is presented in Figure 17-9.

	1968	1969	1970	1971
Sales (net)	$100,000	$95,000	$120,000	$130,000
Cost of Goods Sold	60,000	58,900	69,600	72,800
Gross Margin on Sales	$ 40,000	$36,100	$ 50,400	$ 57,200
Total Selling Expenses	$ 10,000	$ 9,700	$ 11,000	$ 12,000
Net Income Before Income Taxes	$ 5,000	$ 3,800	$ 8,400	$ 10,400

Figure 17-9.
Partial Comparative Income Statements for Four Years

The amounts in Figure 17-9 are converted into trend percentages with 1968 as the base year, as shown in Figure 17-10.

	1968	1969	1970	1971
Sales (net)	100%	95%	120%	130%
Cost of Goods Sold	100	98	116	121
Gross Margin on Sales	100	90	126	143
Total Selling Expenses	100	97	110	120
Net Income Before Income Taxes	100	76	168	208

Figure 17-10.
Comparative Trend Percentages for Four Years

Each item in the 1968 column of Figure 17-9 is assigned a weight of 100 percent. All the amounts in other years are expressed as trend percentages, or percentages of the figures for the base year. Each base year amount is divided into the same item for the other years. Trend percentages for Sales, for example, are calculated as follows: 1969—$95,000 ÷ $100,000 = 95; 1970—$120,000 ÷ $100,000 = 120; and 1971— $130,000 ÷ $100,000 = 130. When the base year amount is larger than the corresponding amount in another year, the trend percentage is less than 100 percent; conversely, when the base year amount is the lesser of the two, the trend percentage is over 100 percent.

The trend percentage statement is an analytical device for condensing the absolute dollar data of comparative statements. The device is especially valuable to management because readability and brevity are achieved by substituting percentages for large dollar amounts, which in themselves are difficult to compare. Trend percentages are generally computed for the major items in the statements; minor amounts are omitted, the objective being to highlight the significant changes.

An evaluation of the trend percentages requires a careful analysis of the interrelated items. Sales, for example, may show increases over a four-year period leading up to a trend percentage of 150 percent for the fourth year. This is unfavorable if it is accompanied by trend percentages of 200 percent for cost of goods sold, 175 percent for selling expenses, and 95 percent for net income before income taxes. Other unfavorable trends include an upward trend in receivables and inventories accompanied by a downward trend in sales and a downward trend in sales accompanied by an upward trend in plant and equipment. Favorable trends would be an increase in sales accompanied by a decrease in cost of goods sold and selling expenses or an increase in current assets accompanied by a decrease in current liabilities.

Trend percentages show the degree of increase and decrease; they do not indicate the causes of the changes. They do, however, single out unfavorable developments for further analysis and investigation by management. A marked change may have been caused by inconsistency in the application of accounting principles, by fluctuating price levels, or by controllable internal factors (for example, an unnecessary increase in merchandise inventory or a decrease in operating efficiency).

Common-Size Statements

Trend percentages provide for *horizontal statement analysis;* common-size statements provide for *vertical analysis* (see Figure 17-11). It is important for the analyst to compare changes on the financial statements that occur from period to period with certain base totals within those periods. Thus total assets, total liabilities and stockholders' equity, and total sales are each converted to a base of 100 percent. Each item within each classification is expressed as a percentage of the base; each asset, for example, is expressed as a percentage of total assets. Since these bases represent 100 percent in all the statements in the comparison, there is a common basis for analysis; therefore the statements are referred to as common-size statements. Comparisons can be made within the company, with other companies in the same industry, or with entire industry figures. Thus, important relationships can be discerned even when comparisons are made with companies of unlike size; and any significant differences may indicate that a decision should be made. The common-size statement, supplemented by additional analytical financial data, are effective tools for an historical financial study of a business or industry. ▶ If comparisons are to be made of one company with one or more other companies or with an entire industry, it must first be carefully established that the data in the comparison are based on reasonably uniform and consistent accounting methods and principles. ◀

Accounting Concept: Uniformity of Data for Comparisons ▶

COMMON-SIZE STATEMENT OF FINANCIAL POSITION. The common-size position statement of the Melvin Company is shown in Figure 17-11. The method of converting dollar amounts into common-size percentages, using data from Figure 17-11, is shown:

$$\frac{\text{Accounts Receivable (1969)}}{\text{Total Assets (1969)}} = \frac{\$34,000}{\$257,000} = 13.2\%$$

Accounts Receivable in 1969 represent 13.2 percent of the total assets. For each dollar of total assets there were 13.2 cents of accounts receivable.

$$\frac{\text{Accounts Payable (1968)}}{\text{Total Liabilities and Stockholders' Equity (1968)}} = \frac{\$26,000}{\$229,000} = 11.4\%$$

MELVIN COMPANY
Comparative Common-Size Statement of Financial Position
December 31, 1969 and 1968

	December 31		Common-Size Percentages December 31	
	1969	1968	1969	1968
Assets				
Current Assets				
Cash	$ 32,000	$ 16,000	12.5	7.0
Accounts Receivable (net)	34,000	26,000	13.2	11.4
Inventories	45,000	36,000	17.5	15.7
Total Current Assets	$111,000	$ 78,000	43.2	34.1
Plant and Equipment				
Store Equipment (net)	$ 23,000	$ 25,000	8.9	10.9
Building (net)	116,000	119,000	45.1	52.0
Land	7,000	7,000	2.8	3.0
Total Plant and Equipment	$146,000	$151,000	56.8	65.9
Total Assets	$257,000	$229,000	100.0	100.0
Liabilities and Stockholders' Equity				
Current Liabilities				
Accounts Payable	$ 34,000	$ 26,000	13.2	11.4
Notes Payable	19,000	20,000	7.4	8.7
Accrued Payables	11,000	8,000	4.3	3.5
Total Current Liabilities	$ 64,000	$ 54,000	24.9	23.6
Long-Term Liabilities				
Mortgage Payable	$ 55,000	$ 60,000	21.4	26.2
Total Liabilities	$119,000	$114,000	46.3	49.8
Stockholders' Equity				
Capital Stock	$109,000	$100,000	42.4	43.7
Retained Earnings	29,000	15,000	11.3	6.5
Total Stockholders' Equity	$138,000	$115,000	53.7	50.2
Total Liabilities and Stockholders' Equity	$257,000	$229,000	100.0	100.0

Figure 17-11.
Comparative Common-Size Statement of Financial Position

Accounts Payable for 1968 represent 11.4 percent of total liabilities and stockholders' equity. For each dollar of total liabilities and stockholders' equity there were 11.4 cents of accounts payable.

Each current asset item has increased both in dollar amount and as a percentage of the total assets. Total current assets for 1969 have increased by 9.1 percent (43.2% − 34.1%) over 1968; total current liabilities for 1969 have increased by only 1.3 percent. Thus, the working capital position has been strengthened. Increases in net income and proceeds from the sale of stock are reflected by increases in each current asset item. The Company did not invest in plant and equipment; the decreases in Store Equipment and Building are due to deductions for annual depreciation charges.

The ratio of stockholders' equity to total assets has increased, with corresponding decreases in the ratio of total liabilities to total assets. On December 31, 1968, the ratio of total liabilities to total assets was 49.8 percent; a year later this decreased to 46.3 percent. The overall financial position of the Melvin Company has improved.

Common-Size Income Statement. The common-size income statement of the Melvin Company is shown in Figure 17-12. Examples of the conversion of income statement dollar amounts into common-size percentages are shown:

$$\frac{\text{Gross Margin on Sales (1969)}}{\text{Net Sales (1969)}} = \frac{\$74,000}{\$197,000} = 37.6\%$$

Gross margin on sales for 1969 represents 37.6 percent of net sales; for each dollar of net sales there was a margin of 37.6 cents.

$$\frac{\text{Total Operating Expenses (1968)}}{\text{Net Sales (1968)}} = \frac{\$33,000}{\$151,000} = 21.8\%$$

Total operating expenses for 1968 represent 21.8 percent of net sales; for each dollar of net sales there were 21.8 cents of total operating expenses.

MELVIN COMPANY
Comparative Common-Size Income Statement
For the Years Ended December 31, 1969 and 1968

Figure 17-12.
*Comparative
Common-Size
Income Statement*

	Year Ended December 31		Common-Size Percentages December 31	
	1969	1968	1969	1968
Sales (net)	$197,000	$151,000	100.0	100.0
Cost of Goods Sold	123,000	92,000	62.4	60.9
Gross Margin on Sales	$ 74,000	$ 59,000	37.6	39.1
Operating Expenses				
Selling Expenses				
Advertising	$ 1,200	$ 1,100	0.6	0.7
Sales Salaries	18,300	17,900	9.3	11.9
Depreciation Expense–Store Equipment	2,000	2,000	1.0	1.3
Total Selling Expenses	$ 21,500	$ 21,000	10.9	13.9
General Expenses				
Depreciation Expense–Building	$ 3,000	$ 3,000	1.5	1.9
Insurance Expense	675	650	0.4	0.4
Miscellaneous General Expenses	425	350	0.2	0.2
General Salaries	7,200	8,000	3.7	5.4
Total General Expenses	$ 11,300	$ 12,000	5.8	7.9
Total Operating Expenses	$ 32,800	$ 33,000	16.7	21.8
Net Operating Margin	$ 41,200	$ 26,000	20.9	17.3
Other Expenses				
Interest Expense	$ 2,750	$ 3,000	1.4	2.0
Net Income Before Income Taxes	$ 38,450	$ 23,000	19.5	15.3
Income Taxes	14,450	7,000	7.3	4.7
Net Income	$ 24,000	$ 16,000	12.2	10.6

A comparison of the cost of goods sold for the two years shows an increase of 1.5 percent (62.4% — 60.9%) and a corresponding decrease in the gross margin. This relatively modest change may indicate an increase in markdowns from original sales prices. Increases in amounts and percentages of inventories accompanied by a decrease in gross margin may indicate an overinvestment in inventories.

The change in total operating expenses is favorable: sales increased by $46,000 ($197,000 — $151,000) while total operating expenses remained approximately the same. The Melvin Company has increased the efficiency of its operations by increasing dollar sales without increasing its operating costs—a favorable development. The amount and ratio of the increase in income taxes is at best a semi-uncontrollable factor.

Use of the Company's Revenue Dollar

Annual reports often include graphic presentations of the disposition of each revenue dollar. These may take the form of a pie-chart, bar graph, or simple statement. Such a presentation is often more meaningful to the reader than a detailed income statement and is popular for its simplicity and effectiveness.

A revenue-dollar statement for Melvin Company is shown:

	1969	1968
Each sales dollar was allocated as follows		
Cost of Goods Sold	$ .624	$ .609
Selling Expenses	.109	.139
General Expenses	.058	.079
Interest Expense	.014	.020
Income Taxes	.073	.047
Net Income	.122	.106
Total Sales Dollar	$1.000	$1.000

Ratios

A tabulation of seventeen significant ratios is shown in Figure 17-13, indicating the range of possibilities in the analysis of financial statements. With the aid of these ratios, the skilled analyst is better able to evaluate the managerial efficiency and financial stability of a company.

Figure 17-13.
Major Ratios

Chapter Reference	Ratio	Computation of Ratio	Indicates
1	Current Ratio	$\dfrac{\text{Current Assets}}{\text{Current Liabilities}}$	The ability of a business to meet its current obligations
1	Acid-Test Ratio	$\dfrac{\text{Quick Assets}}{\text{Current Liabilities}}$	The ability of a business to meet quickly unexpected demands for working capital
4	Creditors' Equity Ratio	$\dfrac{\text{Total Liabilities}}{\text{Total Assets}}$	The amount of the creditor sources of total assets
4	Stockholders' Equity Ratio	$\dfrac{\text{Stockholders' Equity}}{\text{Total Assets}}$	The amount of owner sources of assets
5	Net Income to Stockholders' Equity	$\dfrac{\text{Net Income}}{\text{Average Stockholders' Equity}}$	The profitableness of the business expressed as a rate of return on the stockholders' equity

Chapter Reference	Ratio	Computation of Ratio	Indicates
5	Operating Ratio	$$\frac{\text{Cost of Goods Sold} + \text{Operating Expenses}}{\text{Net Sales Revenue}}$$	The number of cents needed to generate one dollar of sales
5	Merchandise Inventory Turnover	$$\frac{\text{Cost of Goods Sold}}{\text{Average Inventory}}$$	The number of times the merchandise inventory was replenished during the period, or the number of dollars in the cost of goods sold for each dollar of inventory
9	Average Number of Days' Sales Uncollected	$$\frac{\text{Average Accounts Receivable}}{\text{Net Sales}} \times 365$$ OR (1) $$\text{Net Sales} \div 365 = \text{Net Sales Per Day}$$ (2) $$\frac{\text{Average Trade Receivables}}{\text{Net Sales Per Day}}$$	The rapidity with which the accounts receivable are collected; the average number of days elapsing from the time of sale to the time of payment
11	Plant and Equipment to Long-Term Liabilities	$$\frac{\text{Plant and Equipment (net)}}{\text{Long-Term Debt}}$$	The adequacy of protection to long-term creditors
11	Plant and Equipment to Stockholders' Equity	$$\frac{\text{Plant and Equipment (net)}}{\text{Stockholders' Equity}}$$	The extent to which owner sources are being used to finance plant and equipment acquisitions
11	Sales to Plant and Equipment (Plant Turnover)	$$\frac{\text{Net Sales}}{\text{Average Plant and Equipment (net)}}$$	Dollar of sales per dollar of investment in plant and equipment assets
13	Number of Times Preferred Dividend is Earned	$$\frac{\text{Net Income}}{\text{Annual Preferred Dividend}}$$	The primary measure of the safety of an individual's investment in preferred stock—the ability of a firm to meet its preferred dividend requirement
15	Earnings Per Share of Common Stock	$$\frac{\text{Net Income minus Annual Preferred Dividend}}{\text{Outstanding Common Shares}}$$	The company's earning power as related to common stockholders' equity
15	Leverage	(1) $$\frac{\text{Net Income} + \text{Bond Interest}}{\text{Average Total Assets}}$$ $$= \text{\% Earned on Total Investment}$$ (2) $$\frac{\text{Net Income}}{\text{Average Stockholders' Equity}}$$ $$= \text{\% Earned on Stockholders' Equity}$$	Return on prior obligations (bonds) compared with return on stockholders' equity
16	Number of Times Bond Interest is Earned	$$\frac{\text{Net Income} + \text{Income Taxes} + \text{Annual Bond Interest Expense}}{\text{Annual Bond Interest Expense}}$$	The primary measure of the safety of an individual's investment in bonds—the ability of a firm to meet its bond interest requirement

(*Figure 17-13.*
Continued on
following page.)

Chapter Reference	Ratio	Computation of Ratio	Indicates
19	Raw Materials Turnover	$$\frac{\text{Raw Materials Used}}{\text{Average Raw Materials Inventory}}$$	The number of times the raw materials inventory was replaced during the period, or the number of dollars of raw materials used in manufacturing for each dollar of inventory on hand
19	Finished Goods Turnover	$$\frac{\text{Cost of Goods Sold}}{\text{Average Finished Goods Inventory}}$$	The number of times the finished goods inventory was sold and replaced during the period, or the number of dollars of cost of finished goods sold for each dollar of finished goods on hand

FINANCIAL STATEMENT ANALYSIS—INFLUENCES

The techniques and procedures for the analysis of financial statements discussed thus far are useful tools for gaining an insight into the financial affairs of a business. The analyst must, however, evaluate many other influences that, although not specifically reflected in the statements, may nevertheless influence the future of the company. Careful evaluation must be made of the possible effect on the company of sudden changes in key management personnel, shifts in employee or customer loyalty, development of new competing products, as well as broad shifts in the social, political, or economic environment. Another factor that must be evaluated with care is the impact of changing price levels on the statements. Also, differences in financial statements may be due to the wide variations that exist within the framework of generally accepted accounting principles—in the valuation of inventories, the selection of depreciation bases, the treatment of intangibles, and the method of disclosing extraordinary and nonrecurring items, for example.

SUMMARY

One of the fundamental responsibilities of an accounting department is the preparation of various financial reports to be used by management and interested outside parties, including stockholders, potential investors, and grantors of credit.

The increase in the number of stockholders and diversity of ownership that accompanied the immense growth in the size of corporations resulted in the adoption of regulations by the New York Stock Exchange and the Securities Exchange Commission as a means of protecting the investments of these stockholders. As a result of the efforts of these organizations and other groups, the quality of the information included in financial statements has vastly improved. Factors such as large-scale production, wide geographical distribution, the increasing trend toward corporate business expansion with a concomitant delegation of authority, complex income tax legislation, and increasing governmental regulations have necessitated a comprehensible medium of communication within an organization. To satisfy this demand, management has relied upon various accounting and financial reports. To be of maximum usefulness, reports for management must be specifically tailored to fit the decisions to be based on the reports. They should be current, contain sufficient detail of the particular problem to be solved, and present acceptable alternatives. The purpose of financial statements, particularly the annual reports to stockholders, is the communication of the progress made by management, the status of the investment in the business, and the results achieved during the period under review. These statements are not a compilation of absolute truths; rather, they are an incorporation of recorded facts, accounting conventions and principles, and personal judgments. Knowledge of the assumptions upon which the statements are based is mandatory to a thorough understanding of the significance of the statements.

The comprehensibility of financial statements is augmented by these four basic devices: (1) the grouping of similar items to accentuate their resemblance; (2) the arrangement of the items to indicate important relationships; (3) the ordering of the items to focus attention on the most important data; and (4) the description of items in an understandable manner. The statements most commonly included in annual corporate reports are the statement of financial position, the income statement, and the statement of retained earnings.

The statement of financial position is a static statement, showing the resources of an enterprise and the equities in these resources at a specific point of time. This statement may be prepared in the account form, which facilitates financial analysis, or in the report form, which is easily prepared and can be readily expanded. In the statement of financial position, assets are generally classified under Current Assets, Long-Term Investments, Plant and Equipment, Intangible Assets, and Deferred Charges. The use of the caption Deferred Charges has little justification in accounting since the items generally listed in this category may be more appropriately disclosed under another heading. Liabilities are commonly subdivided under Current Liabilities, Long-Term Liabilities, and Deferred Credits. Items that do not fit neatly under another category often appear as deferred credits; they must be reclassified before a meaningful analysis of the statement can be made. On the corporate statement of financial position, the Stockholders' Equity section should reveal the major sources of equity capital as well as certain legal restrictions on capital withdrawals. Adequate disclosure may require the use of footnotes to describe accounting procedures, explain items not readily understandable, or show contingent liabilities.

The appropriate disclosure of extraordinary, nonrecurring gains and losses and corrections of prior years' income has led to the controversy between the current operating performance and all-inclusive concepts of income reporting. The philosophy of the current operating performance concept is that the net income of a period should be an accumulation of items that are related to the ordinary operations of the business. Advocates maintain that extraordinary items and corrections of prior years' income should have no effect on the current income and therefore should appear in the statement of retained earnings. The all-inclusive income statement is prepared to show all the items of gain and loss for the period on the supposition that a series of income statements should reveal the entire income history of a company. Advocates maintain that permitting the deletion of extraordinary items from the income statement may allow the concealment of pertinent information. Also, it is argued that the manipulation of net income is made possible by the omission of certain borderline items from the income statement. A combined statement of income and retained earnings offers the possibility of including both ordinary and extraordinary items in the same statement. A disadvantage of this arrangement is that attention is not focused on net income, which is one of the most significant figures in financial statements. An income statement may be arranged in either the single-step or multiple-step form. The single-step statement is simple to prepare and easy to understand; but it does not facilitate statement analysis as does the multiple-step statement.

An adequate understanding and analysis of financial statement data can be achieved only if the analyst (1) understands the nature and limitations of accounting; (2) understands the terminology of accounting and business; (3) has some knowledge of business; and (4) is acquainted with the nature and tools of financial analysis. The figures in a financial statement are significant (1) as measures of absolute quantity; (2) in relation to similar figures of prior years and comparable companies; and (3) in conjunction with other related figures. The tools of financial analysis are comparative statements, percentage analysis, ratio analysis, and combinations of these. Comparative financial statements, or those covering a period of two or more years, review the progress of a business, thereby emphasizing that statements and the figures contained therein are not isolated data but fragments of a continuous history. The consistent application of generally accepted accounting principles in the comparative statements is a prerequisite for an effective analysis and interpretation of the data contained in the statements. Comparative statements may be made more meaningful by showing, in addition to absolute figures, the dollar amount and the percentage of increase or decrease between the absolute figures. Trend percentages, or the reduction of the absolute figures for different years to a common denominator, highlight significant changes and are thus especially valuable to management in the decision-making process. Trend percentages are often misleading if viewed as isolated figures. To be of maximum benefit, they must be analyzed in the light of the trend percentages of related items.

Common-size financial statements, or those in which a group of items is expressed as percentages of the total of the items, may reveal significant relationships.

Financial ratios and other analytical devices must be considered in relation to the nature of the company, the economical environment, the accounting methods employed, and similar ratios and devices of previous years and similar companies that are relevant to the current situation. Otherwise, the interpretation of the statements will yield useless, if not misleading, results.

☐ **QUESTIONS**

Q17–**1.** (a) What are some limitations of financial statements? (b) List and discuss some factors contributing to the development of financial reporting to outside groups.

Q17–**2.** (a) Discuss the characteristics of a good managerial report. (b) Discuss the purposes of financial statements.

Q17–**3.** Discuss the four basic devices that are commonly used to achieve interpretative statement presentation.

Q17–**4.** What major classifications may be applied to (a) assets, (b) liabilities, and (c) stockholders' equity items? Indicate the nature of the data that are reported within each classification.

Q17–5. 1. Give an example of (a) an asset offset, (b) a liability offset, and (c) a stockholders' equity offset. 2. When is an offset improperly applied?

Q17–6. (a) Define the term *contingent liability*. (b) State three ways in which Notes Receivable Discounted may be disclosed on the financial statements.

Q17–7. What are the advantages and disadvantages of (a) the current operating concept of income reporting and (b) the all-inclusive concept?

Q17–8. "The financial statement analyst should have available comparative statements, showing changes in absolute amounts and percentage changes." Explain.

Q17–9. Comment on the significance of each of the following factors to the financial statement analyst:

1. A steadily increasing price level
2. An increase in inventory
3. An increase in plant and equipment
4. An increase in sales
5. An increase in sales and a decrease in accounts receivable
6. An increase in liabilities

Q17–10. Trend percentages are of limited usefulness because (a) they do not indicate whether the change is favorable or unfavorable, (b) the change may be in relation to a year that is not typical or normal, and (c) they do not measure the effectiveness of management. Discuss.

Q17–11. What are the advantages and limitations to the analyst of the following: (a) comparative statements, (b) trend percentages, and (c) common-size percentages?

Q17–12. Explain how each of the following would be determined:

1. A company's earning power
2. The extent to which internal sources have been used to finance plant and equipment acquisitions
3. The adequacy of protection to long-term debtors
4. The rapidity with which the accounts receivable are collected
5. The ability of a business to meet quickly unexpected demands for working capital

Q17–13. What ratios or other analytical devices will help to answer the following questions?

1. Is there an overinvestment in plant and equipment?
2. Are the assets distributed satisfactorily?
3. Is there adequate protection for creditors?
4. How is the business being financed?
5. Are earnings adequate?
6. Is there a satisfactory relationship between internal and external financing?
7. Are costs and expenses too high? Are sales adequate?

Q17–14. (a) What knowledge must an analyst possess to enable him to evaluate financial statement data successfully? (b) What are some of the influences that are not specifically reflected in financial statements but that an analyst must evaluate to draw correct inferences from his analysis of financial statements?

☐ **EXERCISES**

E17–1. The following items are among those that would appear on the statement of financial position as of December 31, 1969, for the Gloam Company:

1. Marketable Securities
2. Subscriptions Receivable–Common Stock
3. Notes Receivable
4. Notes Receivable Discounted
5. Discount on Notes Payable
6. Discount on Bonds Payable
7. Discount on Common Stock
8. Unearned Interest Included in Face Value of Notes Receivable
9. Treasury Stock–Common
10. Stock Dividend to be Issued–Common

Indicate the statement of financial position classification of each item.

E17–2. The following information is available for the Russell Company as of December 31, 1969:

Gain from Sale of Equipment	$ 30,000
Net Sales Revenue	900,000
Income Taxes–1969	110,000
Selling and Administrative Expenses	225,000
Cost of Goods Sold	440,000
Loss on Write-Off of Abandoned Equipment	4,000
Uninsured Loss through Fire	5,000
Adjustment for Cost of Maintenance and Repairs charged to Plant and Equipment	3,500
Retained Earnings, December 31, 1968 (credit)	60,000
Dividends Paid	50,000
Income Tax Refund for Prior Years	15,000

Prepare (a) an all-inclusive income statement and (b) a statement of retained earnings for the Russell Company for the year ended December 31, 1969.

E17–3. Refer to Exercise E17–2. (a) Prepare a combined all-inclusive statement of income and retained earnings. (b) Prepare an all-inclusive single-step income statement. (c) Prepare an income statement and a statement of retained earnings based on the current operating performance concept.

E17–4. Assume that you have been hired as chief accountant for the Gould Company on December 31, 1969, before the books were closed. In looking back over the accounting records, you discover the following errors:

1. The December 31, 1968, merchandise inventory was overstated by $2,500 because some merchandise items had been included twice.

2. On December 31, 1968, accrued interest payable of $250 had not been recorded; this amount was absorbed as an expense in 1969 when it was paid.

3. The liability for invoices from merchandise suppliers is not recorded until the goods are inspected and marked, although merchandise in the Receiving and Marking department is correctly included in the physical inventory taken at the end of the year. The cost of the uninspected and unmarked merchandise in the Receiving and Marking department at end of 1968 and 1969 was:

December 31, 1968	$3,420
December 31, 1969	$4,500

Assuming that the current operating performance concept is followed, prepare correcting journal entries as of December 31, 1969.

E17–5. The following groups of items are presented for various companies as of December 31, 1969 and 1970, or for the years then ended:

	1970	1969
1. Sales	$ 620,000	$ 480,000
Cost of Goods Sold	400,000	320,000
Operating Expenses	100,000	80,000
Net Income	90,000	60,000
2. Current Liabilities	300,000	200,000
Mortgage Bonds Payable	450,000	500,000
3. Common Stock	1,200,000	1,000,000
Preferred Stock	300,000	400,000
Retained Earnings (deficit)	(10,000)	100,000
4. Cash	142,000	212,000
Accounts Receivable	130,000	140,000
Inventories	60,000	80,000
Other Current Assets	3,000	2,000
Land	20,000	20,000
Buildings	500,000	420,000
Accumulated Depreciation–Buildings	72,000	60,000

Compute the percentage increase or decrease for each item, and indicate possible reasons for the changes.

E17–6. Assume the following transactions:

1. Borrowed cash from the bank; issued a $6,000, 60-day, 5-percent note.
2. Purchased machinery for $60,000; paid $25,000 in cash and issued a 120-day note for the balance.
3. Sold for $25,000 some plant and equipment items that had a book value of $30,000.
4. Wrote off $1,500 of uncollectible accounts.
5. Declared a stock dividend of $35,000.
6. Paid $4,800 to trade creditors.

Indicate the effect of these transactions on the working capital.

E17–7. The following information is given:

	1970	1969
Net Sales	$635,000	$510,000
Cost of Goods Sold	425,000	370,000
Selling Expenses	70,000	55,000
General Expenses	40,000	35,000
Other Revenue	2,000	3,500
Other Expenses	1,000	4,000
Income Taxes	61,000	30,000

(a) Prepare a comparative income statement with common-size percentages. (b) Indicate the favorable and unfavorable changes.

E17–8. The following condensed information is taken from the statements of the Winter Company:

| | December 31 | |
	1970	1969
Current Assets	$228,000	$170,000
Plant and Equipment (net)	290,000	300,000
Current Liabilities	130,000	122,000
Long-Term Liabilities	100,000	120,000
Capital Stock	225,000	200,000
Retained Earnings	63,000	28,000

Prepare a condensed comparative statement of financial position, showing the dollar amounts and the percentages of increase or decrease during 1970.

E17–9. The following balances were taken from the books of the Boxlite Corporation as of June 30, 1969 and 1970:

| | June 30 | |
	1970	1969
Current Assets	$230,000	$170,000
Plant and Equipment	290,000	305,000
Current Liabilities	130,000	110,000
Long-Term Liabilities	115,000	130,000
Common Stock	225,000	200,000
Retained Earnings	50,000	35,000

Prepare a comparative statement of financial position showing common-size percentages.

E17–10. The following revenue and expense data of the Bayou Company for the year 1969 are given:

Sales	$210,000
Cost of Goods Sold	130,000
Selling Expenses	18,000
General Expenses	12,000
Interest Expense	2,500
Income Taxes	23,750
Net Income	23,750

Prepare a revenue-dollar statement.

E17–11. In the left-hand column a series of transactions is listed; in the right-hand column, a series of ratios:

Transaction	Ratio
1. Declaration of a cash dividend	Current ratio
2. Write-off of an uncollectible account receivable	Receivables turnover
3. Purchase of inventory on open account	Acid-test ratio
4. Issuance of 10-year mortgage bonds	Rate of earnings to total assets
5. Issuance of additional shares of stock for cash	Creditor equity ratio
6. Decrease of sales volume at higher unit price	Gross margin percentage

7. Issue of stock dividend on
   common stock   Earnings per share

8. Appropriation of retained earnings   Rate of earnings on
                                          stockholders' equity

9. Purchase of supplies on open
   account   Current ratio

10. Net income increase of 10 percent;
    interest expense increase of
    25 percent   Times interest expense is earned

11. Payment to short-term creditor in full   Acid-test ratio

12. Payment of accounts payable, taking
    the cash discount   Inventory turnover

State whether each transaction will cause the indicated ratio to increase, decrease, or remain unchanged. For the current ratio, receivables turnover, acid-test ratio, and inventory turnover, assume that the ratio is greater than 1 : 1 before each transaction occurred.

☐ **DEMONSTRATION PROBLEMS**

DP17-**1.** (*Statement of financial position*) The following terms appear on various statements of financial position:

> Current Assets   Deferred Charges
> Long-Term Investments   Current Liabilities
> Plant and Equipment   Long-Term Liabilities
> Intangible Assets   Stockholders' Equity

Required: 1. Define and give several examples of each term.
           2. Indicate three ways of grouping the items in formal statements of financial position.

DP17-**2.** (*Correcting errors*) Assume that you are hired as chief accountant of the Erofree Company as of December 31, 1969, before the books are closed. To familiarize yourself with the accounting procedures, you review the records for the two preceding years and discover the following errors:

1. The depreciation on the building was recorded as $1,000 in 1968; it should have been $10,000.

2. The December 31, 1968, inventory was understated by $1,850.

3. The Company purchased a typewriter on July 1, 1968, at a cost of $300. This amount was debited to Office Expense. Normally, the Erofree Company depreciates office equipment by the straight-line method, using a five-year life.

4. The liability for a $2,450 purchase was not recorded as of December 28, 1969, although the amount was correctly included in the December 31, 1969, periodic inventory.

Required: 1. Assuming the use of the current operating performance concept, prepare correcting and adjusting entries as of December 31, 1969.
           2. Assuming the use of the all-inclusive concept, prepare correcting and adjusting entries as of December 31, 1969.

DP17–3. (*Financial statements: current operating performance vs. all-inclusive concept*) The following information is taken from the books of the Brafford Company on December 31, 1969:

Retained Earnings (credit), December 31, 1968	$ 65,000
Loss from Sale of Land	6,000
Sales	560,000
Loss from Flood	8,000
Cost of Goods Sold	280,000
Adjustment for Cost of Machinery Charged to Equipment Repairs	7,000
Income Taxes	85,000
Understatement of Depreciation in Prior Years	12,000
Selling, General, and Administrative Expenses	90,000
Dividends Declared and Paid	50,000

Required: 1. Prepare an income statement and a statement of retained earnings, following the current operating performance concept.
2. Prepare an income statement and a statement of retained earnings, following the all-inclusive concept.
3. Prepare a combined statement of income and retained earnings, following the current operating performance concept.
4. Prepare a combined statement of income and retained earnings, following the all-inclusive concept.
5. Prepare an all-inclusive single-step income statement.

DP17–4. (*Comparative statements: amount and percentage of increase or decrease*) The following condensed comparative statements of Boykins, Inc., are given:

BOYKINS, INC.
Comparative Statement of Financial Position
December 31, 1970 and 1969

	December 31	
	1970	1969
Current Assets	$180,000	$155,000
Plant and Equipment	190,000	205,000
Total Assets	$370,000	$360,000
Current Liabilities	$ 69,000	$ 54,500
Long-Term Liabilities	70,000	75,000
Total Liabilities	$139,000	$129,500
Capital Stock	$200,000	$200,000
Retained Earnings	31,000	30,500
Total Stockholders' Equity	$231,000	$230,500
Total Liabilities and Stockholders' Equity	$370,000	$360,000

BOYKINS, INC.
Comparative Statement of Income and Retained Earnings
For the Years Ended December 31, 1970 and 1969

	Years Ended December 31	
	1970	1969
Sales (net)	$495,000	$550,000
Cost of Goods Sold	376,000	410,000
Gross Margin on Sales	$119,000	$140,000
Operating Expenses	82,000	95,000
Net Income Before Income Taxes	$ 37,000	$ 45,000
Income Taxes	18,500	22,500
Net Income	$ 18,500	$ 22,500
Retained Earnings, January 1	30,500	30,000
Total Net Income and Retained Earnings	$ 49,000	$ 52,500
Dividends Paid	18,000	22,000
Retained Earnings, December 31	$ 31,000	$ 30,500

Required: 1. Prepare a comparative statement of income and retained earnings, showing the amount and percentage of increase or decrease during 1970.
2. Prepare a comparative position statement, showing the amount and percentage of increase or decrease during 1970.
3. Write a report indicating whether the financial condition and operating results are favorable or unfavorable and stating your reasons.

DP17-5. (*Comparative statements—trend percentages*) The following information is taken from the books of the York Company:

	1969	1970	1971	1972
Sales (net)	$135,000	$147,500	$156,250	$168,750
Cost of Goods Sold	78,000	86,840	91,600	98,400
Accounts Receivable	20,000	23,000	24,400	26,800
Merchandise Inventory	35,000	40,600	43,050	45,850
Net Income	12,000	12,240	12,600	12,960

Required: 1. Calculate the trend percentages (1969 is the base year).
2. Point out the favorable and unfavorable tendencies.

DP17-6. (*Common-size statements: revenue-dollar statements*) The comparative condensed financial statements of the Blanton Company are given:

BLANTON COMPANY
Comparative Statement of Financial Position
December 31, 1970 and 1969

	December 31	
	1970	1969
Current Assets	$ 80,000	$ 97,500
Plant and Equipment	210,000	162,500
Total Assets	$290,000	$260,000
Current Liabilities	$ 52,000	$115,000
Long-Term Liabilities	126,000	60,000
Total Liabilities	$178,000	$175,000
Capital Stock	$ 98,000	$ 75,000
Retained Earnings	14,000	10,000
Total Stockholders' Equity	$112,000	$ 85,000
Total Liabilities and Stockholders' Equity	$290,000	$260,000

BLANTON COMPANY
Comparative Income Statement
For the Years Ended December 31, 1970 and 1969

	Years Ended December 31	
	1970	1969
Sales (net)	$320,000	$285,000
Cost of Goods Sold	183,600	161,250
Gross Margin on Sales	$136,400	$123,750
Operating Expenses		
Selling Expenses	$ 68,200	$ 55,000
General Expenses	40,300	27,500
Total Operating Expenses	$108,500	$ 82,500
Net Income	$ 27,900	$ 41,250

Required: 1. Prepare:
    a. A comparative common-size statement of financial position
    b. A comparative common-size income statement
    c. A comparative revenue-dollar statement
2. Discuss the financial condition and operating results of the Company, emphasizing favorable and unfavorable trends.

☐ **PROBLEMS**

P17–1. The post-closing trial balance of the Richard Bose Corporation is given:

RICHARD BOSE CORPORATION
Post-Closing Trial Balance
December 31, 1969

Cash	$ 80,000	
Marketable Securities (at cost; market value is $56,000)	50,000	
Accounts Receivable	144,000	
Allowance for Doubtful Accounts		$ 6,000
Merchandise Inventory	450,000	
Accrued Bond Interest Receivable	12,000	
Prepaid Insurance	6,000	
Bond Sinking Fund	20,000	
Investment in Bonds–Excel Company Bonds	200,000	
Delivery Equipment	16,000	
Accumulated Depreciation–Delivery Equipment		4,000
Machinery and Equipment	900,000	
Accumulated Depreciation–Machinery and Equipment		100,000
Accounts Payable		144,000
Estimated Income Taxes Payable		100,000
Accrued Bond Interest Payable		12,000
First Mortgage 3% Bonds Payable		200,000
Discount on First Mortgage Bonds Payable	2,400	
Second Mortgage 6% Bonds Payable		100,000
Premium on Second Mortgage Bonds Payable		2,000
Preferred Stock, 6%, $100 par value		400,000
Common Stock, $25 par value		600,000
Retained Earnings		116,400
Prepaid Rent	4,000	
Retained Earnings–Restricted for Plant Addition		80,000
Retained Earnings–Restricted for First Mortgage Bond Redemption		20,000
Totals	$1,884,400	$1,884,400

Required: Prepare the statement of financial position for the Richard Bose Corporation as of December 31, 1969, showing working capital and net assets on the left-hand side balanced by stockholders' equity on the right-hand side.

P17-2. Assume that you are hired as chief accountant of the Nudeal Company as of December 31, 1969, before the books are closed. To familiarize yourself with the accounting procedures of the firm, you review the records for the two preceding years and discover the following errors:

1. The depreciation of the building was recorded as $50,000 in 1968; it should have been recorded as $5,000.

2. The December 31, 1968, inventory was overstated by $2,160.

3. An unrecorded bill in the amount of $1,670 for a 1968 purchase was paid in 1969; Purchases was debited.

4. The freight cost of $500 incurred for the purchase of machinery was debited to

Transportation In on July 1, 1968, when the amount was paid. No part of this cost was assigned to the December 31, 1968, inventory. Machinery is depreciated by the straight-line method, assuming a 10-year life.

5. Merchandise costing $1,200 was sold on credit for $1,800 on December 21, 1968; it was returned on December 29, 1968. No entry was made in 1968 to record the return; the entry debiting Sales Returns and Allowances was made on January 5, 1969. The merchandise was included in the December 31, 1968, inventory at the selling price.

Required: Assuming that the current operating performance concept is followed, prepare correcting journal entries.

P17–3. The following information is taken from the books of the Rawson Company on December 31, 1969:

Retained Earnings (credit), December 31, 1968	$ 85,000
Sales	750,000
Dividends Declared and Paid	65,000
Selling, General, and Administrative Expenses	280,000
Loss on Sale of Securities	5,000
Income Taxes	33,000
Cost of Goods Sold	390,000
Loss on Disposal of Equipment	7,000
Overstatement of Depreciation in Prior Years	8,000
Gain from Disposal of Building	15,000

Required: 1. Prepare an income statement and a statement of retained earnings, following the current operating performance concept.

2. Prepare an income statement and a statement of retained earnings, following the all-inclusive concept.

3. Prepare a combined statement of income and retained earnings, following the current operating performance concept.

4. Prepare a combined statement of income and retained earnings, following the all-inclusive concept.

5. Prepare an all-inclusive single-step income statement.

P17–4. The Yorkshire Company presents the following comparative information as of December 31, 1969 and 1970:

	1970	1969
Cash	$ 38,000	$ 35,000
Accounts Receivable	42,000	25,000
Notes Receivable	38,000	10,000
Inventories	65,000	70,000
Machinery and Equipment (net)	90,000	100,000
Building (net)	100,000	120,000
Land	40,000	40,000
Accounts Payable	55,000	47,000
Notes Payable (current)	15,000	29,000
Mortgage Payable (long-term)	70,000	100,000
Capital Stock ($100 par value)	250,000	200,000
Retained Earnings, December 31 (credit)	23,000	24,000
Sales (net)	385,000	300,000
Cost of Goods Sold	250,000	185,000
Operating Expenses	72,000	70,000
Income Taxes	34,000	23,000
Dividends Paid	30,000	18,000

Required: 1. Prepare comparative financial statements, including the amounts and the percentages of change during 1970.
2. Write a report to management indicating the favorable and unfavorable financial and operating trends.

P17-**5.** Condensed comparative financial statements for the Ben Manufacturing Company appear below:

BEN MANUFACTURING COMPANY
Comparative Statements of Financial Position
October 31, 1969, 1970, and 1971
(In thousands of dollars)

	1971	1970	1969
Assets			
Current Assets	$ 1,360	$1,500	$2,000
Plant and Equipment (net of accumulated depreciation)	8,400	7,200	6,000
Intangible Assets	600	800	1,000
Total Assets	$10,360	$9,500	$9,000
Liabilities and Stockholders' Equity			
Liabilities			
Current Liabilities	$ 1,040	$1,000	$ 800
Long-term Liabilities (net of discount)	1,960	1,920	1,880
Stockholders' Equity			
Capital Stock ($50 par)	4,800	4,000	4,000
Capital in Excess of Par Value	360	200	200
Retained Earnings	2,200	2,380	2,120
Total Liabilities and Stockholders' Equity	$10,360	$9,500	$9,000

BEN MANUFACTURING COMPANY
Comparative Income Statements
For the Years Ended October 31, 1969, 1970, and 1971
(In thousands of dollars)

	1971	1970	1969
Net Sales	$28,000	$24,000	$20,000
Cost of Goods Sold	21,000	17,400	14,000
Gross Margin on Sales	$ 7,000	$ 6,600	$ 6,000
Selling Expenses	$ 2,760	$ 2,480	$ 2,000
Administrative Expenses	2,940	2,880	2,800
Interest Expense	98	96	94
Total Expenses	$ 5,798	$ 5,456	$ 4,894
Net Income Before Income Taxes	$ 1,202	$ 1,144	$ 1,106
Provision for Income Taxes	614	592	566
Net Income After Income Taxes	$ 588	$ 552	$ 540

Required: 1. Compute the trend percentages for all statement of financial position items, using 1969 as the base year.

2. Prepare common-size comparative income statements for the three-year period, expressing all items as percentage components of net sales.

3. Comment on the significant trends and relationships revealed by the analytical computations in Requirements 1 and 2.

P17–**6.** In the following schedule, certain items taken from the income statements of the Martin Company have been expressed as percentages of net sales:

	Percentage of Net Sales	
	1970	1969
Net Sales	100	100
Beginning Inventory	10	16
Net Purchases	68	60
Ending Inventory	8	12
Selling Expenses	13	15
Administrative Expenses	8	9
Provision for Income Taxes	2.7	3.6

Net sales were $200,000 in 1969; they increased by 20 percent in 1970. Average accounts receivable were $21,000 in 1970 and $20,000 in 1969. Credit sales were 80 percent of total sales in both years.

Required: 1. Did the net income increase or decrease in 1970 as compared with 1969, and by how much? Prepare a comparative income statement to support your answer.

2. Compute the average length of the Company's receivables turnover days for both years, showing the basis of your computation.

P17–**7.** Statements for the Johnson Company as of December 31, 1969, follow:

JOHNSON COMPANY
Income Statement
For the Year Ended December 31, 1969

Gross Sales	$295,800
Sales Returns and Allowances	4,500
Net Sales	$291,300
Cost of Goods Sold	208,000
Gross Margin on Sales	$ 83,300
Operating Expenses	65,300
Net Income from Operations	$ 18,000
Interest on Mortgage Payable	800
Net Income Before Income Taxes	$ 17,200
Federal Income Taxes	6,200
Net Income After Income Taxes	$ 11,000

JOHNSON COMPANY
Statement of Financial Position
December 31, 1969

Assets

Current Assets			
Cash		$12,000	
Accounts Receivable	$95,000		
Deduct Allowance for Doubtful Accounts	6,000	89,000	
Inventory		80,000	
Total Current Assets			$181,000
Plant and Equipment			
Land		$20,000	
Building	$60,000		
Deduct Accumulated Depreciation	12,000	48,000	
Store Equipment	$15,000		
Deduct Accumulated Depreciation	7,000	8,000	
Total Plant and Equipment			76,000
Total Assets			$257,000

Liabilities and Stockholders' Equity

Current Liabilities			
Accounts Payable		$86,600	
Accrued Expenses Payable		29,000	
Total Current Liabilities			$115,600
Long-Term Liabilities			
Mortgage Payable			20,000
Total Liabilities			$135,600
Stockholders' Equity			
Preferred Stock, 6%, $100 Par Value		$20,000	
Common Stock, $100 Par Value		80,000	
Retained Earnings		21,400	
Total Stockholders' Equity			121,400
Total Liabilities and Stockholders' Equity			$257,000

On December 31, 1968, the inventory was $100,000 and the total stockholders' equity was $115,000.

Required: Compute the following (carry to two decimal places):

> Working capital ratio (current ratio)
> Acid-test ratio
> Inventory turnover
> Percent of year's net sales uncollected
> Ratio of stockholders' equity to total assets
> Ratio of net sales to stockholders' equity
> Ratio of plant and equipment assets to long-term debt
> Earnings per share of common stock
> Percent of net income to average stockholders' equity
> Number of times preferred dividends earned
> Number of times mortgage interest earned

P17–**8**. Certain financial information for the Anson Company and the Battle Company as of the end of 1969, and additional information, are shown:

	Anson Company	Battle Company
Current Assets	$ 240,000	$220,000
Plant and Equipment	1,016,000	770,000
Accumulated Depreciation	(160,000)	(120,000)
Patents	4,000	–0–
Goodwill	–0–	10,000
Total Assets	$1,100,000	$880,000
Current Liabilities	$ 130,000	$ 68,000
Bonds Payable, 5%, due in 10 years	200,000	240,000
Preferred Stock, 7%, $100 par value	240,000	160,000
Common Stock, $25 par value	400,000	300,000
Retained Earnings	90,000	60,000
Retained Earnings Restricted for Contingencies	40,000	–0–
Premium on Common Stock	–0–	52,000
Total Liabilities and Stockholders' Equity	$1,100,000	$880,000
Analysis of Retained Earnings:		
Balance, beginning of year	$ 91,200	$ 49,600
Net Income for year	74,800	39,600
Dividends: Preferred	(16,800)	(11,200)
Dividends: Common	(19,200)	(18,000)
Additions to Retained Earnings Restricted for Contingencies	(40,000)	–0–
	$ 90,000	$ 60,000
Market price of common stock per share	$ 30	$ 30
Market price of preferred stock per share	105	102

Required: Under the assumption that the two Companies are generally comparable, write a brief answer to each of the questions given. Use only the ratios that will most reasonably substantiate your answer and indicate why. Compute the amount of each ratio and percentage indicated (carry your computations to one place beyond the decimal point).

1. Since the market prices of the bonds are not given, what ratios would aid potential investors to determine which bonds would probably sell at the higher price and which bonds would probably yield the higher return?
2. What ratio(s) would aid potential investors in preferred stock to determine which Company's preferred stock is the safer investment?
3. To what extent is each Company benefiting from the leverage factor inherent in the existence of the bonds? of preferred stock?
4. What are the dividend yield rates and earnings per share for the common stock of each Company?

P17–**9**. The Sanders Corporation has issued convertible bonds under an agreement to maintain net assets, defined in the agreement as assets minus all liabilities except the convertible bonds, at an amount not less than 230 percent of the convertible bonds outstanding; to maintain current assets at not less than 200 percent of the current liabilities; and to maintain working capital at not less than 100 percent of the convertible bonds outstanding.

On December 31, 1969, the Corporation's adjusted trial balance was as follows:

SANDERS CORPORATION
Adjusted Trial Balance
December 31, 1969

	Debit	Credit
Cash	$ 10,000	
Marketable Securities	75,000	
Accounts Receivable	74,000	
Allowance for Doubtful Accounts		$ 3,000
Inventory	113,000	
Prepaid Expenses	6,000	
Land	18,000	
Building	156,000	
Accumulated Depreciation–Building		21,000
Equipment	224,000	
Accumulated Depreciation–Equipment		42,000
Accounts Payable		69,000
Notes Payable, 4-year (due 12/20/72)		75,000
Accrued Expenses Payable		6,000
Convertible Bonds Payable		200,000
Common Stock		150,000
Retained Earnings		110,000
Totals	$676,000	$676,000

In January, 1970, it was discovered that title had passed as of December 31, 1969, on incoming merchandise costing $40,000. Since the merchandise was not on hand, it was not included in the inventory. The Corporation had recorded $28,000 of collections from customers received on January 2, 1970, under the date of December 31, 1969, on the theory that such collections in all probability were in the mail before midnight, December 31, 1969. In the afternoon of January 2, 1970, the Corporation wrote and mailed checks to creditors, dating and recording the checks as of December 31, 1969; the checks amounted to $28,000, equal to the collections in transit.

Required: 1. Contrast, by means of comparative ratios, the reported conditions with those you believe more fairly indicate the status of the Corporation. Limit your comparison to the ratios mentioned in the agreement with the bondholders.
2. Comment briefly on your findings.

CASE PROBLEM
Black, Green, Brown, and Smith

You are an analyst for the firm of Black, Green, Brown, and Smith, securities analysts. You have analyzed many financial reports issued annually by publicly owned corporations. Recently, a junior analyst was hired to assist you in the performance of your duties. To give you a basis for judging some of his capabilities, you ask him to analyze the following statements:

ALLRED MERCHANDISING COMPANY
Comparative Statement of Financial Position
December 31, 1970, 1969, and 1968

	1970	1969	1968
Assets			
Current Assets			
Cash	$ 100,320	$ 112,640	$ 63,360
Accounts Receivable (net)	139,700	99,220	86,020
Merchandise Inventory	91,520	62,480	56,320
Prepaid Expenses	2,420	2,200	2,200
Total Current Assets	$ 333,960	$ 276,540	$ 207,900
Land and Depreciable Assets (net)	$ 877,140	$ 918,060	$ 958,980
Total Assets	$1,211,100	$1,194,600	$1,166,880
Liabilities and Stockholders' Equity			
Current Liabilities	$ 176,440	$ 174,900	$ 178,200
Long-Term Liabilities	400,000	400,000	400,000
Total Liabilities	$ 576,440	$ 574,900	$ 578,200
Stockholders' Equity			
Capital Stock, $10 par value	$ 499,800	$ 499,800	$ 499,800
Retained Earnings	134,860	119,900	88,880
Total Stockholders' Equity	$ 634,660	$ 619,700	$ 588,680
Total Liabilities and Stockholders' Equity	$1,211,100	$1,194,600	$1,166,880

ALLRED MERCHANDISING COMPANY
Comparative Statement of Income and Retained Earnings
For the Years Ended December 31, 1970, 1969, and 1968

	1970	1969	1968
Sales (net)	$1,253,560	$1,130,140	$1,128,160
Inventory, Beginning of Year	$ 62,480	$ 56,320	$ 53,680
Purchases (net)	568,040	469,480	442,640
Merchandise Available for Sale	$ 630,520	$ 525,800	$ 496,320
Inventory, End of Year	91,520	62,480	56,320
Cost of Merchandise Sold	$ 539,000	$ 463,320	$ 440,000
Gross Margin	$ 714,560	$ 666,820	$ 688,160
Selling Expenses	$ 207,120	$ 173,480	$ 176,580
Administrative Expenses	138,080	116,300	133,200
Total Operating Expenses	$ 345,200	$ 289,780	$ 309,780
Net Income Before Interest and Taxes	$ 369,360	$ 377,040	$ 378,380
Interest Expense	20,000	20,000	20,000
Net Income Before Income Taxes	$ 349,360	$ 357,040	$ 358,380
Income Taxes	180,400	194,020	185,020
Net Income After Income Taxes	$ 168,960	$ 163,020	$ 173,360
Retained Earnings, Beginning of Year	119,900	88,880	47,520
Total	$ 288,860	$ 251,900	$ 220,880
Dividends	154,000	132,000	132,000
Retained Earnings, End of Year	$ 134,860	$ 119,900	$ 88,880

You instruct your new assistant to compute the following indicators for the Allred Company for each of the three years:

1. Current ratio
2. Acid-test ratio
3. Creditors'-equity ratio
4. Stockholders' equity ratio
5. Net income to stockholders' equity percentage
6. Merchandise inventory turnover
7. Number of days' sales uncollected
8. Average collection period for accounts receivable
9. Plant and equipment to long-term liability ratio
10. Plant and equipment to stockholders' equity percentage
11. Sales to plant and equipment ratio
12. Earnings per share of capital stock
13. Percentage gain or loss from trading on the equity (when determining the return on total assets, compute a hypothetical deduction for income taxes, using a rate of 52.54%)

You also instruct him to indicate whether each of these measurements is improving or regressing, and to indicate the significance of each measurement.

Required: 1. Prepare a solution to your new assistant's assignment, consisting of calculations of indicators 1 through 13, indications of improvement or regression, and statements regarding their significance.
2. What other useful measurements could be applied to these statements?
3. What limitations are inherent in applying some of these measurements?
4. Assuming that the Company experiences constantly rising prices on all acquisitions of merchandise, identify the effect that different inventory costing methods (FIFO and LIFO) would have on the measurements. (Identify the effect and the measurement.)
5. Assuming that the Company constantly expands the size of the physical facilities, identify the effect that different depreciation calculation methods (straight-line and diminishing-balance) would have on the measurements. (Identify the effect and the measurement.)
6. What purpose is served by making calculations based on financial statements?

Chapter Eighteen

Sources and Uses of Funds— Working Capital; Cash

The income statement and the statement of retained earnings disclose the causes of part but not all of the changes that take place in the items appearing in the statements of financial position at the beginning and end of a given period. Businesses engage in a variety of financial transactions, the details of which are not disclosed in either the income statement or the statement of retained earnings. Information regarding the changes in working capital, cash, and other financial items are summarized in various *funds statements*, considered in this chapter.

FUNDS

The term *funds* has a variety of meanings, including cash, cash and securities, working capital, current assets, quick assets, and total resources. One must know the sense in which the term is used when reading or preparing a funds statement. The term funds is used here first in the sense of working capital—current assets minus current liabilities. Alternative uses are discussed later.

The chief sources of funds are operations, additional investments by owners, long-term borrowing, and the sale of assets. The chief uses of funds are to increase noncurrent assets, retire long-term debt, reduce the owner's or stockholders' equity, and pay dividends. The funds statement emphasizes the interrelationship of the sources (*inflows*) and uses (*outflows*) of funds to working capital. A chart of fund inflows and outflows based on an analogy between the flow of funds through a business and the flow of water into and out of a container is shown in Figure 18-1.

THE FUNDS STATEMENT

The income statement and the statement of financial position report the results of operations of a business during a period and the financial condition of that business

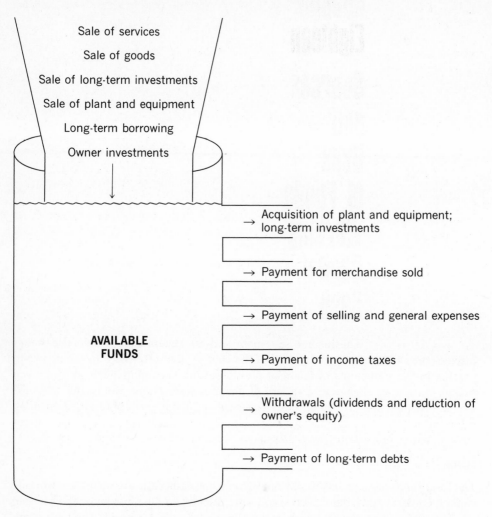

Figure 18-1.
*Fund Inflows
and Outflows.*

Sale of services

Sale of goods

Sale of long-term investments

Sale of plant and equipment

Long-term borrowing

Owner investments

→ Acquisition of plant and equipment;
long-term investments

→ Payment for merchandise sold

→ Payment of selling and general expenses

→ Payment of income taxes

→ Withdrawals (dividends and reduction of
owner's equity)

→ Payment of long-term debts

**AVAILABLE
FUNDS**

as of the end of the period. The *statement of the sources and uses of funds,* also referred to for brevity as the funds statement, supplements the two conventional statements by reporting changes relating to the financial activities of the firm that are not otherwise readily discernible. Its purpose is to show the source of funds from operations and other financing and the use of such funds during the period covered by the statement.

Purpose of the Funds Statement

It is often difficult for management and others to understand how the net income for the period was disposed of and the effect of the flow of funds through the business. Readers of the conventional financial statements often ask such questions as: Where did the funds come from? What was done with them? What happened to the various asset items during the period? Why did working capital decrease although earnings were favorable? Why were dividends not larger? Is the company solvent? Where did the funds for replacement or expansion come from? What kind of financial decisions were made during the period? The funds statement helps to answer these questions.

The smooth flow of funds into and out of a business is the result of a continuing series of managerial decisions, often requiring a high level of skill and judgment. The funds statement helps the reader to understand not only the financial well-being of the company but also the effectiveness of the financial policies of its management.

Understanding the Funds Statement

Proper preparation of the funds statement requires an analysis of the relationships among the items in the financial statements.[1] This involves two basic steps: (1) an analysis of the current accounts—current assets and current liabilities—to determine the net change in working capital during the period and (2) a determination of the causes of the net change in working capital by an analysis of the changes in the noncurrent accounts. The relationships among the various items in a position statement is expressed in the basic accounting equation:

$$\text{Assets} = \text{Liabilities} + \text{Owners' Equity}$$

The equation for a classified position statement is:

$$\text{Current Assets} + \text{Noncurrent Assets}$$
$$= \text{Current Liabilities} + \text{Noncurrent Liabilities} + \text{Owners' Equity}$$

Since the purpose of the funds statement is to show the causes of the changes in working capital, the equation is rewritten to show the current accounts on one side of the equation and the noncurrent accounts on the other side (the initial letters of the terms in the basic equation are used for brevity):

$$CA - CL = NCL + OE - NCA \tag{1}$$

Since the analysis involves comparative position statements, the beginning statement may be represented by:

$$CA_1 - CL_1 = NCL_1 + OE_1 - NCA_1 \tag{2}$$

The subscripts indicate that the amounts in Equation 2 are from the beginning of the period. Similarly, the ending position statement can be represented by:

$$CA_2 - CL_2 = NCL_2 + OE_2 - NCA_2 \tag{3}$$

Equations 2 and 3 may be combined to obtain:

$$\text{Net change in funds} = (CA_2 - CL_2) - (CA_1 - CL_1) = (CA_2 - CA_1) - (CL_2 - CL_1)$$
$$= (NCL_2 - NCL_1) + (OE_2 - OE_1) - (NCA_2 - NCA_1) \tag{4}$$

---

[1]This discussion is based on Ching-Wen Kwang and Albert Slavin, "The Mathematical Unity of Funds-Flow Analyses," *NAA Bulletin*, Section 1, January, 1965, pp. 49–56.

Equation 4 proves that the net change in the current accounts is equal to the algebraic sum of the changes in all noncurrent accounts. All financial transactions for the period can be described within this system of equations. Any single transaction causes a change in one or more items in Equation 2. The cumulative effect of all transactions for the year is to bring about such changes in the terms of Equation 2 that the financial position of the company at the end of the year is shown in Equation 3. The funds statement explains the changes in working capital by listing the changes that appear on the right side of Equation 4. Equations 2, 3, and 4 therefore constitute the analytical framework within which all transactions occurring between the comparative position statement dates can be analyzed in terms of their effect on working capital.

Classification of Transactions

Since there is a great variety of transactions that enter into the inflow and outflow of funds, it is helpful to classify them in distinctive categories, based on their effect on working capital.

1. Transactions that change a current and a noncurrent account. For example, the acquisition of a tract of land for cash changes working capital and is therefore reported in the funds statement.
2. Transactions that change current asset or current liability accounts but have no effect on net working capital. For example, the purchase of merchandise on account and the settlement of an account receivable change the current accounts but do not change the amount of working capital; hence, they are not reported in the funds statement.
3. Transactions that change noncurrent accounts only. For example, the acquisition of a tract of land by a company in exchange for its own stock does not change working capital and is therefore not reported in the funds statement. Other transactions in this category include restrictions on retained earnings, the declaration and issuance of stock dividends, and plant and equipment revaluations.

Funds from Operations

A primary source of funds is the regular operating activities of the business. The determination of funds from this source is complicated by the fact that the change in working capital may be greater than the net income shown in the income statement. To illustrate, assume that the Cowan Company's income statement for the year ended December 31, 1969, is as follows:

Sales		$10,000
Cost of Goods Sold		7,000
Gross Margin on Sales		$ 3,000
Operating Expenses		
Depreciation–Plant and Equipment	$ 400	
Other	2,100	2,500
Net Income		$ 500

An analysis of this statement in terms of the change in working capital resulting from operations shows:

	Income Statement	Working Capital Increase or (Decrease)	Explanation
Sales	$10,000	$10,000	Increase in cash or accounts receivable
Cost of Goods Sold	7,000	(7,000)	Decrease in inventories
Gross Margin on Sales	$ 3,000	$ 3,000	
Operating Expenses			
Depreciation–Plant and Equipment	$ 400	–0–	Decrease in net income and the carrying value of Plant and Equipment
Other	2,100	(2,100)	Decrease in Cash or increase in Accounts Payable
Total Operating Expenses	$ 2,500	$ (2,100)	
Net Income	$ 500		
Net Increase in Working Capital		$ 900	

For brevity, the net increase in working capital from operations may be determined as follows:

Funds Provided by Operations	
Net Income	$500.
Add NonWorking Capital Charges to Revenue and Expense Summary:	
Depreciation Expense–Plant and Equipment	400
Increase in Working Capital	$900

It must not be inferred from the mechanics of this procedure that the $400 depreciation expense increased working capital and is thereby a source of funds. The deduction of depreciation expense merely decreased net income without effecting a corresponding decrease in working capital. An income statement is likely to include several items of this kind—for example, depreciation, amortization of intangible assets, and loss on disposal of plant assets—representing costs and expenses that enter into income determination but do not affect working capital in the current period. The relevant expenditures either were made in a prior period or will be made in a future period. The recognition of depreciation is essential to income measurement, but it does not change the amount of working capital.

To illustrate the preparation of a simple form of funds statement, the position statement of the Fairfield Company, Inc., is given:

FAIRFIELD COMPANY, INC.
Comparative Statement of Financial Position
December 31, 1969 and 1968

	December 31 1969	December 31 1968	Increase or (Decrease)
Assets			
Current Assets			
Cash	$ 30,000	$ 32,000	$ (2,000)
Accounts Receivable (net)	65,000	52,000	13,000
Merchandise Inventory	112,000	92,000	20,000
Unexpired Insurance	3,000	4,000	(1,000)
Total Current Assets	$210,000	$180,000	$ 30,000
Plant and Equipment	$470,000	$438,000	$ 32,000
Deduct Accumulated Depreciation	105,000	98,000	7,000
	$365,000	$340,000	$ 25,000
Total Assets	$575,000	$520,000	$ 55,000
Liabilities and Stockholders' Equity			
Current Liabilities			
Accounts Payable	$ 60,000	$ 81,000	$(21,000)
Bank Loans Payable (short-term)	31,500	26,500	5,000
Accrued Payables	3,500	2,500	1,000
Total Current Liabilities	$ 95,000	$110,000	$(15,000)
Stockholders' Equity			
Capital Stock	$410,000	$350,000	$ 60,000
Retained Earnings	70,000	60,000	10,000
Total Stockholders' Equity	$480,000	$410,000	$ 70,000
Total Liabilities and Stockholders' Equity	$575,000	$520,000	$ 55,000

Step 1 in preparing the funds statement is to determine the changes in working capital:

FAIRFIELD COMPANY, INC.
Schedule of Changes in Working Capital
For the Year Ended December 31, 1969

	December 31 1969	December 31 1968	Changes in Working Capital Increase	Changes in Working Capital Decrease
Current Assets				
Cash	$ 30,000	$ 32,000		$ 2,000
Accounts Receivable (net)	65,000	52,000	$13,000	
Merchandise Inventory	112,000	92,000	20,000	
Unexpired Insurance	3,000	4,000		1,000
Total Current Assets	$210,000	$180,000		
Current Liabilities				
Accounts Payable	$ 60,000	$ 81,000	21,000	
Bank Loans Payable (short-term)	31,500	26,500		5,000
Accrued Payables	3,500	2,500		1,000
Total Current Liabilities	$ 95,000	$110,000		
Working Capital	$115,000	$ 70,000		
Net Increase in Working Capital				$45,000
			$54,000	$54,000

Step 2 is to analyze the changes in all the noncurrent accounts:

FAIRFIELD COMPANY, INC.
Analysis of Changes in Noncurrent Accounts
For the Year Ended December 31, 1969

| | (Debit) or Credit | Effect on Working Capital | |
		Increase	Decrease
Plant and Equipment			
Balance, 12/31/68	$(438,000)		
Acquisitions during 1969	(32,000)		$ 32,000
Balance, 12/31/69	$(470,000)		
Accumulated Depreciation–Plant & Equipment			
Balance, 12/31/68	$ 98,000		
Depreciation for 1969	7,000	$ 7,000*	
Balance, 12/31/69	$ 105,000		
Capital Stock			
Balance, 12/31/68	$ 350,000		
Stock Issued	60,000	60,000	
Balance, 12/31/69	$ 410,000		
Retained Earnings			
Balance, 12/31/68	$ 60,000		
Net Income for 1969	35,000	35,000	
Dividends declared	(25,000)		25,000
Balance, 12/31/69	$ 70,000		
		$102,000	$ 57,000
Net Increase in Working Capital			45,000
		$102,000	$102,000

* Nonworking capital charge to Revenue and Expense Summary.

Step 3 is to prepare a statement summarizing the sources and uses of funds during 1969, as follows:

FAIRFIELD COMPANY, INC.
Statement of Sources and Uses of Funds
For the Year Ended December 31, 1969

Sources of Funds		
Stock Issued		$ 60,000
Operations		
Net Income	$35,000	
Add Depreciation of Plant and Equipment	7,000	42,000
Total		$102,000
Uses of Funds		
Purchase of Equipment	$32,000	
Payment of Dividends	25,000	57,000
Net Increase in Working Capital		$ 45,000

The T-Account Method

Although a statement of sources and uses of funds can be prepared directly from a comparative position statement as in the preceding example, it becomes more difficult as the number of transactions and accounts to be analyzed increases. Some systematic method is needed to facilitate the analysis of the transactions required for the preparation of the formal statement. Several techniques may be used for this purpose, all of which lead to the same result. The technique known as the *direct,* or *T-account,* method[2] is often used because of its relative simplicity and clarity. The basic steps are as follows:

Step 1. A schedule of changes in working capital is prepared.

Step 2. A T account is opened for each noncurrent position statement item and the amount of the net increase or decrease, obtained from the comparative position statement, is entered in each account. Increases in assets and decreases in liabilities and stockholders' equity accounts are debit changes and are entered on the debit side; decreases in assets and increases in liabilities and stockholders' equity accounts are credit changes and are entered on the credit side. A single horizontal line is then drawn under each amount, across the account. The amounts entered in the T accounts are added to make sure that total debits equal total credits.

Step 3. Two additional T accounts, *Funds Summary* and *Revenue and Expense Operating Summary,* are opened. The Funds Summary account represents all the current asset and current liability accounts; the amount entered in this account is, therefore, the net change in working capital as determined in Step 1: it is a debit if there is a net increase; a credit if there is a net decrease. The Revenue and Expense Operating Summary account is used to determine the amount of funds provided by operations. No entry is made in this account at this point.

Step 4. The net changes entered in the T accounts in Steps 2 and 3 represent, in summary form, all the transactions that occurred during the period. These transactions are now reconstructed by separate entries below the horizontal lines in the appropriate T accounts. An offsetting debit or credit to a noncurrent account may be to:

a. Another noncurrent account. Although such a transaction does not affect working capital, the entry is made so that all changes may be explained.

b. Funds Summary. This account is debited or credited for transactions other than revenue and expense that affect working capital and noncurrent accounts.

c. Revenue and Expense Operating Summary. This account is debited or credited for transactions affecting revenue, expense, and noncurrent accounts.

Step 4 is completed only when the balance of the amounts below the horizontal line in each account is equal to the net change entered above the horizontal line in Steps 2 and 3. This ensures that all the transactions that affect working capital have been accounted for. Each entry should be identified by a letter or number, together

---

[2] Based on William J. Vatter, "A Direct Method for the Preparation of Fund Statements," *The Journal of Accountancy,* June, 1946, pp. 479–489.

with a brief notation giving the source of the entry to facilitate the preparation of the formal statement.

Step 5. The balance of Revenue and Expense Operating Summary is transferred to Funds Summary.

Step 6. The formal statement of sources and uses of funds is prepared. Revenue and Expense Operating Summary shows the amount of funds provided by operations. Funds Summary contains details of sources and uses of funds: the debit entries represent sources; the credit entries, uses.

The comparative position statement of the Plymouth Corporation and related supplementary data are used to illustrate the step-by-step T-account method for the preparation of a statement of sources and uses of funds.

PLYMOUTH CORPORATION
Comparative Position Statement
December 31, 1969 and 1968

| | December 31 | | Increase or (Decrease) |
	1969	1968	
Assets			
Current Assets			
Cash	$ 16,000	$ 21,000	$ (5,000)
Accounts Receivable (net)	19,600	16,600	3,000
Merchandise Inventory	31,000	21,000	10,000
Total Current Assets	$ 66,600	$ 58,600	$ 8,000
Long-Term Investments (at cost)	$ 22,000	$ 19,000	$ 3,000
Plant and Equipment			
Machinery	$152,000	$125,000	$27,000
Accumulated Depreciation–Machinery	(37,000)	(25,000)	(12,000)
Buildings	126,000	110,000	16,000
Accumulated Depreciation–Buildings	(38,000)	(35,000)	(3,000)
Land	18,000	18,000	–0–
Total Plant and Equipment	$221,000	$193,000	$28,000
Intangible Assets	$ 9,000	$ 10,000	$ (1,000)
Total Assets	$318,600	$280,600	$38,000
Liabilities and Stockholders' Equity			
Current Liabilities			
Accounts Payable	$ 23,000	$ 19,000	$ 4,000
Notes Payable	3,500	4,000	(500)
Total Current Liabilities	$ 26,500	$ 23,000	$ 3,500
Long-Term Liabilities			
Mortgage Payable	32,000	35,000	$ (3,000)
Total Liabilities	$ 58,500	$ 58,000	$ 500
Stockholders' Equity			
5% Preferred Stock, $100 par value	$ 55,000	$ 50,000	$ 5,000
Common Stock, no-par value, $10 stated value	125,000	110,000	15,000
Premium on Common Stock	13,000	10,000	3,000
Retained Earnings	67,100	52,600	14,500
Total Stockholders' Equity	$260,100	$222,600	$37,500
Total Liabilities and Stockholders' Equity	$318,600	$280,600	$38,000

PLYMOUTH CORPORATION
Income Statement
For the Year Ended December 31, 1969

Sales		$125,000
Cost of Goods Sold		70,000
Gross Margin on Sales		$ 55,000
Operating Expenses		
Depreciation–Machinery	$12,000	
Depreciation–Building	3,000	
Amortization of Intangibles	1,000	
Other	20,675	36,675
Operating Margin		$ 18,325
Gain on Sale of Investments		1,000
Net Income		$ 19,325

An analysis of the income statement, the statement of retained earnings, and the changes in the noncurrent items discloses the following supplementary information:

1. Net income per income statement $19,325
2. Depreciation
   a. Machinery 12,000
   b. Building 3,000
3. Amortization of intangible assets 1,000
4. Dividends declared and paid 4,825
5. Payment on mortgage payable 3,000
6. Investments costing $4,000 were sold for $5,000 (the gain of $1,000 was included in net income). Since investments increased by $3,000, additional investments costing $7,000 ($4,000 + $3,000) must have been acquired.

7. Plant and Equipment
   a. No machinery was sold during the period. Acquisitions, therefore, must have cost $27,000.
   b. No buildings were disposed of during the period. Acquisitions, therefore, must have cost $16,000.
8. Issuance of Stock
   a. Preferred—50 shares at par value
   b. Common—1,500 shares at $12 per share

Step 1. A schedule of changes in working capital is prepared.

PLYMOUTH CORPORATION
Schedule of Changes in Working Capital
For the Year Ended December 31, 1969

	December 31 1969	December 31 1968	Changes in Working Capital Increase	Changes in Working Capital Decrease
Current Assets				
Cash	$16,000	$21,000		$ 5,000
Accounts Receivable	19,600	16,600	$ 3,000	
Merchandise Inventory	31,000	21,000	10,000	
Total Current Assets	$66,600	$58,600		
Current Liabilities				
Accounts Payable	$23,000	$19,000		4,000
Notes Payable	3,500	4,000	500	
Total Current Liabilities	$26,500	$23,000		
Working Capital	$40,100	$35,600		
Net Increase in Working Capital				4,500
			$13,500	$13,500

Step 2. A T account is opened for each noncurrent position statement item and the amount of change during the year is entered. A single horizontal rule is drawn under each amount, as shown:

Long-Term Investments	
3,000	

Mortgage Payable	
3,000	

Machinery	
27,000	

5% Preferred Stock	
	5,000

Accumulated Depr.–Machinery	
	12,000

Common Stock	
	15,000

Buildings	
16,000	

Premium on Common Stock	
	3,000

Accumulated Depr.–Buildings	
	3,000

Retained Earnings	
	14,500

Intangible Assets	
	1,000

Step 3. Two additional T accounts are opened: Funds Summary and Revenue and Expense Operating Summary. The net change in funds is entered in the Funds Summary account, and a rule is drawn.

Revenue and Expense Operating Summary		Funds Summary	
		4,500	
		Increases in working capital	Decreases in working capital

Step 4. All the transactions for the year are reconstructed in separate summary entries below the horizontal rules. The entries indicated by the net changes in the comparative position statements and the supplementary data are made directly to the T accounts. They are shown in general journal form only to facilitate the explanation. They are posted to the T accounts only—*not to the regular general ledger accounts.*

(a)

Revenue and Expense Operating Summary–Net Income	19,325	
Retained Earnings		19,325

This is a summary of all the entries made during the period to the revenue and expense accounts. The amount of $19,325, the net income for the period, was originally recorded as a closing entry by a debit to Revenue and Expense Summary and a credit to Retained Earnings. In this entry, Revenue and Expense Operating Summary is debited in place of Revenue and Expense Summary. Since the balance of the Revenue and Expense Operating Summary account will show the amount of funds provided by operations, this entry assumes a net increase in funds of $19,325 resulting from the revenue and expense transactions for the period.

(b)

Revenue and Expense Operating Summary–Depreciation on Machinery	12,000	
Accumulated Depreciation–Machinery		12,000

This entry represents the annual depreciation charge, the original debit being to Depreciation Expense–Machinery, an expense account. It is evident that the assumption made in Entry a, that all expenses decrease funds, is not valid. Funds are used to acquire machinery but the periodic allocations of this cost as deductions from revenue does not affect funds. The debit in this entry will therefore be added to the debit from Entry a in determining the amount of funds provided by operations.

(c)

Revenue and Expense Operating Summary–Depreciation on Buildings	3,000	
Accumulated Depreciation–Buildings		3,000

The reason for this entry is the same as for Entry b.

(d)

Revenue and Expense Operating Summary–Amortization of Intangibles	1,000	
Intangible Assets		1,000

This entry represents the amortization of a cost incurred in a prior period. The reason for the entry is the same as for Entry b.

(e)

Retained Earnings	4,825	
Funds Summary–Declaration of Dividends		4,825

Dividends were declared and paid, resulting in a decrease in funds. If the dividends were declared but not paid, the credit to Dividends Payable would increase current liabilities and decrease funds; Entry e would therefore be the same.

(f)

Funds Summary	5,000	
Long-Term Investments		4,000
Revenue and Expense Operating Summary–Gain on Sale of		
Investments		1,000

Securities that cost $4,000 were sold for $5,000. The gain on the sale is included in the reported net income of $19,325, and in Revenue and Expense Operating Summary through Entry a. But the effect on the sale was to increase funds by a total of $5,000; hence the debit to Funds Summary for $5,000 in Entry f. Furthermore, the increase in funds resulting from the gain ($1,000) is reported as an integral part of the total increase in funds from sale of investments ($5,000) and not as a part of funds provided by operations. The credit of $1,000 to Revenue and Expense Operating Summary cancels a like amount included in Revenue and Expense Operating Summary through Entry a.

(g)

The T account for Long-Term Investments now appears as shown:

Long-Term Investments

3,000	
	(f) 4,000

Since the balance below the horizontal line must be the same as the balance above the line, a debit entry of $7,000 must be made. It may be assumed that securities costing $7,000 were acquired. In practice, reference would be made to the records to confirm this assumption.

Long-Term Investments	7,000	
Funds Summary–Purchase of Investments		7,000

(h)

Machinery	27,000	
Funds Summary–Purchase of Machinery		27,000

The explanation for Entry h is the same as for Entry g.

Since no machinery was sold during the period, it may be assumed that the net change represents acquisitions.

(i)

Buildings	16,000	
Funds Summary–Acquisition of Building		16,000

(j)

Funds Summary–Issuance of Preferred Stock	5,000	
5% Preferred Stock		5,000

A total of 50 shares of preferred stock were issued at par value.

(k)

Funds Summary–Issuance of Common Stock	18,000	
Common Stock		15,000
Premium on Common Stock		3,000

A total of 1,500 shares of common stock were issued at $12 per share.

(l)

Mortgage Payable	3,000	
Funds Summary–Payment of Mortgage Payable		3,000

The decrease in Mortgage Payable is assumed to be due to a cash payment.

At this point, the balance below the horizontal line in each noncurrent account is equal to the net change above the line, all the transactions affecting funds having been reproduced.

(m)

Step 5. The balance in the Revenue and Expense Operating Summary account is now $34,325, representing the funds provided by operations. This balance is transferred to Funds Summary.

Funds Summary–Funds Provided by Operations	34,325	
Revenue and Expense Operating Summary		34,325

The completeness and accuracy of the work is verified by the equality of the balances above and below the rule of the Funds Summary account.

Long-Term Investments

	3,000		
(g)	7,000	(f)	4,000
(bal. 3,000)			

Mortgage Payable

		3,000	
(l)	3,000		

Machinery

	27,000	
(h)	27,000	

5% Preferred Stock

		5,000	
		(j)	5,000

Accumulated Depr.–Machinery

		12,000	
		(b)	12,000

Buildings

	16,000	
(i)	16,000	

Common Stock

		15,000	
		(k)	15,000

Accumulated Depr.–Buildings

		3,000	
		(c)	3,000

Premium on Common Stock

		3,000	
		(k)	3,000

Intangible Assets

		1,000	
		(d)	1,000

Retained Earnings

		14,500	
(e)	4,825	(a)	19,325
		(bal. 14,500)	

Revenue and Expense Operating Summary

(a)	Net income	19,325	(f) Gain on sale of investments	1,000
(b)	Depreciation on machinery	12,000	(m) Funds provided by operations	34,325
(c)	Depreciation on buildings	3,000		
(d)	Amortization of intangibles	1,000		
		35,325		35,325

Funds Summary (Working Capital)

		4,500		
(f) Sale of investments	5,000	(e) Cash dividends paid		4,825
(j) Issuance of preferred		(g) Purchase of investments		7,000
stock at par value	5,000	(h) Purchase of machinery		27,000
(k) Issuance of common stock		(i) Purchase of buildings		16,000
at premium	18,000	(l) Payment on mortgage		3,000
(m) Funds provided by				
operations	34,325			
(bal. 4,500)				

Step 6. The formal statement of sources and uses of funds can now be prepared directly from the Funds Summary account: the debits represent sources of funds; the credits, uses of funds. Supporting figures for funds received from operations may be taken from the Revenue and Expense Operating Summary account. The statement is shown:

PLYMOUTH CORPORATION
Statement of Sources and Uses of Funds
For the Year Ended December 31, 1969

Sources of Funds		
Operations		$34,325
Sale of Investments		5,000
Issuance of Stock		
Preferred	$ 5,000	
Common	18,000	23,000
Total		$62,325
Uses of Funds		
Purchase of Investments	$ 7,000	
Purchase of Machinery	27,000	
Purchase of Buildings	16,000	
Dividend Payments	4,825	
Payment on Mortgage	3,000	57,825
Net Increase in Working Capital		$ 4,500

THE FUNDS STATEMENT—MANAGERIAL ANALYSIS

The funds statement of the Plymouth Corporation, arranged in common-size form, is shown in Figure 18-2. An analysis in question and answer form to indicate how this statement may be used by management, investors, and other interested persons follows.

1. What was the net change in working capital? An increase of $4,500.
2. What was the effect of plant and equipment acquisitions on working capital? The purchase of additional machinery and buildings decreased available funds by $43,000, or 69 percent of available funds ($43,000 ÷ $62,325). Note, however, that net income per the income statement was $19,325, whereas the funds provided by operations were $34,325; the difference is represented by the deductions from revenue for depreciation on machinery ($12,000) and buildings ($3,000).
3. What funds were made available from investment by owners? from operations?

PLYMOUTH CORPORATION
Statement of Sources and Uses of Funds
For the Year Ended December 31, 1969

Figure 18-2.
Common-Size
Funds Statement.

		Amount	Percent
Sources of Funds			
Operations		$34,325	55.1
Sale of Investments		5,000	8.0
Issuance of Stock			
Preferred	$ 5,000		
Common	18,000	23,000	36.9
Totals		$62,325	100.0
Uses of Funds			
Purchase of Investments		$ 7,000	11.2
Purchase of Machinery		27,000	43.3
Purchase of Buildings		16,000	25.7
Dividend Payments		4,825	7.8
Payment on Mortgage		3,000	4.8
Net Increase in Working Capital		4,500	7.2
Totals		$62,325	100.0

	Amount	Percent of Total
From operations	$34,325	60
From issuance of preferred and common stock	23,000	40
Total	$57,325	100

These two sources thus provided approximately 92 percent of the available funds ($57,325 ÷ $62,325). The remaining 8 percent came from the sale of investments for $5,000.

4. What funds came from outside borrowing? None.

5. What funds came from the sale of noncurrent assets? The sale of investments increased funds by $5,000.

6. What was the effect of the dividend payments on funds? Dividend payments totaled $4,825. These payments represent approximately 25 percent of net income ($4,825 ÷ $19,325) and 8 percent of available funds ($4,825 ÷ $62,325).

ALTERNATIVE DEFINITIONS OF FUNDS

Much of the attention given to the statement of sources and uses of funds in recent years[3] has centered on alternative definitions of the term *funds* and on increasing the flexibility of presentation of the statement. "Types of transactions reflected in the statement of source and application of funds may vary substantially in relative impor-

---

[3] Perry Mason, " 'Cash Flow Analysis' and the Funds Statement," American Institute of Certified Public Accountants, New York: 1961; National Association of Accountants, "Cash Flow Analysis for Managerial Control," Research Report No. 38, New York: October, 1961; Hector R. Anton, *The Flow of Funds,* Houghton-Mifflin Company, Boston: 1962.

tance from one period to another. As a result, consistency of arrangement of items from period to period and uniformity of arrangement as between reporting enterprises are of less significance than in the case of balance sheet or income statement."[4]

The common definition of funds as *working capital* limits the usefulness of the report. Since preparation of the statement involves an analysis of the relationships of the items in the financial statements, the logic of the analysis is the same regardless of the assumed meaning of funds. The mathematical relationships of the accounting quantities are the same; the form of reporting these relationships may vary. A change in the definition of funds simply means a different way of grouping the various items on the right-hand side of Equation 4 (page 613). An important advantage of examining the flow of funds in algebraic terms is that it becomes clearly evident that the underlying mathematical relationships can be readily reported in a variety of statement forms. If, for example, inventories are to be excluded from the definition of funds, Equation 1 (page 613) is rewritten as shown:

$$\text{Funds} = \text{Current Assets (other than inventories)} - \text{Current Liabilities} \qquad (5)$$
$$= \text{Noncurrent Liabilities} + \text{Owners' Equity} - (\text{Noncurrent Assets} + \text{Inventories})$$

Equation 4 now becomes

$$\text{Net change in funds} \qquad (6)$$
$$= [CA_2 \text{ (excluding inventories)} - CA_1 \text{ (excluding inventories)}] - (CL_2 - CL_1)$$
$$= (NCL_2 - NCL_1) + (OE_2 - OE_1) - [(NCA_2 - NCA_1) + (\text{Inventories}_2 - \text{Inventories}_1)]$$

Equation 6 means that a change in inventories will now appear as a specific element in explaining the change in funds.

Funds Defined as Cash

The term *funds* has been used in the preceding pages of this chapter as a synonym for working capital. A funds statement based on this meaning of the term may be too inclusive. The flow of cash—as contrasted with the flow of working capital—is often of particular interest to management, credit grantors, investors, and others. A statement of changes in cash is useful to management and analysts in budgeting cash requirements.

The basic logic of the analysis for a funds-equals-cash statement is the same as for a funds-equals-working-capital statement: an analysis of the relationships of the items in the financial statements. The causes of the changes in cash—the sources and the uses of cash—are determined by analyzing the changes in all accounts other than Cash. Figures from the income statement are used to determine the changes in cash due to operations, and figures from the position statement together with supplementary data will reveal the remaining causes for the changes in cash.

The procedure for analyzing the transactions for a funds-equals-cash statement are the same as for a funds-equals-working-capital statement except that the changes in current asset and current liability accounts are treated separately instead of being

---

[4] *Opinion No. 3 of the Accounting Principles Board,* "The Statement of Source and Application of Funds," New York: American Institute of Certified Public Accountants, October, 1963.

netted as a single amount (working capital). The determination of the cash generated by operations, however, is complicated by the fact that the revenue and expense figures used for income measurement are different from cash receipts and disbursements. The time lag in the settlement of accounts with customers and creditors and the prepayment of certain expenses, for example, make necessary the conversion of accrual-based revenue and expense amounts to the cash equivalent.

The income statement of the Plymouth Corporation (page 620) is analyzed in terms of the changes in cash resulting from operations, as shown:

PLYMOUTH CORPORATION
Income Statement Converted to Show Cash
Generated by Operations
For the Year Ended December 31, 1969

		Income Statement	Cash Increase or (Decrease)
Sales		$125,000	$122,000 (a)
Cost of Goods Sold			
Inventory, 12/31/68	$ 21,000		
Purchases	80,000		
Total	$101,000		
Inventory, 12/31/69	31,000		
Cost of Goods Sold		$ 70,000	$ (76,500) (b)
Operating Expenses			
Depreciation–Machinery	$ 12,000		–0–
Depreciation–Building	3,000		–0–
Amortization of Intangibles	1,000		–0–
Other	20,675	36,675	(20,675)
Total Costs and Expenses		$106,675	$ (97,175)
Operating Margin		$ 18,325	
Gain on Sale of Investments		1,000	
Net Income		$ 19,325	
Cash Generated by Operations			$ 24,825
(a) Sales			$125,000
Accounts Receivable, 12/31/68			16,600
Total			$141,600
Accounts Receivable, 12/31/69			19,600
Cash Collections from Customers			$122,000
(b) Cost of Purchases			$ 80,000
Notes and Accounts Payable, 12/31/68			23,000
Total			$103,000
Notes and Accounts Payable, 12/31/69			26,500
Cash Payments to Creditors			$ 76,500

The T-account method illustrated earlier in this chapter can also be used in the preparation of a sources and uses of cash statement. Again, the data for the Plymouth Corporation are used. Since, by definition, cash is the only fund account, all other accounts are nonfund; hence, T accounts must be opened for those current accounts that are netted under the working capital definition of funds. In the partial T-account ledger shown, only the additional accounts and the two summary accounts are given. All the other accounts would be unchanged from the earlier example (page 625). New entries are designated by double letters; all the other entries carry the original letter notations.

Accounts Receivable				Accounts Payable	
	3,000				4,000
(aa)	3,000		(cc)		4,000

Merchandise Inventory				Notes Payable	
	10,000				500
(bb)	10,000		(dd)	500	

Revenue and Expense Operating Summary (Cash)

(a)	Net Income	19,325	(f)	Gain on sale of investments	1,000
(b)	Depr.–Machinery	12,000	(aa)	Increase–Accts. Rec.	3,000
(c)	Depr.–Buildings	3,000	(bb)	Increase–Mdse. Inv.	10,000
(d)	Amortization–Intangibles	1,000	(dd)	Decrease–Notes Pay.	500
(cc)	Incr.–Accts. Payable	4,000	(m)	Funds provided by operations	24,825
		39,325			39,325

Funds Summary (Cash)

					5,000
(f)	Sale of investments	5,000	(e)	Cash dividends paid	4,825
(j)	Issuance of pfd. stock	5,000	(g)	Purch. of investments	7,000
(k)	Issuance of common stock	18,000	(h)	Purch. of Machinery	27,000
(m)	Funds from operations	24,825	(i)	Purch. of Buildings	16,000
			(l)	Payment on mortgage	3,000

The statement of sources and uses of cash is prepared from the data in the Funds Summary (Cash) account. The Revenue and Expense Operating Summary (Cash) account provides the details of cash received from operations ($24,825).

PLYMOUTH CORPORATION
Statement of Sources and Uses of Cash
For the Year Ended December 31, 1969

Sources of Cash		
Operations	$24,825	
Issuance of stock	23,000	
Sale of investments	5,000	$52,825
Uses of Cash		
Purchase of securities	$ 7,000	
Purchase of machinery	27,000	
Purchase of buildings	16,000	
Dividend payments	4,825	
Mortgage payments	3,000	57,825
Net Decrease in Cash		$ 5,000

SUMMARY

The purpose of the various funds statements is to furnish information regarding sources and uses of working capital, cash, or other financial items.

The chief sources of funds—in the sense of working capital—are operations, long-term borrowing, and the sale of assets. The chief uses are to increase noncurrent assets, retire long-term debt, reduce the stockholders' equity, and pay dividends. The funds statement shows the relationship of the sources and uses of funds to working capital. It supplements the conventional statements.

The preparation of the funds statement requires (1) an analysis of the current assets and current liabilities to determine the net change in working capital during the period and (2) a determination of the causes of the net change by an analysis of the changes in all the other accounts. Transactions that do not change working capital are not reported in the funds statement (for example, transactions that change only current assets or current liabilities and transactions that change only noncurrent accounts). Transactions that change working capital are reported (for example, transactions that change a current and a noncurrent account).

Regular operating activities are a primary source of funds, but the change in working capital may be greater than the net income as shown in the income statement. Adjustments must be made for nonworking capital charges to Revenue and Expense Summary, representing costs and expenses that affect net income but not the working capital of the current period (for example, depreciation, a loss on a disposal of assets, or the amortization of intangible assets).

Preparation of the funds statement requires the following steps:
1. The change in working capital is determined.
2. The changes in all the noncurrent accounts are analyzed.
3. The statement is prepared.

The statement can be prepared directly from a comparative position statement but if there are a number of transactions and accounts to analyze, some systematic method is needed. The T-account method is one.

The flow of cash—as contrasted with the flow of working capital—and a statement of changes in cash is useful to management and analysts in forecasting cash requirements. The causes of the changes in cash are determined by analyzing the changes in all accounts other than Cash. The income statement is converted to determine the changes in cash from operations, and the changes in the position statement together with underlying data reveal the remaining causes for the changes in cash. The procedures for analyzing the transactions for a funds-equals-cash statement are the same as for funds-equals-working capital statement except that the changes in current asset and current liability accounts are treated separately instead of being netted as a single amount (working capital).

☐ **QUESTIONS**

Q18-1. What is the purpose of the statement of sources and uses of funds?

Q18-2. What is meant by the term *funds?*

Q18-3. How may the funds provided by operations be determined?

Q18-4. What are the chief sources of funds from operations? The chief uses?

Q18-5. Certain transactions are eliminated from the funds statement. Why? Give some examples.

Q18-6. How may the statement of sources and uses of funds be used to advantage by management? Investors? Others?

Q18-7. How may the statement of sources and uses of cash be used to advantage by management? Investors? Others?

Q18-8. What are the sources of information for the preparation of the statement of sources and uses of funds?

Q18-9. What is the effect of a dividend declaration on working capital? Of the payment of a dividend?

Q18-10. What is the effect of depreciation of plant and equipment on (a) working capital? (b) cash?

Q18-11. The net income as shown on the income statement and the funds provided by operations are different amounts. Why?

Q18-12. Does the statement of sources and uses of funds eliminate the need for the statement of financial position? The income statement?

Q18-13. What is the effect on funds of a change to an accelerated method of depreciation?

Q18-14. What is the effect on funds of: (a) a gain on sale of equipment; (b) a loss on sale of temporary securities; (c) a collection of accounts receivable; (d) a payment of accounts payable; (e) the issuance of bonds at a premium; (f) an increase in accumulated depreciation; (g) an increase in restrictions of retained earnings; (h) the amortization of intangibles; (i) an uninsured fire loss of merchandise; (j) the settlement of a current debt by the issuance of stock?

Q18-15. In arriving at funds provided by operations, certain items are added to net income and other items are deducted. Illustrate and explain.

Q18-16. It is alleged that cash flow data are helpful to business management. (a) List the areas in which this information would be particularly useful. (b) What are the shortcomings of cash flow data?

☐ **EXERCISES**

E18-1. For each of the following transactions, state whether it (a) was a source of funds, (b) was a use of funds, or (c) had no effect on funds:

1. Purchased U.S. Treasury notes maturing in six months.
2. Issued a stock dividend to common stockholders.
3. Restricted retained earnings for anticipated plant expansion.
4. Issued common stock in exchange for a building.
5. Acquired machinery for $50,000; paid $20,000 in cash and issued a long-term note for the balance.
6. Wrote off an uncollectible account receivable against Allowance for Doubtful Accounts.
7. Reacquired some outstanding preferred stock for retirement.
8. Issued additional common stock at a premium for cash.
9. Wrote off a portion of the Goodwill account.
10. Issued bonds at a discount; the proceeds were used to retire preferred stock.

E18-2. Comparative financial statements of the Flynn Corporation showed the following balances:

	December 31	
	1969	1968
Cash	$ 50,000	$ 52,000
Other Current Assets	110,000	115,000
Plant and Equipment (net)	140,000	110,000
Current Liabilities	110,000	115,000
Stockholders' Equity	190,000	162,000

There were no disposals of plant and equipment during the year. Dividend payments totaled $10,000. Prepare a schedule explaining the cause of the decrease in cash in spite of reported net income of $38,000.

E18-3. The Plant and Equipment section of the Wood Company's comparative statement of financial position shows the following amounts:

	December 31	
	1969	1968
Plant and Equipment		
Machinery	$550,000	$500,000
Deduct Accumulated Depreciation	250,000	240,000
Total Plant and Equipment	$300,000	$260,000

Acquisitions of new machinery during the year totaled $140,000. The income statement shows depreciation charges for the year of $70,000 and a loss from machinery disposals of $24,000. Determine the original cost and accumulated depreciation of machinery sold during the year and the proceeds of the sale; prepare a partial statement of sources and uses of funds.

E18–4. For each of the following cases, compute the funds generated by operations.

	a	b	c	d	e
Net income (loss) per income statement	$10,000	$(10,000)	$50,000	$40,000	$(15,000)
Depreciation of plant and equipment	2,000	2,000	4,500	3,000	1,000
Gain (loss) on sale of long-term investments			(1,000)	2,000	(500)
Periodic amortization of bond discount			1,000	500	250
Periodic amortization of patents				500	300

E18–5. During the year 1969, the changes in the accounts of the Ellery Company were as follows:

	Increases	Decreases
Cash		$10,000
Accounts Receivable	$ 6,000	
Merchandise Inventory	20,000	
Long-Term Investments	6,000	
Plant and Equipment	58,000	
Accumulated Depreciation	4,000	
Accounts Payable	7,500	
Taxes Payable		500
Mortgage Payable		6,000
Common Stock	46,000	
Retained Earnings	29,000	

Additional information is given:
1. Net income per income statement $38,650
2. Dividends declared and paid $ 9,650
3. There were no disposals of plant or equipment during the year.

Prepare a statement of sources and uses of funds.

E18–6. Determine the amount of cash received from customers in each of the following cases:

	1	2
Accounts Receivable–Beginning of Year	$ 17,000	$ 30,000
Accounts Receivable–End of Year	25,000	28,000
Sales	105,000	150,000
Uncollectible Accounts Written Off	500	750
Cash Discounts on Sales	1,000	2,500

E18–7. Determine the amount of cash disbursements for merchandise in each of the following cases:

	1	2
Beginning Inventory	$12,000	$15,000
Ending Inventory	10,000	18,000
Purchases	75,000	85,000
Beginning Accounts Payable	10,000	14,000
Ending Accounts Payable	12,000	10,000
Discounts on Purchases	1,000	1,500

E18-**8.** The comparative statements of financial position of the Simon Company, as of December 31, 1969 and 1968, were as follows:

	1969	1968
Cash	$ 48,000	$ 63,000
Accounts Receivable (net)	58,800	49,800
Merchandise Inventory	85,000	65,000
Long-Term Investments	68,000	60,000
Machinery	350,000	300,000
Buildings	270,000	225,000
Land	50,000	50,000
Patents	18,000	20,000
Totals	$947,800	$832,800
Accumulated Depreciation–Machinery	$ 40,000	$ 30,000
Accumulated Depreciation–Buildings	35,000	20,000
Accounts Payable–Trade	55,000	50,000
Notes Payable–Trade	8,000	10,000
Mortgage Payable	50,000	60,000
Common Stock	550,000	500,000
Retained Earnings	209,800	162,800
Totals	$947,800	$832,800

Additional information is given:
1. Net income for the year was $47,000.
2. There were no sales or disposals of plant or equipment during the year.

Prepare a statement of sources and uses of funds.

E18-**9.** The general journal of the Valin Company shows the following entries:

1969				
Jan. 14		Machinery	100,000	
		Mortgage Payable		75,000
		Cash		25,000
Dec. 31		Patent Amortization	2,000	
		Patents		2,000

Indicate how these transactions would be reflected on a statement of sources and uses of funds.

E18-**10.** From the following data, taken from the ledger of the Winn Company, prepare a partial statement of sources and uses of funds.

Machinery

1969			1969		
Jan. 1	Balance	250,000	Feb. 14	Sale	30,000
July 10	Purchase	33,000	June 21	Sale	25,000

Accumulated Depreciation–Machinery

1969			1969		
Feb. 14	Sale	20,000	Jan. 1		130,000
June 21	Sale	15,000	Dec. 31	Depreciation	42,000

Gain or Loss on Sale of Machinery

1969			1969		
June 21	Sale	3,500	Feb. 14	Sale	2,000

Revenue and Expense Summary

			1969		
			Dec. 31	Net income for year	60,000

E18–11. How would each of the following transactions be reflected in a statement of sources and uses of funds? (Classify each item as a use of funds, a source of funds, or a nonfund, transaction.)

1. Construction of a building
2. Issuance of bonds
3. Recording of depreciation on a building
4. Declaration of a cash dividend
5. Purchase of machinery, giving 60-day note
6. Sale of land for cash at a loss
7. Acquisition of a patent by the issuance of capital stock
8. Amortization of a discount on bonds payable

E18–12. The accounts receivable of a business totaled $15,000 at the beginning of the year and $12,000 at the end of the year. Accounts receivable written off as uncollectible during the year amounted to $1,300, and cash discounts allowed to customers amounted to $600. The sales for the year were $35,000. What were the cash receipts during the year from sales of the current and prior periods?

E18–13. The purchase of merchandise of a business amounted to $50,000 during 1969. Accounts payable at the beginning and end of the year were $16,500 and $14,800, respectively; notes payable given to trade creditors in settlement of open accounts were $4,000 at the beginning of the year and $4,400 at the end of the year. Returns and allowances on purchases were $435. What were the cash payments during 1969 for purchases of 1969 and prior periods?

E18-**14.** For each of the following transactions, indicate whether it (a) was a source of funds, (b) was a use of funds, or (c) had no effect on funds:

1. Restricted retained earnings for contingencies.
2. Issued common stock in exchange for a patent.
3. Wrote off an uncollectible account receivable against the Accumulated Allowance for Doubtful Accounts.
4. Wrote off a portion of the Patent account.
5. Acquired machinery costing $50,000. Paid $20,000 in cash and issued a long-term note for the balance.
6. Declared a cash dividend of $5,000, payable in the following accounting period.
7. Purchased merchandise for cash.
8. Sold for $600 treasury stock purchased in the preceding accounting period at a cost of $500.
9. Sold for $5,000 in cash machinery with a book value of $9,000.
10. Received treasury stock as a donation. The treasury stock had a fair market value of $1,000.
11. Issued common stock for cash.

E18-**15.** The president of the Omar Company, after reviewing his Company's annual financial statements, is puzzled by seeming discrepancies. He notes that although the cash balance increased by $30,000 during the year, the statement of sources and uses of funds shows a decrease in funds. Furthermore, an item in the statement of sources and uses of funds reported Funds Generated by Operations, $15,000, although the income statement reported a net loss of $5,000. Write a letter to the president explaining these matters to him.

E18-**16.** Assume that you are preparing a statement of cash generated by operations for Wear, Inc. One of the problems confronting you is to determine the amount of cash paid out in 1969 in connection with interest transactions. Interest expense of $62,500 is reported on the 1969 income statement. From a comparative statement of financial position, you discover the following items and amounts:

	December 31	
	1969	1968
Prepaid Interest Expense	$2,450	$1,890
Accrued Interest Payable	4,760	5,150

From the information given, compute the amount of cash paid out in 1969 in connection with all interest transactions.

E18-**17.** Assume that you are a prospective investor in the Winter Company and have assembled certain information relating to the operations of the Company. From a comparative statement of financial position and a statement of sources and uses of cash, you decide to reconstruct an income statement on the accrual basis. The first item you desire to determine is Sales for 1969. The 1969 statement of sources and uses of cash reports Cash Received from Customers of $256,410. On the comparative statement of financial position, you find the following items and amounts:

	December 31	
	1969	1968
Accounts Receivable	$50,000	$52,000
Allowance for Doubtful Accounts	3,000	2,000

From other sources, you discover that the Company had written off $1,500 of the accounts receivable at December 31, 1968. You therefore calculated that the bad debts expense for 1969 was $2,500.

From the information given, compute the accrual sales figure for 1969.

☐ **DEMONSTRATION PROBLEMS**

DP18-1. (*Statement of sources and uses of funds*) The December 31, 1968 and 1969, statements of financial position of the Northern Company carried the following debit and credit amounts:

	December 31	
	1969	1968
Debits		
Cash	$ 10,200	$ 12,600
Accounts Receivable (net)	35,100	32,900
Merchandise Inventory	85,200	86,400
Prepaid Expenses	1,500	1,800
Office Equipment	5,000	5,600
Store Equipment	29,800	28,300
Totals	$166,800	$167,600
Credits		
Accumulated Depreciation–Office Equipment	$ 2,500	$ 2,400
Accumulated Depreciation–Store Equipment	7,500	6,500
Accounts Payable	22,400	23,500
Notes Payable	10,000	5,000
Common Stock, $10 par value	110,000	100,000
Premium on Common Stock	6,500	5,500
Retained Earnings	7,900	24,700
Totals	$166,800	$167,600

Additional information is given:

1. The net loss for the year was $1,900.
2. Depreciation expense on office equipment was $500; on store equipment, it was $1,700.
3. Office equipment that was carried at its cost of $600 with accumulated depreciation of $400 was sold for $300. The gain was carried directly to Retained Earnings.
4. Store equipment costing $2,200 was purchased.
5. Fully depreciated store equipment that cost $700 was discarded and its cost and accumulated depreciation were removed from the accounts.
6. Cash dividends of $4,000 were paid during the year.

7. A 1,000-share stock dividend was declared and issued. On the date of declaration, the common stock of the Company had a fair market value of $11 per share.

Required: Prepare a statement of sources and uses of funds.

DP18-2. (*Statement of sources and uses of funds; of cash*) The following data are taken from the books of the Fox Corporation (figures are in thousands of dollars):

	December 31	
	1969	1968
Debits		
Cash	$ 315	$ 285
Marketable Securities	106	50
Receivables (net)	145	125
Inventories	95	70
Long-Term Investments	70	110
Machinery	500	350
Buildings	600	200
Land	35	35
Totals	$1,866	$1,225
Credits		
Accumulated Depreciation	$ 275	$ 150
Accounts Payable	100	75
Notes Payable	50	25
Mortgage Bonds Payable	500	250
Common Stock	550	400
Premium on Stock	55	–0–
Retained Earnings	336	325
Totals	$1,866	$1,225

FOX CORPORATION
Income Statement
For the Year Ended December 31, 1969

Sales		$600
Cost of Goods Sold		337
Gross Margin on Sales		$263
Operating Expenses		
Depreciation–Machinery	$ 50	
Depreciation–Buildings	80	
Other Expenses	100	230
Net Income from Operations		$ 33
Gain on Sale of Long-Term Investments		12
Total		$ 45
Loss on Sale of Machinery (proceeds were $15)		5
Net Income		$ 40

Required: 1. Prepare a statement of sources and uses of funds.
2. Prepare a statement of sources and uses of cash.

DP18–3. (*Funds generated by operations*) You are given the following single-step combined statement of income and retained earnings:

REX COMPANY

Statement of Income and Retained Earnings

For the Year Ended December 31, 1969

Revenue and Other Credits		
Sales		$600,000
Interest Earned		10,500
Correction of Prior Years' Income–		
Overstatement of 1967 Depreciation of		
Machinery		5,000
Total		$615,500
Expenses, Losses, and Other Charges		
Cost of Goods Sold	$470,000	
Salaries and Wages Expense	40,000	
Bad Debts Expense	4,000	
Advertising Expense	10,000	
Depreciation Expense	60,000	
Office Expense	20,000	
Loss on Reduction of Marketable Securities		
to Market	5,000	
Loss on Sale of Machinery	8,000	
Interest Expense	4,000	
Total		621,000
Net Loss for the Year		$ (5,500)
Retained Earnings, December 31, 1968		1,010,500
Total		$1,005,000
Deduct: Dividends declared June 2, 1969		
and paid July 2, 1969	$100,000	
Dividends declared December 2,		
1969 to be paid January 2, 1970	150,000	
Stock dividends declared and		
issued in 1969	200,000	
Total		450,000
Retained Earnings, December 31, 1969		$ 555,000

Interest Earned represents a receipt of $10,000 in cash and the amortization of discount on bonds purchased for investments (long-term) of $500. The Interest Expense figure was increased by $350 for amortization of discount on bonds payable and was decreased by $200 for amortization of a premium on bonds payable.

Required: 1. Starting with the Net Loss for Year compute, in schedule or T-account form, the funds provided (or used) by operations during 1969.

2. Compute the amount of funds provided or used in connection with the dividend policy of the Company.

☐ PROBLEMS

P18–1. The following data of the Holt Company are given in three parts (figures are in thousands of dollars):

Part I

	December 31	
	1969	1968
Debits		
Current Assets	$105	$ 60
Plant and Equipment (net)	150	125
Totals	$255	$185
Credits		
Current Liabilities	$ 40	$ 20
Common Stock	150	150
Retained Earnings	65	15
Totals	$255	$185

Depreciation for period is $5.

Part II

Assume the same facts, except that Plant and Equipment cost and Accumulated Depreciation are itemized as follows:

	December 31	
	1969	1968
Debits		
Current Assets	$105	$ 60
Plant and Equipment	170	140
Totals	$275	$200
Credits		
Accumulated Depreciation	$ 20	$ 15
Current Liabilities	40	20
Common Stock	150	150
Retained Earnings	65	15
Totals	$275	$200

Part III

Assume the same debit and credit amounts as in Part II. Assume further that during the year a machine having an original cost of $10,000 and accumulated depreciation of $5,000 was sold for $7,000.

Required: For each part, prepare a statement of sources and uses of funds.

P18-**2**. Following is the comparative post-closing trial balance of the Treet Company:

TREET COMPANY
Comparative Post-Closing Trial Balance
December 31, 1969 and 1968

	December 31	
	1969	1968
Debits		
Cash	$ 35,000	$ 50,000
Accounts Receivable (net)	95,000	80,000
Merchandise Inventory	260,000	195,000
Marketable Securities		110,000
Prepaid Expenses	4,000	2,500
Plant and Equipment	500,000	300,000
Patents	64,000	68,000
Totals	$958,000	$805,500
Credits		
Accumulated Depreciation–Plant and Equipment	$135,000	$100,000
Accounts Payable	100,000	60,000
Common Stock	500,000	500,000
Retained Earnings	223,000	145,500
Totals	$958,000	$805,500

Additional data are given:

1. Net income for the period was $125,000.
2. Dividends declared and paid were $47,500.
3. The marketable securities were sold at a gain (included in Item 1) of $15,000.
4. Equipment with an original cost of $20,000 and accumulated depreciation of $10,000 was sold at a loss (included in Item 1) of $2,000.
5. Patents are being amortized over their legal life of 17 years.

Required: Prepare a statement of sources and uses of funds.

P18-**3**. The following data of Brandt, Inc., are given:

	December 31	
	1969	1968
Debits		
Cash	$ 60,000	$ 45,000
Accounts Receivable	90,000	80,000
Merchandise Inventory	40,000	32,000
Investments (Long-Term)	30,000	50,000
Machinery	40,000	25,000
Buildings	90,000	75,000
Land	10,000	10,000
Totals	$360,000	$317,000

Credits

Allowance for Doubtful Accounts	$ 3,000	$ 2,000
Accumulated Depreciation–Machinery	7,500	3,000
Accumulated Depreciation–Buildings	18,000	12,000
Accounts Payable	40,000	33,000
Accrued Payables	4,500	3,500
Mortgage Payable	35,000	40,000
Common Stock	200,000	200,000
Retained Earnings	52,000	23,500
Totals	$360,000	$317,000

Additional data are given:

1. Net income for the year was $60,000.
2. Dividends paid during the year were $31,500.
3. Investments that cost $20,000 were sold during the year for $25,000. The gain is included in Item 1.
4. Machinery that cost $5,000, on which $1,000 in depreciation had accumulated, was sold for $6,000. The gain is included in Item 1.

Required: Prepare a statement of sources and uses of funds.

P18-4. The following data of Lite Company are given:

LITE COMPANY
Comparative Position Statements
December 31, 1969 and 1968

	December 31	
	1969	1968
Cash	$ 26,000	$ 37,000
Accounts Receivable (net)	90,000	96,000
Merchandise Inventory	100,000	80,000
Investments (Long-Term)	12,000	10,000
Machinery (net)	200,000	150,000
Buildings (net)	160,000	100,000
Land	20,000	15,000
Totals	$608,000	$488,000
Accounts Payable	$ 75,000	$ 65,000
Accrued Payables	3,000	4,000
Mortgage Payable	70,000	58,000
Common Stock	300,000	250,000
Retained Earnings	160,000	111,000
Totals	$608,000	$488,000

LITE COMPANY
Income Statement
For the Year Ended December 31, 1969

Sales		$810,000
Cost of Goods Sold		480,000
Gross Margin on Sales		$330,000
Operating Expenses		
Depreciation–Machinery	$ 20,000	
Depreciation–Buildings	10,000	
Other Operating Expenses	221,000	251,000
Net Income		$ 79,000

Additional data are given:

1. Dividends paid during year were $30,000.
2. The increase in long-term investments, machinery, buildings, and land were from purchases.
3. Common stock worth $50,000 was issued at par value.

Required: Prepare a statement of sources and uses of cash.

P18–5. You are given the following comparative financial statements and supplementary information for the McGill Company:

McGILL COMPANY
Comparative Position Statement
December 31, 1969, 1968, and 1967

	December 31		
Debits	1969	1968	1967
Cash	$ 30,000	$ 28,000	$ 26,000
Marketable Securities	25,000	18,000	–0–
Accounts Receivable (net)	65,000	79,000	60,000
Inventories	145,000	125,000	134,000
Plant and Equipment	550,000	400,000	435,000
Totals	$815,000	$650,000	$655,000
Credits			
Accumulated Depreciation	$235,000	$200,000	$170,000
Current Liabilities (trade)	130,000	90,000	105,000
Long-Term Liabilities	195,000	125,000	150,000
Common Stock	135,000	125,000	140,000
Retained Earnings	120,000	110,000	90,000
Totals	$815,000	$650,000	$655,000

McGILL COMPANY
Comparative Income Statement
For the Years Ended December 31, 1969 and 1968

	1969	1968
Sales	$735,000	$785,000
Cost of Goods Sold	490,000	510,000
Gross Margin on Sales	$245,000	$275,000
Operating Expenses		
Depreciation	$ 60,000	$ 40,000
Selling and Administrative Expenses	154,000	190,000
Total Operating Expenses	$214,000	$230,000
Net Margin from Operations	$ 31,000	$ 45,000
Gain (Loss) on Disposal of Plant and Equipment	4,000	(5,000)
Net Income	$ 35,000	$ 40,000

Additional data are given:

	1969	1968
Dividends paid	$ 25,000	$20,000
Plant and equipment acquisitions	175,000	50,000

Required: 1. Prepare statements of sources and uses of funds for (a) 1968; (b) 1969.
2. Prepare statements of sources and uses of cash for (a) 1968; (b) 1969.

P18-**6.** You are given the following information from the books of the Atlanta Corporation:

ATLANTA CORPORATION
Statement of Financial Position
December 31, 1969 and 1968

	1969	1968	Increase (Decrease)
Cash	$ 13,200	$ 15,600	$ (2,400)
Accounts Receivable	47,600	32,400	15,200
Merchandise Inventory	22,000	28,000	(6,000)
Machinery	82,400	87,400	(5,000)
Sinking Fund Cash	10,000		10,000
Totals	$175,200	$163,400	$ 11,800
Allowance for Doubtful Accounts	$ 2,800	$ 2,500	$ 300
Accumulated Depreciation–Machinery	16,200	18,200	(2,000)
Accounts Payable	21,000	24,200	(3,200)
Dividends Payable	2,000		2,000
Bonds Payable	20,000		20,000
Premium on Bonds Payable	950		950
Capital Stock	100,000	100,000	
Retained Earnings	2,250	18,500	(16,250)
Retained Earnings–Restricted for Sinking Fund	10,000		10,000
Totals	$175,200	$163,400	$ 11,800

ATLANTA CORPORATION
Statement of Retained Earnings
For the Year Ended December 31, 1969

Balance, December 31, 1968		$18,500
Add: Net Income for year ended December 31, 1969		750
Total		$19,250
Deduct: Dividends Paid in Cash	$ 5,000	
Dividend Declared Payable January 15, 1970	2,000	
Appropriation for Sinking Fund	10,000	17,000
Balance, December 31, 1969		$ 2,250

ATLANTA CORPORATION
Income Statement
For the Year Ended December 31, 1969

Sales		$85,450
Cost of Goods Sold		65,000
Gross Margin on Sales		$20,450
Operating Expenses		
Salaries	$14,700	
Bad Debt Expense	300	
Depreciation of Machinery	3,500	
Taxes	400	
Insurance	300	19,200
Net Income from Operations		$ 1,250
Other Expenses		
Bond Interest Expense	$ 1,050	
Deduct Amortization of Bond Premium	50	
Net Bond Interest Expense	$ 1,000	
Other Income		
Gain on Sale of Machinery	500	500
Net Income to Retained Earnings		$ 750

Additional data are given:

Bonds payable in the amount of $20,000 were sold on April 30, 1968, at 105. Machinery that cost $7,000, and had accumulated depreciation of $5,500, was sold for $2,000 in cash.

Required: Prepare a schedule of working capital changes and a statement of sources and uses of funds by the T-account approach. Submit all supporting computations, including the T accounts.

P18–7. The comparative statements of financial position of the Dexter Company as of December 31, 1969 and 1968, and related supplementary data are as follows:

DEXTER COMPANY
Comparative Position Statements
December 31, 1969 and 1968

	December 31	
	1969	1968
Assets		
Current Assets		
Cash	$ 25,000	$ 23,000
Accounts Receivable (net)	65,000	62,000
Merchandise Inventory	60,000	50,000
Marketable Securities	40,000	35,000
Total Current Assets	$190,000	$170,000
Investments (at cost)	$ 80,000	$ 10,000
Plant and Equipment		
Machinery (net)	$200,000	$140,000
Buildings (net)	225,000	175,000
Land	50,000	50,000
Total Plant and Equipment	$475,000	$365,000
Total Assets	$745,000	$545,000
Liabilities and Stockholders' Equity		
Current Liabilities		
Accounts Payable–Trade	$ 95,000	$ 90,000
Notes Payable–Trade	10,000	25,000
Total Current Liabilities	$105,000	$115,000
Long-Term Liabilities		
Mortgage Bonds Payable	75,000	25,000
Total Liabilities	$180,000	$140,000
Stockholders' Equity		
5% Preferred Stock, $100 par value	$100,000	—
Common Stock, $10 par value	350,000	$350,000
Retained Earnings	115,000	55,000
Total Stockholders' Equity	$565,000	$405,000
Total Liabilities and Stockholders' Equity	$745,000	$545,000

Additional data are given:

1. Net income for the year 1969 was $70,000.
2. Dividends paid during year were $10,000.
3. Depreciation was:

   Machinery $20,000   Buildings   10,000
4. There were no plant and equipment disposals during the year.
5. The Company issued 1000 shares of 5% preferred stock at par value.
6. Investments costing $10,000 were sold for $14,000. The gain is included in Item 1.

   Required: Prepare the following statements:

1. Net change in working capital
2. Funds provided by operations
3. Sources and uses of funds

P18–**8.** You are given the following partial statement and other information for the Keane Company:

	December 31	
Debits	1969	1968
Plant and Equipment	$1,100,000	$800,000

Credits		
Accumulated Depreciation	470,000	400,000
Bonds Payable	100,000	–0–
Premium on Bonds Payable	5,000	–0–

Income Statement Data	1969
Depreciation Expense	$120,000
Gain on Disposal of Plant and Equipment	8,000

Additional data are given:

1. Plant and Equipment acquisitions during the year were $350,000.
2. Bonds Payable were issued on December 31, 1969 at 105 for a total of $105,000.

Required: Set up T accounts for Plant and Equipment, Accumulated Depreciation, Bonds Payable, Premium on Bonds Payable, Revenue and Expense Operating Summary, and Funds Summary. Place the net changes that occurred during 1969 in the first four accounts. Then make all the necessary entries in the accounts to accumulate information for the statement of sources and uses of funds.

P18–**9.** The following information was extracted from the books of the Wheeler Company:

	December 31	
	1969	1968
Working Capital	$366,700	$442,000
Tools	14,000	12,000
Machinery	39,000	45,000
Delivery Equipment	18,000	15,000
Buildings	100,000	100,000
Accumulated Depreciation	90,500	84,500
Land	25,000	40,000
Patents	3,500	4,500
Goodwill		50,000
Discount on Bonds Payable		6,000
Bonds Payable		100,000
Capital Stock	350,000	250,000
Treasury Stock	30,000	
Retained Earnings	155,700	180,000
Retained Earnings Restricted for Bond Retirement		100,000

Retained Earnings

Stock dividend	100,000	Balance, Jan. 1, 1969	180,000
Loss on scrapping of		Gain on sale of land; cost	
machinery; cost $6,000,		$15,000, sold for $18,000	3,000
accumulated depreciation		Gain on trade of delivery	
$4,500	1,500	equipment; cost $4,000,	
Goodwill	50,000	book value $2,500; an	
Unamortized discount		allowance of $3,200 was	
($4,000) and call premium		received on purchased	
($2,500) on bond		new equipment costing	
retirement	6,500	$7,000	700
Cash dividends	10,000	Retained earnings restricted	
Balance, Dec. 31, 1969	155,700	for bond retirement	100,000
		Net income for the year	40,000
	323,700		323,700
		Balance, December 31, 1969	155,700

The income statement reports depreciation of buildings of $6,000; depreciation of machinery of $4,000; depreciation of delivery equipment of $2,000; tools amortization of $4,000; patents amortization of $1,000; and bond discount amortization of $2,000.

Required: 1. Prepare a statement of sources and uses of funds.
2. Based on the information given, which concept of or approach to net income does the Company apply? Support your answer. (The cash basis or the accrual basis is not relevant in answering this question.)
3. Identify the alternative concept or approach, and compute net income according to this other concept.
4. State briefly two arguments supporting each concept.

CASE PROBLEM
Palmer Corporation

You have been employed for several years as a staff accountant in the home office of the Palmer Corporation, a large mail-order firm with offices, stores, and warehouses throughout the country. Upon the recent retirement of the company controller, Arthur Roland was appointed to that position. Since Roland is not acquainted with you or with any of the other employees under his supervision, he decides to conduct his own appraisals of his subordinates.

One morning, he asks you to come into his office. After a few minutes of pleasantries, he tells you that he wishes to make a judgment about you for possible assignment to a higher position in the firm. Thereupon, he hands you copies of the company's most recent financial statements, shown on pages 650 and 651.

After your cursory examination of the statements, Roland poses several questions, which you write on your note pad. He then says that he wishes to have the answers by that afternoon, but that you should plan to confer with him no later than the following morning.

You proceed to your desk and begin studying the statements and the questions, which are given below and in page 651.

PALMER CORPORATION
Comparative Statement of Financial Position
(in millions of dollars)
January 31, 1969 and 1968

	January 31	
	1969	1968
Assets		
Cash	$ 100.8	$ 165.3
Temporary Investments	10.1	12.9
Notes and Accounts Receivable	683.2	602.7
Allowance for Doubtful Notes and Accounts	(17.8)	(15.7)
Inventories (at FIFO cost)	293.3	241.1
Accrued Receivables	2.0	2.1
Prepaid Expenses	.5	.4
Land	37.1	22.3
Depreciable Property	641.4	599.6
Accumulated Depreciation	(388.5)	(379.9)
Leasehold Improvements	112.2	101.8
Long-Term Investments	36.4	31.2
Total Assets	$1,510.7	$1,383.8
Liabilities and Stockholders' Equity		
Accounts Payable	$ 119.3	$ 92.6
Notes Payable	34.7	9.0
Accrued Liabilities	.4	.3
Income Taxes Payable	29.5	25.5
Unearned Revenues	8.6	7.9
Portion of Long-Term Debt Due Within One Year	4.5	4.5
Bonds Payable	194.3	197.3
Mortgages Payable	125.8	95.0
Capital Stock	655.6	629.5
Additional Contributed Capital	10.2	10.0
Retained Earnings	327.8	312.2
Total Liabilities and Stockholders' Equity	$1,510.7	$1,383.8

Roland's questions are as follows:

1. What caused cash to decrease during 1969 by $64.5 million although net income was $52.6 million?
2. What do accountants mean by the term *funds*, how is it computed, and of what significance is it?
3. Prepare a statement of sources and uses of funds for the latest year.
4. What is the relationship between the statement of sources and uses of funds and the other financial statements?

PALMER CORPORATION
Comparative Statement of
Net Income and Retained Earnings
For the Years Ended January 31, 1969 and 1968
(in millions of dollars)

	January 31	
	1969	1968
Net Sales	$2,415.1	$2,210.0
Dividends and Interest Earned	2.4	2.1
Total Revenues	$2,417.5	$2,212.1
Deductions from Revenues		
Amortization of Leasehold Improvements	$ 11.0	$ 10.2
Bad Debts Expense	21.8	19.9
Depreciation	15.3	13.8
Income Taxes	48.6	45.7
Interest	17.1	15.4
Salaries, Wages, Repairs, Maintenance, Rent, and		
Other Operating Expenses	2,251.1	2,057.6
Total deductions	$2,364.9	$2,162.6
Net Income	$ 52.6	$ 49.5
Retained Earnings at Beginning of Year	312.2	299.6
Gain on Disposal of Depreciable Properties	2.0	1.5
Total	$ 366.8	$ 350.6
Cash Dividends Declared and Paid	39.0	38.4
Retained Earnings at End of Year	$ 327.8	$ 312.2

5. Of the total funds that became available for use during 1969, what percentage was produced by operations?
6. Explain the difference(s) between a statement of sources and uses of funds and a statement of sources and uses of cash.

Before answering the questions, you search the records and make the following notes:

1. The change in Temporary Investments resulted from sales of securities at cost.
2. The changes in Notes and Accounts Receivable resulted from increased sales and from a general lengthening of credit terms.
3. The change in Allowance for Doubtful Notes and Accounts resulted from the change in Notes and Accounts Receivable.
4. The change in Inventories resulted from the purchase of a number of bulk shipments at reduced prices.
5. The change in Land resulted from property acquisitions on which new store sites are or will be located.
6. The change in Depreciable Property resulted from property acquisitions costing $60 million (some property was sold).
7. The change in Accumulated Depreciation resulted from the current year's provision and from property disposals.

8. The change in Leasehold Improvements resulted from alterations made to leased buildings.
9. The change in Long-Term Investments resulted from the acquisition of the controlling interest in an insurance company.
10. The change in Accounts and Notes Payable is related to the change in inventory purchases.
11. The change in Income Taxes Payable is simply the result of a larger unpaid liability.
12. The change in Unearned Revenues is related to the change in sales.
13. The change in Bonds Payable resulted from debt retirement.
14. The change in Mortgages Payable is related to the changes in Land and Depreciable Property.
15. The changes in Capital Stock and Additional Contributed Capital resulted from the issuance of common stock.

Required: Answer Roland's six questions.

Part
Four

Cost
Accumulation,
Cost
Control,
and
Financial
Planning

Chapter Nineteen

Cost Accumulation and Control– General Manufacturing Operations

Up to this point, only the accounting for service and trading businesses has been considered. A trading business buys merchandise in finished form and sells it in the same form. A manufacturing company, on the other hand, buys raw materials that it converts into finished products by the application of labor and other factory costs. The accounting principles and procedures, however, are the same for both manufacturing and nonmanufacturing businesses. Additional accounts are opened to record the activities involved in the manufacturing process—the conversion of raw material into finished goods. From these accounts the schedule of cost of goods manufactured may be prepared; this shows the cost of raw materials consumed, direct labor costs, and the other factory costs incurred in the manufacture of the finished product over a stated period.

RAW MATERIALS USED

All materials that are economically traceable to the finished product are classified as *raw materials,* or *direct materials.* The cloth used in the manufacture of a suit, for example, is classified as a direct material. Some materials, although an integral part of the finished product, are not classified as direct materials because the cost or the quantity used is small or because it would be uneconomical to trace and determine the cost and amount of certain materials that are incorporated in the finished product. The thread used in manufacturing a garment, for example, may not be regarded as a direct material although it can otherwise be clearly identified with the end product. The cost of the thread would be accounted for, as are certain other indirect factory costs discussed later in this chapter.

The cost of raw materials used during an accounting period in the manufacture of a product may be determined by the periodic inventory method in the same manner as is the cost of goods sold in a trading business. The procedure necessary to account for raw materials, direct labor, and *manufacturing overhead* in a manufacturing company may be illustrated by the following sequence of transactions.

The Acme Manufacturing Company had raw materials on hand on January 1, 1969, costing $8,200. During the month of January, entries and postings were made as follows (only the general ledger accounts necessary for the illustration are shown):

(1)

Raw Materials Purchased	79,500	
Vouchers Payable		79,500
To record purchases of raw materials on account.		

(2)

Transportation In on Raw Materials Purchased	2,250	
Vouchers Payable		2,250
To record freight charges on raw materials purchased.		

(3)

Vouchers Payable	3,250	
Raw Materials–Purchases Returns and Allowances		3,250
To record credit received for raw materials returned.		

(4)

Vouchers Payable	80,000	
Raw Materials–Purchases Discounts		1,600
Cash		78,400
To record payment of vouchers for raw materials purchased.		

GENERAL LEDGER

Raw Materials Inventory

1969			
Jan. 1	Balance	8,200	

Raw Materials Purchased

1969		
Jan. 31 **(1)**	79,500	

Transportation In on Raw Materials Purchased

1969		
Jan. 31 **(2)**	2,250	

Raw Materials—Purchases Returns and Allowances

	1969	
	Jan. 31 **(3)**	3,250

Raw Materials—Purchases Discounts

	1969	
	Jan. 31 **(4)**	1,600

Raw materials on hand on January 31 were $9,700. The Raw Materials Used section of the schedule of cost of goods manufactured for the month of January is shown in Figure 19-1.

Figure 19-1.
Computation of Raw Materials Used

ACME MANUFACTURING COMPANY
Partial Schedule of Cost of Goods Manufactured
For the Month Ended January 31, 1969   Schedule A-1

Raw Materials Used			
Raw Materials Inventory, January 1, 1969			$ 8,200
Raw Materials Purchased		$79,500	
Transportation In on Raw Materials Purchased		2,250	
Gross Cost of Raw Materials Purchased		$81,750	
Deduct Purchases Returns and Allowances	$3,250		
Purchases Discounts	1,600	4,850	
Net Cost of Raw Materials Purchased			76,900
Cost of Raw Materials Available for Use			$85,100
Deduct Raw Materials Inventory,			
January 31, 1969			9,700
Cost of Raw Materials Used			$75,400

DIRECT LABOR

The wages paid to employees performing operations directly on the product being manufactured are referred to as *direct labor*. Direct labor is the cost of wages paid for work involving the construction, composition, or fabrication of the end product.

The following journal entries demonstrate the recording of direct labor:

(5)

Direct Labor	58,300	
Vouchers Payable (and payroll tax withholding		
liabilities)		58,300
To record the direct labor costs vouchered during		
January (payroll deduction details have been omitted).		

(6)

Direct Labor	2,700	
Accrued Wages and Salaries Payable		2,700
To record direct labor costs accrued.		

The debit total of $61,000 ($58,300 + $2,700) is the direct labor cost for the month. This amount is entered in the schedule of cost of goods manufactured on one line immediately following the amount for raw materials used.

MANUFACTURING OVERHEAD

All factory costs incurred in the manufacturing process other than the cost of raw materials used and direct labor are classified as *manufacturing overhead*. Other terms used for this group of costs are *indirect manufacturing costs* and *manufacturing burden*. For a manufacturing company, manufacturing overhead is a product cost and not a period expense, that is, these costs are incorporated in the inventory of manufactured goods. Selling expenses and general and administrative expenses are not considered manufacturing overhead because they reflect the administrative and distributive functions of the business and are not part of the manufacturing function. Most of the accounts listed in the schedule of cost of goods manufactured (see Figure 19-2) are self-explanatory. Others are explained in the following paragraphs:

Indirect labor is the labor cost for those workers whose efforts are not directly identified with the conversion of specific raw materials into specific finished products. Wages paid to employees who schedule and supervise the work of others, for example, would be classified as indirect labor. The term also includes the wages of repair and maintenance crews, guards, janitors, and cost accounting clerks assigned to the manufacturing function.

Amortization of patents represents that part of the cost of patents allocable to the current accounting period. It is assumed that these patents are for manufacturing processes. The cost of the patents should be amortized over the economically useful life or the remaining legal life of the asset, whichever is shorter. The Patents account may be credited directly for the amortized portion. The amortized portion is debited to Amortization of Patents, listed under Manufacturing Overhead. The unamortized balance of Patents is reported on the statement of financial position as an intangible asset.

Small tools used represents the cost of special small tools used up by workmen during the accounting period. It is possible to depreciate small tools by methods similar to those used for machinery and equipment. This procedure is difficult, however, because of the great variety of tools used and their relatively small value. In addition, small hand tools are easily lost or broken, and their useful life is difficult to predict. To overcome this practical difficulty, small tools may be accounted for as follows: The acquisition cost is debited to the asset account Small Tools; at the end of each accounting period an inventory of tools on hand is taken and priced; the discrepancy between the balance in the asset account and the inventory count represents the cost of tools broken, discarded, or lost. The entry to adjust the Small Tools account to the inventory amount is a debit to Small Tools Used, manufacturing overhead item, and a credit to Small Tools, plant and equipment item.

A separate account may be opened in the general ledger for each manufacturing overhead item; however, if these accounts are numerous, a subsidiary *manufacturing overhead ledger* may be set up. Its controlling account in the general ledger is Manufacturing Overhead.

The journals of the Acme Manufacturing Company showed the following additional entries (Entry 7 was made during the month; the others represent end-of-period adjustments):

(7)

Factory Rent	2,000	
Heat, Light, and Power	12.000	
Indirect Labor	9,100	
Equipment Maintenance and Repairs	2,900	
Miscellaneous Factory Costs	2,950	
Vouchers Payable (and payroll tax withholding liabilities)		28,950

       To record overhead expenses vouchered during the
       month. (There was no accrued indirect labor, and payroll
       deduction details have been omitted.)

(8)

Depreciation–Machinery and Equipment	3,500	
Accumulated Depreciation–Machinery and Equipment		3,500

       To record one month's depreciation of machinery and
       equipment.

(9)

Factory Insurance	1,100	
Prepaid Insurance		1,100

       To record the expiration of one month's insurance.

(10)

Factory Property Tax	1,600	
Accrued Taxes Payable		1,600

       To record property taxes accrued on the factory building.

(11)

Amortization of Patents	950	
Patents		950

       To amortize the patent cost for January.

(12)

Small Tools Used	250	
Small Tools		250

       To adjust the asset account to the inventory valuation.

GENERAL LEDGER

Depreciation–Machinery and Equipment

1969		
Jan. 31 **(8)**	3,500	

GENERAL LEDGER
Factory Rent

1969		
Jan. 31 **(7)**	2,000	

Heat, Light, and Power

1969		
Jan. 31 **(7)**	12,000	

Amortization of Patents

1969		
Jan. 31 **(11)**	950	

Small Tools Used

1969		
Jan. 31 **(12)**	250	

Factory Insurance

1969		
Jan. 31 **(9)**	1,100	

Factory Property Tax

1969		
Jan. 31 **(10)**	1,600	

GENERAL LEDGER
Indirect Labor

1969			
Jan. 31 **(7)**		9,100	

Equipment, Maintenance, and Repairs

1969			
Jan. 31 **(7)**		2,900	

Miscellaneous Factory Costs

1969			
Jan. 31 **(7)**		2,950	

TOTAL PERIOD MANUFACTURING COSTS

Total period manufacturing costs are made up of the costs of raw materials used, direct labor, and manufacturing overhead, as shown:

THE WORK-IN-PROCESS INVENTORY

The fabrication of a product is a continuing and repetitive process. At any time, therefore, partly finished products will be on hand in various stages of completion; they are known as *work in process,* or *goods in process.* At the end of the accounting period, the work in process is inventoried and its value determined. Since the cost of these partly finished units is included in the total period manufacturing costs, the end-of-period work-in-process inventory is deducted from the total costs to arrive at the cost of goods manufactured. Work-in-Process Inventory is classified as a current asset in the statement of financial position. The ending inventory of one period is the beginning inventory of the next period and enters into the cost of goods manufactured for that next period.

The Acme Manufacturing Company had a beginning work-in-process inventory on January 1 of $2,900. On January 31, the ending work-in-process inventory was $3,600. Note that the inventories include the costs of materials, labor, and overhead assignable to the unfinished product.

The completed schedule of cost of goods manufactured is shown in Figure 19-2.

ACME MANUFACTURING COMPANY
Schedule of Cost of Goods Manufactured
For the Month Ended January 31, 1969

Schedule A-1

Figure 19-2.
*Completed Schedule
of Cost of Goods
Manufactured*

Raw Materials Used			
Raw Materials Inventory, January 1, 1969			$ 8,200
Raw Materials Purchased		$79,500	
Transportation In on Raw Materials Purchased		2,250	
Gross Cost of Raw Materials Purchased		$81,750	
Deduct Purchases Returns and Allowances	$3,250		
Purchases Discounts	1,600	4,850	
Net Cost of Raw Materials Purchased			76,900
Cost of Raw Materials Available for Use			$ 85,100
Deduct Raw Materials Inventory,			
January 31, 1969			9,700
Cost of Raw Materials Used			$ 75,400
Direct Labor			61,000
Manufacturing Overhead			
Depreciation–Machinery and Equipment		$ 3,500	
Factory Insurance		1,100	
Factory Rent		2,000	
Factory Property Tax		1,600	
Heat, Light, and Power		12,000	
Indirect Labor		9,100	
Amortization of Patents		950	
Equipment Maintenance and Repairs		2,900	
Small Tools Used		250	
Miscellaneous Factory Costs		2,950	
Total Manufacturing Overhead			36,350
Total Period Manufacturing Costs			$172,750
Add Work-in-Process Inventory, January 1, 1969			2,900
Total			$175,650
Deduct Work-in-Process Inventory,			
January 31, 1969			3,600
Cost of Goods Manufactured			$172,050

FINISHED GOODS AND COST OF GOODS SOLD

The Cost of Goods Sold sections of the income statements of a merchandising business and of a manufacturing business are compared in Figure 19-3. The amounts are from the statements of the King Corporation (Figure 5-1) and the Acme Manufacturing Company. The cost of goods manufactured in the Acme Manufacturing Company statement is equivalent to purchases in the King Corporation statement. The significant difference, however, is that the cost of goods manufactured is supported by a detailed schedule that presents three distinct cost elements, a variety of accounts, and two inventories. The calculation of net purchases, on the other hand, involves only four accounts.

It is assumed in Figure 19-3 that the Acme Manufacturing Company had a beginning finished goods inventory of $12,100 and an ending inventory of $10,150.

The term *finished goods* means the completed goods ready for sale and corresponds to the merchandise inventory of a trading business.

Figure 19-3.
Comparison of Cost of Goods Sold Sections

Merchandising Business			Manufacturing Business		
Cost of Goods Sold			Cost of Goods Sold		
Merchandise Inventory,			Finished Goods Inventory,		
1/1/1969		$15,400	1/1/1969		$ 12,100
Purchases (net)		63,280	Cost of Goods Manufactured (Schedule A-1)		172,050
Cost of Merchandise			Cost of Finished Goods		
Available for Sale		$78,680	Available for Sale		$184,150
Merchandise Inventory,			Deduct Finished Goods		
12/31/1969		11,480	Inventory, 1/31/1969		10,150
Total Cost of Goods Sold		$67,200	Total Cost of Goods Sold		$174,000

MANUFACTURING SUMMARY

It is possible to close all the manufacturing accounts directly into the Revenue and Expense Summary account. However, since the determination of the cost of goods manufactured is in part a process of adjusting, it is helpful to indicate this fact by showing the cost of goods manufactured in a temporary general ledger account called *Manufacturing Summary*. All account balances that enter into the calculation of the cost of goods manufactured are transferred to this account. In turn, the final balance of this account, which is the cost of goods manufactured, is closed into the Revenue and Expense Summary account. The closing entries are entered in the general journal, and the procedure followed is the same as for a trading concern. The closing entries may be made directly from the worksheet.

The closing entries for the Acme Manufacturing Company are given:

Closing Entries

(13)

Manufacturing Summary	190,200	
Raw Materials Inventory (beginning)		8,200
Work-in-Process Inventory (beginning)		2,900
Raw Materials Purchased		79,500
Transportation In on Raw Materials Purchased		2,250
Direct Labor		61,000
Depreciation–Machinery and Equipment		3,500
Factory Insurance		1,100
Factory Rent		2,000
Factory Property Tax		1,600
Heat, Light, and Power		12,000
Indirect Labor		9,100
Amortization of Patents		950
Equipment Maintenance and Repairs		2,900
Small Tools Used		250
Miscellaneous Factory Costs		2,950
To close all the manufacturing accounts with debit balances.		

(14)

Raw Materials Inventory (ending)	9,700	
Work-in-Process Inventory (ending)	3,600	
Raw Materials–Purchases Returns and Allowances	3,250	
Raw Materials–Purchases Discounts	1,600	
Manufacturing Summary		18,150
To record the ending inventories and to close all the		
manufacturing accounts with credit balances.		

(15)

Revenue and Expense Summary	172,050	
Manufacturing Summary		172,050
To close the Manufacturing Summary account and to		
transfer the cost of goods manufactured to Revenue		
and Expense Summary.		

(16)

Revenue and Expense Summary	12,100	
Finished Goods Inventory (beginning)		12,100
To close the beginning finished goods inventory into		
Revenue and Expense Summary.		

(17)

Finished Goods Inventory (ending)	10,150	
Revenue and Expense Summary		10,150
To record the ending finished goods inventory.		

Entries 16 and 17 may be recorded as part of the compound entries closing out the remaining income statement accounts. If they are made separately, the balance of Revenue and Expense Summary after Entries 16 and 17 are posted shows the cost of goods sold.

GENERAL LEDGER
Manufacturing Summary

1969			1969			
Jan. 31 **(13)**		190,200	Jan. 31 **(14)**			18,150
			31 **(15)**			172,050
		190,200				190,200

Finished Goods Inventory

1969			1969		
Jan. 1 Bal.		12,100	Jan. 31 **(16)**		12,100
31 **(17)**		10,150			

GENERAL LEDGER (continued)
Revenue and Expense Summary

1969			1969		
Jan. 31	**(15)**	172,050	Jan. 31	**(17)**	10,150
31	**(16)**	12,100			

The $174,000 balance of the Revenue and Expense Summary account is the cost of goods sold, as shown in Figure 19-3. The remaining closing entries for the Acme Manufacturing Company are the same as for a merchandising business.

THE WORKSHEET FOR A MANUFACTURING COMPANY

There is only one essential difference between a worksheet for a manufacturing company and one for a merchandising company. In the worksheet for a manufacturing company, a pair of columns is added, headed Manufacturing, into which are extended the debit and credit account balances representing the elements of the cost of manufacturing; that is, all the accounts that enter into the preparation of the schedule of cost of goods manufactured. The difference between the totals of these columns is the cost of goods manufactured, which is then transferred to the Income Statement Debit column.

The function of the other worksheet columns is the same as in a merchandising company. The remaining illustrations and discussion in this chapter are based on the worksheet of the Carol Manufacturing Company, shown in Figure 19-4.

Ending Inventories on the Manufacturing Worksheet

The raw materials inventory on December 31, 1969, was $51,500. This amount is entered on the Raw Materials Inventory line as a debit in the Position Statement columns and as a credit in the Manufacturing columns. The ending inventory is a current asset; furthermore, it must be deducted from the cost of raw materials available to determine the cost of raw materials used. This deduction is effected on the worksheet by entering the amount in the Manufacturing Credit column.

The work-in-process inventory at the end of the year was $47,000; it is entered on the Work-in-Process Inventory line. The debit in the Position Statement columns sets up the new inventory (a current asset), and the credit in the Manufacturing columns is used in computing the cost of goods manufactured.

The finished goods inventory on December 31, 1969, was $19,600; it is entered on the Finished Goods Inventory line. Again, the debit in the Position Statement columns establishes the new inventory (a current asset); the credit in the Income Statement columns is deducted from the cost of goods available to derive the cost of goods sold.

CAROL MANUFACTURING COMPANY
Worksheet
For the Year Ended December 31, 1969

Account Title	Trial Balance Dr.	Trial Balance Cr.	Adjustments Dr.	Adjustments Cr.	Manufacturing Dr.	Manufacturing Cr.	Income Statement Dr.	Income Statement Cr.	Position Statement Dr.	Position Statement Cr.
Cash	12,000								12,000	
Accounts Receivable	78,350								78,350	
Allowance for Doubtful Accounts		650		(1) 1,037						1,687
Raw Materials Inventory	58,300				58,300	51,500			51,500	
Work-in-Process Inventory	31,725				31,725	47,000			47,000	
Finished Goods Inventory	23,200						23,200	19,600	19,600	
Prepaid Insurance	2,100			(2) 1,500					600	
Office Equipment	6,050								6,050	
Accumulated Depreciation–Office Equipment		2,000		(4) 605						2,605
Store Equipment	10,000								10,000	
Accumulated Depreciation–Store Equipment		4,000		(4) 1,000						5,000
Machinery and Equipment	51,000								51,000	
Accumulated Depreciation–Machinery and Equipment		10,000		(3) 10,200						20,200
Accounts Payable		29,200								29,200
Capital Stock		180,000								180,000
Retained Earnings		12,855								12,855
Dividends	10,000								10,000	
Sales		420,000						420,000		
Sales Returns and Allowances	5,200						5,200			
Sales Discounts	2,400						2,400			
Raw Materials Purchased	91,000				91,000					
Raw Materials–Purchases Returns and Allowances		2,800				2,800				
Raw Materials–Purchases Discounts		2,650				2,650				
Direct Labor	98,530		(5) 3,500		102,030					
Indirect Labor	21,200		(5) 1,400		22,600					
Rent	12,000				9,600		{ 1,800 S { 600 G			
Heat, Light, and Power	8,100				7,290		{ 405 S { 405 G			
Advertising Expense	6,500						6,500			
Salesmen's Salaries Expense	50,000		(5) 5,100				55,100			
Executive Salaries Expense	60,500						60,500			
Office Salaries Expense	26,000						26,000			
	664,155	664,155								
Bad Debts Expense			(1) 1,037				1,037			
Insurance			(2) 1,500		1,050		{ 300 S { 150 G			
Depreciation–Machinery and Equipment			(3) 10,200		10,200					
Depreciation Expense–Office Equipment			(4) 605				605			
Depreciation Expense–Store Equipment			(4) 1,000				1,000			
Accrued Wages and Salaries Payable				(5) 10,000						10,000
Income Tax Expense			(6) 7,368				7,368			
Income Taxes Payable				(6) 7,368						7,368
			31,710	31,710	333,795	103,950				
Cost of Goods Manufactured						229,845	229,845			
					333,795	333,795	422,415	439,600	286,100	268,915
Net Income							17,185			17,185
							439,600	439,600	286,100	286,100

Legend: S = Selling expenses
G = General and Administrative Expenses

Figure 19-4.
*Worksheet for
a Manufacturing
Company*

Adjusting Entries on the Manufacturing Worksheet

The entries in the Adjustments columns of the worksheet are based on the information that follows. The numbers correspond to those used on the worksheet.

(1)

The Bad Debts Expense was estimated at ¼ of 1 percent of gross sales less sales returns and allowances. The amount of the adjustment was computed as follows:

Gross Sales	$420,000
Deduct Sales Returns and Allowances	5,200
	$414,800
Bad Debts Expense Percentage	× .0025
Bad Debts Expense	$ 1,037

The entry is as shown:

```
1969
Dec. 31   Bad Debts Expense                         1,037
               Allowance for Doubtful Accounts                1,037
```

The debit records the estimated bad debts charge; the credit increases Allowance for Doubtful Accounts to $1,687 ($650 + $1,037).

(2)

Insurance of $1,500 has expired; this is recorded by the following entry.

```
1969
Dec. 31   Insurance                              1,500
               Prepaid Insurance                            1,500
```

The debit records the cost of the lapsed insurance; the credit decreases the asset account.

(3)

The annual depreciation rate for factory machinery and equipment is 20 percent. Since all the equipment was acquired prior to 1969, a full year's depreciation is taken, based on the amount shown in the trial balance. The computation is as follows:

Cost of machinery and equipment	$51,000
Annual depreciation rate	× .20
Depreciation for 1969	$10,200

The entry is as shown:

```
1969
Dec. 31   Depreciation—Machinery and Equipment          10,200
               Accumulated Depreciation—Machinery and
                  Equipment                                       10,200
```

The debit records the depreciation of the machinery and equipment; the credit increases the Accumulated Depreciation–Machinery and Equipment account.

(4)

The annual depreciation rate for both office equipment and store equipment is 10 percent. All the office and store equipment was acquired prior to 1969; consequently, a full year's depreciation is taken, based on the amount of each account shown in the trial balance. The computations are as follows:

	Office Equipment	Store Equipment
Cost	$6,050	$10,000
Annual depreciation rate	×.10	×.10
Depreciation for 1969	$ 605	$ 1,000

The entry is as shown:

```
1969
Dec. 31   Depreciation Expense–Office Equipment        605
          Depreciation Expense–Store Equipment       1,000
                Accumulated Depreciation–Office Equipment         605
                Accumulated Depreciation–Store Equipment        1,000
```

The debits record the depreciation expense for the office and store equipment; the credits increase the corresponding Accumulated Depreciation accounts.

(5)

The accrued wages and salaries payable as of December 31, 1969, were:

Direct labor	$ 3,500
Indirect labor	1,400
Salesmen's salaries	5,100
Total	$10,000

The entry is as shown:

```
1969
Dec. 31   Direct Labor                                3,500
          Indirect Labor                              1,400
          Salesmen's Salaries Expense                 5,100
                Accrued Wages and Salaries Payable            10,000
```

The debits record all the wages and salaries incurred but not paid; the credit records the accrued liability.

(6)

The estimated income tax liability is $7,368. The entry is as shown:

```
1969
Dec. 31   Income Tax Expense              7,368
                Income Taxes Payable                7,368
```

The debit records the estimated income tax; the credit records the estimated income tax liability.

Allocation of Costs and Expenses on the Worksheet

In the Trial Balance and Adjustments columns there are certain accounts representing costs incurred partly in the manufacturing processes and partly in the selling and general administrative functions. Assume that a study was made late in 1968 to find an equitable method for allocating these items. As a result of this study, the following bases for allocation were decided upon:

Item	Basis for Allocation
Rent	Square footage of building space used
Heat, light, and power	Actual readings from meters in the factory and in the general and administrative areas
Insurance	Cost of comprehensive policies covering the buildings allocated on the basis of square footage; other insurance costs charged directly to manufacturing, selling, or general expense

From these bases, converted to percentages, the following allocations were made:

		Manufacturing		Selling		General	
Item	Total	%	Amount	%	Amount	%	Amount
Rent	$12,000	80	$9,600	15	$1,800	5	$600
Heat, light, and power	8,100	90	7,290	5	405	5	405
Insurance	1,500	70	1,050	20	300	10	150

On the line of the worksheet for each of these items, the total of the Trial Balance and Adjustments columns is extended to the appropriate column. The Rent debit balance of $12,000, for example, is distributed as follows: $9,600 ($12,000 × .80) is extended to the Manufacturing Debit column; $1,800 ($12,000 × .15) and $600 ($12,000 × .05) are extended to the Income Statement Debit column. Note that the $9,600 is classified as manufacturing overhead under Factory Rent (Figures 19-4 and 19-6); the $1,800 is classified as a selling expense, Rent Expense (Figures 19-4 and 19-5). The $9,600 portion is carried as a product cost and not as an expense because it is part of the cost of the finished product; it becomes an expense only when the product is sold. Until such time, overhead costs are assets; that is, they are part of either work in process (asset) or finished goods (asset). The $1,800 portion of the rent is classified as Rent Expense because it does not enter into the cost of goods manufactured (finished goods) but is rather an expense of the period in which it is incurred. This distinction also applies to heat, light, and power and to insurance. All the overhead accounts and all the portions of accounts allocated to manufacturing are product cost accounts.

The letters S and G after the amounts identify the specific income statement classifications of selling or general and administrative expenses. These letters may be further used for amounts extended as lump sums in a single column to facilitate the precise classification of the accounts if the formal income statement is prepared directly from the worksheet.

FINANCIAL STATEMENTS

The Manufacturing columns of the worksheet contain all the amounts required for the preparation of the schedule of cost of goods manufactured in their proper debit or credit relationship; each amount is used once. Similarly, the Income Statement and Position Statement columns of the worksheet contain all the figures needed for the preparation of the income statement, statement of retained earnings, and statement of financial position. The financial statements are illustrated in Figures 19-5, 19-6, 19-7, and 19-8.

CAROL MANUFACTURING COMPANY · Exhibit A
Income Statement
For the Year Ended December 31, 1969

Figure 19-5.
Income Statement

Sales Revenue		
Sales		$420,000
Deduct Sales Returns and Allowances	$ 5,200	
Sales Discounts	2,400	7,600
Net Sales Revenue		$412,400
Cost of Goods Sold		
Finished Goods Inventory, January 1, 1969	$ 23,200	
Add Cost of Goods Manufactured (Schedule A-1)	229,845	
Cost of Finished Goods Available for Sale	$253,045	
Deduct Finished Goods Inventory,		
December 31, 1969	19,600	
Cost of Goods Sold		233,445
Gross Margin on Sales		$178,955
Operating Expenses		
Selling		
Rent Expense	$ 1,800	
Heat, Light, and Power Expense	405	
Advertising Expense	6,500	
Salesmen's Salaries Expense	55,100	
Insurance Expense	300	
Depreciation Expense–Store Equipment	1,000	
Total Selling Expenses	$ 65,105	
General and Administrative		
Rent Expense	$ 600	
Heat, Light, and Power Expense	405	
Executive Salaries Expense	60,500	
Office Salaries Expense	26,000	
Bad Debts Expense	1,037	
Insurance Expense	150	
Depreciation Expense–Office Equipment	605	
Total General and Administrative Expenses	89,297	
Total Operating Expenses		154,402
Net Income Before Income Taxes		$ 24,553
Income Tax Expense		7,368
Net Income After Income Taxes		$ 17,185

Figure 19-6.
*Schedule of Cost
of Goods Manufactured*

CAROL MANUFACTURING COMPANY   Schedule A-1
Schedule of Cost of Goods Manufactured
For the Year Ended December 31, 1969

Raw Materials Used			
Raw Materials Inventory, January 1, 1969			$ 58,300
Raw Materials Purchased		$91,000	
Deduct: Purchases Returns and Allowances	$2,800		
Purchases Discounts	2,650	5,450	
Net Cost of Raw Materials Purchased			85,550
Cost of Raw Materials Available for Use			$143,850
Deduct Raw Materials Inventory,			
December 31, 1969			51,500
Cost of Raw Materials Used			$ 92,350
Direct Labor			102,030
Manufacturing Overhead			
Indirect Labor		$22,600	
Factory Rent		9,600	
Heat, Light, and Power		7,290	
Factory Insurance		1,050	
Depreciation—Machinery and Equipment		10,200	
Total Manufacturing Overhead			50,740
Total Period Manufacturing Costs			$245,120
Add Work-in-Process Inventory,			
January 1, 1969			31,725
Total			$276,845
Deduct Work-in-Process Inventory,			
December 31, 1969			47,000
Cost of Goods Manufactured (to Exhibit A)			$229,845

MANUFACTURING ACCOUNTING—MANAGERIAL ANALYSIS

A company must control its inventories and its cost of operations. Excessive inventories must be avoided because they may result in losses due to changes in style, obsolescence, and price fluctuations. Several ratios and comparisons are indicators of such losses. Ratios and trends vary from industry to industry, but within any given industry, or especially within a single company, valuable trends and ratios can be established. Amounts for the year 1968 for the Carol Manufacturing Company have been assumed. Amounts for 1969 are from the statements in Figures 19-5, 19-6, 19-7, and 19-8.

Turnover of Raw Materials

An overinvestment or underinvestment in raw materials may be brought to management's attention by comparing the raw materials turnover with that of prior periods or of other similar companies. An overinvestment in raw materials inventory should be avoided because it ties up working capital and storage space and creates the possibility of loss through shrinkage, style and price changes, and so on. Conversely, an underinvestment in inventory must be avoided to ensure a steady flow of raw materials into production and to prevent the possible incurrence of higher costs through a "shoe-string" buying policy. The turnover of raw materials inventories is shown in Figure 19-9.

CAROL MANUFACTURING COMPANY Exhibit B
Statement of Financial Position
December 31, 1969

Figure 19-7.
Statement of Financial Position

Assets

Current Assets			
Cash		$ 12,000	
Accounts Receivable	$78,350		
Deduct Allowance for Doubtful Accounts	1,687	76,663	
Raw Materials Inventory		51,500	
Work-in-Process Inventory		47,000	
Finished Goods Inventory		19,600	
Prepaid Insurance		600	
Total Current Assets			$207,363
Plant and Equipment			
Office Equipment	$ 6,050		
Deduct Accumulated Depreciation	2,605	$ 3,445	
Store Equipment	$10,000		
Deduct Accumulated Depreciation	5,000	5,000	
Machinery and Equipment	$51,000		
Deduct Accumulated Depreciation	20,200	30,800	
Total Plant and Equipment			39,245
Total Assets			$246,608

Liabilities and Stockholders' Equity

Current Liabilities			
Accounts Payable		$ 29,200	
Accrued Wages and Salaries Payable		10,000	
Income Taxes Payable		7,368	
Total Current Liabilities			$ 46,568
Stockholders' Equity			
Capital Stock		$180,000	
Retained Earnings (Exhibit C)		20,040	
Total Stockholders' Equity			200,040
Total Liabilities and Stockholders' Equity			$246,608

CAROL MANUFACTURING COMPANY Exhibit C
Statement of Retained Earnings
For the Year Ended December 31, 1969

Figure 19-8.
Statement of Retained Earnings

Retained Earnings, January 1, 1969	$12,855
Net Income for the Year (Exhibit A)	17,185
Total	$30,040
Deduct Dividends	10,000
Retained Earnings, December 31, 1969	$20,040

Figure 19-9.
Raw Materials
Turnover

		1969	1968
Raw materials used	**(a)**	$92,350	$86,670
Raw materials inventories			
Beginning of year		$58,300	$61,900
End of year		51,500	58,300
Average	**(b)**	$54,900	$60,100
Raw materials turnovers (a ÷ b)		1.68	1.44

In 1969, for every $1 in the average raw materials inventory there was $1.68 worth of raw materials used in the manufacture of the finished products. The numbers 1.68 and 1.44 represent the number of times the raw materials were replaced during the year. These turnover rates may be converted to days by dividing the number of days in a year by the turnover, as shown:

		1969	1968
Number of days in year	**(a)**	360	360
Turnover (from Figure 19-9)	**(b)**	1.68	1.44
Number of days' inventory (a ÷ b)		214	250

The number 214 for 1969 means that during that year the Company had, on the average, raw materials on hand sufficient for 214 days' use. This information, together with such factors as available sources of supply and the length of time required to obtain the material, makes it possible to recognize and to initiate action to control overstocking or understocking of inventories.

Turnover of Finished Goods

The computation of the finished goods turnovers for the Carol Manufacturing Company for the years 1969 and 1968 is shown in Figure 19-10.

Figure 19-10.
Turnover of
Finished Goods

		1969	1968
Cost of goods sold	**(a)**	$233,445	$197,142
Finished goods inventories			
Beginning of year		$ 23,200	$ 24,650
End of year		19,600	23,200
Average	**(b)**	$ 21,400	$ 23,925
Finished goods turnovers (a ÷ b)		10.91	8.24

In 1969, for every $1 in the average finished goods inventory there was $10.91 worth of finished goods sold. The computation for converting these turnover rates to days is:

		1969	1968
Number of days in year	**(a)**	360	360
Turnover (from Figure 19-10)	**(b)**	10.91	8.24
Number of days' inventory (a ÷ b)		33	44

The Carol Manufacturing Company has improved the finished goods inventory turnover in 1969 as compared to 1968. In terms of the number of days' sales requirements, the inventory has been decreased from 44 days to 33 days.

There are a variety of factors that influence the finished goods inventory turnover trend and that must be considered before any conclusions are drawn. The ratio is influenced by actual or anticipated changes in prices, volume, basis of inventory valuation, the presence of obsolete or unsalable goods in the inventory, and so on. If, for example, a higher turnover is the result of an increased volume of sales due to lowered prices, gross margin may not increase. If, however, the amount of the inventory and the rate of gross margin are relatively stable, an increased turnover will result in an increase in gross margin. Again, such increases in gross margin may not result in increased earnings if the more rapid turnover is accompanied by increases in advertising and other costs of distributing the product.

Manufacturing Costs

The percentage relationships of raw materials used, direct labor, and manufacturing overhead to total period manufacturing costs also provide significant information about the business. These percentages may indicate to management the need for investigation if they are disproportionate to those of prior periods or similar companies. The computations for the relationships for the Carol Manufacturing Company for 1969 are:

$$\frac{\text{Raw materials used}}{\text{Total period manufacturing costs}} = \frac{\$92,350}{\$245,120} = \quad 38$$

$$\frac{\text{Direct labor}}{\text{Total period manufacturing costs}} = \frac{\$102,030}{\$245,120} = \quad 41$$

$$\frac{\text{Manufacturing overhead}}{\text{Total period manufacturing costs}} = \frac{\$50,740}{\$245,120} = \quad \underline{21}$$

Total $\qquad\qquad\qquad\qquad\qquad\qquad\qquad\quad \underline{\underline{100}}$

Percentage

Each dollar of the total period cost of manufacturing consisted of raw materials, 38 cents; direct labor, 41 cents; and manufacturing overhead, 21 cents.

Unit Cost Analysis

An important measure of management efficiency is the cost to manufacture each unit. It is in the interest of management to keep the unit cost of the product as low as possible. Any increase in unit cost results in either a decrease in gross margin or an increase in the selling price. Assume that the Carol Manufacturing Company manufactures a single product and that it manufactured 20,000 units in 1969. The unit cost is computed as shown in Figure 19-11.

$$\frac{\text{Cost of goods manufactured}}{\text{Number of units manufactured}} = \frac{\$229,845}{20,000} = \$11.49 \text{ (cost per unit)}$$

Figure 19-11.
Unit Cost Computation

Measuring and Recording Inventories

To determine operating results in manufacturing accounting, it is necessary to take physical inventories of raw materials, work in process, and finished goods. The pricing of the work-in-process and finished goods inventories is difficult to accomplish because the cost of the components that are incorporated in these inventories cannot be easily associated with the physical articles. The next two chapters deal with the more elaborate methods used in cost accounting, which enable management to trace the flow of unexpired costs directly to the products.

If the Carol Manufacturing Company produced only a single product and manufactured 20,000 units (see Figure 19-11), management could price each inventory unit at $11.49. However, if the Company produced several different products it would have to install a device for pricing the ending work-in-process and finished goods inventories. The cost of raw materials per unit of the product can usually be measured accurately by reference to materials requisitions.[1] Direct labor cost per unit can also be determined satisfactorily by observation coupled with an occasional keeping of time and cost records. The unit cost of factory overhead is difficult to determine directly. It is necessary to calculate an equitable relationship between factory overhead cost and some common measure to the commodities produced. Direct labor cost is usually a fair indicator because the passage of time is an element in both direct labor and factory overhead costs. More direct labor time implies more use of factory facilities, which results in more factory overhead cost for that product. This relationship of factory overhead and direct labor cost—called the *predetermined overhead rate*—for the Carol Manufacturing Company (see Figure 19-6) is as shown:

$$\frac{\text{Total manufacturing overhead}}{\text{Direct labor}} = \frac{\$50,740}{\$102,030} = 49.7\%$$

For each dollar of direct labor cost incurred on a given product, 49.7 cents worth of manufacturing overhead will be allocated to it. For example, the per unit cost of the ending inventories of finished goods and work in process of Products A and B were computed as shown:

Finished-Goods Inventory

	Product A	Product B
Raw materials (from requisitions)	$ 5.00	$ 4.00
Direct labor (from payroll records)	4.00	6.00
Manufacturing overhead ($4 × .497)	1.99	
($6 × .497)		2.98
Total inventory cost per unit	$10.99	$12.98

Work-in-Process Inventory

	Product A	Product B
Raw materials (from requisitions)	$ 3.00	$ 2.00
Direct labor (from payroll records)	2.30	1.20
Manufacturing overhead ($2.30 × .497)	1.14	
($1.20 × .497)		.60
Total inventory cost per unit	$ 6.44	$ 3.80

SUMMARY

The accounting system for a manufacturing firm is an elaboration of the system employed in trading concerns. Since a manufacturing firm purchases raw materials and

---

[1] A materials requisition is a written request for materials from the storeroom.

converts them into finished products, additional accounts must be employed for costing the conversion process. General accounting for a manufacturing firm utilizes the periodic inventory system; the cost accounting systems discussed in subsequent chapters use the perpetual inventory system.

Direct materials are all the raw materials of a significant nature that are incorporated in the finished product. Raw Materials Used represents the cost of the direct materials consumed during a given period of time. Direct labor is the cost of all the wages paid to employees performing operations directly on the product being manufactured. Manufacturing overhead is all the manufacturing costs other than direct materials and direct labor. Raw materials used, direct labor, and manufacturing overhead are product costs since they reflect the cost of the finished product and become expenses only when the product is sold; that is, when they become a part of cost of goods sold. General and administrative expenses, and selling expenses are period expenses since they are deducted from revenues in the period in which they are incurred.

A manufacturing concern has three inventory accounts: Raw Materials, Work-in-Process, and Finished Goods. All are classified as current assets in the statement of financial position. The total period manufacturing costs are the costs of all materials and efforts expended in the manufacturing process during the period. The cost of goods manufactured is the cost of all goods that were completed during the period, regardless of the period in which the costs were incurred. The computation of the cost of goods manufactured is shown in the manufacturing schedule, which supplements the income statement. The only difference in the computation of the cost of goods sold for a manufacturing concern and for a trading concern is that the cost of goods manufactured is substituted for the net cost of purchases.

Manufacturing Summary is a temporary intermediary account into which all the account balances that enter into the determination of the cost of goods manufactured are closed at the end of an accounting period. The balance of Manufacturing Summary is then closed to Revenue and Expense Summary.

The only essential difference between the worksheet of a manufacturing concern and that of a nonmanufacturing concern is the addition of Manufacturing Debit and Credit columns, in which all the amounts for the determination of the cost of goods manufactured are entered. The balance of these columns is transferred to the Income Statement columns. Certain costs that are incurred partially in the manufacturing process and partially in the administrative or selling functions must be allocated in a reasonable manner between the Manufacturing and Income Statement columns of the worksheet.

Comparisons of the turnover of raw materials and the turnover of finished goods with the ratios of previous years and the equivalent ratios of similar firms yield valuable information to management concerning the propriety of the investment in inventories. The percentage relationships of raw materials used, direct labor, and manufacturing overhead to total period manufacturing costs may reveal useful information to management when compared with the relationships of previous years and of similar companies.

The valuation of the work-in-process and finished goods inventories is a difficult task when the periodic inventory system is employed. If more than one product is manufactured, an estimation of the raw materials, direct labor, and manufacturing overhead incorporated in the inventories must be made. These estimates, which are inherently inexact, may result in a material over or understatement of the inventories and thus a corresponding error in net income.

☐ **QUESTIONS**

Q19-1. "The accounting principles and procedures are the same for both the manufacturing and the nonmanufacturing types of business." Justify this statement by showing that accounting in the two types of business is the same in regard to inventory items.

Q19-2. Explain each of the following terms: (a) raw materials used, (b) direct labor, and (c) manufacturing overhead.

Q19-3. What are the criteria for distinguishing between direct labor and indirect labor?

Q19-4. (a) How is the cost of a patent determined? (b) What part of the cost of the patent should be assigned to the current accounting period? (c) Discuss the nature of the Amortization of Patents account.

Q19-5. Describe the purpose and function of the Manufacturing columns in the worksheet. Where in the worksheet would the amounts normally contained in the Manufacturing columns be entered if the Manufacturing columns were eliminated?

Q19-6. The following accounts appear on the ledger of Halsey Company, Inc.:

Manufacturing Summary		Revenue and Expense Summary	
96,000	23,200	72,800	14,200
	72,800	10,600	

Reconstruct in summary form the journal entries that resulted in these postings.

Q19-7. The books of the Smith Corporation showed the following information:

Inventories	12/31/1969	12/31/1968
Finished goods	$16,000	$12,000
Work in process	11,500	7,000
Raw materials	10,600	12,700

Explain how each amount will be shown in (a) the worksheet, (b) the schedule of cost of goods manufactured, (c) the income statement, and (d) the statement of financial position.

Q19-8. When a given cost is applicable partly to manufacturing and partly to the administrative or selling function, how is the amount allocated in the worksheet? Discuss a possible alternative method.

Q19-9. State the formula and purpose of (a) the turnover of raw materials and (b) the turnover of finished goods.

Q19-10. Identify some of the problems involved in the measurement of the periodic inventories of work in process and finished goods.

☐ EXERCISES

E19-1. Compute the missing amounts in the following tabulation:

	Beginning Inventory of Raw Materials	Raw Materials Purchases	Transportation In on Raw Materials	Raw Materials Purchases Returns And Allowances	Raw Materials Purchases Discounts	Net Cost of Raw Materials Purchased	Cost of Raw Materials Available for Use	Ending Inventory of Raw Materials	Cost of Raw Materials Used
1.	$1,500	$8,600	$?	$300	$150	$9,500	$?	$?	$8,500
2.	?	2,500	300	200	?	2,500	5,500	?	3,600
3.	3,500	?	700	200	400	?	19,900	5,000	?

E19-2. Compute the missing amounts in the following tabulation:

	Net Sales	Beginning Inventory of Finished Goods	Cost of Goods Manufactured	Cost of Finished Goods Available for Sale	Ending Inventory of Finished Goods	Cost of Goods Sold	Gross Margin on Sales
1.	$41,000	$?	$30,000	$40,000	$?	$25,500	$?
2.	?	25,000	?	?	10,000	81,000	20,000
3.	60,000	?	40,000	60,000	?	?	10,500

E19-3. Compute the missing amounts in the following tabulation:

	Cost of Raw Materials Used	Direct Labor	Manufacturing Overhead	Total Period Cost of Manufacturing	Beginning Work-in-Process Inventory	Ending Work-in-Process Inventory	Cost of Goods Manufactured
1.	$ 10,500	$?	$ 12,000	$ 37,000	$ 5,000	$?	$ 35,000
2.	?	50,000	60,000	135,500	100,000	125,000	110,500
3.	250,500	400,000	300,000	?	100,000	150,000	?

E19-4. The Barrow Corporation acquired certain patent rights for $90,000 and spent an additional $46,000 in further developing them.

1. Record the acquisition and development of the patents.
2. Record the patent amortization for one year, based on a full legal life.
3. Record the patent amortization, based on an assumed useful economic life of eight years.

E19-5. The following Small Tools account is from the books of the Wilding Corporation:

Small Tools

1969			
Jan.	1	Balance	10,400
Aug.	3	Purchase	2,600

The inventory of small tools on hand on December 31, 1969, was priced at $6,750, based on a physical count.

1. How is the cost of small tools used determined? What part of the Small Tools account is allocated to the current accounting period?
2. Prepare the entry to adjust the Small Tools account.

E19-**6.** The adjusted trial balance of the Hale Corporation included the following items:

Rent	$3,500
Heat, light, and power	2,100
Insurance	1,200
Taxes	1,000
Depreciation	2,000

The accountant for the Hale Corporation determined the following allocation percentages:

	Manufacturing	Selling	General
Rent	80%	15%	5%
Heat, light, and power	83%	10%	7%
Insurance (plant & equipment)	60%	20%	20%
Taxes	70%	20%	10%
Depreciation	77%	12%	11%

Enter the account balances in the Adjusted Trial Balance columns of a manufacturing worksheet and, using the allocation percentages given, extend the items to the appropriate columns of the worksheet.

E19-**7.** The following information is available for the Farrell Corporation:

	12/31/1968	1969	12/31/1969
Inventories			
Raw Materials	$12,000		$11,000
Work in Process	14,000		18,000
Finished Goods	22,000		21,500
Raw materials purchased during year		$37,000	
Direct labor		22,000	
Manufacturing overhead		17,000	

Prepare a schedule of cost of goods manufactured for 1969.

E19-**8.** The following data are taken from the books of the Adell Manufacturing Company:

	1969	1968
Raw materials used	$ 47,000	$ 45,000
Raw materials inventories		
Beginning of year	29,000	32,000
End of year	26,000	29,000
Cost of goods sold	117,000	112,000
Finished goods inventories		
Beginning of year	13,750	14,500
End of year	11,500	13,750

1. Compute the turnover of raw materials and finished goods.
2. What were the average inventories in terms of days, on the basis of a 365-day year?

E19-**9.** The following data are revealed by the financial statements of the Rumley Corporation:

Raw Materials Inventory, December 31, 1968	$232,000
Raw Materials Purchased, 1969	364,000
Raw Materials Inventory, December 31, 1969	204,000
Direct Labor, 1969	400,000
Manufacturing Overhead, 1969	200,000
Work-in-Process Inventory, December 31, 1968	132,000
Work-in-Process Inventory, December 31, 1969	170,000
Finished Goods Inventory, December 31, 1968	92,000
Finished Goods Inventory, December 31, 1969	80,000

What significant relationships may be determined from these figures?

E19-**10.** The following data were taken from the books of the Guthrie Company for the year 1969:

Raw materials purchased	$100,000
Direct labor	200,000
Manufacturing overhead	200,000
Raw materials inventory change (amount of increase of ending inventory over beginning inventory)	30,000
Work-in-process inventory (net change–decrease)	20,000
Finished goods inventory (net change–increase)	10,000

Determine (a) the cost of goods manufactured and (b) the cost of goods sold.

☐ DEMONSTRATION PROBLEMS

DP19-**1.** (*Computation of raw materials used*) The following information is available from the records of the Random Manufacturing Company:

Raw materials inventory, December 31, 1968	$ 12,750
Raw materials inventory, December 31, 1969	10,000
Raw materials purchased in 1969	200,000
Transportation in on raw materials purchased, 1969	4,000
Raw materials purchases returns and allowances, 1969	5,000
Raw materials purchases discounts, 1969	3,500

Required: In schedule form, compute the cost of raw materials used in 1969.

DP19-**2.** (*Computation of cost of goods sold*) The following information is available from the records of the Sagmaw Company:

Finished goods inventory, December 31, 1968	$ 25,000
Cost of goods manufactured in 1969	300,000
Finished goods inventory, December 31, 1969	30,000
Work-in-process inventory, December 31, 1968	10,500
Work-in-process inventory, December 31, 1969	12,650

Required: In schedule form, compute the cost of goods sold in 1969.

DP19-**3.** (*Journal entries; schedule of cost of goods manufactured; analysis*) The Gugenhiem Manufacturing Company uses a voucher register. During 1969, the firm completed certain transactions as follows:

1. Purchased raw materials on account for $154,000.
2. Paid transportation charges amounting to $5,100 on raw materials.

3. Received $8,000 credit for raw materials returned.
4. Issued checks for $133,000 in payment of vouchers for raw materials purchased for $135,000 (discounts taken were $2,000).
5. Paid direct labor wages of $80,000. (Ignore payroll taxes.)
6. Paid the following items: factory rent, $6,000; heat, light, and power, $7,000; indirect labor, $5,000; and miscellaneous factory costs, $1,500.
7. Made year-end adjusting entries to record expired factory insurance of $2,000; small tools costs of $2,000; and depreciation on machinery and equipment of $8,000.

Required: 1. Journalize the transactions and post to T accounts.
2. Prepare a schedule of cost of goods manufactured for the Gugenhiem Manufacturing Company. Inventories were as follows:

	Beginning	Ending
Raw materials	$11,000	$9,000
Work-in-process	3,000	4,000

3. Journalize the entries to close the nominal manufacturing accounts.
4. Compute the raw materials turnover in terms of (a) rate and (b) days.
5. Determine the percentage relationship of raw materials used, direct labor, and manufacturing overhead to total period manufacturing costs.

DP19–4. (*Worksheet, statements and closing entries*) The condensed adjusted trial balance of the Anderson Corporation on December 31, 1969, after adjustment, consisted of the following:

Cash	$20,000
Accounts Receivable	14,000
Finished Goods, December 31, 1968	12,000
Work-in-Process, December 31, 1968	8,000
Raw Materials, December 31, 1968	10,000
Plant and Equipment	50,000
Accumulated Depreciation–Plant and Equipment	10,000
Vouchers Payable	24,000
Common Stock	50,000
Retained Earnings	18,000
Sales	84,000
Raw Materials Purchases	30,000
Direct Labor	20,000
Manufacturing Overhead	16,000
Selling Expenses	4,000
General Expenses	2,000

Inventories on December 31, 1969, were:

Finished goods	$10,000
Work-in-process	12,000
Raw materials	14,000

Required: Prepare (a) a manufacturing worksheet, (b) a schedule of cost of goods manufactured, (c) an income statement, (d) a statement of financial position, and (e) the closing entries.

☐ **PROBLEMS**

P19-1. The Tyrrell Manufacturing Company's partial statement of financial position as of December 31, 1968, is given:

Raw Materials Inventory		$ 6,300
Work-in-Process Inventory		8,200
Finished Goods Inventory		9,500
Prepaid Insurance		950
Patents		2,000
Machinery and Equipment	$25,000	
Deduct Accumulated Depreciation	3,000	22,000
Office Equipment	$10,000	
Deduct Accumulated Depreciation	1,000	9,000

Condensed transactions for 1969 are shown:

1. Sales on account for the year were $250,000.

2. Collections from customers were:

Accounts receivable	$210,000
Deduct discounts taken	2,400
Total	$207,600

3. Raw materials purchased on account were $78,300.

4. Freight and other transportation charges on raw materials purchases were $2,300.

5. Credit received for materials returned was $3,750.

6. Vouchers payable were paid as follows:

Vouchers payable	$60,000
Deduct discounts taken	1,500
Checks issued	$58,500

7. Direct labor vouchered and paid for the year was $62,000 (ignore payroll taxes).

8. Insurance vouchered and paid for the year was $4,500.

9. The following additional items were vouchered and paid for:

Rent	$ 5,200
Property taxes	1,100
Indirect labor (ignore payroll taxes)	9,300
Building maintenance and repairs	3,000
Miscellaneous factory overhead costs	1,500
Office salaries	10,400
Heat, light, and power	6,500
Salesmen's salaries (ignore payroll taxes)	13,800

Inventory and adjustment data are given:

a. Depreciation rates are: machinery and equipment, 5%; office equipment, 4%.

b. Amortization of patents is $500.

c. Prepaid insurance is $800.

d. Wages and salaries payable (not yet recognized) were:

Direct labor	$ 850
Indirect labor	150
Salesmen's salaries	1,200
Office salaries	1,000

e. Ending Inventories include raw materials, $6,600; work-in-process, $7,500; and finished goods, $8,800.

f. Allocation data:

Item	Allocation		
	Manufacturing	Selling	General
Rent	80%	15%	5%
Property Taxes	85%	10%	5%
Maintenance and Repairs	90%	5%	5%
Heat, light, and power	70%	10%	20%
Insurance	80%	5%	15%

Required: 1. Enter the December 31, 1968, balances in T accounts.
2. Record the transactions for 1969, including the adjusting entries, in general journal form and post to the T accounts.
3. Prepare a schedule of cost of goods manufactured.
4. Prepare the closing entries to accumulate the cost of goods manufactured and to transfer the balance to the appropriate account.

P19–2. The Gayolde Manufacturing Company was created on January 1, 1969. Selected transactions that took place during the year are given:

1. Received a charter authorizing the issuance of 30,000 shares of $75 par value common stock.

2. Issued 20,000 shares of common stock at $79 per share for cash.

3. Purchased machinery and equipment for $41,250 in cash. (Assume that this purchase was made on January 1, 1969.)

4. Purchased raw materials on account for $260,000.

5. Paid $8,500 in transportation charges on raw materials.

6. Received $7,250 credit for raw materials returned.

7. Issued checks for $240,000 in payment of vouchers for $248,000 (discounts taken were $8,000).

8. Paid the following factory payrolls (use an assumed rate of 5% for the F.I.C.A. taxes):

	Gross Wages	F.I.C.A. Taxes Withheld	Employees' Federal Income Taxes Withheld	Employees' State Income Taxes Withheld
Direct labor	$100,000	$5,000	$15,150	$3,100
Indirect labor	10,000	500	1,200	300

Record the employer's payroll taxes.

The gross wages were subject to all payroll taxes. Debit Payroll Taxes–Factory for the total and include this in manufacturing overhead.

9. Paid factory rent of $8,950 and miscellaneous factory costs of $12,000.

10. Made year-end adjustments to record expired factory insurance of $4,500 and depreciation of machinery and equipment, computed under the sum of the years-digits method, assuming a 10-year life and no salvage value.

11. The December 31, 1969, inventories were: raw materials, $14,000; work in process, $4,500; and finished goods, $16,400.

> Required: 1. Journalize the transactions, assuming that general manufacturing operations use periodic inventories.
>
> 2. Prepare the journal entries to record the three ending inventories.

P19-3. Following are the Manufacturing columns from the worksheet of the Byrd Corporation for the year ended December 31, 1969:

	Manufacturing	
	Dr.	Cr.
Raw Materials Inventory	$ 30,000	$ 29,000
Work-in-Process Inventory	20,000	25,000
Raw Materials Purchases	70,000	
Direct Labor	35,000	
Indirect Labor	7,500	
Rent	3,200	
Heat, Light, and Power	2,400	
Depreciation–Plant and Equipment	3,000	
Miscellaneous Factory Costs	2,500	
	$173,600	$ 54,000
Cost of Goods Manufactured (40,000 units)		119,600
	$173,600	$173,600

> Required: 1. Prepare a schedule of cost of goods manufactured for 1969.
>
> 2. Compute the significant ratios and percentages.
>
> 3. Journalize the closing entries pertaining to the manufacturing functions.

P19-4. The following accounts and amounts, arranged in alphabetical order, were taken from the completed worksheet of the California Manufacturing Corporation:

Accounts Receivable	$ 28,500
Accumulated Depreciation–Machinery and Equipment	9,800
Advertising Expense	1,450
Allowance for Doubtful Accounts	600
Bad Debts Expense	550
Cash	2,550
Depreciation–Machinery and Equipment	1,100
Direct Labor	15,500
Factory Insurance	1,500
Factory Rent	3,000
Finished Goods Inventory, December 31, 1968	23,500
Finished Goods Inventory, December 31, 1969	21,200

Heat, Light, and Power–Factory	1,450
Indirect Labor	4,300
Machinery and Equipment	23,000
Miscellaneous Factory Costs	1,970
Prepaid Insurance	1,100
Purchases–Raw Materials	46,150
Purchases Discounts–Raw Materials	1,500
Purchases Returns and Allowances–Raw Materials	1,200
Raw Materials Inventory, December 31, 1968	18,500
Raw Materials Inventory, December 31, 1969	18,750
Sales	148,500
Sales Discounts	2,100
Salesmen's Salaries Expense	13,500
Sales Returns and Allowances	1,400
Small Tools	6,200
Small Tools Used	650
Transportation In–Raw Materials	750
Work-in-Process Inventory, December 31, 1968	15,000
Work-in-Process Inventory, December 31, 1969	12,000

Required: 1. Prepare the schedule of cost of goods manufactured for 1969.
2. Prepare a partial income statement through Gross Margin on Sales for 1969.
3. Prepare the Current Assets section of the statement of financial position.

P19-5. The adjusted trial balance of the Eastern Company for the year ended December 31, 1969, is shown on page 686.

Additional data:

The December 31, 1969, inventories were:

Raw Materials	$12,525
Work-in-Process	1,125
Finished Goods	28,600

Allocation percentages are:

Item	Manufacturing	Selling	General
Rent	80	10	10
Heat, light, and power	85	10	5
Insurance	70	20	10

Required: 1. Prepare a schedule of cost of goods manufactured for 1969.
2. Prepare an income statement.
3. Prepare a statement of financial position.

EASTERN COMPANY
Adjusted Trial Balance
December 31, 1969

	Debit	Credit
Cash	$ 16,300	
Accounts Receivable	39,890	
Allowance for Doubtful Accounts		$ 1,200
Raw Materials Inventory	29,600	
Work-in-Process Inventory	1,590	
Finished Goods Inventory	12,100	
Prepaid Insurance	425	
Machinery and Equipment	45,300	
Accumulated Depreciation–Machinery and Equipment		20,320
Office Equipment	8,010	
Accumulated Depreciation–Office Equipment		3,800
Accounts Payable		14,600
Income Taxes Payable		3,500
Accrued Wages and Salaries Payable		5,500
Capital Stock		60,000
Retained Earnings		35,100
Sales		220,000
Sales Returns and Allowances	2,700	
Sales Discounts	1,250	
Purchases—Raw Materials	45,800	
Purchases Returns and Allowances— Raw Materials		1,375
Purchases Discounts—Raw Materials		1,500
Direct Labor	51,070	
Depreciation–Machinery and Equipment	5,200	
Indirect Labor	10,900	
Rent	7,200	
Heat, Light, and Power	4,600	
Insurance	1,750	
Advertising Expense	3,800	
Salesmen's Salaries Expense	51,300	
Executive Salaries Expense	22,700	
Bad Debts Expense	1,100	
Depreciation–Office Equipment	810	
Income Taxes Expense	3,500	
Totals	$366,895	$366,895

P19-**6.** The post-closing trial balance of the Orange Manufacturing Company on December 31, 1968, is shown at the top of page 687.

Condensed transactions for 1969 were:

1. The accrued wages and salaries payable as of December 31, 1968, consisted of (no entry is required; this detailed information is needed for a later entry):

Direct Labor	$2,000
Indirect Labor	1,500
Salesmen's Salaries	1,200
Executive Salaries	1,300

ORANGE MANUFACTURING COMPANY
Post-Closing Trial Balance
December 31, 1968

	Debit	Credit
Cash	$ 25,250	
Accounts Receivable	13,000	
Allowance for Doubtful Accounts		$ 650
Raw Materials Inventory	18,000	
Work-in-Process Inventory	24,000	
Finished Goods Inventory	22,000	
Prepaid Insurance	1,200	
Supplies Inventory	425	
Patents	1,000	
Small Tools	675	
Machinery and Equipment	25,000	
Accumulated Depreciation		8,000
Vouchers Payable		28,000
Accrued Wages and Salaries Payable		6,000
Dividends Payable		20,000
Income Taxes Payable		13,500
Common Stock, $100 par value; issued 400 shares		40,000
Retained Earnings		14,400
Totals	$130,550	$130,550

2. Sales on account for the year were $150,000.

3. Collections from customers were:

Accounts receivable	$130,000
Deduct discounts allowed	1,300
Amount collected	$128,700

4. Purchased raw materials on account for $36,000.

5. Dividends due stockholders were paid in the amount of $20,000.

6. Freight and other transportation charges on raw materials were vouchered and paid in the amount of $600.

7. Credit received for raw materials returned totaled $1,100.

8. Vouchers for raw materials were paid as follows:

Vouchers payable	$39,500
Deduct discounts earned	790
Amount paid	$38,710

9. Payrolls vouchered and paid during year were (ignore the payroll taxes):

Direct labor	$16,000
Indirect labor	7,300
Salesmen's salaries	9,500
Executive salaries	10,300

10. The following items were also vouchered and paid:

Small Tools	$ 300
Insurance (debit Prepaid Insurance)	1,200
Supplies	720
Rent	6,000
Repairs and Maintenance	2,500
Miscellaneous General Expenses	1,200
Miscellaneous Selling Expenses	420
Heat, Light, and Power	1,800

11. Dividends declared by the board of directors were $8,000.

12. Accounts receivable written off during year amounted to $900.

13. Merchandise returned by customers and credit granted totaled $2,300.

14. Vouchered and paid income taxes were $13,500.

Inventory and adjustment data are given:

1. Depreciation of machinery and equipment is 10 percent of original cost.

2. All patents had a legal and economic life of 10 years as of the beginning of the year.

3. Prepaid Insurance as of December 31, 1969, was $950.

4. Provision for doubtful accounts is estimated at ½ percent of net sales.

5. The small tools inventory as of December 31, 1969, was $810.

6. Supplies on hand as of December 31, 1969, amounted to $350.

7. Estimated income taxes were $26,500.

8. The December 31, 1969, inventories were:

Raw Materials	$19,000
Work-in-Process	21,000
Finished Goods	20,000

9. Allocation percentages are as follows:

Item	Manufacturing	Selling	General
Insurance	85	10	5
Supplies	80	10	10
Rent	80	15	5
Repairs and Maintenance	90	5	5
Heat, light, and power	80	15	5

Required: 1. Enter the December 31, 1968, post-closing trial balance amounts in the appropriate ledger T accounts.
2. Record the condensed transactions for 1969 and post to T accounts (omit dates and posting references).
3. Prepare:
   a. A worksheet
   b. A schedule of cost of goods manufactured
   c. An income statement
   d. A statement of retained earnings
   e. A statement of financial position
4. Compute the turnover of raw materials.
5. Compute the turnover of finished goods.

6. Determine the percentage relationship of raw materials used, direct labor, and factory overhead to the total period costs of manufacturing.
7. Assume that the Orange Manufacturing Company produced a single product. Determine the unit cost based on 50,000 units manufactured during the year.

P19–7. The following information is from the books of the Catawba Company:

Inventories

	June 30, 1968	June 30, 1969	Year Ended June 30, 1969
Raw Materials	$20,000	$23,000	
Work-in-Process	29,800	28,700	
Finished Goods	73,500	70,900	
Raw Materials Purchased			$275,500
Transportation In–Raw Materials			13,700
Direct Labor			310,000
Manufacturing Overhead			263,000

Required: 1. Compute the total period cost of manufacturing.
2. Compute the cost of goods manufactured.
3. Compute the cost of goods sold.

P19–8. The following information is from the books of the Forsythe Company as of December 31, 1969:

Cost of goods sold	$186,000
Total manufacturing overhead	36,000
Direct labor	72,000
Cost of goods manufactured	190,000
Raw materials inventory, 12/31/1968	17,000
Transportation in–raw materials	10,000
Work-in-process inventory, 12/31/1968	14,600
Raw materials used in production	90,000
Finished goods inventory, 12/31/1968	17,800
Raw materials purchased	84,000

Required: Compute the inventories of raw materials, work in process, and finished goods as of December 31, 1969.

P19–9. The Wake Manufacturing Company produces a single commodity. A summary of its activities for 1969 follows:

	Units	Amount
Sales	60,000	$600,000
Raw materials inventory, 12/31/1968		32,000
Work-in-process inventory, 12/31/1968		40,000
Finished goods inventory, 12/31/1968	12,000	48,000
Raw materials inventory, 12/31/1969		24,000
Work-in-process inventory, 12/31/1969		50,000
Finished goods inventory, 12/31/1969	16,000	?
Raw materials purchased		128,000
Direct labor		90,000
Manufacturing overhead costs		72,000

Required: 1. Prepare a schedule of cost of goods manufactured for 1969. Indicate on the schedule the number of units completed for the year and the cost per unit of finished goods.
2. Determine the gross margin on sales for the year, assuming that the transfer of the cost of finished goods to cost of goods sold is on the last-in, first-out basis. Show all your computations.

P19–**10.** The accountant for the Russell Manufacturing Company made several errors during 1969 and previous years as indicated:

1. Purchases of raw materials are not recorded until payment is made, although the Company purports to be on the accrual basis. In January, 1969, $4,600 was paid for raw materials received in 1968. As of December 31, 1969, $2,750 worth of raw materials for which payment had not been made were on hand.

2. The December 31, 1968, inventory of raw materials was understated by $3,000.

3. Machinery used in manufacturing was purchased on January 1, 1968, at a cost of $5,500. This machinery was debited to Repairs and Maintenance and was reported as a part of the operating expenses for 1968. No depreciation has been taken on this machinery. Normally, the Company depreciates factory machinery under the sum of the years'-digits method, using a 10-year life.

Required: Assuming that the current operating performance concept is followed and that the books have not been closed for 1969, prepare correcting and adjusting entries as of December 31, 1969.

CASE PROBLEM
Bow, Incorporated

Bow, Incorporated, is a manufacturer of men's and women's shirts. It purchases materials and supplies from a number of suppliers, then manufactures many different styles and designs of dress and sports shirts, and finally sells these shirts in various quantities directly to retailers and mail-order houses.

Bertram Eason, the production manager, is endeavoring to increase the turnover of uncut cloth (raw materials) and manufacturing supplies. In fact, he is engaged in competition with Raymond Gordon, the sales manager, in attempting to produce a greater improvement in the turnover of items for which he is responsible than Gordon produces in finished shirts turnover.

The accountant has been instructed to provide the data that will indicate the degree of success or failure of this competition. Accordingly, the following partially adjusted balances have been taken from the general ledger on the dates indicated.

	Cumulative Amounts from January 1		
	July 31	August 31	September 30
Inventory–Finished Shirts, 1/1	$240,000	$240,000	$240,000
Inventory–Shirts in Production, 1/1	44,000	44,000	44,000
Inventory–Uncut Cloth, 1/1	88,000	88,000	88,000
Inventory–Supplies, 1/1	12,000	12,000	12,000
Direct Labor	520,000	590,000	672,000
Purchases of Raw Materials (uncut cloth)	510,000	580,000	650,000
Manufacturing Overhead–Supplies Purchased	84,000	98,000	116,000
Manufacturing Overhead–Other	430,000	496,000	566,000

Departmental records maintained by Gordon and Eason disclose that the actual inventories on these dates were:

	July 31	August 31	September 30
Finished shirts	$268,000	$260,000	$220,000
Shirts in production	60,000	56,000	66,000
Uncut cloth	80,000	76,000	78,000
Supplies	14,000	18,000	16,000

Required: 1. Prepare a comparative schedule of cost of goods manufactured for the following five periods:
  a. The seven months ended July 31, 1969
  b. The eight months ended August 31, 1969
  c. The nine months ended September 30, 1969
  d. The month of August, 1969
  e. The month of September, 1969

2. Prepare a comparative schedule of cost of goods sold for the five periods listed in Requirement 1.

3. For each of the five periods, compute the raw materials (uncut cloth) turnover, the supplies turnover, and the finished goods (finished shirts) turnover. (Note: It is necessary to annualize the numerator before making the calculation. Carry your computations to two decimal places and round to one.)

4. For each of the five periods, calculate the percentage relationships of raw materials used, direct labor, and manufacturing overhead costs to total period manufacturing costs. (Carry to four decimal places and round to three.)

5. Indicate which turnovers are improving and which are deteriorating. Give possible reasons for these changes.

6. Which competitor, Eason or Gordon, has shown the greatest improvement in the turnover of items for which he is responsible? Explain.

7. Establish rules that the accountant can use in deciding how the debits relating to production can be treated. (What are the characteristics of raw materials, direct labor, and manufacturing overhead?)

8. Explain how the cost of individual shirts can be determined.

Chapter Twenty

Cost Accumulation and Control— Job Order and Process Cost Systems

Cost accounting, a tool of management, is concerned with three basic objectives: (1) unit cost determination, (2) cost control, and (3) cost analysis. The calculation of relevant unit product costs enables management to obtain better cost information which in turn, enables management to determine more exactly the net income figure. In addition, this information helps management in making many decisions, particularly those involved in the determination of profitable selling prices and the development of means of reducing costs. The control of costs is achieved by the establishment and use of a system of perpetual inventory accounts, budgets, and other predetermined cost information. For example, when subsidiary perpetual inventory records related to the general ledger accounts are maintained, control is more constant and systematic, and inventory valuations are more accurate. Cost information is available at any time for managerial analysis, thereby permitting the observation and control of cost trends and cost movements.

COST ACCOUNTING SYSTEMS

The flow of the product and its related costs through the factory can be determined by a *job order cost system* or a *process cost system.* The job order cost system is used when each unit maintains its identity and costs can be specifically associated with the physical units in the job order, as in job printing. A process cost system is used for manufacturing processes in which one unit cannot be distinguished from another unit and production is largely continuous, as in the petroleum industry. Costs for the total output of a productive operation are determined over a period of time, and the unit cost is determined by dividing the total cost by the number of units produced.

A cost system under the job order or process approach may be either *historical* or *standard.* In a historical cost system, the actual costs of materials requisitioned and labor expended are recorded when they are used on the job. Manufacturing overhead is usually allocated on the basis of a predetermined overhead rate.

On the other hand, when a standard cost system is employed predetermined costs are incorporated in the inventory accounts. Each product has an established standard cost for materials, labor, and overhead. The flow of costs through the production process is measured at both standard cost and actual cost and all variations are recorded in *variance accounts*. By constantly analyzing the variance accounts, management can quickly determine the reasons for variances and initiate proper remedial action. Standard costs are discussed in more detail in Chapter 21. The remainder of this chapter is concerned with the examination of historical cost systems.

GENERAL ACCOUNTING COMPARED WITH COST ACCUMULATION FOR A MANUFACTURING COMPANY

A manufacturing company may accumulate costs under a general accounting system as described in the preceding chapter, or it may accumulate costs under a cost accounting system. The difference between the two systems is the method of cost determination and control. In a general accounting system for a manufacturing firm, the cost of goods manufactured in any particular period is determined by assembling appropriate account balances in a schedule of cost of goods manufactured. The shortcoming of this procedure is that the cost of each product, process, job, unit, or department is not known. Furthermore, the use of a periodic inventory does not provide a satisfactory means of controlling the cost of raw materials used in manufacturing.

The title of the Raw Materials Inventory account is usually shortened to Materials Inventory or Stores Inventory. In the remaining chapters, it will be referred to as Materials Inventory.

A cost accounting system involves the use of the perpetual inventory plan, which provides for (1) a system of inventory control through controlling accounts and (2) a flow of costs through ledger accounts for Materials Inventory, Direct Labor, and Manufacturing Overhead, culminating in cost accumulations for work in process, finished goods, and cost of goods sold. In this flow and accumulation, it is necessary to distinguish between *product costs* and expenses. Product costs are initially assets; they have been reclassified in form but maintain their basic identity. These asset costs become expenses when they expire and are released from the company, becoming deductions from revenue. In a trading business, sales salaries and all selling and general expenses are expired costs and are expenses of the period in which they are incurred. Factory wages and all other costs of manufacturing, on the other hand, are initially unexpired product costs (assets, not expenses) in the form of the finished product. When the finished product is sold, it becomes an expired cost, or an expense —cost of goods sold.

There are three stages in the flow of costs: (1) *Recognition* (asset); (2) *transference*, or internal reclassification (asset)—transference of materials, direct labor, and manufacturing overhead through work in process into finished goods; and (3) *expiration*, or conversion of asset into expense—finished goods are sold and become expired costs or expenses; that is, the cost of goods sold.

THE JOB ORDER COST SYSTEM

Figure 20-1 shows the flow of job order costs through the general ledger accounts. The debits and credits represent current transactions; balances represent ending inventories.

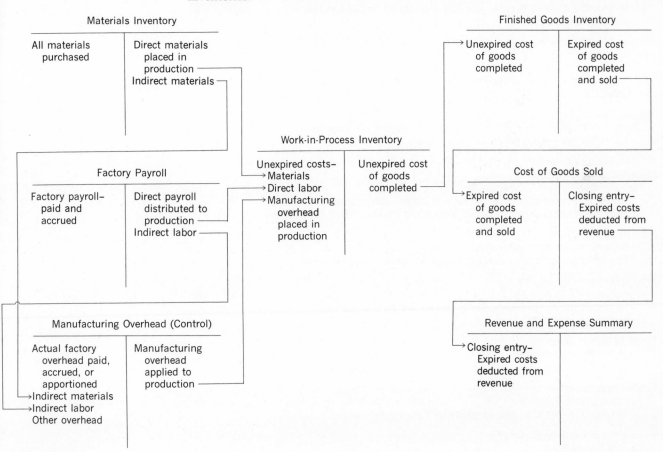

Figure 20-1.
*Flow Chart for
Job Order Cost System*

The debits to Materials Inventory, Factory Payroll, and Manufacturing Overhead in Figure 20-1 reflect the recognition of assets. Transference, or the internal regrouping of assets, is reflected by the three debits to Work-in-Process Inventory with offsetting credits to Materials Inventory, Factory Payroll, and Manufacturing Overhead; the debit to Finished Goods Inventory and the credit to Work-in-Process Inventory are for the cost of work completed. Expiration is reflected by the debit to a *Cost of Goods Sold* account, set up to accumulate expired manufacturing costs, and the credit to Finished Goods Inventory for the cost of work completed and sold. The debit to Revenue and Expense Summary and the credit to Cost of Goods Sold for the expired cost of finished goods sold during the period is a closing entry and reflects the deduction of expired costs—expenses—from realized revenues for the period.

The flow of costs illustrated in Figure 20-1 can be summarized in journal form, as follows:

Materials Inventory	xx	
Vouchers Payable		xx
To record purchase of materials and supplies to be used in the manufacturing process.		
Work-in-Process Inventory	xx	
Manufacturing Overhead	xx	
Materials		xx
To record the issuance of direct and indirect materials to production.		
Factory Payroll	xx	
Cash or Accrued Factory Wages Payable (and payroll tax liabilities)		xx
To record the factory payroll for the period.		
Work-in-Process Inventory	xx	
Manufacturing Overhead	xx	
Factory Payroll		xx
To record the distribution of all factory wages—direct wages to production and indirect wages to Manufacturing Overhead.		
Manufacturing Overhead	xx	
Various Accounts (Cash, Accumulated Depreciation, and so on)		xx
To record actual factory overhead paid, accrued, or apportioned.		
Work-in-Process Inventory	xx	
Manufacturing Overhead		xx
To record the overhead applied to production by the use of a predetermined rate.		
Finished Goods Inventory	xx	
Work-in-Process Inventory		xx
To record the cost of goods completed in the current period.		
Cost of Goods Sold	xx	
Finished Goods Inventory		xx
To record the expired cost of goods sold during the period.		
Revenue and Expense Summary	xx	
Cost of Goods Sold		xx
To close the Cost of Goods Sold account at the end of the period.		

Cost Control Accounts

Cost control accounts are controlling accounts used with a cost system. The function of the cost control accounts is the same as that of the controlling accounts in a general accounting system—Accounts Receivable and Accounts Payable, for example. Some commonly used cost control accounts and the related subsidiary ledgers or records are:

Cost Control Accounts	Subsidiary Ledgers or Records
Work-in-Process Inventory	Job order cost sheets
Finished Goods Inventory	Finished goods ledger cards
Materials Inventory	Material ledger cards
Factory Payroll	Individual employee payroll records
Manufacturing Overhead	Manufacturing overhead ledger cost accounts

Many forms and documents are used in conjunction with the flow and accumulation of costs. These are omitted here—except for the basic *job order cost sheet* (Figure 20-2)—because they are usually tailored to meet specific needs and therefore vary widely in scope and content.

Quantity and Description	2 Type B Motors		Job No.	53
Date Started	1/2/1969		Date Completed	1/19/1969
For	Stock			

| Direct Materials | | | Direct Labor | | | |
Date	Requisition Number	Amount	Date	Time Ticket No.	Hours	Amount
1969			1969			
1/2	475	125.00	1/2	892	8	40.00
1/5	481	75.50	1/4	901	8	34.00
1/19	490	225.00	1/10	909	6	25.50
			1/11	915	8	40.00
			1/12	917	6	24.00
			1/15	920	8	34.00
			1/19	925	6	30.00
	Total	425.50		Totals	50	227.50

Summary

	Amount	Per Unit
Materials	$425.50	$212.75
Labor	227.50	113.75
Overhead 50 hrs. at $2.00	100.00	50.00
Totals	$753.00	$376.50

Figure 20-2.
Job Order
Cost Sheet

WORK IN PROCESS. The Work-in-Process Inventory account and its subsidiary job order cost sheets accumulate the production cost data for single items or group of items. A job order cost sheet is kept for each job in process. During the accounting period, the costs of material, labor, and manufacturing overhead are entered on a cost sheet for each job in production. Work-in-Process Inventory is a summary controlling account, the details of which are shown on the job order cost sheets. A job order cost sheet for the Wilson Company is shown in Figure 20-2 (the amounts are assumed). The amount of manufacturing overhead costs applied is explained later in this chapter.

The summary entry to record the data on the cost sheet in Figure 20-2 is:

Work-in-Process Inventory	753.00	
Materials		425.50
Factory Payroll		227.50
Manufacturing Overhead		100.00

The balance of the Work-in-Process Inventory account should correspond to the total charges for materials, labor, and overhead entered on the job order cost sheets for all jobs started but not yet completed.

The job order cost sheet provides management with each element of the cost per unit. Once the variances between actual and budgeted costs and their causes are known, required remedial action may be initiated. In addition, the job order cost sheets may serve as guides for future budgeting and pricing policies.

FINISHED GOODS. The entry to record the transfer of work completed to the Finished Goods Inventory account is (two Type B Motors at $376.50 each):

Finished Goods Inventory	753	
Work-in-Process Inventory		753

A corresponding debit entry for $753 is made on the subsidiary *finished goods ledger card* for two Type B Motors. When finished goods are sold, entries are made to record (1) the selling price and (2) the cost of goods sold. The entries to record the sale by the Wilson Company of one Type B motor for $750 are as shown:

Accounts Receivable	750.00	
Sales		750.00
Cost of Goods Sold	376.50	
Finished Goods Inventory		376.50

Corresponding entries would be made in the subsidiary finished goods ledger and the accounts receivable ledger.

The perpetual inventory records for finished goods are of value to management in furnishing current inventory data and in inventory control. The availability of goods to fill telephone or across-the-counter orders, for example, may be determined without delay by reference to the perpetual inventory cards. The taking of a complete physical inventory at one time with its attendant interruption of normal operational activities is not necessary; the count of inventory items on hand may be compared with the finished goods ledger cards on a continuing basis.

MATERIALS. Control of materials involves the recording, reconciling, efficient use, and verification of quantitative data; it is essential to effective management. The receipt of material is recorded from the approved vendor's invoice by a debit to Materials Inventory and a credit to Vouchers Payable or Accounts Payable; each different type of item purchased is entered on an individual *materials ledger card*. Transfer of materials from the storeroom is effected by an authorized *materials requisition form*, which shows quantity, stock and job numbers, unit price, and total price; a requisition for indirect material refers to an identifying account in the manufacturing overhead ledger. Work-in-Process Inventory or Manufacturing Overhead is debited and Materials Inventory is credited for the transfers. On the subsidiary records, appropriate charges are made either to the job order cost sheet or to the manufacturing overhead ledger, with corresponding credits to the materials ledger cards. The pricing procedure used may be FIFO, LIFO, or any other acceptable method. The selected pricing method must be used consistently. The reconciliation aspect of material control is effected when the balances of the individual materials ledger cards agree in total with the balance of the Materials Inventory controlling account.

Under the perpetual inventory system for the control of materials, quantities of stock on hand may be determined readily from the records at any time; this eliminates the need for a complete physical inventory at the end of each accounting period. Verification by physical count of goods on hand and comparison with materials ledger cards can be a continuing process resulting in a minimum of interruption to plant operation.

FACTORY PAYROLL. *Time cards*, or *time tickets*, showing daily hours worked by employees are sorted by type of labor—direct and indirect. If an employee changes jobs during the day, a new time card is prepared. Time cards serve as the basis for the distribution of employee wages either to job order cost sheets (direct labor) or to manufacturing overhead accounts (indirect labor, such as supervision, factory clerical, idle time, or overtime). At the end of each pay period, a summary entry of the total labor costs incurred is made, usually from the factory payroll register, debiting Factory Payroll and crediting Accrued Factory Wages Payable. Payroll details are entered regularly on individual employees' earnings record cards from the factory payroll register. The total debits to the Factory Payroll controlling account should agree with the total earnings on the individual employees' earnings record cards. A summary entry is also made at the end of the accounting period, debiting Work-in-Process Inventory for direct labor and Manufacturing Overhead for indirect labor and crediting Factory Payroll, to distribute the total factory payroll costs. The Factory Payroll account thus serves as a *clearing* account—the charges to it are redistributed to other accounts.

MANUFACTURING OVERHEAD. Manufacturing overhead includes all costs incurred in the manufacturing process other than the costs of materials and labor charged directly to job order cost sheets. Generally, all actual manufacturing overhead costs incurred are first debited to the Manufacturing Overhead controlling account. Individual overhead items—factory supplies used, indirect labor, depreciation of factory machinery, and so on—are also debited to the various accounts in the subsidiary manufacturing overhead ledger.

The specific identification of the direct material and labor costs incurred on a given job order can be determined readily. Manufacturing overhead, however, cannot be economically identified with a specific job order. Some manufacturing overhead items—depreciation, insurance, rent, and property taxes, for example—are related to the passage of time and are not affected by production volume, whereas other manufacturing overhead costs—power, cutting oil, and small tools, for example —vary with the volume of production. If completed product costs are to be currently available to management, it becomes necessary to apply manufacturing overhead to job order cost sheets on a predetermined, or estimated, basis.

The calculation of a predetermined overhead rate is based on (1) expected manufacturing overhead based on budgeted production and (2) an estimated cost factor related to expected future production. A cause and effect relationship should exist between the cost factor selected and the manufacturing overhead cost. To illustrate, assume that the Wilson Company estimates manufacturing overhead costs at $800,000 and expects a production level of 400,000 direct labor hours during 1969. In this plant, there is a close relationship between direct labor hours and manufacturing overhead. The predetermined overhead rate for 1969 is calculated as follows:

$$\frac{\text{Estimated manufacturing overhead}}{\text{Estimated direct labor hours}} = \frac{\$800,000}{400,000} = \$2 \text{ per direct labor hour}$$

If a given job requires 50 labor hours (see Figure 20-2), a charge of $100 (50 hours × $2) would be recorded on that job order cost sheet for overhead. The entry would be:

Work-in-Process Inventory	100	
Manufacturing Overhead		100

If actual direct labor hours during 1969 are 400,000, as estimated, the Wilson Company will have charged $800,000 (400,000 hours × $2) in manufacturing overhead costs to the various job order cost sheets. If, as is likely, a variance exists between the actual and the estimated amounts, there will be a balance in the Manufacturing Overhead account—a debit balance indicates overhead *underapplied* (actual overhead more than overhead applied) and a credit balance indicates overhead *overapplied* (actual overhead less than overhead applied). The under or overapplied manufacturing overhead, although affecting work in process, finished goods, and cost of goods sold, may in practice be treated as an adjustment to the largest of these items, the cost of goods sold, and is therefore closed into that account. The amount of over or underapplied overhead should be relatively small at all times. Variances arise through variations in actual volume of production from budgeted volume, variations in actual price levels from budgeted, and errors or waste. Persistent variations may necessitate a revision of the predetermined rate. This, in turn, may involve adjustments of the sales price of the product, revisions of purchase commitments (for overhead services and supplies), and so on. Careful investigation should be made to trace specific causes so that proper remedial steps may be taken.

Other bases for applying manufacturing overhead are (1) material cost, (2) machine hours, (3) direct labor dollars, and (4) units of production. The computation of a predetermined overhead rate using any of these bases is the same as for direct labor hours. Assume that the Wilson Company selects the material cost basis and estimates the direct material cost to be $3,200,000 for budgeted production in 1969. The computation of the predetermined overhead rate based on material cost is as follows:

$$\frac{\text{Estimated manufacturing overhead}}{\text{Estimated material cost}} = \frac{\$800,000}{\$3,200,000} = 25\% \text{ of material cost}$$

The overhead to be applied to Job Order 53 (Figure 20-2) would be $106.38 (direct material cost of $425.50 × 0.25 predetermined overhead rate).

Selecting the Basis of Allocation. An important management decision is the selection of the proper basis for allocating overhead. The basis that should be selected is one that charges the job with an amount of manufacturing overhead most nearly corresponding to the actual manufacturing overhead costs incurred on the job. Each available basis—with due consideration for economy and practicability in application—has particular merits under particular circumstances. A detailed analysis should be made of all cost and production factors involved prior to the selection of a base, and should be continuously reconsidered. The direct labor hours method, for example, is used widely because it recognizes the causal relationship of time and overhead cost; an increase in direct labor hours on a job will result in a corresponding increase in the factory overhead charged to that job. Some may object to its use because of certain added clerical costs in recording and reconciling hours of direct labor by jobs.

The direct labor dollars method is economical to administer. Direct labor costs are readily available from the payroll records. Reference to direct labor hours may therefore be omitted from the job order cost sheets for clerical simplicity. The method may, however, result in an inequitable overhead charge when there are differentials in wage rates for employees performing the same type of operation with the same degree of skill. Assume, for example, that a factory with a predetermined overhead rate of 50 percent of labor costs has the following identical jobs in process concurrently:

Job No.	Materials	Labor	Overhead	Total Cost
110	$50	$30 (10 hrs. × $3)	$15 ($30 × 0.50)	$ 95
111	50	40 (10 hrs. × $4)	20 ($40 × 0.50)	110

Assume that the production process primarily uses automatic machines, with the cost of depreciation on machinery and equipment representing approximately 80 percent of the total overhead cost. Overhead is most equitably charged to production in this instance by using a machine hours basis. Additional clerical costs are incurred, however, in recording machine hours and allocating them to jobs.

A satisfactory predetermined rate should accomplish two objectives in distributing overhead to job order cost sheets: (1) accuracy, resulting in a minimization of over or underapplied manufacturing overhead; (2) equitability, resulting in a charge to each job of a logically defensible share of overhead. If these objectives are met, the overhead applied to each job will correspond closely to the actual overhead costs incurred on those jobs.

DEPARTMENTALIZATION OF MANUFACTURING OVERHEAD. Up to this point, a single predetermined overhead rate, or *blanket rate*, has been used to distribute factory overhead costs to jobs. If the operations are organized by departments, predetermined departmental overhead rates are desirable to achieve closer control of overhead costs and more accurate product and unit cost figures. Costs are accumulated for each department—both *service* and *producing*. Producing departments are the departments that are in actual contact with the job or product—milling, cutting, assembling, and so on. A service, or *indirect,* department services the producing departments—power, maintenance, and storage, for example. Overhead rates are calculated only for the producing departments.

To establish predetermined overhead rates, each department head submits a budget of his anticipated direct overhead costs (costs incurred within the department) for the budget period. Estimated indirect overhead costs (costs incurred in more than one department) are then allocated to the producing and service departments. The allocation of indirect costs to all the departments and the reallocation of service department costs to the producing departments require the selection of appropriate bases for such allocations. The resulting estimated total is the budgeted departmental overhead. Total budgeted departmental overhead is then divided by the anticipated total direct labor dollars, probable total machine hours, and so on, to arrive at the predetermined rate to be used.

The preparation of a schedule for the computation of departmental overhead rates involves four steps: (1) estimating direct and indirect overhead costs; (2) allocating indirect overhead costs to departments; (3) allocating service department costs to producing departments; and (4) calculating a predetermined overhead rate for each producing department. In Step 3, service department overhead costs are prorated to producing departments so that they may be incorporated in the costs applied to jobs. Service department totals may be closed directly into producing departments either by an arbitrary allocation or on some selected basis of distribution. An alternative—and more equitable—procedure is to transfer service department costs to the producing departments based on relative serviceability: the costs of the department rendering the greatest amount of service are closed first to the remaining service and producing departments, followed by closing out the costs of the department rendering the next greatest amount of service, and so on. If serviceability cannot be measured accurately, then the service department with the largest cost is closed out first. The assumption is that the department with the largest cost has rendered the greatest service.

The Atlas Machine Company has two producing departments, Assembling and Machining, and one service department, Maintenance. The factory survey discloses the following data:

Department	Square Footage	Number of Employees	Kilowatt Hours	Direct Labor Cost	Machine Hours
Assembling	2,000	35	80,000	$150,000	–0–
Machining	7,000	20	200,000	120,000	50,000
Maintenance	1,000	5	20,000	–0–	–0–
Totals	10,000	60	300,000	$270,000	50,000

The computation of predetermined overhead rates for the Atlas Machine Company is illustrated in Figure 20-3. The three departmental budgets for direct and indirect overhead costs are estimated in total and by departments. The indirect costs are then prorated to producing and servicing departments. From a survey of actual use, it is determined that the apportionment of the overhead cost for March, 1969, of the Maintenance Department ($10,550) is ⅖ to the Assembling Department and ⅗ to the Machining Department. Overhead rates for the producing departments are to be predetermined on the basis of budgeted direct labor cost for the Assembling Department ($150,000) and on the basis of budgeted machine hours (50,000) for the Machining Department.

ATLAS MACHINE COMPANY
Computation of Departmental Overhead Rates
For the Month Ending March 31, 1969

	Distribution Base	Total	Department Assembling	Machining	Maintenance
Estimated direct overhead					
Small tools cost	Direct	$ 6,000	$ 2,000	$ 1,000	$ 3,000
Other indirect labor	Direct	15,000	7,500	6,000	1,500
Depreciation–Machinery and Equipment	Direct	25,000	3,000	20,000	2,000
Estimated indirect overhead					
Factory rent	Square Feet	20,000	4,000	14,000	2,000 (a)
Supervision	No. of Employees	15,000	8,750	5,000	1,250 (b)
Light and power	Kilowatt Hours	12,000	3,200	8,000	800 (c)
Total overhead		$93,000	$ 28,450	$54,000	$10,550
Maintenance		$10,550	4,220	6,330	(d)
Estimated overhead costs (total budgeted overhead)		$93,000	$ 32,670	$60,330	
Budgeted direct labor cost			$150,000		
Budgeted machine hours				50,000	
Predetermined overhead rate			21.78% of direct labor dollars (e)	$1.2066 per machine hour (f)	

Figure 20-3.
Departmental Overhead Rates

▶ Computations:

(a) $\dfrac{\$20,000}{10,000}$ = $2 per square foot: 2,000 × $2 = $4,000, and so on.

(b) $\dfrac{\$15,000}{60}$ = $250 per employee: 35 × $250 = $8,750, and so on.

(c) $\dfrac{\$12,000}{300,000}$ = $.04 per kilowatt hour: 80,000 × $.04 = $3,200 and so on.

(d) $10,550 × 2/5 = $4,220: $10,550 × 3/5 = $6,330.

(e) $\dfrac{\$32,670}{\$150,000}$ = 21.78%

(f) $\dfrac{\$60,330}{50,000}$ = $1.2066

Using the predetermined rates from Figure 20-3, the cost of a job is computed in summary form as shown in Figure 20-4.

Job No. 123

Figure 20-4.
Cost of a Given Job

Materials	$ 90.00
Direct labor	
Assembling	100.00
Machining	20.00
Overhead	
Assembling ($100 × .2178)	21.78
Machining (5 M.H. × $1.2066)	6.03
Total	$237.81

Managerial Control of Budgeted Data

At the end of the accounting period, another worksheet similar in form to Figure 20-3 is prepared to show the actual overhead costs. The worksheet is completed by following the same step-by-step sequence; an item-by-item analysis and comparison is made to determine variances between the budgeted amounts and the actual amounts and their causes. This analysis points up operating efficiencies and inefficiencies and indicates the scope or direction of remedial action. The computation of over and under-applied manufacturing overhead for the Atlas Machine Company is shown. Amounts and hours are assumed.

	Department	
	Assembling	Machining
Total actual overhead	$32,900.00	$60,500.00
Total applied overhead		
Actual direct labor dollars ($148,000 × .2178)	32,234.40	
Actual machine hours (50,300 × $1.2066)		60,691.98
Underapplied overhead	$ 665.60	
Overapplied overhead		$ 191.98

THE PROCESS COST SYSTEM

The process cost system is used by companies in which the manufacturing process is continuous and uniform; that is, where there is a continuous flow of units of a product through successive departments. Process costing is used by firms engaged in such diverse industries as pharmaceuticals, chemicals, petroleum, gas, electricity, plastics, and mining. There are two basic differences between job order costing and process costing: in job order costing, all costs are identified with specific jobs, and unit costs are computed when the job is completed; in process costing, there is a continuous flow of units of a product unrelated to specific jobs, and emphasis is placed on homogeneous output for a given period of time. Unit costs are computed for time intervals rather than for specific jobs. Material, labor, and manufacturing overhead costs are charged to the manufacturing department where they are used, and at the end of a period—usually a month—the unit cost of the product in that department is determined by dividing the total manufacturing cost by the total number of units of the product processed through that department.

Flow of Costs in a Process Cost System

The distinction between direct and indirect materials and labor in a process cost system may be different from that in a job order cost system. In many cases, what was an indirect cost in a job order cost system may now be a direct cost since it can be specifically identified with a particular department; if not, the cost becomes an element of manufacturing overhead.

In a number of cases, actual manufacturing overhead may be charged directly to the departments, thus eliminating the application of overhead by a predetermined rate; however, if certain manufacturing overhead costs—particularly those of a company that operates a seasonal business—cannot be assigned directly to departments, a predetermined rate may be used.

The flow of the three elements of cost through a hypothetical two-process pharmaceutical company that manufactures a single homogeneous product called Allegrow is illustrated in Figure 20-5. Certain basic raw materials used in the manufacture of this product are started first in the Cooking Department. After the drug is cooked for several hours, it is transferred to the Finishing Department, where additional materials are added and the product is finished and bottled in pint jars for sale.

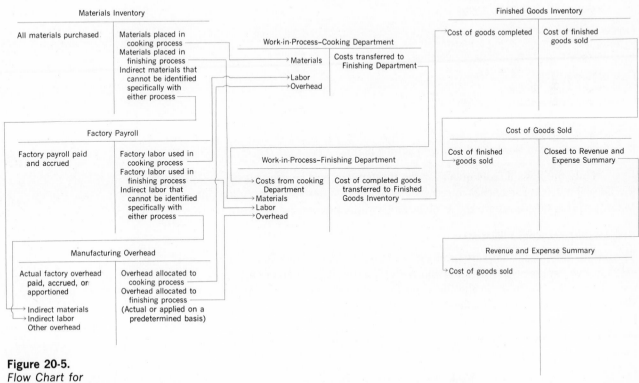

Figure 20-5.
*Flow Chart for
Process Cost System*

The flow of costs illustrated in Figure 20-5 can be summarized in the following journal entries:

Work-in-Process–Cooking Department	xx	
Work-in-Process–Finishing Department	xx	
Manufacturing Overhead	xx	
Materials		xx
To record materials issued to processes and Manufacturing Overhead.		

Work-in-Process–Cooking Department	xx	
Work-in-Process–Finishing Department	xx	
Manufacturing Overhead	xx	
Factory Payroll		xx
To record the distribution of factory wages incurred during the period.		

Work-in-Process–Cooking Department	xx	
Work-in-Process–Finishing Department	xx	
Manufacturing Overhead		xx
To record the allocation of actual overhead to the producing departments.		

Work-in-Process–Finishing Department	xx	
Work-in-Process–Cooking Department		xx
To record the cost of Allegrow transferred to the Finishing Department from the Cooking Department.		

Finished Goods Inventory	xx	
Work-in-Process–Finishing Department		xx
To record the cost of Allegrow finished.		

Cost of Goods Sold	xx	
Finished Goods Inventory		xx
To record the cost of Allegrow sold.		

Revenue and Expense Summary	xx	
Cost of Goods Sold		xx
To close Cost of Goods Sold at the end of the period.		

Only the flow of costs involving the three major cost accounts is illustrated in the journal entries. The entries to record the debits to Materials, Factory Payroll, and Manufacturing Overhead are the same as those in the job order cost illustrations.

Process Cost Accounting Illustration

The Atkins Chemical Company produces a single product, Bettergum, which is processed in two departments, Blending and Aging. On July 1, 1969, there is no beginning work-in-process inventory in the Blending Department. During July, 50,000 units of Bettergum are started in the Blending Department; of this amount 40,000 units are finished and transferred to the Aging Department. Ten thousand units are still in process at July 31—these are 100 percent complete as to materials and 50 percent complete as to labor and overhead. The July costs added in the Blending Department are:

Materials	$10,000
Labor	13,500
Overhead	11,250

In the Aging Department, there is a beginning work-in-process inventory of 4,000 units, 75 percent complete as to labor and overhead; no materials are added in the Aging Department. During July, 40,000 units are received from the Blending Department. Of the 44,000 units of Bettergum to be accounted for in the Aging Department, 38,000 units are finished and transferred to Finished Goods Inventory and on July 31, 6,000 units are in process, 33⅓ percent complete as to labor and overhead. The work-in-process inventory and costs added in July in the Aging Department are:

July 1 work-in-process inventory	$ 5,300
July costs	
Materials	–0–
Labor	14,800
Overhead	13,320

Generally, the detailed information regarding a process cost system is summarized on a *cost of production report*. The individual items that appear on this report are discussed separately first; then the entire cost of production report for July, 1969, is presented and summarized.

QUANTITY SCHEDULE—BLENDING. A *quantity schedule* is prepared for each department, showing the number of units of the product processed during a given period of time. Such a schedule for the Blending Department is illustrated in Figure 20-6.

Figure 20-6.
Quantity Schedule,
Blending Department

	Units
Quantity to be accounted for	
Units in process at beginning of period	–0–
Units started in process	50,000
Total	50,000
Quantity accounted for	
Transferred to Aging Department	40,000
Units still in process at end of period	10,000 (all material–1/2 L and O)
Total	50,000

The stage of completion for the July 31 work-in-process inventory is an average estimate; in other words, the Bettergum that has just entered the Blending Department has material added but no labor or overhead; the Bettergum that is almost ready to leave the department has almost all the labor and overhead absorbed; thus, the average work in process in this case has all the material cost and one-half the labor and overhead cost.

SCHEDULE OF EQUIVALENT PRODUCTION—BLENDING. *Equivalent production* is the finished unit equivalent of the units completely and partially processed in a given period; in other words, it is the finished number of whole units that could have been completed if all the effort and costs for the period had been applied only to wholly finished units. The conversion of work-in-process units to equivalent whole units is necessary when computing unit costs because there may be a different number of units—called *equivalent production units*—for material, for labor, and for overhead.

The schedule of equivalent production for the Blending Department is illustrated in Figure 20-7.

Figure 20-7.
Schedule of
Equivalent Production,
Blending Department

	Materials	L and O
Beginning work-in-process inventory (to complete)	–0–	–0–
Units started and finished (this period)	40,000	40,000
Equivalent whole units contained in ending work-in-process inventory (stage of completion)	10,000	5,000 (10,000 units × 1/2)
Equivalent production units	50,000	45,000

In the Blending Department, there is no beginning work-in-process inventory to complete; hence zeros are entered in the Materials column and in the L and O column (Figure 20-7). Units started and finished in this period (July) totaled 40,000 and are shown in both the Materials column and the L and O column. The ending work-in-process inventory consists of 10,000 units; its stage of completion is such that all the materials have been received (10,000 is entered in the Materials column), and one-half labor and overhead has been absorbed (5,000 is entered in the L and O column). This is based on the assumption that the costs expended in completing one-half the work on 10,000 units are the same as the costs of completing 5,000 units.

UNIT COST COMPUTATION—BLENDING. Unit costs are computed for each element—materials, labor, and overhead. Each cost element in the Total Cost column is divided by the corresponding equivalent units produced to derive the unit costs indicated in Figure 20-8.

Figure 20-8.
Unit Cost
Computation,
Blending Department

Element	Total Cost Amount	Equivalent Units	Unit Cost
Materials	$10,000	50,000	$.20
Labor	13,500	45,000	.30
Overhead	11,250	45,000	.25
Totals	$34,750		$.75

ACCUMULATED COST DISTRIBUTION—BLENDING. The total accumulated cost distribution of the Blending Department ($34,750) is accounted for by the $30,000 (40,000 units × $.75) transferred to the Aging Department and the $4,750 that appears in the ending work-in-process inventory; this is computed as follows:

Materials	10,000 units × $.20	$2,000
Labor	10,000 units × ½ × $.30	1,500
Overhead	10,000 units × ½ × $.25	1,250
Work-in-Process Inventory–Blending Dept. (July 31, 1969)		$4,750

The same schedules and computations are now made for the second process in the Aging Department. Note that there is an added complication in this process, a beginning work-in-process inventory of 4,000 units.

QUANTITY SCHEDULE—AGING. The quantity schedule for the Aging Department is shown in Figure 20-9.

	Units*
Figure 20-9.	
Quantity Schedule,	
Aging Department	

Quantity to be accounted for	
Units in process at beginning of period	4,000 (3/4 L and O)
Units received from Blending Department	40,000
Total	44,000

Quantity accounted for	
Transferred to Finished Goods Inventory	38,000
Units still in process at end of period	6,000 (1/3 L and O)
Total	44,000

*No materials are added in the Aging Department.

SCHEDULE OF EQUIVALENT PRODUCTION—AGING. The 4,000 units in the beginning work-in-process inventory were three-fourths complete as to the elements of labor and overhead on July 1. Therefore, these 4,000 units receive one-fourth of their labor and overhead during this cost period; they should each be equated with one-fourth of a unit of labor and of overhead. Consequently, 1,000 units (4,000 units × ¼) are entered in the L and O column, as shown in Figure 20-10. The number of units started and finished during this period is determined as follows:

Units transferred to finished goods inventory	−	Units in beginning work-in-process inventory	=	Units started and finished
38,000	−	4,000	=	34,000

These 34,000 units are recorded in the L and O column. Each unit in the ending work-in-process inventory of 6,000 units received one-third of its labor and overhead this month. The stage of completion of the ending work-in-process inventory, expressed in terms of whole units, is 2,000 (6,000 units × ⅓); this figure is recorded in the L and O column. The total of the L and O column (37,000 units) represents equivalent production units for the month of July.

	Materials	L and O
Figure 20-10.		
Schedule of		
Equivalent Production,		
Aging Department		
Beginning work-in-process inventory (to complete)	–0–	1,000 (4,000 units × 1/4)
Units started and finished	–0–	34,000
Equivalent whole units contained in ending work-in-process inventory (stage of completion)	–0–	2,000 (6,000 units × 1/3)
	–0–	37,000

UNIT COST COMPUTATION—AGING. Since no materials are added in the Aging Department, the departmental unit cost is computed by dividing the cost of labor and overhead added in July by the equivalent production for July. This computation is shown in Figure 20-11.

Element	Total Cost Amount	Equivalent Production	Unit Cost
Labor	$14,800	37,000	$.40
Overhead	13,320	37,000	.36
Totals	$28,120		$.76

Figure 20-11.
Unit Cost Computation, Aging Department

It should be noted, however, that the total unit cost of goods started this period completed and transferred to the finished goods inventory during July is $1.51 (the unit cost of $.75 from the Blending Department plus the unit cost of $.76 from the Aging Department).

ACCUMULATED COST DISTRIBUTION—AGING. The beginning work-in-process inventory and the new production are typically recorded separately and costed on the first-in, first-out basis; that is, the beginning work-in-process inventory is completed before the new production is costed. To determine the cost of completing this inventory, which has flowed in during June from the Blending Department and has had added to it in the Aging Department three-fourths of the labor and overhead for a total cost of $5,300, the cost of the additional one-fourth of the labor and overhead used during July is added. Labor added amounted to $400 (4,000 units in process × ¼ × $.40) and overhead was $360 (4,000 units in process × ¼ × $.36). The total cost of the 4,000 units transferred to finished goods is $6,060, or $1.515 per unit. It should be observed that these finished units have a different cumulative unit cost from the cumulative unit cost ($1.51) for units started and finished during July, representing a variance in unit cost elements. During July, 34,000 units were started and finished at a cost of $51,340 (34,000 units × $1.51); added to $6,060 (4,000 units × $1.515), this totals $57,400 for 38,000 units transferred to Finished Goods Inventory. The ending work-in-process inventory includes a cost of $4,500 for work done on these 6,000 units in the Blending Department (6,000 × $.75); plus labor in process, $800, one-third complete (6,000 units × ⅓ × $.40); and overhead in process, $720, one-third complete (6,000 units × ⅓ × $.36). Therefore, the total cost of the ending work-in-process inventory is $6,020 ($4,500 + $800 + $720); added to $57,400, this equals $63,420, the accumulated cost to be distributed.

Cost of Production Report

All the information described separately in the preceding paragraphs is combined in the cost of production report. This report for the Atkins Chemical Company is shown in Figure 20-12.

Flow of Process Costs—Summary Journal Entries

Summary entries to record the flow of costs for the Atkins Chemical Company are shown:

(a)

Work-in-Process Inventory–Blending Department	10,000	
Materials Inventory		10,000

Figure 20-12.
Cost of Production Report

ATKINS CHEMICAL COMPANY
Cost of Production Report
For the Month Ended July 31, 1969

	Blending Department Total Cost	Unit Cost	Comments and Computations	Aging Department Total Cost	Unit Cost	Comments and Computations
Accumulated costs						
Beginning work-in-process inventory	-0-			$ 5,300		(Given as June cost)
Costs from preceding department transferred in during period				$30,000	$ .75	($30,000 ÷ 40,000 units)
Costs added within department						
Materials	$10,000	$ .20	($10,000 ÷ 50,000 units)	$14,800	.40	($14,800 ÷ 37,000 units)
Labor	13,500	.30	($13,500 ÷ 45,000 units)	13,320	.36	($13,320 ÷ 37,000 units)
Overhead	11,250	.25	($11,250 ÷ 45,000 units)			
Total costs within department	$34,750	$ .75		$28,120	$ .76	
Total costs accumulated	$34,750	$ .75		$63,420	$ 1.51	
Accumulated costs distributed						
Transferred to next department or finished goods inventory						
From beginning work-in-process inventory						
Inventory value				$ 5,300		(Value brought down from preceding section)
Labor added				400		(4,000 units × 1/4 × $.40)
Overhead added				360		(4,000 units × 1/4 × $.36)
(subtotal)					$ 6,060	
From current production, units started and finished	$30,000		(40,000 units × $.75)	51,340		(34,000 units × $1.51)
Total		$30,000			$57,400	
Ending work-in-process inventory						
Costs from preceding department				$ 4,500		(6,000 units × $.75)
Materials	$ 2,000		(10,000 units × $.20)			
Labor	1,500		(10,000 units × 1/2 × $.30)	800		(6,000 units × 1/3 × $.40)
Overhead	1,250		(10,000 units × 1/2 × $.25)	720		(6,000 units × 1/3 × $.36)
(subtotal)		4,750			6,020	
Accumulated cost distribution		$34,750			$63,420	

Quantity Schedule

	Blending Department Units	Aging Department Units	Comments
Quantity to be accounted for			
Units in process at beginning	-0- L and O	4,000	(3/4 L and O)
Units started in process or received from preceding department	40,000	40,000	
Total	50,000	44,000	
Quantity accounted for			
Transferred to next department or finished goods inventory	40,000	38,000	(1/3 L and O)
Units still in process	10,000	6,000	
Total	50,000	44,000	

Schedule of Equivalent Production

	Blending Materials	Blending L and O	Comments	Aging L and O	Comments
Beginning work in process inventory (to complete)	-0-	-0-		1,000	(4,000 units × 1/4)
Started and finished (this period)	40,000	40,000		34,000	(38,000 units − 4,000 units)
Ending work in process inventory (stage of completion)	10,000	5,000	(10,000 units × 1/2)	2,000	(6,000 units × 1/3)
Equivalent production units	50,000	45,000		37,000	

(b)

Work-in-Process Inventory–Blending Department	13,500	
Work-in-Process Inventory–Aging Department	14,800	
Factory Payroll		28,300

(c)

Work-in-Process Inventory–Blending Department	11,250	
Work-in-Process Inventory–Aging Department	13,320	
Manufacturing Overhead		24,570

(d)

Work-in-Process Inventory–Aging Department	30,000	
Work-in-Process Inventory–Blending Department		30,000

(e)

Finished Goods Inventory	57,400	
Work-in-Process Inventory–Aging Department		57,400

(f)

Cost of Goods Sold	57,400	
Finished Goods Inventory		57,400

Work-in-Process Inventory–Aging Department has a debit balance on July 1 of $5,300, which is the value of the beginning work-in-process inventory. Entry d transfers costs from the Blending Department to the Aging Department. When the finished goods are sold, the costs are transferred to Cost of Goods Sold—Entry f—and the customers are billed for the sales.

It should be noted that the accountant of the Atkins Chemical Company was able to assign all materials and labor costs to the applicable department; hence none of these costs had to be considered as manufacturing overhead.

Managerial Uses of the Cost of Production Report

The cost of production report is a valuable aid in controlling costs; it may be used for comparisons with prior company costs, current industry costs, and predetermined estimates. The report can be expanded to include the description and total cost of each item of material, each labor operation, and each item of overhead, together with corresponding unit costs. A careful study and analysis of day-to-day variations in unit costs as shown on daily cost reports may reveal losses or inefficiencies that might otherwise continue for an indefinite period.

SUMMARY

Although a manufacturing concern could use a general accounting system similar to the one discussed in the previous chapter, it should use a perpetual inventory system as a means of better controlling materials and the provision of unit cost information of finished goods. A job order cost system is used if the units maintain their identity and the costs can be specifically associated with the physical units in the job order. A process cost system is used for manufacturing processes in which one unit cannot be distinguished from another unit and production is largely continuous. The three stages in the flow of manufacturing costs for either system are (1) recognition (asset); (2) transference, or internal reclassification (asset); and (3) expiration or conversion of assets into expense.

In a job order cost system, total production costs are debited to the Work-in-Process Inventory controlling account. In a subsidiary ledger consisting of separate job order cost sheets, the total cost of each job is accumulated. Thus, in the production process entries must be made in both the control accounts and the subsidiary records. With the use of a perpetual inventory system, a materials ledger card is maintained, showing the quantity and cost of each item of material. When materials are purchased, Materials Inventory is debited for the total cost, and the quantity and price of each item are entered on the various materials ledger cards. As direct materials are withdrawn on the basis of materials requisitions, the costs are entered on job order cost sheets and credited to the materials ledger cards to reflect the transfer. The total cost of the materials withdrawn is credited to Materials Inventory and debited to Work-in-Process Inventory for direct materials and Manufacturing Overhead for indirect materials. During the period, the job order cost sheets (for direct labor) and Manufacturing Overhead (for indirect labor) are debited for an amount based on the time cards of all employees. At the end of each pay period, a summary of the total labor costs is made and debited to Factory Payroll. At the end of the accounting period, factory payroll costs are distributed by debiting Work-in-Process Inventory (for direct labor) or Manufacturing Overhead (for indirect labor) and crediting Factory Payroll. During the period, the total actual manufacturing overhead costs are debited to Manufacturing Overhead and the individual overhead costs are debited to the appropriate accounts in the Manufacturing Overhead subsidiary ledger. Since most items of manufacturing overhead cannot be identified specifically with a single job, it is necessary to apply overhead to the jobs on a predetermined basis if the costs of completed products are to be currently available to management. The calculation of a predetermined overhead rate is based on (1) expected manufacturing overhead cost based on budgeted production and (2) an estimated cost factor related to expected future production. The basis chosen for distributing overhead to jobs should be accurate, resulting in a minimization of over or underapplied manufacturing overhead; and equitable, resulting in a charge to each job with a logically defensible share of overhead. As a practical expediency at the end of an accounting period, over or underapplied overhead is closed to Cost of Goods Sold.

If business operations are organized by departments, more effective control over manufacturing overhead and more accurate product costs can be obtained if overhead costs are allocated on a departmental basis. Overhead costs are accumulated in service and producing departments, the service department overhead costs are allocated to the producing departments, and the overhead costs of the producing departments are applied to the products on a predetermined basis. As each job is completed, its cost is entered on a subsidiary finished goods ledger card, and the total cost of jobs completed is debited to Finished Goods Inventory and credited to Work-in-Process Inventory. When a job is sold, an entry is made on the finished goods ledger card and the sale is recorded in the controlling accounts as it would be in a nonmanufacturing concern using the perpetual inventory system.

In process costing, costs are associated with departments or processes and not with specific jobs as in job order costing, and unit costs are computed for a specific period and not for a specific job. The unit cost of a product in a specific department is computed by dividing the total manufacturing costs incurred in that department by the total number of units of product processed through that department. Direct process costs are those that are economically traceable to the related department or process. All costs that are not direct process costs are included in factory overhead. In many instances, costs that are indirect in a job order cost system may be direct in a process cost system if they can be specifically identified with a department. The cost of all direct materials and direct labor are charged to the associated department's Work-in-Process Inventory account. Actual manufacturing overhead costs often can be allocated to departments on some reasonable basis.

At the end of a specified time period, the unit cost of each product in each department is computed for each cost component. If there is a beginning or ending work-in-process inventory in a department, the production of that department must first be converted to equivalent production, which is the number of whole units that could have been completed if all efforts and costs for the period had been applied to wholly finished units only. This must be done separately for each cost component since the work-in-process inventories may be in different stages of completion for each component. After completing the equivalent production, the unit cost of each component is computed by dividing the total cost of each component by the equivalent production for that component. The finished cost of items in the beginning work-in-process inventory is computed by adding the previous period's costs to the costs required to complete the goods in the current period. The cost of the items that were started and finished during the current period is computed by multiplying the units completed by the previously determined cost per unit. The cost of the ending inventory of each department is computed by (1) multiplying the unit cost of each component by the equivalent production of that component and (2) totaling the costs.

A cost of production report, which summarizes the detailed information in a process cost system, is a valuable aid in controlling costs. It serves as a basis for comparisons of actual costs with prior company costs, current industry costs, and predetermined estimates.

□ **QUESTIONS**

Q20–**1.** Name two types of cost systems. Which produces more meaningful information for management? Explain.

Q20–**2.** The three stages in the flow of costs are recognition, transference, and expiration. Explain these stages.

Q20–**3.** What is the difference between *product cost* and *expense*?

Q20–**4.** What subsidiary ledgers or records are controlled by each of the following general ledger accounts: (a) Work-in-Process Inventory; (b) Materials Inventory; (c) Factory Payroll; (d) Manufacturing Overhead; and (e) Finished Goods Inventory?

Q20–**5.** (a) What is the function of a job order cost sheet? (b) What documents may furnish direct material and direct labor costs for the job order cost sheet? (c) How is manu-

facturing overhead applied? (d) What controlling account in the general ledger controls the data on the job order cost sheets?

Q20–**6.** (a) Define the term *manufacturing overhead*. (b) What are the debit and credit
functions of the Manufacturing Overhead controlling account? (c) Why is a predetermined overhead rate used in applying overhead to job order cost sheets?
(d) Explain the causes and the significance of over- and underapplied overhead.

Q20–**7.** (a) How is a predetermined overhead rate computed? (b) What bases may be used
in applying manufacturing overhead to job order cost sheets? (c) What are the
objectives in distributing overhead to job order cost sheets?

Q20–**8.** (a) Distinguish between producing and service departments. (b) What are the
advantages of departmental overhead rates? (c) Distinguish between direct and
indirect overhead costs.

Q20–**9.** (a) What types of industry are likely to use a process cost system? (b) What are
the differences between a job order cost system and a process cost system? (c) Describe the accumulation of costs when a process cost system is used.

Q20–**10.** A given manufacturing cost may be indirect if a job order cost system is used, but
may be direct if a process cost system is used. Explain and give two examples.

☐ **EXERCISES**

E20–**1.** The following ledger accounts show certain cost flows for a period:

Materials Inventory

Inventory	36,000	Returned to vendors	1,800
Purchases	44,000	Direct	70,000
Returned from jobs	4,000	Indirect	2,000

Factory Payroll			Manufacturing Overhead		
60,000	Direct	54,000	Materials	2,000	
	Indirect	6,000	Labor	6,000	
			Other	29,100	

Finished Goods Inventory

145,620

Manufacturing overhead is applied to production on the basis of 70 percent of
direct labor cost.

Reconstruct the journal entries affecting the Work-in-Process Inventory
account and post to a Work-in-Process Inventory T account.

E20–**2.** The following are among the transactions of the Rex Manufacturing Company:

1. Issued $80,000 worth of materials for use on jobs and $4,000 for general factory use.

2. Distributed factory payroll, consisting of $100,000 to direct labor and $8,000
to indirect labor.

3. Applied manufacturing overhead at 60% of direct material cost.

4. Completed jobs that cost $96,000.

Prepare journal entries to record the transactions.

E20–3. The work-in-process inventory as of the end of a period is as follows:

Work-in-Process Inventory

Direct materials	40,000	Finished goods	116,000
Direct labor	56,000		
Manufacturing overhead	28,000		

There is one job in process at the end of the month. The direct materials charged to this job total $2,000.

Determine the amount charged to this job for direct labor and manufacturing overhead. Assume that manufacturing overhead is applied to production on the basis of direct labor cost.

E20–4. The following account is from the ledger of the Sun Manufacturing Company:

Manufacturing Overhead (Control)

1969 Actual	204,670	1969 Applied	203,250

(a) Before this account is closed, three accounts are understated because of underapplied overhead. Name these three accounts. (b) Give the entry to close the account.

E20–5. Various cost data for the Jobber Company are given:

Direct labor for 1969	$55,000
Direct material for 1969	20,000
Manufacturing overhead for 1969	55,550
Materials inventory, 12/31/69	12,000
Work-in-process inventory, 12/31/69	8,000
Finished goods inventory, 12/31/69	15,000

(a) Based on direct labor cost, what was the manufacturing overhead rate? (b) If the direct labor cost in the finished goods inventory was $6,000, what did the direct materials cost?

E20–6. The predetermined overhead rates for the three producing departments of the O'Roark Manufacturing Company are:

Department X	20% of direct labor cost
Department Y	$2 per machine hour
Department Z	$1.50 per direct labor hour

The cost sheet for Job 12 shows:

	Dept. X	Dept. Y	Dept. Z
Materials	$250	$100	$20
Direct labor			
20 hours at $3.50	$ 70		
8 hours at $3.00		$ 24	
4 hours at $2.50			$10
Machine hours		16	

Compute the total cost of this job.

E20–**7.** The following information is taken from the records of a firm that produces one standardized product in a single process:

Beginning work-in-process inventory: 1,000 units, 75% complete as to materials and 40% complete as to direct labor and manufacturing overhead.

Finished and transferred to finished goods inventory: 30,000 units during the period.

Ending work-in-process inventory: 500 units, 60% complete as to materials and 20% complete as to direct labor and manufacturing overhead.

Compute the equivalent production for each element of cost for the period.

E20–**8.** The following information is taken from the books of the Procex Company in May, 1969:

Schedule of Equivalent Production

	Materials	L and O
Equivalent production of Zum	10,000	8,000

The beginning work-in-process inventory consisted of 1,000 units, 70-percent complete as to materials and 40-percent complete as to direct labor and overhead. The May, 1969, cost to manufacture was:

Materials	$30,000
Direct Labor	24,000
Manufacturing Overhead	20,000
Total	$74,000

Cost of the beginning work-in-process inventory was $5,600. There were 5,000 units of Zum started and finished during May.

Compute the total cost of only the 5,000 units that were started and finished during May, 1969.

E20–**9.** The Western Chemical Company manufactures its product in a single processing department. The costs of production for 1969 were:

Materials	$200,000
Direct labor	$141,000
Manufacturing overhead	$117,500

During the year, 100,000 units were started in process, of which 92,000 units were transferred to the finished goods inventory. On December 31, 1969, 8,000 units were still in process, having received all materials and ¼ of labor and over-head. The finished goods inventory on December 31, 1968, consisted of 20,000 units costing $4.95 each. On December 31, 1969, there were 12,000 finished units on hand. There was no work-in-process inventory as of December 31, 1968. The finished goods inventory is costed on the first-in, first-out basis.

Calculate the cost of the December 31, 1969, inventories of finished goods and work in process.

E20–10. The Rensen Manufacturing Company produces a single product requiring a single process. Following are data for the month of May, 1969:

> Beginning work-in-process inventory: 12,000 units, 100% complete as to materials and 50% complete as to direct labor and manufacturing over-head; cost $18,000
>
> Started in process: 48,000 units
>
> Added within department during the period: materials, $144,000; direct labor, $48,000; overhead, $24,000
>
> Completed: 54,000 units
>
> Units in process on May 31, 6,000: all material; and ⅓ completed as to labor and overhead.

Compute (a) the unit cost of material, direct labor, and overhead for May, 1969; (b) the total cost to be accounted for; (c) the cost of completed units; and (d) the cost of the ending work-in-process inventory.

☐ **DEMONSTRATION PROBLEMS**

DP20–1. (*Job order cost system*) The Albermarle Manufacturing Company completed the following transactions during the month of April, 1969:

1. Purchased materials for $50,000.

2. Requisitioned materials for production as follows:

Job 1	$12,000
Job 2	8,000
Job 3	5,000
Job 4	3,000
Total	$28,000

3. Requisitioned materials for general factory use for $4,000 (charge Manufac-turing Overhead).

4. Paid a factory payroll totaling $48,000 (ignore payroll taxes). The direct factory labor cost was distributed as follows:

	Hours	Amount
Job 1	5,000	$10,000
Job 2	3,000	6,000
Job 3	7,000	15,750
Job 4	6,000	13,500
Total		$45,250

   Indirect labor cost $2,750.

5. Incurred additional overhead costs of $42,750 (credit Vouchers Payable).

6. Applied manufacturing overhead to job order cost sheets at the rate of $1.75 per direct labor hour.

7. Completed Jobs 1, 2, and 3 and transferred them to finished goods.

8. Sold Jobs 1 and 2 on account for $90,000.

9. Transferred the balance of Manufacturing Overhead to Cost of Goods Sold.

Required: 1. Prepare journal entries to record the transactions.
2. Post to a Work-in-Process Inventory T account.
3. Post to a T account for each of the four jobs.
4. Verify the ending work-in-process inventory.

DP20-**2**. (*Computation of predetermined overhead rates*) The Durham Manufacturing Company prepared the following budgeted data for the year 1969:

Manufacturing overhead	$300,000
Direct material cost	$150,000
Machine hours	600,000
Direct labor hours	100,000
Direct labor cost	$300,000
Units of production	900,000

Required: 1. Calculate the predetermined overhead rate for the Company for 1969 on each of the following bases: (a) direct material cost, (b) machine hours, (c) direct labor hours, (d) direct labor cost, and (e) units of production.
2. Data on Job 30, which was completed during 1969, are as follows: direct materials cost, $320; direct labor hours, 680; direct labor cost, $2,220; machine hours, 1,330; units, 2,000. (a) Compute the cost of Job 30, using each of the bases from Requirement 1. (b) Which method of applying overhead do you recommend? (c) Why?

DP20-**3**. (*Departmental overhead rates—computation and application*) The Chappelle Manufacturing Company departmentalizes all manufacturing overhead for its two producing departments, Cutting and Packing, and its one service department, Maintenance. The following survey of plant facilities and other budgeted data were prepared for use in establishing departmental overhead rates for the year:

Department	Square Footage	Number of Employees	Direct Labor Cost	Investment in Machinery	Indirect Materials	Direct Labor Hours	Other Indirect Labor
Cutting	6,000	24	$60,000	$100,000	$1,000		$2,400
Packing	4,000	12	40,000	80,000	2,600	20,000	1,600
Maintenance	2,000	4		20,000	400		1,200

Budgeted manufacturing overhead items and distribution bases are:

	Amount	Basis for Distribution
Indirect materials	$ 4,000	Direct
Other indirect labor	5,200	Direct
Depreciation on machinery and equipment	10,000	Direct—5% of investment
Supervision	20,000	Number of employees
Factory rent	6,000	Square footage
Miscellaneous factory overhead	8,000	Number of employees

Maintenance Department costs are distributed to the Cutting and Packing Departments on the basis of area occupied.

Required: 1. Determine the predetermined overhead rate for each producing department on the basis of (a) direct labor costs in
the Cutting Department and (b) direct labor hours in the
Packing Department.
2. The cost sheet for a particular job showed direct materials
of $3,000, direct labor costs in the Cutting Department of
$700 and direct labor costs in the Packing Department of
$600, and 300 direct labor hours in the Packing Depart-
ment. What was the total cost of this job?
3. At the end of the year the following information was
available:

	Department	
	Cutting	Packing
Total actual overhead (direct and indirect)	$32,510	$21,900
Actual direct labor cost	60,500	
Actual direct labor hours		20,800

Determine the under or overapplied overhead for each department.

DP20–4. (*Process cost system with a single process*) The Gnu Manufacturing Company
began operations on January 1, 1969. It plans to manufacture a single standardized product called Zex, which requires a single process.

During January it started and finished 8,000 units of Zex. There was no
January 31 work-in-process inventory. The Company's costs for January were:

Materials	$ 52,000
Direct labor	68,000
Manufacturing overhead	81,600
Total	$201,600

During February, the Company started and finished 9,000 units of Zex;
it had 400 units in process as of February 28, 1969, in the following stage of
completion:

Materials	75%
Direct labor and manufacturing overhead	50%

Costs for February were:

Materials	$ 57,660
Direct labor	75,440
Manufacturing overhead	90,528
Total	$223,628

During March, the Company completed 10,000 units, including the beginning
work-in-process inventory. It had 500 units in process as of March 31, in the following stage of completion:

Materials	100%
Direct labor and manufacturing overhead	60%

Costs for March were:

Materials	$ 61,200
Direct labor	80,800
Manufacturing overhead	96,960
Total	$238,960

Required: For each month, where applicable, (a) prepare a schedule of equivalent production; (b) compute the unit cost of materials, direct labor, and manufacturing overhead; (c) compute the total cost to be accounted for; (d) compute the cost of completed units; and (e) compute the cost of the ending work-in-process inventory.

DP20–5. (*Process cost system with two processes*) The Zang Company manufactures a product in two processes. In Process 1, all the material is added when the units of the product are started in process; in Process 2, materials are added as the last step in the processing. During July, 1969, the Company started 8,000 units in Process 1; 6,000 units were completed and sent to Process 2. The remaining 2,000 were ½ complete in Process 1. There were 1,000 units ¾ complete in Process 2 at the beginning of the month; at the end of the month 1,800 were on hand, ⅔ complete. The following costs were incurred:

	Process 1	Process 2
Beginning work-in-process inventory	$ –0–	$8,670
Materials	24,000	2,600
Labor	11,200	5,650
Manufacturing overhead	15,400	4,520

Required: 1. Calculate the equivalent units produced.
2. Calculate the unit cost for the month.
3. Calculate the cost of the work-in-process and finished goods inventories in each process.

☐ PROBLEMS

P20–1. The following were among the transactions completed by the Powell Manufacturing Company during the month of December:

1. Purchased materials for $72,000.
2. Requisitioned materials worth:

Job 80	$16,000
Job 81	14,000
Job 82	18,000
Job 83	10,000
Total	$58,000

3. Requisitioned materials for general factory use for $6,000 (charge Manufacturing Overhead).
4. Paid the factory payroll for December of $84,000 (ignore payroll taxes). Direct labor was distributed as follows:

Job 80	$20,000
Job 81	18,000
Job 82	23,000
Job 83	15,000
Total	$76,000

Indirect labor used cost $8,000.

5. Recorded additional actual overhead costs for December of $72,000 (credit Vouchers Payable).
6. Applied manufacturing overhead to job order cost sheets at the rate of 150% of direct material cost.

7. Completed Jobs 80, 81, and 83 and transferred them to finished goods inventory.

8. Sold Jobs 80 and 83 on account for $140,000.

9. Closed the balance of Manufacturing Overhead into Cost of Goods Sold.

> Required: 1. Journalize the transactions.
> 2. Post to a Work-in-Process Inventory T account.
> 3. Post to T accounts for each of the jobs.
> 4. Verify the ending work-in-process inventory.

P20-2. The Dare Manufacturing Company completed the following transactions during October:

1. Purchased materials on account for $104,000.

2. Requisitioned direct materials totaling $60,000 for job orders.

3. Used indirect materials worth $6,000.

4. Returned materials worth $2,000 to the vendor during October.

5. Returned materials to the storeroom: from job orders, $2,400; from indirect materials issued, $1,000.

6. Paid a total factory payroll for October of $130,000 (ignore payroll taxes).

7. Distributed the factory payroll as follows: direct labor, $128,400; indirect labor, $1,600.

8. Recorded additional actual overhead costs for October of $58,000.

9. Applied manufacturing overhead to production at 50% of direct labor cost.

10. Completed jobs during the month costing $230,000.

11. Sold finished goods on account as follows: selling price, $370,000; cost of finished goods sold, $222,000.

12. Allowed credit for finished goods returned by customers, $3,000. These finished goods cost $1,800.

13. Closed out the over or underapplied manufacturing overhead to Cost of Goods Sold.

> Required: Journalize the transactions.

P20-3. The Trent Company uses a job order cost system for assigning manufacturing costs to its products. Management has decided to change from a system of allocating actual manufacturing overhead to jobs at the end of each month to a system of allocating overhead at a predetermined rate.

At the beginning of 1969, the following estimates of production costs for the year were made:

Direct materials	$ 750,000
Direct labor	900,000
Manufacturing overhead	1,350,000

There was no work-in-process on January 1, 1969. During the first three months of 1969, actual production costs were:

	January	February	March
Direct materials	$30,000	$44,250	$44,550
Direct labor	40,500	48,750	60,750
Manufacturing overhead	60,000	75,000	90,000

Required: 1. The Company uses the direct labor dollar method to allocate manufacturing overhead to the various jobs. Based on the estimated production cost for 1969, what should the predetermined rate for allocating manufacturing overhead be? In light of the actual costs for the three months given, is this rate realistic? Support your answer by computations.

2. In summary form, record the materials requisitioned for the various jobs; the distribution of the direct labor payroll; and, using the rate derived in Requirement 1, the assignment of manufacturing overhead to the various jobs for the month of January.

3. All goods worked on during the three-month period were completed except for Job 1247, which had accumulated direct materials costing $1,200, and direct labor costing $900. All goods completed during the period were sold except for Job 1114, which had a total assigned cost of $3,000. Record, in general journal entry form, the completion of work during the period and the cost of goods sold during the period.

P20–**4.** The Ashe Company has two producing departments and one service department. Budget and plant survey data for 1969 are as follows:

Department	Square Footage	Number of Employees	Kilowatt Hours	Direct Labor Cost	Value of Machinery	Small Tools Cost	Machine Hours	Other Indirect Labor
A	16,000	16	600,000	$100,000	$160,000	$1,200		$5,000
B	12,000	6	400,000	60,000	120,000	600	80,000	3,000
Service	4,000	4	200,000		40,000	200		1,000

Budgeted manufacturing overhead costs and distribution bases are:

	Amount	Basis for Distribution
Small tools cost	$ 2,000	Direct
Other Indirect labor	9,000	Direct
Depreciation on machinery and equipment	32,000	Direct—10% of investment
Light and power	36,000	Kilowatt hours
Supervision	39,000	Number of employees
Factory rent	96,000	Square footage

The costs of the Service Department were distributed ⅗ to Department A and ⅖ to Department B.

Required: 1. Compute predetermined departmental overhead rates, based on direct labor cost for Department A and machine hours for Department B.

2. The cost sheet for Job 80 showed direct materials of $4,000, direct labor costs of $1,600 and $1,320 in Departments A and B, respectively, and 72 machine hours in Department B. Compute the cost of this job.

3. Actual costs and machine hours for the year were:

	Department A	Department B
Total actual overhead (direct and indirect)	$127,800	$83,980
Actual direct labor costs	99,200	
Actual machine hours		79,300

What was the under or overapplied overhead for each department?

P20–**5**. The Vino Extract Company produces a product in a single process. Following are data for the month of May:

In process as of April 30: 2,000 units, 60% complete as to materials and 10% complete as to direct labor and manufacturing overhead

Started in process during May: 26,000 units

In process on May 31: 3,000 units, 75% complete as to materials and 20% complete as to direct labor and manufacturing overhead.

Required: Prepare a schedule in good form showing the equivalent units produced in May.

P20–**6**. The cost of production report for Department 2 of the Rangoon Company for June is reproduced in part, (there was no beginning work-in-process inventory):

	Total Cost	Unit Cost
Production costs		
Costs from preceding department	$180,000	$1.80
Costs added in within Department		
Materials	$ 40,000	
Direct labor	55,200	
Manufacturing overhead	18,400	
Total costs added	$113,600	
Total costs	$293,600	

	Units
Quantity to be accounted for	
Units transferred from Department 1	100,000
Quantity accounted for	
Units completed and transferred to storeroom	88,000
Units unfinished at end of month	12,000
	100,000

The work in process in Department 2 at the end of June is complete as to materials and one-third complete as to direct labor and manufacturing overhead.

Required: 1. Compute the equivalent units produced in June.
2. Compute the unit cost of production in Department 2 for materials, labor, and manufacturing overhead added in Department 2.
3. Compute the total cost and unit cost of goods transferred to finished goods inventory.

4. Compute the cost of the work-in-process inventory in Department 2 at the end of June. Show computations in good form.

P20-**7.** The Sandran Company started manufacturing a new product on November 1; it required processing in two departments, Baking and Drying. Total cost and unit data for the month were:

	Department	
	Baking	Drying
Costs		
Materials	$ 92,160	$ –0–
Labor	50,032	84,185
Overhead	33,072	76,735
Totals	$175,264	$160,920
	Units	*Units*
Quantity to be accounted for		
Started in process	96,000	
Received from preceding department		82,000
Totals	96,000	82,000
Quantity accounted for		
Transferred to next department	82,000	72,000
Units in process (all materials added)		
1/5 complete as to labor and overhead	14,000	
1/4 complete as to labor and overhead		10,000
Totals	96,000	82,000

Required: Prepare a cost of production report for November.

P20-**8.** The Rasputin Chemical Company manufactures a product in two processes: preparation and blending. Materials are complete when a unit is started in the Preparation Department, but are added continuously in the Blending Department. During September, the Company started 24,000 units in the Preparation Department; 4,000 of them were in the work-in-process inventory, ¼ complete, at the end of the month. The others went to the Blending Department where there were 6,000 units ⅓ complete at the start of the month and 8,000 units ¾ complete at the end. Costs were as follows:

	Department	
	Preparation	Blending
Work-in-process, August 31	$ –0–	$18,240
Direct materials	26,400	11,000
Direct labor	14,700	17,600
Manufacturing overhead	10,500	14,300

Required: Prepare a cost of production report for the two departments for the month of September.

CASE PROBLEM
Quality Clothing Company—Part I

The Quality Clothing Company is a manufacturer of the popular Wear-Well brand of men's suits. Suits of different sizes, styles, and materials are made according to management's conception of future consumers' demands.

Production supervisors have identified the requirements of an average suit as follows:

Basic cloth—5 yards (45″ width)

Secondary cloth, for coat lining and pockets—2 yards (45″ width)

Direct labor, cutting and sewing—3 hours

Manufacturing overhead, which includes supplies such as thread, buttons, zippers, and labels, is expected to be about 90% of direct labor costs.

When bolts of the basic and secondary cloth are released by the custodian of the materials to the cutters, prompt notification is given to the accounting department to debit Suits-in-Process Inventory and to credit Materials Inventory, even though several days may pass before all the cloth is cut and started through the sewing cycle. A single bolt of cloth contains forty yards. The cutters and sewers punch timeclocks, thereby recording their working hours on time cards. The payroll clerk makes daily calculations of direct labor costs, resulting in a debit to Suits-in-Process Inventory and a credit to Accrued Payroll Payable. The monthly charge to Suits-in-Process Inventory for manufacturing overhead is made at a predetermined rate of 90 percent of the month's total direct labor costs.

At the beginning of the month of April, the following analysis was prepared of the status of Style 127-J suits:

Material, basic	300 bolts @ $78.00 =	$23,400
Material, secondary	121 bolts @ 36.00 =	4,356
Total materials inventory		$27,756

Suits-in-process inventory—40 suits
  All basic cloth has been cut and started
    100% × 40 suits × 5 yds × $1.95 = $ 390
  One-half the secondary cloth has been cut and started
    50% × 40 suits × 2 yds × $.90 =   36
  An average of 1/3 of the direct labor has been done
    33-1/3% × 40 suits × 3 hrs × $3.50 =   140
  Manufacturing overhead is considered complete to the same degree
  as direct labor
    90% × $140 =   126
    Total suits-in-process inventory $ 692

Completed suits inventory (none has been sold)
  120 suits @ $31.50 = $ 3,780

At the end of April, the Suits-in-Process Inventory account appeared as shown. (Even though journal entries are prepared daily, postings are made in summary form at the end of the month.)

Suits-in-Process Inventory

April	1	Beginning inventory	692.00	April 30	To Completed	
	30	Basic cloth	21,840.00		Suits Inventory	66,780.00
	30	Secondary cloth	3,852.00			
	30	Direct labor	22,624.00			
	30	Manufacturing overhead	20,361.60			

Additional materials have not been acquired and none of the completed suits inventory has been sold. The actual requirements were in agreement with the expected requirements as regards both materials and direct labor.

At the end of April, 160 suits were in process and their stages of completion were estimated to be as follows:

Basic cloth	100%
Secondary cloth	25%
Direct labor	30%
Manufacturing overhead	30%

Early in the month of May, production of Style 127-J was completed and all the materials had been used.

Required: 1. Prepare an analysis of Style 127-J as of the end of the month of April comparable to the analysis given as of the beginning of April.
2. As a manager, how would you expect to use this analysis?
3. Prepare a schedule of equivalent production for the month of April.
4. What is the purpose of computing equivalent production?
5. Verify the correctness of each April 30 posting to the Suits-in-Process account.
6. State whether the purchasing agent acquired a proper balance of quantities of the two materials. Explain.
7. Prepare a complete job order cost sheet as it would appear if a job order cost system were used when the production of Style 127-J was completed early in May. Include the production of all the suits.
8. What are some similarities and differences between the process cost system and the job order cost system?
9. How may wasteful cutting and sewing of materials be detected?
10. How may slow cutting and sewing be detected?
11. Explain the functions and purposes of a cost system.

Chapter Twenty-One

Cost Accumulation and Control— Standard Costs; Direct Costing

A historical cost system furnishes information that often becomes available too late for many decisions. If data are to be received in time for a large number of decisions, a system must be designed to yield predetermined or precomputed costs, the output of a *standard cost system*. This chapter deals with the rudiments of standard costs and the controversial question of direct costing.

STANDARD COSTS

Standard costs are precomputed costs used as a basis for comparison with actual costs, thereby serving as a criterion of the adequacy of a company's performance. Standard costs are similar to budgets in that both are estimates. Both standard costs and budgets aim at the same objective—managerial control. Standard costs are the anticipated costs of a product; to be useful to management they must be computed with great care.

Each product has a standard cost card that shows what costs should be incurred under normal operating conditions. Actual costs of the product may also be recorded on the card. The basic objective is to compare each element of standard cost with each element of actual cost so that differences may be identified for study and remedial action.

The Principle of Management by Exception

Accounting Concept: Management by Exception ▶

Job order and process costing procedures, as described in the previous chapter, deal with actual historical costs except for the use of predetermined overhead rates. In many industries, the use of predetermined costs has been extended to all costs of manufacturing through the use of standard costs. ▶ The comparison of actual costs with standard costs or the analysis of actual cost variances from standard costs makes possible *management by exception*. It is the exceptions and their causes that must be determined and remedied. ◀ Costs can be controlled better when variances and their causes are known promptly. Standard costs may be used with either job order costing or process costing. They also may be used effectively for the control of selling and administrative costs of a company to measure the efficiency of those functions.

The use of overhead standards is related to the grouping of costs in the overhead budget. Budgetary control results when budgets and standards are harmonized effectively. One cannot function properly without the other, for the budget is, in effect, a summary of standard costs. The materials purchases budget, for example, can be prepared readily when production requirements are known and the standard quantity of material required for the end product has been determined.

The Fixed Manufacturing Overhead Budget

Budgeted overhead is sometimes based on the assumption of a *fixed* budget; that is, it is based on a predetermined level of production. The individual items in such a budget are often not classified even as to fixed or variable elements. A fixed overhead budget based on a production level of 10,000 units of the finished product of the Stetson Manufacturing Company is shown in Figure 21-1.

STETSON MANUFACTURING COMPANY
Fixed Manufacturing Overhead Budget
For the Month Ending July 31, 1969

Item	Amount
Depreciation–Factory Building	$ 3,000
Factory Property Taxes	200
Insurance–Factory Building	300
Other Fixed Costs	16,500
Factory Supplies	500
Light and Power	800
Indirect Labor	600
Other Variable Costs	8,100
Total	$30,000

Figure 21-1.
Fixed Manufacturing Overhead Budget

Such a budget is of limited use to management in its control-exercising function because variations of actual costs from budgeted costs arise whenever the total number of units produced is different from that on which the budget was based.

The Flexible Budget

A budget that gives recognition to varying levels of production and to the costs that change with these levels, often called the *flexible budget*, overcomes the shortcomings of the fixed budget by providing management with a basis for analyzing—and therefore controlling—the variances between budgeted and actual costs. This is accomplished by comparing actual expenditures with previously established budgeted amounts, adjusted for varying levels of production. A series of budgets is prepared, showing estimated or standard costs at various levels of production. Since it is not practicable to set up budgets for every possible level of operation, interpolation may be necessary if, for example, the flexible budgets are at 5,000 unit intervals and actual production falls at a point between the intervals. The preparation of a flexible budget involves an analysis of the degree and extent to which each item of overhead cost is affected by changes in volume of production. The flexible budget, therefore, is essentially a series of fixed budgets. The preparation of any one budget in the series is the same as for a single fixed budget. Basic to the preparation of a flexible budget is the careful analysis of the effect on cost of each different level of activity being budgeted.

FIXED AND VARIABLE COSTS. A fixed manufacturing overhead cost is one that is unaffected by changes in volume of production. Typical examples are depreciation, property taxes, fire insurance, and rent. Fixed costs may vary independently of volume changes as a result of certain management decisions. Variable overhead costs, on the other hand, are those that vary in proportion to the volume of production. Typical examples are indirect materials, fuel, and power. Semivariable overhead costs are costs that are affected by changes in the volume of production but not proportionately; they contain both fixed and variable elements. Such costs vary in steps. Two quality control inspectors, for example, may be adequate for an output of 1,000 units per 40-hour week. If the volume exceeds that point and overtime work is not feasible, an additional inspector must be hired. When a flexible budget is prepared, the fixed and variable component of each semivariable cost must be resolved.

To illustrate, assume that the Stetson Manufacturing Company produces a single, uniform product. The flexible manufacturing overhead budget for the month of July is shown in Figure 21-2.

Figure 21-2.
Flexible Manufacturing Budget

	90%	95%	100%	105%
Direct Labor Hours	27,000	28,500	30,000	31,500
Fixed Costs				
Depreciation–factory building	$ 3,000	$ 3,000	$ 3,000	$ 3,000
Factory property taxes	200	200	200	200
Insurance–factory building	300	300	300	300
Other costs	16,500	16,500	16,500	16,500
Total fixed costs	$20,000	$20,000	$20,000	$20,000
Variable costs				
Factory supplies	$ 450	$ 475	$ 500	$ 525
Light and power	720	760	800	840
Indirect labor	540	570	600	630
Other costs	7,290	7,695	8,100	8,505
Total variable costs	$ 9,000	$ 9,500	$10,000	$10,500
Total costs	$29,000	$29,500	$30,000	$30,500

The 100 percent of capacity level used in Figure 21-2 is not intended to indicate the maximum plant capacity. Rather, it is the level at which it is considered theoretically sound to charge all fixed overhead costs to the finished products as being properly utilized; that is, no part of the fixed overhead costs should be considered as *idle time cost*, a lost cost. Hence, the Stetson Manufacturing Company may select 90 percent, 95 percent, or some other actual level as the standard level of output on which to base its predetermined overhead rate and the point from which to measure overapplied or underapplied overhead. It may be assumed that the level of 30,000 direct labor hours or 10,000 units of output represents the Company's average operating capacity over a relatively long period of time.

Figure 21-2 indicates that (1) fixed costs are constant at all four levels of capacity, (2) overhead is to be applied with direct labor hours as a basis, and (3) variable costs are in direct proportion to capacity levels. This is evident from the following computations relating to the 100% and 95% columns:

$$30,000 \text{ direct labor hours} \times 95\% = 28,500 \text{ hours}$$
$$\$500 \text{ in factory supplies} \times 95\% = \$475$$
$$\$10,000 \text{ in total variable costs} \times 95\% = \$9,500$$

The Stetson Manufacturing Company produces 10,000 units at its 100 percent of capacity level. Each unit requires three hours of direct labor.

Illustration of Standard Cost Accounting

A standard cost accounting system is illustrated by the continuation of the activities of the Stetson Manufacturing Company for the month of July, 1969.

THE STANDARD COST CARD. The accountant working with engineers develops standards usually based on what the cost of each element should be, assuming average performance of laborers working under normal operating conditions. The standard cost card of the Stetson Manufacturing Company reveals the following standard cost per unit:

Materials: 2 pieces of Material K-12 at $5	$10
Labor: 3 hours at $3	9
Overhead: 3 hours at $1 (See Figure 21-3)	3
	$22

The predetermined overhead rate for the month of July, based on the 100 percent column (from Figure 21-2), is shown in Figure 21-3.

$$\frac{\text{Total Budget Manufacturing Overhead}}{\text{Total Budgeted Direct Labor Hours}} = \frac{\$30,000}{30,000} = \$1 \text{ per hour}$$

The hourly rate also may be computed as follows:

$$\text{Variable cost per hour} = \frac{\text{Variable costs}}{\text{Total hours}} = \frac{\$10,000}{30,000} = \$0.33\tfrac{1}{3}$$

$$\text{Fixed cost per hour} = \frac{\text{Fixed costs}}{\text{Total hours}} = \frac{\$20,000}{30,000} = \frac{\$0.66\tfrac{2}{3}}{\$1.00}$$

Figure 21-3.
Predetermined Overhead Rate

THE FLOW CHART OF A STANDARD COST SYSTEM. Figure 21-4 shows the flow of standard cost through the hypothetical Stetson Manufacturing Company. Each of these indicated steps is illustrated and discussed in conjunction with the accounting for the activities and transactions described below.

JULY COST INFORMATION FOR THE STETSON MANUFACTURING COMPANY. During July, 10,000 units were started and 9,880 units were completed; the be-

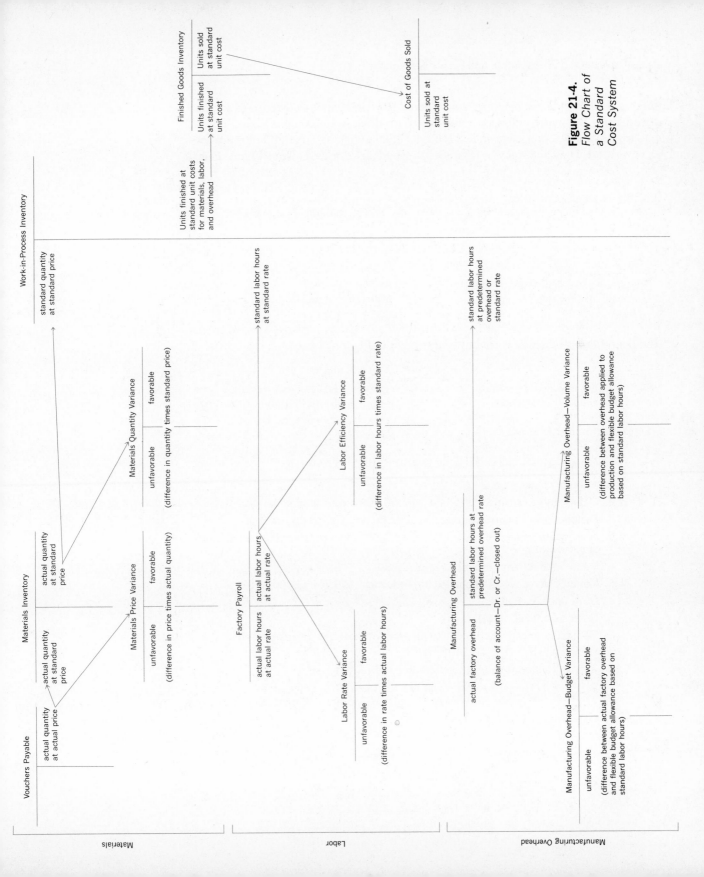

Figure 21-4.
Flow Chart of a Standard Cost System

ginning work-in-process inventory consisted of 80 units, which had received all the material and one-fourth of the labor and overhead; there were 200 units in the ending work-in-process inventory, which had received all materials and one-fifth of the labor and overhead. These data may be expressed in schedule form, as shown in Figure 21-5.

	Units	
Quantity to be accounted for		
Units in process at beginning	80 (all material–¼ L and O)	**Figure 21-5.** *Quantity Schedule for July*
Units started in process	10,000	
Total	10,080	
Quantity accounted for		
Transferred to finished goods inventory	9,880	
Units still in process	200 (all material–⅕ L and O)	
Total	10,080	

The equivalent production is computed as shown in Figure 21-6.

	Materials	L and O	
Beginning work-in-process inventory	–0–	60 (80 units × ¾)	**Figure 21-6.** *Schedule of Equivalent Production for July*
Started and finished this period	9,800	9,800 (9,880 units − 80 units)	
Units still in process	200	40 (200 × ⅕)	
Equivalent production units	10,000	9,900	

A summary of transactions for the month of July is given:

a. Materials purchased: 20,200 pieces of Material K-12 at $4.98
b. Materials requisitioned for production: 20,100 pieces of Material K-12
c. Factory payroll incurred during July: 29,600 hours at $3.05 per hour
d. Direct labor applied: standard hours for 9,900 units of finished product times standard rate
e. Manufacturing overhead incurred: $29,850
f. Manufacturing overhead applied to production: $29,700 (9,900 × $3)
g. Units finished: 9,880
h. Units sold: 9,500 at $30
i. Manufacturing Overhead controlling account closed and variances entered in budget and volume variance accounts

The entries to record the transactions for the month are:

(a)

Materials Inventory	101,000	
Materials Price Variance		404
Vouchers Payable		100,596

Quantity	Price	Amount
Actual–20,200 × Standard–$5.00		$101,000
Actual–20,200 × Actual–$4.98		100,596
Materials price variance (favorable)		$ 404

(b)

Work-in-Process Inventory	100,000	
Materials Quantity Variance	500	
Materials Inventory		100,500

Quantity	Price	Amount
Actual—20,100 × Standard—$5.00		$100,500
Standard—20,000 × Standard—$5.00		100,000
Materials quantity variance (unfavorable)		$ 500

 10,000 equivalent production units (see Figure 21-6)
   ×2 standard pieces per unit
20,000 standard units of material

(c)

Factory Payroll	90,280	
Vouchers Payable (and payroll tax liabilities)		90,280

     29,600 actual hours × $3.05 = $90,280

(d)

Work-in-Process Inventory	89,100	
Labor Rate Variance	1,480	
Labor Efficiency Variance		300
Factory Payroll		90,280

Rate Variance

Hours	Rate	Amount
Actual—29,600 × Actual—$3.05		$90,280
Actual—29,600 × Standard—$3.00		88,800
Labor rate variance (unfavorable)		$ 1,480

Efficiency Variance

Hours	Rate	Amount
Standard—29,700 × Standard—$3.00		$89,100
Actual—29,600 × Standard—$3.00		88,800
Labor efficiency variance (favorable)		$ 300

 9,900 equivalent production units (see Figure 21-6)
   ×3 standard hours per unit
29,700 total standard labor hours

(e)

Manufacturing Overhead	29,850	
Prepaid Insurance and other accounts		29,850

(f)

Work-in-Process Inventory	29,700	
Manufacturing Overhead		29,700

   29,700 standard labor hours × $1 per hour
    predetermined overhead rate = $29,700

(g)

Finished Goods Inventory	217,360	
Work-in-Process Inventory		217,360

9,880 completed units × $22 standard unit cost =
$217,360

(h)

Cost of Goods Sold	209,000	
Accounts Receivable	285,000	
Finished Goods Inventory		209,000
Sales		285,000

9,500 units × $22 standard unit cost = $209,000
9,500 units × $30 unit selling price = $285,000

(i)

Manufacturing Overhead–Volume Variance	200	
Manufacturing Overhead–Budget Variance		50
Manufacturing Overhead		150

The Manufacturing Overhead controlling account after Entry i is posted appears as follows:

Manufacturing Overhead

Entry e	29,850	Entry f	29,700
		Entry i	150
	29,850		29,850

The actual manufacturing overhead incurred ($29,850) exceeded the overhead applied ($29,700); therefore, the debit balance of $150 represents underapplied overhead. Further analysis indicates that the $150 is made up of (1) a credit budget variance of $50 and (2) a debit volume variance of $200. In deriving these two amounts, reference must be made to the flexible budget to determine the budget allowance based on standard labor hours for the actual work completed (29,700 hours). Since a breakdown of the fixed and variable elements in the predetermined overhead rate is available, computations for the flexible budget allowances for 29,700 labor hours on work completed may be made as follows (see Figure 21-3):

Fixed costs	$20,000
Variable costs 29,700 hours × $.33⅓	9,900
Flexible budget allowance	$29,900

If a breakdown of the fixed and variable elements is not available, the $29,900 may be derived directly from the flexible budget schedule (Figure 21-2):

$$\frac{\text{Standard labor hours for work done}}{\text{Budgeted direct labor hours}} = \frac{29,700}{30,000} = 99\%$$

The flexible budget allowance at this 99-percent level may now be interpolated as follows:

95% (28,500 hours)	$29,500
100% (30,000 hours)	30,000
5% difference	$ 500
1% difference	100
4%	$ 400

The flexible budget allowance at 99% level is:

95%	$29,500
4%	400
99%	$29,900

The underapplied overhead of $150 may be analyzed as follows:

1. Budget variance:

Flexible budget allowance for 99% capacity attained	$29,900
Actual overhead incurred	29,850
Budget variance (favorable)	$ 50

2. Volume variance:

Flexible budget allowance for 99% capacity attained	$29,900
Overhead applied during July (29,700 hrs. × $1)	29,700
Volume variance (unfavorable)	$ 200

The budget variance is favorable because the actual overhead costs incurred are less than the flexible budget allowance at the 99 percent of actual capacity level. The volume variance is unfavorable because a portion (1%) of the available plant facilities were not used, resulting in a loss of $200, computed as follows:

Budgeted hours	30,000
Standard hours for capacity attained	29,700
Idle capacity hours	300
Fixed overhead rate per hour	$ .66⅔
Cost of idle capacity	$ 200

The idle capacity, or unfavorable volume variance, represents the portion of the fixed costs that was not absorbed due to the failure to achieve full production (30,000 hours). Had the volume of activity exceeded 100 percent (30,000 standard labor hours), an excess capacity, or favorable volume variance, would have resulted.

Practice varies with respect to the disposition of the variance accounts. One method is to treat the variances as costs of the period in which they are incurred; that is, to close all the variance accounts into Cost of Goods Sold. This may either be done monthly or be deferred until the end of the annual accounting period. Deferral may be practical if the variances tend to offset each other owing to seasonal volume fluctuations. Other accountants view standard costs as being realistic costs; therefore, they view the variances as losses or if they are favorable, gains. They would close the variances to the Revenue and Expense Summary account.

The Stetson Manufacturing Company computes the value of the 80 units (all material and ¼ of labor and overhead) in the beginning work-in-process inventory as follows:

Materials: 80 units × $10 standard cost   = $ 800
Labor: 80 units × ¼ × $9 standard cost   =   180
Overhead: 80 units × ¼ × $3 standard cost =   60
Total $1,040

The Work-in-Process Inventory ledger account appears as shown:

Work-in-Process Inventory

Beginning balance	1,040	Entry g: finished goods	217,360
Entry b: materials	100,000		
Entry d: labor	89,100		
Entry f: overhead (2,480)	29,700		

The $2,480 debit balance in the account represents the standard cost of 200 units in the ending work-in-process inventory, which is verified as follows:

Cost Element	Units in Process	Stage of Completion	Standard Unit Cost	Total Standard Cost
Materials	200	100%	$10	$2,000 (200 × $10)
Labor	200	20%	9	360 (200 × ⅕ × $9)
Overhead	200	20%	3	120 (200 × ⅕ × $3)
Total work in process				$2,480

MANAGERIAL INTERPRETATION OF VARIANCES

As a first step in the managerial interpretation of variances, it is necessary to identify who has primary responsibility for each of the variances. For example, the purchasing department is responsible, in part at least, for the materials prices variance. Supervisory factory personnel, however, may have some influence on materials prices when these individuals specify certain brand-named materials or materials of certain grade and quality. Factory supervisory personnel have primary responsibility for the materials quantity and labor efficiency variances. The personnel department is partly responsible for the labor rate variance (although others in the factory may have some influence here—for example, hiring policies). Top factory heads are responsible for the overhead volume variance; those who acquire and use overhead items are responsible for the overhead budget variance.

When any variance is large enough, an investigation should be made to see if corrective action should be taken. For example, if the price of materials is substantially above the standard, a study should be made—possibly by the accountant working with the individual (or individuals) who has primary responsibility for the materials price variance—to see if this cost could be reduced by buying in larger quantities, by the substitution of other materials, and by taking other measures. The other variances are analyzed in a similar manner. It is important, also, to know what variances *are not* large enough to justify an investigation, as these studies may be extremely costly and hence, for small differences, unprofitable for management.

DIRECT COSTING

A primary purpose of cost accounting is to furnish management with meaningful accounting data for use in decision-making. With this in view, a number of companies are using the principle of direct costing. Direct costing will be contrasted with *absorption,* or conventional, costing. Under direct costing, all manufacturing costs are segregated into product costs and period expenses, based on the variability of costs with volume. For direct costing purposes, costs that vary with changes in volume are considered product costs; those that do not vary are treated as period expenses. The cost of goods sold and the cost of goods in inventory are valued on the basis of product costs alone—direct labor, direct material, and variable manufacturing overhead. Fixed manufacturing overhead costs are reported as expenses for the period and deducted from the gross margin. Thus, the reported excess of revenue over variable costs and expenses, or *marginal income,* under direct costing reflects directly the effect of sales volume. Costs that are incurred to make a given level of plant productive facilities available—that is, costs that do not vary with the amount of work done but expire with the passage of time—are excluded in valueing both the cost of goods sold and the cost of goods on hand. Absorption costing, which treats *all* manufacturing costs as product costs, on the other hand, reflects the factors of both sales and production volume.

The ledger accounts under direct costing provide for the segregation of costs into their fixed and variable elements; the income statement is prepared to show *marginal income*—sales minus variable costs—from which fixed costs are deducted to arrive at net income. This is in contrast to absorption costing, under which the fixed and variable elements are mingled within the individual accounts. The separation of costs into their fixed and variable elements enables management to analyze the effect of volume changes on these cost elements and on net income. Under direct costing, fixed costs are deducted in the period when they are incurred, whereas under absorption costing, a portion of the fixed costs remains in inventory; hence the reported net income will differ under the two systems. When production exceeds sales, a portion of the fixed costs will remain in inventory under the absorption costing method, cost of goods sold will be less, and net income will be higher than under the direct costing method. The results are reversed when sales exceed production. Reported earnings under absorption costing may therefore rise with falling sales volume if production volume is increased, and fall with rising sales volume if production falls.

The operating data of the Crane Corporation for the three years 1967 through 1969 are used to compare absorption costing with direct costing:

Sales price per unit		$13
Normal capacity		20,000 units per year
Manufacturing costs at normal capacity		
	Total	Per Unit
Fixed	$ 80,000	$4.00
Variable (% of production)	105,000	5.25
Total	$185,000	$9.25

Selling and administrative expenses

Fixed	$ 9,000	$ .45
Variable (% of sales)	8,000	.40
Total	$ 17,000	$ .85

Inventories, production, and sales, in units, are shown in Figure 21-7.

	Units			For the 3-Year Period
	1969	1968	1967	
Beginning finished goods inventory	6,000	10,000	–0–	–0–
Production	21,000	11,000	20,000	52,000
Sales	27,000	15,000	10,000	52,000
Ending finished goods inventory	–0–	6,000	10,000	–0–

Figure 21-7.
Inventories, Production, and Sales in Units

The beginning and ending work-in-process inventories for each year were zero.

Comparative income statements based on the data in Figure 21-7 under the two cost reporting methods are shown in Figures 21-8 and 21-9. The statements are prepared under the assumptions that (1) volume is the only factor that had an influence on net income or loss; (2) selling prices remain constant; (3) fixed costs of production and selling and administrative costs remain unchanged; (4) variable costs are directly proportionate to sales at any level, hence constant in terms of cost per unit; (5) volume variances (under and overapplied costs) are closed to Revenue and Ex-

Figure 21-8.
Comparative Income Statement—Absorption Costing

CRANE CORPORATION
Comparative Income Statement—Absorption Costing
For the Years Ended December 31, 1969, 1968, and 1967

	Year			For the 3-Year Period
	1969	1968	1967	
Sales	$351,000	$195,000	$130,000 (10,000 units × $13)	$676,000
Cost of Goods Sold (standard)				
Beginning Finished Goods Inventory	$ 55,500	$ 92,500	–0–	–0–
Cost of Goods Manufactured	194,250	101,750	$185,000 (20,000 units × $9.25)	$481,000
Total Goods Available for Sale	$249,750	$194,250	$185,000	$481,000
Ending Finished Goods Inventory	–0–	55,500	92,500 (10,000 units × $9.25)	–0–
Cost of Goods Sold	$249,750	$138,750	$ 92,500	$481,000
Gross Margin on Sales (standard)	$101,250	$ 56,250	$ 37,500 ($130,000 − $92,500)	$195,000
Selling and Administrative Expenses				
Variable Selling and Administrative Expenses	$ 10,800	$ 6,000	$ 4,000 (10,000 units × $.40)	$ 20,800
Fixed Selling and Administrative Expenses	9,000	9,000	9,000	27,000
Total	$ 19,800	$ 15,000	$ 13,000	$ 47,800
Net Income (standard)	$ 81,450	$ 41,250	$ 24,500 ($37,500 − $13,000)	$147,200
Deduct Underapplied Manufacturing Costs	–0–	36,000 (a)	–0–	32,000 (c)
Add Overapplied Manufacturing Costs	4,000 (b)	–0–	–0–	–0–
Net Income (actual)	$ 85,450	$ 5,250	$ 24,500	$115,200

(a) 9,000 units (20,000 units − 11,000 units) × $4 = $36,000
(b) 1,000 units (21,000 units − 20,000 units) × $4 = $ 4,000

(c) 8,000 units (9,000 units − 1,000 units) × $4 = $32,000

CRANE CORPORATION
Comparative Income Statement—Direct Costing
For the Years Ended December 31, 1969, 1968, and 1967

	Year				For the 3-Year Period
	1969	1968	1967		
Sales	$351,000	$195,000	$130,000	(10,000 units × $13)	$676,000
Cost of Goods Sold–Variable Costs	141,750	78,750	52,500	(10,000 units × $5.25)	273,000
Marginal Income from Manufacturing	$209,250	$116,250	$ 77,500		$403,000
Variable Selling and Administrative Expenses	10,800	6,000	4,000	(10,000 units × $.40)	20,800
Marginal Income	$198,450	$110,250	$ 73,500		$382,200
Fixed Operating Costs and Expenses					
Manufacturing Costs	$ 80,000	$ 80,000	$ 80,000		$240,000
Selling and Administrative Expenses	9,000	9,000	9,000		27,000
Total	$ 89,000	$ 89,000	$ 89,000		$267,000
Net Income (or Loss)	$109,450	$ 21,250	$ (15,500)	($89,000 − $73,500)	$115,200

Figure 21-9.
Comparative Income Statement—Direct Costing

pense Summary rather than apportioned between the cost of goods sold and the ending inventories; and (6) finished goods inventories are valued at standard costs.

The statements of the Crane Corporation show the effect of the two costing methods on the relationship of sales, volume of production, and cost of goods sold, as follows:

1. In any given year when units produced are greater than units sold, reported net income under direct costing is less than under absorption costing. Results for 1967 are:

Absorption costing–net income (Figure 21-8)	$24,500
Direct costing–net loss (Figure 21-9)	(15,500)
Variation between methods	$40,000

The $40,000 variation results from the difference in the valuation of the ending finished goods inventories, which are:

Absorption costing (10,000 units × $9.25)	$92,500
Direct costing (10,000 units × $5.25)	52,500
Difference	$40,000

This difference is due, in turn, to the $4 fixed manufacturing cost per unit:

Inventory including fixed manufacturing costs (10,000 × $9.25)	$92,500
Inventory excluding fixed manufacturing costs (10,000 × $5.25)	52,500
Difference	$40,000

2. When units produced are less than units sold, reported income under direct costing is greater than under absorption costing. Results for 1968 under these assumptions are:

Direct costing (Figure 21-9)	$21,250
Absorption costing (Figure 21-8)	5,250
Variation between methods	$16,000

The variation is due to the difference in inventory valuations resulting from the inclusion (absorption) or exclusion (direct) of the $4 fixed manufacturing overhead cost per unit, as follows:

Beginning finished goods inventory		
Absorption costing (10,000 units × $9.25)		$92,500
Direct costing (10,000 units × $5.25)		52,500
Difference		$40,000
Ending finished goods inventory		
Absorption costing (6,000 units × $9.25)	$55,500	
Direct costing (6,000 units × $5.25)	31,500	24,000
Difference		$16,000

3. When units sold and units produced are the same, reported income is the same under both methods. This is evident from the tabulation that follows, in which the data for the three years are combined. Units produced and units sold were equal over the three years.

	Year			For the 3-Year Period
	1969	1968	1967	
Units produced	21,000	11,000	20,000	52,000
Units sold	27,000	15,000	10,000	52,000
Net income–absorption costing (Figure 21-8)	$ 85,450	$ 5,250	$24,500	$115,200
Net income (or loss)–direct costing (Figure 21-9)	$109,450	$21,250	($15,500)	$115,200

4. Under direct costing, increases and decreases in units sold result in proportionate increases and decreases in marginal income because only variable costs are assigned to the cost of units produced.

		Per Unit
Sales price		$13.00
Variable costs		
Manufacturing	$5.25	
Selling and Administrative	.40	5.65
Marginal income		$ 7.35

Year	Units Sold	Marginal Income Per Unit	Marginal Income on Income Statement
1967	10,000	$7.35	$ 73,500
1968	15,000	7.35	110,250
1969	27,000	7.35	198,450

5. Under direct costing, the emphasis is on the number of units sold, and the net income or net loss will therefore move in the same direction as the sales volume. Net income or net loss cannot increase or decrease, however, in direct proportion to sales volume because unit fixed costs do not stay constant. Under absorption costing, emphasis is both on production and on sales, and the net income and net loss do not, therefore, show the expected relationship to sales. This is illustrated by the comparison that follows of sales and net income (or loss) data for the Crane Corporation:

	Direct Costing			Absorption Costing		
	1969	1968	1967	1969	1968	1967
Sales	$351,000	$195,000	$130,000	$351,000	$195,000	$130,000
Net Income (or Loss)	109,450	21,250	(15,500)	85,450	5,250	24,500

Although sales during the second year increased by $65,000 ($195,000 − $130,000), net income under absorption costing decreased by $19,250 ($24,500 − $5,250).

6. Under direct costing, inventory valuations are determined with fixed costs excluded and are always smaller than inventory valuations computed under absorption costing, which includes fixed costs. Therefore, working capital (current assets less current liabilities) reported on the statement of financial position under the direct costing method will always be smaller. Ending finished goods inventories reported on the statement of financial position under both methods for 1967 and 1968 are as follows:

December 31	Direct Costing	Absorption Costing
1967	$52,500 (10,000 units × $5.25)	$92,500
1968	31,500 (6,000 units × $5.25)	55,500

In conclusion, note that the difference between the results under direct costing and absorption costing stems from the amount of fixed manufacturing costs allocated to finished goods and work-in-process inventories. The advocates of direct costing argue that these fixed costs are not a part of the cost of goods manufactured during a given period. Rather, these are the costs of having the capacity to produce; hence they are expenses and should be charged against revenue irrespective of physical production. Proponents of absorption costing argue that fixed manufacturing costs are as essential to the production of goods as are variable costs. Also, net income from the sale of any unit of a product does not emerge until after the total cost of bringing that product to the point of sale has been recovered.

Unquestionably, the delineation of costs into their fixed and variable components is useful to management in studying cost-volume-income relationships; but to include only variable costs in finished goods and work-in-process inventories leaves some doubt about the validity of the valuation of those items for such purposes as securing loans and issuing capital stock. Also, the undervaluation of inventories leaves some doubt about the validity of subsequent income measurement. For these reasons, direct costing has not attained the status of a generally accepted accounting procedure. Some firms, however, have set up their records on a direct costing basis; then for financial reporting and tax purposes they convert their statements to an absorption cost basis.

SUMMARY

A standard cost is a predetermined estimate of the cost of each element of a product, based on an analysis of past experience and expected future developments. It shows what each product should cost if the assumptions on which the standard costs are based prove to be true. Standard costs provide a basis for comparison with actual costs and, therefore, serve as a criterion in measuring the adequacy or inadequacy of the actual performance.

To utilize standard costs effectively in connection with manufacturing overhead costs, a flexible budget that shows the expected standard cost of overhead at various levels of production should be used. A fixed budget is of little value, since variations of actual costs from budgeted costs will arise if actual production differs from budgeted production. To prepare a flexible budget, the behavior of each overhead cost in relation to changes in volume must be examined. A fixed overhead cost is unaffected by volume changes; a variable overhead cost varies proportionately with volume changes. A semivariable overhead cost changes with volume changes, but not proportionately; in a flexible budget, the semivariable costs must be divided into their fixed and variable components. If a flexible budget is employed, one volume of production must be chosen upon which to apply overhead to the various products during the period. Once the volume is selected, the overhead rate may be divided into two components, the variable overhead rate and the fixed overhead rate. During the period, actual overhead costs are accumulated in the Manufacturing Overhead account but overhead is charged to products based on the standard overhead rates. At the end of the period, the difference between the budgeted overhead at the standard volume and the actual overhead incurred can be broken down into the following variances: (1) Budget variance—the difference between the budgeted amount at the attained capacity and the actual overhead incurred during the period. (2) Volume variance— the difference between the budgeted amount at the attained capacity and the overhead applied during the period.

Under a standard cost system, purchased materials are charged to Materials Inventory at standard prices, and Work-in-Process Inventory is charged for the standard quantity of materials used at their standard prices. The difference between the standard cost and the actual cost of materials purchased is the materials price variance, and the difference between the actual quantity used and the standard quantity at the standard cost is the materials quantity variance.

Work-in-Process Inventory is charged for the standard number of labor hours at the standard rate under a standard cost system. The labor rate variance is the difference between the actual hours worked at the actual rate and at the standard rate. The labor efficiency variance is the difference between the standard labor hours and the actual labor hours at the standard rate.

The most common method of disposing of the variances is to close them to the Cost of Goods Sold account at the end of the accounting period.

Absorption costing, or conventional financial costing, is based on the assumption that all factory costs, fixed and variable, should be charged to Cost of Goods Manufactured during the period and should be recognized as expenses only as the related goods are sold. Since all manufacturing costs are treated as product costs, the gross margin reflects the effect of both sales and production volume. Direct costing rejects the assumption that all manufacturing costs are product costs and limits product costs to those that vary with changes in the volume of production; that is, direct materials, direct labor, and variable manufacturing overhead. Fixed costs are reported as expenses of the period. Thus, the marginal income (excess of sales revenue over variable costs) reflects only the effect of sales volume. Direct costing is often more valuable to management for decision-making purposes than absorption costing since variable cost and marginal income data are readily available from the accounting records and statements. It also helps to clarify the relationship between costs, volume, and income. When production exceeds sales, net income will be higher under absorption costing than under direct costing since a portion of the fixed costs will be charged to the Inventory account instead of being charged to expense during the period. When sales exceed production, the results are reversed. Under direct costing, reported earnings move in the same direction as sales volume; if the volume of sales increases, reported earnings increase, and if the volume of sales decreases, reported earnings decrease. However, under absorption costing, reported earnings do not necessarily move in the same direction as sales volume; for example, an increase in earnings may accompany a decrease in sales volume if production volume increases. The difference in reported net income under direct costing and absorption costing is due to the difference in inventory valuations resulting from the inclusion (absorption costing) or exclusion (direct costing) of the fixed overhead costs.

□   **QUESTIONS**

Q21-**1.** How does a standard cost system make possible the application of the principle of management by exception?

Q21-**2.** (a) What is the difference between a fixed budget and a flexible budget? (b) Why must all costs ultimately be classified either as fixed or variable when preparing a flexible budget? (c) Why is it desirable to establish the variable and fixed factors of the predetermined overhead rate?

Q21-**3.** (a) What is meant by the standard cost of a unit? (b) Why is a standard cost system an effective means of cost control? (c) Identify and explain six variance accounts used in a standard cost system.

Q21-**4.** (a) What is meant by "budget allowance based on standard costs"? (b) How may interpolation be applied when a flexible budget is used? (c) How may the budget and volume variances be analyzed? (d) When should the standard costs be changed?

Q21-**5.** Standard cost as discussed in this text applies to a manufactured product; is it possible to extend the general principle of standard cost to the cost of services? Explain and give examples.

Q21-**6.** What is the basic difference between an income statement based on direct costing procedures and one based on the absorption costing method?

Q21-7. Give the advantages and the disadvantages of direct costing to management.

Q21-8. On January 1, 1969, the Directee Company had on hand 1,000 units of a given product; it manufactured 10,000 units and sold 6,000 units. Which costing method—direct or absorption—will produce the smaller net income for 1969? Explain the reason for the difference.

Q21-9. State the production circumstances under which the absorption method as compared to the direct costing method will yield the lower net income figure for a given year.

Q21-10. When a nonmanufacturing trading firm determines the cost of its purchases by taking invoice price less cash discounts plus an applicable part of direct transportation cost, but ignoring any fixed cost of the purchasing department, is it not applying a direct costing principle? Identify and explain the appropriate absorption costs for purchases.

☐ **EXERCISES**

E21-1. The budgeted data for the Timothy Company at 100 percent of capacity are:

Direct labor hours	120,000
Variable overhead costs	$60,000
Fixed overhead costs	$90,000

1. Prepare a flexible overhead budget at 85, 90, 95, 100, and 105 percent of capacity.
2. Compute the overhead rate at each capacity.

E21-2. Five pounds of a given material at $.65 per pound are standard for the production of a given product manufactured by the James Company. During August, 14,000 pounds of the particular materials were purchased at $.66 a pound; 12,000 pounds were put into process; 2,470 equivalent units of the finished product were produced.

Determine the materials price and quantity variances.

E21-3. Three gallons of a given material at $1.10 per gallon are standard for the production of a given product manufactured by the Mallory Company. During March, 1969, the following transactions (in summary form) took place:

1. Materials purchased were 17,000 gallons at $1.08 per gallon.
2. Materials requisitioned for production totaled 15,765 gallons.
3. Equivalent production for March was 5,250 equivalent units of the finished product.

Journalize the transactions involving materials, including the materials price and quantity variances.

E21-4. The Levin Company's standard cost card for one of its products showed the following direct labor charge:

Direct labor: 2 hours at $2.75 per hour

Standard direct labor hours for production for the month of April were 2,400; actual direct labor hours were 2,360 at a total cost of $6,608.

Determine (a) the labor rate variance and (b) the labor efficiency variance.

E21-**5.** The Bordeaux Company's standard cost card for its product, Zoxine, showed the following direct labor charge:

Direct labor: 3½ hours at $2.00 per hour

The following were among the transactions that occurred during June, 1969:

1. Factory payroll incurred during June was 30,460 hours, at a total cost of $60,615.
2. The standard direct labor cost was assigned to 8,680 equivalent finished units.

Journalize the transactions involving direct labor, including the labor rate variance and the labor efficiency variance.

E21-**6.** The Davidson Company maintains a standard cost system and a flexible overhead budget, as shown:

	70%	80%	90%	100%
Variable costs	$ 56,000	$ 64,000	$ 72,000	$ 80,000
Fixed costs	100,000	100,000	100,000	100,000
Total costs	$156,000	$164,000	$172,000	$180,000

Normal capacity is budgeted at the 100-percent level of 400,000 direct labor hours; the standard overhead rate is $.45 an hour. During the period, the Company worked 392,000 actual direct labor hours. Overhead was applied to production on the basis of 394,000 standard hours. Actual overhead incurred was $176,000.

Determine the manufacturing overhead (a) volume variance and (b) budget variance. (c) Prove the volume variance, using alternative computations.

E21-**7.** The Luther Company produced 20,000 units of a new product during 1969. 16,000 units were sold at $25 each. Costs of production and operating expenses were as follows:

Direct materials	$ 60,000
Direct labor	40,000
Manufacturing overhead–fixed	100,000
Manufacturing overhead–variable	120,000
(There was no ending work-in-process inventory)	
Selling and administrative expenses–fixed	30,000
Selling and administrative expenses–variable	20,000

Prepare an income statement, using the direct costing method.

E21-**8.** The Wagstaff Company reported the following results for the year 1969: sales, $200,000; variable cost of goods sold, $96,000; variable selling expenses, $12,000; fixed manufacturing overhead, $64,000; and fixed selling expenses, $8,400.

Prepare an income statement, using the direct costing method.

E21-**9.** The Bates Company, which began operations on January 1, 1969, produced 2,000 more units than it sold in 1969. Its fixed manufacturing overhead cost was $5 per unit, and the variable manufacturing cost was $7 per unit. There was no ending work-in-process inventory.

From this information, compute the difference between the net income that would be reported under direct costing and compare it to the income that would be reported under absorption costing.

E21–10. The Randall Company had a finished goods inventory of 3,000 units of a given product as of January 1, 1969, with a cost of $24,300 under the absorption costing method, or a cost of $15,000 under the direct costing method. There was no beginning work-in-process inventory.

      During 1969, the Randall Company manufactured 56,500 units of the particular product. The fixed manufacturing overhead cost totaled $169,500 during 1969 and the variable unit cost was the same as in 1968. The Company sold 50,000 units of the product at $10 each and used the FIFO method of assigning costs to the cost of goods sold. There was no ending work-in-process inventory.

      Operating expenses for the year were:

Selling and administrative expenses–fixed	$16,400
Selling and administrative expenses–variable	22,000

      Prepare an income statement for 1969 using (a) the direct cost method and (b) the absorption cost method.

☐ . DEMONSTRATION PROBLEMS

DP21–1. (*Standard cost accounting with a flexible budget*) The Allied Products Company used a standard cost system and a fixed manufacturing overhead budget in 1968, as follows:

Direct labor hours	40,000
Fixed costs	
Depreciation–factory building	$ 8,000
Factory taxes	600
Depreciation–machinery and equipment	16,000
Other costs (item data omitted)	35,400
Total fixed costs	$60,000
Variable costs	
Light and power	$ 2,000
Factory supplies	1,000
Other costs (item data omitted)	17,000
Total Variable Costs	$20,000
Total Manufacturing Overhead	$80,000

      In 1969, the management decided to prepare a flexible overhead budget at 80, 90, 100, and 110 percent of capacity levels of production. The 1968 budget represents a normal capacity of 100 percent. The standard unit cost of the product is:

Materials: 1 piece of Material Y-37	$ 3
Direct labor: 2 hours at $2.50	5
Manufacturing overhead: 2 hours at $2	4
Total	$12

Production data for 1969 were:

  There was no beginning work-in-process inventory.

  19,800 units started in production.

  19,000 units completed.

    800 units in process (all materials added and ¼ of labor and overhead).

Condensed transactions for 1969 were:

1. Materials purchased totaled 20,000 pieces at $3.02.
2. Materials requisitioned for production were 19,810 pieces.
3. Direct labor was 38,500 hours at $2.48 per hour.
4. Manufacturing overhead totaled $77,200.
5. Manufacturing overhead was applied to production on the basis stated.
6. Units finished were 19,000.
7. Units sold were 18,800 at $22 each.
8. Manufacturing Overhead control account was closed and variances were entered in budget and volume variance accounts.

Required: 1. Construct the flexible budget.
2. Record the transactions for 1969.
3. Post to a Work-in-Process Inventory T account and prove the ending balance.
4. Prepare a schedule analyzing the volume variance.

DP21-2. (*Direct costing*) The Graham Manufacturing Company produced 40,000 units of a new product during 1969 and sold 30,000 units at $25 each. Costs for 1969 were as follows:

	Fixed Costs	Variable Costs
Direct materials		$100,000
Direct labor		80,000
Manufacturing overhead	$220,000	160,000
Selling and administrative expenses	140,000	40,000

There was no ending work-in-process inventory.

Required: 1. Prepare comparative income statements for the year 1969, using: (a) the absorption cost method and (b) the direct cost method.
2. Give the reasons for the difference in reported net income or net loss in Requirements a and b.

☐ **PROBLEMS**

P21-1. Following are the budgeted data for the Rossell Company for the first three months of 1969, based on a normal capacity level of 100 percent:

Units	60,000
Direct materials	$180,000
Direct labor cost	$120,000
Direct labor hours	60,000
Fixed overhead costs	
Depreciation—machinery and equipment	$10,000
Factory taxes	4,000
Factory insurance	6,000
Miscellaneous	10,000
Variable overhead costs	
Light and power	5,000
Factory supplies	2,000
Miscellaneous	8,000

Required: 1. Construct a flexible manufacturing overhead budget at levels of 85, 90, 95, 100, and 105 percent.
2. Prepare standard cost cards for the product at each level of activity; compute separate variable and fixed cost rates per direct labor hour.

P21-2. The standard cost card for the Fraissure Company showed the following information in regard to its commodity, Plamb:

Materials: 2 gallons of Zunk at $2 each	$ 4
Direct labor: 3 hours at $3	9
Total materials and direct labor cost	$13

Production data for 1969 were:

Beginning work-in-process inventory: 100 units, 60% complete as to materials and 40% complete as to direct labor and manufacturing overhead

Completed during 1969: 20,000 units

Ending work-in-process inventory: 2,000 units, 80% complete as to materials and 50% complete as to direct labor and manufacturing overhead.

Transactions involving materials and labor during 1969 were:

1. Purchased 48,000 gallons of Zunk at $2.02 per gallon.
2. Requisitioned 43,120 gallons of Zunk for production.
3. Factory payroll incurred during the period was 61,920 hours at a total cost of $186,379.20. In recording the factory payroll, ignore payroll taxes.
4. A standard direct labor cost was assigned to production on the basis of information contained on the standard cost card.

Required: Record in journal form the foregoing information clearly establishing all material and labor variances in appropriate accounts.

P21-3. The Ennis Company manufactures a single product in several styles, all of which are uniform as to material quantity and production time requirements. The standard cost sheet for all products is as follows:

Materials: 16 pieces at $2	$ 32
Direct labor: 20 hours at $3	60
Manufacturing overhead: 20 hours at $1	20
Total	$112

The standard cost was the same for July and August. Overhead distribution is based on direct labor hours. The condensed flexible overhead budget for August, 1969, is:

	50%	75%	100%	125%
Direct labor hours	1,200	1,800	2,400	3,000
Variable costs	$ 600	$ 900	$1,200	$1,500
Fixed costs	1,200	1,200	1,200	1,200
Total costs	$1,800	$2,100	$2,400	$2,700

Production data for August were as follows:

Beginning work-in-process inventory: 10 units, 80% complete as to materials and 50% complete as to direct labor and manufacturing overhead.

Completed during the period: 122 units

Ending work-in-process inventory: 6 units, 100% complete as to materials and 50% complete as to direct labor and manufacturing overhead.

Transactions for the month included the following:

1. Materials purchased totaled 2,050 pieces at $1.98.
2. Materials issued for production totaled 2,040 pieces.
3. Labor costs incurred were 2,510 direct labor hours at $2.95; standard labor cost was transferred to the work-in-process inventory.
4. Manufacturing overhead incurred was $2,600.
5. Manufacturing overhead was applied to production.
6. Recorded units completed.
7. Sold 130 units for $200 each.
8. Closed the Manufacturing Overhead controlling account and entered the variances in budget and volume variances accounts.

Required: 1. Give the journal entries for the month.
2. Post to a Work-in-Process Inventory T account and verify the ending balance.
3. Prepare a schedule to account for the volume variance.

P21–**4.** The Nu-Standard Company manufactures a single product in several styles, all of which are uniform as to quantity of materials and production time requirements. The standard cost card for all products reveals the following quantities and costs:

Materials:	6 pieces × $1	$ 6
Direct labor:	8 hours × $4	32
Manufacturing overhead:	8 hours × $4	32
Total		$70

The normal (100%) standard budgeted overhead costs consist of:

Direct labor hours	2,000
Variable costs	$2,000
Fixed costs	6,000
Total costs	$8,000

Production data for July, 1969, are given (there was no June 30, 1969, work-in-process inventory):

Completed: 250 units

In process as of July 31: 10 units, 40% complete as to materials and 30% complete as to labor and overhead

Selected transactions for the month of July, 1969 included the following:

1. Materials purchased were 1,600 pieces at $.98.
2. Materials issued for production totaled 1530 pieces.
3. Manufacturing overhead incurred was $8,200.
4. Manufacturing overhead was applied to production.

5. Closed the Manufacturing Overhead controlling account and entered the variances in budget and volume variance accounts.

  Required: 1. Prepare the journal entries to record the transactions.
      2. Prepare the end-of-period entries to close the four established variances.

P21–5. The standard cost card for the Ellett Company shows the following information in regard to its commodity, Zamblam:

Materials: 4 pounds of Dunker at $1.50	$ 6
Direct labor: 2 hours at $2	4
Total	$10

The schedule of equivalent production reveals the following figures:

	Materials	Direct Labor
Equivalent production	52,000 units	51,600 hours

Selected transactions for the month of November, 1969, included the following:

1. Purchased 215,600 pounds of Dunker at $1.49 per pound.

2. Requisitioned for production 207,950 pounds of Dunker.

3. Factory payroll incurred during the period was 103,100 hours at a total cost of $205,100.

4. Standard direct labor costs were assigned to production at the standard rate.

  Required: 1. Prepare the journal entries to record the transactions.
      2. Prepare the end-of-period entries to close the four established variances.

P21–6. The Christopher Manufacturing Company, having completed its first year of operations on December 31, 1969, reported the following:

Units sold		24,000
Units produced		36,000
Sales price per unit	$	20.00
Variable manufacturing cost per unit		8.00
Fixed manufacturing overhead		216,000.00
Fixed manufacturing overhead cost per unit		6.00
(There was no ending work-in-process inventory)		
Variable selling and administrative expenses per unit sold		.60
Fixed selling and administrative expenses		80,000.00

  Required: 1. Prepare income statements for the year 1969, using (a) the absorption costing method and (b) the direct costing method.
      2. Prepare a schedule to account for the difference in net income or net loss.

P21–7. On January 1, 1969, the London Manufacturing Company began the manufacture of a new product. Management is disturbed because, in spite of a substantial increase in sales, profits decreased during 1970. The cost accountant explains that reported marginal income does not necessarily fluctuate in proportion to sales unless the statements are prepared on the direct costing basis. Operating data for 1969 and 1970 are:

	1969	1970
Units sold	60,000	80,000
Units produced	100,000	50,000
Sales price per unit	$ 18.00	$ 18.00
Variable manufacturing cost per unit	6.00	6.00
Fixed manufacturing overhead	400,000.00	400,000.00
(There was no ending work-in-process inventory)		
Variable selling and administrative expenses per unit sold	.20	.20
Fixed selling and administrative expenses	32,000.00	32,000.00

Required: 1. Prepare income statements for 1969 and 1970, using the absorption costing method. In a parallel column, prepare an income statement for 1970 only, assuming sales of 90,000 units. Assume the use of FIFO.

2. Prepare income statements for 1969 and 1970, using the direct costing method. In a parallel column, prepare an income statement for 1970 only, assuming sales of 90,000 units.

3. Under what conditions will the net income be the same under either method?

P21-**8.** On January 1, 1969, the Beaufort Company had a finished goods inventory of 5,600 units of its commodity, Ortogum, which had a cost of $61,600 under the absorption costing method and a cost of $42,000 under the direct costing method.

During 1969, the Beaufort Company manufactured 175,650 units of Ortogum. The fixed manufacturing overhead costs totaled $702,600 during 1969 and the variable unit cost was the same as in 1968. The Company sold 100,000 units of Ortogum at $20 each and used the LIFO method of assigning costs to the cost of goods sold.

Operating expenses for the year were:

Selling and administrative expenses–fixed	$20,000
Selling and administrative expenses–variable	18,000

Required: 1. Prepare income statements for 1969, using (a) the absorption costing method and (b) the direct costing method.

2. Prepare a schedule to account for the difference in net income or net loss.

CASE PROBLEM
Quality Clothing Company—Part II

Earl Braxton, the controller of the Quality Clothing Company (see Case Problem for Chapter 20), has decided to incorporate standard costs in the accounting records. In the production of one suit, Style 127-J, he has computed standard costs as follows:

Basic cloth for suit exterior: 4⅔ yds × $1.95	$ 9.10
Secondary cloth for coat lining and pockets: 2⅓ yards × $.90	2.10
Direct labor for cutting and sewing: 3¼ hours × $3.60	11.70
Variable manufacturing overhead–supplies and supervision	1.30

Fixed manufacturing overhead–depreciation, insurance, utilities, and so on:

70% of direct labor $8.19

During a given period, 3,600 equivalent units of the suits were made, and the following actual costs were incurred:

17,550 yards of basic cloth	$34,047
7,800 yards of secondary cloth	7,215
11,160 hours of direct labor	39,618
Variable manufacturing overhead	4,626
Fixed manufacturing overhead	29,484

Required:
1. As an assistant to Braxton, prepare a short report that he can submit to the president of the Company, justifying the decision to incorporate standard costs into the accounting records.
2. Include in your report the calculations of the following variances and indicate whether each variance is favorable or unfavorable:
   a. Basic cloth price variance: per yard, per suit, and total
   b. Basic cloth usage variance, quantity and cost: per suit and total
   c. Secondary cloth price variance: per yard, per suit, and total
   d. Secondary cloth usage variance, quantity and cost: per suit and total
   e. Direct labor rate variance: per hour, per suit, and total
   f. Direct labor efficiency variance, quantity and cost: per suit and total
   g. Variable manufacturing overhead variance: per suit and total
3. Explain how the knowledge of these variances can be useful.
4. How are standard costs determined?
5. Verify the calculation of the allocated fixed manufacturing overhead.
6. Why is the fixed manufacturing overhead variance very difficult to determine?
7. Prepare the journal entries to record the completion of the 3,600 suits at standard costs. Transfer each variance listed in Requirement 2 to a separate account. Consider the actual costs as having been debited to Suits in Process, and standard costs as being debited to Finished Suits.
8. What are the full costs of making one suit (actual and standard)? What are the direct costs of making one suit (actual and standard)?
9. What is the minimum amount for which a suit could be sold and have a positive effect on net income? Why and under what conditions would the management be willing to sell some of the output at that price?
10. Is it permissible for Finished Suits Inventory to be reported on the statement of financial position at direct cost? Why?

Chapter Twenty-Two

Special Cost Analysis and Control in Management Decisions

Before costs can be analyzed and interpreted for managerial use, a specific conception of the nature and content of various costs must be known. Therefore, certain basic cost concepts are defined and reviewed here.

Fixed costs are the costs that, without change in present productive capacity, are not affected by changes in volume of output. For instance, rent on a factory building is a fixed cost because it does not change when productive volume increases or decreases.

Variable costs are costs that are affected in total by changes in the volume of output. The cost of raw materials, for example, is a variable cost because it increases in direct proportion to the increase in the number of units produced.

Marginal costs (or *differential costs*) are the differences in cost between two levels of output, or the additional cost necessary to produce an additional unit.

Opportunity cost is the cost of foregoing one thing to get its next best alternative; for example, a company may make a large investment in plant and equipment, thereby giving up an opportunity to invest in bonds.

Out-of-pocket costs are costs that give rise to cash expenditures, such as wages, in contrast to depreciation, which requires no cash disbursement in the current period.

Sunk costs are costs that do not involve new cash expenditures and that therefore should not enter into a specific management decision. The difference between the undepreciated original cost of an old machine and what it would bring in the secondhand market is such a cost.

As a general rule, no single cost concept is relevant for all the decisions that must be made. Different kinds of decisions require different kinds of cost calculations. The problems of determining periodic net income are different from the problems met by management in day-to-day operations. Cost calculations that serve one purpose will not always serve another.

Business decisions are made after alternative courses of action are considered; the identification of the alternatives to be considered is itself a very important aspect of decision-making. A rational decision depends on a determination of the expected consequences of each of the various alternatives. It is only the prospective differences in consequences that influence the choice. Only those factors that are affected by the choice should be viewed as relevant to the decision.

If a cost is the same for each alternative under consideration, that cost should have no bearing on the outcome of the decision. As a general rule, fixed costs are common to all alternatives and hence have little meaning to many managerial problems. The relevant costs for the majority of business decisions are variable costs; however, it must be realized that in the long run all costs are variable; hence, for long-run decisions all costs are relevant. Also, in those short- and intermediate-run decisions involving the addition of an element of fixed cost, the cost that is added becomes, in effect, a variable cost for the particular decision to be made. In other words, marginal cost as defined is simply that cost which is variable for the specific decision under consideration; that is the variable cost as such plus any additional fixed cost per unit, due to new facilities, that will be incurred in implementing the decision.

The average total absorption cost described in Chapters 20 and 21 is acceptable for measuring the amount of inventories for statement presentation, for the calculation of net income, and for decisions of long-run effect; for example, a firm would not build a new plant unless it were sure of earning a return after the recovery of total expired costs. As a general rule, however, these average unit cost figures are unacceptable as a guide to short-run decisions.

In decision-making, all relevant differences are necessarily future differences, starting from the moment of decision. Past events cannot be changed by a decision made today. Past costs in dollars of any size are not relevant costs. Present and estimated future costs are the only relevant costs. It should be emphasized, however, that sometimes the only guide to present and future costs are past book figures.

Some of the specific managerial decisions for which special cost analyses must be prepared are discussed in this chapter. As will be shown in the following discussion, these analyses may require the use of data that are not readily available from regular accounting records.

BREAK-EVEN ANALYSIS

The *break-even point* is the volume of sales at which the business will neither earn income nor incur a loss; it is the point at which expired costs, or expenses, and revenue are exactly equal. The break-even point indicates to management the volume of sales needed to cover total variable and fixed costs and expenses. Sales in excess of the break-even point result in a net income because fixed costs have been recovered at the break-even sales volume.

Break-even analysis is an aid to management in policy-making because it highlights the effect on income of changes in selling prices, volume of sales, *product mix* (changes in the type of products sold), variable costs, and fixed costs. An understanding of the interaction of these factors assists management in budgeting and income-planning and in evaluating the effects of alternative courses of action.

Computation of the Break-Even Point

Since the break-even point is the volume of sales at which the business will neither earn net income nor incur a loss, the following basic formula is indicated:

$$S_{BEP} - (FC + VC_{BEP}) = 0, \text{ where}$$

S_{BEP} = Sales at break-even point
FC = Total fixed costs
VC_{BEP} = Variable costs at break-even point

Further, since S_{BEP} is the unknown element in the equation and since VC_{BEP} depends upon a knowledge of the sales at break-even point, VC_{BEP} has to be stated as a percentage of sales. With this in mind, the equation can be restated as follows:

$$S_{BEP} = FC + VC_{BEP}$$

$$VC_{BEP} = \frac{TVC}{TS} S_{BEP}, \text{ where}$$

TVC = Total variable cost for whatever volume of actual or budgeted sales is used in the computation
TS = The total sales volume that corresponds to the total variable cost.

Then the equation may be further restated, thus:

$$S_{BEP} = \frac{FC}{1 - \dfrac{TVC}{TS}}$$

To illustrate, assume that the budgeted data of Jackson Corporation are as shown in Figure 22-1.

Figure 22-1.
Data for Break-Even Computation

	Fixed	Variable	
Budgeted sales: 20,000 units $15 each			$300,000
Budgeted costs			
Direct materials		$ 25,000	
Direct labor		35,000	
Factory overhead	$ 50,000	40,000	
Selling expenses	30,000	15,000	
Administrative expense	25,000	5,000	
Totals	$105,000	$120,000	$225,000
Budgeted Net Income			$ 75,000

The break-even point is $175,000, computed as follows:

$$\frac{\$105,000}{1 - \dfrac{\$120,000}{\$300,000}} = \frac{\$105,000}{1 - .40} = \frac{\$105,000}{.60} = \$175,000$$

The mechanics of the break-even computation are further illustrated by the following equation:

$$VC_{BEP} = \frac{\text{Total variable costs}}{\text{Total sales}} = \frac{\$120,000}{\$300,000} = .40$$

or, 40 percent of sales is required to cover the variable costs.

	Percent
Break-even sales	100
Variable costs	40
Fixed costs at break-even point	60

Thus, 60 percent of each sales dollar (the *contribution percentage*) is available to cover the fixed costs.

$$S_{BEP} = \frac{\text{Fixed costs}}{\text{Percent of fixed costs to sales at break-even point}} = \frac{\$105{,}000}{.60} = \$175{,}000 = \frac{\text{Volume of sales at}}{\text{break-even point}}$$

The proof of this equation is as follows:

Break-even sales		$175,000
Costs		
Variable (40%)	$ 70,000	
Fixed (60%)	105,000	175,000
Net income		–0–

The Break-Even Chart

One effective means of presenting the relationship of fixed and variable costs to sales at different volume levels is the *break-even chart*. Two charts as shown (Figures 22-2 and 22-3) are based on data in Figure 22-1. In Figure 22-2, the vertical line (*y* axis) represents dollars from which both total sales and various costs can be read; the horizontal line (*x* axis) represents sales unit volume and percent of plant capacity. The fixed costs, assumed to be unaffected by volume changes, are therefore represented by a horizontal line running parallel to the *x* axis. Total costs, which are affected by volume changes, are represented by a straight line starting at the fixed cost point on the *y* axis and rising to the right of the chart. The point at which the two lines meet is the break-even point; at this point costs equal sales so that there is neither income nor loss. The spread between the lines above the intersection measures the amount of income; the spread between the lines below the intersection measures the amount of loss.

In Figure 22-2, the Fixed Costs line is below the Variable Costs line. In Figure 22-3, an inverted break-even chart, the Fixed Costs line is above the Variable Costs line to show clearly the portion of the fixed costs remaining to be recovered (Loss area) before income is realized. The break-even point in the two forms is, of course, the same.

The charts are based on certain assumptions regarding the relationship between prices and costs and the relative proportions of the various products sold. Further assumptions are that costs are either fixed or variable and that variable costs are affected proportionately by volume changes; and that beginning and ending inventories, price levels, product mix, and technical plant and labor efficiency will remain essentially unchanged. The degree and the effect of these factors on actual and assumed conditions must be carefully balanced and evaluated in break-even analysis. Break-even charts may be prepared from budgeting data as a forecast of costs and

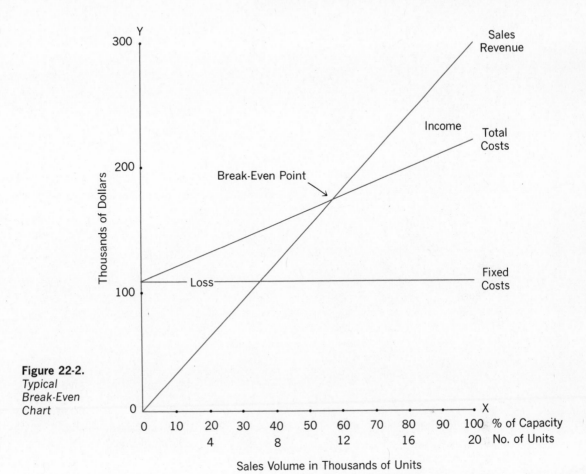

Figure 22-2.
*Typical
Break-Even
Chart*

Sales Volume in Thousands of Units

income, or they may be based on data taken from the books as a historical presentation of cost-volume-income relationships.

The break-even point in terms of units or in terms of percentage of plant capacity used may be determined from the x axis scale. The amounts at the break-even point are as shown (see Figure 22-2):

Break-even percent of plant capacity	58.3
Break-even units (assuming a single product or a constant mix)	11,667

The break-even percentage of operating capacity may also be verified mathematically as follows:

$$\frac{\text{Break-even sales volume}}{\text{Budgeted sales volume}} = \frac{\$175,000}{\$300,000} = 58.3\%$$

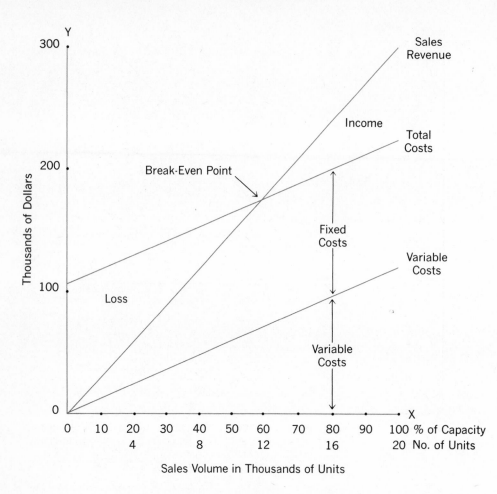

Figure 22-3.
*Inverted
Break-Even
Chart*

The break-even point in units is proven as shown:

$$x = \text{number of units sold at break-even point at \$15 each}$$
$$15x = 15(0.4x) + 105{,}000$$
$$9x = 105{,}000$$
$$x = 11{,}667$$

The same computation may be made in the following terms:

Line		
1	Unit sales price (see Figure 22-1)	$ 15
2	Unit variable cost (0.40 × $15)	6
3	Unit contribution (amount available for the recovery of fixed costs and profit)	$ 9
4	Fixed costs	$105,000
5	Unit break-even sales (Line 4 ÷ Line 3)	11,667

The proof of this calculation is:

Sales (11,667 × $15)		$175,000*
Costs		
Variable (11,667 × $6)	$ 70,000*	
Fixed	105,000	175,000
Net Income		–0–

*Adjusted for rounding.

This discussion of cost variability in break-even analysis has been based on the rather convenient assumption that costs can be segregated into two groups—those that vary directly with volume and those that are unaffected by volume changes. This assumption is an oversimplification, and care must be taken against reaching possible erroneous conclusions. The course of many costs is quite erratic in relation to volume. This is particularly true of second-shift costs, fringe benefits, and so on. Few if any costs are uniform in terms of units of output or time except within relatively limited volume ranges.

Other limitations, in summary, are: (1) If the break-even chart is based on data of only one or just a few periods, the results obtained may not be typical of the company's experience, and (2) the chart is not well designed for firms that sell a great variety of products, the proportions of which may change.

Marginal Income Statements

Marginal income, or contribution to fixed cost, is the excess of revenue over variable costs and variable expenses. The marginal income statement, therefore, separates costs and expenses into their fixed and variable elements. It is a convenient means of presenting data to management when charts or other forms might not be as serviceable. The break-even sales volume can be calculated readily from such a statement. A marginal income statement and break-even computation for the Jackson Corporation is shown in Figure 22-4 (see Figure 22-1 for supporting data).

Figure 22-4.
Marginal Income Statement

Sales (net): 20,000 units × $15 each	$300,000
Variable costs and expenses	120,000
Marginal income	$180,000
Fixed costs and expenses	105,000
Net income	$ 75,000
Marginal income percentage	60%
Break-even point: $105,000 ÷ 0.60	$175,000
Break-even point in units: $\dfrac{\$105,000}{\$15 - 0.4\,(\$15)}$	11,667

From this, the following basic equations may be derived:

$$\text{Sales} - \text{Variable costs} = \text{Marginal income}$$
$$\text{Marginal income} - \text{Fixed costs} = \text{Net income}$$
$$\text{Marginal income} \div \text{Sales} = \text{Marginal income, or contribution, percentage}$$
$$\text{Fixed costs} \div \text{Contribution percentage} = \text{Break-even point in sales dollars}$$
$$\text{Fixed costs} \div \text{Contribution per unit} = \text{Break-even point in units}$$

A marginal income statement is prepared to emphasize the contribution of each sales dollar toward the recovery of fixed costs and toward net income. Marginal income must equal fixed costs for the firm to break even; marginal income must exceed fixed costs if a net income is to be realized. Thus, in Figure 22-4, 60 cents out of each sales dollar contributes to the recovery of fixed costs up to sales of $175,000; out of each dollar of sales thereafter, 60 cents contributes to net income.

Margin of Safety

The *margin of safety* is the dollar volume of sales above the break-even point, or the amount or percentage by which sales may decrease before losses are incurred. The margin of safety for the Jackson Corporation is:

Sales	$300,000
Deduct break-even sales	175,000
Margin of Safety	$125,000

A loss will not be incurred unless sales decrease by more than $125,000. The percentage of safety is computed as follows:

$$\frac{\text{Margin of safety}}{\text{Net sales}} = \frac{\$125,000}{\$300,000} = 0.4167$$

Any decreases in sales up to 41.67 percent can be absorbed before a loss is incurred.

Marginal Income Planning

The effect of any prospective changes in operations can be determined rapidly when data on costs are divided between the fixed and variable elements. This kind of evaluation and analysis is demonstrated in the following two cases.

Case 1. The Excel Manufacturing Company is considering the possibility of expanding the present plant facilities at a time when the plant is operating at full capacity. Two important factors that must be known before the decision is made are the sales volume required with the planned expansion to earn the current income and an appraisal from the marketing department of whether this figure can be reached and exceeded.

Assume the following data for the Excel Manufacturing Company:

	Under Present Plant Facilities		Under Proposed Plant Facilities	
Sales		$600,000		$800,000
Variable costs	$180,000		$240,000	
Fixed costs	350,000	530,000	462,000	702,000
Net income		$ 70,000		$ 98,000

The following basic formula (expanded from the break-even formula) is appropriate to determine the sales volume required with the planned expansion to earn the current income:

$$S = VC_S + FC + I, \text{ where}$$
$$I = \text{Current income}$$
$$VC_S = \text{Variable costs at the specifically required sales volume}$$

Thus, the formula can be stated:

$$S = \frac{FC + I}{1 - \dfrac{TVC}{TS}}$$

Since $1 - \dfrac{TVC}{TS}$ is the contribution, or marginal income, percentage, which may be designated as C, then for purposes of clarity the formula may be restated as follows:

$$S = \frac{FC + I}{C}$$

The data for the Company may be substituted in the second formula, as shown:

$$S = \frac{462,000 + 70,000}{1 - \dfrac{240,000}{800,000}} = \$760,000$$

This is verified in conventional income statement form as follows:

Sales (S)		$760,000
Variable costs (.30S)	$228,000	
Fixed costs	462,000	690,000
Net income (currently being earned)		$ 70,000

It is assumed in this illustration that the variable cost rate will continue to be 30 percent of sales. It is possible that the additional facilities may permit an increase in the productivity of labor or purchasing economies, thus causing a decrease in the variable cost rate. Other factors must be considered in determining whether the proposed expansion is warranted. The acquisition of additional plant and equipment involves long-term investments, possible long-term financing, and increased taxes, insurance, maintenance, and other costs. Management should be reasonably assured that it will be able to make sustained use of the added facilities.

Case 2. A corporation is considering whether to purchase some special machines. Management will buy the machines if their cost can be recovered in three years; that is, if the marginal income (less out-of-pocket related fixed costs other than depreciation) generated by these machines over a three-year period is equal to their cost. Assume the following facts:

1. The machines cost $180,000.
2. The annual revenue generated by the machines will total $200,000.
3. The variable cost is 60 percent of sales.

The marginal income is $80,000 per year, computed as shown:

$$[(1.00 - 0.60) \times \$200,000] = \$80,000$$

If the annual fixed cost on these machines other than depreciation—property taxes, insurance, and so on—amounts to $6,000 per year, then the remainder, or $74,000 ($80,000 − $6,000), per year is a recovery of the cost of the machines. At this rate, the cost of the machines will be recouped in approximately 2.4 years, determined as follows:

$$\frac{\$180,000}{\$74,000} = 2.4 \text{ years}$$

If this is the only variable upon which the decision rests, then the special machines should be purchased. A more complete discussion of this and other problems involving investments in plant assets may be found in Chapter 23.

SPECIAL ORDERS

A decision with which management is often confronted is whether or not to accept a special order involving the production of additional units beyond outstanding commitments. An analysis of pre-existing cost patterns will not necessarily furnish the required data for such a decision. Each new situation requires a new cost analysis. The probable effect of the additional order on fixed manufacturing costs, selling and administrative expenses, selling price, and possible reduction in direct material costs resulting from increased volume buying must be analyzed carefully.

If the price of the special order exceeds its marginal costs—which will equal variable costs if unused capacity is available—and there are no alternative uses for this available capacity, the offer should be accepted. To illustrate, assume the following total unit cost data for the Jason Company, based on a budgeted annual production of 60,000 units:

Direct materials	$2.00
Direct labor	2.50
Variable overhead costs	1.50
Total variable costs	$6.00
Fixed overhead costs ($180,000 ÷ 60,000 units)	3.00
Total unit cost	$9.00

The Jason Company has been offered a long-term contract for 20,000 additional units annually at a unit price of $8.50. Since the purchaser is to attach his own label to the product, the Jason Company's established price of $15 each will not be affected. Since fixed costs are not affected by the volume of production, fixed manufacturing, fixed selling, and fixed administrative expenses, $280,000 in this case, will not be increased by the new order. Therefore, since the special offer price of $8.50 exceeds the marginal costs of $6, the regular sales are not affected, and a gain of $50,000 is realized on the additional order, the offer should be accepted. The comparative budget data shown at the top of page 765 verify this conclusion:

The data also indicate the possibility of developing a new market through price reductions made possible by the absorption of fixed costs in the regular volume of business. This may be particularly effective when a product is sold in a foreign market, or in any decisions involving levels of output or the cost of additional volume.

PRODUCT PRICING

An intricate relationship exists between the factors of price, cost, and volume. An understanding of this relationship is imperative because it underlies virtually every

JASON COMPANY
Budgeted Comparative Income Statement
For the Year Ending December 31, 1969

	Budgeted Production	Additional Order	Totals
Sales			
60,000 units @ $15.00	$900,000		
20,000 units @ 8.50		$170,000	$1,070,000
Variable Costs			
60,000 units @ $ 6.00	360,000		
20,000 units @ 6.00		120,000	480,000
Marginal Income	$540,000	$ 50,000	$ 590,000
Fixed Costs	280,000		280,000
Net Income	$260,000	$ 50,000	$ 310,000

decision confronting management. It is essential, therefore, that management make continuing analyses of its selling prices, particularly for competitive products.

One of the knottiest problems is calculating the effect of price on the volume of sales in terms of both short-run and long-run effects. The cost analyst plays a significant role in pricing policy decisions by projecting the effect on costs and income of the sales volumes that may be expected at different prices.

The method of accumulating costs to arrive at total costs has been discussed in previous chapters. Total costs consist of direct costs (direct materials and labor), variable manufacturing overhead (power, supplies, maintenance), and fixed manufacturing overhead (insurance, taxes, depreciation). The process of establishing a predetermined overhead rate involves an allocation of the fixed manufacturing overhead on some arbitrary basis as well as an estimated volume factor that becomes the denominator in the overhead rate formula. The pricing of the product on this total cost basis is often considered unsatisfactory (1) because the allocation of overhead items is inherently imprecise, (2) because the projected volume on which the overhead rate is based is also imprecise, and (3) because total cost is not relevant to short-run decisions.

In general, however, the unit price that yields the greatest marginal income is the price that should be used for a particular product. Following this approach, therefore, a schedule should be prepared based on variable costs only, such as the one in Figure 22-5 showing the probable volume of sales and the marginal income that will result at each of the several price levels under consideration. It may be assumed that the volume-price relationships are estimated from the results of a market survey based on test sales in selected areas and on questionnaires.

Figure 22-5.
Marginal Income at Various Prices

Quantity	Sales Price Per Unit	Projected Sales	Variable Costs ($40 per unit)	Marginal Income
40,000	$80.00	$3,200,000	$1,600,000	$1,600,000
45,000	78.00	3,510,000	1,800,000	1,710,000
55,000	75.00	4,125,000	2,200,000	1,925,000
57,000	72.50	4,132,500	2,280,000	1,852,500
65,000	67.00	4,355,000	2,600,000	1,755,000

A sales price of $75 per unit will provide the greatest marginal income—$1,925,000. The $75 selling price does not provide the greatest margin on each unit sold; the unit marginal income is $35 compared with $40 at the $80 selling price. The increased sales volume at the lower price, however, results in a greater total marginal income.

When more than one product is priced, it is necessary to find a combination of price and volume that results in the greatest marginal income. Assume, for example, that the Baker Company manufactures two different products, X and Y, that require nearly identical production processes. Variable unit costs are $10 for Product X and $12 for Product Y. Facilities are available to produce a combined total of 11,000 units. The following schedule was prepared to aid management in its pricing policy.

Product X

Quantity	Sales Price Per Unit	Projected Sales	Variable Cost	Marginal Income
4,000	$22	$ 88,000	$40,000	$48,000
5,000	20	100,000	50,000	50,000
7,000	16	112,000	70,000	42,000

Product Y

Quantity	Sales Price Per Unit	Projected Sales	Variable Cost	Marginal Income
3,000	$26	$ 78,000	$36,000	$42,000
5,000	23	115,000	60,000	55,000
7,000	22	154,000	84,000	70,000

A combination of 5,000 units of Product X and 7,000 units of Product Y results in the largest possible marginal income ($50,000 + $70,000 = $120,000). If, however, plant capacity cannot be efficiently expanded beyond the previously assumed level of 11,000 units, the most profitable combination is 4,000 units of Product X and 7,000 units of Product Y for a total marginal income of $118,000 ($48,000 + $70,000).

The establishment of prices based on marginal income is customary practice in retailing. Prices are set on the basis of a percentage markup on cost. The markup must be delicately adjusted to gauge the responsiveness of consumer demand. Studies may be made to determine the percentage of change that results from each percentage price change (elasticity of demand) for products whose sales potential fluctuates inversely with changes in price.

In these examples, is it assumed that fixed costs remain the same at all the indicated sales levels and that net income is therefore maximized at prices that provide the greatest marginal income. Total unit costs (fixed and variable) depend, however, on total volume, and total volume in turn depends on the price charged. It is for this reason that cost studies also should be made showing estimates of total cost and net income at the various sales levels. Such studies might indicate maximum net income at levels different from the marginal income studies. In the last analysis, a firm must recover total costs, not just variable costs. Long-term pricing based on marginal income might result in prices set too close to the marginal income point, possibly resulting in needless cutthroat competition within the industry.

Another factor is that the firm may not be motivated exclusively by the maximum income objective. In the long run—or even in the short run—a just price resulting in a reasonable income may prove ultimately to be the best price. A short-run price based on maximized income may operate adversely in the long run by depressing future demand. There is also the possibility that competing costs and prices are such as to permit setting a price above the level indicated by the marginal income analysis, should the firm so decide.

DECIDING TO MAKE OR TO BUY

Management must often decide whether to make or to buy a particular part, product, or plant asset. If the plant facilities have already been acquired, the capacity is available, quality can be assured, and there are no negative factors, the decision depends upon a comparison of variable costs with the outside purchase price of the item. (If other fixed costs have to be added, then marginal cost would be the relevant cost.) If the variable production cost of the item is less than the quoted purchase price, then the item should be manufactured; if the quoted purchase price is less than the variable cost of the item, it should be purchased.

Assume that the Ames Company manufactures a particular part at a unit cost of $6.80, and that this cost consists of the following:

Direct materials	$1.50
Direct labor	2.50
Variable overhead costs	1.20
Total variable costs	$5.20
Fixed overhead costs	1.60
Total unit cost	$6.80

The Ames Company can purchase this part from a reliable manufacturer for $6.05. If the available plant facilities represent sunk costs that cannot be recovered by some other use of the facilities represented by the fixed overhead unit cost of $1.60, then the firm should continue to make the part. The variable costs of $5.20 are less than the quoted purchase price of $6.05 and the difference might be used to defray part of fixed overhead costs. If, on the other hand, the Ames Company can make an alternative and profitable use of those facilities for other purposes, it should buy the part. Under this assumption, fixed overhead costs must be included in the total cost of the part because the Company is foregoing the opportunity of making an alternate use of the facilities. With fixed overhead costs included, the unit cost to make is greater than the cost to buy—$6.80 compared with $6.05.

This involves a decision whether to continue making a product or to buy it. The parallel problem—whether to manufacture a part or a product that is currently being purchased—involves essentially the same factors for consideration, together with such other relevant factors as the effect of the change on inventories and on working capital, on net income before and after taxes, on the rate of return on capital employed, and on the rate of return on sales. Finally, intangible factors at the top management level would also enter into the decision to make or buy.

DEPARTMENT, TERRITORY, OR PRODUCT ABANDONMENT

The decision whether or not to abandon a supposedly unprofitable department, territory, or product involves a careful analysis of the effect of the abandonment on the fixed and variable costs and the marginal income. If a department, territory, or product produces any marginal income it should not be abandoned unless the newly created capacity—that is, a substituted new department, territory, or product— could be committed to a more profitable use.

The departmental income statement of the Stevens Clothing Company is shown in Figure 22-6. The accountant for the Company has been asked by the management to study the probable effect on total costs if the Children's Department is eliminated. Management is aware that, although closing the department will eliminate sales, cost of goods sold, and gross margin entirely, certain other costs currently chargeable to the department will continue.

Figure 22-6.
*Departmental
Income Statement*

STEVENS CLOTHING COMPANY
Income Statement
For the Year Ended December 31, 1969

	Men's Department	Women's Department	Children's Department	Combined
Sales (net)	$78,910	$128,000	$34,400	$241,310
Cost of Goods Sold	53,656	90,444	26,630	170,730
Gross Margin on Sales	$25,254	$ 37,556	$ 7,770	$ 70,580
Deduct Operating Expenses				
Advertising Expense	$ 981	$ 1,590	$ 429	$ 3,000
Salesmen's Salaries	9,050	12,030	3,515	24,595
Commissions Expense	750	1,100	240	2,090
Rent Expense	2,160	3,600	1,440	7,200
Depreciation Expense–Store Equipment	400	500	100	1,000
Supervisor's Salary	2,603	5,196	1,301	9,100
Office Salary	1,158	2,313	579	4,050
Insurance Expense	480	600	120	1,200
Bad Debts Expense	75	175	50	300
Miscellaneous General Expenses	400	500	100	1,000
Heat and Light Expense	450	750	300	1,500
Total Operating Expenses	$18,507	$ 28,354	$ 8,174	$ 55,035
Net Operating Income or (Loss)	$ 6,747	$ 9,202	$ (404)	$ 15,545

A careful analysis reveals the cost tabulation shown in Figure 22-7.
As a result of this study, the effect of discontinuing the Children's Department can be reasonably forecast as follows:

Net operating income of all departments (Figure 22-6)		$15,545
Reduction in gross margin on sales (Figure 22-6)	$7,770	
Reduction in variable costs (Figure 22-7)	4,454	
Reduction in net operating income		3,316
Combined net operating income with Children's Department eliminated		$12,229

Based on this calculation, the Children's Department should not be eliminated even though it shows a net loss. The department contributed to the earnings of the Com-

	Operating Costs Charged to Children's Dept.	Effect of Elimination of Children's Dept.	
		Eliminated	Not Eliminated
Variable Costs			
Advertising	$ 429	$ 429	
Salesmen's Salaries	3,515	3,515	
Commissions	240	240	
Insurance	120	120	
Bad Debts	50	50	
General	100	100	
Fixed Costs			
Rent	1,440		$1,440
Depreciation–Store Equipment	100		100
Supervisor's Salary	1,301		1,301
Office Salaries	579		579
Heat and Light	300		300
Totals	$8,174	$4,454	$3,720

Figure 22-7.
Effect on Costs of Elimination of Children's Department

pany by absorbing a part of the fixed expenses. Elimination of the department will reduce net operating income by $3,316.

Children's Department fixed costs (Figure 22-7)	$3,720
Deduct net loss (Figure 22-6)	404
Reduction in net operating income	$3,316

If this department were discontinued, the other departments would have to absorb the remaining $3,316 of fixed costs, resulting in a comparable decrease in the combined net income.

Another way of verifying this information is to compute the marginal income earned by the Children's Department: revenue of $34,400, less variable costs of $31,084 (cost of goods sold of $26,630 plus variable operating expenses of $4,454), equals $3,316, the advantage to the total firm of continuing the Children's Department.

In this example, the information used is net operating income (or income before income taxes and other expenses and revenue). Since a loss reduces income taxes, the value of the Children's Department to the total firm would be in reality larger than the $3,316 indicated. The effect of income taxes on the decision was ignored to simplify the problem. Of course, income taxes are pertinent to the problem, but their inclusion in this instance will not change the final decision.

There are, in addition, certain intangible factors that would result from the elimination of the Children's Department and that cannot be measured by an analysis of the income statement. This department brings in customers; business may be lost because some customers will not be able to buy clothing for the entire family in one location. Furthermore, customers who intend to purchase children's clothing only are exposed to the displays of the other two departments, which may result in additional purchases from these other departments. Also, the reduction in the volume of purchases may have a negative effect on the ability of the Company to get quantity discounts.

SUMMARY

Although useful in measuring periodic net income, the costs reported in financial statements are often meaningless in the solution of short-run business decisions; therefore, other costs must be developed to satisfy management's requirements.

The word *cost* has many different meanings, some of which are: (1) Fixed costs are those costs that, without change in present productive capacity, are not affected by changes in volume of output. (2) Variable costs are those that change in proportion to changes in volume of output. (3) Marginal, or differential, cost is the difference in cost between two levels of output, or the additional cost necessary to produce an additional unit. In other words, the marginal cost for a specific decision is the variable cost plus any additional fixed cost that will result from the decision to be made. (4) Opportunity cost is the sacrifice involved in accepting one alternative under consideration rather than following another course of action. (5) Out-of-pocket costs are costs that require cash expenditures. (6) Sunk cost are costs that do not involve a new cash expenditure but have arisen from actions taken in the past, and thus are unaffected by a current decision.

There is no cost that is acceptable for all decision-making purposes; cost calculations that serve one purpose do not always serve another purpose. The calculation, therefore, must be tailored to fit the specific decision being analyzed. Most business decisions are results of comparisons of alternative courses of action. In comparing alternatives, costs that are the same under each alternative should be ignored; only those costs that are different under the alternatives are relevant to the decision. In decision-making, all relevant costs are present costs or expected future costs; past events cannot be affected by a current decision and thus are irrelevant to current decisions.

The break-even point is the volume of sales at which a company neither realizes a net income nor incurs a net loss. The break-even chart graphically depicts the relationships between variable and fixed costs, revenue, and income. Break-even analysis is an aid to management in budgeting, income planning, and other decisions because it spotlights the effect on income of changes in volume, product mix, variable costs, and fixed costs. The use of break-even analysis is subject to certain limitations: (1) The assumption that all costs are either fixed or variable is an oversimplification since many costs behave erratically with changes in volume, especially outside a relatively limited volume range; (2) if the break-even chart is based on one period or only a few periods, the results obtained may not be typical of the company's experience; and (3) a break-even chart assumes a specific product mix; any change in the product mix invalidates the previous break-even chart.

In a marginal income statement, costs are divided into fixed and variable, rather than by the nature of the expenditure, as in the conventional income statement. Thus, the contribution of sales revenue toward the recovery of fixed costs and the earning of income is emphasized. The separation of costs in such a manner is useful for decision-making purposes, since the effect of any prospective changes can be quickly determined. The margin of safety is the dollar volume of sales above the break-even point or the percentage by which sales may decrease before a loss is incurred.

A special offer to produce additional units beyond outstanding plans and commitments should be accepted if there is a resultant marginal income (excess of revenue from the offer over the marginal cost of producing the additional units) and if there are no adverse effects on regular sales and business operations.

The determination of the optimum selling price of a product involves a thorough analysis of the intricate relationships between price, cost, and volume. Generally, the unit price of a product should be the one that yields the greatest marginal income.

If the marginal cost of producing an item is less than its outside purchase price of an item, the item should be manufactured. Fixed costs (other than the additional fixed costs created by the production of the item) should be omitted from the determination of the marginal cost if the available productive capacity cannot be utilized in any other manner.

A seemingly unprofitable department, product, or territory should be discontinued or abandoned only if it produces no marginal income or the capacity presently devoted to it could be committed to a more profitable use.

Decision-making can seldom be reduced to simplified quantitative computations. Many intangible and qualitative factors that cannot be expressed in quantitative terms must also be analyzed and considered in conjunction with quantitative measures to reach the most appropriate decisions.

☐   **QUESTIONS**

Q22–1. Define the following terms: (a) sunk costs, (b) variable costs, and (c) out-of-pocket costs.

Q22–2. What is meant by the saying "Different costs for different purposes"? Illustrate by explaining how an element of depreciation might be treated differently, as a cost, for different purposes.

Q22–3. (a) Costs relevant to a decision must be present or estimated future costs. Explain. (b) Can past costs ever be relevant to a given decision?

Q22–4. (a) What is meant by the term *break-even point?* (b) How is it computed? (c) What are its practical applications? (d) What are its limitations?

Q22–5. Define the following terms: (a) operating capacity, (b) product mix, (c) margin of safety, and (d) marginal income statement.

Q22–6. Under what circumstances would it be advantageous for a manufacturer in this country to accept a long-term contract for his product from a foreign buyer?

Q22–7. The sales price of a product should be the amount that will result in the largest marginal income. Comment.

Q22–8. Is maximum income the sole objective in determining the sales price of a new product?

Q22–9. (a) What use does management make of cost data in deciding whether to make or buy a certain part? (b) Should fixed costs enter into the decision?

Q22–10. (a) Is it possible for one of three departments in a retail store to show a net loss even though its elimination would decrease the total net income of the entire store? (b) What other intangible factors must be considered when deciding whether or not a certain department should be eliminated?

□ **EXERCISES**

E22–1. The Windham Company estimates its costs at full capacity as follows:

| Fixed | $210,000 |
| Variable | 120,000 |

Fixed costs are constant at all levels of operation; variable costs vary in direct proportion to sales. Sales at full capacity are estimated at $400,000.

1. Calculate the break-even point.
2. Determine the break-even percentage of operating capacity.
3. Prepare a marginal income statement assuming full capacity sales.
4. Compute the margin of safety, expressed as a dollar amount.
5. Compute the margin of safety, expressed as percentage.

E22–2. For the year 1969, the Taylor Company estimates fixed costs at $195,000 and variable costs at $1.30 per unit.

1. How many units must be sold to break even, assuming a unit sales price of $3.25?
2. Prepare an income statement in proof of your answer.

E22–3. The Runmoor Company has fixed costs of $440,000 per year. Its variable costs are $6.60 per unit and its sales price is $11 per unit. It is considering the purchase of machinery that will increase the fixed costs to $512,000 per year, but will enable the Company to reduce variable costs to $4.84 per unit.

1. Compute the break-even point before and after the acquisition of the new machinery, giving it in both sales dollars and units of product.
2. If net income before the acquisition is $88,000, how many units will have to be sold after the machinery is acquired to maintain the net income?

E22–4. The fixed costs in the Eastern Division of the Longhorn Company are now $736,000 per year. They are expected to increase to $760,000 next year. Variable costs will also go up from $4.40 to $4.80 per unit. Its product sells for $9.60 per unit.

How much sales revenue must be obtained to have a net income (before taxes) of $72,000 next year?

E22–5. A new machine costing $320,000 is under consideration. The product it makes sells for $10 per unit and requires materials costing $2.20, direct labor of $3.20, and other variable costs of $.30 per unit. Sales of 40,000 units per year are assumed. Applicable annual fixed costs other than depreciation amount to $12,000.

Over what period of time would this investment be recovered?

E22–6. The Jason Company manufactures and sells 1,500,000 units of its product in the United States annually. The selling price per unit is $20, variable costs are $8 per unit, and fixed costs are $10 per unit.

Should the Company accept an additional order to sell 500,000 units abroad at (a) $7.50 per unit? (b) $7.90 per unit; (c) $9.00 per unit; (d) $10.50 per unit? Explain your answer to each question.

E22–7. The Jaxrow Company was organized early in 1969. During 1969, it produced 6,000 units and sold 5,600 units; costs for the year were:

Variable costs	
Direct materials	$21,600
Direct labor	28,800
Manufacturing overhead	34,500
Selling and administrative expenses	9,000
Fixed costs	
Manufacturing overhead	13,500
Selling and administrative expenses	6,000

The selling price per unit is $22.

1. Calculate the break-even point.
2. Prepare a marginal income statement.
3. Compute the margin of safety, expressed as a dollar amount.

E22–8. Rambler, Inc., can sell 22,000 units of its product at $8 per unit. The variable costs of this product are $3 per unit. However, a reduction in sales price to $6 per unit would increase units sold to 35,000. The greater volume of production would reduce variable costs to $2.50 per unit: fixed costs are expected to increase by $15,000.

Should Rambler, Inc., reduce its selling price? Explain and support with computations.

E22–9. The Colonial Company manufactures Parzine; unit costs are as follows:

Direct materials	$ 6
Direct labor	4
Variable overhead costs	2
Subtotal	$12
Fixed overhead costs	3
Total	$15

The Colonial Company can purchase this part for $13.40.

Should Parzine be purchased if: (a) fixed overhead unit cost of $3 is a sunk cost? (b) an alternative and profitable use can be made of the plant facilities now devoted to making Parzine?

E22–10. The following operational information is available for the Glass Department Store for 1969:

	Department			
	1	2	3	Total
Net operating income or (loss)	$10,000	$20,000	$(5,000)	$25,000
Marginal income	22,000	37,600	2,000	61,600

1. Should Department 3 be eliminated?
2. If Department 3 is eliminated and 1970's operating results for Departments 1 and 2 are the same as in 1969, how much higher (or lower) will the 1970 net operating income be?

☐ **DEMONSTRATION PROBLEMS**

DP22–1. (*Break-even sales; income planning in conjunction with expansion of plant facilities*) The Hall Manufacturing Company is operating at full capacity. It has under consideration a plan for the expansion of its plant facilities. Current and projected income statement data are as shown:

	Under Present Plant Facilities		Under Proposed Plant Facilities	
Sales		$1,000,000		$1,500,000
Variable costs	$400,000		$600,000	
Fixed costs	480,000	880,000	720,000	1,320,000
Net income		$ 120,000		$ 180,000

Required: 1. What is the present break-even point?
2. What is the break-even point under the proposed plan?
3. What will be the amount of sales necessary to realize the current net income of $120,000 under the proposed plan?
4. Prepare an income statement to prove your answer to Requirement 3.

DP22–2. (*Acceptance or rejection of an offer*) The Bootery Company is operating at 70 percent of capacity, producing 140,000 pairs of men's fancy boots annually. Actual unit cost and selling price data for the year 1969 are as follows:

Direct materials	$ 6
Direct labor	4
Variable overhead costs	2
Total variable costs	$12
Fixed overhead costs ($700,000 ÷ 140,000)	5
Total unit cost	$17
Selling price	$32

The Company has been offered a long-term contract to sell 50,000 pairs of men's boots annually to a Mexican importing firm at $14.50 per pair. This will not affect domestic sales. Fixed overhead costs of $700,000 as well as fixed selling and administrative costs of $1,000,000 will not be affected by the new order.

Required: Prepare comparative statements for management indicating whether or not this long-term contract should be accepted.

DP22–3. (*Product pricing*) After conducting a market survey of its new product, the Calvin Company prepared the following estimates:

Sales Price Per Unit	Estimated Sales (units)
$25	36,000
$24	46,000
$22	54,000
$21	58,000
$16	64,000

Variable costs are estimated at $5 per unit.

Required: Determine the price that will result in the maximum marginal income and the maximum net income.

DP22–4. (*Make or buy decision*) The Benjamin Manufacturing Company can produce a part for the following costs:

Direct materials	$ 4.50
Direct labor	6.00
Variable overhead costs	2.50
Subtotal	$13.00
Fixed overhead costs	4.00
Total unit costs	$17.00

The Company can purchase the part for $14.

Required: Should the part be purchased if: (a) fixed overhead unit cost of $4 is a sunk cost? (b) an alternative and profitable use can be made of those plant facilities now devoted to making the part?

DP22-5. (*Department abandonment*) The following condensed marginal income statement is available for the Slavino Department Store for 1969:

| | Department | | | |
	A	B	C	Total
Sales (net)	$350,000	$300,000	$250,000	$900,000
Variable costs	180,000	270,000	120,000	570,000
Marginal income	$170,000	$ 30,000	$130,000	$330,000
Fixed costs	100,000	80,000	68,000	248,000
Net operating income (or loss)	$ 70,000	$ (50,000)	$ 62,000	$ 82,000

Required: 1. Should Department B be eliminated? Explain.
2. Assume that none of the fixed costs can be eliminated if Department B is abandoned, and that the 1970 operational results for Departments A and C are the same as in 1969. Prepare a condensed marginal income statement for 1970, assuming that Department B is eliminated.

☐ **PROBLEMS**

P22-1. The management of the Murrell Corporation prepared the following budgeted income statement for the year 1969:

	Fixed	Variable	
Estimated sales (70,000 units at $25)			$1,750,000
Estimated costs			
Direct materials		$266,000	
Direct labor		140,000	
Factory overhead	$410,000	320,000	
Selling	80,000	41,000	
Administrative	60,000	20,500	
	$550,000	$787,500	1,337,500
Estimated net income			$ 412,500

Required: 1. (a) Compute the break-even point.
(b) Prove the break-even point.
(c) Compute the break-even point expressed as a percentage of operating capacity.
(d) Compute the break-even point in units, assuming a constant product mix.

(e) Compute the margin of safety, expressed both as a percentage and as a dollar amount.

2. Prepare a marginal income statement.

3. Prepare a break-even chart.

P22-**2.** The estimate of the Kozy Korner Manufacturing Company is that fixed costs will total $720,000 during 1969 and that variable costs will be $7 per unit.

Required: 1. At a selling price of $15 per unit, at what level of revenue will the Company break even?

2. At a selling price of $16 per unit, at what level of revenue will the Company break even?

3. In order to earn $500,000 before taxes, how many units will have to be sold at a price of $15.50?

P22-**3.** The Eason Company can sell 44,000 units of its product at $16 per unit. The variable costs of this product are $6 per unit. However, a reduction in sales price to $14 per unit would increase units sold to 50,000. The greater volume of production would reduce variable costs to $5 per unit; fixed costs are expected to increase by $60,000.

Required: Should the Eason Company reduce its selling price? Explain, showing supporting computations.

P22-**4.** The condensed income statement for Kings, Inc., is given:

KINGS, INC.
Condensed Income Statement
For the Year Ended December 31, 1969

Net Sales		$500,000
Deduct Costs and Expenses		
Variable	$250,000	
Fixed	150,000	400,000
Net Income		$100,000

The directors of Kings, Inc., are considering a plant expansion program from the present 100-percent sales capacity of $500,000 to $750,000. The expansion would increase annual fixed costs by $75,000. Variable costs would remain directly proportional to sales, and the expansion would not change the current relationship of variable costs to sales.

Required: 1. What is the current break-even point?

2. What will the break-even point be under the proposed plan?

3. What dollar amount of sales is required under the proposed plan to equal the current net income of $100,000?

4. Prepare an income statement to prove your answer to Requirement 3.

P22-**5.** The Brandnu Corporation is considering whether to purchase some special machines. Management does not wish to buy the machines unless their cost can be recovered in three years. The following information is available:

1. Cost of the machines is $360,000.

2. Sales revenue generated by new machines is estimated to be $400,000.

3. Variable cost is 60% of sales.
4. Annual fixed costs other than depreciation total $12,000.

> Required: 1. Based on the criterion of the three-year recovery period, should the special machines be purchased? Support your answer with a computation of the period of time required for the investment of $360,000 to be recovered.
> 2. Discuss briefly any other factors that should be considered by management in deciding whether to acquire the special machines.

P22-**6.** The Langenderfer Company is currently operating at its full capacity of 200,000 units annually. Costs are as follows:

Direct materials	$400,000
Direct labor	200,000
Variable overhead	100,000
Fixed overhead	60,000
Variable selling and administrative expenses	40,000
Fixed selling and administrative expenses	30,000

The product is sold under Langenderfer Company brand for $6.15. Humphrey Distributors, Inc.; offers to purchase 50,000 units annually for the next five years at $4.10 per unit. This offer, if accepted, will not affect the current selling price because Humphrey Distributors will sell under its own brand name. Acceptance of the offer will have the following results:

1. Labor costs on the additional 50,000 units will be 1½ times the regular rate.
2. Variable selling and administrative expenses will increase by $0.05 per unit on the additional units only.
3. The required additional materials can be purchased at a 5% volume discount.
4. All other cost factors will remain the same.

> Required: Should Langenderfer Company accept the offer? Show all your computations in support of your conclusion.

P22-**7.** The Harding Company has the facilities to produce two additional products, Florex and Byxine, which require approximately the same production processes. The following data were made available to management to aid in establishing sales prices and product mix:

Florex		Byxine	
Estimated Sales Units	Sales Price Per Unit	Estimated Sales Units	Sales Price Per Unit
6,000	$65	4,500	$76
7,250	61	7,500	70
10,250	47	10,500	65
Variable costs per unit are $25.		Variable costs per unit are $35.	

> Required: What product mix of Florex and Byxine will result in the largest marginal income?

P22-**8.** The Roosevelt Company is presently purchasing five parts used in the manufacture of its finished product. Comparative costs to manufacture the parts and to
buy them outside are as shown:

Part No.	Estimated Materials, Labor, and Variable Overhead to Make	Cost to Buy
1	$20.00	$18.00
2	7.50	8.50
3	5.50	6.50
4	7.00	5.00
5	10.00	9.00
Totals	$50.00	$47.00

The Roosevelt Company has the capacity to produce these parts, and at the present time it has no alternative profitable use for the facilities. Making the parts will
not increase fixed costs.

Required: 1. What is the proper decision?
2. Assume that the Roosevelt Company is presently purchasing 20,000 units of each part annually, that it can use the
available plant facilities to make and sell annually 10,000
units of a new product without increasing fixed costs, and
that this will result in an estimated marginal income of
$6.50 per unit. What is the proper decision under these
circumstances?

P22-**9.** The management of the Wright Company is considering the elimination of Department B. The departmentalized income statement follows:

WRIGHT COMPANY
Income Statement
For the Year Ended December 31, 1969

	Dept. A	Dept. B	Combined
Sales (net)	$134,000	$45,000	$179,000
Cost of Goods Sold	68,000	30,000	98,000
Gross Margin on Sales	$ 66,000	$15,000	$ 81,000
Operating Expenses			
Advertising Expense	$ 4,200	$ 1,200	$ 5,400
Salesmen's Salaries	10,000	6,000	16,000
Office Salaries	3,500	1,700	5,200
Insurance Expense	900	600	1,500
Bad Debts Expense	1,000	500	1,500
Miscellaneous General Expenses	1,800	900	2,700
Rent Expense	11,000	5,000	16,000
Depreciation Expense–Store Equipment	2,000	1,200	3,200
Total Operating Expenses	$ 34,400	$17,100	$ 51,500
Net Operating Income or (Loss)	$ 31,600	$ (2,100)	$ 29,500

The following additional data have been submitted to management relative to the proposed elimination of Department B:

1. There will be a 10% decline in the sales of Department A. The cost of goods sold varies directly with the sales volume.
2. The operating expenses of Department A will decrease as follows:
   a. Insurance Expense by 5%
   b. Bad Debts Expense by 8%
   c. Miscellaneous General Expenses by 10%
3. The elimination of Department B will have the following effect on the operating expenses of Department B:
   a. Advertising Expense, Salesmen's Salaries, Insurance Expense, and Bad Debts Expense will be eliminated.
   b. Of the apportioned Miscellaneous General Expenses, 80% will not be incurred.
   c. Office salaries will be reduced by $900 through the dismissal of some part-time employees.
   d. There will be no reduction in Rent Expense or in Depreciation Expense–Store Equipment.

Required: 1. Prepare a statement showing the probable effect on operating costs if Department B is eliminated.
2. Prepare a statement showing the effect on net income if Department B is eliminated.

P22–10. The Taylor Company has three sales territories, X, Y, and Z. Management is considering the elimination of Territory X. The following condensed information has been prepared to aid in making this decision:

TAYLOR COMPANY
Marginal Income Statement
For the Year Ended December 31, 1969

| | Territory | | | |
	X	Y	Z	Total
Sales (net)	$175,000	$200,000	$300,000	$675,000
Variable Costs	105,000	80,000	120,000	305,000
Marginal Income	$ 70,000	$120,000	$180,000	$370,000
Fixed Costs	100,000	50,000	75,000	225,000
Net Operating Income (or Loss)	$ (30,000)	$ 70,000	$105,000	$145,000

None of the fixed costs of Territory X can be eliminated.

Required: Prepare a report to aid management in deciding whether to discontinue Territory X.

CASE PROBLEM
Parham Oil Company

The Parham Oil Company operates a chain of service stations throughout the local area. Each station sells the usual service station products: gasoline, oil, tires, batteries, automobile accessories, and so on. All the products are purchased in bulk by the home office and delivered on a scheduled basis to each station. If a station manager foresees that the quantities he will need will vary by more than 5 percent from the scheduled quantities, he calls the home office at least twenty-four hours in advance of the anticipated delivery time and changes the standing order.

Being an astute businessman, Otis Lester, the president and major stockholder of the Company, has the accountant of the Company prepare a separate income statement for each station. Also, he often asks for income statements by product line within each station. However, his main concern at this time is the poor overall operating results of the station located in Johnson City. This station was once considered profitable, but since a nearby military base was closed, business has declined. The most recent income statement is typical of each of the past three years.

Sales		$110,632
Cost of Goods Sold		86,293
Gross Margin on Sales		$ 24,339
Operating Expenses (listed alphabetically)		
Advertising (Company-oriented and allocated equally to each station)	$ 950	
Attendants' Salaries (the number of attendants is adequate for the current volume)	10,500	
Depreciation–Building and Equipment	5,000	
Home Office Expenses (allocated to each station based on station sales)	4,500	
Insurance (fire and public liability)	700	
Interest on Average Book Investment (a book charge only; all long-term funds are provided by the stockholders)	4,800	
Local Property Taxes and Privilege Licenses	382	
Manager's Bonus	400	
Manager's Salary	4,800	
Payroll Taxes (attendants' salaries and manager's salary and bonus)	1,042	
Repairs and Maintenance (on building and equipment)	275	
Station Supplies	3,500	
Utilities (electricity, heat, telephone, and water)	310	
Total Operating Expenses		37,159
Net Loss		$ (12,820)

Required: 1. As a management consultant with the local certified public accounting firm, what would you recommend to Lester as the course of action regarding the station in Johnson City? Some possibilities are (a) to continue to operate as is, (b) to discontinue operation, (c) to initiate local advertising, and (d) to sell the station. If your recommendation is to sell the station, what is the minimum amount that Lester should accept?

2. Give the reason(s) for your recommendation.

3. What overall business objective will your recommendation help to achieve? Justify this objective.

4. Support your recommendation with appropriate computations.

5. Identify some nonaccounting factors that could influence a decision of this type.

6. Which accounting techniques, if any, do you think should be changed? How should they be changed? Why should they be changed?
7. If the division into variable and fixed costs remains as it is and current accounting procedures are continued, by how much must sales increase in order for this station to break even?
8. How much must sales be in order for this station to report a net income of $10,000?

Chapter
Twenty-Three

Capital
Budgeting

Measurement techniques used in capital budget decision-making give effect to the *time value of money;* that is, to the factor of compound interest. For this reason, the first part of this chapter includes a summary of the fundamentals of compound interest. The second part of the chapter deals with the systematic evaluation of long-term capital investment projects.

SIMPLE INTEREST

Simple interest is earned in direct proportion to the time during which the amount of money, or principal, is used. The simple interest on $100 for four years at 6 percent per year is:

Principal	$ 100
Multiply by rate of interest	0.06
Equals interest for one year	$ 6
Multiply by number of years principal is used	4
Simple interest on $100 for 4 years at 6%	$ 24

The interest rate is applied to the principal at the beginning; the fact that the amount is increased at the end of each interest period by the interest for that period is ignored.

COMPOUND INTEREST

Compound interest is interest earned on a principal sum that is increased at the end of each period by the interest for that period. The interest compounded annually on $100 for four years at 6 percent per year is:

1	2	3	4
		Annual	Accumulated Amount
	Amount at	Amount	at End
	Beginning	of Interest	of Year
Year	of Year	(Col. 2 × 0.06)	(Col. 2 + Col. 3)
1	$100.00	$ 6.00	$106.00
2	106.00	6.36	112.36
3	112.36	6.74	119.10
4	119.10	7.15	126.25
Total		$26.25	

The principal of $100 at the beginning of year 1 has by year 4 grown to $126.25, the *compound amount.*

Each amount in Column 4 is 106 percent of the corresponding amount in Column 2. This means that 106 percent, or 1.06, has been used as a multiplier four times; 1.06 has been raised to the fourth power. The compound amount is therefore $100 multiplied by 1.06 to the fourth power, as shown:

$$1.06^4 \qquad\qquad 1.2625$$
$$\text{Multiplied by principal} \qquad \$\ \ \ 100$$
$$\text{Compound amount} \qquad \$126.25$$

The compound amount of 1 for n periods is expressed by the following formula:

$$a = (1 + i)^n, \text{ where}$$

$a = $ Compound amount of 1 ($1, or any other monetary unit) at interest for n periods
$n = $ Number of periods
$i = $ Periodic interest rate

The difference between the compound amount and the original principal is the compound interest. The compound interest (I) on 1 for four periods at 6 percent is computed as follows:

$$I = (1 + i)^n - 1$$
$$= (1 + .06)^4 - 1$$
$$= 1.2625 - 1$$
$$= 0.2625$$

The calculation of compound interest on $100 for four years at 6 percent compounded annually is shown:

$$\$100 \times 0.2625 = \$26.25$$

Present Value

If $100 is worth $126.25 when it is left at 6 percent compound interest each year for four years, then it follows that $126.25 four years from now is worth $100 now; that is, $100 is the *present value* of $126.25. The present value is the amount that must be invested now to produce the known future value. In compound-amount problems, the future value of a known present value must be determined; in present-value problems, the present value of a known future value must be determined. If the known future value is $126.25, then the amount that must be invested now at 6 percent compounded annually to produce $126.25 is $100. The computation is as shown:

$$\frac{\$126.25}{(1 + 0.06)^4} = \frac{\$126.25}{1.2625} = \$100$$

The general formula for the present value (p) of 1 due in any number of periods is as follows:

$$p = \frac{1}{(1 + i)^n}$$

The present value of 1 at 6-percent interest compounded annually for four years is computed as shown:

$$p = \frac{1}{(1 + i)^n} = \frac{1}{(1 + 0.06)^4} = \frac{1}{1.2625} = 0.79208$$

If the present value of 1 is 0.79208, then the present value of $126.25 is computed as follows:

$$\$126.25 \times 0.79208 = \$100$$

If $100 is deposited at 6 percent interest compounded annually, it will amount to $126.25 in four years.

Compound Discount

Compound discount (D) is the difference between the future value and the present value; it is expressed by the following formula:

$$D = 1 - \frac{1}{(1 + i)^n}$$

The compound discount on 1 at 6 percent interest, compounded annually, is:

$$D = 1 - \frac{1}{(1 + i)^n} = 1 - 0.79208 = 0.20792$$

Ordinary Annuity—Amount

An *ordinary annuity* is the sum of a series of equal payments or deposits at the end of equal intervals of time plus compound interest on these payments. The value of the annuity at the end of the successive time periods is the *amount of the annuity*. The calculation of the amount of an ordinary annuity of four payments of $100 each at 6 percent is shown in Figure 23-1.

1	2	3	4	5
Period	Beginning Balance	Interest Earned (6% × Col. 2)	Periodic Payment	Accumulated at End of Period (Col. 2 + Col. 3 + Col. 4)
1	$ -0-	$ -0-	$100	$100.00
2	100.00	6.00	100	206.00
3	206.00	12.36	100	318.36
4	318.36	19.10	100	437.46

Figure 23-1.
Amount of an Ordinary Annuity

The formula for finding the amount (A) of an ordinary annuity of 1 is as follows:

$$A = \frac{(1 + i)^n - 1}{i}$$

Since the numerator of this equation is the compound interest (I), the equation may be restated as:

$$A = \frac{I}{i}$$

The amount of an ordinary annuity of $100 for four years at 6 percent interest compounded annually may be computed directly as follows:

$$A = \frac{I}{i} = \frac{0.2625}{0.06} \times \$100 = \$437.50$$

Figure 23-1 shows the amount to be $437.46. The $0.04 difference is due to rounding.

Ordinary Annuity—Present Value

The present value of an ordinary annuity is the present value of a series of payments to be made at equal intervals in the future. That is, it is the single sum that, if invested at compound interest now, provides for a stated series of payments or withdrawals at equal time intervals. The formula for the present value of an ordinary annuity of 1 is as follows:

$$P = \frac{1 - \dfrac{1}{(1 + i)^n}}{i}$$

Since the numerator of this equation is the compound discount, the equation may be restated as shown:

$$P = \frac{D}{i}$$

The present value of an ordinary annuity of four payments of $100 at 6 percent is calculated as shown:

$$P = \frac{D}{i} = \frac{0.20792}{0.06} \times \$100 = \$346.53$$

The proof that the present value of an ordinary annuity of four payments of $100 at 6 percent is $346.53 is shown:

Amount invested	$346.53
Interest earned, 1st period (6% × $346.53)	20.79
Amount at end of 1st period	$367.32
Deduct 1st payment	100.00
Balance of investment at beginning of 2d period	$267.32
Interest earned, 2d period (6% × $267.32)	16.04
Amount at end of 2d period	$283.36
Deduct 2d payment	100.00
Balance of investment at beginning of 3d period	$183.36
Interest earned, 3d period (6% × $183.36)	11.00
Amount at end of 3d period	$194.36
Deduct 3d payment	100.00
Balance of investment at beginning of 4th period	$ 94.36

Interest earned, 4th period (6% × $94.36)	5.66
Amount at end of 4th period	$100.02
Deduct 4th payment	100.00
Total (difference is due to rounding)	$000.02

The four basic formulas may be summarized in chart form, using the abbreviated notations, as follows:

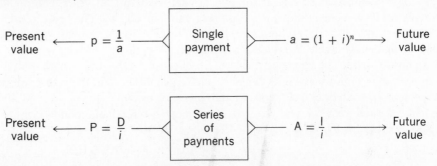

Since $p = 1/a$, $D = 1 - p$, and $I = a - 1$, the formula for the amount of 1, $a = (1 + i)^n$ is the source for the derivation of the other formulas. (Present value and future value tables are available and are in common use in banking, industry, and elsewhere.)

Present Value Tables

Table A shows the present value of $1 for interest rates ranging from 8 to 25 percent and for interest periods ranging from 1 to 25. For example, the figure in the 10% column for Period 10 is 0.386. This means that $1 due at the end of ten years, compounded annually at 10-percent interest, if discounted, has a present value of $.386; that is, if $.386 were invested today at 10-percent interest compounded annually, it

Table A

Present Value of $1

$$p = \frac{1}{(1 + i)^n}$$

Period	8%	10%	12%	14%	16%	18%	20%	25%
1	0.926	0.909	0.893	0.877	0.862	0.847	0.833	0.800
2	0.857	0.826	0.797	0.769	0.743	0.718	0.694	0.640
3	0.794	0.751	0.712	0.675	0.641	0.609	0.579	0.512
4	0.735	0.683	0.636	0.592	0.552	0.516	0.482	0.410
5	0.681	0.621	0.567	0.519	0.476	0.437	0.402	0.328
6	0.630	0.564	0.507	0.456	0.410	0.370	0.335	0.262
7	0.583	0.513	0.452	0.400	0.354	0.314	0.279	0.210
8	0.540	0.467	0.404	0.351	0.305	0.266	0.233	0.168
9	0.500	0.424	0.361	0.308	0.263	0.225	0.194	0.134
10	0.463	0.386	0.322	0.270	0.227	0.191	0.162	0.107
15	0.315	0.239	0.183	0.140	0.108	0.084	0.065	0.035
20	0.215	0.149	0.104	0.073	0.051	0.037	0.026	0.012
25	0.146	0.092	0.059	0.038	0.024	0.016	0.010	0.004

would accumulate to $1 in ten years. The figures in the table are *discount factors* that, when multiplied by any known future amount, produce the present value equivalent of that amount. For example, to produce $6,750 ten years from now, at 10-percent interest compounded annually, $6,750 × 0.386, or $2,605.50, must be deposited.

Table B shows the present values of series of payments to be made at equal intervals in the future. For example, the figure in the 10% column for Period 10 is 6.145. This means that $1 due at the end of each year for ten years, compounded annually at 10-percent interest, has a present value of $6.145. The same result can be obtained by using the discount factors from Table A to accumulate each present value in the series. Table B shortens the process by giving a single discount factor for an entire series. The figures in Table B are discount factors that, when multiplied by any series of uniform amounts due at regular equal intervals in the future, produce the present equivalent of that series of amounts. For example, to produce $1,250 at the end of each year for ten years at 10 percent interest compounded annually, $1,250 × 6.145, or $7,681.25, must be deposited.

Table B

Present Value of $1 Received Annually for N Years $P = \dfrac{1 - \dfrac{1}{(1 + i)^n}}{i}$

Period	8%	10%	12%	14%	16%	18%	20%	25%
1	0.926	0.909	0.893	0.877	0.862	0.847	0.833	0.800
2	1.783	1.736	1.690	1.647	1.605	1.566	1.528	1.440
3	2.577	2.487	2.402	2.322	2.246	2.174	2.106	1.952
4	3.312	3.170	3.037	2.914	2.798	2.690	2.589	2.362
5	3.993	3.791	3.605	3.433	3.274	3.127	2.991	2.689
6	4.623	4.355	4.111	3.889	3.685	3.498	3.326	2.951
7	5.206	4.868	4.564	4.288	4.039	3.812	3.605	3.161
8	5.747	5.335	4.968	4.639	4.344	4.078	3.837	3.329
9	6.247	5.759	5.328	4.946	4.607	4.303	4.031	3.463
10	6.710	6.145	5.650	5.216	4.833	4.494	4.192	3.571
15	8.559	7.606	6.811	6.142	5.575	5.092	4.675	3.859
20	9.818	8.514	7.469	6.623	5.929	5.353	4.870	3.954
25	10.675	9.077	7.843	6.873	6.097	5.467	4.948	3.985

BUDGETING CAPITAL EXPENDITURES

Capital budgeting refers to the allocation and commitment of funds to long-term capital investment projects. Such investments or expenditures are usually large in amount and are made in expectation of benefits to be received over a number of years. Capital budgeting concerns itself with the development, selection, and evaluation of proposals for plant expansion and modernization, equipment replacement, product development, and so on. The nature of these investments and their effect on the long-range welfare of a company make it imperative that they be analyzed and evaluated with the utmost care.

Types of Capital Expenditure

The types of capital expenditure can perhaps best be illustrated by questions involving capital investment decisions, such as the following:

1. *Expansion.* Shall we buy additional equipment to supply the actual or anticipated increase in demand for our product? Shall we expand our facilities to produce new products? Shall we acquire the necessary facilities to make parts that we are now buying from outside sources? Shall we conduct a new type of advertising campaign to boost our product?
2. *Replacement.* Shall we replace present equipment with new and more efficient equipment? Shall we automate our production lines? Shall we buy Machine A or Machine B? Shall we lease the new equipment or shall we buy it?
3. *Other.* Some investments are made on noneconomic grounds. Expenditures for recreational facilities for use by employees, for example, are not made to reduce costs or increase revenue, but rather to improve employer-employee relations. An investment to eliminate sound nuisances or smoke hazards may be made in compliance with local ordinances; but even if it is not mandatory, a company may choose to make such an investment to improve its relations with the local community.

Rate of Return

Businessmen make investments to get a satisfactory return. What constitutes a satisfactory rate of return depends on a number of factors, including available funds, available investment opportunities, the cost of obtaining funds, and the degree of uncertainty and risk. In the long run, the rate of return must be adequate to attract new capital.

The choice of an appropriate rate of return is central to the capital budgeting decision since it has a direct influence on the decision. The choice may be based on the *investment opportunity* concept, which is a subjective evaluation of the available investment opportunities and their respective earnings rates. The selected rate of return is the rate that the funds could earn if they were invested in the best available alternative project. Since funds used on Project A, for example, are not available for use on Project B, the amount that could have been earned on Project B is sacrificed. The amount or rate so sacrificed constitutes an opportunity cost, or the minimum rate that must be earned on Project A, the project chosen.

The choice of a cutoff rate may be based on a different concept, the *cost of capital.* The premise for the use of the cost of capital as the minimum rate of return is that the project ought to earn at least as much as the cost of the funds invested in the project. The measurement of the cost of capital is complex. It is a weighted average of the cost of funds—dividends and interest—obtained from shareholders and long-term debtors. The implication is that all funds, external debts as well as stockholders' equity (including retained earnings), have a cost. Since the quantity and the cost of the different forms of capital vary, a weighted average is used in the cost of capital computation.

Budgeting Decisions

The capital budgeting decision involves making a choice among alternatives. Available proposals usually exceed available funds, so that a system must be established for ranking the proposals and selecting the most desirable ones. Since the capital budgeting decision is an investment decision, it may be subjected to the same criterion that any prudent investor uses; that is, the gain or the rate of return to be realized on the investment. This, in turn, furnishes the rationale for the selection once the desired minimum rate of return has been fixed.

Present Value Concept

The present value concept refers to the conversion of cash inflows and outflows over a period of time to a common point in time for purposes of comparing capital expenditures. The concepts of compound amounts and present values are used in this conversion process: Since dollar amounts can be moved forward in time by compounding or backward in time by discounting, direct comparisons can be made of cash flows occurring in different periods. If, for example, an investment in a piece of equipment will reduce operating costs by $100 a year for four years, and the company has opportunities to invest its funds in other projects yielding a return of 10 percent a year, it can afford to pay $317 for this piece of equipment and still realize a 10-percent rate of return on the investment. The factor comes from the 10% column for Period 4 in Table B. The computation is as follows:

$$\$100 \times 3.170 = \$317$$

The Company could pay $317 for the equipment even if it had to borrow the $317 at 10-percent interest. The fact that the company could repay the loan and interest with the funds derived from the annual $100 costs savings and still be as well off as it would be before the equipment was purchased is demonstrated by the following calculation:

Amount borrowed	$317.00
Interest for 1st year	31.70
Total	$348.70
First payment	100.00
Amount due at beginning of 2d period	$248.70
Interest for 2d year	24.87
Total	$273.57
Second payment	100.00
Amount due at beginning of 3d period	$173.57
Interest for 3d year	17.36
Total	$190.93
Third payment	100.00
Amount due at beginning of 4th period	$ 90.93
Interest 4th year	9.09
Total	$100.02
Fourth payment	100.02

The discrepancy of $0.02 is due to rounding. Payments are assumed to have been made at the end of each year. The assumed saving of $100 each year in operating costs enables the company to recover the loan or the investment of $317 plus annual interest of 10 percent on the unrecovered balance.

Capital expenditures are subject to the same test as any other kind of investment: the earning of a satisfactory profit. Investments in government securities are, of course, qualitatively different from investments in machinery because the element of certainty of return on the investment is greater. But the essential objectives of the two types of investment are the same: a satisfactory rate of return. Since sums moved forward or backward in time can be converted to a comparable basis by the factor $(1 + i)^n$ or its reciprocal, $\dfrac{1}{(1 + i)^n}$, the application of present value factors to the solution of capital budgeting problems follows logically. The formulas that apply to the analysis of financial investments apply equally to the analysis of capital expenditures.

COMPARING CAPITAL EXPENDITURES

DETERMINING THE RELEVANT CASH FLOWS. A capital investment generates a flow of cash into and out of the business over a period of time. A comparison of several investment projects from which the best choice is to be made involves a comparison of the expected cash flows under the several alternatives. The concern is with future—not past—costs, and with relevant costs; that is, the costs that will be different. Clearly, a cost or revenue amount that will be the same under all the alternatives from which a choice is to be made is not relevant since it will not change the decision. The appropriateness for the emphasis on cash flow to the exclusion of valuations based on generally accepted accounting principles must be considered within the context of the capital budgeting problem. The measurement of revenue and expense—the measurement of net income—*is not* relevant to the timing of the related cash flows. The measurement of a rate of return on a specific investment proposal *is* affected by the timing of the cash flows due to the time value of money. There is no conflict between conventional income measurements and rate of return measurements; the goals and end-uses of each are different.

Present Value Method

The measurement of a proposed capital expenditure by the present value method requires a determination of the following:

1. The net cash investment
2. The net cash inflows
3. The estimated useful life of the investment
4. Excess present value

For example, assume that the West Company is planning to buy a new press for $25,000, with an estimated useful life of ten years. Freight and installation costs will be $1,500. The press being replaced originally cost $20,000, has a carrying value of $8,000 and a remaining life of ten years, and can be sold for $4,000. The new press is not expected to change revenue but is expected to reduce labor costs, including fringe benefits, by $5,500, and to increase power costs by $1,000. Maintenance, taxes, and insurance will be unchanged. The advisability of the replacement is being questioned. The Company's cost of capital is 14 percent.

Step 1: Net Cash Investment. The initial step in the measurement of the rate of return is to determine the net amount of the initial cash investment required by the specific capital expenditure proposed. This usually consists of the purchase price of the asset, transportation, installation, and any other costs incurred to prepare the asset for operation. If the project involves the replacement of an old asset, the proceeds from the sale of the old asset are deducted in arriving at the amount of the net investment.

The net cash investment for the West Company is computed as follows:

Purchase price of new press	$25,000
Freight and installation	1,500
Total	$26,500
Deduct proceeds from sale of old press	4,000
Net investment	$22,500

The carrying value of the old press is irrelevant because it represents a past, or sunk, cost, not a future cost. Whatever the carrying value, the net investment is $22,500. What is relevant is the selling price of the old machine because it represents a future cash flow.

Step 2: Net Cash Inflows. The West Company proposal falls into the cost reduction category. The relevant cash outflows are those costs that will be different— the *differential costs*—if the proposal is adopted. The expected change in annual operating cash flows will be as follows:

Cost decreases—labor	$5,500
Deduct cost increases—power	1,000
Net annual saving	$4,500

This step involves a careful analysis of all operating costs to determine which costs will be increased and which decreased. Only those cost changes that will change cash flows are relevant. Changes in costs due, for example, to changes in cost allocations without corresponding changes in cash flow are irrelevant for this purpose even though they are essential to the accounting process.

Step 3: Estimated Useful Life. The rate of return on an investment project is directly affected by the estimated useful life of the project. The serviceable life of an asset cannot be definitely known at the time of its acquisition, and it may be difficult to estimate, but an approximation or judgment must be made. The estimate is based not on physical life but on economic life. The question to be answered is: How long will the project contribute earnings to the firm? A machine with an estimated physical life of ten years may have to be replaced after only one year due to changes in the nature of the business—method of manufacture; location, type, or design of product; and so on. Advances in technology may necessitate replacement of an existing machine even if it is in perfect condition. The relevant factor is earning power, not necessarily physical life, the life used for financial reporting, or the life used for Federal income tax reporting.

Step 4: Excess Present Value. The relative desirability of an investment is indicated by the difference, at a common point of time, between the cost of the investment and the expected earnings from that investment discounted at the desired minimum rate. The greater the excess of the present value of the earnings over the net cash investment, the more desirable is the investment. Using the West Company figures, the excess present value is calculated as follows:

Present value of earnings at 14% rate: $4,500 × 5.216 (Table B)	$23,472
Net cash investment	22,500
Excess present value	$ 972

Since the present value of the earnings exceeds the investment, the project is desirable. If, however, the desired minimum is increased to 16 percent, the present value of the earnings is less than the investment; at 16 percent, therefore, the investment is undesirable. The computation is as follows:

Net cash investment	$22,500
Present value of earnings at 16%: $4,500 × 4.833 (Table B)	21,749
Excess of investment over present value	$ 751

EXCESS PRESENT VALUE INDEX. The excess present value index is the ratio of the present value of the earnings to the required investment. This ratio, or *profitability index*, is useful as a ranking device for investments varying in size and economic life. An index of 1.00 or more indicates that the earnings equal or exceed the desired minimum rate. The higher the index, the more desirable is the project. The indexes for the West Company at 14 percent and 16 percent are shown:

$$\frac{\text{Present value of earnings at 14\%}}{\text{Investment}} = \frac{\$23,472}{\$22,500} = 1.04$$

$$\frac{\text{Present value of earnings at 16\%}}{\text{Investment}} = \frac{\$21,749}{\$22,500} = 0.967$$

The index at 16 percent, being less than 1.00, indicates that the earnings are not high enough to earn a 16-percent return on the $22,500 investment.

Rate of Return Method

The net cash investment of the West Company ($22,500), the annual net cash earnings ($4,500), and the economic life (10 years) having been determined, these relationships can now be combined to compute a rate of return on the investment and, concurrently, the return of the investment. In the language of compound interest, the rate of return will be that rate—the *internal rate of return* or the *time-adjusted rate of return*—at which the present values of the cash inflows and outflows offset each other. The computation on page 790 shows, for example, that an investment of $317 now is exactly equal to a future inflow of $100 at the end of each year for four years at 10 percent interest. That is, the present value of the inflows exactly offsets the present outflow. This means that the rate of return on the $317 investment is exactly 10 percent.

The rate of return computation for the West Company involves finding a discount rate that, applied to the net cash inflows of $4,500 over the ten-year period, equals $22,500, the net cash investment. This can be found by the process of trial and error. When positive and negative present values are found, the exact rate can be discovered by interpolation. This procedure is illustrated later in this chapter. However, when the cash flows are *uniform*, as in the West Company problem, the time-consuming trial and error method can be avoided. The predicted annual earnings of $4,500 must, in each of the ten years, contribute to the recovery of a portion of the net cash investment of $22,500 and a return on the yet unrecovered portion of the investment. What is needed is a present value factor that, when applied to the annual cash inflows of $4,500, equals $22,500. This factor must be the net cash investment divided by the net cash inflow, or $22,500 ÷ $4,500 = 5

The quotient, 5, is the ratio of the investment to the annual earnings. The factors in Table B are likewise ratios of investments to earnings: of an investment of $1 to various rates and lives of earnings. Since the problem is to find a discount factor that, when applied to the earnings, exactly equals the investment, then that factor must be the investment (numerator) divided by the earnings (denominator).

Table B lists combinations of three elements: (1) economic life, (2) interest rate, and (3) discount factor. Given any two of these elements, the third element can be read off directly. Given the factor, 5, and the economic life, ten years, the third element, the rate, can be read directly from the table.

The rate of return can now be found by looking at Table B, in the row corresponding to the economic life, and for the factor closest to 5, the quotient of the investment divided by the earnings. The column heading under which this figure is found is the approximate rate. The factors in the 14% and 16% columns are 5.216 and 4.833. The rate may therefore be estimated at roughly 15 percent.

The trial-and-error method yields the same result. Assuming that the first rate tried was 14 percent and the next was 16 percent, the results would be as shown:

Net cash investment	$22,500
Present value of earnings at 14%: $4,500 × 5.216	23,472
Difference	$ 972

Net cash investment	$22,500
Present value of earnings at 16%: $4,500 × 4.833	21,749
Difference	$ (751)

The positive difference at 14 percent indicates a rate above 14 percent; the negative difference at 16 percent indicates a rate below 16 percent; the true rate is therefore between 14 percent and 16 percent. If an investment of $22,500 is made today with an estimated life of ten years, and if the required minimum rate of return is 15 percent, then the project will have to produce annual cash earnings of $4,500 to repay the investment.

Depreciation, Income Taxes, and Capital Budgeting

For financial and income tax reporting, the costs of plant and equipment assets are amortized over the useful lives of the assets; a portion of the cost of the assets is deducted from revenue in measuring net income. Such revenue deductions, although essential to the income measurement process, are irrelevant to the capital budgeting decision because they do not represent actual cash outflows. The inclusion of the entire net cash investment as a cash outflow makes it unnecessary to allocate portions of the cost over the asset's useful life as revenue deductions. Only the actual acquisition of the asset—not its allocation to income—involves cash. But the periodic depreciation deduction does reduce net income and therefore the amount of the income tax, which does represent a cash outflow. Furthermore, the use of accelerated depreciation methods has a direct effect on the pattern of the income tax cash outflows and thereby influences the rate of return.

Assuming that the West Company is subject to an income tax rate of 50 percent, the loss on the sale of the old press will result in a $2,000 tax benefit as shown below.

Carrying value	$8,000
Selling price	4,000
Deductible loss	$4,000
Tax rate	0.50
Tax deduction	$2,000

Although the book loss is $4,000, the net after-tax effect of the sale is a loss of only $2,000 since if the sale did not take place, the West Company's cash outflow for income taxes would be $2,000 greater. In this case, the net cash investment would be as shown:

Cost of new press		$26,500
Proceeds from sale of old press	$4,000	
Tax deduction from loss on sale of old press	2,000	6,000
Net cash investment		$20,500

If the old press were sold at a gain, the tax on the gain would be deducted from the proceeds in computing the net cash investment.

The depreciation deduction and income taxes affect not only the net investment but also the net cash outflow. The change in the annual depreciation deduction changes taxable net income, which, in turn, changes the net cash earnings after taxes. The net cash earnings after taxes for the West Company, assuming the use of the straight-line depreciation method, is as follows:

Annual cash savings before taxes		$4,500	$4,500
Increase in annual depreciation deduction			
On new press: 10% of $26,500	$2,650		
On old press: 10% of $20,000	2,000	650	
Increase in taxable net income		$3,850	
Income taxes: 50% of $3,850			1,925
Net cash earnings after taxes			$2,575

Irregular Cash Flow Patterns

The capital budgeting proposals discussed thus far involved a single present net cash investment and uniform savings over the entire life span. Some projects, however, produce irregular cash flow patterns. The present value of a stream of earnings is influenced directly by both the amount and the timing of the inflow. The rate of discount increases with time, so that cash inflows of early years have a higher present value than corresponding inflows of later years. The analysis must, therefore, identify both the amount and the time pattern by years. To illustrate, assume that a company makes an immediate investment of $100,000 in a plant to manufacture a new product.

796

Cost Accumulation, Cost Control, and Financial Planning

Earnings rise in the second year as the market for the product is developed, then fall in the third year under the impact of competition. An additional investment is made in year 3 for an intensive advertising campaign. Because of the uneven cash flow, each amount must be multiplied by the appropriate present value of 1 factor, as shown (assumed cost of capital is 20 percent):

Year	Cash Inflow (Outflow)	Present Value of $1 Discounted at 20% (Table A)	Present Value
1	$40,000	0.833	$ 33,320
2	50,000	0.694	34,700
3	25,000	0.579	14,475
	(10,000)	0.579	(5,790)
4	45,000	0.482	21,690
5	30,000	0.402	12,060
Total			$110,455

The excess present value and index are computed as follows:

Present value of cash flows	$110,455
Present value of original investment	100,000
Excess present value	$ 10,455
Excess present value index: $110,455 ÷ 100,000	1.10455

The exact rate of return may be found by trial and error. The cash flows are discounted, using different trial rates, until a rate is found at which the net present value is zero. At this rate the net inflows equal the amount of the investment. The trial-and-error computation, using trial rates of 20 and 25 percent, follows:

Year	Cash Inflow (Outflow)	Present Value Factors 20%	25%	Present Values of Cash Flows 20%	25%
1	$40,000	0.833	0.800	$ 33,320	$32,000
2	50,000	0.694	0.640	34,700	32,000
3	25,000	0.579	0.512	14,475	12,800
	(10,000)	0.579	0.512	(5,790)	(5,120)
4	45,000	0.482	0.410	21,690	18,450
5	30,000	0.402	0.328	12,060	9,840
Net Present Values				$110,455	$99,970

The second trial rate of 25 percent shows present value inflows of $99,970, which when compared with the net investment of $100,000 gives an approximate rate of return of 25 percent.

Annual Cost of an Investment

Businessmen customarily think in terms of annual costs. Statements of financial position and earnings reports are in annual terms. Capital budgeting problems may also be expressed in terms of annual costs. This is useful not only because it is a customary way of thinking but also because it provides a common basis for the comparison of two projects with different economic lives. The decision is based on whether the annual earnings expected from the investment exceed the annual cost of the investment over the estimated life.

The annual cost of an investment may be found by dividing the net investment by the present value factor corresponding to the desired rate of return and estimated life. Returning to the West Company proposal, if the Company used a cutoff rate of 16 percent, the annual cost, given the net investment of $22,500 and a useful life of ten years, is (refer to Table B):

$$\frac{\text{Investment}}{\text{Present value factor for } i = 16\%, n = 10} = \frac{\$22,500}{4.833} = \$4,655$$

Since the estimated savings are $4,500, the project will not earn the 16-percent rate. If, however, the desired minimum is 14 percent, the annual cost becomes:

$$\frac{\text{Investment}}{\text{Present value factor for } i = 14\%, n = 10} = \frac{\$22,500}{5.216} = \$4,314$$

The annual cost at 14 percent is $4,314; this is less than the estimated annual earnings of $4,500. The project therefore meets the 14-percent minimum rate test.

Annual cost computations are useful for a variety of capital expenditure problems. To illustrate, assume that a company is considering the advisability of investing in data processing equipment that will reduce annual clerical costs from $30,000 to $18,000. The equipment costs $60,000 and has an estimated useful life of ten years. Assuming that the desired rate of return is 10 percent, the annual cost comparison is as shown:

Present costs		$30,000
Proposed costs		
Clerical	$18,000	
Equipment	9,764	27,764
Annual saving		$ 2,236

The computation of the annual cost of the equipment is as follows:

$$\frac{\text{Investment}}{\text{Present value factor for } i = 10\%, n = 10} = \frac{\$60,000}{6.145} = \$9,764$$

The annual saving indicates (1) that the rate of return is greater than 10 percent, (2) that the 10 percent rate of return can be realized even if proposed costs increase by $2,236, or (3) that the company could pay up to $73,740 [($30,000 − $18,000) × 6.145] for the equipment and still realize a 10-percent rate of return, as shown:

Present costs		$30,000
Proposed costs		
Clerical	$18,000	
Equipment	12,000	30,000
Annual saving		$ -0-

In this situation, the computation of the annual cost of the equipment is as follows:

$$\frac{\text{Investment}}{\text{Present value factor for } i = 10\%, n = 10} = \frac{\$73,740}{6.145} = \$12,000$$

Payback

Payback, or *payout*, is a method of measuring the desirability of a project in terms of a single criterion: How soon will the cash invested in the project be returned? It is a measure of the time required for the accumulated cash earnings from a project to equal the cash investment, or:

$$\frac{\text{Investment}}{\text{Annual net cash flow}} = \text{Payback}$$

In theory, the shorter the payback time, the less the risk. The popularity of payback is due to its simplicity and to its effectiveness as an initial screening measure, especially for high-risk investments in which the useful life is difficult to project. It is also useful in evaluating projects of such obvious merit that refined analysis is not needed, and projects showing no financial merit. Its limitations are that it ignores (1) the useful life, (2) the amount and pattern of cash flows beyond the payback point, (3) disposal values, (4) the time value of money, and (5) the profitability of the investment. To illustrate, assume the following figures:

Project	Net Investment	Annual Net Cash Savings
A	$10,000	$ 5,000
B	20,000	10,000

The payback on both projects is two years; on this basis they are equally desirable. However, if it is further assumed that Project A has a two-year life and Project B a five-year life, it becomes obvious that these proposals are not equally desirable.

LIMITATIONS

The primary objective of this chapter is to present an approach to the quantification of capital expenditures. The concept of present values has theoretical validity and practicability in the capital budgeting process. It provides the basis for a systematic analysis of available alternative investment proposals. But sophistication and refinement of procedure cannot insure a best choice if the data are wrong. The data used are projections of expectations—often long-range—involving revenue, costs, equipment life, human and material performance, and so on. Under such conditions of uncertainty, skillful managerial judgment is imperative. Finally, there are irreducible factors that cannot be quantified. An investment may have a direct or indirect effect on employee morale or on relations with the community, which, if not carefully judged, could cause irreparable harm. There is usually no single right answer. Sophisticated analytical procedures will not mitigate the effects of poor judgment as to market potential, available resources, and environmental factors—economic, political, and social.

SUMMARY

Capital budgeting refers to the allocation and commitment of funds to long-term investment projects, most commonly involving the acquisition of plant and equipment. The measurement techniques give effect to the time value of money at compound interest—interest based on a principal sum that is increased at the end of each period by the interest for that period.

The concept of present value is especially relevant to capital budgeting. The present value of an amount is the amount that must be invested in the present to produce the known future value; the present value of a series of amounts is the present value of a series of payments to be made at equal intervals in the future. Tables of present value discount factors are commonly available to facilitate their application to capital budgeting valuations. Of especial relevance are the discount factors (1) for a single amount to be received at the end of n periods from the present, discounted at various interest rates, and (2) for a stream of uniform amounts to be received at the end of each period for the next n periods. The present value is the product of the discount factor multiplied by the amount.

The choice of an appropriate rate of return is central to the capital budgeting decision. This rate may be (1) the rate that the funds could earn if invested in the next best available alternative project and (2) the cost of capital—a weighted average of the cost of the funds obtained from the stockholders and the long-term debtors. Once the desired minimum rate of return has been fixed, the choice can be made based on the highest return.

The analysis of the cash flows must identify both amounts and the time pattern by years since these have a direct bearing on the present value.

Investments and earnings are reduced to a net amount after taxes. Revenue deductions that do not represent actual cash outflows are irrelevant to the capital budgeting decision but the depreciation deduction reduces net income and therefore the amount of the cash outflow for income taxes. It is for this reason only that depreciation is significant in capital budgeting.

Discounting cash flows is a method of applying present value factors to convert cash inflows and outflows over time to present values for comparisons. The relative desirability of an investment is indicated by the magnitude of the excess of the cost of the investment and the expected earnings from that investment discounted at the desired minimum rate to facilitate comparisons. The excess may be expressed as an index by dividing the present value of the earnings by the investment. This index is useful as a ranking device for investments varying in size and economic life.

Comparison may be based on the internal rate of return or the time-adjusted rate of return. This is the rate at which the present values of the cash inflows and outflows offset each other and can be found by a process of trial and error. The cash flows are discounted, using different trial rates, until a rate is found at which the net present value is zero.

A crude measure of the desirability of an investment is payback, or the time required for the accumulated cash earnings to equal the cash investment.

☐ **QUESTIONS**

Q23-**1.** What is capital budgeting? Why are the principles of compound interest relevant to capital budgeting?

Q23-**2.** What is meant by (a) simple interest? (b) compound interest? (c) present value? (d) compound discount? (e) ordinary annuity amount? (f) present value of an ordinary annuity?

Q23-**3.** What kind of investment problems lend themselves to rate of return measurement techniques?

Q23-**4.** What constitutes a satisfactory rate of return? How is a rate selected? How is it determined?

Q23-**5.** What is meant by the term *discounted cash flow?*

Q23-**6.** Why is it appropriate in making capital budgeting decisions to emphasize the relevant cash flows rather than revenue and expense valuations based on generally accepted accounting principles?

Q23-**7.** What are the steps to be taken in measuring the rate of return on a proposed capital expenditure?

Q23-**8.** How is the annual cost of an investment measured? Of what use is such a measurement?

Q23-**9.** What is meant by (a) excess present value? (b) excess present value index?

Q23-**10.** What is the relevance of depreciation and income taxes to capital budgeting problems?

Q23-**11.** (a) Define *payback.* (b) What are its advantages? (c) Its disadvantages?

Q23-**12.** What limitations are inherent in the application of present value to capital budgeting problems?

Q23-**13.** "The excess present value method is wrong because it ignores depreciation." Comment on this statement.

Q23-**14.** "The method of depreciation does not affect the capital budgeting decision." Comment on this statement.

☐ **EXERCISES**

Note: *For all exercises and problems, use an interest rate of 10 percent unless otherwise instructed.*

E23-**1.** Students A and B have expressed contrary views to you regarding each of the following matters and ask your help in settling their differences:

1. The amount of $70 today is more valuable than $100 five years from today.

2. It is worthwhile to invest $4,000 now in a canteen operation that will earn about $1,000 a year for the next five years.

3. It is better to invest $5,000 in food vending machines that will earn about $2,000 a year for five years than to invest $8,800 in a similar business that will earn about $3,000 a year for five years.

4. An investment of $30,000 in a business that will earn $5,000 a year for ten years will not earn a 10% return.

5. To justify a $50,000 investment in a ten-year concession operation, earnings would have to be at least $8,200 annually.

6. Projects A and B each involve a $2,000 investment but the net cash proceeds for the first year are $2,400 and $2,000, respectively. Project A should therefore be selected.

E23-2. What is the approximate rate of return on an investment with an initial cash outlay of $10,000 and net cash inflows of $2,770 a year for five years?

E23-3. A machine that costs $15,000 will reduce present operating costs by $3,000 a year (net). What is the approximate rate of return if the life of the machine is (a) 8 years? (b) 15 years? (c) What must the minimum useful life of the machine be if the required rate of return is 10%?

E23-4. A company has an opportunity to make one of three possible investments, as follows:

	1	2	3
Investment	$44,500	$57,300	$62,500
Estimated net cash inflow			
Year 1	12,000	18,000	22,000
Year 2	18,000	25,000	30,000
Year 3	25,000	35,000	40,000

Determine, for each investment: (a) the payback period, (b) the excess present value, (c) the excess present value index, and (d) the time-adjusted rate of return.

E23-5. The engineer for the Sloan Corporation has proposed the installation of certain equipment that he estimates will produce the following net after-tax savings over a five-year period:

Year	Savings
1	$1,500
2	1,800
3	2,000
4	2,200
5	2,200

What is the maximum amount that should be paid for the equipment? (Assume a minimum rate of return of 12%.)

E23-6. The Swing Machine Company is considering replacing a machine presently in use and carried on the books at $10,000 with a new machine costing $20,000. The new machine will make possible cost reductions of $3,800 annually for ten years. The old machine, which could otherwise be continued in use for another ten years, can be sold for about $5,000. Assuming the use of straight-line depreciation, a desired rate of return of 10 percent, and an income tax rate of 50 percent, should the replacement be made?

E23-7. What is the maximum amount that should be paid for a business that will earn $10,000 a year for five years, at the end of which time it can be sold for about $25,000?

☐ **DEMONSTRATION PROBLEMS**

DP23-1. (*Payback; excess present value; internal rate of return*) Climax, Inc., plans to invest $200,000 in certain improved metal fabrication equipment that is expected to save $70,000 (net after taxes) annually for ten years. Additional working capital of $20,000 will be required. Assume a 50-percent income tax rate and straight-line depreciation with no salvage value.

> Required: 1. Compute the payback period.
> 2. Compute the excess present value.
> 3. Compute the internal rate of return.

DP23-**2**. (*Payback; excess present value; rates of return*) The American Machine Company plans to spend $50,000 on land for the construction of a factory and an adjoining warehouse. Preparation of the site for construction (deductible as an expense) will be $25,000, construction of buildings will cost $825,000 and additional working capital of $50,000 will be needed. The new facilities are expected to bring savings of $200,000 (before taxes and depreciation) annually for ten years. The sum of the years-digits method of depreciation is used. Assume a 50-percent income tax rate.

> Required: Determine whether the plan should be undertaken.

DP23-**3**. (*Payback, excess present value; rates of return*) The W. J. Cavanagh Company is considering a proposal to add an electro-zinc plating unit for finishing work now being done by outside contractors at an average cost of $0.027 per pound. Annual requirements are 2,000,000 pounds. Two types are available.

	Semiautomatic	Fully Automatic
Purchase price	$25,000	$50,000
Operating costs per unit	0.024	0.01955
Economic life	8 years	8 years

> Required: Determine which type of unit is preferable.

☐ PROBLEMS

P23-**1**. The Travers Chemical Company is considering the advisability of buying a new reactor that can handle products at high temperatures. The reactor will make possible annual savings in labor and maintenance costs of about $10,000. Data regarding the new reactor are as follows:

Purchase price	$75,000
Salvage value	5,000
Estimated life	15 years

> Required: Determine whether the reactor should be purchased.

P23-**2**. The Kane Corporation owns 32 concrete block buildings that house certain metering and control equipment. To maintain good public relations with the residents and officials of the towns in which the buildings are located, it is necessary to paint the buildings regularly at an annual cost of $6,400. It has been proposed that the buildings be covered with aluminum siding at a cost of $51,200; this will eliminate all further maintenance. The guarantee period is 20 years.

> Required: Determine whether the proposal should be approved.

P23-**3**. The C. C. Bach Company is planning to buy a continuous gelatin dryer to replace the hand nets currently used to perform the drying operation. The useful life of the dryer is ten years and its installed cost is $300,000. The old equipment has a carrying value of $50,000 and can be sold for $20,000.

The new dryer will reduce labor costs and fringe benefits by $70,000 annually and will eliminate the need for nets at a saving of $20,000 each year. Maintenance costs will increase by $10,000 annually. The new dryer is expected to improve the quality of the product and eliminate some presently existing sanitation problems.

The Company uses the straight-line method of depreciation and is subject to a combined Federal and state income tax of 50 percent. The present equipment could have been used for another ten years.

Required: Determine whether the dryer should be purchased to replace the old equipment.

P23-**4.** J. W. Owen, the plant engineer for the Smith Company, has been asked to procure equipment that will improve the present method used by the Company for shearing bar stock. He finds three different systems, each of which will improve present methods and reduce space requirements. The costs of the systems are as follows:

A $56,100
B 86,100 (includes $30,000 for unscrambler)
C 94,100 (includes $38,000 for unscrambler and unloading conveyor)

The work to be done by the new equipment currently requires 2,200 hours annually at an hourly variable cost of $24.02. The new systems will do the same work in 733 hours at the following rates:

A $28.77
B 25.90
C 21.03

The Company plans to depreciate the new equipment over eight years, using the straight-line method, and is subject to a 50-percent combined state and Federal income tax rate. No salvage value is expected.

The old equipment, which has a carrying value of $5,000, can be sold for $2,000. The new system will not require increased working capital.

Required: 1. Compute the payback period.
2. Compute the internal rate of return.

P23-**5.** The Rosenberg Company is considering the replacement of conventional drilling equipment with a numerically controlled drilling machine. The purchase price of the machine, including controls, is $54,560. Freight and installation costs are $1,643. Other first-year expenses include a programmer at $8,500 and training fees of $1,500. The useful life of the machine is ten years. Projected annual savings are as follows:

Reduction in tooling costs	$13,857
Reduction in tool wear and tear	600
Reduced scrap and rework costs	494
Reduced floor space: 160 square feet × $2.92 per square foot	467
Reduced maintenance	600
Reduction in labor and fringe benefits	7,775

After the first year, the part-time services of a programmer will be needed at an annual cost of $2,830.

Required: Compute the internal rate of return, assuming no salvage value, a 50-percent income tax rate, and straight-line depreciation.

P23-**6.** The D. J. Crowley Company needs equipment to produce about 1,400 microcircuits per week for the next five years. Rapidly evolving microcircuit technology makes projections for any period longer than five years hazardous. Two methods are being considered, as follows:

	A	B
Investment for equipment	$24,000	$30,000
Variable costs per 1-inch microcircuit (exclusive of transistors and diodes)	0.80	0.77

The choice of method will not affect sales volume because the microcircuits are incorporated into a larger piece of equipment. No salvage value is expected. Required: Determine which investment should be made.

CASE PROBLEM
Gaynor Corporation

The Gaynor Corporation performs accurate light machining operations on numerous small parts for certain scientific instruments. Orders are for small lots, each requiring special jigs and fixtures. The Company has been investigating the possible use of numerically controlled machining techniques, which would make possible multiple machining operations in one setup and eliminate the need for the special jigs and fixtures. This, in turn, would lessen the problems of quality control and reduce inventory requirements. Companies now using numerically controlled equipment report reductions in machining time of from 50 to 80 percent and can produce parts of a higher quality than with conventional machinery. Subsequent studies by the Gaynor Corporation indicate possible savings in the following areas:

1. Labor hours
2. Variable overhead
3. Inventory carrying costs
4. Scrap and rework
5. Inspection
6. Tooling costs

The Company has made a study of the savings that would result on 195 parts suitable for numerically controlled machining to be phased into the new program in two stages: 98 parts at the beginning of the first year and the remainder at the beginning of the second year.

Labor Hours. The 195 parts currently require 11,000 machining hours annually at an average hourly rate of $2.80 (including fringe benefits). The same parts can be machined on numerically controlled equipment in 6,000 hours.

Variable Overhead. The present overhead rate is $7 per direct labor hour. This amount includes $0.20 for fringe benefits and $0.41 for depreciation and other nonvariable costs.

Inventory Carrying Costs. The average inventory cost of the 195 parts is $50,000, with an annual turnover ratio of 4:1. Use of numerically controlled equipment would require an average inventory cost of $16,250. Inventory carrying charges are presently 20 percent, but since present storage space and stores personnel would remain unchanged, annual savings of about $5,000 are anticipated.

Scrap and Rework. A review of the quality control records and monthly rework reports showed rework costs due to shop errors for the 195 parts of about $3,000. The built-in self-monitoring devices of the numerically controlled equipment should eliminate at least 90 percent of rework costs.

Inspection. Since the numerically controlled equipment is highly accurate within the guaranteed limits, it will be necessary to inspect only the first piece of each lot and one or two other pieces, instead of every piece. This will reduce inspection costs by $3,000 annually.

Tooling Costs. Anticipated savings relating to tooling result from (1) design and fabrication of tools for new parts and (2) maintenance of existing tools. Design and fabrication of new parts suitable for the numerically controlled equipment is expected to number 43, 85, and 85, respectively, for the first three years of use, after which the two-shift capacity of the machine will have been reached. Numerically controlled tooling is $75 per part, compared with $300 per part currently. Savings from general tool maintenance would continue on an annual basis at $5,000 yearly.

The cost of the numerically controlled equipment is $140,000, consisting of the following:

Basic machine price	$112,000
Tool holders and accessories	20,000
Installation	8,000
Total	$140,000

In addition, one-time costs of $11,000 would be incurred for the basic program for producing tapes and for training programmers and operators.

It is estimated that the equipment will be worth $14,000 at the end of its expected six-year life. The Company uses the sum-of-the-years'-digits method of depreciation and is subject to a 50-percent income tax rate. Its cost of capital is 10 percent.

Required: Write a report to management, giving your recommendations and reasons for the action you recommend, together with supporting schedules and exhibits.

Chapter
Twenty-Four
Federal
Income
Taxes

The major justification for the inclusion of an introduction to Federal income taxes in an elementary text is the need to emphasize the primary differences between traditional business income and taxable income. Accordingly, in this chapter, consideration is given to (1) high lights of Federal income taxation and (2) income tax planning problems as a foundation for observing some examples of differences between book net income and taxable income.

THE FEDERAL INCOME TAX

To acquaint the student with a few of the intricacies of the Federal income tax structure, this section includes discussions of (1) classes of taxpayers, (2) tax accounting methods, (3) individual income taxes, (4) the partnership informational return, and (5) corporate income taxes.

Classes of Taxpayers

Four kinds of separate entities are subject to the income tax: individuals, corporations, estates, and trusts—each must file a return and, if applicable, pay a tax on its taxable income.[1] Single proprietorships and partnerships are not taxed as separate entities. Rather, the single proprietor reports his business income along with all his personal income on Form 1040, the U.S. Individual Income Tax Return. The partnership files a separate informational return, Form 1065, but each partner reports his share of net income together with his personal nonpartnership income on his Form 1040.

---

[1] Some trusts, all of whose income goes to beneficiaries, file tax returns for information purposes only. The income received from these trusts by the individual beneficiaries should be reported on their individual tax returns. Under these circumstances, the trust would not pay any income taxes.

Tax Accounting Methods

The Internal Revenue Code sets forth rules and the Internal Revenue Service establishes regulations regarding the inclusion and exclusion of certain revenue and expense items and the use of certain methods and procedures in computing taxable income.

The Internal Revenue Code, however, permits taxpayers to select certain options, among them the alternative to choose the cash or accrual basis of computing net income under certain circumstances. To reiterate, on the cash basis, income is recognized when cash is received and expenses are considered to be incurred when the cash expenditure is made. Although the cash basis is not a satisfactory method of measuring net business income, for tax purposes it is well-suited for individuals not engaged in business and also, to a lesser extent, for businesses in which inventories, payables, and receivables are not a major factor. An individual whose only income is a salary is required to use the cash basis.

The cash basis allowed for income tax purposes is modified in two ways: (1) the cost of a long-lived asset cannot be deducted in the year of its purchase: the taxpayer must treat the item as an asset and apportion its cost over its useful service life and (2) revenue is recognized when it is constructively received; that is, when the revenue is in the control of the taxpayer. For example, interest credited to a savings and loan account is deemed to be constructively received even though the cash is not yet in the hands of the taxpayer.

The taxpayer should choose the method permissible under the law that will postpone and avoid taxes, thereby conserving working capital and achieving the lowest long-run tax cost.

The accrual basis of measuring income has been discussed in preceding chapters of this text. Under this method, revenue is recognized in the period when a sale is made or a service is rendered, irrespective of when cash is received; and expenses are recognized in the period when services are received and utilized in the production of revenue. The accrual basis is required of those businesses in which production, purchases, and sales of merchandise are significant factors. Any taxpayer other than a salaried individual who maintains a set of accounting records may elect to use the accrual basis.

The Individual Income Tax

The individual taxpayer computes his tax by following the outline provided on the U.S. Individual Income Tax Return, Form 1040. Figure 24-1 presents the basic content of Form 1040 and shows the tax formula for individuals.

Gross Income. All income not specifically excluded by law is includable in gross income. In addition to the items mentioned in Figure 24-1, gambling winnings and income from illegal activities must be included in gross income.

The following are specifically excluded by law, Treasury regulations, or court decisions:

1. Interest on state and municipal bonds and notes
2. Qualified dividends received by each spouse who actually owns stock, not to exceed $100 for each owner

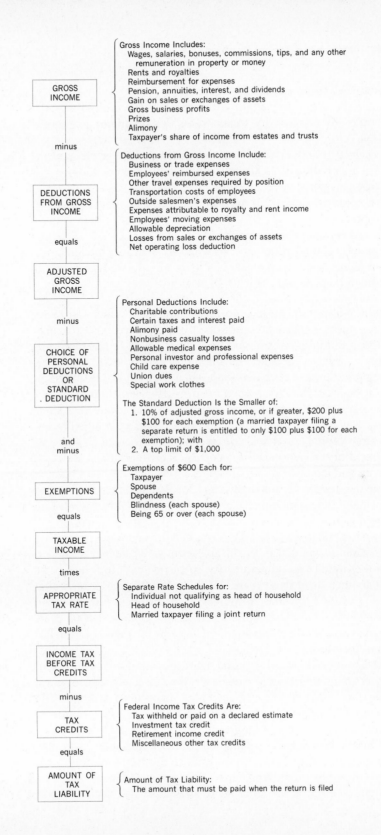

Figure 24-1.
*Individual
Income
Tax Chart*

GROSS INCOME

Gross Income Includes:
   Wages, salaries, bonuses, commissions, tips, and any other
      remuneration in property or money
   Rents and royalties
   Reimbursement for expenses
   Pension, annuities, interest, and dividends
   Gain on sales or exchanges of assets
   Gross business profits
   Prizes
   Alimony
   Taxpayer's share of income from estates and trusts

minus

DEDUCTIONS FROM GROSS INCOME

Deductions from Gross Income Include:
   Business or trade expenses
   Employees' reimbursed expenses
   Other travel expenses required by position
   Transportation costs of employees
   Outside salesmen's expenses
   Expenses attributable to royalty and rent income
   Employees' moving expenses
   Allowable depreciation
   Losses from sales or exchanges of assets
   Net operating loss deduction

equals

ADJUSTED GROSS INCOME

minus

CHOICE OF PERSONAL DEDUCTIONS OR STANDARD DEDUCTION

Personal Deductions Include:
   Charitable contributions
   Certain taxes and interest paid
   Alimony paid
   Nonbusiness casualty losses
   Allowable medical expenses
   Personal investor and professional expenses
   Child care expense
   Union dues
   Special work clothes

The Standard Deduction Is the Smaller of:
   1. 10% of adjusted gross income, or if greater, $200 plus
      $100 for each exemption (a married taxpayer filing a
      separate return is entitled to only $100 plus $100 for each
      exemption); with
   2. A top limit of $1,000

and
minus

EXEMPTIONS

Exemptions of $600 Each for:
   Taxpayer
   Spouse
   Dependents
   Blindness (each spouse)
   Being 65 or over (each spouse)

equals

TAXABLE INCOME

times

APPROPRIATE TAX RATE

Separate Rate Schedules for:
   Individual not qualifying as head of household
   Head of household
   Married taxpayer filing a joint return

equals

INCOME TAX BEFORE TAX CREDITS

minus

TAX CREDITS

Federal Income Tax Credits Are:
   Tax withheld or paid on a declared estimate
   Investment tax credit
   Retirement income credit
   Miscellaneous other tax credits

equals

AMOUNT OF TAX LIABILITY

Amount of Tax Liability:
   The amount that must be paid when the return is filed

3. Gifts, inheritances, and bequests received
4. Life insurance proceeds received upon the death of the insured
5. Insurance proceeds for casualty losses when the premiums paid were nondeductible
6. Amounts received from workmen's compensation and other kinds of insurance, with a limitation of $100 per week under certain conditions
7. Social security receipts
8. Return of investment portion of annuity receipts and other returns of capital investments
9. GI benefits and certain veteran's payments
10. Income earned by United States citizens while resident in a foreign country and from foreign sources up to $20,000 per year, provided the taxpayer remains in the foreign country at least 18 months

CAPITAL GAINS AND LOSSES. The income tax treatment of gains and losses on sale of capital assets—stocks, bonds, and other qualifying property—is extremely important because net long-term capital gains are taxed at one-half, or less than one-half, the rates applicable to ordinary income. The amount of gain or loss is the difference between the selling price and the tax basis—cost when the asset was acquired by purchase, the basis in the hands of the donor when the property was acquired by gift, fair market value at date of death (or at the election of the recipient, one year later) when the property was acquired by inheritance, and other legally specified bases.

Gains or losses from capital assets held for six months or less are classified as short-term and 100 percent of the gain must be reported. Short-term gains are taxed as ordinary income. Gains and losses arising from capital assets held for more than six months are classified as long-term; only one-half of net long-term gains are included in adjusted gross income, and the maximum rate of tax applicable to the gross (before the 50-percent reduction) gain is 25 percent.

Capital losses, whether short-term or long-term, may be deducted from other gross income up to a maximum of $1,000, or the taxable income, whichever is smaller. The unused portion of the capital loss, however, may be carried over to future years and offset against ordinary income of those years, not to exceed the maximum limitations per year as stated. The 1964 Revenue Act removed the five-year limit that had been in effect on loss carryovers. On those capital losses arising from post-1963 years there is no limit on carryover, and the carried-over loss retains its original character; that is, it is short-term or long-term.

The income tax law requires that long- and short-term transactions be combined in a certain way in computing taxable income. In the first place, all long-term gains and long-term losses must be offset against each other in order to determine the net long-term gain or loss. In a similar manner, short-term gains and losses must be combined. The combination and netting of long-term and short-term items produce a number of situations that require further explanation. For example, a taxpayer may have both a net long-term gain and a net short-term gain. In this case, he would treat the two items separately: the entire short-term gain would be included in gross income and treated as ordinary income. If, on the other hand, a taxpayer had net short-term losses and net long-term losses he would combine these into one figure, and up to $1,000 would be deducted in the computation of adjusted gross income. Still further, it is possible for a taxpayer to have gains of either type greater than losses of either type. These must be combined to arrive at either a net long-term gain or a net short-term gain, depending upon the characteristic of the dominant gain. These rules are illustrated in Figure 24-2.

Figure 24-2.
*Capital Gain
and
Loss Rules*

Case A		Case B	
Net LTCG	$5,000	Net LTCL	$3,500
Net STCG	1,000	Net STCL	1,500
		Total Capital Loss	$5,000

Includable in AGI:	Deductible from Gross Income:
All of the STCG is included, but only half of LTCG; the total included in AGI is $3,500.	$1,000 is deductible in the current year to arrive at AGI; balance is carried over to future years.

Case C		Case D	
Net LTCG	$4,000	Net LTCL	$4,200
Net STCL	2,500	Net STCG	5,600
Net capital gain (long-term)	$1,500	Net capital gain (short-term)	$1,400

Includable in AGI:	Includable in AGI:
50 percent of the $1,500, or $750, is included.	The entire $1,400 would be included and taxed as ordinary income.

Abbreviations used in this illustration are:
Net LTCG—Net long-term capital gain
Net STCG—Net short-term capital gain
Net LTCL—Net long-term capital loss
Net STCL—Net short-term capital loss
AGI—Adjusted gross income

DEDUCTIONS FROM GROSS INCOME. The various classes of deductions from gross income are indicated in Figure 24-1. In general, they are self-explanatory. A brief word about a few should suffice.

Business expenses are the ordinary and necessary expenses of carrying on a trade, business, or profession. In actual practice, business expenses are deducted from business revenue on a separate Schedule C to Form 1040, and only the net income from business is included in adjusted gross income.

Allowable employee expenses are necessary and actually incurred in connection with the employment.

Losses from sales or exchanges may qualify as capital losses and hence would follow the rules summarized in Figure 24-2.

PERSONAL DEDUCTIONS OR STANDARD DEDUCTION. A taxpayer has the option of itemizing the personal deductions listed in Figure 24-1 or taking the standard deduction, whichever will benefit him most. Some of the personal deductions have limits. For example, contributions to recognized charitable, religious, educational, and other eleemosynary organizations are limited to a percentage that may vary from 20 to 30 percent of adjusted gross income. If the contributions to churches, hospitals, educational organizations, governmental units, and public charities such as the Red Cross are at least 10 percent of adjusted gross income, the limit is 30 percent; but if these special contributions are not 10 percent of adjusted gross income, the limit is 20 percent of adjusted gross income plus the amount of the special contributions.

Gross medical expenses include doctor, hospital, and dental fees, travel to hospital, and the cost of medicines and drugs in excess of 1 percent of adjusted gross income.

The allowable medical expense for all taxpayers for post-1966 tax years is the amount of medical and dental expense in excess of 3 percent of adjusted gross income, with no maximum limits. Prior to 1967, the undeductable 1-percent and 3-percent limitations were dropped for taxpayers over 65. The Social Security Amendment Act of 1965 (the so-called Medicare Act), in effect amends the Internal Revenue Code by reinstating the 1-percent and 3-percent medical expense limitations for elderly taxpayers for taxable years after 1966.

The 1964 Revenue Act modified the optional standard deduction by adding a minimum limit. The current standard deduction is 10 percent of adjusted gross income, with a minimum of $200 plus $100 for each exemption, or $1,000, whichever is smaller. However, a married taxpayer filing a separate return is entitled to only $100 plus $100 for each exemption claimed.

EXEMPTIONS. A personal exemption in the amount of $600 is allowed for the taxpayer, for his spouse if a joint return is filed, and for each person who qualifies as a *dependent* of the taxpayer. The taxpayer and spouse may claim special exemptions if he or she is blind, or if either is 65 years old or over.

Under the law, a dependent is a person who receives over one-half his support from the taxpayer, is closely related to the taxpayer or lives in his home, and has received less than $600 in gross income during the year, unless the dependent is a child of the taxpayer who is under 19 years of age or a full-time student.

INDIVIDUAL INCOME TAX RATES. Once the taxable income is properly determined, the income tax before credits is computed by multiplying the appropriate tax rates by the net taxable income. The tax rates that are applied depend upon the rate-qualification of the taxpayer. There is a separate tax schedule for a single person who does not qualify as head of household, another schedule for an individual who does qualify as head of household, and still another schedule for a married couple filing a joint return. All these rates are progressive in nature; that is, those with the lowest taxable income are taxed at the lowest rate and those with larger taxable incomes are taxed at progressively higher rates. The progressive character of the individual tax rate can be observed from Figure 24-3, which shows the rates for a single person who does not qualify as head of household or as a surviving spouse, starting at 14 percent and rising gradually to 70 percent. (The taxpayer must consult the latest rates, which are furnished by the Internal Revenue Service, before he prepares his Federal income tax return.)

INCOME TAX RATES FOR INDIVIDUAL TAXPAYERS
1967

Figure 24-3.
*Individual Taxpayers'
Tax Rate Schedule*

(Single person not qualifying as Head of Household or Surviving Spouse; and for a married person filing a separate return)

Taxable Income	Tax (Before Credits)
Not over $500	14% of the taxable income
$ 500 to $ 1,000	$ 70 plus 15% of excess over $ 500
1,000 to 1,500	145 plus 16% of excess over 1,000
1,500 to 2,000	225 plus 17% of excess over 1,500
2,000 to 4,000	310 plus 19% of excess over 2,000
4,000 to 6,000	690 plus 22% of excess over 4,000
6,000 to 8,000	1,130 plus 25% of excess over 6,000
8,000 to 10,000	1,630 plus 28% of excess over 8,000
10,000 to 12,000	2,190 plus 32% of excess over 10,000
12,000 to 14,000	2,830 plus 36% of excess over 12,000
14,000 to 16,000	3,550 plus 39% of excess over 14,000
16,000 to 18,000	4,330 plus 42% of excess over 16,000
18,000 to 20,000	5,170 plus 45% of excess over 18,000
20,000 to 22,000	6,070 plus 48% of excess over 20,000
22,000 to 26,000	7,030 plus 50% of excess over 22,000
26,000 to 32,000	9,030 plus 53% of excess over 26,000
32,000 to 38,000	12,210 plus 55% of excess over 32,000
38,000 to 44,000	15,510 plus 58% of excess over 38,000
44,000 to 50,000	18,990 plus 60% of excess over 44,000
50,000 to 60,000	22,590 plus 62% of excess over 50,000
60,000 to 70,000	28,790 plus 64% of excess over 60,000
70,000 to 80,000	35,190 plus 66% of excess over 70,000
80,000 to 90,000	41,790 plus 68% of excess over 80,000
90,000 to 100,000	48,590 plus 69% of excess over 90,000
Over $100,000	55,490 plus 70% of excess over 100,000

The separate tax schedule for married taxpayers is designed to eliminate tax inequity for married couples in states having community property laws that permit them to divide gross income and couples in states that do not have such laws. Married couples filing a joint return, in effect, pay a tax that can first be computed on one-half of their combined taxable income, using the rates shown in Figure 24-3, and doubling this amount to arrive at the final tax liability. Generally, however, they determine their income tax before credits by applying the rates indicated in Figure 24-4, the tax rates that are specifically applicable to married taxpayers filing joint returns. In this way, a married couple earning a taxable income of $60,000—where the final tax liability is twice the tax on $30,000—will pay far less in taxes than will an unmarried individual earning the same amount.

INCOME TAX RATES FOR MARRIED TAXPAYERS FILING JOINT RETURNS
1967

Taxable Income	Tax (Before Credits)	
Not over $1,000	14% of the taxable income	
$ 1,000 to $ 2,000	$ 140 plus 15% of excess over $ 1,000	
2,000 to 3,000	290 plus 16% of excess over 2,000	
3,000 to 4,000	450 plus 17% of excess over 3,000	
4,000 to 8,000	620 plus 19% of excess over 4,000	
8,000 to 12,000	1,380 plus 22% of excess over 8,000	
12,000 to 16,000	2,260 plus 25% of excess over 12,000	
16,000 to 20,000	3,260 plus 28% of excess over 16,000	
20,000 to 24,000	4,380 plus 32% of excess over 20,000	
24,000 to 28,000	5,660 plus 36% of excess over 24,000	
28,000 to 32,000	7,100 plus 39% of excess over 28,000	
32,000 to 36,000	8,660 plus 42% of excess over 32,000	
36,000 to 40,000	10,340 plus 45% of excess over 36,000	
40,000 to 44,000	12,140 plus 48% of excess over 40,000	
44,000 to 52,000	14,060 plus 50% of excess over 44,000	
52,000 to 64,000	18,060 plus 53% of excess over 52,000	
64,000 to 76,000	24,420 plus 55% of excess over 64,000	
76,000 to 88,000	31,020 plus 58% of excess over 76,000	
88,000 to 100,000	37,980 plus 60% of excess over 88,000	
100,000 to 120,000	45,180 plus 62% of excess over 100,000	
120,000 to 140,000	57,580 plus 64% of excess over 120,000	
140,000 to 160,000	70,380 plus 66% of excess over 140,000	
160,000 to 180,000	83,580 plus 68% of excess over 160,000	
180,000 to 200,000	97,180 plus 69% of excess over 180,000	
Over $200,000	110,980 plus 70% of excess over 200,000	

Figure 24-4.
Married Taxpayers' Tax Rate Schedule

It should be noted that marital status is determined as of December 31 of a given taxable year. For example, if a couple were married on December 31, 1967, they would qualify to file a joint return for the entire taxable year of 1967.

The special tax schedule for head of household provides an element of relief for widows or widowers and others who qualify as head of household to partially compensate them for the additional family burden that they must carry. Only the following persons may qualify as head of household: (1) one who is unmarried (or legally separated) at the end of the taxable year, or (2) one who is married at the end of the year to an individual who was a nonresident alien at any time during the taxable year. In addition, the individual must have furnished over half the cost of maintaining as the taxpayer's home a household that during the entire year, except for temporary absences, was occupied as the principal place of abode and as a member of such household by (1) any related person, other than the taxpayer's unmarried child or stepchild for whom the taxpayer is entitled to a deduction for an exemption, unless the deduction arises from a multiple support agreement, or (2) the taxpayer's unmarried child, grandchild, or stepchild, even though such child is not a dependent. The rates, as shown in Figure 24-5, are lower than for nonhead-of-household unmarried individuals but are higher than those for married couples filing joint returns.

INCOME TAX RATES FOR HEAD OF HOUSEHOLD
1967

Figure 24-5.
Head of Household Tax Rate Schedule

Taxable Income	Tax (Before Credits)
Not over $1,000	14% of the taxable income
$ 1,000 to $ 2,000	$ 140 plus 16% of excess over $ 1,000
2,000 to 4,000	300 plus 18% of excess over 2,000
4,000 to 6,000	660 plus 20% of excess over 4,000
6,000 to 8,000	1,060 plus 22% of excess over 6,000
8,000 to 10,000	1,500 plus 25% of excess over 8,000
10,000 to 12,000	2,000 plus 27% of excess over 10,000
12,000 to 14,000	2,540 plus 31% of excess over 12,000
14,000 to 16,000	3,160 plus 32% of excess over 14,000
16,000 to 18,000	3,800 plus 35% of excess over 16,000
18,000 to 20,000	4,500 plus 36% of excess over 18,000
20,000 to 22,000	5,220 plus 40% of excess over 20,000
22,000 to 24,000	6,020 plus 41% of excess over 22,000
24,000 to 26,000	6,840 plus 43% of excess over 24,000
26,000 to 28,000	7,700 plus 45% of excess over 26,000
28,000 to 32,000	8,600 plus 46% of excess over 28,000
32,000 to 36,000	10,440 plus 48% of excess over 32,000
36,000 to 38,000	12,360 plus 50% of excess over 36,000
38,000 to 40,000	13,360 plus 52% of excess over 38,000
40,000 to 44,000	14,400 plus 53% of excess over 40,000
44,000 to 50,000	16,520 plus 55% of excess over 44,000
50,000 to 52,000	19,820 plus 56% of excess over 50,000
52,000 to 64,000	20,940 plus 58% of excess over 52,000
64,000 to 70,000	27,900 plus 59% of excess over 64,000
70,000 to 76,000	31,440 plus 61% of excess over 70,000
76,000 to 80,000	35,100 plus 62% of excess over 76,000
80,000 to 88,000	37,580 plus 63% of excess over 80,000
88,000 to 100,000	42,620 plus 64% of excess over 88,000
100,000 to 120,000	50,300 plus 66% of excess over 100,000
120,000 to 140,000	63,500 plus 67% of excess over 120,000
140,000 to 160,000	76,900 plus 68% of excess over 140,000
160,000 to 180,000	90,500 plus 69% of excess over 160,000
Over $180,000	104,300 plus 70% of excess over 180,000

USE OF THE TAX TABLES. The Internal Revenue Service provides tax tables for taxpayers who have adjusted gross income of less than $5,000. The use of these tax tables is simply a short-cut method of figuring the income tax. The tables are based on the taxpayer's personal exemptions and the relevant standard deduction in place of itemized personal deductions and certain credits. The special tax tables are prepared by the Internal Revenue Service and are mailed to the taxpayer at the same time Form 1040 is mailed.

Although there are four different classes of income tax payers, there are only two different basic rate structures, the individual and corporate structures. An estate or trust is subject to the income tax rates applicable to a single individual who does not qualify as head of household; that is, at the rates shown in Figure 24-3. The corporate rate structure is considered in connection with the discussion of the corporate income tax.

TAX CREDITS. After the income tax has been computed, certain special credits may be deducted from this amount in computing the amount of the tax liability currently outstanding. Typical tax credits are:

1. Income Tax Withheld or Paid on Declared Estimate. A taxpayer takes credit for all salary withholding income taxes and for advance payments made on the basis of his Declaration of Estimated Income Tax, Form 1040-ES.

2. Retirement Income Credit. Persons who have worked for at least ten years, in which at least $600 was earned in each year, who are now receiving retirement pay and individuals over 65 who meet the same earnings test and who receive primarily rents, interest, and dividends are entitled to a tax credit of 15 percent of qualifying retirement income—rents, interest, dividends, and other—up to $1,524, or a maximum credit of $228.60; however, if a husband and wife, both 65 or over, file a joint return and if either one meets the ten-year work test, then the tax credit of 15 percent may be applied to qualifying retirement income up to $2,286, or a maximum credit of $342.90.

3. Investment Credit. A tax credit is allowed in the amount of 7 percent of qualifying investment in new—and, to a limited extent, used—depreciable property placed in service during the year.

In general, for a taxpayer to get the 7 percent tax credit, the property acquired must have a useful life of eight years or more. If the useful life is six or seven years, the 7 percent is allowed on only two-thirds of the cost of the asset; if useful life is four or five years, only one-third of the asset cost qualifies; but if the life is four years and under, no credit is allowed.

4. Miscellaneous Tax Credits. A few other rather infrequent tax credits are allowed. For example, a credit is allowed for taxes paid to foreign countries on income that is also taxed by the United States.

Illustrative Problem—Individual Income Tax

The following hypothetical case illustrates the major features of the individual Federal income tax computation:

John Thompson, who is 44 years old, is married to Faye Thompson, who is 40 years old. They have two children: a son, John, Jr., 10 years old; and Mary Kay, 20 years old, who is attending college. The Thompsons furnish over one-half the support of both their children, although Mary Kay works as a summer camp counselor and earned $900 in 1967.[2] Thompson owns and operates a grocery store under the name of Thompson Groceries. Mrs. Thompson did not earn any income in 1967. Relevant business and personal information for the family is shown in Figure 24-6.

---

[2] The year 1967 rather than 1969 is used in the discussion in this chapter because statements made are based on the law in effect during 1967. The Federal tax rates are subject to change at any time.

Income
    Net income from Thompson Groceries (sales of $50,000 less operating
        expenses of $40,000) $10,000
    Interest on U.S. Bonds   1,000
    Interest on State of Massachusetts Bonds   1,800
    Dividends on stock jointly owned   3,200
    Net long-term capital gain from sale of 100 shares of National
        Carbon Company stock:

Date Acquired	Date Sold	Tax Basis (Cost)	Selling Price	
2/10/59	3/6/67	$4,000	$5,000	1,000

    Net short-term capital gain from sale of 200 shares of United
        Widgets Company stock:

Date Acquired	Date Sold	Tax Basis (Cost)	Selling Price	
1/10/67	4/1/67	$2,000	$2,500	500

Expenditures
    Contributions to church and university $ 800
    Contribution to Community Chest   200
    Interest paid on personal loans   300
    Property taxes paid to town and county   692
    State taxes paid
        Sales tax   158
        Automobile license tags   24
        Gasoline tax   100
    Family medical expenses
        Doctor and hospital fees   200
        Drugs and medicine   100
    Amount paid in 1967 as a result of filing Form 1040-ES,
        Declaration of Estimated Income Tax   1,700

Figure 24-6.
*1967 Tax Information—
John and Faye Thompson*

The computation of the tax liability on a joint return filed by the Thompsons appears, in summary form, in Figure 24-7. Supporting information is shown in Schedules 1 through 5.

JOHN AND FAYE THOMPSON
Computation of Income Tax Liability
Taxable Year 1967

Gross Income (Schedule 1)		$15,000
Deductions from Gross Income (The only allowable deductions are the operating expenses of the grocery store. Since only the net income from the store is included, there are no separate deductions from gross income.)		–0–
Adjusted Gross Income		$15,000
Personal Deductions (Schedule 2)	$2,250	
Personal Exemptions (Schedule 3)	2,400	4,650
Taxable Income		$10,350
Federal Income Tax for 1967 (Schedule 4)		$ 1,897
Tax Credits (Schedule 5)		1,700
Net Tax Liability		$ 197

Figure 24-7.
*Computation of the Tax
Liability*

(Continued on next page)

Schedule 1—Gross Income

Net income from Thompson Groceries	$10,000
Interest on U.S. Bonds	1,000
Dividends received ($100 per owner-spouse is excluded)	3,000
Net long-term capital gains (only 50% included)	500
Net short-term capital gains (100% included)	500
(Interest on State of Massachusetts Bonds is 100% excludable)	
Total Gross Income	$15,000

Schedule 2—Personal Deductions

Contributions (both apply since they do not exceed allowable limitation— all are qualifying special contributions)	$1,000
Interest paid on personal loans	300
Property taxes	692
Sales tax	158
Gasoline tax	100

(The $24 paid for license tags is not a deductible item in post-1963 years, and the medical expenses are not large enough to be included—only that part of the drugs that exceed $150 (1% of AGI of $15,000) would qualify as a gross medical expense and further only the medical expenses that exceed $450 (3% of AGI of $15,000) would qualify as a personal deduction.)

Total Personal Deductions	$2,250

Schedule 3—Personal Exemptions

John Thompson	1
Faye Thompson	1
Mary Kaye (Under a special relief provision of the tax law, she qualifies as an exemption for Thompson even though she earned over $600 income— she would have to file a return and could claim an exemption for herself; but Thompson may also claim her as an exemption)	1
John, Jr.	1
Total	4

Value of Personal Exemptions; $4 \times \$600 = \$2,400$

Schedule 4—Computation of Federal Income Tax

Referring to tax schedule, Figure 24-4, for married couples filing joint returns:	
Income tax on first $8,000	$1,380
Plus 22% × $2,350	517
Total Federal Income Tax for 1967 .	$1,897

Schedule 5—Tax Credits

Amount Paid in 1967 as a result of filing Form 1040-ES, Declaration of Estimated Income Tax for Individuals	$1,700

Figure 24-7.
Computation of Tax Liability
(Continued)

THE PARTNERSHIP INFORMATIONAL RETURN

Partnerships are not taxed as separate entities. Rather, the relevant revenues and expenses of the partnership are reported on an informational return, Form 1065, and the individual partners report their respective shares of operating income, net long-term and short-term capital gains, dividends received, contributions, tax-exempt income, and any other items that require special treatment on their own U.S. Individual Income Tax Returns.

Consider the partnership firm of Warren and Baker, which has an ordinary taxable income of $100,000 after salaries of $8,000 to George Warren and $10,000 to Peter Baker. Relevant items belonging to each partner are indicated in Figure 24-8.

WARREN AND BAKER PARTNERSHIP
Tax Information—Taxable Year 1967

Figure 24-8.
*Partnership
Tax Information*

	Total	Warren's Share	Baker's Share
Partnership ordinary income	$100,000	$70,000	$30,000
Net long-term capital gains	2,000	1,400	600
Net short-term capital gains	1,000	700	300
Dividends received	10,000	7,000	3,000
Contributions	(2,200)	(1,540)	(660)
Interest received on municipal bonds	1,100	770	330
Total partnership income per books	$111,900	$78,330	$33,570

On his U.S. Individual Income Tax Return, Warren, for example, would consolidate the following items with his own personal income and deductions: salary received from partnership, $8,000; ordinary income from partnership, $70,000; net long-term capital gains (only 50% included), $700; net short-term capital gains, $700; dividends received (net of $100 exclusion, assuming that Warren is single and does not own any stocks personally), $6,900; and contributions, $1,540. The interest received on municipal bonds is tax-exempt and hence would be excluded from Warren's gross income. Warren's individual Federal income tax would then be computed in the manner described in Figure 24-7.

CORPORATE INCOME TAXES

The income of business corporations is subject to a separate income tax, and the corporations are not allowed to deduct dividends that are paid to stockholders. Also, the dividends are partially taxed to the individual stockholders who receive them. The special corporate tax rate schedule is a simple two-step progressive structure:

Taxable Income	Tax Rate
$0 to $25,000	22%
$25,000 and over	48%

In general, the taxable income of a corporation is computed in the same manner as the taxable income of an individual. Among the exceptions is the fact that a corporation may not take certain personal deductions allowed to individuals. For example, a corporation is not entitled to personal exemptions, the standard deduction, or such deductions as medical expenses. Since personal deductions are not allowed, the concept of adjusted gross income would be meaningless and, therefore, is not applicable to the corporation.

The $100 dividend exclusion is not applicable to corporations. Normally, they may deduct from gross income 85 percent of dividends received from domestic corporations. Under certain conditions, when a consolidated return is filed for qualifying affiliates, the consolidated group may, in effect, deduct 100 percent of dividends received by members of the group from each other; that is, the intercompany dividend amount.

Capital losses of a corporation can be deducted only against capital gains. Capital losses may be carried over and offset against any capital gains during the succeeding five years, not counting the year of the loss. The unlimited carryover of losses rules included in the 1964 Revenue Act apply only to individuals; carryovers by corporations are still limited to five years.

Net long-term capital gains are 100 percent includable in taxable income of corporations, but are subject to a maximum tax rate of 25 percent. For example, if the Carter Corporation reported a taxable income of $100,000, composed entirely of net long-term capital gains, its tax would be only $25,000; but if it reported a normal business income of $100,000 its tax would be $41,500.

A maximum limit of 5 percent of taxable income, figured without regard to the contribution deduction, for corporate contributions is imposed on corporations. Any contribution in excess of this limit may be carried over, however, to the two succeeding years and deducted, provided the total contributions including the carried over amounts are within the 5 percent limit of the appropriate years.

The Corporate Income Tax Return, Form 1120, must be filed two and one-half months after the end of taxable fiscal year. Corporations whose tax liability for the forthcoming year is expected to be in excess of $100,000 must file declarations of estimated tax on Form 1120-ES and prepay their income tax.

The major features of the corporate income tax are illustrated by the tax computation for the Dickens Corporation, shown in Figure 24-9.

DICKENS CORPORATION
Tax Computation—Taxable Year 1967

Revenue			
Net Sales			$500,000
Expenses			
Cost of Goods Sold	$250,000		
Operating Expenses	100,000		350,000
Net Income per Books			$150,000
Add Items not Deductible for Tax Purposes			
Capital Losses Deducted as a Part of Operating Expenses		$ 7,200	
Charitable Contributions in Excess of 5% Limit		2,800	10,000
Net Taxable Income			$160,000
Tax Computation			
Tax on First $25,000 of Taxable Income at 22%			$ 5,500
Tax on Income over $25,000 ($135,000 × 48%)			64,800
Total Corporate Income Tax			$ 70,300

Figure 24-9. *Corporate Income Tax Computation*

INCOME TAX PLANNING

Since 1913, the weight of the income tax has become heavier and heavier on individuals, estates, trusts, and corporations. Today, a large part of the income dollar of all taxpayers goes to various governmental agencies in the form of taxes, with the income tax taking one of the largest bites. Therefore, it behooves the management of taxpaying entities to plan certain controllable transactions in a manner that will minimize the tax cost in the long run. In other words, management should avoid all income taxes possible by the legal method of preventing a tax liability from coming into existence, referred to as *avoidance;* but it should never evade taxes by failure to report, illegal reporting, or the nonpayment of taxes.

The essence of tax planning is the predetermination of the income tax effect of transactions; with the effect thus determined, the taxpayer can make those transactions that will result in the minimization of the income tax. For example, the timing of revenue receipts and expenses is an excellent way of controlling taxable income. A few general rules illustrate this point: a taxpayer should avoid bunching taxable revenue in one year with related expenses falling in another; if he anticipates high revenue in a succeeding year, he should hold off discretionary expenses and make these in the high-revenue year in order to minimize taxable income; if a change in income tax rates is anticipated, he should accelerate or postpone revenue and expenses accordingly; and he should avoid, if possible, the offsetting of long-term capital losses against long-term capital gains in the same year, for only 50 percent of net long-term capital gains are includable in taxable income.

There are many relief provisions in the income tax law, which should be used by taxpayers to the fullest extent possible. Some examples are:

1. The use of LIFO in inventory valuation when prices are rising (permission must be obtained from the Internal Revenue Service for a company to switch inventory pricing methods)
2. The use of allowable accelerated depreciation methods
3. The deduction of the current market price of stock, with no attendant taxable gain, when stock, the price of which has risen substantially above the original cost, is donated to a charitable organization
4. The required use of the percentage depletion allowance (a percent authorized by the Internal Revenue Service multiplied by revenue) if it exceeds cost depletion (explained in Chapter 11). The taxpayer has no option to choose between these two methods; he must use the method that yields the larger deduction.

In summary, these guidelines should be observed:

1. All controllable transactions should be planned in light of the tax consequences—a taxpayer may be able to do something about the tax effect before a transaction occurs, but he can legally do nothing except follow the tax law after the transaction has already taken place.
2. Evidence of transactions should be preserved; in other words, a set of books should be maintained. Even a cash-basis salaried individual taxpayer should

establish as a minimum a simple columnar journal of cash receipts and expenditures. In case of an audit by a representative of the Internal Revenue Service, this kind of record would be invaluable.

DIFFERENCES BETWEEN BUSINESS INCOME AND TAXABLE INCOME

Taxable income should be computed in accordance with statutes and administrative regulations of the Federal government, whereas the computation of business income should be based on generally accepted accounting principles. Any feature of the tax law that increases taxable income also increases the amount of tax; likewise, any feature of the law that decreases the amount of taxable income decreases the amount of tax. A summary of the major differences between traditional business income and taxable income follows:

1. Some items not considered to be revenue by generally accepted accounting principles are taxed as revenue by the law.
2. Some items considered as business expenses are not deductible for tax purposes.
3. Some items generally considered to be business revenue are exempt from tax by law.
4. Some items not generally considered to be business expenses are deductible for tax purposes.

A brief discussion of each of these differences is illustrated by examples. In general, the corporate net income is the basis for the comparison; however, many of the statements apply to net income earned by a single proprietor.

Taxable Nonbusiness Revenues

The most important taxable receipts that are not generally considered to be business revenues are the unearned revenue items, such as advance receipts of rent, interest, or royalties. The Federal government levies the tax in the year of receipt, when the cash is presumably available for payment of the tax. Sound accounting, on the other hand, recognizes these items as revenue in the year in which they are earned. An exception to the general tax rule stated is the unearned subscriptions revenue received by publishing companies. These particular entities are permitted to report taxable revenue on the basis of the earning process as opposed to the time of cash receipt.

Nondeductible Business Expenses

Representative examples of items that would normally be considered business expenses but that are not allowed for tax purposes are as follows:

1. As indicated in the discussion of corporate income tax, charitable contributions in excess of 5 percent of applicable income are not deductible even when they are made for an ostensible business purpose.
2. Interest on money borrowed to purchase tax-exempt securities is not deductible.
3. Premiums paid on life insurance policies carried by the corporation on the

lives of its key personnel are not deductible if the corporation names itself as beneficiary—sound accounting would require that the amount of the premium in excess of increases in cash surrender value (the investment in the policies) should be considered an expense.
4. The Federal income tax itself is not an expense for tax purposes.
5. Any amortization of an indefinite-life intangible fixed asset, particularly goodwill, is not deductible.

Business Revenue Items Exempt from Taxation

There are several revenue items that are exempt from taxation because of various reasons ranging from social desirability to administrative expedience. Representative examples of items specifically exempted by the Internal Revenue Code are:

1. Interest received on state and municipal bonds and notes is specifically exempt from taxation.
2. Gains on plant assets traded in for similar assets to be held for the same purpose as the old assets are exempt; the basis of the new plant assets is reduced by the amounts of the nonrecognized gain (see page 389).
3. A portion of net long-term capital gains, in effect, is exempt since the maximum tax rate is 25 percent of such gains.
4. Life insurance proceeds received upon the death of the insured are not taxed.

Deductions Allowed by Tax Law That Are Not
Generally Considered to be Expenses

The tax law provides special relief provisions and investment incentives that are not generally deducted from business revenue to measure net income. Among these are:

1. The part of depletion usually determined on a percentage of revenue basis that is in excess of cost.
2. In a similar manner, the part of allowable accelerated depreciation that is in excess of sound depreciation expense.
3. The net operating loss deduction—a special feature of the tax law designed to give taxpayers who suffer a loss in a given bad year some relief from taxes paid in the three years immediately preceding, or the five years following, the year of the loss.

FINANCIAL REPORTING PROBLEMS

The differences between taxable income and business income fall into two classes: (1) those that tend to result in a near-permanent difference between taxable and business income, and (2) those for which the difference between taxable income and business income is washed out in time. The latter class has caused some financial reporting problems that are magnified by the size of the current income tax. The controversy centers around the proper measurement of the Federal income tax expense. If the Federal income tax is a business expense, it appears that the matching concept dictates that it be computed on the basis of reported business income, taking into consideration the items in Class 2.

If the assumption is valid, the accountants of those companies which have material differences between taxable income and reported business income that tend to wash out in time should give serious consideration to the allocation of the income tax expense among the relevant periods. Since the problem is such a complex one and also since it is typically treated in depth in intermediate accounting texts, it is not further developed here.

SUMMARY

As provided by the Internal Revenue Code, Federal income taxes are levied on individuals, corporations, estates, and trusts. These taxes consume a significant portion of the taxpayer's income and therefore should be considered in all decisions of any consequence. The subject is broad and complicated; however, it is essential to realize the impact of taxes on individuals and various forms of business organizations and the problems its creates in financial reporting.

A taxpayer in certain instances may elect to report income for Federal income tax purposes on either the cash basis or accrual basis of accounting. When confronted with this decision, he should choose the method that postpones the payment of taxes for the longest period of time. The accrual basis is required of businesses in which production, purchases, and sales of merchandise are significant factors, and the cash basis is required of taxpayers whose only income is a salary. For income tax purposes, a taxpayer using the cash basis may not deduct the cost of long-lived assets in the year of purchase but must apportion the cost through depreciation deductions over the useful life of the assets. Revenue must be recognized when it is constructively received; that is, when it is in the control of the taxpayer.

All items of income except those specifically excluded by law must be included in gross income. Among the more common exclusions are interest on state and municipal bonds, the dividend exclusion, and gifts and inheritances. Deductions from gross income include expenses incurred in a trade or business or in the production of royalty or rental revenue, travel and entertainment expenses, certain expenses of employees, and the capital gains deduction. The distinction between these deductions and deductions from adjusted gross income is important since each may have a different effect on the income tax liability.

Capital gains and losses result from the sale of stocks, bonds, and other capital assets. If a capital asset held for over six months is sold, a long-term capital gain or loss results; if the capital asset was held for a shorter period of time its sale results in a short-term capital gain or loss. A deduction of 50 percent of the net long-term capital gain is allowed for tax purposes. If short-term or long-term capital losses exceed the capital gains, the excess may be deducted from gross income up to a maximum of $1,000 or the taxable income, whichever is smaller. If the capital losses exceed this limitation, the excess may be carried to future years and offset against capital gains, or gross income not to exceed the maximum limitation.

A taxpayer has the option of taking the standard deduction or itemizing personal deductions, whichever will benefit him the most. The standard deduction is the greater of 10 percent of adjusted gross income or the minimum standard deduction, which is $200 plus $100 for each exemption. The standard deduction can never exceed $1,000. Itemized deductions include charitable contributions, medical expenses, interest, specific taxes, and various expenses of employees. Many of these deductions are subject to limitations specified by the Internal Revenue Code. Regardless of whether a taxpayer elects to take the standard deduction or to itemize personal deductions, a personal exemption of $600 is allowed for the taxpayer, for his spouse if a joint return is filed, and for each person qualifying as a dependent. Additional exemptions are allowed if the taxpayer or his spouse is 65 years old or blind.

The income tax before credits is determined by multiplying the taxable income by the appropriate rates. The tax rates are progressive; that is, the applicable rate increases as the taxable income increases. Different rate structures apply to married couples filing a joint return, a single person qualifying as head of household, and a single person not qualifying as head of household. Tax credits are deducted from the taxable income to determine the Federal income taxes payable. Common tax credits are withheld taxes, payments made on declared estimates, the retirement income credit, and the investment credit.

Although a partnership is not taxed as a separate entity, it is required to file an information return. Each partner reports his share of profits, dividends received, capital gains and losses, charitable contributions, and other items on his personal return.

The computation of the taxable income of a corporation is similar to that of the taxable income of an individual; however, a corporation is not allowed personal deductions, such as the standard deduction, or personal exemptions. An exclusion of 85 percent of the dividends received by a corporation is provided by law, and charitable contributions in any year are limited to 5 percent of applicable income. Net long-term capital gains are 100 percent includable in taxable income, but are subject to a maximum tax rate of 25 percent. The capital losses of a corporation can only be offset against capital gains and any unused capital losses may be carried forward and offset against capital gains during the succeeding five years.

Because of the existing high income tax rates, taxpayers should plan their financial affairs in such a manner as to avoid as much income taxes as possible by the legal method of preventing tax liabilities from coming into existence. If the income tax effects on proposed transactions are predetermined, then the taxpayer may choose the transaction or form of transaction that will result in the minimum tax. Tax planning also encompasses the full utilization of all relief provisions in the income tax law that are available to the taxpayer.

Since net income for accounting purposes is computed following generally accepted accounting principles, whereas taxable net income is computed according to statutes and regulations of the Federal government, in many cases the two net income figures will differ. The differences are primarily caused by one or more of the following: (1) Items that are not considered to be revenue by generally accepted accounting principles but are taxed as revenue by the tax laws. (2) Items that are considered as business expenses but are not deductible for tax purposes. (3) Items that are generally considered to be business revenue but are exempt from tax by law. (4) Items that are not generally considered to be business expenses but are deductible for tax purposes.

Some of these factors may result in near-permanent differences; others result in differences that are washed out over a period. This latter class has caused a controversy concerning the proper measurement of Federal income tax expenses for financial accounting and the proper handling of the complex problem of income tax allocation, which is not discussed in this text.

☐ QUESTIONS

Q24-1. (a) Distinguish between the cash and accrual bases of accounting. (b) What is a modified cash basis?

Q24-2. (a) Define the term *gross income* from an individual income tax point of view. (b) List six items that must be reported as gross income. (c) List four items that are excludable from gross income.

Q24-3. (a) What is the individual income tax standard deduction? (b) State its maximum and minimum limits.

Q24-4. Smith, a bachelor, earned $20,000 in taxable income in 1967. What amount of Federal income tax would be saved if he were to marry on December 31, 1967, a woman who had no taxable income in 1967?

Q24-5. (a) For tax purposes, what are capital assets? (b) Distinguish between short-term and long-term capital gains. (c) The timing of capital gains and losses is important in tax planning. Discuss.

Q24-6. John Allen, aged 21, is attending the State University. During the summer of 1967, he worked as a construction laborer and earned $850. His parents contributed $1,850 toward his support in 1967. Can Allen's parents claim him as an exemption?

Q24-7. Samuel Shuster elected to use the cash basis for tax purposes. During 1967, he collected $12,000 from clients for services rendered in prior years, and billed clients for $30,000 for services rendered in 1967. His accounts receivable as of December 31, 1967, totaled $8,700. What is the amount of gross income he should report on his Form 1040 for 1967?

Q24-8. John and Susan Adams owned some shares of stock. During 1967, they received $700 in dividends. Dividends of $610 were received on stock owned by John Adams only. The remainder was received on stock owned by Susan Adams. What would be the dividends included in gross income on a joint return?

Q24-9. List and briefly discuss the computational differences between the individual income tax and the corporation income tax.

Q24-10. (a) State the objective of tax planning. (b) Discuss ways and means of accomplishing tax planning.

Q24-11. In outline form, state four ways that traditional business income may differ from taxable income, and under each way give two specific illustrations.

☐ EXERCISES

E24-1. Samuel Adden, a bachelor, had the following cash receipts during 1967:

Salary earned as a professor	$14,000
Receipt of insurance proceeds for fire damages to personal car	500
Dividends from domestic companies	2,000
Interest on U.S. Government bonds	600
Interest on North Carolina State bonds	700
Total Cash Receipts	$17,800

Compute the amount of gross income subject to the individual income tax.

E24-**2.** Robert and Alice Baker had the following income and related information for 1967:

Salary to Robert Baker	$10,000
Dividends on stock owned by Robert Baker	2,000
Dividends on stock owned by Alice Baker	1,000
Alice Baker sold some stock she had acquired on April 1, 1960, on March 15, 1967, at a gain of	4,000
Robert Baker sold some stock he had acquired on July 1, 1967, on November 15, 1967, at a loss of	1,500

Compute the adjusted gross income subject to tax on a joint return filed by Robert and Alice Baker.

E24-**3.** David and Phyllis Carter filed a joint return in 1967. They had the following taxable income after deductions and exemptions:

Ordinary taxable income	$ 50,000
Net capital gains (long-term)	50,000
Total	$100,000

Compute the 1967 Federal income tax. Remember that the income tax on net long-term capital gains cannot exceed 25 percent of the long-term gain.

E24-**4.** Scott and Sarah Dawson filed a joint return in 1967, on which they reported an adjusted gross income of $12,000. The couple had allowable personal deductions of $1,500; they are both under 65 and have two small children, aged six and eight. Compute the 1967 Federal income tax.

E24-**5.** Philip and Rose Eason filed a joint return in 1967, on which they reported an adjusted gross income of $5,000. The couple's itemized deductions totaled $600; they are both under 65 and have five children, aged one, three, five, seven, and nine. Compute the 1967 Federal income tax.

E24-**6.** Thomas and Amy Fields filed a joint return and reported a 1967 correct income tax before credits of $4,600. Includable in taxable income was $1,000 of qualifying dividends—the couple had received $1,200 on stock jointly owned. They paid $4,100 in 1967 on a declaration of estimated tax for 1967. Compute the amount of the remaining tax liability for 1967.

E24-**7.** The Goodson Corporation reported a net income per books of $360,000. In addition, its records show capital losses deducted as operating expenses of $8,000 and charitable contributions in excess of the 5-percent limit of $3,000. Compute the 1967 Federal income tax.

☐ **DEMONSTRATION PROBLEMS**

DP24-**1.** (*Individual income tax computation*) Amos Kidder, who is 66 years old, is married to Susan Kidder, who is 63 years old. They have two children: Jacob, 16 years old, and Sandra, 21 years old, who is attending a university. The Kidders furnish over one-half the support for both their children, although Sandra works as a sales-clerk in the summer and earned $950 in 1967. Kidder owns and operates a service station under the name of Kidder Service Station. Mrs. Kidder did not have any earned income in 1967.

Relevant business and personal information for the family is shown:

Cash Receipts

Gross revenue from Kidder Service Station	$100,000
Interest on U.S. bonds	1,000
Interest on State of Virginia bonds	3,450
Dividends on stock jointly owned	4,200
Cash proceeds from insurance policy for fire damage on nonbusiness property	1,800

Capital gains

Sale of 200 shares of National Fruit Company common stock:

Date Acquired	Date Sold	Cost	Selling Price
3/4/65	5/2/67	$24,000	$28,000

Sale of 100 shares of United Fusbits Company common stock:

Date Acquired	Date Sold	Cost	Selling Price
4/2/67	8/10/67	$10,000	$10,600

Expenditures

Cost of goods sold and operating expenses of Kidder Service Station	$70,000
Contributions to church and university	2,000
Contribution to Community Chest	800
Interest paid on personal loans	600
Property taxes paid to town and county	800
State taxes paid	
Sales tax	160
Automobile license tags	24
Gasoline tax	100
Family medical expenses	
Doctor and hospital fees	300
Drugs and medicine	120
Amount paid in 1967 on declared estimated tax for 1967	7,000

Required: In an orderly schedule form, compute the income tax liability remaining to be paid for 1967, assuming that a joint return is filed.

DP24-2. (*Information to be reported on partnership informational return*) Cabot and Nixon are partners sharing profits 2:1, respectively. The following information has been taken from the partnership records for the year 1967:

Taxable ordinary income	$60,000
Long-term capital gains	9,000
Short-term capital gains	3,600
Short-term capital losses	(3,000)
Dividends received	1,800
Charitable contributions	(2,100)
Interest on Orange County bonds	900
Salaries to partners ($5,000 to Cabot and $4,000 to Nixon)	9,000
Net income per books before partner's salaries	$79,200

Assume that Cabot is 40 years old and single, and that he has the following tax information from sources other than the partnership:

Dividends received	$8,000
Long-term capital losses	3,000
Itemized deductions	1,500

Required: 1. Prepare a schedule showing the information that should be presented on the partnership informational return.
2. Compute the 1967 income tax for Cabot.

DP24-**3.** (*Corporate income tax computation*) The Lawson Corporation reported the following information for 1967:

Sales	$2,000,000
Cost of goods sold	1,100,000
Operating expenses other than capital losses	500,000
Capital losses	20,000
Charitable contributions	25,000

Required: Compute the corporate income tax for 1967.

☐ **PROBLEMS**

P24-**1.** Ronald Paison, who is 45 years old, is married to Ann Paison, who is 41 years old. They have two children: a son, David, 9 years old, and a daughter, Sarah, 14 years old. Paison owns and operates a hardware store under the name of the Paison Hardware Company. Mrs. Paison did not have any earned income in 1967.

Tax and other information for 1967 is as follows:

Cash Receipts	
Gross sales of Paison Hardware Company	$200,000
Interest on Dare County bonds	2,000
Dividends on stock owned by Ann Paison	6,000
Cash inherited by Ann Paison	20,000
Capital gains on stock sold by Ann Paison	
Long-term gains	10,000
Short-term gains	1,200
Expenditures	
Cost of goods sold and operating expenses of Paison Hardware Company	140,000
Contribution to church	8,000
Contribution to Community Chest	1,000
Interest paid on personal loans	800
Personal property taxes	1,000
State taxes paid	
Sales taxes	175
Automobile license tags	30
Gasoline tax	120
Family medical expenses	
Doctor and hospital fees	1,200
Drugs and medicine	500
Amount paid in 1967 on declared estimated tax for 1967	20,000

Required: Compute the income tax liability remaining to be paid for 1967, assuming that a joint return is filed.

P24–2. Paul Queens, who is 67 years old, and his wife Mary Queens, who is 64 years old, file a joint return. They have two children, Paul, Jr., who is 30 years old, and Veronica, who is 21 years old and is attending college full time. Mr. and Mrs. Queens furnish over one-half the support for Veronica, although she earned $1,150 on a summer job in 1967. Various receipts and expenditures of Mr. and Mrs. Queens are listed:

Mr. Queens

Cash Receipts
Withdrawal by proprietor from business (sales, $260,000; cost of goods sold, $154,000; operating expenses, $52,000)	$20,000
Cash dividends received	2,600
Gain on sale of stock purchased five years ago	4,000
Interest received on school district bonds	2,000

Expenditures
Contribution to church and university	6,000
Contribution to Community Chest	200
Personal property taxes	1,000
Insurance on residence	200
Automobile license plates	24
State sales taxes	150
State gasoline tax	100
Medical expenses	
Drugs and medicines	380
Doctor and hospital bills	950
Interest on personal loans	700
Payment on declaration of estimated tax	18,500

Mrs. Queens

Cash Receipts
Rental of apartment building	$10,000
Dividends received on stock	850
Received from sale of stock purchased for $3,600 four months previously	2,900

Expenditures
Apartment building (original cost on January 1, 1959, was $63,000. Sum of the years'-digits depreciation is used for tax purposes, with an assumed life of 20 years and no salvage value)
Interest on business indebtedness	900
Property taxes	1,600
Insurance for 1967	210
Repairs and maintenance	1,800
Contribution to church	300

Required: Compute the remaining tax liability for 1967 for Mary and Paul Queens on a joint return.

P24–3. Each of the following five cases represents a possible situation with respect to capital gains and losses. Assume that Albert Sykes, a bachelor, has a salary income of $10,000 in addition to the items shown:

1. Long-term capital gains of $8,000; long-term capital losses of $4,000; short-term capital gains of $6,000; short-term capital losses of $3,000

2. Long-term capital gains of $8,000; short-term capital losses of $16,000

3. Long-term capital gains of $4,000; long-term capital losses of $8,000; short-term capital gains of $2,000; short-term capital losses of $7,000

4. Long-term capital gains of $10,000; short-term capital losses of $6,000

5. Long-term capital gains of $1,000; long-term capital losses of $500; short-term capital loss of $1,200

Required: Compute Albert Sykes's adjusted gross income in each case for the year 1967.

P24-**4.** George Slading is single, aged 47, and uses the standard deductions. He reported the following tax information for 1966 and 1967:

1966	
Ordinary income	$30,000
Net long-term capital gains	1,000
1967	
Ordinary income	$ 5,000
Net long-term capital gains	40,000

Required: Compute the amount of Slading's income tax for each year. (Remember that the tax on long-term capital gains cannot exceed 25 percent of the long-term gain.)

P24-**5.** The following information relates to a taxpayer:

Gross revenue (including $1,000 in interest received on South Carolina bonds and $1,000 in dividends)	$12,900
Deductions to arrive at adjusted gross income	800
Payments made on declaration of estimated tax for 1967	1,200
Long-term capital gains	1,500
Short-term capital losses	2,900
Itemized deductions	1,060

Required: 1. Compute the remaining income tax liability, assuming that the taxpayer is married, that both he and his wife are under 65, that they have three dependent children, and that the wife did not receive any separate income.

2. Compute the remaining income tax liability, assuming that the taxpayer is single and under 65.

P24-**6.** King and Johnson are partners; they share profits 3:1, respectively. The following information has been taken from the partnership records for the year 1967:

Taxable ordinary income	$24,000
Long-term capital gains	10,000
Short-term capital losses	(4,000)
Dividends received	2,000
Charitable contributions	(800)
Interest on Florida State bonds	1,000
Salaries to partners ($6,000 to King; $4,000 to Johnson)	10,000
Net income per books before partners' salaries	$42,200

Assume that King is 68 years old and single, and that he has the following tax information from sources other than the partnership:

Dividends received	$6,000
Long-term capital losses	1,600
Itemized deductions	2,000

Required: 1. Prepare a schedule showing the information that should be presented on the partnership informational return.
2. Compute King's 1967 income tax.

P24-**7.** The Heller Corporation reported the following information for 1967:

Sales	$1,860,000
Cost of goods sold	920,000
Operating expenses, other than capital losses	380,000
Capital losses	18,000
Charitable contributions	21,000

Required: Compute the corporate income tax for 1967.

CASE PROBLEM
Cannady Production Company

The Cannady Production Company, a textile manufacturer, has recently had a change in ownership and top management. Robert James, the new president, is a retired military officer and is noted for being an excellent organizer and administrator. James is gaining a reputation around the office for asking hard questions and for requiring complete and logical answers.

During one of the mornings that James is devoting to familiarizing himself with the workings of the accounting department, he reviews the latest federal corporate tax return and the latest income statement in the corporate annual report. He immediately notices that the taxable income of $136,495 on the tax return and the net income before income taxes of $219,400 on the income statement are not the same amount. On closer examination he observes that the following items are not the same on each report.

1. Depreciation expense is $92,510 on the income statement and $147,250 on the tax return.
2. Cost of goods sold is $929,180 on the income statement and $951,200 on the tax return.
3. Interest earned is $1,200 on the income statement and $880 on the tax return.
4. Gain on disposal of machinery is $5,790 on the income statement and does not appear on the tax return.
5. Bad debt expense is $6,400 on the income statement and $6,350 on the tax return.
6. Amortization of organization costs does not appear on the income statement and is $85 on the tax return.

He also notes that the income tax expense on the income statement is not the same as the income tax on the tax report.

By this time he is confused and bewildered. He approaches you, an assistant accountant in the tax division, and questions the discrepancies. (He has a dual purpose in asking you questions. He wishes answers to his questions and he wishes to evaluate your knowledge of tax accounting.)

Required: 1. Reconcile the two different income amounts.
2. Identify what might be a complete and logical reason for each of the six differences. (Remember that you wish to convince the new president of your competence.)
3. (a) Why does income tax expense on the income statement differ from

the income tax on the tax report? (b) What is the basis for each calculation? (c) Which would you expect to be the larger? Why?

4. What is the justification for permitting differences between business income and taxable income?

5. Identify the separate objectives of business accounting and tax accounting.

6. How would you explain to Mr. James that mistakes have not been made and that everything is correct?

Index

Absorption costing, compared with direct costing, 739–744
  see also Cost accounting
Accounting, functions, 3–4
Accounting concepts, bookkeeping function, 6
  comparability of data, 580
  conservation, 549
  consistency, 355, 359, 580
  cost allocation, 376
  cost basis for assets, 70, 341
  depreciation, 114, 383
  depreciation and investment, 384
  design of accounting system, 217
  dividend recognition, 552
  entity, 4
  expenses and costs compared, 61
  fair presentation, 127–129
  financial statements, purpose, 569
  full disclosure, 127–129, 269–270
  income measurement, 61
  internal control, 199
  lower of cost or market, 352
  management by exception, 729
  matching revenue and expenses, 62, 108, 314
  materiality, 127–129
  personal judgment, 569
  reports basis, 569
  securities cost, 546
  stock dividends, 487
Accounting cycle, see Accounting sequence
Accounting equation, 5–6
  debit and credit rules and, 63
  expanded, 29–30

Accounting flow, 419
Accounting methods, 107–108
Accounting sequence, 39, 65, 134–135
  comprehensive illustration, 67–89
Accounting systems, cost and general compared, 694
  design, 197, 213, 217
  need, 25
Accounts, after closing, 130–134
  asset valuation, 114
  balance form, 36, 219
  capital, 442
  chart of, 65, 67–68
  contra, 114
  controlling, 64–65, 408–409, 696
  cost control, 696
  drawing, 87–88, 446
  entering transactions, 32–34
  expense, 60–61
  form, 31–32, 36
  ledger, 35–36
  machine accounting, 219
  manufacturing summary, 663–665
  merchandising business, 157–164
  mixed, 109–113
  nominal, 80
  numbering, 31, see also Chart of accounts
  open charge, 8–9, 247
  permanent, 80
  real, 80
  revenue, 59
  summary; manufacturing, 663–665, revenue and expense, 80–81, 129
  T, 34–35

Accounts (continued)
  temporary, 80
  three-money-column, 36, 219
  titles, 67
  valuation, 114
Accounts payable, defined, 10
  notes to settle, 253
  schedule, 77–78
Accounts payable ledger, 64–65, 66
  debit balances, 323–324
  posting, from business documents, 216–217
    from cash disbursements journal, 212
    from general journal, 65, 66
    from purchases journal, 202, 203
  replaced in voucher system, 416
Accounts receivable, aging, 317
  average collection period, 324–325
  classification, 313–314
  defined, 8–9, 313–314
  forecast of collections, 298
  internal control, 325
  notes to settle, 258–259
  schedule, 77
  turnover, 324–325
  uncollectible, *see* Bad debts
Accounts receivable ledger, 64, 66
  credit balances, 323–324
  posting, from business documents, 216–217
    from cash receipts journal, 206–208
    from general journal, 65, 66
    from sales journal, 200, 201
Accrual basis, 108
Accrued assets, defined, 118
Accrued expenses, *see* Accrued liabilities
Accrued liabilities, defined, 10, 118
  interest, 117–118
  payment, 136–137
  on position statement, 10
  wages, 116–117
Accrued revenue, defined, 118
  receipt, 137
Acid-test ratio, 14
Adjusted trial balance, 122, 123
Adjustments, accrued interest, 117–118
  accrued liabilities, 116–118
  accrued wages, 116–117, 425–426, 668
  bad debts, 314–316, 318–320, 667
  bonds payable, 524–525
  defined, 107
  depreciation, 113–116, 667–668
  income tax liability, 118–119, 668–669
  manufacturing worksheet, 667–669
  mixed accounts, 109–113
  nature, 109

Adjustments (continued)
  need, 108–109
  notes payable, 117–118, 255–257
  notes payable discounted, 254
  notes receivable, 261–262
  prepaid insurance, 108–109, 111–112, 667
  prepaid rent, 110–111
  recording, 109–119, in journal, 127, 128
  result, 127
  unearned rent, 112–113
  worksheet section, 120–121
All-inclusive concept, 576–577, 578–579
Allowance for doubtful accounts, *see* Bad debts
American Accounting Association, opinion on
  historical cost, 352
  inventory pricing, 354
American Institute of Certified Public Accountants,
    comments and quotations concerning
  comparative statements, 580
  current assets, 571
  definition of accounting, 3
  definition of current liabilities, 10
  definition of value, 341
  funds statement, 627–628
  inventory cost, 340, 341
  lower of cost or market, 352–353
  purpose of financial statements, 569
  stock dividends, 487
Amortization, bond discount, 521–522
  bond premium, 518–520, 523–525
  defined, 377
  intangible assets, 392–393
  organization costs, 393, 452
  patents, 392, 658
  procedure, 392
Analysis of financial statements, *see* Financial
    statement analysis
Analyzing transactions, 68–71
Annuity, amount, 785
  defined, 785
  present value, 786–788
Articles of copartnership, 443
Asset expirations, *see* Depreciation
Asset valuation account, 114
Assets, accrued, defined, 118
  book value, 114
  carrying value, 114
  classification, 8–10
  current, 8–9, 571–572
  defined, 4–5
  fixed, *see* Plant and equipment
  intangible, 392–393, 572
  net, 6
  quick, 14, 572

Assets (continued)
  recording basis, 70
  revaluation, 479
  trading, 572
  valuation, 341
Automatic data processing, 217–222
  bookkeeping machines, 218–219
  electronic, 221–222
  flow of information, 218
  punched-card equipment, 219–220
Average costing, inventory, 347–348

Bad debts, 176–177, 314–323
  adjustment, 314–316, 318–320, 667
  comparison of methods, 323
  direct write-off method, 321–322
  estimating, 316–318
  on financial statements, 314–315
  recognition of losses, 314–322
  recovery, allowance method, 320–321
    direct write-off method, 322
  writing off, allowance method, 320
    direct write-off method, 321–322
Balance, account, 34
  defined, 31
Balance-form ledger account, 36, 219
Balance sheet, *see* Position statement
Balancing, open accounts, 84–86
Bank charges, 413
Bank reconciliation, 289–295
  entries, 294–295
  illustrated, 291–292, 293
Bank statement, 288–295
Bearer bonds, 512
Bill of lading, 267
Board of directors, 453
  dividend declaration, 481–482
Bonds, and capital stock compared, 511, 512–514
  convertible, 512, 528–529
  defined, 11, 510
  entries of issuer and investor compared, 554
  long-term investment, 553–556
  serial, 512, 525
  temporary investment, 546–547
  times interest earned ratio, 556–557
  types, 511–512
  yield table, 517
  see also Bonds payable
Bonds payable, 510–531
  authorizing, 514–515
  callable, 512; retirement, 526–528
  and capital stock compared, 511, 512–514
  convertible, 512, 528–529
  defined, 11, 510

Bonds payable (continued)
  indenture, 512
  issue price, 515, 516–517
  issued at discount, 516–517, 520–522
    interest, 521–522
    issuance, 520–521
    retirement, 522
  issued at face value, 516
  issued between interest dates, 523–525
  issued at premium, 516–520, 523–525
    interest, 518–520, 523
    issuance, 518, 523
    retirement, 520
  nominal interest, 514, 515
  reasons for issuing, 512–514
  refunding, 528
  restricted retained earnings, 530–531
  retirement, callable, 526–528
    convertible, 528–529
    methods, 525
    refunding, 528
  serial, 512, 525
  sinking fund, 512, 529–530
Book of final entry, defined, 37
Book of original entry, defined, 37
Book value
  assets, 114
  stock, 457, 492–493
Bookkeeping
  function, 6
  machines, 218–219
Break-even analysis, 756–764
  chart, 758–761
  margin of safety, 762
  marginal income statement, 761–762
Break-even point, computation, 757–758
  defined, 756
Budgeting, capital, 788–798
    decisions, 789–790
    depreciation and, 793–794
    discounted cash flow, 790–793
    irregular cash flow, 794–795
    limitations, 798
    taxes and, 393–394
    see also Investments
  cash, 296–299, 790–795
Buildings, on position statement, 9–10
  see also Plant and equipment
Business documents, direct posting from, 216–217
  role in accounting system, 417–418, 419
Business organization, forms, 11, 441–442

Callable bonds, 512, 526–528
Capital, accounts, 442

Capital (continued)
  budgeting, *see* Budgeting, capital
  legal, 457
  sources, 454
  stated, 457
  working, *see* Working capital
Capital assets, *see* Plant and equipment
Capital expenditures, budgeting, 788–798
  defined, 384–385
  types, 788–789
Capital stock, *see* Stocks
Carrying charge, 268–269, *see also* Interest
Carrying value, 114
Cash, composition, 285
  control, 286–287
  defined, 8
  flow, 628–631
    discounted, 790–793
    irregular, 794–795
  forecast, 296–299
  petty, *see* Petty cash
  short or over, 295–296
  statement of sources and uses, 628–631
Cash basis, 107–108
Cash disbursements, control, 407–418
  see also Voucher system
Cash disbursements journal, 198, 208–212
  form, 208
  with Other Accounts section, 214
  posting flow, 211
  posting from, 211–212
  proving, 210
  recording, 208–210
Cash receipts journal, 198, 202–208
  form, 202–203
  with Other Accounts section, 213–214
  posting flow, 207
  posting from, 206–208
  proving, 206
  recording, 204–206
Cashiers checks, 266–267
Certified checks, 266, 288
Chain discounts, 177
Charge accounts, 8–9, 247
Chart of accounts, 65, 67–68
Check register, 409–410, 412
  design, 412
  posting, 412, 415
Checks, 266–267
Circular E, 420–421
Circulating capital, *see* Working capital
Claims, creditors', *see* Liabilities
  primary, 5
  residual, 5

Closing, entries, 80–83, 129
  merchandising business, 171, 172
  general ledger after, 130–134
Common-size statements, 585–588
  defined, 176, 580
Common stock, 454, 455, *see also* Stocks
Comparative statements, 580–583
Composite depreciation, 381–382
Compound entry, 40
Computers, 221–222
Conservatism, accounting concept, 549
Consistency, accounting concept, 355, 359, 580
Contingencies, restriction of retained earnings, 480–481
Contingent liabilities, defined, 262
  disclosure, 264
Contra account, 114
Contract interest, 514, 515
Contributed capital, 441–464
  corporation, 450–464, 477–479
  defined, 477
  partnership, 443–450
  on position statement, 493–496
  single proprietorship, 441–443
Control, internal, *see* Internal control
  management, exception principle, 177–178, 729–730
Controlling accounts, accounts payable, 64–65
  accounts receivable, 64
  cost system, 696
  defined, 65
  general and administrative expenses, 409
  selling expense, 409
  vouchers payable, 408–409
Convertible bonds, 512, 528–529
Copartnership, articles of, 443
Copyrights, 392–393
Corporations, advantages, 11
  characteristics, 450–452
  contributions to, 478
  defined, 11
  disadvantages, 451
  donations to, 478
    stock, 491–492
  legal capital, 457
  organization costs, 452
  organizing, 452–453
  ownership, 451–452
Corrections, of depreciation, 390–391
  in journals, 215–216
  in voucher system, 413–414
Cost, basis for recording assets, 70
  distinguished from expense, 61
  historical, 352

Cost (continued)
  inventory, 340–341, *see also* Inventory costing
  replacement, 351–352
  undepreciated, 114
Cost accounting, absorption and direct compared,
    739–744
  direct, 739–744
  and general accounting compared, 694
  job order, 695–704
    controlling accounts, 696
    cost sheet, 697
    defined, 693
    departments, 701–704
    factory payroll, 699
    finished goods, 698
    flow of costs, 695–696
    materials, 698–699
    overhead, 699–704
    work in process, 697–698
  objectives, 693
  process, 704–712
    cost of production reports, 707–710, 711–712
    defined, 693
    equivalent production, 707–708
    flow of costs, 705–706, 710–712
    summary entries, 710–712
  standard, 729–739
    comprehensive illustration, 732–738
    cost card, 732
    defined, 694, 729
    fixed budget, 730
    fixed costs, 731–732
    flexible budget, 730–732
    flow of costs, 733
    variable costs, 731–732
    variances, 736–737
    variances, interpretation, 738–739
  systems, 693–694
Cost analysis, 755–770
  abandonment of product or department, 767–770
  break-even, 756–764
Cost of goods manufactured, 662, 671
Cost of goods sold, 157, 164–166
  in manufacturing, 662–663
Cost of production report, 707–710
  analysis, 712
  illustrated, 711
Costing, inventory, *see* Inventory costing
Costs, allocation of manufacturing, 669–670
  concepts, 755–756
  flow of, job order system, 695–696
    process cost system, 705–706, 710–712
    standard cost system, 733
Coupon bonds, 511

Credit, defined, 35
Creditors' ledger, *see* Accounts payable ledger
Current assets, 8–9, 571–572
Current liabilities, 10, 509–510, 573
Current operating performance concept, 575–576
Current ratio, 13–14
Customers' ledger, *see* Accounts receivable ledger

Data processing, *see* Automatic data processing
Debenture bonds, 512
Debit, defined, 35
Debit and credit, rules, 35, 63
Declining-balance depreciation method, 379–381
Deferred charges, 572–573
Deferred credits, 573
Delivery equipment, 10
Depletion, 376–377, 391–392
Deposits in transit, 290
Depreciation, 376–384
  adjustments, 113–116, 667–668
  and capital budgeting, 793–794
  composite rates, 381–382
  declining-balance method, 379–381
  defined, 114
  as element of expense, 62
  estimated useful life, 377
  group rates, 381–382
  methods, 377–384
    compared, 380–381, 383–384
  partial accounting periods, 382–383
  on position statement, 116
  production methods, 378–379
  production-unit method, 378–379
  purpose, 383
  recording, 113–116
  revision of rate, 390–391
  salvage value, 377
  straight-line method, 114–115, 378
  sum of the years-digits method, 379–381
  working-hours method, 378
Direct costing, 739–744
Direct labor, 657–658, 699
Direct write-off, bad debts, 321–322
Disbursements, defined, 61–62
Disclosure, *see* Full disclosure
Discounts, bonds, 520
  chain, 177
  compound, 785
  lost, 178–179, 412–413
  notes payable, 253, 254
  notes receivable, 262–266
  purchases, gross price method, 160–161
    lost, 178–179, 412–413
    net price method, 178–179

Discounts, purchases (continued)
  terms, 177
  sales, 158–159, 162
    allowance, 322–323
    gross price method, 158–159
    net price method, 178
    not taken, 178
    terms, 177
  trade, 177
Dividends, 62, 481–488
  declaration, 62, 482–483
  defined, 11, 481
  earned, 547–548
  liquidating, 482
  payment, 62, 483
  preferred, 483–486
  receivable, 551–552
  record date, 481–482
  recording, 62, 483
  stock, 482, 486–488, 552–553
Documents, direct posting from, 216–217
  role in accounting system, 417–418, 419
Dollar, values of, 572
Dollar signs in financial statements, 8
Dollar statement, 176
Double-entry accounting, 40
Doubtful accounts, see Bad debts
Drafts, 266–268
Drawing accounts, partnership, 446
  single proprietorship, 87–88

Electronic data processing, 221–222
Employee's Withholding Exemption Certificate, 421
Employer's Tax Guide, 420–421
End-of-period procedures, 106–135, see also
    Adjustments; Worksheet
Endorsement, checks, 286
  notes, 248
Entity concept, 4
Equation, accounting, 5–6
  debit and credit rules and, 63
  expanded, 29–30
Equipment, see Plant and equipment
Equivalent production, 707–708
Errors, in depreciation rate, 390–391
  in journals, 215–216
  in voucher system, 413–414
Estimated useful life, 377
  revision, 390–391
Exception, management by, 177–178, 729–730
Expenditures, defined, 384–385
Expense analysis sheets, 409
Expenses, accounts, 60–61, 63–64
  accrued, see Accrued liabilities

Expenses (continued)
  allocation of manufacturing, 669–670
  defined, 60
  distinguished from costs, 61
  general and administrative, 166, 409
  matching with revenue, 62, 107–108, 314
  other, 166–167

Fair Labor Standards Act, 419–420
Fair presentation, 127–129
Federal Depositary Receipt, 424
Federal Insurance Contributions Act, see F.I.C.A.
Federal unemployment compensation tax, 420,
    422, 425
Federal Wage and Hour Law, 419–420
F.I.C.A. taxes, employer's, 422
  recording, 423–424
  reporting, 424–425
  employee's, 420–421
FIFO, 343–345
  periodic method, 344–345
  perpetual inventory, 343–344
Final entry, book of, defined, 37
Financial position, statement of, see Position
    statement
Financial statement analysis, 12–16, 579–590
  horizontal, 583–585
  influences, 590
  manufacturing costs, 674
  percentage, 137–138, 175–176
  ratio, see Ratio analysis
  tools of, 579–580
  trend percentages, 583–585
  vertical, 175–176, 585–588
Financial statements, comparative, 580–583
  development, 567–568
  dollar signs on, 8
  full disclosure, 127–129, 269–270
  heading, 8
  interim, 171–172
  interpretive presentation, 570
  interrelationship, 89–91
  manufacturing company, 670–671
  merchandising company, 170–171
  partnership, 449–450
  preparation, 78–80
  purpose, 569
  rules on, 8
Financing, long-term
  choice of methods, 512–514
  mortgages, 532
  notes, 532
  see also Bonds payable
  short-term, 247–270

Financing, short-term (continued)
    choice of method, 247, 268–269
    see also Notes payable
Finished goods, 662–663
  job order system, 698
  measuring and recording, 674–675
  process system, 705–706
  turnover, 673–674
First in, first out, *see* FIFO
Fixed assets, *see* Plant and equipment
Fixed costs, defined, 755
Fixed liabilities, *see* Long-term liabilities
Flow, accounting, 419
  cash, 628–631
  cost, *see* Cost accounting
  discounted, 790–793
  irregular, 794–795
  posting, 38–39
F.O.B., defined, 160
Folio column, 35
Footing, defined, 34
Footnotes, position statement, 264, 574–575
Forecasts, cash, 296–299
    see also Budgeting
Form 450, 424
Form 941, 424
Form W-2, 425
Form W-4, 421
Franchises, 393
Freight charges, 159–160, 163
Full disclosure, 127–129, 269–270
  contingent liabilities, 264
  footnotes, 574–575
  inventory valuation basis, 355
Funds, as cash, 628–631
  defined, 611
  from operations, 614–617
  other than working capital, 627–631
  petty cash, 287–288
  sinking, 512, 529–530
  see also Funds statement; Working capital
Funds statement, 611–627
  analysis, 626–627
  equations, 613–614
  preparation, 615–618
  purpose, 612–613
  simplified, 617
  T-account method, 618–626

General and administrative expenses, 166
  controlling account, 409
General journal, 71–73
  correcting entries in, 215
  entering transactions, 37

General journal (continued)
  form, 37
  unusual current transactions, 214–215
General ledger, after closing, 130–134
  defined, 64
Goodwill, 393
Gross margin, defined, 166
  determination, 168
  inventory estimating method, 355–357
Group depreciation, 381–382

Heading, financial statement, 8
Historical cost, 352

Imprest system, 288
Income, business and taxable contrasted, 822–824
  marginal, 761–762
    direct costing, 739
  net, 61, 62
  on worksheet, 122–123
Income statement, 62, 125–126
  all-inclusive concept, 576–577, 578–579
  bad debts, 314–315
  cash short or over, 296
  classified, illustrated, 165
  common-size, 176, 587–588
  comparative, 582–583
  current operating performance concept, 575–576
  dollar, 176
  gain or loss on equipment disposal, 386, 387
  manufacturing company, 670–671
  merchandising company, 157
    illustrated, 165
  multiple-step, 578
  partnership, 450
  preparation, 78–79
  single-step, 578, 579
  and statement of retained earnings combined, 577–578
  worksheet section, 122–125
Income taxes, 807–824
  accounting methods, 808
  business and taxable income contrasted, 822–824
  and capital budgeting, 793–794
  classes of taxpayers, 807
  corporate, 819–820
  depreciation rates, 379
  estimated liability, 118–119, 668–669
  exchanges of assets, 389–390
  individual, 810–818
  lower of cost or market, 354–355
  partnerships, 819
  planning, 821–822
  withholding, 421, 424–425, *see also* Payroll

Indenture, bond, 512
Installment loans, 268–269
Insurance, prepaid, 9
   adjustment, 108–109, 111–112, 667
Intangible assets, 392–393, 572
Interest, 249–250
   accrued, 117–118
      bonds payable, 523–525
   actual, 268–269
   bond, times earned ratio, 556–557
      yield table, 517
      see also Bonds payable
   compound, 783–788
   contract, 514, 515
   effective, 254–255, 268–269
      bonds issued at discount, 522
      bonds issued at premium, 520
   formula, 117, 249
   installment loans, 268–269
   nominal, 514, 515
   notes payable, adjustments, 255–257
   notes receivable, adjustments, 261–262
   to partners, 447–449
   payable, adjustment, 117–118
   present value, 784–785
   receivable, accrued, 118, 137
   simple, 783
   6-percent, 60-day method, 250
   unearned, 259
Interim statements, 171–172
Internal control, 4, 285–286
   accounting concept, 199
   accounts receivable, 325
   cash, 286–287
   voucher system, 407–408
Internal Revenue Service
   Circular E, Employer's Tax Guide, 420–421
   depreciation guidelines, 377
   exchange of assets, 389–390
   see also Income taxes
Inventory, 339–363
   control, 359–361
   cost, 340–341, 351–352
   economical buying quantities, 360–361
   estimating, gross margin method, 355–357
      retail method, 357–358
   finished goods, 662–663, 674–675, 698
   manufacturing, measuring and recording, 674–675
      on worksheet, 665–666
   materials, 655–657, 698–699, 705–706
   merchandise, account, 161, 163
      defined, 9
      on worksheet, 167–168
   periodic, 341

Inventory (continued)
      compared with perpetual, 349–350
      procedures, 361–362
   perpetual, 342
      compared with periodic, 349–350
   physical, *see* Inventory, periodic
   ratio to working capital, 360
   retail method, 357–358
   turnover, 174–175, 360
   work in process, 661–662, 674–675, 697–698
   on worksheet, 167–168
Inventory card, 348, 350
Inventory costing, FIFO, 343–345
      periodic method, 344–345
      perpetual method, 343–344
   LIFO, 345–347
      periodic method, 346–347
      perpetual method, 345–346
   moving average, 347, 348
   specific identification, 348–349
   weighted average, 347–348
Inventory valuation, basis, 340–341
   importance, 339–340
   lower of cost or market, 352–355
      application, 353, 354
      arguments against, 354
      evaluation, 353–355
   methods compared, 350–352
Investment register, 546
Investments, annual cost, 796–798
   classification, 545
   cost of capital, 789
   long-term, 550–556
      bonds, 553–556
      mortgage notes, 556
      notes, 556
      on position statement, 572
      stocks, 551–553
   payback, 798
   rate of return, 789
      measuring, 795–796
   short-term, *see* Marketable securities
   temporary, *see* Marketable securities
Invoices, in automatic data processing, 218
   defined, 159, 418
   posting from, 216–217
   terms, 177
   in voucher system, 408, 418–419

Job order cost accounting, *see* Cost accounting, job order
Journal, *see* General journal
Journalizing, 71–73
   compound entry, 40

Journalizing (continued)
  defined, 36
  results, 39
  split entry, 136–137

Labor, direct, 657–658
  factory payroll, 699
  indirect, 658
  see also Payroll
Land, on position statement, 9–10
  see also Plant and equipment
Last in, first out, *see* LIFO
Leaseholds, amortization, 393
Ledgers, in automatic data processing, 219
  defined, 36
  manufacturing overhead, 659
  stockholders, 454
  subsidiary, 64–65, 66
Leverage, 512–513
Liabilities, accrued, 116–118
    defined, 10, 118
    payment, 136–137
    on position statement, 10
  classification, 10–11
  contingent, defined, 262
    disclosure, 264
  current, 10, 509–510, 573
  defined, 5
  long-term, 532
    defined, 10–11
    on position statement, 573
    see also Bonds payable
LIFO, 345–347
  periodic method, 346–347
  perpetual method, 345–346
Liquidation, defined, 10
Liquidity, defined, 8
Loans, to officers, 313
Long-term liabilities, 10–11, 532, 573
  see also Bonds payable
Loss, net, 61, 62
Lower of cost or market, 352–355
  application, 353, 354
  arguments against, 354
  evaluation, 353–355
  income tax requirements, 354–355
  marketable securities, 549–550

Make or buy decisions, 767
Managerial reports, 568–569
Manufacturing, cost accumulation, 655–675
  overhead, *see* Overhead
  summary, 663–665
  worksheet, 665–670
  see also Cost accounting

Marginal costs, defined, 755
Marginal income
  defined, 761–762
  direct costing, 739
  planning, 762–764
  pricing and, 764–767
  statements, 761–762
Markdown, 357–358
Market value, 457, 493
Marketable securities, 545–550
  bonds, 546–547
  cost, 546
  defined, 8
  on position statement, 549, 550
  stock, 547–548
  valuation, 548–550
Markon, 358
Markup, 357–358
Marshall, John, 450
Matching revenue and expenses, 62, 107–108, 314
Materiality concept, 127–129
Materials, 655–657
  control, 674–675, 698–699
  direct, 655
  job order system, 698–699
  process system, 705–706
  turnover, 671–673
Maturity date, 117, 248–249
Merchandise, issuance of notes for, 252–253
  inventory, *see* Inventory
Merchandising business
  accounts for, 157–164
    functions, 161–164
  closing entries, 171, 172
  financial statements, 170–171
  income statement, 165
  worksheet, 167–169
Minute book, 453
Mixed accounts, adjusting, 109–113
  defined, 109
Mortgage bonds, 512
Mortgage notes
  long-term investment, 556
  payable, 11, 532
Multiple-step income statement, 578

Natural resources, 376–377, 391–392
Net assets, defined, 6
Net income, 61, 62
  on worksheet, 122–123
Net loss, 61, 62
Net operating margin, defined, 166
  ratio, 174
Net purchases, defined, 164

New York Stock Exchange, 567–568
Nominal accounts, 80
Nominal interest, defined, 514, 515
No-par value, defined, 456
Notes, characteristics, 248
  defined, 247
  endorsement, 248
  illustrated, 248
  interest, 249–250
  maturity date, 248–249
  term, 248–249
Notes payable, 250–257
  adjustments, 117–118, 255–257
  to banks, 253
  defined, 10
  discounted, 253, 254
  for long-term financing, 532
  for merchandise, 252–253
  for plant and equipment, 251–252
  recording, 250–255
  to settle account payable, 253
  in voucher system, 414–415
Notes receivable, 313–314
  accounting for, 257–261
  adjustments, 261–262
  defined, 9
  discounted, 262–266
    determining proceeds, 263
    dishonored, 265–266
    payment, 264–265
    on position statement, 264, 269–270
    recording proceeds, 264
  dishonored, 260–261
  long-term investment in, 556
  recording, 257–261
  renewal, 259–260

Office supplies, 9
Open charge accounts, 8–9, 247
  issuance of notes to settle, 253
Operating cycle, defined, 571
Operating expenses, accounts, 166
Operating ratio, 174
Opportunity cost, defined, 755
Order bill of lading, 267
Organization costs, 393, 452
Original entry, book of, defined, 37
Other expenses, 166–167
Other revenue, 166–167
Out-of-pocket costs, defined, 755
Overdrafts, 289
Overhead, 658–661, 699–704
  allocation, 700–701
  departmental, 701–704

Overhead (continued)
  fixed budget, 730
  fixed costs, 731–732
  flexible budget, 730–732
  ledger, 659
  overapplied, 700
  rates, 700–701
  underapplied, 700
  variable costs, 731–732
Owner's equity, statement of, 89

Paid-in capital, *see* Contributed capital
Par value, defined, 455
Participating preferred stock, 484
Partners' equity, 12, 445–450
Partnerships, 443–450
  advantages, 12, 444
  defined, 12, 443
  disadvantages, 12, 444–445
  distribution of profit, 446–449
    if no agreement, 443, 446–447
  drawing accounts, 446
  equity accounts, 445–450
  formation, 445
  position statement, 12, 450
  statement of partners' equities, 449–450
  types, 443–444
Patents, 392, 658
Payables, *see* Accounts payable; Notes payable
Payback of investment, 798
Payroll, 418–426
  accrued, 116–117, 425–426
  control, 418
  deductions, 418–419
  employer's taxes, 422–423
    recording, 423–424
  factory, 699
  Fair Labor Standards Act, 419–420
  F.I.C.A. taxes, employee's, 420–421
    recording, 423–424
    reporting, 424–425
  F.U.T.A., 420, 422, 425
  Federal Wage and Hour Law, 419–420
  income tax withholding, 421
    reporting, 424–425
  merit rating, 423
  other deductions, 421
  recording, 422
  state unemployment compensation tax, 422–423
    reporting and paying, 425
  voucher system, 426
Pension contracts, 532
Permanent accounts, 80
Petty cash, 287–288

Petty cash (continued)
   analysis sheet, 287–288
   in voucher system, 413
Plant, defined, 9
Plant assets, *see* Plant and equipment
Plant and equipment, 375–397
   classification, 9–10
   cost, 375–376
   defined, 9–10, 375
   depreciation, *see* Depreciation
   discard, 385–386
   disposal, 385–390
   issuance of notes for, 251–252
   on position statement, 9–10, 572
   ratios, 393–395
   replacement considerations, 395–396
   sale, 385–387
   trade-in, 387–390
   turnover, 395
Position statement, 42, 125–126, 567–590
   account form, 6
   allowance for doubtful accounts on, 315
   analysis, *see* Financial statement analysis;
      Ratio analysis
   bad debts on, 314–315, 319–320
   classified, 8–11, 170, 571–574
   common-size, 585–587
   comparative, 581–582
   contingent liabilities on, 264
   contributed capital on, 493–496
   current assets on, 8–9, 571–572
   current liabilities on, 10, 573
   deferred charges on, 572–573
   deferred credits on, 573
   defined, 6–7
   depreciation on, 116
   discount on stock on, 459–460
   dollar signs on, 8
   doubtful accounts on, 319–320
   effect of transactions, 26–29
   footnotes, 264, 574–575
   form, 6–7, 570–571
   heading, 8
   intangible assets on, 572
   inventory valuation on, 355
   long-term investments on, 572
   long-term liabilities on, 573
   marketable securities on, 549, 550
   notes receivable discounted on, 264
   owner's equity section, 11–12, 443
   partnership, 12, 450
   plant and equipment on, 9–10, 572
   premium on stock on, 459–460
   preparation, 79–80

Position statement (continued)
   receivables on, 314
   report form, 7
   rules on, 8
   single proprietorship, 12, 88–89
   stock subscription on, at discount, 464
      at par, 461
      at premium, 463
   stockholders' equity section, 454–455, 493–496,
      573–574
   treasury stock on, 490
   worksheet section, 122–125
Post-closing trial balance, 86, 134, 135
Posting, 73–76
   from business documents, 216–217
   from cash disbursements journal, 211–212
   from cash receipts journal, 206–208
   from check register, 412, 415
   defined, 36
   flow chart, 38–39
   machine, 218–219
   method of, 37–39
   from purchases journal, 202, 203
   results, 39–40
   from sales journal, 200–201
   to subsidiary ledgers, 65, 66
   timing of, 37, 73
   from voucher register, 409, 415
Pre-emptive right, 453
Preferred stock, *see* Stock, preferred
Premium, bonds, 518
Prepaid insurance, 9
   adjustments, 108–109, 111–112, 667
Prepaid items, defined, 9
Prepaid rent, 110–111
Present value, 784–785
Pricing, inventory, *see* Inventory valuation
   product, 764–767
Process cost accounting, *see* Cost Accounting,
   process
Profit, defined, 61, 62
Promissory notes, *see* Notes
Proprietorship, *see* Single proprietorship
Protest fee, 264
Proxies, 453
Punched-card equipment, 219–220
Purchase allowances, 160, 164
Purchase discounts
   account, 160–161, 164
   gross price method, 160
   net price method, 178–179
   ratio to purchases, 176
Purchase order, 418
Purchases, account, 159, 163

Purchases (continued)
  forecast of payments, 298
  journal, 198, 202, 203
  net, defined, 164
Purchases returns and allowances, account, 160, 164
  journal, 198, 213
  ratio to purchases, 176
  in voucher system, 414

Quick assets, 14, 572

Ratio analysis, acid-test ratio, 14
  average collection period, 324–325
  creditors' equity, 138
  current ratio, 13–14
  equity ratios, 138
  finished goods turnover, 673–674
  inventory turnover, 174–175, 360
  inventory to working capital, 360
  limitations, 15–16
  net income to stockholders' equity, 173
  net operating margin ratio, 174
  net sales to plant and equipment, 394–395
  number days' sales uncollected, 324–325
  operating ratio, 174
  plant and equipment to long-term liabilities, 394–395
  plant and equipment to stockholders' equity, 395
  plant and equipment turnover, 395
  purchases discounts to purchases, 176
  purchases returns to purchases, 176
  raw materials turnover, 671–673
  receivables turnover, 324–325
  return on stockholders' equity, 173
  return on total equities, 173
  sales discounts to sales revenue, 176
  sales returns to sales revenue, 176
  stockholders' equity, 138
  summarized, 588–590
  times bond interest earned, 556–557
  working capital turnover, 175
Raw materials, see Materials
Real accounts, 80
Receivables, 313–327
  average collection period, 324–325
  classification, 313–314
  sources, 313–314
  turnover, 324–325
  see also Accounts receivable; Notes receivable
Receiving report, 418
Reconciliation, bank, 289–295
Record date, 481–482
Registered bonds, 511
Registrar, 454

Rent, prepaid, 110–111
  unearned, 112–113
Replacement cost, 351–352
Residual value, 113
Retail inventory method, 357–358
Retained earnings, defined, 11–12, 479
  restricted, 479–481
    for bond redemption, 530–531
    for contingencies, 480–481
    contractual, 481
    legal, 481
    for plant expansion, 480
    for retirement of preferred stock, 481
  statement, 79, 125–127, 171
    all-inclusive concept, 576–577
    current operating performance concept, 575–576
    and income statement combined, 577–578
Revaluation of assets, 479
Revenue, accounts, 59
  accrued, defined, 118
  defined, 59
  matching with expenses, 62, 107–108, 314
  other, 166–167
Revenue expenditure, defined, 384–385
Revenue and expense summary, 80–81, 129
Ruling, closed accounts, 82–84
  on financial statements, 8
  open accounts, 84–86

Safety, margin of, 762
Salaries, to partners, 448–449
  see also Payroll
Sales, account, 157–158, 162
  allowances, 158, 162
  discounts, 158–159, 162
    allowance for, 322–323
    gross price method, 158–159
    net price method, 178
    ratio to sales revenue, 176
  journal, 198–201
    posting from, 200–201
    recording in, 199–200
  returns and allowances, account, 158, 162
    allowance for, 322–323
    journal, 198, 212–213
    ratio to sales revenue, 176
Salvage value, 113, 377
Schedule of accounts payable, 77–78
Schedule of accounts receivable, 77
Schedule of cost of goods manufactured, 662, 671
Schedule of vouchers payable, 415–416
Securities and Exchange Commission, 456, 568
Selling expenses, 166

Selling expenses (continued)
  controlling account, 409
Serial bonds, 512, 525
Service business, defined, 25
Service department, 701–702
Sight draft, 267
Single proprietorship, accounting procedures, 42–43
  accounting sequence, 87–89
  advantages, 11
  capital accounts, 88–89, 441–443
  defined, 12
  position statement, 12, 88–89
Single-step income statement, 578, 579
Sinking fund bonds, 512, 529–530
Social Security Act, 420–421, see also Payroll
Source documents, in automatic data processing, 218
  posting from, 216–217
Special journals, 197–217
  advantages, 198–199
  equality of debits and credits, 206
  forwarding totals, 216
  kinds, 198
  need, 198
  use of general journal with, 214–216
  see also specific journal
Special orders, 764
Specific identification costing, 348–349
Split entries, 136–137
Standard cost accounting, see Cost accounting, standard
State unemployment compensation, 422–423, 425
Stated value, defined, 456
Statement analysis, see Financial statement analysis
Statement of financial position, see Position statement
Statement of owner's equity, 89, 443
Statement of partners' equities, 449–450
Statement of retained earnings, 79, 125–127, 171
  all-inclusive concept, 576–577
  current operating performance concept, 575–576
  and income statement combined, 577–578
Statement of sources and uses of funds, see Funds statement
Statements, bank, 288–295
  financial, see Financial statements
Stock, authorization, 458
  and bonds compared, 511, 512–514
  book value, 457, 492–493
  certificate, 454
  classes, 455
  common, 453, 455
  conversion of bonds to, 528–529

Stock (continued)
  discount, 455
  dividends, see Dividends
  entries for, 457–460
  issuance, 458–460
  long-term investment in, 551–553
  market value, 457, 493
  no-par value, 456–457
  par value, 455–456
  preferred, 455
    dividends, 483–486
    restriction of retained earnings for, retirement, 481
  premium, 477
  sale, 456–457
  shares, 451–452
  split-ups, 488–489
  stated value, 456–457
  subscription, 460–464
    at discount, 463–464
    at par, 460–461
    preferred, 464
    at premium, 462–463
  temporary investment in, 547–548
  transactions, 457–560
  transfer, 451
  treasury, 489–492
    donated, 491–492
    legal restrictions, 492
    purchase, 489–490
    reissue, 490–491
  unissued, 454–455
  value, 457, 492–493
  watered, 456
Stockholders, 451, 453
Stockholders' equity, per share, 492–493
  on position statement, 493–496, 573–574
  return on, 173
  sources, 477, 478
Stockholders' ledger, 454
Store equipment, 10
Store supplies, 9
Straight-line depreciation, 114–115, 378
Subscriptions, stock, see Stock, subscriptions
Subsidiary ledgers, 64–65, 66, 659, see also Accounts payable ledger; Accounts receivable ledger
Sum of the years-digits depreciation, 379–381
Summary accounts
  manufacturing, 663–665
  revenue and expense, 80–81, 129
Sunk costs, defined, 755
Supplies, 9
  adjustments, 109
Supporting documents, 417–418, 419

T accounts, 34–35
Tangible assets, *see* Plant and equipment
Taxes, *see* Income taxes; Payroll
Taxpayers, classes of, 807
Temporary accounts, 80
Terms, discount, 177
Time cards, 699
Time drafts, 267
Trade acceptances, 267–268
Trade discounts, 177
Trade-in, 387–390
Trade payables, *see* Accounts payable; Notes payable
Trade receivables, *see* Accounts receivable; Notes receivable; Receivables
Trading assets, 572
Transactions
    analyzing, 68–71
    effects on accounting equation, 29–30
Transfer agent, 454
Transportation in account, 159–160, 163
Treasury stock, 489–492
Trial balance, 34, 110
    adjusted, 122, 123
    locating errors, 41–42
    post-closing, 86, 134, 135
    preparing, 76–77
    purpose, 41
    worksheet section, 119–120

Uncollectible accounts, *see* Bad debts
Undepreciated cost, 114
Underwriter, 525
Unearned interest, 259
Unearned rent, 112–113
Unpaid voucher file, 409, 415–416

Valuation, account, 114
    asset, 341
    inventory, *see* Inventory valuation
Value, defined, 4–5, 341
Variable costs, defined, 755
Variances, calculation, 736–737
    cash forecast, 296
    interpretation, 738–739
Vertical analysis, 175–176, 585–588
Voucher check, 416–417
Voucher jacket, 408
Voucher register, 408–409, 410–411
    design, 412
    posting from, 409, 415
Voucher system, 407–417
    advantages, 417

Voucher system (continued)
    described, 407–408
    discounts, 412–413
    expense analysis sheets, 409
    installment payments, 415
    limitations, 417
    partial payments, 415
    payroll, 426
    supporting documents, 417–418
    voucher check, 416–417
Vouchers, defined, 408
    petty cash, 287
    recording and paying, 413–415
    unpaid, 408–409, 415–416
Vouchers payable
    account, 408–409
    schedule of, 416

Wage and Hour Law, 419–420
Wages, *see* Payroll
Watered stock, 456
Withholding, income tax, *see* Payroll
Withholding statement, 425
Working capital, defined, 14–15
    flow, 15
    from operations, 614–617
    ratio of inventory to, 360
    schedule of changes in, 616, 620
    turnover, 175
    see also Funds; Funds statement
Work-in-process inventory, 661–662
    job order, 697–698
    measuring and recording, 674–675
    process, 705–706
Worksheet, 119–127
    adjusted trial balance section, 122, 123
    adjusting entries in, 109
    adjustments section, 109, 120–121, 127
    defined, 107
    income on, 122–123
    income statement section, 122–125
    manufacturing, 665–670
        adjustments, 667–669
        allocation of costs and expenses, 669–670
        ending inventories, 665–666
        illustrated, 666
    merchandise inventory on, 167–168
    for merchandising business, 167–169
    net income, 122–123
    position statement section, 122–123
    preparation of financial statements, 125–127
    trial balance section, 119–120

Yield table, bond, 517